History of Medieval India
543 BCE to 16th Century

Compiled by
Bailee Skeen

Scribbles

Year of Publication 2018

ISBN : 9789352979189

Book Published by

Scribbles

(An Imprint of Alpha Editions)

email - alphaedis@gmail.com

Produced by: PediaPress GmbH
Limburg an der Lahn
Germany
http://pediapress.com/

The content within this book was generated collaboratively by volunteers. Please be advised that nothing found here has necessarily been reviewed by people with the expertise required to provide you with complete, accurate or reliable information. Some information in this book may be misleading or simply wrong. Alpha Editions and PediaPress does not guarantee the validity of the information found here. If you need specific advice (for example, medical, legal, financial, or risk management) please seek a professional who is licensed or knowledgeable in that area.

Sources, licenses and contributors of the articles and images are listed in the section entitled "References". Parts of the books may be licensed under the GNU Free Documentation License. A copy of this license is included in the section entitled "GNU Free Documentation License"

The views and characters expressed in the book are those of the contributors and his/her imagination and do not represent the views of the Publisher.

Contents

Articles 1

Introduction 1
Middle kingdoms of India 1
Medieval India 40

Early medieval 47
Chalukya dynasty 47
Harsha 70
Karkoṭa Empire 75
Umayyad campaigns in India 77
Tripartite Struggle 87
Gurjara-Pratihara dynasty 89
Rashtrakuta dynasty 100
Pala Empire 123
Medieval Cholas 142
Western Chalukya Empire 148
Pallava dynasty 173
Chola dynasty 187
Western Ganga dynasty 221
Kakatiya dynasty 244
Sena dynasty 261

Late medieval — 269

- Delhi Sultanate 269
- Mamluk dynasty (Delhi) 289
- Khalji dynasty 296
- Tughlaq dynasty 306
- Sayyid dynasty 329
- Lodi dynasty 333
- Pandyan dynasty 338
- Vijayanagara Empire 361
- Bengal Sultanate 388
- Ahom kingdom 403
- Reddy dynasty 416
- Gajapati Kingdom 432

Appendix — 435

- References 435
- Article Sources and Contributors 481
- Image Sources, Licenses and Contributors 484

Article Licenses — 491

Index — 493

Introduction

Middle kingdoms of India

Human history
↑ **Prehistory**
Recorded history
Ancient
<ul><li>Earliest records</li><li>Africa</li><li>Americas</li><li>Oceania</li><li>East Asia</li><li>South Asia</li><li>Southeast Asia</li><li>West Asia</li><li>Europe</li></ul>
Postclassical
<ul><li>Africa</li><li>Americas</li><li>Oceania</li><li>East Asia</li><li>South Asia</li><li>Southeast Asia</li><li>West Asia</li><li>Europe</li></ul>
Modern
<ul><li>Early modern</li><li>Late modern</li></ul>
See also
<ul><li>Contemporary</li><li>Modernity</li><li>Futurology</li></ul>
↓ **Future**
<ul><li>v</li><li>t</li><li>e[1]</li></ul>

The **Middle kingdoms of India** were the political entities in India from the 3rd century BCE to the 13th century CE. The period begins after the decline of the Maurya Empire, and the corresponding rise of the Satavahana dynasty, beginning with Simuka, from 230 BCE. The "Middle" period lasted for about 1500 years and ended in the 13th century, with the rise of the Delhi Sultanate, founded in 1206, and the end of the Later Cholas (Rajendra Chola III, who died in 1279 CE).

This period encompasses two eras: **Classical India**, from the Maurya Empire up until the end of the Gupta Empire in the 6th century CE, and early Medieval India from the 6th century onwards. It also encompasses the era of classical Hinduism, which is dated from 200 BCE to 1100 CE. From 1 CE until 1000 CE, India's economy is estimated to have been the largest in the world, having between one-third and one-quarter of the world's wealth. It is followed by the late Medieval period in the 13th century.

The Northwest

During the 2nd century BCE, the Maurya Empire became a collage of regional powers with overlapping boundaries. The whole northwest attracted a series of invaders between 200 BCE and 300 CE. The Puranas speak of many of these tribes as foreigners and impure barbarians (Mlecchas). First the Satavahana dynasty and then the Gupta Empire, both successor states to the Maurya Empire, attempt to contain the expansions of the successive before eventually crumbling internally due pressure exerted by these wars.

The invading tribes were influenced by Buddhism which continued to flourish under the patronage of both invaders and the Satavahanas and Guptas and provides a cultural bridge between the two cultures. Over time, the invaders became "Indianized" as they influenced society and philosophy across the Gangetic plains and were conversely influenced by it. This period is marked by both intellectual and artistic achievements inspired by cultural diffusion and syncretism as the new kingdoms straddle the Silk Road.

The Indo-Scythian Sakas

The Indo-Scythians are a branch of the Sakas who migrated from southern Siberia into Bactria, Sogdia, Arachosia, Gandhara, Kashmir, Punjab, and into parts of Western and Central India, Gujarat, Maharashtra and Rajasthan, from the middle of the 2nd century BCE to the 4th century CE. The first Saka king in India was Maues or Moga who established Saka power in Gandhara and gradually extended supremacy over north-western India. Indo-Scythian rule

Middle kingdoms of India

Figure 1: *Silver coin of the founder of the Indo-Greek Kingdom, Demetrius (r. c. 205–171 BC).*

in India ended with the last of the Western Satraps, Rudrasimha III, in 395 CE.

The invasion of India by Scythian tribes from Central Asia, often referred to as the "Indo-Scythian invasion", played a significant part in the history of India as well as nearby countries. In fact, the Indo-Scythian war is just one chapter in the events triggered by the nomadic flight of Central Asians from conflict with Chinese tribes which had lasting effects on Bactria, Kabul, Parthia and India as well as far off Rome in the west. The Scythian groups that invaded India and set up various kingdoms, included besides the Sakas[2] other allied tribes, such as the Medes,[3] WP:NOTRS Wikipedia:Citation needed Scythians,[4] Massagetae, Wikipedia:Citation needed Getae,[5] Parama Kamboja Kingdom, Avars, Wikipedia:Citation needed Bahlikas, Rishikas and Parada Kingdom.

The Indo-Greeks

The Indo-Greek Kingdom covered various parts of the Northwestern South Asia during the last two centuries BCE, and was ruled by more than 30 Hellenistic kings, often in conflict with each other.

The kingdom was founded when Demetrius I of Bactria invaded the Hindu Kush early in the 2nd century BCE. The Greeks in India were eventually divided from the Greco-Bactrian Kingdom centered in Bactria (now the border between Afghanistan and Uzbekistan).

The expression "Indo-Greek Kingdom" loosely describes a number of various dynastic polities. There were numerous cities, such as Taxila[6] Pakistan's Punjab, or Pushkalavati and Sagala.[7] These cities would house a number of dynasties in their times, and based on Ptolemy's *Geography* and the nomenclature of later kings, a certain Theophila in the south was also probably a satrapal or royal seat at some point.

Euthydemus I was, according to Polybius[8] a Magnesian Greek. His son, Demetrius, founder of the Indo-Greek kingdom, was therefore of Greek descent from his father at minimum. A marriage treaty was arranged for Demetrius with a daughter of Antiochus III the Great, who had partial Persian descent.[9] The ethnicity of later Indo-Greek rulers is less clear.[10] For example, Artemidoros Aniketos (80 BCE) may have been of Indo-Scythian descent. Intermarriage also occurred, as exemplified by Alexander the Great, who married Roxana of Bactria, or Seleucus I Nicator, who married Apama of Sogdia.

During the two centuries of their rule, the Indo-Greek kings combined the Greek and Indian languages and symbols, as seen on their coins, and blended Greek, Hindu and Buddhist religious practices, as seen in the archaeological remains of their cities and in the indications of their support of Buddhism, pointing to a rich fusion of Indian and Hellenistic influences.[11] The diffusion of Indo-Greek culture had consequences which are still felt today, particularly through the influence of Greco-Buddhist art. The Indo-Greeks ultimately disappeared as a political entity around 10 CE following the invasions of the Indo-Scythians, although pockets of Greek populations probably remained for several centuries longer under the subsequent rule of the Indo-Parthians and Kushan Empire.[12]

The Yavanas

The **Yavana** or **Yona** people, literally "Ionian" and meaning "Western foreigner", were described as living beyond Gandhara. Yavanas, Sakas, the Pahlavas and Hunas were sometimes described as *mleccha*s, "barbarians". Kambojas and the inhabitants of Madra, the Kekeya Kingdom, the Indus River region and Gandhara were sometimes also classified as *mleccha*s. This name was used to indicate their cultural differences with the culture of the Kuru Kingdom and Panchala.Wikipedia:Citation needed

The Indo-Parthians

The Indo-Parthian Kingdom was founded by Gondophares around 20 BCE. The kingdom lasted only briefly until its conquest by the Kushan Empire in the late 1st century CE and was a loose framework where many smaller dynasts maintained their independence.

The Pahlavas

The **Pahlavas** are a people mentioned in ancient Indian texts like the *Manusmṛti*, various Puranas, the *Ramayana*, the *Mahabharata*, and the *Brhatsamhita*. In some texts the Pahlavas are synonymous with the Pallava dynasty of South India. While the *Vayu Purana* distinguishes between *Pahlava* and *Pahnava*, the *Vamana Purana* and *Matsya Purana* refer to both as *Pallava*. The *Brahmanda Purana* and *Markendeya Purana* refer to both as *Pahlava* or *Pallava*. The *Bhishama Parava* of the Mahabharata does not distinguish between the Pahlavas and Pallavas. The Pahlavas are said to be same as the Parasikas, a Saka group. According to P. Carnegy,[13] the Pahlava are probably those people who spoke Paluvi or Pehlvi, the Parthian language. Buhler similarly suggests Pahlava is an Indic form of *Parthava* meaning "Parthian".[14] In a 4th-century BCE, the *Vartika* of Kātyāyana mentions the *Sakah-Parthavah*, demonstrating an awareness of these Saka-Parthians, probably by way of commerce.[15]

The Western Satraps

The Western Satraps (35-405 CE) were Saka rulers of the western and central part of India (Saurashtra and Malwa: modern Gujarat, southern Sindh, Maharashtra, Rajasthan and Madhya Pradesh states). Their state, or at least part of it, was called "Ariaca" according to the *Periplus of the Erythraean Sea*. They were successors to the Indo-Scythians and were contemporaneous with the Kushan Empire, which ruled the northern part of the Indian subcontinent and were possibly their overlords, and the Satavahana dynasty of Andhra who ruled in Central India. They are called "Western" in contrast to the "Northern" Indo-Scythian satraps who ruled in the area of Mathura, such as Rajuvula, and his successors under the Kushans, the "Great Satrap" Kharapallana and the "Satrap" Vanaspara.[16] Although they called themselves "Satraps" on their coins, leading to their modern designation of "Western Satraps", Ptolemy's *Geography* still called them "Indo-Scythians".[17] Altogether, there were 27 independent Western Satrap rulers during a period of about 350 years.

The Kushans

The Kushan Empire (c. 1st–3rd centuries) originally formed in Bactria on either side of the middle course of the Amu Darya in what is now northern Afghanistan, Tajikistan and Uzbekistan; during the 1st century CE, they expanded their territory to include the Punjab and much of the Ganges basin, conquering a number of kingdoms across the northern part of the Indian subcontinent in the process.[18,19] The Kushans conquered the central section of the main Silk Road and, therefore, had control of the overland trade between India, and China to the east, and the Roman Empire and Persia to the west.

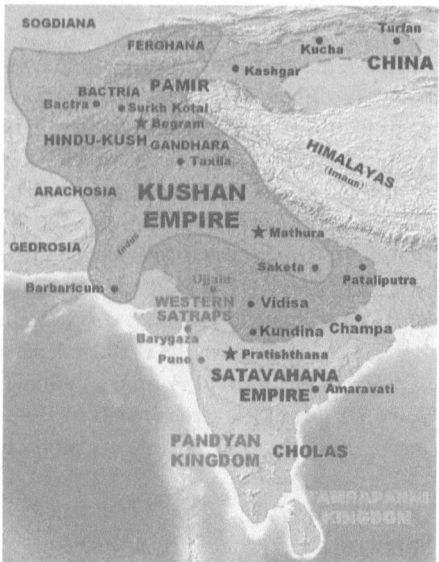

Figure 2: *Kushan Empire*

Emperor Kanishka was a great patron of Buddhism; however, as Kushans expanded southward toward the Indian subcontinent the deities of their later coinage came to reflect its new Hindu majority.

The Indo-Sasanians

The rise of new Persian power, the Sasanian Empire, saw them exert their influence into the Indus region and conquer lands from the Kushan Empire, setting up the Indo-Sasanians around 240 CE. They were to maintain their influence in the region until they were overthrown by the Rashidun Caliphate. Afterwards, they were displaced in 410 CE by the invasions of the Hephthalite Empire.

The Hephthalite Hunas

The Hephthalite Empire was another Central Asian nomadic group to invade. They are also linked to the Yuezhi who had founded the Kushan Empire. From their capital in Bamyan (present-day Afghanistan) they extended their rule across the Indus and North India, thereby causing the collapse of the Gupta Empire. They were eventually defeated by the Sasanian Empire allied with Turkic peoples.

Figure 3: *Billon drachma of the Huna King Napki Malka (Afghanistan or Gandhara, c. 475–576).*

The Rais

The Rai dynasty of Sindh were patrons of Buddhism even though they also established a huge temple of Shiva in Sukkur close to their capital, Aror.

The Gandharan Kambojas

The **Gandhara** Satrapy became an independent kingdom based from Afghanistan and vied with the Tang dynasty, Tibetan Empire, the Islamic Caliphate and Turkic tribes for domination in the region.

The Karkotas

The Karkota Empire was established around 625 CE. During the eighth century they consolidated their rule over Kashmir.[22] The most illustrious ruler of the dynasty was Lalitaditya Muktapida. According to Kalhana's *Rajatarangini*, he defeated the Tibetans and Yashovarman of Kanyakubja, and subsequently conquered eastern kingdoms of Magadha, Kamarupa, Gauda, and Kalinga. Kalhana also states that he extended his influence of Malwa and Gujarat and defeated Arabs at Sindh.[23,24] According to historians, Kalhana highly exaggerated the conquests of Lalitaditya.[20,21]

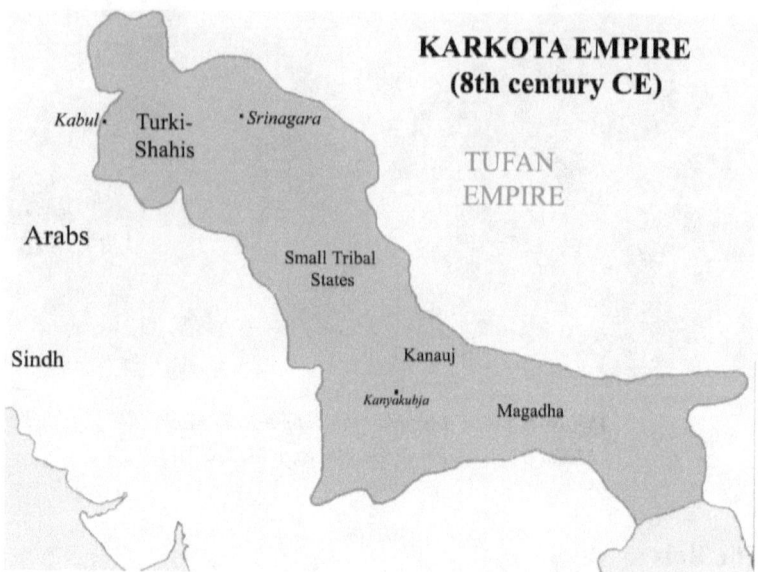

Figure 4: *Extent of the Karkota Empire during the reign of Lalitaditya Muktapida (8th century), according to Kalhana's Rajatarangini. Note that Kalhana highly exaggerated the conquests of Lalitaditya.*[20,21]

The Kabul Shahis

The Kabul Shahi dynasties ruled portions of the Kabul valley and Gandhara from the decline of the Kushan Empire in the 3rd century to the early 9th century.[25] The kingdom was known as the Kabul Shahan or Ratbelshahan from 565 CE-670 CE, when the capitals were located in Kapisa and Kabul, and later Udabhandapura, also known as Hund[26] for its new capital. In ancient time, the title Shahi appears to be a quite popular royal title in Afghanistan and the northwestern areas of the Indian subcontinent. Variants were used much more priorly in the Near East,[27] but as well later on by the Sakas, Kushans Hunas, Bactrians, by the rulers of Kapisa/Kabul and Gilgit.[28] In Persian form, the title appears as *Kshathiya, Kshathiya Kshathiyanam*, Shao of the Kushanas and the *Ssaha* of Mihirakula (Huna chief).[29] The Kushanas are stated to have adopted the title *Shah-in-shahi* (*"Shaonano shao"*) in imitation of Achaemenid practice.[30] The Shahis are generally split up into two eras—the Buddhist Shahis and the Hindu Shahis, with the change-over thought to have occurred sometime around 870 CE.

The Gangetic Plains and Deccan

Following the demise of the Mauryan Empires the Satavahanas rose as the successor state to check and contend with the influx of the Central Asian tribes from the Northwest. The Satavahanas straddling the Deccan plateau also provided a link for transmission of Buddhism and contact between the Northern Gangetic plains and the Southern regions even as the Upanishads were gaining ground. Eventually weakened both by contention with the northwestern invaders and internal strife they broke up and gave rise to several nations around Deccan and central India regions even as the Gupta Empire arose in the Indo-Gangetic Plain and ushered in a **"Golden Age"** and rebirth of empire as decentralized local administrative model and the spread of Indian culture until collapse under the Huna invasions. After the fall of Gupta Empire the Gangetic region broke up into several states temporarily reunited under Harsha then giving rise to the Rajput dynasties. In the Deccan, the Chalukyas arose forming a formidable nation marking the migration of the centers of cultural and military power long held in the Indo-Gangetic Plain to the new nations forming in the southern regions of India.

The Satavahana Empire

The **Sātavāhana dynasty** began as feudatories to the Maurya Empire but declared independence with its decline. They were the first Indic rulers to issue coins struck with their rulers embossed and are known for their patronage of Buddhism, resulting in Buddhist monuments from the Ellora Caves to Amaravathi village, Guntur district. They formed a cultural bridge and played a vital role in trade and the transfer of ideas and culture to and from the Gangetic plains to the southern tip of India.

The Sātavāhanas had to compete with the Shunga Empire and then the Kanva dynastys of Magadha to establish their rule. Later they had to contend in protecting their domain from the incursions of Sakas, Yonas and the Pahlavas. In particular their struggles with the Western Satraps weakened them and the empire split into smaller states.

The Mahameghavahana dynasty

The Mahameghavahana dynasty (c. 250s BCE-400s CE) was an ancient ruling dynasty of Kalinga after the decline of the Mauryan Empire. The third ruler of the dynasty, Khārabēḷa, conquered much of India in a series of campaigns at the beginning of the common era.[31] Kaḷingan military might was reinstated by Khārabēḷa: under Khārabēḷa's generalship, the Kaḷinga state had a formidable maritime reach with trade routes linking it to the then-Simhala

Figure 5: *Silver coin of the Gupta King Kumara Gupta I (414–455).*

(Sri Lanka), Burma (Myanmar), Siam (Thailand), Vietnam, Kamboja (Cambodia), Borneo, Bali, Samudra (Sumatra) and Jabadwipa (Java). Khārabēḷa led many successful campaigns against the states of Magadha, Anga, the Satavahanas and the South Indian regions ruled by the Pandyan dynasty (modern Andhra Pradesh) and expanded Kaḷinga as far as the Ganges and the Kaveri.

The Kharavelan state had a formidable maritime empire with trading routes linking it to Sri Lanka, Burma, Thailand, Vietnam, Cambodia, Borneo, Bali, Sumatra and Java. Colonists from Kalinga settled in Sri Lanka, Burma, as well as the Maldives and Maritime Southeast Asia. Even today Indians are referred to as Keling in Malaysia because of this.[32]

Although religiously tolerant, Khārabēḷa patronised Jainism, and was responsible for the propagation of Jainism in the Indian subcontinent but his importance is neglected in many accounts of Indian history. The main source of information about Khārabeḷa is his famous seventeen line rock-cut Hātigumphā inscription in the Udayagiri and Khandagiri Caves near Bhubaneswar, Odisha. According to the Hathigumpha inscription, he attacked Rajagriha in Magadha, thus inducing the Indo-Greek king Demetrius I of Bactria to retreat to Mathura.[33]

The Bharshiva dynasty

Before the rise of the Guptas, Bharshiva Kings ruled most of the Indo-Gangetic plains. They perform ten Ashvamedha sacrifices on the banks of Ganga River. Samudragupta mention Naga rulers in his Allahabad pillar.[34]

The Guptas

The **Classical Age** refers to the period when much of the Indian Subcontinent was reunited under the Gupta Empire (ca. 320 CE–550 CE).[35] This period is called the Golden Age of India and was marked by extensive achievements in science, technology, engineering, art, dialectic, literature, logic, mathematics, astronomy, religion and philosophy that crystallized the elements of what is generally known as Hindu culture.[36] The decimal numeral system, including the concept of zero, was invented in India during this period.Wikipedia:Citation needed The peace and prosperity created under Guptas leadership enabled the pursuit of scientific and artistic endeavors in India.[37]

The high points of this cultural creativity is seen in Gupta architecture, sculpture and painting.[38] The Gupta period produced scholars such as Kalidasa, Aryabhata, Varahamihira, Vishnu Sharma, and Vatsyayana who made advances in a variety of academic fields.[39] Science and political administration advanced during the Gupta era.Wikipedia:Citation neededWikipedia:Please clarify Trade ties made the region an important cultural center and set the region up as a base that would influence nearby kingdoms and regions in Burma, Sri Lanka, and both maritime and mainland Southeast Asia.

The Guptas performed Vedic sacrifices to legitimize their rule, but they also patronized Buddhism, which continued to provide an alternative to Brahmanical orthodoxy.Wikipedia:Citation needed The military exploits of the first three rulers - Chandragupta I (ca. 319–335), Samudragupta (ca. 335–376), and Chandragupta II (ca. 376–415) —brought much of India under their leadership.[40] They successfully resisted the North-Western Kingdoms until the arrival of the Hunas who established themselves in Afghanistan by the first half of the 5th century, with their capital at Bamiyan. Nevertheless, much of the Deccan and southern India were largely unaffected by this state of flux in the north.Wikipedia:Citation needed

The Vakatakas

The **Vakataka Empire** was the contemporaries of the Gupta Empire and the successor state of the Satavahanas they formed the southern boundaries of the north and ruled over today's modern-day states of Madhya Pradesh and Maharashtra during the 3rd and 5th centuries. The rock-cut Buddhist viharas and chaityas of Ajanta Caves (a UNESCO World Heritage Site), built under the patronage of the Vakataka rulers. They were eventually overrun by the Chalukyas.

Figure 6: *The rock-cut Buddhist viharas and chaityas of Ajanta Caves, built under the patronage of the Vakataka rulers.*

The Harsha Vardhana

After the collapse of the Gupta Empire, the gangetic plains fractured into numerous small nations. Harsha of Kannauj was able to briefly bind them together under his rulership as the Empire of Harsha. Only a defeat at the hands of the Chalukyas (Pulakeshin II) prevented him from expanding his reign south of the Narmada River. This unity did not last long beyond his reign and his empire fractured soon after his death in 647 AD.

The Gurjars

From 550 to 1018 AD, the **Gurjars** played a great part in history of Northern India nearly for 500 years.[41] Present day Rajasthan was under the rule of Gurjars for centuries with capital at Bhilmal (Bhinmal or Srimal), situated nearly 50 miles to the north west of Mount Abu. The Gurjars of Bhilmal conquered Kannuaj on the Ganges at the beginning of the 9th century and transferred their capital to Kannuaj and founded an empire which at its peak was bounded on the east by Bihar, on the west by the *lost river*, the Hakra, and the Arabian Sea, on the North By the Himalaya and Sutlaj, and on the South by the Jumna and Narmada. The region round Broach, which was offshoot of this kingdom, was also ruled by the Gurjaras of Nandipuri (or Nadol).

The Vishnukundinas

The **Vishnukundina Empire** was an Indian dynasty that ruled over the Deccan, Odisha and parts of South India during the 5th and 6th centuries carving land out from the Vakataka Empire. The Vishnukundin reign came to an end with the conquest of the eastern Deccan by the Chalukya, Pulakeshin II. Pulakeshin appointed his brother Kubja Vishnuvardhana as Viceroy to rule over the conquered lands. Eventually Vishnuvardhana declared his independence and started the Eastern Chalukya dynasty.

The Maitrakas

The **Maitraka Empire** ruled Gujarat in western India from the c. 475 to 767 CE. The founder of the dynasty, *Senapati* (general) Bhatarka, was a military governor of Saurashtra peninsula under Gupta Empire, who had established himself as the independent ruler of Gujarat approximately in the last quarter of the 5th century. The first two Maitraka rulers Bhatarka and Dharasena I used only the title of *Senapati* (general). The third ruler Dronasimha declared himself as the *Maharaja*.[42] King Guhasena stopped using the term *Paramabhattaraka Padanudhyata* along his name like his predecessors, which denotes the cessation of displaying of the nominal allegiance to the Gupta overlords. He was succeeded by his son Dharasena II, who used the title of *Mahadhiraja*. His son, the next ruler Siladitya I, Dharmaditya was described by Hiuen Tsang as a "monarch of great administrative ability and of rare kindness and compassion". Siladitya I was succeeded by his younger brother Kharagraha I.[43] Virdi copperplate grant (616 CE) of Kharagraha I proves that his territories included Ujjain.

The Gurjara Pratiharas

The **Gurjara Pratihara Empire** (Hindi: गुर्जर प्रतिहार) formed an Indian dynasty that ruled much of Northern India from the 6th to the 11th centuries. At its peak of prosperity and power (c. 836–910 CE), it rivaled the Gupta Empire in the extent of its territory.[44]

Pointing out the importance of the Gurjara Pratihara empire in the history of India Dr. R. C. Majumdar has observed, "the *Gurjara Pratihara Empire* which continued in full glory for nearly a century, was the last great empire in Northern India before the Muslim conquest." This honour is accorded to the empire of Harsha by many historians of repute but without any real justification, for the Pratihara empire was probably larger, certainly not less in extent rivalled the Gupta Empire and brought political unity and its attendant blessings upon a large part of Northern India. But its chief credit lies in its succecessful resistance to the foreign invasions from the west, from the days of Junaid. This was frankly recognised by the Arab writers themselves.

Historians of India, since the days of Eliphinstone, has wondered at slow progress of Muslim invaders in India compared to their rapid advance in other parts of the world. Arguments of doubtful validity have often been put forward to explain this unique phenomenon. Now there can be little doubt that it was the power of the Gurjara Pratihara army that effectively barred the progress of the Muslims beyond the confines of Sindh, their first conquest for nearly three hundred years. In the light of later events this might be regarded as the "chief contribution of the Gurjara Pratiharas to the history of India".

The Rajputs

The **Rajput** were a Hindu clan who rose to power across a region stretching from the gangaetic plains to the Afghan mountains, and refer to the various dynasties of the many kingdoms in the region in the wake of the collapse of the Sassanid Empire and Gupta Empire and marks the transition of Buddhist ruling dynasties to Hindu ruling dynasties.

Katoch Dynasty

The **Katoch** were a Hindu Rajput clan of the Chandravanshi lineage; with recent research suggests that Katoch may be one of the oldest royal dynasty in the world.[45]

The Chauhans

The **Chauhan dynasty** flourished from the 8th to 12th centuries CE. It was one of the three main Rajput dynasties of that era, the others being Pratiharas and Paramaras. Chauhan dynasties established themselves in several places in North India and in the state of Gujarat in Western India. They were also prominent at Sirohi in the southwest of Rajputana, and at Bundi and Kota in the east. Inscriptions also associate them with Sambhar, the salt lake area in the Amber (later Jaipur) district (the Sakhambari branch remained near lake Sambhar and married into the ruling Gurjara–Pratihara, who then ruled an empire in Northern India). Chauhans adopted a political policy that saw them indulge largely in campaigns against the Chalukyas and the invading Muslim hordes. In the 11th century, they founded the city of Ajayameru (Ajmer) in the southern part of their kingdom, and in the 12th century, the Chauhans captured Dhilika (the ancient name of Delhi) from the Tomaras and annexed some of their territory along the Yamuna River.

The **Chauhan Kingdom** became the leading state in Northern India under King Prithviraj III (1165–1192 CE), also known as **Prithvi Raj Chauhan** or

Middle kingdoms of India

Figure 7: *Statue of Prithvi Raj Chauhan at Ajmer*

Rai Pithora. Prithviraj III has become famous in folk tales and historical literature as the Chauhan king of Delhi who resisted and repelled the invasion by Mohammed of Ghor at the first Battle of Tarain in 1191. Armies from other Rajput kingdoms, including Mewar, assisted him. The Chauhan kingdom collapsed after Prithviraj and his armies fled[46,47] from Mohammed of Ghor in 1192 at the Second Battle of Tarain.

The Kachwaha

The **Kachwaha** originated as tributaries of the preceding powers of the region. Some scholars point out that it was only following the downfall, in the 8th-10th century, of Kannauj (the regional seat-of-power, following the break-up of Harsha's empire), that the Kacchapaghata state emerged as a principal power in the Chambal valley of present-day Madhya Pradesh.[48]

The Paramaras

The **Paramara dynasty** was an early medieval Indian dynasty who ruled over Malwa region in central India. This dynasty was founded by Upendra in c. 800 CE. The most significant ruler of this dynasty was Bhoja I who was a philosopher king and polymath. The seat of the Paramara kingdom was *Dhara Nagari* (the present day Dhar city in Madhya Pradesh state).[49]

Figure 8: *Modhera Sun Temple built by the Chaulukyas.*

Chalukyas

The **Chaulukyas** (also called Solankis) in vernacular literature) were Hindu. In Gujarat, Anhilwara (modern Siddhpur Patan) served as their capital. Gujarat was a major center of Indian Ocean trade, and Anhilwara was one of the largest cities in India, with population estimated at 100,000 in the year 1000. The Chaulukyas were patrons of the great seaside temple of Shiva at Somnath Patan in Kathiawar; Bhima Dev helped rebuild the temple after it was sacked by Mahmud of Ghazni in 1026. His son, Karna, conquered the Bhil king Ashapall or Ashaval, and after his victory established a city named Karnavati on the banks of the Sabarmati River, at the site of modern Ahmedabad.

Tomaras of Delhi

During 9th-12th century, the Tomaras of Delhi ruled parts of the present-day Delhi and Haryana.[50] Much of the information about this dynasty comes from bardic legends of little historical value, and therefore, the reconstruction of their history is difficult.[51] According to the bardic tradition, the dynasty's founder Anangpal Tuar (that is Anangapala I Tomara) founded Delhi in 736 CE.[52] However, the authenticity of this claim is doubtful.[51] The bardic legends also state that the last Tomara king (also named Anangapal) passed on the throne of Delhi to his maternal grandson Prithviraj Chauhan. This claim is

Figure 9: *Buddha and Bodhisattvas, 11th century, Pala Empire*

also inaccurate: historical evidence shows that Prithviraj inherited Delhi from his father Someshvara.[51] According to the Bijolia inscription of Someshvara, his brother Vigraharaja IV had captured Dhillika (Delhi) and Ashika (Hansi); he probably defeated a Tomara ruler.[53]

The Pratihars

Pratihars ruled from Mandore, near present day Jodhpur, they held the title of Rana before being defeated by Guhilots of Chittore.

The Palas

Pala Empire was a Buddhist dynasty that ruled from the north-eastern region of the Indian subcontinent. The name *Pala* (Modern Bengali: পাল *pal*) means *protector* and was used as an ending to the names of all Pala monarchs. The Palas were followers of the Mahayana and Tantric schools of Buddhism. Gopala was the first ruler from the dynasty. He came to power in 750 CE in Gaur by a democratic election. This event is recognized as one of the first democratic elections in South Asia since the time of the Mahā Janapadas. He reigned from 750-770 CE and consolidated his position by extending his control over all of Bengal. The Buddhist dynasty lasted for four centuries (750-1120 CE) and ushered in a period of stability and prosperity in Bengal. They created many temples and works of art as well as supported the Universities of Nalanda and Vikramashila. Somapura Mahavihara built by Dharmapala is the greatest Buddhist Vihara in the Indian Subcontinent.

The empire reached its peak under Dharmapala and Devapala. Dharmapala extended the empire into the northern parts of the Indian Subcontinent. This triggered once again the power struggle for the control of the subcontinent. Devapala, successor of Dharmapala, expanded the empire to cover much of South Asia and beyond. His empire stretched from Assam and Utkala in the east, Kamboja (modern-day Afghanistan) in the north-west and Deccan in the south. According to Pala copperplate inscription Devapala exterminated the Utkalas, conquered the Pragjyotisha (Assam), shattered the pride of the Huna, and humbled the lords of Pratiharas, Gurjara and the Dravidas.

The death of Devapala ended the period of ascendancy of the Pala Empire and several independent dynasties and kingdoms emerged during this time. However, Mahipala I rejuvenated the reign of the Palas. He recovered control over all of Bengal and expanded the empire. He survived the invasions of Rajendra Chola and the Chalukyas. After Mahipala I the Pala dynasty again saw its decline until Ramapala, the last great ruler of the dynasty, managed to retrieve the position of the dynasty to some extent. He crushed the Varendra rebellion and extended his empire farther to Kamarupa, Odisha and Northern India.

The Pala Empire can be considered as the golden era of Bengal. Palas were responsible for the introduction of Mahayana Buddhism in Tibet, Bhutan and Myanmar. The Palas had extensive trade as well as influence in south-east Asia. This can be seen in the sculptures and architectural style of the Sailendra Empire (present-day Malaya, Java, Sumatra).

The Candras

The **Candra Dynasty** who ruled over eastern Bengal and were contemporaries of the Palas.

The Eastern Gangas

The **Eastern Ganga dynasty** rulers reigned over Kalinga which consisted of the parts of the modern-day Indian states of Odisha, West Bengal, Jharkhand, Chhattisgarh, Madhya Pradesh and Andhra Pradesh from the 11th century to the early 15th century.[54] Their capital was known by the name Kalinganagar, which is the modern Srimukhalingam in Srikakulam District of Andhra Pradesh bordering Odisha. Today they are most remembered as the builders of the Konark Sun Temple a World Heritage site at Konark, Odisha. It was

Middle kingdoms of India

Figure 10: *Konark Sun Temple at Konark, Odisha, built by King Narasimhadeva I (1236–1264 AD) also a World Heritage site.*

built by King Narasimhadeva I (1238–1264 CE). During their reign (1078–1434 CE) a new style of temple architecture came into being, commonly called as Indo-Aryan architecture. This dynasty was founded by King Anantavarma Chodaganga Deva (1078–1147 CE). He was a religious person and a patron of art and literature. He is credited for having built the famous Jagannath Temple of Puri in Odisha.

King Anantavarman Chodagangadeva was succeeded by a long line of illustrious rulers such as Narasimhadeva I (1238–1264 CE). The rulers of Eastern Ganga dynasty not only defended their kingdom from the constant attacks of the Muslim rulers from both northern and southern India but were perhaps one of the few empires to have successfully invaded and defeated their Muslim adversaries. The Eastern Ganga King Narasimha Deva I invaded the Muslim kingdom of Bengal and handed a heavy defeat to the Sultan. This ensured that Sultanate never encroached upon the domains of the Ganga Emperors for nearly a century. His military exploits still survive today as folklore in Odisha. This kingdom prospered through trade and commerce and the wealth was mostly used in the construction of temples. The rule of the dynasty came to end under the reign of King Bhanudeva IV (1414–1434 CE), in the early 15th century.

The Senas

The Palas were followed by the Sena dynasty who brought Bengal under one ruler during the 12th century. Vijay Sen the second ruler of this dynasty defeated the last Pala emperor Madanapala and established his reign. Ballal Sena introduced Kulīna System in Bengal and made Nabadwip the capital. The fourth king of this dynasty Lakshman Sen expanded the empire beyond Bengal to Bihar, Assam, northern Odisha and probably to Varanasi. Lakshman was later defeated by the Muslims and fled to eastern Bengal where he ruled few more years. The Sena dynasty brought a revival of Hinduism and cultivated Sanskrit literature in India.

The Varmans

The **Varman Dynasty** (not to be confused with the Varman dynasty of Kamarupa) ruled over eastern Bengal and were contemporaries of the Senas.

The Northeast

Kamarupa

The **Kāmarūpa**, also called **Pragjyotisha**, was one of the historical kingdoms of Assam alongside Davaka,[55] that existed from 350 to 1140 CE. Ruled by three dynasties from their capitals in present-day Guwahati, North Guwahati and Tezpur, it at its height covered the entire Brahmaputra Valley, North Bengal, Bhutan and parts of Bangladesh, and at times portions of West Bengal and Bihar.

The Varmans

The **Varman dynasty** (350-650 CE), the first historical rulers of Kamarupa; was established by Pushyavarman, a contemporary of Samudragupta.[56,57] This dynasty became vassals of the Gupta Empire, but as the power of the Guptas waned, Mahendravarman (470-494 CE) performed two horse sacrifices and threw off the imperial yoke.[58] The first of the three Kamarupa dynasties, the Varmans were followed by the Mlechchha and then the Pala dynasties.

The Mlechchhas

The **Mlechchha dynasty** succeeded the Varman dynasty and ruled to the end of the 10th century. They ruled from their capital in the vicinity of the Harrupeshwara (Tezpur). The rulers were aboriginals, with lineage from Narakasura. According to historical records, there were ten rulers in this dynasty. The Mlechchha dynasty in Kamarupa was followed by the Pala kings.

Figure 11:
9th-10th century lion sculpture representing powerful Kamarupa-Palas, Madan Kamdev

The Palas

The **Pala dynasty** of Kamarupa succeeded the Mlechchha dynasty, ruled from its capital at Durjaya (North Gauhati). Dynasty reigned till the end of the 12th century.

Brahma Pala (900-920 CE), was founder Pala dynasty (900–1100 CE) of Kamarupa. Dynasty ruled from its capital Durjaya, modern-day North Guwahati. The greatest of the Pala kings, Dharma Pala had his capital at Kamarupa Nagara, now identified with North Guwahati. Ratna Pala was another notable sovereign of this line. Records of his land-grants have been found at Bargaon and Sualkuchi, while a similar relic of Indra Pala, has been discovered at Guwahati. Pala dynasty come to end with Jaya Pala (1075-1100 CE).

The Twipra

The **Twipra Kingdom** ruled ancient Tripura. Kingdom was established around the confluence of the Brahmaputra river with the Meghna and Surma rivers in today's Central Bangladesh area. The capital was called Khorongma and was along the Meghna river in the Sylhet Division of present-day Bangladesh.

The Deccan plateau and South

In the first half of the millennium the South saw various smalled kingdoms rise and fall mostly independent to the turmoil in the Gangetic plains and the spread of the Buddhism and Jainism to the southern tip of India. During the second half of the millennium after the fall of the Gupta Empire we see a gradual shift of the balance of power both military and cultural from the northern states to the rise of large southern states.

In fact, from the mid-seventh to the mid-13th centuries, regionalism was the dominant theme of political or dynastic history of the Indian subcontinent. Three features commonly characterize the sociopolitical realities of this period.

- First, the spread of Brahmanical religions was a two-way process of Sanskritization of local cults and localization of Brahmanical social order.
- Second was the ascendancy of the Brahman priestly and landowning groups that later dominated regional institutions and political developments.
- Third, because of the seesawing of numerous dynasties that had a remarkable ability to survive perennial military attacks, regional kingdoms faced frequent defeats but seldom total annihilation.

Peninsular India was involved in an 8th-century tripartite power struggle among the Chalukyas (556–757 CE), the Pallavas (300–888 CE) of Kanchipuram, and the Pandyas. The Chalukya rulers were overthrown by their subordinates, the Rashtrakutas (753-973 CE). Although both the Pallava and Pandya kingdoms were enemies, the real struggle for political domination was between the Pallava and Chalukya realms.

The emergence of the Rashtrakutas heralded a new era in the history of South India. The idiom of a Pan-Indian empire had moved to south. South Indian kingdoms had hitherto ruled areas only up to and south of the Narmada River. It was the Rashtrakutas who first forged north to the Gangetic plains and successfully contested their might against the Palas of Bengal and the Rajput Prathiharas of Gujarat.

Despite interregional conflicts, local autonomy was preserved to a far greater degree in the south where it had prevailed for centuries. The absence of a highly centralized government was associated with a corresponding local autonomy in the administration of villages and districts. Extensive and well-documented overland and maritime trade flourished with the Arabs on the west coast and with Southeast Asia. Trade facilitated cultural diffusion in Southeast Asia, where local elites selectively but willingly adopted Indian art, architecture, literature, and social customs.

The interdynastic rivalry and seasonal raids into each other's territory notwithstanding, the rulers in the Deccan and South India patronized all three religions - Buddhism, Hinduism, and Jainism. The religions vied with each other for royal favor, expressed in land grants but more importantly in the creation of monumental temples, which remain architectural wonders. The cave temples of Elephanta Island (near Mumbai or Bombay, as it was known formerly), Ajanta, and Ellora (in Maharashtra), and structural temples of Pattadakal, Aihole, Badami in Karnataka and Mahaballipuram and Kanchipuram in Tamil Nadu are enduring legacies of otherwise warring regional rulers.

By the mid-7th century, Buddhism and Jainism began to decline as sectarian Hindu devotional cults of Shiva and Vishnu vigorously competed for popular support.

Although Sanskrit was the language of learning and theology in South India, as it was in the north, the growth of the bhakti (devotional) movements enhanced the crystallization of vernacular literature in Dravidian languages: Kannada and Tamil; they often borrowed themes and vocabulary from Sanskrit but preserved much local cultural lore. Examples of Tamil literature include two major poems, Cilappatikaram (The Jewelled Anklet) and Manimekalai (The Jewelled Belt); the body of devotional literature of Shaivism and Vaishnavism—Hindu devotional movements; and the reworking of the Ramayana by Kamban in the 12th century. A nationwide cultural synthesis had taken place with a minimum of common characteristics in the various regions of South Asia, but the process of cultural infusion and assimilation would continue to shape and influence India's history through the centuries.

The Sangam Era Kingdoms

Farther south were three ancient Tamil states — Chera (on the west), Chola (on the east), and Pandya (in the south). They were involved in internecine warfare seeking regional supremacy. They are mentioned in Greek and Ashokan sources as important Indian kingdoms beyond the Mauryan Empire. A corpus of ancient Tamil literature, known as Sangam (academy) works, provides much useful information about life in these kingdoms in the era 300 BCE to 200 CE.

Dravidian social order was based on different ecoregions rather than on the Aryan varna paradigm, although the Brahmans had a high status at a very early stage. Segments of society were characterized by matriarchy and matrilineal succession—which survived well into the 19th century—cross-cousin marriage, and strong regional identity. Tribal chieftains emerged as "kings" just as people moved from pastoralism toward agriculture sustained by irrigation based on rivers by small-scale water tanks (as man-made ponds are called in India) and wells, as well as maritime trade with Rome and Southeast Asia.

Discoveries of Roman gold coins in various sites attest to extensive South Indian links with the outside world. As with Pataliputra in the northeast and Taxila in the northwest (in modern Pakistan), the city of Madurai, the capital of the Pandyan Kingdom (in modern Tamil Nadu), was the center of intellectual and literary activity. Poets and bards assembled there under royal patronage at successive concourses to composed anthologies of poems and expositions on Tamil grammar. By the end of the 1st century BCE, South Asia was crisscrossed by overland trade routes, which facilitated the movements of Buddhist and Jain missionaries and other travelers and opened the area to a synthesis of many cultures.

The Cheras

From early pre-historic times, Tamil Nadu was the home of the four Tamil states of the Chera, Chola, Pandya and Pallavas. The oldest extant literature, dated between 300 BCE and 600 CE mentions the exploits of the kings and the princes, and of the poets who extolled them. Cherans, who spoke Tamil language ruled from the capital of Karur in the west and traded extensively with West Asian kingdoms.

An unknown dynasty called Kalabhras invaded and displaced the three Tamil kingdoms between the 4th and the 7th centuries. This is referred to as the Dark Age in Tamil history. They were eventually expelled by the Pallavas and the Pandyas.

The Kalabhras

Little of their origins or the time during which they ruled is known beyond that they ruled over the entirety of the southern tip of India during the 3rd to the 6th century, overcoming the Sangam era kingdoms. The appear to be patrons of Jainism and Buddhism as the only source of information on them is the scattered mentions in the many Buddhist and Jain literature of the time. They were contemporaries of the Kadambas and the Western Ganga Dynasty. They were overcome by the rise of the Pallavas and the resurgence of the Pandyan Kingdom.

The Kadambas

The **Kadamba Dynasty** (Kannada: ಕದಂಬರು) (345–525 CE) was an ancient royal family of Karnataka that ruled from Banavasi in present-day Uttara Kannada district. The dynasty later continued to rule as a feudatory of larger Kannada empires, the Chalukya and the Rashtrakuta empires for over five hundred years during which time they branched into Goa and Hanagal. At the peak of their power under King Kakushtavarma, they ruled large parts of Karnataka.

Figure 12: *Kadamba tower at Doddagaddavalli*

During the pre-Kadamba era the ruling families that controlled Karnataka, the Mauryas, Satavahanas and Chutus were not natives of the region and the nucleus of power resided outside present day Karnataka. The Kadambas were the first indigenous dynasty to use Kannada, the language of the soil at an administrative level. In the history of Karnataka, this era serves as a broad based historical starting point in the study of the development of region as an enduring geo-political entity and Kannada as an important regional language.

The dynasty was founded by Mayurasharma in 345 which at times showed the potential of developing into imperial proportions, an indication to which is provided by the titles and epithets assumed by its rulers. One of his successors, Kakusthavarma was a powerful ruler and even the kings of imperial Gupta Dynasty of northern India cultivated marital relationships with his family, giving a fair indication of the sovereign nature of their kingdom. Tiring of the endless battles and bloodshed, one of the later descendants, King Shivakoti adopted Jainism. The Kadambas were contemporaries of the Western Ganga Dynasty of Talakad and together they formed the earliest native kingdoms to rule the land with absolute autonomy.

Figure 13: *Statue of Bahubali as Gommateshvara built by the Western Ganga is one of the largest monolithic statues in the world.*

The Western Gangas

The **Western Ganga Dynasty** (350–1000 CE) (Kannada: ಪಶ್ಚಿಮ ಗಂಗ ಸಂಸ್ಥಾನ) was an important ruling dynasty of ancient Karnataka in India. They are known as **Western Gangas** to distinguish them from the Eastern Gangas, who in later centuries ruled over modern Odisha. The general belief is the Western Gangas began their rule during a time when multiple native clans asserted their freedom due to the weakening of the Pallava dynasty of South India, a geo-political event sometimes attributed to the southern conquests of Samudragupta. The Western Ganga sovereignty lasted from about 350 to 550 CE, initially ruling from Kolar and later moving their capital to Talakad on the banks of the Kaveri in modern Mysore district.

After the rise of the imperial Chalukya dynasty of Badami, the Gangas accepted Chalukya overlordship and fought for the cause of their overlords against the Pallavas of Kanchipuram. The Chalukyas were replaced by the Rashtrakutas of Manyakheta in 753 CE as the dominant power in the Deccan. After a century of struggle for autonomy, the Western Gangas finally accepted Rashtrakuta overlordship and successfully fought alongside them against their foes, the Chola dynasty of Tanjavur. In the late 10th century, north of Tungabhadra river, the Rashtrakutas were replaced by the emerging Western Chalukya

Empire and the Chola Dynasty saw renewed power south of the Kaveri. The defeat of the Western Gangas by Cholas around 1000 resulted in the end of Ganga influence over the region.

Though territorially a small kingdom, the Western Ganga contribution to polity, culture and literature of the modern south Karnataka region is considered important. The Western Ganga kings showed benevolent tolerance to all faiths but are most famous for their patronage towards Jainism resulting in the construction of monuments in places such as Shravanabelagola and Kambadahalli. The kings of this dynasty encouraged the fine arts due to which literature in Kannada and Sanskrit flourished. Chavundaraya's writing, *Chavundaraya Purana* of 978 CE, is an important work in Kannada prose. Many classics were written on subjects ranging from religious topics to elephant management.

The Badami Chalukyas

The **Chalukya Empire**, natives of the Aihole and Badami region in Karnataka, were at first a feudatory of the Kadambas.[59,60,61,62,63] They encouraged the use of Kannada in addition to the Sanskrit language in their administration.[64,65] In the middle of the 6th century the Chalukyas came into their own when Pulakeshin I made the hill fortress in Badami his center of power.[66] During the rule of Pulakeshin II a south Indian empire sent expeditions to the north past the Tapti River and Narmada River for the first time and successfully defied Harshavardhana, the King of Northern India (*Uttarapatheswara*). The Aihole inscription of Pulakeshin II, written in classical Sanskrit language and old Kannada script dated 634,[67,68] proclaims his victories against the Kingdoms of Kadambas, Western Gangas, Alupas of South Canara, Mauryas of Puri, Kingdom of Kosala, Malwa, Lata and Gurjaras of southern Rajasthan. The inscription describes how King Harsha of Kannauj lost his *Harsha* (joyful disposition) on seeing a large number of his war elephants die in battle against Pulakeshin II.[69,70,71,72,73]

These victories earned him the title *Dakshinapatha Prithviswamy* (lord of the south). Pulakeshin II continued his conquests in the east where he conquered all kingdoms in his way and reached the Bay of Bengal in present-day Odisha. A Chalukya viceroyalty was set up in Gujarat and Vengi (coastal Andhra) and princes from the Badami family were dispatched to rule them. Having subdued the Pallavas of Kanchipuram, he accepted tributes from the Pandyas of Madurai, Chola dynasty and Cheras of the Kerala region. Pulakeshin II thus became the master of India, south of the Narmada River.[74] Pulakeshin II is widely regarded as one of the great kings in Indian history.[75,76] Hiuen-Tsiang, a Chinese traveller visited the court of Pulakeshin II at this time and Persian emperor Khosrau II exchanged ambassadors.[77] However, the continuous wars with Pallavas took a turn for the worse in 642 when the Pallava

Figure 14: *Badami Cave Temples No 3. (Vishnu)*

king Narasimhavarman I avenged his father's defeat, conquered and plundered the capital of Pulakeshin II who may have died in battle.[78] A century later, Chalukya Vikramaditya II marched victoriously into Kanchipuram, the Pallava capital and occupied it on three occasions, the third time under the leadership of his son and crown prince Kirtivarman II. He thus avenged the earlier humiliation of the Chalukyas by the Pallavas and engraved a Kannada inscription on the victory pillar at the Kailasanatha Temple.[79,80,81,82] He later overran the other traditional kingdoms of Tamil country, the Pandyas, Cholas and Keralas in addition to subduing a Kalabhra ruler.[83]

The Kappe Arabhatta record from this period (700) in *tripadi* (three line) metre is considered the earliest available record in Kannada poetics. The most enduring legacy of the Chalukya dynasty is the architecture and art that they left behind.[84] More than one hundred and fifty monuments attributed to them, built between 450 and 700, have survived in the Malaprabha basin in Karnataka.[85] The constructions are centred in a relatively small area within the Chalukyan heartland. The structural temples at Pattadakal, a UNESCO World Heritage Site, the cave temples of Badami, the temples at Mahakuta and early experiments in temple building at Aihole are their most celebrated monuments. Two of the famous paintings at Ajanta cave no. 1, "The Temptation of the Buddha" and "The Persian Embassy" are also credited to them.[86] Further,

Figure 15: *Shore Temple in Mamallapuram built by the Pallavas. (c. eighth century CE)*

they influenced the architecture in far off places like Gujarat and Vengi as evidenced in the Nava Brahma temples at Alampur.[87]

The Pallavas

The 7th century Tamil Nadu saw the rise of the Pallavas under Mahendravarman I and his son *Mamalla* Narasimhavarman I. The Pallavas were not a recognised political power before the 2nd century.[88] It has been widely accepted by scholars that they were originally executive officers under the Satavahana Empire.[89] After the fall of the Satavahanas, they began to get control over parts of Andhra and the Tamil country. Later they had marital ties with the Vishnukundina who ruled over the Deccan. It was around 550 AD under King Simhavishnu that the Pallavas emerged into prominence. They subjugated the Cholas and reigned as far south as the Kaveri River. Pallavas ruled a large portion of South India with Kanchipuram as their capital. Dravidian architecture reached its peak during the Pallava rule.Wikipedia:Citation needed Narasimhavarman II built the Shore Temple which is a UNESCO World Heritage Site. Many sources describe Bodhidharma, the founder of the Zen school of Buddhism in China, as a prince of the Pallava dynasty.[90]

The Eastern Chalukyas

Eastern Chalukyas were a South Indian dynasty whose kingdom was located in the present day Andhra Pradesh. Their capital was Vengi and their dynasty lasted for around 500 years from the 7th century until c. 1130 CE when the Vengi kingdom merged with the Chola empire. The Vengi kingdom was continued to be ruled by Eastern Chalukyan kings under the protection of the Chola empire until 1189 CE, when the kingdom succumbed to the Hoysalas and the Yadavas. They had their capital originally at Vengi now (Pedavegi, Chinavegi and Denduluru) near Eluru of the West Godavari district end later changed to Rajamahendravaram (Rajamundry).

Eastern Chalukyas were closely related to the Chalukyas of Vatapi (Badami). Throughout their history they were the cause of many wars between the more powerful Cholas and Western Chalukyas over the control of the strategic Vengi country. The five centuries of the Eastern Chalukya rule of Vengi saw not only the consolidation of this region into a unified whole, but also saw the efflorescence of Telugu culture, literature, poetry and art during the later half of their rule. It can be said to be the golden period of Andhra history.

The Pandyas

Pallavas were replaced by the Pandyas in the 8th century. Their capital Madurai was in the deep south away from the coast. They had extensive trade links with the Southeast Asian maritime empires of Srivijaya and their successors. As well as contacts, even diplomatic, reaching as far as the Roman Empire. During the 13th century of the Christian era Marco Polo mentioned it as the richest empire in existence.Wikipedia:Citation needed Temples like Meenakshi Amman Temple at Madurai and Nellaiappar Temple at Tirunelveli are the best examples of Pandyan Temple architecture.[91,92] The Pandyas excelled in both trade as well as literature and they controlled the pearl fisheries along the South Indian coast, between Sri Lanka and India, which produced some of the finest pearls in the known ancient world.

The Rashtrakutas

In the middle of the 8th century the Chalukya rule was ended by their feudatory, the Rashtrakuta family rulers of Berar (in present-day Amravati district of Maharashtra). Sensing an opportunity during a weak period in the Chalukya rule, Dantidurga trounced the great Chalukyan "Karnatabala" (power of Karnata).[93,94] Having overthrown the Chalukyas, the Rashtrakutas made Manyakheta their capital (modern Malkhed in Gulbarga district).[95,96] Although the origins of the early Rashtrakuta ruling families in central India and the Deccan in the 6th and 7th centuries is controversial, during the eighth

Middle kingdoms of India

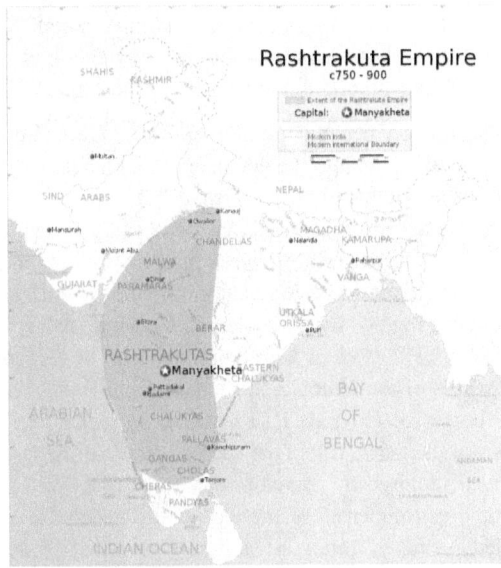

Figure 16: *Rashtrakuta Empire in 800 CE, 915 CE.*

Figure 17: *Kailash Temple in Ellora Caves*

through the 10th centuries they emphasised the importance of the Kannada language in conjunction with Sanskrit in their administration. Rashtrakuta inscriptions are in Kannada and Sanskrit only. They encouraged literature in both languages and thus literature flowered under their rule.[97,98,99,100]

The Rashtrakutas quickly became the most powerful Deccan empire, making their initial successful forays into the doab region of Ganges River and Jamuna River during the rule of Dhruva Dharavarsha.[101] The rule of his son Govinda III signaled a new era with Rashtrakuta victories against the Pala Dynasty of Bengal and Gurjara Pratihara of north western India resulting in the capture of Kannauj. The Rashtrakutas held Kannauj intermittently during a period of a tripartite struggle for the resources of the rich Gangetic plains.[102] Because of Govinda III's victories, historians have compared him to Alexander the Great and Pandava Arjuna of the Hindu epic Mahabharata.[103] The Sanjan inscription states the horses of Govinda III drank the icy water of the Himalayan stream and his war elephants tasted the sacred waters of the Ganges River.[104] Amoghavarsha I, eulogised by contemporary Arab traveller Sulaiman as one among the four great emperors of the world, succeeded Govinda III to the throne and ruled during an important cultural period that produced landmark writings in Kannada and Sanskrit.[105,106] The benevolent development of Jain religion was a hallmark of his rule. Because of his religious temperament, his interest in the arts and literature and his peace-loving nature,[107] he has been compared to emperor Ashoka.[108] The rule of Indra III in the 10th century enhanced the Rashtrakuta position as an imperial power as they conquered and held Kannauj again.[109] Krishna III followed Indra III to the throne in 939. A patron of Kannada literature and a powerful warrior, his reign marked the submission of the Paramara of Ujjain in the north and Cholas in the south.[110]

An Arabic writing *Silsilatuttavarikh* (851) called the Rashtrakutas one among the four principle empires of the world.[111] *Kitab-ul-Masalik-ul-Mumalik* (912) called them the "greatest kings of India" and there were many other contemporaneous books written in their praise.[112] The Rashtrakuta empire at its peak spread from Cape Comorin in the south to Kannauj in the north and from Banaras in the east to Broach (Bharuch) in the west.[113] While the Rashtrakutas built many fine monuments in the Deccan, the most extensive and sumptuous of their work is the monolithic Kailasanatha temple at Ellora, the temple being a splendid achievement.[114] In Karnataka their most famous temples are the Kashivishvanatha temple and the Jain Narayana temple at Pattadakal. All of the monuments are designated UNESCO World Heritage Sites.

The Western Chalukyas

In the late 10th century, the Western Chalukyas, also known as the Kalyani Chalukyas or 'Later' Chalukyas rose to power by overthrowing the Rashtrakutas under whom they had been serving as feudatories. Manyakheta was their capital early on before they moved it to Kalyani (modern Basavakalyan). Whether the kings of this empire belonged to the same family line as their namesakes, the Badami Chalukyas is still debated.[115,116] Whatever the Western Chalukya origins, Kannada remained their language of administration and the Kannada and Sanskrit literature of their time was prolific.[117,118,119,120] Tailapa II, a feudatory ruler from Tardavadi (modern Bijapur district), re-established the Chalukya rule by defeating the Rashtrakutas during the reign of Karka II. He timed his rebellion to coincide with the confusion caused by the invading Paramara of Central India to the Rashtrakutas capital in 973.[121,122,123] This era produced prolonged warfare with the Chola dynasty of Tamilakam for control of the resources of the Godavari River–Krishna River doab region in Vengi. Someshvara I, a brave Chalukyan king, successfully curtailed the growth of the Chola Empire to the south of the Tungabhadra River region despite suffering some defeats[124,125] while maintaining control over his feudatories in the Konkan, Gujarat, Malwa and Kalinga regions.[126] For approximately 100 years, beginning in the early 11th century, the Cholas occupied large areas of South Karnataka region (Gangavadi).[127]

In 1076 CE, the ascent of the most famous king of this Chalukya family, Vikramaditya VI, changed the balance of power in favour of the Chalukyas.[128] His fifty-year reign was an important period in Karnataka's history and is referred to as the "Chalukya Vikrama era".[129] His victories over the Cholas in the late 11th and early 12th centuries put an end to the Chola influence in the Vengi region permanently. Some of the well known contemporaneous feudatory families of the Deccan under Chalukya control were the Hoysalas, the Seuna Yadavas of Devagiri, the Kakatiya dynasty and the Southern Kalachuri.[130] At their peak, the Western Chalukyas ruled a vast empire stretching from the Narmada River in the north to the Kaveri River in the south. Vikramaditya VI is considered one of the most influential kings of Indian history.[131,132] Important architectural works were created by these Chalukyas, especially in the Tungabhadra river valley, that served as a conceptual link between the building idioms of the early Badami Chalukyas and the later Hoysalas.[133,134] With the weakening of the Chalukyas in the decades following the death of Vikramaditya VI in 1126, the feudatories of the Chalukyas gained their independence.

The Kalachuris of Karnataka, whose ancestors were immigrants into the southern deccan from central India, had ruled as a feudatory from Mangalavada (modern Mangalavedhe in Maharashtra).[135] Bijjala II, the most powerful ruler of this dynasty, was a commander (*mahamandaleswar*) during the reign of

Figure 18: *Gadag style pillars, Western Chalukya art.*

Chalukya Vikramaditya VI.[136] Seizing an opportune moment in the waning power of the Chalukyas, Bijjala II declared independence in 1157 and annexed their capital Kalyani.[137] His rule was cut short by his assassination in 1167 and the ensuing civil war caused by his sons fighting over the throne ended the dynasty as the last Chalukya scion regained control of Kalyani. This victory however, was short-lived as the Chalukyas were eventually driven out by the Seuna Yadavas.[138]

The Yadavas

The **Seuna**, *Sevuna* or **Yadava dynasty** (Marathi: देवगिरीचे यादव, Kannada: ಸೇವುಣರು) (c. 850–1334 CE) was an Indian dynasty, which at its peak ruled a kingdom stretching from the Tungabhadra to the Narmada rivers, including present-day Maharashtra, north Karnataka and parts of Madhya Pradesh, from its capital at Devagiri (present-day Daulatabad in Maharashtra). The Yadavas initially ruled as feudatories of the Western Chalukyas. Around the middle of the 12th century, they declared independence and established rule that reached its peak under Singhana II. The foundations of Marathi culture was laid by the Yadavas and the peculiarities of Maharashtra's social life developed during their rule.Wikipedia:Citation needed

Figure 19: *Sangamanatha temple at Kudalasangama, North Karnataka*

The Kakatiyas

The Kakatiya dynasty was a South Indian dynasty that ruled parts of what is now Telangana, India from 1083 to 1323 CE. They were one of the great Telugu kingdoms that lasted for centuries.

The Kalachuris

Kalachuri is this the name used by two kingdoms who had a succession of dynasties from the 10th-12th centuries, one ruling over areas in Central India (west Madhya Pradesh, Rajasthan) and were called Chedi or *Haihaya (Heyheya)* (northern branch) and the other southern Kalachuri who ruled over parts of Karnataka. They are disparately placed in time and space. Apart from the dynastic name and perhaps a belief in common ancestry, there is little in known sources to connect them.Wikipedia:Citation needed

The earliest known Kalachuri family (550–620 CE) ruled over northern Maharashtra, Malwa and western Deccan. Their capital was Mahismati situated in the Narmada river valley. There were three prominent members; Krishnaraja, Shankaragana and Buddharaja. They distributed coins and epigraphs around this area.[139]

Kalachuris of Kalyani or the southern Kalachuris (1130–1184 CE) at their peak ruled parts of the Deccan extending over regions of present-day North

Figure 20: *Shilabalika, Chennakeshava temple, Belur.*

Karnataka and parts of Maharashtra. This dynasty rose to power in the Deccan between 1156 and 1181 CE. They traced their origins to *Krishna* who was the conqueror of *Kalinjar* and Dahala in Madhya Pradesh. It is said that *Bijjala* a viceroy of this dynasty established the authority over Karnataka. He wrested power from the Chalukya king Taila III. Bijjala was succeeded by his sons Someshwara and Sangama but after 1181 CE, the Chalukyas gradually retrieved the territory. Their rule was a short and turbulent and yet very important from the socio-religious movement point of view; a new sect called the Lingayat or Virashaiva sect was founded during these times.

A unique and purely native form of Kannada literature-poetry called the *Vachanas* was also born during this time. The writers of *Vachanas* were called *Vachanakaras* (poets). Many other important works like Virupaksha Pandita's *Chennabasavapurana*, Dharani Pandita's *Bijjalarayacharite* and Chandrasagara Varni's *Bijjalarayapurana* were also written.

Kalachuris of Tripuri (Chedi) ruled in central India with its base at the ancient city of Tripuri (Tewar); it originated in the 8th century, expanded significantly in the 11th century, and declined in the 12th–13th centuries.

The Hoysalas

The Hoysalas had become a powerful force even during their rule from Belur in the 11th century as a feudatory of the Chalukyas (in the south Karnataka region).[140] In the early 12th century they successfully fought the Cholas in the south, convincingly defeating them in the battle of Talakad and moved their capital to nearby Halebidu.[141,142] Historians refer to the founders of the dynasty as natives of Malnad Karnataka, based on the numerous inscriptions calling them *Maleparolganda* or "Lord of the Male (hills) chiefs" (*Malepas*).[143,144,145,146,147] With the waning of the Western Chalukya power, the Hoysalas declared their independence in the late 12th century.

During this period of Hoysala control, distinctive Kannada literary metres such as *Ragale* (blank verse), *Sangatya* (meant to be sung to the accompaniment of a musical instrument), *Shatpadi* (seven line) etc. became widely accepted.[148,149,150] The Hoysalas expanded the Vesara architecture stemming from the Chalukyas,[151] culminating in the Hoysala architectural articulation and style as exemplified in the construction of the Chennakesava Temple at Belur and the Hoysaleswara temple at Halebidu.[152] Both these temples were built in commemoration of the victories of the Hoysala Vishnuvardhana against the Cholas in 1116.[153,154] Veera Ballala II, the most effective of the Hoysala rulers, defeated the aggressive Pandya when they invaded the Chola kingdom and assumed the titles "Establisher of the Chola Kingdom" (*Cholarajyapratishtacharya*), "Emperor of the south" (*Dakshina Chakravarthi*) and "Hoysala emperor" (*Hoysala Chakravarthi*).[155] The Hoysalas extended their foothold in areas known today as Tamil Nadu around 1225, making the city of Kannanur Kuppam near Srirangam a provincial capital. This gave them control over South Indian politics that began a period of Hoysala hegemony in the southern Deccan.[156,157]

In the early 13th century, with the Hoysala power remaining unchallenged, the first of the Muslim incursions into South India began. After over two decades of waging war against a foreign power, the Hoysala ruler at the time, Veera Ballala III, died in the battle of Madurai in 1343.[158] This resulted in the merger of the sovereign territories of the Hoysala empire with the areas administered by Harihara I, founder of the Vijayanagara Empire, located in the Tungabhadra region in present-day Karnataka. The new kingdom thrived for another two centuries with Vijayanagara as its capital.[159]

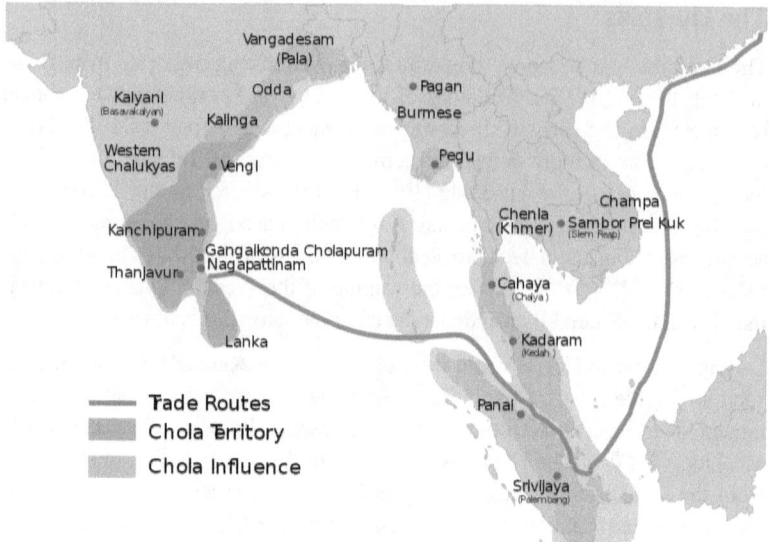

Figure 21: *Chola Empire under Rajendra Chola c. 1030 CE*

The Cholas

By the 9th century, under Rajaraja Chola and his son Rajendra Chola, the Cholas rose as a notable power in south Asia. The Chola Empire stretched as far as Bengal. At its peak, the empire spanned almost 3,600,000 km^2 (1,389,968 sq mi). Rajaraja Chola conquered all of peninsular South India and parts of the Sri Lanka. Rajendra Chola's navies went even further, occupying coasts from Burma (now Myanmar) to Vietnam, the Andaman and Nicobar Islands, Lakshadweep, Sumatra, Java, Malaya in South East Asia and Pegu islands. He defeated Mahipala, the king of the Bengal, and to commemorate his victory he built a new capital and named it Gangaikonda Cholapuram.Wikipedia:Citation needed

The Cholas excelled in building magnificent temples. Brihadeshwara Temple in Thanjavur is a classical example of the magnificent architecture of the Chola kingdom. Brihadshwara temple is an UNESCO Heritage Site under "Great Living Chola Temples."[160] Another example is the Chidambaram Temple in the heart of the temple town of Chidambaram.

References

Sources

<templatestyles src="Template:Refbegin/styles.css" />

Books

- Agarwala, V. S. (1954). *India as Known to Panini*.
- Barstow, A.E., *The Sikhs: An Ethnology*, Reprinted by B.R. Publishing Corporation, Delhi, India, 1985, first published in 1928.
- Alexander Cunningham (1888) *Coins of the Indo-Scythians, Sakas, and Kushans*, Reprint: Indological Book House, Varanasi, India, 1971.
- D. C. Ganguly (1981). R. S. Sharma, ed. *A Comprehensive History of India (A. D. 300-985)*[161]. 3, Part 1. Indian History Congress / Orient Longmans.
- Dilip Kumar Ganguly (1984). *History and Historians in Ancient India*[162]. Abhinav. ISBN 978-0-391-03250-7.
- Hill, John E. 2004. *The Peoples of the West from the Weilüe* 魏略 *by Yu Huan* 魚豢 *: A Third Century Chinese Account Composed between 239 and 265 CE*. Draft annotated English translation. Weilue: The Peoples of the West[163]
- Hill, John E. (2009) *Through the Jade Gate to Rome: A Study of the Silk Routes during the Later Han Dynasty, 1st to 2nd Centuries CE*. BookSurge, Charleston, South Carolina. ISBN 978-1-4392-2134-1.
- Latif, S.M., (1891) *History of the Panjab*, Reprinted by Progressive Books, Lahore, Pakistan, 1984.
- Chadurah, Haidar Malik (1991). *History of Kashmir*[164]. Bhavna Prakashan.
- Hasan, Mohibbul (1959). *Kashmir Under the Sultans*[165]. Aakar. ISBN 9788187879497.
- Sailendra Nath Sen (1999). *Ancient Indian History and Civilization*[166]. New Age. ISBN 9788122411980.
- Upinder Singh (2008). *A History of Ancient and Early Medieval India: From the Stone Age to the 12th Century*[167]. Pearson Education India. ISBN 978-81-317-1120-0.
- Bharatiya Vidya Bhavan (Bombay, Inde), Majumdar, R. C., Pusalker, A. D., & Majumdar, A. K. (1988). The history and culture of the Indian people: 3. (History and culture of the Indian people.) Bombay: Bharatiya Vidya Bhavan.

Website

- ⓐ This article incorporates public domain material from the Library of Congress Country Studies website http://lcweb2.loc.gov/frd/cs/[168]. - India[169]

Medieval India

Medieval India refers to a long period of the history of the Indian subcontinent between the "ancient period" and "modern period". Definitions of the period itself vary widely, and partly for this reason, many historians now prefer to avoid the term completely.[170]

One definition, used in the rest of this article, includes the period from the 8th century to the 16th century, essentially the same period as the Middle Ages of Europe. It may be divided into two periods: The 'early medieval period' which lasted from the 6th to the 13th century and the 'late medieval period' which lasted from the 13th to the 16th century, ending with the start of the Mughal Empire in 1526. The Mughal era, from the 16th century to the 18th century, is often referred to as the early modern period, but is sometimes also included in the 'late medieval' period.

An alternative definition, often seen in those more recent authors who still use the term at all, brings the start of the medieval period forward, either to about 1,000, or to the 12th century. The end may be pushed back to the 18th century, making the period in effect that between the start of Muslim domination (at least in northern India) and British India. Or the "early medieval" period is begun in the 8th century, ending with the 11th.[171]

The use of "medieval" at all as a term for periods in Indian history has often been objected to, and is probably becoming more rare (there is a similar discussion in terms of the history of China).[172] It is argued that neither the start nor the end of the period really mark fundamental changes in Indian history, comparable to the European equivalents.[173] Burton Stein still used the concept in his *A History of India* (1998, referring to the period from the Guptas to the Mughals), but most recent authors using it are Indian. Understandably, they often specify the period they cover within their titles.[174] The critic Peter Hardy argues that Muslim historiography on medieval India is often motivated by Islamic apologetics, which tries to justify "the life of medieval Muslims to the modern world".[175]

Early medieval period

The start of the period is typically taken to be the slow collapse of the Gupta Empire from about 480 to 550,[176] ending the "classical" period, as well as "ancient India",[177] although both these terms may be used for periods with widely different dates, especially in specialized fields such as the history of art or religion.[178] At least in northern India, there was no comparably large state until perhaps the Delhi Sultanate, or certainly the Mughal Empire,[179] but there were several different dynasties ruling large areas for long periods, as well as many other dynasties ruling smaller areas, often paying some form of tribute to larger states. John Keay puts the typical number of dynasties within the subcontinent at any one time at between 20 and 40,[180] not including local rajas.

- Rashtrakuta dynasty, was a Kannada Dynasty ruling large parts of the Indian subcontinent between the 6th and the 10th centuries and one who built World Heritage center Ellora, Maharashtra.
- Eastern Chalukyas, 7th to 12th centuries, a South Indian Kannada dynasty whose kingdom was located in the present-day Andhra Pradesh they were the descendants of Western Chalukyas.
- Pallava dynasty, rulers of Telugu and some Tamil areas from the 6th to 9th centuries.
- Pala Empire, the last major Buddhist rulers, from the 8th to 12th centuries in Bengal. Briefly controlled most of north India in the 9th century.
- Chola Empire, a South Indian empire which ruled from Tamil Nadu and extended to include South-east Asian territories at its height. From 9th century to 13th century.
- Empire of Harsha, a brief period of control of most of north India, from 601 to 647, under Harsha of the Vardhana dynasty.
- Western Chalukya Empire, ruled most of the western Deccan and some of South India, between the 10th and 12th centuries. Kannada-speaking, with capital at Badami.
- Kalachuri dynasty, ruled areas in Central India during 10th-12th centuries.
- Western Ganga dynasty, was an important ruling dynasty of ancient Karnataka, often under the overlordship of larger states, from about 350 to 1000 AD. The large monolithic Bahubali of Shravanabelagola was built during their rule.
- Eastern Ganga dynasty, was a royal dynasty ruling Odisha region who are descendants of Kannada Western Ganga Dynasty and Tamil Chola Empire. They have built famous Konark Sun Temple and Jagannath Temple, Puri.
- Hoysala Empire, a prominent South Indian Kannadiga empire that ruled most of the modern day state of Karnataka between the 10th and the 14th centuries. The capital of the Hoysalas was initially located at Belur but was later moved to Halebidu.
- Kakatiya Kingdom, a Telugu dynasty that ruled most of current day Andhra Pradesh, India from 1083 to 1323 CE.
- The Sena dynasty, was a Hindu dynasty that ruled from Bengal through the 11th and 12th centuries. The empire at its peak covered much of the north-eastern region of the Indian subcontinent. The rulers of the Sena Dynasty traced their origin to the south Indian region of Karnataka.

Late medieval era

- Delhi Sultanate, five short-lived dynasties, based in Delhi, from 1206 to 1526, when it fell to the Mughal Empire.
- Bengal Sultanate, 1352 to 1576, ruled over Bengal and much of Burma.
- Ahom Kingdom, 1228–1826, Brahmaputra valley in Assam, resisted the Mughals, eventually taken by the British.
- Reddy Kingdom, 1325 to 1448, in Andhra Pradesh.
- Seuna (Yadava) dynasty, 1190-1315, an old Kannada-Maratha dynasty, which at its peak ruled a kingdom stretching from the Tungabhadra to the Narmada rivers, including present-day Maharashtra, north Karnataka and parts of Madhya Pradesh, from its capital at Devagiri.
- Rajput States, were a group of Rajput Hindu states that ruled present-day Rajasthan, and at times much of Madhya Pradesh, Gujarat, Uttaranchal, Himachal Pradesh, Western Uttar Pradesh and Central Uttar Pradesh. Many Rajput kingdoms continued under the Mughals and as Princely States in British India until Indian independence.
- Vijayanagara Empire, 1336–1646, a Hindu-Kannadiga empire based in Karnataka, in the Deccan Plateau region. UNESCO World Heritage site Hampi in Karnataka district of Bellary was their capital city.
- Gajapati Kingdom, was a medieval Hindu dynasty that ruled over Kalinga (the present day Orissa).

Early modern era

The start of the Mughal Empire in 1526 marked the beginning of the early modern period of Indian history, often referred to as the Mughal era. Sometimes, the Mughal era is also referred to as the 'late medieval' period.

- Mughal Empire, was an imperial state founded by Babar, who had Turco-Mongol origin from Central Asia. The empire ruled most of the Indian subcontinent from 16th to 18th century, though it lingered for another century, formally ending in 1857.
- Maratha Empire, was an imperial power based in modern-day Maharashtra in western India. Marathas replaced the Mughal rule over large parts of India in the 18th century, but lost the Anglo-Maratha Wars in the early 19th century, and became rulers of Princely States.
- Kingdom of Mysore, was a Kannada kingdom have been founded in 1399 in the vicinity of the modern city of Mysore. Fully independent after the fall of the Vijayanagara Empire in 1646, reduced in size by the British, but ruled until 1947.

- Nayak dynasty of Kannada, Telugu, Tamil kings ruled parts of south India after the fall of the Vijayanagara Empire in 1646. Their contribution can be seen in Ikkeri, Sri Ranga, Madurai, and Chitradurga.
- Sikh Empire, was a major power in the Northwestern part of the Indian subcontinent, which arose under the leadership of Maharaja Ranjit Singh in the Punjab region. They were usurped by the British East India Company between early and mid 19th century, following the British victory in the Anglo-Sikh wars.

References

- Avari, Burjor, *India: The Ancient Past: A History of the Indian Subcontinent from C. 7000 BCE to CE 1200*, 2016 (2nd edn), Routledge, ISBN 1317236734, 9781317236733, google books[181]
- Farooqui, Salma Ahmed, *A Comprehensive History of Medieval India: From Twelfth to the Mid-Eighteenth Century*, 2011, Pearson Education India, ISBN 8131732029, 9788131732021, google books[182]
- Harle, J.C., *The Art and Architecture of the Indian Subcontinent*, 2nd edn. 1994, Yale University Press Pelican History of Art, ISBN 0300062176
- Keay, John, *India, a History*, 2000, HarperCollins, ISBN 0002557177
- Michell, George, (1977) *The Hindu Temple: An Introduction to its Meaning and Forms*, 1977, University of Chicago Press, ISBN 978-0-226-53230-1
- Rowland, Benjamin, *The Art and Architecture of India: Buddhist, Hindu, Jain*, 1967 (3rd edn.), Pelican History of Art, Penguin, ISBN 0140561021

Further reading

<templatestyles src="Template:Refbegin/styles.css" />

- Satish Chandra; Historiography, Religion and State in Medieval India, Har-Anand Publications, 2010.
- Elliot and Dowson: The History of India as told by its own Historians, New Delhi reprint, 1990.
- Elliot, Sir H. M., Edited by Dowson, John. The History of India, as Told by Its Own Historians. The Muhammadan Period; published by London Trubner Company 1867–1877. (Online Copy: The History of India, as Told by Its Own Historians. The Muhammadan Period; by Sir H. M. Elliot; Edited by John Dowson; London Trubner Company 1867–1877[183] – This online Copy has been posted by: The Packard Humanities Institute; Persian Texts in Translation; Also find other historical books: Author List and Title List[184])

- Gommans, Jos J. L. (2002), Mughal Warfare: Indian Frontiers and Highroads to Empire, 1500-1700, Routledge, ISBN 0-415-23989-3.
- Lal, K. S. (1999). Theory and practice of Muslim state in India. New Delhi: Aditya Prakashan.
- Majumdar, Ramesh Chandra; Pusalker, A. D.; Majumdar, A. K., eds. (1960). *The History and Culture of the Indian People*. VI: The Delhi Sultanate. Bombay: Bharatiya Vidya Bhavan.
- Majumdar, Ramesh Chandra; Pusalker, A. D.; Majumdar, A. K., eds. (1973). *The History and Culture of the Indian People*. VII: The Mughal Empire. Bombay: Bharatiya Vidya Bhavan.
- Misra, R. G. (1993). Indian resistance to early Muslim invaders up to 1206 AD. Meerut City: Anu Books.
- Sarkar, Jadunath. (1997). Fall of the Mughal Empire: Vol. 1-4. Hyderabad: Orient Longman.
- Sarkar, Jadunath. (1975). Studies in economic life in Mughal India. Delhi: Oriental Publishers & Distributors.; (1987). Mughal economy: Organization and working. Calcutta, India: Naya Prokash.
- Srivastava, A. L. (1970). The Mughal Empire, 1526-1803 A.D. ... Seventh revised edition. Agra: Shiva Lal Agarwala & Co.
- Srivastava, A. L. (1975). Medieval Indian culture. Agra: Agarwala.
- Wink, André (2004). *Indo-Islamic society: 14th - 15th centuries*[185]. Volume 3 of Al-Hind Series. BRILL. ISBN 9004135618. Retrieved 24 April 2014.
- Wink, André (1996). Al-Hind: The Making of the Indo-Islamic Worlds Vol 1. E. J. Brill. ISBN 0-391-04173-8.

Primary Sources

- Babur, ., & Thackston, W. M. (2002). The Baburnama: Memoirs of Babur, prince and emperor. New York: Modern Library.
- Muḥammad, A. K., & Pandit, K. N. (2009). A Muslim missionary in mediaeval Kashmir: Being the English translation of Tohfatu'l-ahbab.
- V. S. Bhatnagar (1991). *Kānhaḍade Prabandha, India's Greatest Patriotic Saga of Medieval Times: Padmanābha's Epic Account of Kānhaḍade*. Aditya Prakashan. ISBN 978-81-85179-54-4.
- Jain, M. The India They Saw : Foreign Accounts (4 Volumes) Delhi: Ocean Books, 2011.

External links.com

- Online Copy: The History of India, as Told by Its Own Historians. The Muhammadan Period; by Sir H. M. Elliot; Edited by John Dowson; London Trubner Company 1867–1877[183] – This online Copy has been postesd by: The Packard Humanities Institute; Persian Texts in Translation; Also find other historical books: Author List and Title List[184]

Early medieval

Chalukya dynasty

Chalukya dynasty	
Empire (Subordinate to Kadamba Dynasty until 543)	
543–753	
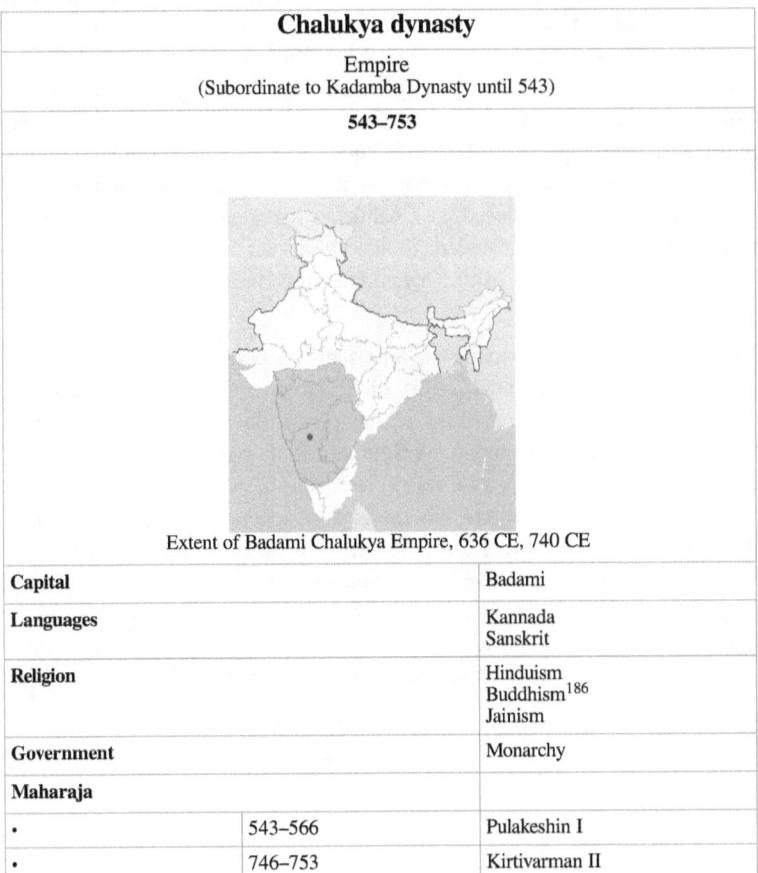 Extent of Badami Chalukya Empire, 636 CE, 740 CE	
Capital	Badami
Languages	Kannada Sanskrit
Religion	Hinduism Buddhism[186] Jainism
Government	Monarchy
Maharaja	
• 543–566	Pulakeshin I
• 746–753	Kirtivarman II

History		
•	Earliest records	543
•	Established	543
•	Disestablished	753
	Preceded by	**Succeeded by**
	Kadamba dynasty	Rashtrakuta dynasty Eastern Chalukyas
Today part of		India

The **Chalukya dynasty** ([tʃaːlukjə]) was an Indian royal dynasty that ruled large parts of southern and central India between the 6th and the 12th centuries. During this period, they ruled as three related yet individual dynasties. The earliest dynasty, known as the "Badami Chalukyas", ruled from Vatapi (modern Badami) from the middle of the 6th century. The Badami Chalukyas began to assert their independence at the decline of the Kadamba kingdom of Banavasi and rapidly rose to prominence during the reign of Pulakeshin II. After the death of Pulakeshin II, the Eastern Chalukyas became an independent kingdom in the eastern Deccan. They ruled from Vengi until about the 11th century. In the western Deccan, the rise of the Rashtrakutas in the middle of the 8th century eclipsed the Chalukyas of Badami before being revived by their descendants, the Western Chalukyas, in the late 10th century. These Western Chalukyas ruled from Kalyani (modern Basavakalyan) until the end of the 12th century.

The rule of the Chalukyas marks an important milestone in the history of South India and a golden age in the history of Karnataka. The political atmosphere in South India shifted from smaller kingdoms to large empires with the ascendancy of Badami Chalukyas. A Southern India-based kingdom took control and consolidated the entire region between the Kaveri and the Narmada rivers. The rise of this empire saw the birth of efficient administration, overseas trade and commerce and the development of new style of architecture called "Chalukyan architecture". Kannada literature, which had enjoyed royal support in the 9th century Rashtrakuta court found eager patronage from the Western Chalukyas in the Jain and Veerashaiva traditions. The 11th century saw the birth of Telugu literature under the patronage of the Eastern Chalukyas.

Figure 22: *Old Kannada inscription of Chalukya King Mangalesha dated 578 CE at Badami cave temple no.3*

Origins

Natives of Karnataka

While opinions vary regarding the early origins of the Chalukyas, the consensus among noted historians such as John Keay, D.C. Sircar, Hans Raj, S. Sen, Kamath, K. V. Ramesh and Karmarkar is the founders of the empire at Badami were native to the modern Karnataka region.[187,188,189,190,191,192,193,194,195,196]

A theory that they were descendants of a 2nd-century chieftain called Kandachaliki Remmanaka, a feudatory of the Andhra Ikshvaku (from an Ikshvaku inscription of the 2nd century) was put forward. This according to Kamath has failed to explain the difference in lineage. The Kandachaliki feudatory call themselves *Vashisthiputras* of the *Hiranyakagotra*. The Chalukyas, however, address themselves as *Harithiputras* of *Manavyasagotra* in their inscriptions, which is the same lineage as their early overlords, the Kadambas of Banavasi. This makes them descendants of the Kadambas. The Chalukyas took control of the territory formerly ruled by the Kadambas.[197]

A later record of Eastern Chalukyas mentions the northern origin theory and claims one ruler of Ayodhya came south, defeated the Pallavas and married a Pallava princess. She had a child called Vijayaditya who is claimed to be the Pulakeshin I's father. However, according to the historians K.

Figure 23: *Old Kannada inscription on victory pillar, Virupaksha Temple, Pattadakal, 733–745 CE*

V. Ramesh, Chopra and Sastri, there are Badami Chalukya inscriptions that confirm Jayasimha was Pulakeshin I's grandfather and Ranaraga, his father.[198,199,200,201] Kamath and Moraes claim it was a popular practice in the 11th century to link South Indian royal family lineage to a Northern kingdom. The Badami Chalukya records themselves are silent with regards to the Ayodhya origin.[202,203]

While the northern origin theory has been dismissed by many historians, the epigraphist K. V. Ramesh has suggested that an earlier southern migration is a distinct possibility which needs examination.[204] According to him, the complete absence of any inscriptional reference of their family connections to Ayodhya, and their subsequent Kannadiga identity may have been due to their earlier migration into present day Karnataka region where they achieved success as chieftains and kings. Hence, the place of origin of their ancestors may have been of no significance to the kings of the empire who may have considered themselves natives of the Kannada speaking region.[205] The writing of 12th century Kashmiri poet Bilhana suggests the Chalukya family belonged to the Shudra caste while other sources claim they were Kshatriyas.[206]

The historians Jan Houben and Kamath, and the epigraphist D.C. Sircar note the Badami Chalukya inscriptions are in Kannada and Sanskrit.[207,208,209] According to the historian N. L. Rao, their inscriptions call them *Karnatas* and their names use indigenous Kannada titles such as *Priyagallam* and *Noduttagelvom*. The names of some Chalukya princes end with the pure Kannada term *arasa* (meaning "king" or "chief").[210,211] The Rashtrakuta inscriptions call the Chalukyas of Badami *Karnatabala* ("Power of Karnata"). It has been proposed by the historian S. C. Nandinath that the word "Chalukya" originated from *Salki* or *Chalki* which is a Kannada word for an agricultural implement.[212,213]

Historical sources

Inscriptions in Sanskrit and Kannada are the main source of information about Badami Chalukya history. Among them, the Badami cave inscriptions of Mangalesha (578), Kappe Arabhatta record of c. 700, Peddavaduguru inscription of Pulakeshin II, the Kanchi Kailasanatha Temple inscription and Pattadakal Virupaksha Temple inscription of Vikramaditya II (all in Kannada language) provide more evidence of the Chalukya language.[214,215] The Badami cliff inscription of Pulakeshin I (543), the Mahakuta Pillar inscription of Mangalesha (595) and the Aihole inscription of Pulakeshin II (634) are examples of important Sanskrit inscriptions written in old Kannada script.[216] The reign of the Chalukyas saw the arrival of Kannada as the predominant language of inscriptions along with Sanskrit, in areas of the Indian peninsula outside what is known as Tamilaham (Tamil country).[217] Several coins of the Badami Chalukyas with Kannada legends have been found. All this indicates that Kannada language flourished during this period.[218]

Travelogues of contemporary foreign travellers have provided useful information about the Chalukyan empire. The Chinese traveller Xuanzang had visited the court of Pulakeshin II. At the time of this visit, as mentioned in the Aihole record, Pulakeshin II had divided his empire into three *Maharashtrakas* or great provinces comprising 99,000 villages each. This empire possibly covered present day Karnataka, Maharashtra and coastal Konkan.[219,220] Xuanzang, impressed with the governance of the empire observed that the benefits of the king's efficient administration was felt far and wide. Later, Persian emperor Khosrau II exchanged ambassadors with Pulakeshin II.[221,222,223]

Legends

Court poets of the Western Chalukya dynasty of Kalyani narrate:

"Once when Brahma, the creator, was engaged in the performance of the *sandhya* (twilight) rituals, Indra approached and beseeched him to create a hero who could put to an end the increasing evil on earth. On being thus requested, Brahma looked steadily into the *Chuluka-jala* (the water of oblation in his palm) and out sprang thence a great warrior, the progenitor of the Chalukyas".[224] The Chalukyas claimed to have been nursed by the *Sapta Matrikas* ("seven divine mothers") and were worshippers of many gods including Siva, Vishnu, Chamundi, Surya, Kubera, Parvati, Vinayaka and Kartikeya.

Some scholars connect the Chalukyas with the Chaulukyas (Solankis) of Gujarat. According to a myth mentioned in latter manuscripts of Prithviraj Raso, Chaulukyas were born out of fire-pit (Agnikund) at Mount Abu. However it has been reported that the story of Agnikula is not mentioned at all in the original version of the Prithviraj Raso preserved in the Fort Library at Bikaner.

According to the Nilagunda inscription of King Vikramaditya VI (11th century or later), the Chalukyas originally hailed from Ayodhya where fifty-nine kings ruled, and later, sixteen more of this family ruled from South India where they had migrated. This is repeated by his court poet Bilhana, who claims that the first member of the family, "Chalukya", was so named as he was born in the "hollow of the hands" of God Brahma.[225,226]

According to a theory put forward by Lewis, the Chalukya were descendants of the "Seleukia" tribe of Iraq and that their conflict with the Pallava of Kanchi was, but a continuation of the conflict between ancient Seleukia and "Parthians", the proposed ancestors of Pallavas. However, this theory has been rejected by Kamath as it seeks to build lineages based simply on similar-sounding clan names.[227]

Periods in Chalukya history

Chalukya dynasties
• $\underline{v}$ • $\underline{t}$ • $\underline{e}^{228}$

The Chalukyas ruled over the Deccan plateau in India for over 600 years. During this period, they ruled as three closely related, but individual dynasties. These are the "Chalukyas of Badami" (also called "Early Chalukyas"), who ruled between the 6th and the 8th century, and the two sibling dynasties, the "Chalukyas of Kalyani" (also called Western Chalukyas or "Later Chalukyas") and the "Chalukyas of Vengi" (also called Eastern Chalukyas).

Figure 24: *Bhutanatha temple complex, at Badami*

Chalukyas of Badami

In the 6th century, with the decline of the Gupta dynasty and their immediate successors in northern India, major changes began to happen in the area south of the Vindhyas – the Deccan and Tamilaham. The age of small kingdoms had given way to large empires in this region.[229] The Chalukya dynasty was established by Pulakeshin I in 543.[230,231,232] Pulakeshin I took Vatapi (modern Badami in Bagalkot district, Karnataka) under his control and made it his capital. Pulakeshin I and his descendants are referred to as "Chalukyas of Badami". They ruled over an empire that comprised the entire state of Karnataka and most of Andhra Pradesh in the Deccan.

Pulakeshin II, whose pre-coronation name was Ereya,[233] commanded control over the entire Deccan and is perhaps the most well-known emperor of the Badami dynasty.[234,235] He is considered one of the notable kings in Indian history.[236,237,238] His queens were princess from the Alupa Dynasty of South Canara and the Western Ganga Dynasty of Talakad, clans with whom the Chalukyas maintained close family and marital relationships.[239,240] Pulakeshin II extended the Chalukya Empire up to the northern extents of the Pallava kingdom and halted the southward march of Harsha by defeating him on the banks of the river Narmada. He then defeated the Vishnukundins in the south-eastern Deccan.[241,242,243,244] Pallava Narasimhavarman however reversed this victory in 642 by attacking and occupying Badami temporarily. It is presumed Pulakeshin II, "the great hero", died fighting.[245]

The Badami Chalukya dynasty went into a brief decline following the death of Pulakeshin II due to internal feuds when Badami was occupied by the Pallavas for a period of thirteen years.[246,247] It recovered during the reign of Vikramaditya I, who succeeded in pushing the Pallavas out of Badami and restoring order to the empire. Vikramaditya I took the title "Rajamalla" (*lit* "Sovereign of the *Mallas*" or Pallavas).[248] The thirty-seven year rule of Vijayaditya (696–733) was a prosperous one and is known for prolific temple building activity.[249,250]

The empire was its peak again during the rule of the illustrious Vikramaditya II (733–744) who is known not only for his repeated invasions of the territory of Tondaimandalam and his subsequent victories over Pallava Nandivarman II, but also for his benevolence towards the people and the monuments of Kanchipuram, the Pallava capital.[251,252] He thus avenged the earlier humiliation of the Chalukyas by the Pallavas and engraved a Kannada inscription on the victory pillar at the Kailasanatha Temple.[253,254] During his reign Arab intruders of the Umayyad Caliphate invaded southern Gujarat which was under Chalukya rule but the Arabs were defeated and driven out by Pulakesi, a Chalukya governor of Navsari.[255] He later overran the other traditional kingdoms of Tamil country, the Pandyas, the Cholas and the Cheras in addition to subduing a Kalabhra ruler.[256] The last Chalukya king, Kirtivarman II, was overthrown by the Rashtrakuta King Dantidurga in 753.[257] At their peak, the Chalukyas ruled a vast empire stretching from the Kaveri in the south to the Narmada in the north.

Chalukyas of Kalyani

The Chalukyas revived their fortunes in 973 after over 200 years of dormancy when much of the Deccan was under the rule of the Rashtrakutas. The genealogy of the kings of this empire is still debated. One theory, based on contemporary literary and inscriptional evidence plus the finding that the Western Chalukyas employed titles and names commonly used by the early Chalukyas, suggests that the Western Chalukya kings belonged to the same family line as the illustrious Badami Chalukya dynasty of the 6th century[258,259] while other Western Chalukya inscriptional evidence indicates they were a distinct line unrelated to the Early Chalukyas.[260]

Tailapa II, a Rashtrakuta feudatory ruling from Tardavadi – 1000 (Bijapur district) overthrew Karka II, re-established the Chalukya rule in the western Deccan and recovered most of the Chalukya empire.[261,262] The Western Chalukyas ruled for over 200 years and were in constant conflict with the Cholas, and with their cousins, the Eastern Chalukyas of Vengi. Vikramaditya VI is widely considered the most notable ruler of the dynasty.[263,264] Starting from the very beginning of his reign, which lasted fifty years, he abolished the original *Saka* era and established the *Vikrama Era*. Most subsequent Chalukya inscriptions are dated in this new era.[265,266] Vikramaditya VI was an ambitious and skilled military leader. Under his leadership the Western Chalukyas were able to end the Chola influence over Vengi (coastal Andhra) and become the dominant power in the Deccan.[267,268] The Western Chalukya period was an important age in the development of Kannada literature and Sanskrit literature.[269,270] They went into their final dissolution towards the end of the 12th century with the rise of the Hoysala Empire, the Pandyas, the Kakatiya and the Seuna Yadavas of Devagiri.[271]

Chalukyas of Vengi

Pulakeshin II conquered the eastern Deccan, corresponding to the coastal districts of modern Andhra Pradesh in 616, defeating the remnants of the Vishnukundina kingdom. He appointed his brother Kubja Vishnuvardhana as Viceroy in 621.[272,273] Thus the Eastern Chalukyas were originally of Kannada stock.[274] After the death of Pulakeshin II, the Vengi Viceroyalty developed into an independent kingdom and included the region between Nellore and Visakhapatnam.[275]

After the decline of the Badami Chalukya empire in the mid-8th century, territorial disputes flared up between the Rashtrakutas, the new rulers of the western deccan, and the Eastern Chalukyas. For much of the next two centuries, the Eastern Chalukyas had to accept subordination towards the Rashtrakutas.[276] Apart from a rare military success, such as the one by Vijayaditya II(c.808–847), it was only during the rule of Bhima I (c.892–921) that these Chalukyas were able to celebrate a measure of independence. After the death of Bhima I, the Andhra region once again saw succession disputes and interference in Vengi affairs by the Rashtrakutas.

The fortunes of the Eastern Chalukyas took a turn around 1000. Danarnava, their king, was killed in battle in 973 by the Telugu Choda King Bhima who then imposed his rule over the region for twenty-seven years. During this time, Danarnava's two sons took refuge in the Chola kingdom. Choda Bhima's invasion of Tondaimandalam, a Chola territory, and his subsequent death on the battlefield opened up a new era in Chola–Chalukya relations. Saktivarman I, the elder son of Danarnava was crowned as the ruler of Vengi in 1000, though under the control of king Rajaraja Chola I.[277] This new relationship between the Cholas and the coastal Andhra kingdom was unacceptable to the Western Chalukyas, who had by then replaced the Rashtrakutas as the main power in the western Deccan. The Western Chalukyas sought to brook the growing Chola influence in the Vengi region but were unsuccessful.[278]

Initially, the Eastern Chalukyas had encouraged Kannada language and literature, though, after a period of time, local factors took over and they gave

Figure 25: *Virupaksha temple in Dravidian style at Pattadakal, built 740 CE*

importance to Telugu language.[279,280] Telugu literature owes its growth to the Eastern Chalukyas.[281]

Architecture

The Badami Chalukya era was an important period in the development of South Indian architecture. The kings of this dynasty were called *Umapati Varlabdh* and built many temples for the Hindu god Shiva.[282] Their style of architecture is called "Chalukyan architecture" or "Karnata Dravida architecture".[283,284] Nearly a hundred monuments built by them, rock cut (cave) and structural, are found in the Malaprabha river basin in modern Bagalkot district of northern Karnataka.[285] The building material they used was a reddish-golden Sandstone found locally. These cave temples are basically excavations, cut out of the living rock sites they occupy. They were not built as their structural counterparts were, rather created by a special technique known as "subtraction" and are basically sculptural.[286] Though they ruled a vast empire, the Chalukyan workshops concentrated most of their temple building activity in a relatively small area within the Chalukyan heartland – Aihole, Badami, Pattadakal and Mahakuta in modern Karnataka state.[287]

Their temple building activity can be categorised into three phases. The early phase began in the last quarter of the 6th century and resulted in many cave temples, prominent among which are three elementary cave temples at Aihole (one Vedic, one Jain and one Buddhist which is incomplete), followed by four developed cave temples at Badami (of which cave 3, a Vaishnava temple, is dated accurately to 578 CE). These cave temples at Badami are similar, in that, each has a plain exterior but an exceptionally well finished interior consisting of a pillared verandah, a columned hall (*mantapa*) and a cella (shrine, cut deep into rock) which contains the deity of worship.[288] In Badami, three caves temples are Vedic and one in Jain. The Vedic temples contain large well sculpted images of Harihara, Mahishasuramardhini, Varaha, Narasimha, Trivikrama, Vishnu seated on Anantha (the snake) and Nataraja (dancing Shiva).[289]

The second phase of temple building was at Aihole (where some seventy structures exist and has been called "one of the cradles of Indian temple architecture"[290]) and Badami. Though the exact dating of these temples has been debated, there is consensus that the beginnings of these constructions are from c. 600.[291,292,293] These are the Lad Khan Temple (dated by some to c. 450 but more accurately to 620) with its interesting perforated stone windows and sculptures of river goddesses; the Meguti Jain Temple (634) which shows progress in structural design; the Durga Temple with its northern Indian style tower (8th century) and experiments to adapt a Buddhist *Chaitya* design to a brahminical one (its stylistic framework is overall a hybrid of north and south Indian styles.); the Huccimalli Gudi Temple with a new inclusion, a vestibule, connecting the sanctum to the hall.[294] Other *dravida* style temples from this period are the Naganatha Temple at Nagaral; the Banantigudi Temple, the Mahakutesvara Temple and the Mallikarjuna Temple at Mahakuta; and the Lower Sivalaya Temple, the Malegitti Sivalaya Temple (upper) and the Jambulingesvara Temple at Badami. Located outside the Chalukyan architectural heartland, 140 km south-east of Badami, with a structure related to the Early Chalukya style is the unusual Parvati Temple at Sanduru which dates to the late 7th century. It is medium-sized, 48 ft long and 37 ft wide. It has a *nagara* (north Indian) style *vimana* (tower) and *dravida* (south Indian) style parts, has no mantapa (hall) and consists of an *antarala* (vestibule) crowned with a barrel-vaulted tower (*sukhanasi*). The "staggered" base plan of the temple became popular much later, in the 11th century.[295,296]

The structural temples at Pattadakal, built in the 8th century and now a UNESCO World Heritage Site, marks the culmination and mature phase of Badami Chalukyan architecture. The Bhutanatha group of temples at Badami are also from this period. There are ten temples at Pattadakal, six in southern *dravida* style and four in the northern *nagara* style. Well known among these are the Sangamesvara Temple (725), the Virupaksha Temple (740–745) and the Mallikarjuna Temple (740–745) in the southern style. The Papanatha temple (680) and Galaganatha Temple (740) are early attempts in the *nagara* –

dravida fusion style.[297] Inscriptional evidence suggests that the Virupaksha and the Mallikarjuna Temples were commissioned by the two queens of King Vikramaditya II after his military success over the Pallavas of Kanchipuram. Some well known names of Chalukyan architects are Revadi Ovajja, Narasobba and Anivarita Gunda.[298]

The reign of Western Chalukyas was an important period in the development of Deccan architecture. Their architecture served as a conceptual link between the Badami Chalukya architecture of the 8th century and the Hoysala architecture popularised in the 13th century.[299,300] The centre of their cultural and temple-building activity lay in the Tungabhadra region of modern Karnataka state, encompassing the present-day Dharwad district; it included areas of present-day Haveri and Gadag districts.[301,302] Here, large medieval workshops built numerous monuments.[303] These monuments, regional variants of pre-existing dravida temples, defined the *Karnata dravida* tradition.[304]

The most notable of the many buildings dating from this period are the Mahadeva Temple at Itagi in the Koppal district,[305,306] the Kasivisvesvara Temple at Lakkundi in the Gadag district,[307,308] the Mallikarjuna Temple at Kuruvatti, and the Kallesvara Temple at Bagali,[309] both in the Davangere district.[310] Other notable constructions are the Dodda Basappa Temple at Dambal (Gadag district),[311,312] the Siddhesvara Temple at Haveri (Haveri district),[313,314] and the Amrtesvara Temple at Annigeri (Dharwad district).[315,316] The Eastern Chalukyas built some fine temples at Alampur, in modern eastern Andhra Pradesh.[317,318]

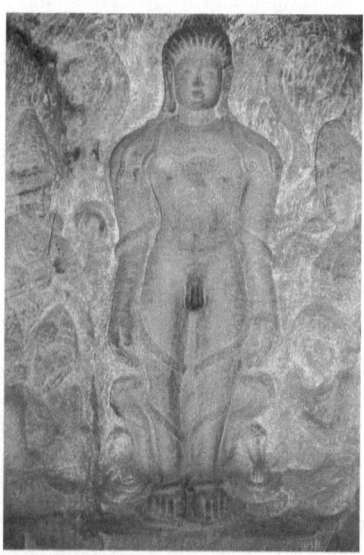

Figure 26: *Bahubali at Jain Cave temple No. 4 at Badami, 6th century*

Figure 27: *Vishnu image in Cave temple No. 3*

Figure 28: *Bhutanatha group of temples facing the Badami tank*

Figure 29: *The Parvati Temple, located about 140 km southeast to the Badami*

Figure 30: *Aihole – Durga Temple Front View*

Figure 31: *Aihole – Meguti Jain Temple*

Figure 32: *Mallikarjuna temple in dravidian style and Kashi Vishwanatha temple in nagara style at Pattadakal, built 740 CE*

Figure 33: *Dancing Shiva in cave no. 1 in Badami*

Figure 34: *Papanatha temple at Pattadakal – fusion of southern and northern Indian styles, 680 CE*

Literature

The Aihole inscription of Pulakeshin II (634) written by his court poet Ravikirti in Sanskrit language and Kannada script is considered as a classical piece of poetry.[319] A few verses of a poet named Vijayanaka who describes herself as the "dark Sarasvati" have been preserved. It is possible that she may have been a queen of prince Chandraditya (a son of Pulakeshin II).[320] Famous writers in Sanskrit from the Western Chalukya period are Vijnaneshwara who achieved fame by writing Mitakshara, a book on Hindu law, and King Someshvara III,

Figure 35: *Poetry on stone at the Meguti temple (Aihole inscription) dated 634 CE, in Sanskrit language and old Kannada script, with a Kannada language endorsement of about the same date at the bottom.*

a noted scholar, who compiled an encyclopedia of all arts and sciences called *Manasollasa*.[321]

From the period of the Badami Chalukyas, references are made to the existence of Kannada literature, though not much has survived.[322] Inscriptions however refer to Kannada as the "natural language".[323] The Kappe Arabhatta record of c. 700 in *tripadi* (three line) metre is the earliest available work in Kannada poetics.[324] *Karnateshwara Katha*, which was quoted later by Jayakirti, is believed to be a eulogy of Pulakeshin II and to have belonged to this period.[325] Other probable Kannada writers, whose works are not extant now but titles of which are known from independent references[326] are Syamakundacharya (650), who is said to have authored the *Prabhrita*, and Srivaradhadeva (also called Tumubuluracharya, 650 or earlier), the possible author of the *Chudamani* ("Crest Jewel"), a lengthy commentary on logic.[327,328,329]

The rule of the Western and Eastern Chalukyas, however, is a major event in the history of Kannada and Telugu literatures respectively. By the 9th–10th centuries, Kannada language had already seen some of its most notable writers. The "three gems" of Kannada literature, Adikavi Pampa, Sri Ponna and Ranna belonged to this period.[330,331] In the 11th century, Telugu literature was born under the patronage of the Eastern Chalukyas with Nannaya Bhatta as its first writer.[332]

Badami Chalukya country

Army

The army was well organised and this was the reason for Pulakeshin II's success beyond the Vindyas.[333] It consisted of an infantry, a cavalry, an elephant corps and a powerful navy. The Chinese traveller Hiuen-Tsiang wrote that the Chalukyan army had hundreds of elephants which were intoxicated with liquor prior to battle.[334] It was with their navy that they conquered *Revatidvipa* (Goa), and Puri on east coast of India. Rashtrakuta inscriptions use the term *Karnatabala* when referring to the powerful Chalukya armies.[335]

Land governance

The government, at higher levels, was closely modelled after the Magadhan and Satavahana administrative machinery. The empire was divided into *Maharashtrakas* (provinces), then into smaller *Rashtrakas* (*Mandala*), *Vishaya* (district), *Bhoga* (group of 10 villages) which is similar to the *Dasagrama* unit used by the Kadambas. At the lower levels of administration, the Kadamba style prevailed fully. The Sanjan plates of Vikramaditya I even mentions a land unit called *Dasagrama*.[336] In addition to imperial provinces, there were autonomous regions ruled by feudatories such as the Alupas, the Gangas, the Banas and the Sendrakas.[337] Local assemblies and guilds looked after local issues. Groups of *mahajanas* (learned brahmins) looked after *agraharas* (called *ghatika* or "place of higher learning") such as at Badami which was served by 2000 *mahajans* and Aihole which was served by 500 *mahajanas*. Taxes were levied and were called the *herjunka* – tax on loads, the *kirukula* – tax on retail goods in transit, the *bilkode* – sales tax, the *pannaya* – betel tax, *siddaya* – land tax and the *vaddaravula* – tax levied to support royalty.

Coinage

The Badami Chalukyas minted coins that were of a different standard compared to the coins of the northern kingdoms.[338] The coins had *Nagari* and Kannada legends. The coins of Mangalesha had the symbol of a temple on the obverse and a 'sceptre between lamps' or a temple on the reverse. Pulakeshin II's coins had a caparisoned lion facing right on the obverse and a temple on the reverse. The coins weighed 4 grams and were called, in old-Kannada, *hun* (or *honnu*) and had fractions such as *fana* (or *fanam*) and the *quarter fana* (the modern day Kannada equivalent being *hana* – which literally means "money"). A gold coin called *gadyana* is mentioned in a record at the Vijayeshwara Temple at Pattadakal, which later came to be known as *varaha* (their royal emblem).

Figure 36: *Vaishnava Cave temple No. 3 at Badami, 578 CE*

Religion

Part of a series on the
History of Karnataka

- Political history of medieval Karnataka
- Origin of Karnataka's name
- Kadambas and Gangas
- Chalukya Empire
- Rashtrakuta Empire
- Western Chalukya Empire
- Southern Kalachuri
- Hoysala Empire
- Vijayanagara Empire
- Bahmani Sultanate

• Bijapur Sultanate
• Kingdom of Mysore
• Nayakas of Keladi
• Nayakas of Chitradurga
• Haleri Kingdom
• Unification of Karnataka
Categories
• Architecture • Forts • Economies • Societies
• v̲ • t̲ • e̲[339]

Both Shaivism and Vaishnavism flourished during the Badami Chalukya period, though it seems the former was more popular.[340] Famous temples were built in places such as Pattadakal, Aihole and Mahakuta, and priests (*archakas*) were invited from northern India. Vedic sacrifices, religious vows (*vrata*) and the giving of gifts (*dana*) was important.[341] The Badami kings were followers of Vedic Hinduism and dedicated temples to popular Hindu deities in Aihole. Sculptures of deities testify to the popularity of Hindu Gods such as Vishnu, Shiva, Kartikeya, Ganapathi, Shakti, Surya and *Sapta Matrikas* ("seven mothers"). The Badami kings also performed the Ashwamedha ("horse sacrifice").[342] The worship of Lajja Gauri, a fertility goddess is known. Jainism too was a prominent religion during this period. The kings of the dynasty were however secular and actively encouraged Jainism. One of the Badami Cave temples is dedicated to the Jain faith. Jain temples were also erected in the Aihole complex, the temple at Maguti being one such example.[343] Ravikirti, the court poet of Pulakeshin II was a Jain. Queen Vinayavati consecrated a temple for the Trimurti ("Hindu trinity") at Badami. Sculptures of the Trimurti, Harihara (half Vishnu, half Shiva) and *Ardhanarishwara* (half Shiva, half woman) provide ample evidence of their tolerance. Buddhism was on a decline, having made its ingress into Southeast Asia. This is confirmed by the writings of Hiuen-Tsiang. Badami, Aihole, Kurtukoti and Puligere (modern Lakshmeshwar in the Gadag district) were primary places of learning.

Society

The Hindu caste system was present and devadasis were recognised by the government. Some kings had concubines (*ganikas*) who were given much respect,[344] and Sati was perhaps absent since widows like Vinayavathi and

Vijayanka are mentioned in records. Devadasis were however present in temples. Sage Bharata's *Natyashastra*, the precursor to Bharatanatyam, the classical dance of South India, was popular and is seen in many sculptures and is mentioned in inscriptions.[345] Some women from the royal family enjoyed political power in administration. Queen Vijayanka was a noted Sanskrit poet, Kumkumadevi, the younger sister of Vijayaditya (and queen of Alupa King Chitravahana) made several grants and had a Jain basadi called Anesajjebasadi constructed at Puligere,[346] and the queens of Vikramaditya II, Lokamahadevi and Trailokyamahadevi made grants and possibly consecrated the Lokesvara Temple (now called Virupaksha temple) but also and the Mallikarjuna temple respectively at Pattadakal.[347]

In popular culture

The Chalukya era may be seen as the beginning of the fusion of cultures of northern and southern India, making way for the transmission of ideas between the two regions. This is seen clearly in the field of architecture. The Chalukyas spawned the *Vesara* style of architecture which includes elements of the northern *nagara* and southern *dravida* styles. During this period, the expanding Sanskritic culture mingled with local Dravidian vernaculars which were already popular. Dravidian languages maintain these influences even today. This influence helped to enrich literature in these languages.[348] The Hindu legal system owes much to the Sanskrit work *Mitakshara* by Vijnaneshwara in the court of Western Chalukya King Vikramaditya VI. Perhaps the greatest work in legal literature, *Mitakshara* is a commentary on *Yajnavalkya* and is a treatise on law based on earlier writings and has found acceptance in most parts of India. Englishman Henry Thomas Colebrooke later translated into English the section on inheritance, giving it currency in the British Indian court system.[349] It was during the Western Chalukya rule that the Bhakti movement gained momentum in South India, in the form of Ramanujacharya and Basavanna, later spreading into northern India.

A celebration called *Chalukya utsava*, a three-day festival of music and dance, organised by the Government of Karnataka, is held every year at Pattadakal, Badami and Aihole. The event is a celebration of the achievements of the Chalukyas in the realm of art, craft, music and dance. The program, which starts at Pattadakal and ends in Aihole, is inaugurated by the Chief Minister of Karnataka. Singers, dancers, poets and other artists from all over the country take part in this event. In the 26 February 2006 celebration, 400 art troupes took part in the festivities. Colorful cutouts of the *Varaha* the Chalukya emblem, *Satyashraya* Pulakeshin (Pulakeshin II), famous sculptural masterpieces such as Durga, Mahishasuramardhini (Durga killing demon Mahishasura) were present everywhere. The program at Pattadakal is named *Anivaritacharigund vedike* after the famous architect of the Virupaksha temple, Gundan Anivaritachari. At Badami it is called *Chalukya Vijayambika Vedike* and at Aihole, *Ravikirti Vedike* after the famous poet and minister (Ravikirti) in the court of Pulakeshin II. *Immadi Pulakeshi*, a Kannada movie of the 1960s starring Dr. Rajkumar celebrates the life and times of the great king.

References

Books <templatestyles src="Template:Refbegin/styles.css" />

- Bolon, Carol Radcliffe (1 January 1979). "The Mahākuṭa Pillar and Its Temples". **41** (2/3): 253–268. doi: 10.2307/3249519[350]. JSTOR 3249519[351].
- Chopra, P.N.; Ravindran, T.K.; Subrahmanian, N (2003) [2003]. *History of South India (Ancient, Medieval and Modern) Part 1*. New Delhi: Chand Publications. ISBN 81-219-0153-7.
- Cousens, Henry (1996) [1926]. *The Chalukyan Architecture of Kanarese Districts*. New Delhi: Archaeological Survey of India. OCLC 37526233[352].
- Foekema, Gerard (1996). *Complete Guide to Hoysala Temples*. New Delhi: Abhinav. ISBN 81-7017-345-0.
- Foekema, Gerard (2003) [2003]. *Architecture decorated with architecture: Later medieval temples of Karnataka, 1000–1300 AD*. New Delhi: Munshiram Manoharlal Publishers Pvt. Ltd. ISBN 81-215-1089-9.
- Hardy, Adam (1995) [1995]. *Indian Temple Architecture: Form and Transformation-The Karnata Dravida Tradition 7th to 13th Centuries*. Abhinav Publications. ISBN 81-7017-312-4.
- Houben, Jan E.M. (1996) [1996]. *Ideology and Status of Sanskrit: Contributions to the History of the Sanskrit language*. Brill. ISBN 90-04-10613-8.
- Kamath, Suryanath U. (2001) [1980]. *A concise history of Karnataka: from pre-historic times to the present*. Bangalore: Jupiter books. LCCN 80905179[353]. OCLC 7796041[354].
- Karmarkar, A.P. (1947) [1947]. *Cultural history of Karnataka: ancient and medieval*. Dharwad: Karnataka Vidyavardhaka Sangha. OCLC 8221605[355].
- Keay, John (2000) [2000]. *India: A History*. New York: Grove Publications. ISBN 0-8021-3797-0.
- Michell, George (2002) [2002]. *Pattadakal – Monumental Legacy*. Oxford University Press. ISBN 0-19-566057-9.
- Moraes, George M. (1990) [1931]. *The Kadamba Kula, A History of Ancient and Medieval Karnataka*. New Delhi, Madras: Asian Educational Services. ISBN 81-206-0595-0.

- Mugali, R.S. (1975) [1975]. *History of Kannada literature*. Sahitya Akademi. OCLC 2492406[356].
- Narasimhacharya, R (1988) [1988]. *History of Kannada Literature*. New Delhi, Madras: Asian Educational Services. ISBN 81-206-0303-6.
- Ramesh, K.V. (1984). *Chalukyas of Vatapi*. Delhi: Agam Kala Prakashan. OCLC 567370037[357]. 3987-10333.
- Sastri, Nilakanta K.A. (2002) [1955]. *A history of South India from prehistoric times to the fall of Vijayanagar*. New Delhi: Indian Branch, Oxford University Press. ISBN 0-19-560686-8.
- Sen, Sailendra Nath (1999). *Ancient Indian History and Civilization*. New Age Publishers. ISBN 81-224-1198-3.
- Thapar, Romila (2003) [2003]. *The Penguin History of Early India*. New Delhi: Penguin Books. ISBN 0-14-302989-4.
- Vaidya, C.V. *History of Mediaeval Hindu India (Being a History of India from 600 to 1200 A.D.)*. Poona: Oriental Book Supply Agency. OCLC 6814734[358].
- Various (1988) [1988]. *Encyclopaedia of Indian literature – vol 2*. Sahitya Akademi. ISBN 81-260-1194-7.

Web <templatestyles src="Template:Refbegin/styles.css" />

- "APOnline – History of Andhra Pradesh-ancient period-Eastern Chalukyas by Tata Consultancy Services"[359]. Archived from the original[360] on 6 December 2006. Retrieved 12 November 2006.
- "Architecture of Indian Subcontinent, Takeyo Kamiya, 20 September 1996, Published by Gerard da Cunha-Architecture Autonomous, Bardez, Goa, India"[361]. Retrieved 2006-11-12.
- "Badami Chalukyans' magical transformation, an article by Azmathulla Shariff in Deccan Herald, Spectrum, 26 July 2005"[362]. Archived from the original[363] on 2007-02-10. Retrieved 2006-11-12.

<indicator name="featured-star"> ★ </indicator>

External links

 Wikimedia Commons has media related to *Chalukya dynasty*.

- "Chalukyan Art by Dr. Jyotsna Kamat, Kamat's Potpourri, 4 November 2006"[364]. Retrieved 2006-11-10.
- "History of the Kannada Literature, Dr. Jyotsna Kamat, on Kamat's Potpourri, Timeless Theater-Karnataka-History of Kannada, 4 November 2006"[365]. Retrieved 2006-11-12.

- "Aihole Temples, Photographs by Michael D. Gunther, 2002"[366]. Retrieved 2006-11-10.
- "Badami Cave Temples, Photographs by Michael D. Gunther, 2002"[367]. Retrieved 2006-11-10.
- "Pattadakal Temples, Photographs by Michael D. Gunther, 2002"[368]. Retrieved 2006-11-10.
- Chalukyas of Kalyana (973–1198 CE)[369] by Dr. Jyotsna Kamat
- "Coins of Alupas"[370]. Archived from the original[371] on 2006-08-15. Retrieved 2006-11-10.

Harsha

Harsha	
Maharajadhiraja	
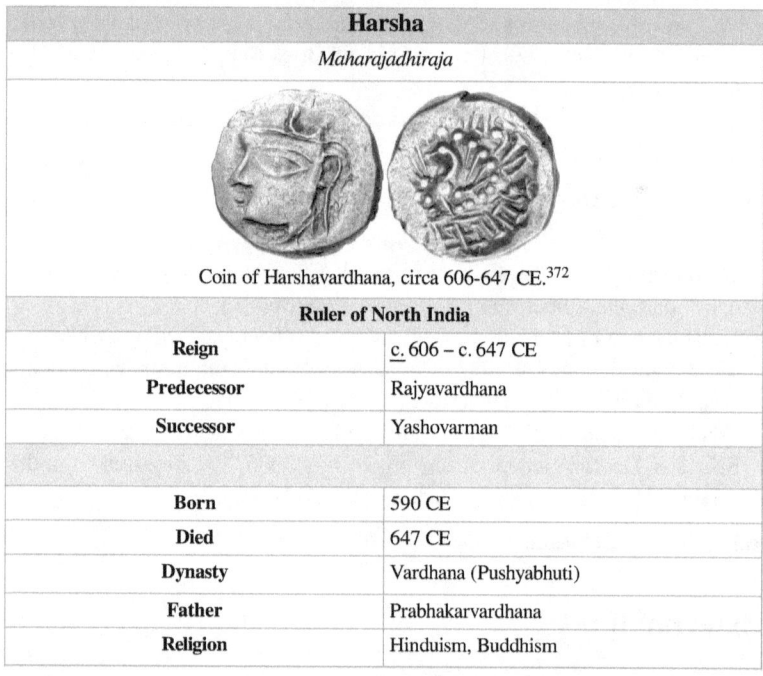	
Coin of Harshavardhana, circa 606-647 CE.[372]	
Ruler of North India	
Reign	c. 606 – c. 647 CE
Predecessor	Rajyavardhana
Successor	Yashovarman
Born	590 CE
Died	647 CE
Dynasty	Vardhana (Pushyabhuti)
Father	Prabhakarvardhana
Religion	Hinduism, Buddhism

Harsha (c. 590–647 CE), also known as **Harshavardhana**, was an Indian emperor who ruled North India from 606 to 647 CE. He was a member of the Vardhana dynasty; and was the son of Prabhakarvardhana who defeated the Alchon Huna invaders,[373] and the younger brother of Rajyavardhana, a king of Thanesar, present-day Haryana. At the height of Harsha's power, his Empire covered much of North and Northwestern India, extended East till Kamarupa, and South until Narmada River; and eventually made Kannauj (in present Uttar Pradesh state) his capital, and ruled till 647 CE.[374] Harsha was defeated by the

Figure 37: *Palace ruins at "Harsh ka tila" mound area spread over 1 km*

south Indian Emperor Pulakeshin II of the Chalukya dynasty, when Harsha tried to expand his Empire into the southern peninsula of India.[375]

The peace and prosperity that prevailed made his court a centre of cosmopolitanism, attracting scholars, artists and religious visitors from far and wide. The Chinese traveller Xuanzang visited the court of Harsha and wrote a very favourable account of him, praising his justice and generosity. His biography *Harshacharita* ("Deeds of Harsha") written by Sanskrit poet Banabhatta, describes his association with Thanesar, besides mentioning the defence wall, a moat and the palace with a two-storied *Dhavalagriha* (white mansion).

Origins

After the downfall of the Gupta Empire in the middle of the 6th century, North India was split into several independent kingdoms. The northern and western regions of India passed into the hands of a dozen or more feudatory states. Prabhakara Vardhana, the ruler of Sthanvisvara, who belonged to the Vardhana family, extended his control over neighbouring states. Prabhakar Vardhana was the first king of the Vardhana dynasty with his capital at Thaneswar. After Prabhakar Vardhana's death in 605, his eldest son, Rajya Vardhana, ascended the throne. Harsha Vardhana was Rajya Vardhana's younger brother. This

Figure 38: *Territorial reach of Harsha.*

period of kings from the same line has been referred to as the Vardhana dynasty in many publications.[376,377,378,379]

According to major evidences, Harsha, like the Guptas, was of the *Vaishya* Varna. The Chinese traveler Xuanzang mentions an emperor named Shiladitya, who had been claimed to be Harsha. Xuanzang mentions that this king belonged to "Fei-she". This word is generally restored as "Vaishya" (a varna or social class).

Ascension

Rajya Vardhana's and Harsha's sister Rajyashri had been married to the Maukhari king, Grahavarman. This king, some years later, had been defeated and killed by king Devagupta of Malwa and after his death Rajyashri had been cast into prison by the victor. Harsha's brother, Rajya Vardhana, then the king at Thanesar, could not stand this affront on his family, marched against Devagupta and defeated him. But it so happened at this moment that Shashanka, king of Gauda in Eastern Bengal, entered Magadha as a friend of Rajyavardhana, but in secret alliance with the Malwa king. Accordingly, Shashanka treacherously murdered Rajyavardhana. On hearing about the murder of his brother, Harsha resolved at once to march against the treacherous king of

Gauda and killed Shashanka in a battle. Harsha ascended the throne at the age of 16.

Reign

As North India reverted to small republics and small monarchical states ruled by Gupta rulers after the fall of the prior Gupta Empire, Harsha united the small republics from Punjab to central India, and their representatives crowned him king at an assembly in April 606 giving him the title of Maharaja. Harsha established an empire that brought all of northern India under his control.[374] The peace and prosperity that prevailed made his court a center of cosmopolitanism, attracting scholars, artists and religious visitors from far and wide. The Chinese traveler Xuanzang visited the court of Harsha, and wrote a very favourable account of him, praising his justice and generosity.

Pulakeshin II defeated Harsha on the banks of Narmada in the winter of 618-619 CE. Pulakeshin entered into a treaty with Harsha, with the Narmada River designated as the border between the Chalukya Empire and that of Harshavardhana.

Xuanzang describes the event thus:

> "Shiladityaraja (i.e., Harsha), filled with confidence, himself marched at the head of his troops to contend with this prince (i.e., Pulakeshin); but he was unable to prevail upon or subjugate him".

In 648, Tang dynasty emperor Tang Taizong sent Wang Xuance to India in response to Harsha sending an ambassador to China. However once in India he discovered Harsha had died and the new king attacked Wang and his 30 mounted subordinates. This led to Wang Xuance escaping to Tibet and then, mounting a joint force of over 7,000 Nepalese mounted infantry and 1,200 Tibetan infantry attacked the Indian state on June 16. The success of this attack brought Wang Xuance the prestigious title of the "Grand Master for the Closing Court." He also secured a reported Buddhist relic for China.

Religion

Like many other ancient Indian rulers, Harsha was eclectic in his religious views and practices. His seals describe his ancestors as sun-worshippers, his elder brother as a Buddhist, and himself as a Shaivite. His land grant inscriptions describe him as *Parama-maheshvara* (supreme devotee of Shiva), and his play *Nagananda* is dedicated to Shiva's consort Gauri. His court poet Bana also describes him as a Shaivite.

According to the Chinese Buddhist traveler Xuanzang, Harsha became a devout Buddhist at some point in his life. Xuanzang states that Harsha banned animal slaughter for food, and built monasteries at the places visited by Gautama Buddha. He erected several thousand 100-feet high stupas on the banks of the Ganges river, and built well-maintained hospices for travelers and poor people on highways across India. He organized an annual assembly of global scholars, and bestowed charitable alms on them. Every five years, he held a great assembly called Moksha. Xuanzang also describes a 21-day religious festival organized by Harsha in Kannauj; during this festival, Harsha and his subordinate kings performed daily rituals before a life-sized golden statue of the Buddha.

Since Harsha's own records describe him as Shaivite, his conversion to Buddhism would have happened, if at all, in the later part of his life. Even Xuanzang states that Harsha patronized scholars of all religions, not just Buddhist monks.

Author

Harsha is widely believed to be the author of three Sanskrit plays Ratnavali, Nagananda and Priyadarsika. While some believe (e.g., Mammata in Kavyaprakasha) that it was Bana, Harsha's court poet who wrote the plays as a paid commission, Wendy Doniger is "persuaded, however, that king Harsha really wrote the plays ... himself."

Further reading

Wikisourcehas the text of the 1911 *Encyclopædia Britannica*article ***Harsha***.

- Reddy, Krishna (2011), Indian History[380], Tata McGraw-Hill Education Private Limited, New Delhi
- Price, Pamela (2007), Early Medieval India, HIS2172 - Periodic Evaluation[381], University of Oslo
- "Conquests of Siladitya in the south"[382] by S. Srikanta Sastri

Karkoṭa Empire

Karkota Empire	
625 CE–885 CE	
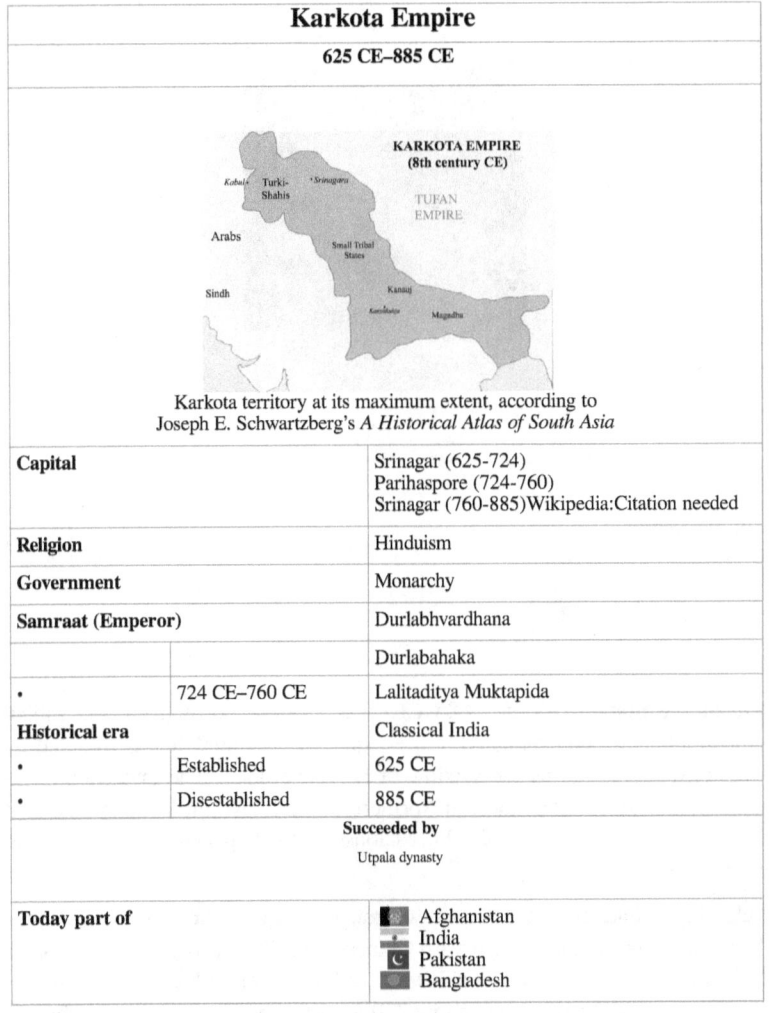 Karkota territory at its maximum extent, according to Joseph E. Schwartzberg's *A Historical Atlas of South Asia*	
Capital	Srinagar (625-724) Parihaspore (724-760) Srinagar (760-885)Wikipedia:Citation needed
Religion	Hinduism
Government	Monarchy
Samraat (Emperor)	Durlabhvardhana
	Durlabahaka
• 724 CE–760 CE	Lalitaditya Muktapida
Historical era	Classical India
• Established	625 CE
• Disestablished	885 CE
Succeeded by Utpala dynasty	
Today part of	Afghanistan India Pakistan Bangladesh

Part of a series on the
History of India

- v
- t
- e[383]

Karkota Empire (c. 625 - 885 CE) was a major power from the Indian subcontinent; which originated in the region of Kashmir. It was founded by Durlabhvardhana during the lifetime of Harshavardhan. The dynasty marked the rise of Kashmir as a power in Northern India.[384] Avanti Varman ascended the throne of Kashmir on 855 A.D., establishing the Utpala dynasty and ending the rule of Karkota dynasty.

Lalitaditya Muktapida, the dynasty's strongest ruler captured parts of Central Asia, Afghanistan and Punjab with Chinese help.[385] According to Kalhana's *Rajatarangini*, Lalitaditya was able to extend the power of Kashmir beyond the normal mountain limits and in about 740 AD inflicted a defeat upon Yashovarman, the King of Kannauj. Lalitaditya was able to vanquish the Turks, Tibetans, Bhutias, Kambojas and others. According to some historians, Kalhana highly exaggerated the conquests of Lalitaditya.[386,387]

The Karkota emperors were primarily Hindu. They built spectacular Hindu temples in their capital Parihaspur. They however also allowed Buddhism to flourish under them. Stupa, Chaitya and Vihara can be found in the ruins of their capital. Martand Sun Temple in the Anantnag district were built by

Lalitaditya. It is the oldest known Sun temple in India and was also one of the biggest temple complexes at the time.

Notes
References
- Wink, André (2002), *Al-Hind, the Making of the Indo-Islamic World*[388], 1, BRILL, ISBN 9780391041738
- Chadurah, Haidar Malik (1991), *History of Kashmir*[389], Bhavna Prakashan
- Hasan, Mohibbul (1959), *Kashmir Under the Sultans*[390], Aakar, ISBN 9788187879497

Umayyad campaigns in India

Umayyad campaigns in India	
Sindh and neighbouring kingdoms	
Date	712–740 CE
Location	Rajasthan and Gujarat, India
Result	Victory of Indian kingdoms, Arab expansion checked
Territorial changes	Umayyad expansion checked and contained to Sindh.
Belligerents	
Chalukya dynasty Gurjara-Pratihara dynasty	Umayyad Caliphate
Commanders and leaders	
Nagabhata I Vikramaditya II Bappa Rawal	Junayd ibn Abd al-Rahman al-Murri Tamim ibn Zaid al-Utbi† Al Hakam ibn Awana†

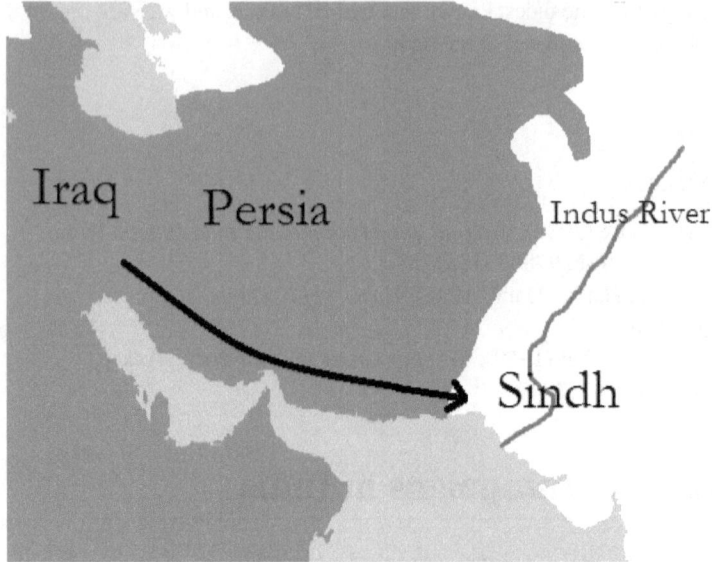

Figure 39: *A map of Muhammad bin Qasim's expedition into Sindh in 711 AD*

In the first half of the 8th century CE, a series of battles took place between the Umayyad Caliphate and the Indian kingdoms to the east of the Indus river.[391]

Subsequent to the Arab conquest of Sindh in present-day Pakistan in 712 CE, Arab armies engaged kingdoms further east of the Indus. Between 724 and 810 CE, a series of battles took place between the Arabs and the north Indian Emperor Nagabhata I of the Gurjara-Pratihara dynasty, the south Indian Emperor Vikramaditya II of the Chalukya dynasty, and other small Indian kingdoms. In the north, Nagabhata of the Gurjara Pratihara Dynasty defeated a major Arab expedition in Malwa. From the South, Vikramaditya II sent his general Pulakesi, who defeated the Arabs in Gujarat.[392] Later in 776 CE, a naval expedition by the Arabs was defeated by the Saindhava naval fleet under Agguka I.

The Arab defeats led to an end of their eastward expansion, and later manifested in the overthrow of Arab rulers in Sindh itself and the establishment of indigenous Muslim Rajput dynasties (Soomras and Sammas) there.

Background

After the reign of Emperor Harshavardhana, by the early 8th century, North India was divided into several kingdoms, small and large. The Northwest was controlled by the Kashmir-based Karkota dynasty, and the Hindu Shahis based in Kabul. Kanauj, the *de facto* capital of North India was held by Yashovarman, Northeast India was held by the Pala dynasty, and South India by the powerful Chalukyas. Western India was dominated by the Rai dynasty of Sindh, and several kingdoms of Gurjara clans, based at Bhinmal (Bhillamala), Mandor, Nandol-Broach (Nandipuri-Bharuch) and Ujjain. The last of these clans, who called themselves Pratiharas were to be the eventually dominating force. Altogether, the combined region of southern Rajasthan and northern Gujarat was called Gurjaratra (Gurjara country), before it got renamed to *Rajputana* in later medieval times. The Kathiawar peninsula (Saurashtra) was controlled by several small kingdoms, such as Saindhavas, dominated by Maitrakas at Vallabhi.

The third wave of military expansion of the Umayyad Caliphate lasted from 692 to 718 CE. The reign of Al-Walid I (705–715 CE) saw the most dramatic Marwanid Umayyad conquests, in a period of barely ten years, as North Africa, Spain, Transoxiana, and Sindh were subdued and colonised.[393] Sindh, controlled by King Raja Dahir of the Rai dynasty, was captured by the Umayyad general Muhammad bin Qasim.[394] While Sindh, now a second-level province of the Caliphate (*iqlim*) with capital Al Mansura, was a suitable base from where excursions into India could be launched, after bin Qasim's departure most of his captured territories were recaptured by the Indian kings.[395]

During the reign of Yazid II (720 to 724 CE), the fourth expansion was launched to all the warring frontiers, including India. The campaign lasted from 720 to 740 CE. During Yazid's times, there was no significant check to the Arab expansion. However, the advent of Hisham ibn Abd al-Malik (r. 691–743 CE), the 10th Umayyad Caliph, saw a turn in the fortune of the Umayyads which resulted in eventual defeat on all the fronts and the complete halt of Arab expansionism. The hiatus from 740 to 750 CE due to military exhaustion, also saw the advent of the third of a series of civil wars, which resulted in the collapse of the Umayyad Caliphate.[396]

Campaign by Muhammad bin Qasim (712–715)

After taking full control of Sindh, Muhammad bin Qasim wrote to 'the kings of Hind' calling upon them to surrender and accept the faith of Islam.[397] He dispatched a force against *al-Baylaman* (Bhinmal), which is said to have offered submission. The *Mid* people of *Surast* (Maitrakas of Vallabhi) also made peace.[398] Bin Qasim then sent a cavalry of 10,000 to Kanauj, along with a decree from the Caliph. He himself went with an army to the prevailing frontier of Kashmir called *panj-māhīyāt* (in west Punjab).[399] Nothing is known of the

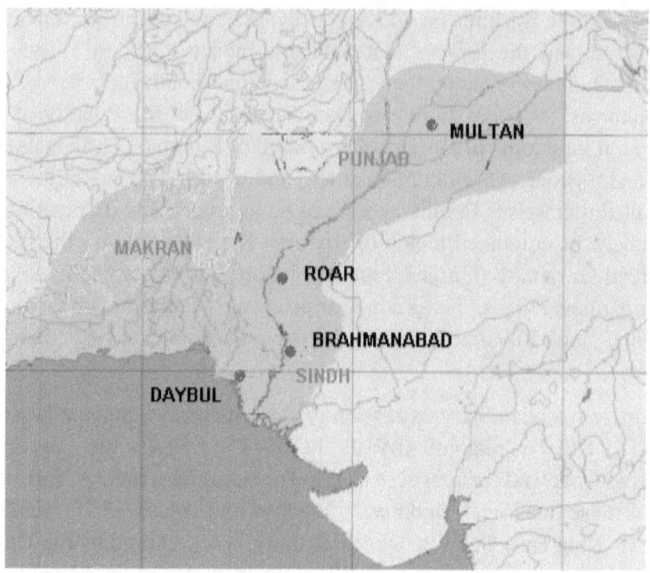

Figure 40: *Extent and expansion of Umayyad rule under Muhammad bin Qasim in medieval India (modern state boundaries shown in red).*

Kanauj expedition. The frontier of Kashmir might be what is referred to as *al-Kiraj* in later records (Kira kingdom in Kangra Valley, Himachal Pradesh[400]), which was apparently subdued.[401]

Bin Qasim was recalled in 715 CE and died *en route*. Al-Baladhuri writes that, upon his departure, the kings of *al-Hind* had come back to their kingdoms. The period of Caliph Umar II (r. 717–720) was relatively peaceful. Umar invited the kings of "al-Hind" to convert to Islam and become his subjects, in return for which they would continue to remain kings. Hullishah of Sindh and other kings accepted the offer and adopted Arab names.[402] During the caliphates of Yazid II (r. 720–724) and Hisham (r. 724–743), the expansion policy was resumed. *Junayd ibn Abd ar-Rahman al-Murri* (or Al Junayd) was appointed the governor of Sindh in 723 CE.Wikipedia:Citation needed

Campaign by Al Junayd (723–726)

After subduing Sindh, Junayd sent campaigns to various parts of India. The justification was that these parts had previously paid tribute to Bin Qasim but then stopped. The first target was *al-Kiraj* (possibly Kangra valley), whose conquest effectively put an end to the kingdom. A large campaign was carried out in Rajasthan which included *Mermad* (Maru-Mala, in Jaisalmer and

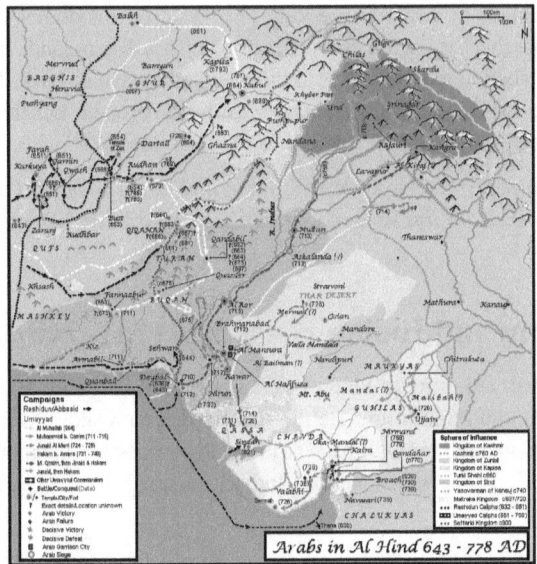

Figure 41: *Arab Campaigns in Indian Sub Continent. A generic representation, not to exact scale.*

north Jodhpur), *al-Baylaman* (Bhillamala or Bhinmal) and *Jurz* (Gurjara country—southern Rajasthan and north Gujarat). Another force was sent against *Uzayn* (Ujjain), which made incursions into its country (Avanti) and some parts of it were destroyed (the city of *Baharimad*, unidentified). Ujjain itself may not have been conquered. A separate force was also sent against *al-Malibah* (Malwa, to the east of Ujjain), but the outcome is not recorded.[403]

Towards the North, Umayyads attempted to expand into Punjab but were defeated by Lalitaditya Muktapida of Kashmir. Another force was dispatched south. It subdued *Qassa* (Kutch), *al-Mandal* (perhaps Okha), *Dahnaj* (unidentified), *Surast* (Saurashtra) and *Barus* or *Barwas* (Broach).

The kingdoms weakened or destroyed included the Bhattis of Jaisalmer, the Gurjaras of Bhinmal, the Mauryas of Chittor, the Guhilots of Mewar, the Kacchelas of Kutch, the Maitrakas of Saurashtra and Gurjaras of Nandipuri. Altogether, Al-Junayd might have conquered all of Gujarat, a large part of Rajasthan and some parts of Madhya Pradesh. Blankinship states that this was a full-scale invasion carried out with the intent of founding a new province of the Caliphate.[404]

In 726 CE, the Caliphate replaced Al-Junayd by *Tamim ibn Zayd ibn Hamal al-Qayni* (Tamim) as the governor of Sindh. During the next few years, all of the gains made by Junayd were lost. The Arab records do not explain why, except to state that the Caliphate troops, drawn from distant lands such as Syria and Yemen, abandoned their posts in India and refused to go back. Blankinship admits the possibility that the Indians must have revolted, but thinks it more likely that the problems were internal to the Arab forces.[405]

Governor Tamim is said to have fled Sindh and died *en route*. The Caliphate appointed *al-Hakam ibn Awana al-Kalbi* (Al-Hakam) in 731 who governed till 740.

Al-Hakam and Indian resistance (731–740)

Al-Hakam restored order to Sindh and Kutch and built secure fortifications at Al-Mahfuzah and Al-Mansur. He then proceeded to retake Indian kingdoms previously conquered by Al-Junayd. The Arab sources are silent on the details of the campaigns. However, several Indian sources record victories over the Arab forces.[406]

The Gurjara king of Nandipuri, Jayabhata IV, documented, in an inscription dated to 736 CE, that he went to the aid of the king of Vallabhi and inflicted a crushing defeat on a *Tājika* (Arab) army. The Arabs then overran the kingdom of Jayabhata himself and proceeded on to Navsari in southern Gujarat.[407] The Arab intention might have been to make inroads into South India. However, to the south of the Mahi River lay the powerful Chalukyan empire. The Chalukyan viceroy at Navsari, Avanijanashraya Pulakeshin, decisively defeated the invading Arab forces as documented in a Navsari grant of 739 CE. The *Tājika* (Arab) army defeated was, according to the grant, one that had attacked "Kacchella, Saindhava, Saurashtra, Cavotaka, Maurya and Gurjara" kings. Pulakesi subsequently received the titles "Solid Pillar of Deccan" (*Dakshināpatha-sādhāra*) and the "Repeller of the Unrepellable" (*Anivartaka-nivartayitr*). The Rashtrakuta prince Dantidurga, who was subsidiary to Chalukyas at this time, also played an important role in the battle.[408]

The kingdoms recorded in the Navsari grant are interpreted as follows: *Kacchelas* were the people of Kutch. The *Saindhavas* are thought to have been emigrants from Sindh, who presumably moved to Kathiawar after the Arab occupation of Sindh in 712 CE. Settling down in the norther tip of Kathiawar, they had a ruler by the name of Pushyadeva. The *Cavotakas* (also called *Capotaka* or *Capa*) were also associated with Kathiawar, with their capital at Anahilapataka. *Saurashtra* is south Kathiawar. The *Mauryas* and *Gurjaras* are open to interpretation. Blankinship takes them to be the Mauryas of Chittor and Gurjaras of Bhinmal whereas Baij Nath Puri takes them to be a subsidiary line of Mauryas based in Vallabhi and the Gurjaras of Bharuch under Jayabhata IV. In Puri's interpretation, this invasion of the Arab forces was limited to the southern parts of modern Gujarat with several small kingdoms, which got terminated when it reached the Chalukya empire.

Indications are that Al-Hakam was overstretched. An appeal for reinforcements from the Caliphate in 737 is recorded, with 600 men being sent, a surprisingly small contingent. Even this force was absorbed in its passage through Iraq for quelling a local rebellion.[409] The defeat at the hands of Chalukyas is believed to have been a blow to the Arab forces with large costs in men and arms.[409]

The weakened Arab forces were driven out by the subsidiaries of the erstwhile kings. The Guhilot prince Bappa Rawal (r. 734–753) drove out the Arabs who had put an end to the Maurya dynasty at Chittor. A Jain *prabandha* mentions a king *Nahada*, who is said to have been the first ruler of his family at Jalore, near Bhinmal, and who came into conflict with a Muslim ruler whom he defeated.[410] Nahada is identified with Nagabhata I (r. 730–760), the founder of the Gurjara-Pratihara dynasty, which is believed to have started from the Jalore-Bhinmal area and spread to Avanti at Ujjain.[411] The Gwalior inscription of the king Bhoja I, says that Nagabhata, the founder of the dynasty, defeated a powerful army of *Valacha Mlecchas* (foreigners called "Baluchs"[412]) around 725 CE.[413] Even though many historians believe that Nagabhata repulsed Arab forces at Ujjain.

Baij Nath Puri states that the Arab campaigns to the east of Indus proved ineffective. However, they had the unintended effect of integrating the Indian kingdoms in Rajasthan and Gujarat. The Chalukyas extended their empire to the north after fighting off the Arabs successfully. Nagabhata I secured a firm position and laid the foundation for a new dynasty, which would rise to become the principal deterrent against Arab expansion.[414] Blankinship also notes that Hakam's campaigns caused the creation of larger, more powerful kingdoms, which was inimical to the caliphate's interests.[415] Al-Hakam died in battle in 740 CE while fighting the *Meds* of north Saurashtra (Maitrakas, probably under the control of Chalukyas at this time).[416]

Aftermath

Following Hakam's death, the Muslim presence had effectively ended in the Indian subcontinent excluding Sindh. Al-Hakam's successor 'Amr bin Muhammad bin al-Qasim al-Thaqafi (740-43) didn't have the opportunity to undertake any offensive. The Sindhis revolted perhaps with the help of Indian kingdoms, elected a king and besieged 'Amr in the capital al-Mansura. He wrote to Yusub bin Umar, governor of Iraq, for assistance and was provided with 4,000 men to subdue the revolt which he was able to do. The next governor is said to have undertaken eighteen campaigns. If so, they were probably insignificant because the only source that reports about them gives no details and the Muslims never expanded beyond Sindh again.

The death of Al-Hakam effectively ended the Arab presence to the east of Sindh. In the following years, the Arabs were preoccupied with controlling Sindh. They made occasional raids to the sea ports of Kathiawar to protect their trading routes but did not venture inland into Indian kingdoms. Dantidurga, the Rashtrakuta chief of Berar turned against his Chalukya overlords in 753 and became independent. The Gurjara-Pratiharas immediately to his north became his foes and the Arabs became his allies, due to the geographic logic as well as the economic interests of sea trade. The Pratiharas extended their influence throughout Gujarat and Rajasthan almost to the edge of the Indus river, but their push to become the central power of north India was repeatedly thwarted by the Rashtrakutas. This uneasy balance of power between the three powers lasted till the end of the caliphate.Wikipedia:Citation needed

Later in 776 CE, a naval expedition by the Arabs was defeated by the Saindhava naval fleet under Agguka I.

List of major battles

The table below lists some of the major military conflicts during the Arab expeditions in Gujarat and Rajasthan.

| Arab | Indian |

(Colour legend for victor)

Year	Aggressor	Location	Commander	Details
636	Arab	Tanah, near Mumbai	Caliph Umar	Major naval raid.
713	Arab	Multan	Muhammad ibn Qasim	Muslim conquest of urban Sindh completed
715	Indian	Alor	Hullishah, al-Muhallab	Indian army retakes major city from Muslims.
715	Indian	Mehran	Hullishah, al-Muhallab	Muslims stall the Hindu counter-offensive
718	Indian	Brahmanabadh	Hullishah, al-Muhallab	Indian attacks resume
721	Arab	Brahmanabadh	al-Muhallab, Hullishah	Hullishah becomes a Muslim, likely due to military reversals.

724–740	Arab	Uzain, Mirmad, Dahnaj, others	Junayd of Sindh	Raiding India as part of Umayyad policy in India.
725	Arab	Avanti	Junayd, Nagabhata I	Defeat of large Arab expedition against Avanti.[417]
740	Arab	Chittor	Maurya of Chittor	Indians repulse an Arab siege[418]
743?	Arab	al-Bailaman, al-Jurz	Junayd	Annexed by Arabs.[419]
750	Arab	Vallabhi		Maitraka capital sacked in Arab raid.[420]
776–778	Arab	Saurashtra	Agguka I, Caliph Al-Mahdi	Arab amphibious assault annihilated.[421]
780–787	Arab	Fort Tharra, Bagar, Bhaqmbur	Haji Abu Turab	Vigorous Arab offensive captures several important Indian outposts.[422]
800–810	Indian	Sindh border	Nagabhata II, Caliph Al-Amin	Several Arab outposts fall to Pratihara incursions.[423]
820–830	Arab	Fort Sindan	al-Fadl ibn Mahan	Sindan captured, but Indian riots make pacification of the region impossible.
839	Indian	Fort Sindan	Mihira Bhoja	Indians expel Arab garrison.
845	Indian	Yavana	Dharmpala?	Arab principality becomes vassal of Pratiharas.
845–860	Indian	Pratihara-Sindh	Mihira Bhoja	Uneasy truce between Sindh and Rajputana.
860	Indian	Rajputana-Sindh	Kokkalla I	Kalachuri raids into Sindh to finance war with Pratihara kingdom

Bibliography

- Al-Baladhuri, Abul Abbas Ahmad ibn-Jabir (1924). *Kitab Futuh Al-Buldan [The Origins of Islamic State]*. **2**. Translated by Francis Clark Murgotten. Columbia University.
- Bhandarkar, D. R. (1929). "Indian Studies No. I: Slow Progress of Islam Power in Ancient India". *Annals of the Bhandarkar Oriental Research Institute*. **10** (1/2): 25–44. JSTOR 41682407[424].
- Blankinship, Khalid Yahya (1994). *The End of the Jihad State: The Reign of Hisham Ibn 'Abd al-Malik and the Collapse of the Umayyads*[425]. SUNY Press. ISBN 978-0-7914-1827-7.
- Chattopadhyaya, B. D. (1998), *Representing the Other? Sanskrit Sources and the Muslims*, New Delhi: Manohar, ISBN 8173042527
- Elliot, Henry Miers (1869). *History of India, as told by its own historians*[426]. London.

- Majumdar, R. C., ed. (1955). *History and Culture of Indian People*. Bombay.
- Majumdar, R. C. (1977). *Ancient India* (Eighth ed.). Delhi: Motilal Banarsidass. ISBN 81-208-0436-8.
- Puri, Baij Nath (1986). *The History of the Gurjara-Pratiharas*. Delhi: Munshiram Manoharlal.
- Ray, Hem Chandra (1973) [first published 1931]. *The Dynastic History of Northern India, I. Early Medieval Period*. Munshiram Manoharlal.
- Rāya, Panchānana (1939). *A historical review of Hindu India: 300 B. C. to 1200 A. D.*[427] I. M. H. Press.
- Sen, Sailendra Nath (1999). *Ancient Indian History and Civilisation*. New Delhi: New Age International Publishers. ISBN 81-224-1198-3.
- Sharma, Sanjay (2006). "Negotiating Identity and Status Legitimation and Patronage under the Gurjara-Pratīhāras of Kanauj". *Studies in History*. **22** (22): 181–220. doi: 10.1177/025764300602200202[428].
- Tripathi, Rama Shankar (1989), *History of Kanauj: To the Moslem Conquest*[429], Motilal Banarsidass Publ., ISBN 978-81-208-0404-3
- Vaidya, C. V. (2013) [first published 1921]. *History of Medieval Hindu India*. HardPress Publishing. ISBN 1313363294.
- Wink, André (2002) [first published 1996], *Al-Hind: The Making of the Indo-Islamic World*[430] (Third ed.), Brill, ISBN 0391041738

Further reading

- Atherton, Cynthia Packert (1997). *The Sculpture of Early Medieval Rajasthan*. BRILL. ISBN 9004107894.
- Bose, Mainak Kumar (1988). *Late classical India*. Calcutta: A. Mukherjee & Co. OL 1830998M[431].
- O'Brien, Anthony Gordon (1996). *The Ancient Chronology of Thar: The Bhattika, Laulika and Sindh Eras*. Oxford University Press India. ISBN 1582559309.

Tripartite Struggle

The **Tripartite Struggle** for control of northern India took place in the ninth century. The struggle was between the Pratihara Empire, the Pala Empire and the Rashtrakuta Empire.[432]:20

Part of a series on the
History of India

- v
- t
- e[433]

Towards the end of the successor of Nagabhata II, the ruler of pratiharas successfully attacked Kanauj and established control there. This was short-lived as he was soon after defeated by the Rastrakuta ruler, Govinda III. However the Rastrakutas also formed a matrimonial relationship with the Gangas and defeated the kingdom of Vengi. By the end of the 9th Century the power of the Rastrakutas started to decline along with the Palas. This was seen as an ideal opportunity by the feudal king Taila II who defeated the Rastrakuta ruler and declared his kingdom there. This came to be known the Later Chalukya dynasty. Their kingdom included the states of Karnataka, Konkan and northern Godavari. By the end of the tripartite struggle, the Pratiharas emerged victorious and established themselves as the rulers of central India.

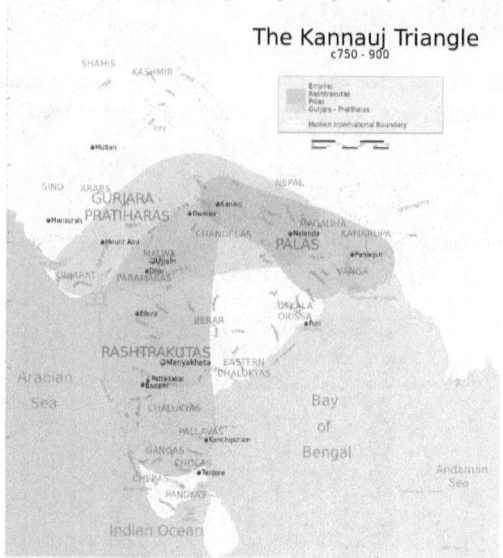

Figure 42: *Kanauj Triangle*

History

Not much is known about the kingdom of the Kannauj after Emperor Harsha's death in 647 AD resulting in a great confusion due to the absence of his heirs. Kannauj came for a short period under the hands of Arunasva who attacked Wang Hstian-tse who came to the court of king Harsha as ambassador of the Chinese emperor Tai-tsung. However Wang Hstian-tse succeeded in capturing Arunasva who was taken back to China to spend his days in attendance on the Tang Emperor.

About AD 730, Yashovarman established a kingdom at Kannauj. His invasion of Gauda (Bengal) formed the subject of the Prakrit poem *Gaudavaho* (Slaying of the king of Gauda), composed by his courtier Vakapatiraja in the 8th century.

After Yashovarman, three kings — Vijrayudha, Indrayudha and Chakrayudha — ruled over Kannauj between close of the 8th century till the 820s. Taking advantage of the weakness of these Ayudha rulers and attracted by the immense strategic and economic potentialities of the kingdom of Kannauj, the Gurjara-Pratiharas of Bhinmal (Rajasthan), the Palas of Bengal and Bihar and the Rashtrakutas of the Manyakheta (Karnataka) fought against each other. This tripartite struggle for Kannauj lingered for almost two centuries and ultimately ended in favour of the Gurjara-Pratihara ruler Nagabhata II who made the city the capital of the Gurjara-Pratihara state, which ruled for nearly three centuries.

References

- Majumdar, Ramesh Chandra (1977) [1952], *Ancient India*[434] (Reprinted ed.), Motilal Banarsidass, ISBN 9788120804364

Gurjara-Pratihara dynasty

Gurjara-Pratihara dynasty	
mid-8th century CE–1036 CE	
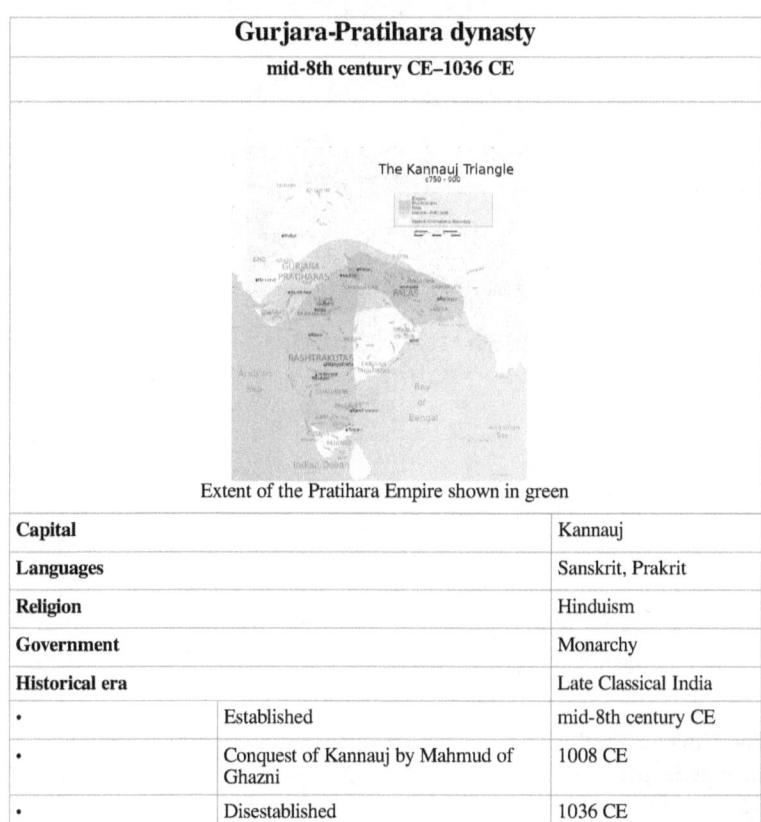 Extent of the Pratihara Empire shown in green	
Capital	Kannauj
Languages	Sanskrit, Prakrit
Religion	Hinduism
Government	Monarchy
Historical era	Late Classical India
• Established	mid-8th century CE
• Conquest of Kannauj by Mahmud of Ghazni	1008 CE
• Disestablished	1036 CE

Preceded by	Succeeded by
Empire of Harsha	Chandela
	Paramara dynasty
	Kalachuris of Tripuri
	Ghurid Sultanate
	Chavda dynasty
	Chahamanas of Shakambhari
Today part of	India

- v
- t
- e[435]

The **Gurjara-Pratihara dynasty**, also known as the **Pratihara Empire**, was an imperial power during the Late Classical period on the Indian subcontinent, that ruled much of Northern India from the mid-8th to the 11th century. They ruled first at Ujjain and later at Kannauj.[436]

The Gurjara-Pratiharas were instrumental in containing Arab armies moving east of the Indus River. Nagabhata I defeated the Arab army under Junaid and Tamin during the Caliphate campaigns in India. Under Nagabhata II, the Gurjara-Pratiharas became the most powerful dynasty in northern India. He was succeeded by his son Ramabhadra, who ruled briefly before being succeeded by his son, Mihira Bhoja. Under Bhoja and his successor Mahendrapala I, the Pratihara Empire reached its peak of prosperity and power. By the time of Mahendrapala, the extent of its territory rivalled that of the Gupta Empire stretching from the border of Sindh in the west to Bengal in the east and from the Himalayas in the north to areas past the Narmada in the south.[437,438] The expansion triggered a tripartite power struggle with the Rashtrakuta and Pala empires for control of the Indian Subcontinent. During this period, Imperial Pratihara took the title of *Maharajadhiraja of Āryāvarta* (*Great King of Kings of India*).

Gurjara-Pratihara are known for their sculptures, carved panels and open pavilion style temples. The greatest development of their style of temple building was at Khajuraho, now a UNESCO World Heritage Site.[439]

The power of the Pratiharas was weakened by dynastic strife. It was further diminished as a result of a great raid led by the Rashtrakuta ruler Indra III who, in about 916, sacked Kannauj. Under a succession of rather obscure rulers, the Pratiharas never regained their former influence. Their feudatories became more and more powerful, one by one throwing off their allegiance until, by the end of the 10th century, the Pratiharas controlled little more than the Gangetic Doab. Their last important king, Rajyapala, was driven from Kannauj by Mahmud of Ghazni in 1018.[438]

Etymology and origin

The origin of the dynasty and the meaning of the term "Gurjara" in its name is a topic of debate among historians. The rulers of this dynasty used the self-designation "Pratihara" for their clan, and never referred to themselves as Gurjaras.[440] The *Imperial* Pratiharas could have emphasized their Kshatriya, instead of Gurjara, identity for political reasons. However, at local levels *Pratiharas* were not wary of projecting their tribal (Gurjara) identity.[441] They claimed descent from the legendary hero Lakshmana, who is said to have acted as a *pratihara* ("door-keeper") for his brother Rama.[442,443] K. A. Nilakanta Sastri theorized that the ancestors of the Pratiharas served the Rashtrakutas, and the term "Pratihara" derives from the title of their office in the Rashtrakuta court.

Multiple inscriptions of their neighbouring dynasties describe the Pratiharas as "Gurjara".[444] The term "Gurjara-Pratihara" occurs only in the Rajor inscription of a feudatory ruler named Mathanadeva, who describes himself as a "Gurjara-Pratihara". Another Pratihara king named Hariraja is also mentioned as a "ferocious Gurjara" (garjjad gurjjara meghacanda) in the Kadwaha inscription.[445] According to one school of thought, Gurjara was the name of

Figure 43: *Nilgund inscription (866) of Amoghavarsha mentions that his father Govinda III subjugated the Gurjaras of Chitrakuta*

the territory (see Gurjara-desha) originally ruled by the Pratiharas; gradually, the term came to denote the people of this territory. An opposing theory is that Gurjara was the name of the tribe to which the dynasty belonged, and Pratihara was a clan of this tribe.[446] Several historians consider Gurjaras to be the ancestors of the modern Gurjar or Gujjar tribe.[447] The proponents of the tribal designation theory argue that the Rajor inscription mentions the phrase: "all the fields cultivated by the Gurjaras". Here, the term "Gurjara" obviously refers to a group of people rather than a region.[448,449] The *Pampa Bharata* refers the Gurjara-Pratihara king Mahipala as a Gurjara king. Rama Shankar Tripathi argues that here Gurjara can only refer to the king's ethnicity, and not territory, since the Pratiharas ruled a much larger area of which Gurjara-desha was only a small part.[448] Critics of this theory, such as D. C. Ganguly, argue that the term "Gurjara" is used as a demonym in the phrase "cultivated by the Gurjaras".[450] Several ancient sources including inscriptions clearly mention "Gurjara" as the name of a country.[451,452,453] Shanta Rani Sharma notes that an inscription of Gallaka in 795 CE states that Nagabhata I, the founder of the Imperial Pratihara dynasty, conquered the "invincible Gurjaras," which makes it unlikely that the Pratiharas were themselves Gurjaras.[454] However, she does concede that Imperial Pratiharas were indeed known as Gurjaras, on account of their nationality. She mentions two groups of people who were known as Gurjaras, and draws a line between them; i.e. Gurjaras who were an *ethnic* people and Gurjaras who were *nationals* of Gurjaradesa (Gurjara Country).[455] According to her, Gujjars are the descendants of ethnic Gurjaras, and have nothing to do with imperial Pratiharas and Chalukyas who were also known as Gurjaras (due to their Gurjara nationality).[454]

Among those who believe that the term Gurjara was originally a tribal designation, there are disagreements over whether they were native Indians or foreigners.[456] The proponents of the foreign origin theory point out that the Gurjara-Pratiharas suddenly emerged as a political power in north India around 6th century CE, shortly after the Huna invasion of that region.[457] Critics of the foreign origin theory argue that there is no conclusive evidence of their foreign origin: they were well-assimilated in the Indian culture. Moreover, if they invaded Indian through the north-west, it is inexplicable why would they choose to settle in the semi-arid area of present-day Rajasthan, rather than the fertile Indo-Gangetic Plain.[458]

According to the Agnivansha legend given in the later manuscripts of *Prithviraj Raso*, the Pratiharas and three other Rajput dynasties originated from a sacrificial fire-pit (agnikunda) at Mount Abu. Some colonial-era historians interpreted this myth to suggest a foreign origin for these dynasties. According to this theory, the foreigners were admitted in the Hindu caste system after performing a fire ritual.[459] However, this legend is not found in the earliest available copies of *Prithviraj Raso*. It is based on a Paramara legend; the 16th century Rajput bards probably extended the original legend to include other dynasties including the Pratiharas, in order to foster Rajput unity against the Mughals.[460]

History

The original centre of Pratihara power is a matter of controversy. R. C. Majumdar, on the basis of a verse in the Harivamsha-Purana, AD 783, the interpretation of which he conceded was not free from difficulty, held that Vatsaraja ruled at Ujjain . Dasharatha Sharma, interpreting it differently located the original capital in the Bhinmala Jalor area. M. W. Meister and Shanta Rani Sharma concur with his conclusion in view of the fact that the writer of the Jaina narrative Kuvalayamala states that it was composed at Jalor in the time of Vatsaraja in AD 778, which is five years before the composition of Harivamsha-Purana.

Early rulers

Nagabhata I (730–756) extended his control east and south from Mandor, conquering Malwa as far as Gwalior and the port of Bharuch in Gujarat. He established his capital at Avanti in Malwa, and checked the expansion of the Arabs, who had established themselves in Sind. In this battle (738 CE) Nagabhata led a confederacy of Gurjara-Pratiharas to defeat the Muslim Arabs who had till then been pressing on victorious through West Asia and Iran. Nagabhata I

Figure 44: *Varaha (the boar-headed Vishnu avatar), on a Gurjara-Pratihara coin. 850–900 CE. British Museum.*

was followed by two weak successors, who were in turn succeeded by Vatsraja (775–805).

Conquest of Kannauj and further expansion

The metropolis of Kannauj had suffered a power vacuum following the death of Harsha without an heir, which resulted in the disintegration of the Empire of Harsha. This space was eventually filled by Yashovarman around a century later but his position was dependent upon an alliance with Lalitaditya Muktapida. When Muktapida undermined Yashovarman, a tri-partite struggle for control of the city developed, involving the Pratiharas, whose territory was at that time to the west and north, the Palas of Bengal in the east and the Rashtrakutas, whose base lay at the south in the Deccan. Vatsraja successfully challenged and defeated the Pala ruler Dharmapala and Dantidurga, the Rashtrakuta king, for control of Kannauj.

Around 786, the Rashtrakuta ruler Dhruva (c. 780–793) crossed the Narmada River into Malwa, and from there tried to capture Kannauj. Vatsraja was defeated by the Dhruva Dharavarsha of the Rashtrakuta dynasty around 800. Vatsraja was succeeded by Nagabhata II (805–833), who was initially defeated by the Rashtrakuta ruler Govinda III (793–814), but later recovered Malwa from the Rashtrakutas, conquered Kannauj and the Indo-Gangetic Plain as far as Bihar from the Palas, and again checked the Muslims in the west. He rebuilt the great Shiva temple at Somnath in Gujarat, which had been demolished in an Arab raid from Sindh. Kannauj became the center of the Gurjara-Pratihara state, which covered much of northern India during the peak of their power, c. 836–910.Wikipedia:Citation needed

Rambhadra (833-c. 836) briefly succeeded Nagabhata II. Mihira Bhoja (c. 836–886) expanded the Pratihara dominions west to the border of Sind, east to Bengal, and south to the Narmada. His son, Mahenderpal I (890–910), expanded further eastwards in Magadha, Bengal, and Assam.Wikipedia:Citation needed

Decline

Bhoj II (910–912) was overthrown by Mahipala I (912–944). Several feudatories of the empire took advantage of the temporary weakness of the Gurjara-Pratiharas to declare their independence, notably the Paramaras of Malwa, the Chandelas of Bundelkhand, the Kalachuris of Mahakoshal, the Tomaras of Haryana, and the Chauhans of Rajputana. The south Indian Emperor Indra III (c. 914–928) of the Rashtrakuta dynasty briefly captured Kannauj in 916, and although the Pratiharas regained the city, their position continued to weaken in the 10th century, partly as a result of the drain of simultaneously fighting off Turkic attacks from the west, the attacks from the Rashtrakuta dynasty from the south and the Pala advances in the east. The Gurjara-Pratiharas lost control of Rajasthan to their feudatories, and the Chandelas captured the strategic fortress of Gwalior in central India around 950. By the end of the 10th century the Gurjara-Pratihara domains had dwindled to a small state centered on Kannauj.Wikipedia:Citation needed

Mahmud of Ghazni captured Kannauj in 1018, and the Pratihara ruler Rajapala fled. He was subsequently captured and killed by the Chandela ruler Vidyadhara. The Chandela ruler then placed Rajapala's son Trilochanpala on the throne as a proxy. Jasapala, the last Gurjara-Pratihara ruler of Kannauj, died in 1036.Wikipedia:Citation needed

Gurjara-Pratihara art

Vishnu Trivikrama, an 11th-century Pratihara stone sculpture from Kashipur, kept at the National Museum, New Delhi.

Teli ka Mandir is a 8-9th century Hindu Temple built by the Pratihara emperor Mihira Bhoja.

There are notable examples of architecture from the Gurjara-Pratihara era, including sculptures and carved panels. Their temples, constructed in an open pavilion style, were particularly impressive at Khajuraho.

Māru-Gurjara architecture

Māru-Gurjara architecture was developed during Gurjara Pratihara Empire.

Bateshwar Hindu temples complex

Bateshwar Hindu temples, Madhya Pradesh was constructed during the Gurjara-Pratihara Empire between 8th to 11th century.[461]

Caliphate campaigns in India

Junaid, the successor of Qasim, finally subdued the Hindu resistance within Sindh. Taking advantage of the conditions in Western India, which at that time was covered with several small states, Junaid led a large army into the region in early 738 CE. Dividing this force into two he plundered several cities in southern Rajasthan, western Malwa, and Gujarat.

Indian inscriptions confirm this invasion but record the Arab success only against the smaller states in Gujarat. They also record the defeat of the Arabs at two places. The southern army moving south into Gujarat was repulsed at Navsari by the south Indian Emperor Vikramaditya II of the Chalukya dynasty and Rashtrakutas. The army that went east, after sacking several places, reached Avanti whose ruler Nagabhata (Gurjara-Pratihara) trounced the invaders and forced them to flee. After his victory Nagabhata took advantage of the disturbed conditions to acquire control over the numerous small states up to the border of Sindh.

Junaid probably died from the wounds inflicted in the battle with the Gurjara-Pratihara. His successor Tamin organized a fresh army and attempted to avenge Junaid's defeat towards the close of the year 738 CE. But this time Nagabhata, with his Chauhan and Guhilot feudatories, met the Muslim army before it could leave the borders of Sindh. The battle resulted in the complete rout of the Arabs who fled broken into Sindh with the Gurjara-Pratihara close behind them.

The Arabs crossed over to the other side of the Indus River, abandoning all their lands to the victorious Hindus. The local chieftains took advantage of these conditions to re-establish their independence. Subsequently, the Arabs constructed the city of Mansurah on the other side of the wide and deep Indus, which was safe from attack. This became their new capital in Sindh. Thus began the reign of the imperial Gurjara-Pratiharas.

In the Gwalior inscription, it is recorded that Gurjara-Pratihara emperor Nagabhata "crushed the large army of the powerful Mlechcha king." This large army consisted of cavalry, infantry, siege artillery, and probably a force of camels. Since Tamin was a new governor he had a force of Syrian cavalry from Damascus, local Arab contingents, converted Hindus of Sindh, and foreign mercenaries like the Turkics. All together the invading army may have had anywhere between 10–15,000 cavalry, 5000 infantry, and 2000 camels.Wikipedia:Citation needed

The Arab chronicler Sulaiman describes the army of the Pratiharas as it stood in 851 CE, "The ruler of Gurjars maintains numerous forces and no other Indian prince has so fine a cavalry. He is unfriendly to the Arabs, still he acknowledges that the king of the Arabs is the greatest of rulers. Among the princes of India there is no greater foe of the Islamic faith than he. He has got riches, and his camels and horses are numerous."

Legacy

Historians of India, since the days of Elphinstone, have wondered at the slow progress of Muslim invaders in India, as compared with their rapid advance in other parts of the world. The Arabs possibly only stationed small invasions independent of the Caliph. Arguments of doubtful validity have often been put forward to explain this unique phenomenon. Currently it is believed that it was the power of the Gurjara-Pratihara army that effectively barred the progress of the Muslims beyond the confines of Sindh, their first conquest for nearly three hundred years. In the light of later events this might be regarded as the "Chief contribution of the Gurjara Pratiharas to the history of India".

List of rulers

- Nagabhata I (730–760)
- Kakustha and Devaraja (760–780)
- Vatsaraja (780–800)
- Nagabhata II (800–833)
- Ramabhadra (833–836)
- Mihira Bhoja or Bhoja I (836–885)
- Mahendrapala I (885–910)
- Bhoja II (910–913)
- Mahipala I (913–944)
- Mahendrapala II (944–948)
- Devapala (948–954)
- Vinayakapala (954–955)
- Mahipala II (955–956)
- Vijayapala II (956–960)
- Rajapala (960–1018)
- Trilochanapala (1018–1027)
- Yasahpala (1024–1036)

References

Bibliography

<templatestyles src="Template:Refbegin/styles.css" />

- Avari, Burjor (2007). *India: The Ancient Past. A History of the Indian-Subcontinent from 7000 BC to AD 1200*[462]. New York: Routledge. ISBN 978-0-203-08850-0.
- Sircar, Dineschandra (1971). *Studies in the Geography of Ancient and Medieval India*[463]. Motilal Banarsidass Publ. ISBN 9788120806900.
- Ganguly, D. C. (1935), Narendra Nath Law, ed., "Origin of the Pratihara Dynasty", *The Indian Historical Quarterly*, Caxton, **XI**: 167–168
- Majumdar, R. C. (1981), "The Gurjara-Pratiharas", in R. S. Sharma and K. K. Dasgupta, *A Comprehensive history of India: A.D. 985-1206*[464], 3 (Part 1), Indian History Congress / People's Publishing House, ISBN 978-81-7007-121-1
- Majumdar, R.C. (1955). The Age of Imperial Kanauj (First ed.). Bombay: Bharatiya Vidya Bhavan.
- Mishra, V. B. (1954), "Who were the Gurjara-Pratīhāras?", *Annals of the Bhandarkar Oriental Research Institute*, **35** (¼): 42–53, JSTOR 41784918[465]
- Meister, M.W (1991). Encyclopaedia of Indian Temple Architecture, Vol. 2, pt.2, North India: Period of Early Maturity, c. AD 700-900 (first ed.). Delhi: American Institute of Indian Studies. p. 153. ISBN 0195629213
- Puri, Baij Nath (1957), *The history of the Gurjara-Pratīhāras*[466], Munshiram Manoharlal
  - Puri, Baij Nath (1986) [first published 1957], *The History of the Gurjara-Pratiharas*, Delhi: Munshiram Manoharlal
- Sharma, Dasharatha (1966). Rajasthan through the Ages. Bikaner: Rajasthan State Archives
- Sharma, Sanjay (2006), "Negotiating Identity and Status Legitimation and Patronage under the Gurjara-Pratīhāras of Kanauj", *Studies in History*, **22** (22): 181–220, doi: 10.1177/025764300602200202[467]
- Sharma, Shanta Rani (2012), "Exploding the Myth of the Gūjara Identity of the Imperial Pratihāras", *Indian Historical Review*, **39** (1): 1–10, doi: 10.1177/0376983612449525[468]
- Singh, R. B. (1964), *History of the Chāhamānas*[469], N. Kishore
- Sharma, Shanta Rani (2017). Origin and Rise of the Imperial Pratihāras of Rajasthan: Transitions, Trajectories and Historical Change (First ed.). Jaipur: University of Rajasthan. p. 77-78. ISBN 978-93-85593-18-5.
- Tripathi, Rama Shankar (1959). *History of Kanauj: To the Moslem Conquest*[470]. Motilal Banarsidass. ISBN 978-81-208-0478-4.
- Yadava, Ganga Prasad (1982), *Dhanapāla and His Times: A Sociocultural Study Based Upon His Works*[471], Concept

Wikimedia Commons has media related to *Gurjara-Pratihara dynasty*.

 Wikiquote has quotations related to: *Gurjara-Pratihara dynasty*

Rashtrakuta dynasty

Rashtrakutas of Manyakheta		
Empire		
753–982		
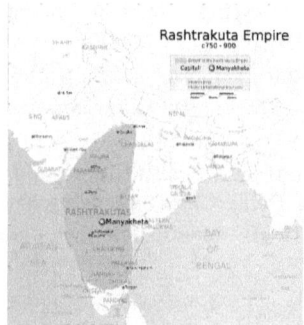 Extent of Rashtrakuta Empire, 800 CE, 915 CE		
Capital		Manyakheta
Languages		Kannada Sanskrit
Religion		Hinduism Jainism Buddhism[472]
Government		Monarchy
Maharaja		
•	735–756	Dantidurga
•	973–982	Indra IV
History		
•	Earliest Rashtrakuta records	753
•	Established	753
•	Disestablished	982

Preceded by	Succeeded by
Chalukya dynasty	Western Chalukya Empire

Today part of	India

Rashtrakuta Emperors (753-982)	
Dantidurga	(735 - 756)
Krishna I	(756 - 774)
Govinda II	(774 - 780)
Dhruva Dharavarsha	(780 - 793)
Govinda III	(793 - 814)
Amoghavarsha	(814 - 878)
Krishna II	(878 - 914)
Indra III	(914 -929)
Amoghavarsha II	(929 - 930)
Govinda IV	(930 – 936)
Amoghavarsha III	(936 – 939)
Krishna III	(939 – 967)
Khottiga	(967 – 972)
Karka II	(972 – 973)
Indra IV	(973 – 982)
Tailapa II (*Western Chalukyas*)	(973-997)

Rashtrakuta (IAST: *rāṣṭrakūṭa*) was a royal dynasty ruling large parts of the Indian subcontinent between the sixth and 10th centuries. The earliest known Rashtrakuta inscription is a 7th-century copper plate grant detailing their rule from Manapura, a city in Central or West India. Other ruling Rashtrakuta clans from the same period mentioned in inscriptions were the kings of Achalapur (modern Elichpur in Maharashtra) and the rulers of Kannauj. Several controversies exist regarding the origin of these early Rashtrakutas, their native home and their language.

The Elichpur clan was a feudatory of the Badami Chalukyas, and during the rule of Dantidurga, it overthrew Chalukya Kirtivarman II and went on to build an empire with the Gulbarga region in modern Karnataka as its base. This clan came to be known as the Rashtrakutas of Manyakheta, rising to power in South India in 753. At the same time the Pala dynasty of Bengal and the Prathihara dynasty of Malwa were gaining force in eastern and northwestern India respectively. An Arabic text, *Silsilat al-Tawarikh* (851), called the Rashtrakutas one of the four principal empires of the world.[473]

This period, between the eighth and the 10th centuries, saw a tripartite struggle for the resources of the rich Gangetic plains, each of these three empires annexing the seat of power at Kannauj for short periods of time. At their peak the Rashtrakutas of Manyakheta ruled a vast empire stretching from the Ganges River and Yamuna River doab in the north to Cape Comorin in the south, a fruitful time of political expansion, architectural achievements and famous literary contributions. The early kings of this dynasty were influenced by Hinduism and the later kings by Jainism.

During their rule, Jain mathematicians and scholars contributed important works in Kannada and Sanskrit. Amoghavarsha I, the most famous king of this dynasty wrote *Kavirajamarga*, a landmark literary work in the Kannada language. Architecture reached a milestone in the Dravidian style, the finest example of which is seen in the Kailasanath Temple at Ellora in modern Maharashtra. Other important contributions are the Kashivishvanatha temple and the Jain Narayana temple at Pattadakal in modern Karnataka, both of which are UNESCO World Heritage Sites.

History

The origin of the Rashtrakuta dynasty has been a controversial topic of Indian history. These issues pertain to the origin of the earliest ancestors of the Rashtrakutas during the time of Emperor Ashoka in the 2nd century BCE,[474] and the connection between the several Rashtrakuta dynasties that ruled small kingdoms in northern and central India and the Deccan between the 6th and 7th centuries. The relationship of these medieval Rashtrakutas to the most famous later dynasty, the Rashtrakutas of Manyakheta (present day Malkhed in the Gulbarga district, Karnataka state), who ruled between the 8th and 10th centuries has also been debated.[475,476]

The sources for Rashtrakuta history include medieval inscriptions, ancient literature in the Pali language,[477] contemporaneous literature in Sanskrit and Kannada and the notes of the Arab travellers.[478] Theories about the dynastic lineage (*Surya Vamsa*—Solar line and *Chandra Vamsa*—Lunar line), the native region and the ancestral home have been proposed, based on information gleaned from inscriptions, royal emblems, the ancient clan names such as "Rashtrika", epithets (*Ratta, Rashtrakuta, Lattalura Puravaradhiswara*), the names of princes and princesses of the dynasty, and clues from relics such as coins.[479,480] Scholars debate over which ethnic/linguistic groups can claim the early Rashtrakutas. Possibilities include the north western ethnic groups of

Figure 45: *Shiva sculpture in Kailasanath Temple, Ellora Caves*

Figure 46: *Three-storied monolithic Jain cave temple at Ellora*

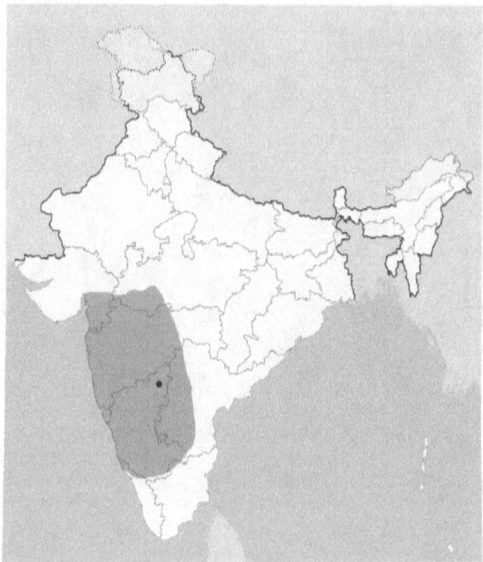

Figure 47: *Core territory of the empire of Manyakheta*

India,[481] the Kannadiga,[482,483] Reddi,[484] the Maratha,[485,486] or the tribes from the Punjab region.[487]

Scholars however concur that the rulers of the imperial dynasty in the 8th to 10th century made the Kannada language as important as Sanskrit. Rashtrakuta inscriptions use both Kannada and Sanskrit (historians Sheldon Pollock and Jan Houben claim they are mostly in Kannada),[488,489,490,491,492] and the rulers encouraged literature in both languages. The earliest existing Kannada literary writings are credited to their court poets and royalty.[493,494,495,496] Though these Rashtrakutas were Kannadigas,[497,498,499,500] they were conversant in a northern Deccan language as well.

The heart of the Rashtrakuta empire included nearly all of Karnataka, Maharashtra and parts of Andhra Pradesh, an area which the Rashtrakutas ruled for over two centuries. The Samangadh copper plate grant (753) confirms that the feudatory King Dantidurga, who probably ruled from Achalapura in Berar (modern Elichpur in Maharashtra), defeated the great Karnatic army (referring to the army of the Badami Chalukyas) of Kirtivarman II of Badami in 753 and took control of the northern regions of the Chalukya empire.[501,502,503] He then helped his father-in-law, Pallava King Nandivarman regain Kanchi from the Chalukyas and defeated the Gurjaras of Malwa, and the rulers of Kalinga, Kosala and Srisailam.[504,505]

Dantidurga's successor Krishna I brought major portions of present-day Karnataka and Konkan under his control.[506,507] During the rule of Dhruva Dharavarsha who took control in 780, the kingdom expanded into an empire that encompassed all of the territory between the Kaveri River and Central India.[508,509,510] He led successful expeditions to Kannauj, the seat of northern Indian power where he defeated the Gurjara Pratiharas and the Palas of Bengal, gaining him fame and vast booty but not more territory. He also brought the Eastern Chalukyas and Gangas of Talakad under his control.[511] According to Altekar and Sen, the Rashtrakutas became a pan-India power during his rule.[512]

Expansion

The ascent of Dhruva Dharavarsha's third son, Govinda III, to the throne heralded an era of success like never before.[513] There is uncertainty about the location of the early capital of the Rashtrakutas at this time.[514,515,516] During his rule there was a three way conflict between the Rashtrakutas, the Palas and the Pratiharas for control over the Gangetic plains. Describing his victories over the Pratihara Emperor Nagabhatta II and the Pala Emperor Dharmapala, the Sanjan inscription states the horses of Govinda III drank from the icy waters of the Himalayan streams and his war elephants tasted the sacred waters of the Ganges.[517,518] His military exploits have been compared to those of Alexander the Great and Arjuna of Mahabharata.[519] Having conquered Kannauj, he travelled south, took firm hold over Gujarat, Kosala (Kaushal), Gangavadi, humbled the Pallavas of Kanchi, installed a ruler of his choice in Vengi and received two statues as an act of submission from the king of Ceylon (one statue of the king and another of his minister). The Cholas, the Pandyas and the Cheras all paid him tribute.[520,521,522] As one historian puts it, the drums of the Deccan were heard from the Himalayan caves to the shores of the Malabar. The Rashtrakutas empire now spread over the areas from Cape Comorin to Kannauj and from Banaras to Bharuch.[523,524]

The successor of Govinda III, Amoghavarsha I made Manyakheta his capital and ruled a large empire. Manyakheta remained the Rashtrakutas' regal capital until the end of the empire.[525,526,527] He came to the throne in 814 but it was not until 821 that he had suppressed revolts from feudatories and ministers. Amoghavarsha I made peace with the Western Ganga dynasty by giving them his two daughters in marriage, and then defeated the invading Eastern Chalukyas at Vingavalli and assumed the title *Viranarayana*.[528,529] His rule was not as militant as that of Govinda III as he preferred to maintain friendly relations with his neighbours, the Gangas, the Eastern Chalukyas and the Pallavas with whom he also cultivated marital ties. His era was an enriching one for the arts, literature and religion. Widely seen as the most famous of the Rashtrakuta Emperors, Amoghavarsha I was an accomplished scholar in Kannada and Sanskrit.[530] His *Kavirajamarga* is considered an important landmark in Kannada poetics and *Prashnottara Ratnamalika* in Sanskrit is a writing of high merit and was later translated into the Tibetan language.[531] Because of his religious temperament, his interest in the arts and literature and his peace-loving nature, he has been compared to the emperor Ashoka and called "Ashoka of the South".[532]

During the rule of Krishna II, the empire faced a revolt from the Eastern Chalukyas and its size decreased to the area including most of the Western Deccan and Gujarat.[533] Krishna II ended the independent status of the Gujarat branch and brought it under direct control from Manyakheta. Indra III recovered the dynasty's fortunes in central India by defeating the Paramara and then invaded the doab region of the Ganges and Jamuna rivers. He also defeated the dynasty's traditional enemies, the Pratiharas and the Palas, while maintaining his influence over Vengi.[534,535] The effect of his victories in Kannauj lasted several years according to the 930 copper plate inscription of Emperor Govinda IV.[536,537] After a succession of weak kings during whose reigns the empire lost control of territories in the north and east, Krishna III the last great ruler consolidated the empire so that it stretched from the Narmada River to Kaveri River and included the northern Tamil country (Tondaimandalam) while levying tribute on the king of Ceylon.[538,539,540,541,542]

Decline

In 972 A.D., during the rule of Khottiga Amoghavarsha, the Paramara King Siyaka Harsha attacked the empire and plundered Manyakheta, the capital of the Rashtrakutas. This seriously undermined the reputation of the Rastrakuta Empire and consequently led to its downfall. The final decline was sudden as Tailapa II, a feudatory of the Rashtrakuta ruling from Tardavadi province in modern Bijapur district, declared himself independent by taking advantage of this defeat.[543,544] Indra IV, the last emperor, committed Sallekhana (fasting unto death practised by Jain monks) at Shravanabelagola. With the fall of the Rashtrakutas, their feudatories and related clans in the Deccan and northern India declared independence. The Western Chalukyas annexed Manyakheta and made it their capital until 1015 and built an impressive empire in the Rashtrakuta heartland during the 11th century. The focus of dominance shifted to the Krishna River – Godavari River doab called Vengi. The former feudatories of the Rashtrakutas in western Deccan were brought under control of the Chalukyas, and the hitherto-suppressed Cholas of Tanjore became their arch enemies in the south.[545]

In conclusion, the rise of Rashtrakutas of Manyakheta had a great impact on India, even on India's north. Sulaiman (851), Al Masudi (944) and Ibn Khurdadba (912) wrote that their empire was the largest in contemporary India and Sulaiman further called it one among the four great contemporary empires of the world.[546,547,548] According to the travelogues of the Arabs Al Masudi and Ibn Khordidbih of the 10th century, "most of the kings of Hindustan turned their faces towards the Rashtrakuta king while they were praying, and they prostrated themselves before his ambassadors. The Rashtrakuta king was known as the "King of kings" (*Rajadhiraja*) who possessed the mightiest of armies and whose domains extended from Konkan to Sind."[549] Some historians have called these times an "Age of Imperial Kannauj". Since the Rashtrakutas successfully captured Kannauj, levied tribute on its rulers and presented themselves as masters of North India, the era could also be called the "Age of Imperial Karnataka". During their political expansion into central and northern India in the 8th to the 10th centuries, the Rashtrakutas or their relatives created several kingdoms that either ruled during the reign of the parent empire or continued to rule for centuries after its fall or came to power much later. Well-known among these were the Rashtrakutas of Gujarat (757–888),[550] the Rattas of Saundatti (875–1230) in modern Karnataka,[551] the Gahadavalas of Kannauj (1068–1223),[552] the Rashtrakutas of Rajasthan (known as Rajputana) and ruling from Hastikundi or Hathundi (893–996),[553] Dahal (near Jabalpur),[554] Mandore (near Jodhpur), the Rathores of Dhanop,[555] Rashtraudha dynasty of Mayuragiri in modern Maharashtra[556] and Rashtrakutas of Kannauj.[557] Rajadhiraja Chola's conquest of the island of Ceylon in the early 11th century CE led to the fall of four kings there. According to historian K. Pillay, one of them, King Madavarajah of the Jaffna kingdom, was an usurper from the Rashtrakuta Dynasty.

Administration

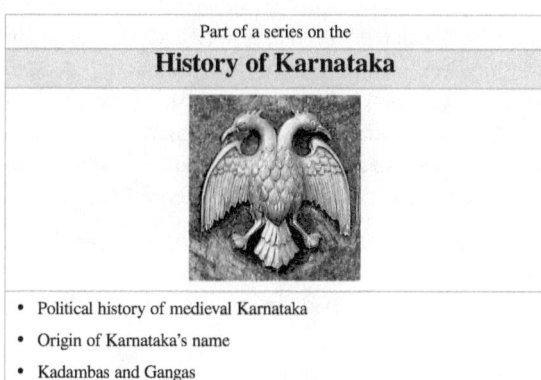

Part of a series on the
History of Karnataka

- Political history of medieval Karnataka
- Origin of Karnataka's name
- Kadambas and Gangas

- Chalukya Empire
- Rashtrakuta Empire
- Western Chalukya Empire
- Southern Kalachuri
- Hoysala Empire
- Vijayanagara Empire
- Bahmani Sultanate
- Bijapur Sultanate
- Kingdom of Mysore
- Nayakas of Keladi
- Nayakas of Chitradurga
- Haleri Kingdom
- Unification of Karnataka

Categories
• Architecture • Forts • Economies • Societies
• v • t • e[558]

Inscriptions and other literary records indicate the Rashtrakutas selected the crown prince based on heredity. The crown did not always pass on to the eldest son. Abilities were considered more important than age and chronology of birth, as exemplified by the crowning of Govinda III who was the third son of king Dhruva Dharavarsha. The most important position under the king was the Chief Minister (*Mahasandhivigrahi*) whose position came with five insignia commensurate with his position namely, a flag, a conch, a fan, a white umbrella, a large drum and five musical instruments called *Panchamahashabdas*. Under him was the commander (*Dandanayaka*), the foreign minister (*Mahakshapataladhikrita*) and a prime minister (*Mahamatya* or *Purnamathya*), all of whom were usually associated with one of the feudatory kings and must have held a position in government equivalent to a premier.[559] A *Mahasamantha* was a feudatory or higher ranking regal officer. All cabinet ministers were well versed in political science (*Rajneeti*) and possessed military training. There were cases where women supervised significant areas as when Revakanimaddi, daughter of Amoghavarsha I, administered Edathore *Vishaya*.

The kingdom was divided into *Mandala* or *Rashtras* (provinces). A *Rashtra* was ruled by a Rashtrapathi who on occasion was the emperor himself. Amoghavarsha I's empire had sixteen *Rashtras*. Under a *Rashtra* was a *Vishaya* (district) overseen by a Vishayapathi. Trusted ministers sometimes ruled more than a *Rashtra*. For example, Bankesha, a commander of Amoghavarsha I headed Banavasi-12000, Belvola-300, Puligere-300, Kunduru-500 and Kundarge-70, the suffix designating the number of villages in that territory. Below the *Vishaya* was the *Nadu* looked after by the Nadugowda or Nadugavunda; sometimes there were two such officials, one assuming the position through heredity and another appointed centrally. The lowest division was a *Grama* or village administered by a *Gramapathi* or *Prabhu Gavunda*.[560]

The Rashtrakuta army consisted of large contingents of infantry, horsemen, and elephants. A standing army was always ready for war in a cantonment (*Sthirabhuta Kataka*) in the regal capital of Manyakheta. Large armies were also maintained by the feudatory kings who were expected to contribute to the defense of the empire in case of war. Chieftains and all the officials also served as commanders whose postings were transferable if the need arose.[561]

The Rashtrakutas issued coins (minted in an *Akkashale*) such as *Suvarna*, *Drammas* in silver and gold weighing 65 grains, *Kalanju* weighing 48 grains, *Gadyanaka* weighing 96 grains, *Kasu* weighing 15 grains, *Manjati* with 2.5 grains and *Akkam* of 1.25 grain.[562]

Economy

The Rashtrakuta economy was sustained by its natural and agricultural produce, its manufacturing revenues and moneys gained from its conquests. Cotton was the chief crop of the regions of southern Gujarat, Khandesh and Berar. Minnagar, Gujarat, Ujjain, Paithan and Tagara were important centres of textile industry. Muslin cloth were manufactured in Paithan and Warangal. The cotton yarn and cloth was exported from Bharoch. White calicos were manufactured in Burhanpur and Berar and exported to Persia, Turkey, Poland, Arabia and Egypt.[563] The Konkan region, ruled by the feudatory Silharas, produced large quantities of betel leaves, coconut and rice while the lush forests of Mysore, ruled by the feudatory Gangas, produced such woods as sandal, timber, teak and ebony. Incense and perfumes were exported from the ports of Thana and Saimur.

The Deccan was rich in minerals, though its soil was not as fertile as that of the Gangetic plains. The copper mines of Cudappah, Bellary, Chanda, Buldhana, Narsingpur, Ahmadnagar, Bijapur and Dharwar were an important source of income and played an important role in the economy.[564] Diamonds were mined in Cudappah, Bellary, Kurnool and Golconda; the capital Manyakheta and Devagiri were important diamond and jewellery trading centres. The leather industry and tanning flourished in Gujarat and some regions

Figure 48: *Kashivishvanatha temple at Pattadakal, Karnataka*

of northern Maharashtra. Mysore with its vast elephant herds was important for the ivory industry.[565]

The Rashtrakuta empire controlled most of the western sea board of the subcontinent which facilitated its maritime trade.[566] The Gujarat branch of the empire earned a significant income from the port of Bharoch, one of the most prominent ports in the world at that time.[567] The empire's chief exports were cotton yarn, cotton cloth, muslins, hides, mats, indigo, incense, perfumes, betel nuts, coconuts, sandal, teak, timber, sesame oil and ivory. Its major imports were pearls, gold, dates from Arabia, slaves, Italian wines, tin, lead, topaz, storax, sweet clover, flint glass, antimony, gold and silver coins, singing boys and girls (for the entertainment of the royalty) from other lands. Trading in horses was an important and profitable business, monopolised by the Arabs and some local merchants.[568] The Rashtrakuta government levied a shipping tax of one golden *Gadyanaka* on all foreign vessels embarking to any other ports and a fee of one silver *Ctharna* (a coin) on vessels travelling locally.

Artists and craftsman operated as corporations (guilds) rather than as individual business. Inscriptions mention guilds of weavers, oilmen, artisans, basket and mat makers and fruit sellers. A Saundatti inscription refers to an assemblage of all the people of a district headed by the guilds of the region.[569] Some guilds were considered superior to others, just as some corporations were, and received royal charters determining their powers and privileges. Inscriptions suggest these guilds had their own militia to protect goods in transit and, like village assemblies, they operated banks that lent money to traders and businesses.[570]

The government's income came from five principal sources: regular taxes, occasional taxes, fines, income taxes, miscellaneous taxes and tributes from feudatories.[571] An emergency tax was imposed occasionally and were applicable when the kingdom was under duress, such as when it faced natural calamities, or was preparing for war or overcoming war's ravages. Income tax included taxes on crown land, wasteland, specific types of trees considered valuable to the economy, mines, salt, treasures unearthed by prospectors.[572] Additionally, customary presents were given to the king or royal officers on such festive occasions as marriage or the birth of a son.[573]

The king determined the tax levels based on need and circumstances in the kingdom while ensuring that an undue burden was not placed on the peasants.[574] The land owner or tenant paid a variety of taxes, including land taxes, produce taxes and payment of the overhead for maintenance of the Gavunda (village head). Land taxes were varied, based on type of land, its produce and situation and ranged from 8% to 16%. A Banavasi inscription of 941 mentions reassessment of land tax due to the drying up of an old irrigation canal in the region. The land tax may have been as high as 20% to pay for expenses of a military frequently at war.[575] In most of the kingdom, land taxes were paid in goods and services and rarely was cash accepted.[576] A portion of all taxes earned by the government (usually 15%) was returned to the villages for maintenance.[577]

Taxes were levied on artisans such as potters, sheep herders, weavers, oilmen, shopkeepers, stall owners, brewers and gardeners. Taxes on perishable items such as fish, meat, honey, medicine, fruits and essentials like fuel was as high as 16%.[578] Taxes on salt and minerals were mandatory although the empire did not claim sole ownership of mines, implying that private mineral prospecting and the quarrying business may have been active.[579] The state claimed all such properties whose deceased legal owner had no immediate family to make an inheritance claim.[580] Other miscellaneous taxes included ferry and house taxes. Only Brahmins and their temple institutions were taxed at a lower rate.[581]

Figure 49: *Kailasanatha Temple*

Culture

Religion

The Rashtrakuta kings supported the popular religions of the day in the traditional spirit of religious tolerance.[582] Scholars have offered various arguments regarding which specific religion the Rashtrakutas favoured, basing their evidence on inscriptions, coins and contemporary literature. Some claim the Rashtrakutas were inclined towards Jainism since many of the scholars who flourished in their courts and wrote in Sanskrit, Kannada and a few in Apabhramsha and Prakrit were Jains.[583] The Rashtrakutas built well-known Jain temples at locations such as Lokapura in Bagalkot district and their loyal feudatory, the Western Ganga Dynasty, built Jain monuments at Shravanabelagola and Kambadahalli. Scholars have suggested that Jainism was a principal religion at the very heart of the empire, modern Karnataka, accounting for more than 30% of the population and dominating the culture of the region.[584] King Amoghavarsha I was a disciple of the Jain acharya Jinasena and wrote in his religious writing, *Prashnottara Ratnamalika*, "having bowed to Varaddhamana (Mahavira), I write Prashnottara Ratnamalika". The mathematician Mahaviracharya wrote in his *Ganita Sarasangraha*, "The subjects under Amoghavarsha are happy and the land yields plenty of grain. May the kingdom of King Nripatunga Amoghavarsha, follower of Jainism ever increase far and wide." Amoghavarsha may have taken up Jainism in his old age.[585,586] However, the Rashtrakuta kings also patronized Hinduism's followers of the Shaiva, Vaishnava and Shakta faiths. Almost all of their inscriptions begin with an invocation to god Vishnu or god Shiva. The Sanjan inscriptions tell of King Amoghavarsha I sacrificing a finger from his left hand at the Lakshmi temple at Kolhapur to avert a calamity in his kingdom. King Dantidurga performed the *Hiranyagarbha* (horse sacrifice) and the Sanjan and Cambay plates of King Govinda IV mention Brahmins performing such rituals as *Rajasuya*, *Vajapeya* and *Agnishtoma*.[587] An early copper plate grant of King Dantidurga (753) shows an image of god Shiva and the coins of his successor, King Krishna I (768), bear the legend *Parama Maheshwara* (another name for Shiva). The kings' titles such as *Veeranarayana* showed their Vaishnava leanings. Their flag had the sign of the Ganges and Yamuna rivers, perhaps copied from the Badami Chalukyas.[588] The famous Kailasnatha temple at Ellora and other rock-cut caves attributed to them show that the Hinduism was flourishing. Their family deity was a goddess by name *Latana* (also known as *Rashtrashyena*, *Manasa Vindyavasini*) who took the form of a falcon to save the kingdom.[589] They built temples with icons and ornamentation that satisfied the needs of different faiths. The temple at Salotgi was meant for followers of Shiva and Vishnu and the temple at Kargudri was meant for worshipers of Shiva, Vishnu and Bhaskara (Surya, the sun god).

In short, the Rashtrakuta rule was tolerant to multiple popular religions, Jainism, Vaishnavaism and Shaivism. Buddhism too found support and was popular in places such as Dambal and Balligavi, although it had declined significantly by this time.[472] The decline of Buddhism in South India began in the 8th century with the spread of Adi Shankara's Advaita philosophy.[590] Islamic contact with South India began as early as the 7th century, a result of trade between the Southern kingdoms and Arab lands. Jumma Masjids existed in the Rashtrakuta empire by the 10th century[591] and many Muslims lived and mosques flourished on the coasts, specifically in towns such as Kayalpattanam and Nagore. Muslim settlers married local women; their children were known as Mappilas (*Moplahs*) and were actively involved in horse trading and manning shipping fleets.[592]

Society

Chronicles mention more castes than the four commonly known castes in the Hindu social system, some as many as seven castes.[593] One traveller's account mentions sixteen castes including the four basic castes of Brahmins, Kshatriya, Vaishya and Sudras.[594] The *Zakaya* or *Lahud* caste consisted of communities specialising in dance and acrobatics.[595] People in the professions of sailing, hunting, weaving, cobblery, basket making and fishing belonged to specific castes or subcastes. The *Antyajas* caste provided many menial services to the wealthy. Brahmins enjoyed the highest status in Rashtrakuta society; only those Kshatriyas in the *Sat-Kshatriya* sub-caste (noble Kshatriyas) were higher in status.[596,597]

The careers of Brahmins usually related to education, the judiciary, astrology, mathematics, poetry and philosophy[598] or the occupation of hereditary administrative posts.[599] Also Brahmins increasingly practiced non-Brahminical professions (agriculture, trade in betel nuts and martial posts).[600] Capital punishment, although widespread, was not given to the royal Kshatriya sub-castes or to Brahmins found guilty of heinous crimes (as the killing of a Brahmin in medieval Hindu India was itself considered a heinous crime). As an alternate punishment to enforce the law a Brahmin's right hand and left foot was severed, leaving that person disabled.[601]

By the 9th century, kings from all the four castes had occupied the highest seat in the monarchical system in Hindu India.[602] Admitting Kshatriyas to Vedic schools along with Brahmins was customary, but the children of the Vaishya and Shudra castes were not allowed. Landownership by people of all castes is recorded in inscriptions[603] Intercaste marriages in the higher castes were only between highly placed Kshatriya girls and Brahmin boys,[604] but was relatively frequent among other castes.[605] Intercaste functions were rare and dining together between people of various castes was avoided.[606]

Joint families were the norm but legal separations between brothers and even father and son have been recorded in inscriptions.[607] Women and daughters had rights over property and land as there are inscriptions recording the sale of land by women.[608] The arranged marriage system followed a strict policy of early marriage for women. Among Brahmins, boys married at or below 16 years of age and the brides chosen for them were 12 or younger. This age policy was not strictly followed by other castes.[609] Sati (a custom in which a dead man's widow would immolate herself on her husband's funeral pyre) was practiced but the few examples noted in inscriptions were mostly in the royal families.[610] The system of shaving the heads of widows was infrequent as epigraphs note that widows were allowed to grow their hair but decorating it was discouraged.[611] The remarriage of a widow was rare among the upper castes and more accepted among the lower castes.[612]

In the general population men wore two simple pieces of cloth, a loose garment on top and a garment worn like a *dhoti* for the lower part of the body. Only kings could wear turbans, a practice that spread to the masses much later.[613] Dancing was a popular entertainment and inscriptions speak of royal women

Figure 50: *Jain Narayana temple at Pattadakal, Karnataka*

being charmed by dancers, both male and female, in the king's palace. Devadasis (girls were "married" to a deity or temple) were often present in temples.[614] Other recreational activities included attending animal fights of the same or different species. The Atakur inscription (hero stone, *virgal*) was made for the favourite hound of the feudatory Western Ganga King Butuga II that died fighting a wild boar in a hunt.[615] There are records of game preserves for hunting by royalty. Astronomy and astrology were well developed as subjects of study, and there were many superstitious beliefs such as catching a snake alive proved a woman's chastity. Old persons suffering from incurable diseases preferred to end their lives by drowning in the sacred waters of a pilgrim site or by a ritual burning.[616]

Literature

Kannada became more prominent as a literary language during the Rashtrakuta rule with its script and literature showing remarkable growth, dignity and productivity. This period effectively marked the end of the classical Prakrit and Sanskrit era. Court poets and royalty created eminent works in Kannada and Sanskrit that spanned such literary forms as prose, poetry, rhetoric, the Hindu epics and the life history of Jain tirthankars. Bilingual writers such as Asaga gained fame,[617] and noted scholars such as the Mahaviracharya wrote on pure mathematics in the court of King Amoghavarsha I.[618,619]

ಪದನಱಿದು ನುಡಿಯಲುಂ ನುಡಿದುದ
ನಱಿಯಲುಮಾರ್ಪರಾ ನಾಡವರ್ಗಳ್
ಚದುರರ್ ನಿಜದಿಂ ಕುರಿತೋದದೆಯುಂ
ಕಾವ್ಯಪ್ರಯೋಗ ಪರಿಣತಮತಿಗಳ್

Figure 51: *A stanza from the 9th century Kannada classic Kavirajamarga, praising the people for their literary skills*

Kavirajamarga (850) by King Amoghavarsha I is the earliest available book on rhetoric and poetics in Kannada,[620] though it is evident from this book that native styles of Kannada composition had already existed in previous centuries.[621] *Kavirajamarga* is a guide to poets (*Kavishiksha*) that aims to standardize these various styles. The book refers to early Kannada prose and poetry writers such as Durvinita, perhaps the 6th-century monarch of Western Ganga Dynasty.[622,623,624]

The Jain writer Adikavi Pampa, widely regarded as one of the most influential Kannada writers, became famous for *Adipurana* (941). Written in champu (mixed prose-verse style) style, it is the life history of the first Jain *tirthankara* Rishabhadeva. Pampa's other notable work was *Vikramarjuna Vijaya* (941), the author's version of the Hindu epic, Mahabharata, with Arjuna as the hero.[625] Also called *Pampa Bharata*, it is a eulogy of the writer's patron, King Chalukya Arikeseri of Vemulawada (a Rashtrakuta feudatory), comparing the king's virtues favorably to those of Arjuna. Pampa demonstrates such a command of classical Kannada that scholars over the centuries have written many interpretations of his work.[626]

Another notable Jain writer in Kannada was Sri Ponna, patronised by King Krishna III and famed for *Shantipurana*, his account of the life of Shantinatha, the 16th Jain tirthankara. He earned the title *Ubhaya Kavichakravathi* (supreme poet in two languages) for his command over both Kannada and Sanskrit. His other writings in Kannada were *Bhuvanaika-ramaabhyudaya*, *Jinaksharamale* and *Gatapratyagata*.[627] Adikavi Pampa and Sri Ponna are called "gems of Kannada literature".

Prose works in Sanskrit was prolific during this era as well. Important mathematical theories and axioms were postulated by Mahaviracharya, a native of Gulbarga, who belonged to the Karnataka mathematical tradition and was patronised by King Amoghavarsha I. His greatest contribution was *Ganitasarasangraha*, a writing in 9 chapters. Somadevasuri of 950 wrote in the court of Arikesari II, a feudatory of Rashtrakuta Krishna III in Vemulavada. He was the author of *Yasastilaka champu, Nitivakyamrita* and other writings. The main aim of the *champu* writing was to propagate Jain tenets and ethics. The second writing reviews the subject matter of *Arthashastra* from the standpoint of Jain morals in a clear and pithy manner.[628] Ugraditya, a Jain ascetic from Hanasoge in the modern Mysore district wrote a medical treatise called *Kalyanakaraka*. He delivered a discourse in the court of Amoghavarsha I encouraging abstinence from animal products and alcohol in medicine.[629,630]

Trivikrama was a noted scholar in the court of King Indra III. His classics were *Nalachampu* (915), the earliest in champu style in Sanskrit, *Damayanti Katha*, *Madalasachampu* and Begumra plates. Legend has it that Goddess Saraswati helped him in his effort to compete with a rival in the king's court. Jinasena was the spiritual preceptor and guru of Amoghavarsha I. A theologian, his contributions are *Dhavala* and *Jayadhavala* (written with another theologian Virasena). These writings are named after their patron king who was also called Athishayadhavala. Other contributions from Jinasena were *Adipurana*, later completed by his disciple Gunabhadra, *Harivamsha* and *Parshvabhyudaya*.

Architecture

The Rashtrakutas contributed much to the architectural heritage of the Deccan. Art historian Adam Hardy categorizes their building activity into three schools: Ellora, around Badami, Aihole and Pattadakal, and at Sirval near Gulbarga.[631] The Rashtrakuta contributions to art and architecture are reflected in the splendid rock-cut cave temples at Ellora and Elephanta, areas also occupied by Jain monks, located in present-day Maharashtra. The Ellora site was originally part of a complex of 34 Buddhist caves probably created in the first half of the 6th century whose structural details show Pandyan influence. Cave temples occupied by Hindus are from later periods.

The Rashtrakutas renovated these Buddhist caves and re-dedicated the rockcut shrines. Amoghavarsha I espoused Jainism and there are five Jain cave temples at Ellora ascribed to his period. The most extensive and sumptuous of the Rashtrakuta works at Ellora is their creation of the monolithic Kailasanath Temple, a splendid achievement confirming the "Balhara" status as "one among the four principal Kings of the world". The walls of the temple have marvellous sculptures from Hindu mythology including Ravana, Shiva and Parvathi while the ceilings have paintings.

The Kailasanath Temple project was commissioned by King Krishna I after the Rashtrakuta rule had spread into South India from the Deccan. The architectural style used is *Karnata Dravida* according to Adam Hardy. It does not

Figure 52: *Kailasanath Temple at Ellora, Maharashtra*

contain any of the *Shikharas* common to the *Nagara* style and was built on the same lines as the Virupaksha temple at Pattadakal in Karnataka.[632] According to art historian Vincent Smith, the achievement at the Kailasanath temple is considered an architectural consummation of the monolithic rock-cut temple and deserves to be considered one of the wonders of the world.[633] According to art historian Percy Brown, as an accomplishment of art, the Kailasanath temple is considered an unrivalled work of rock architecture, a monument that has always excited and astonished travellers.[634]

While some scholars have claimed the architecture at Elephanta is attributable to the Kalachuri, others claim that it was built during the Rashtrakuta period.[635] Some of the sculptures such as *Nataraja* and *Sadashiva* excel in beauty and craftsmanship even that of the Ellora sculptures.[636] Famous sculptures at Elephanta include *Ardhanarishvara* and *Maheshamurthy*. The latter, a three faced bust of Lord Shiva, is 25 feet (8 m) tall and considered one of the finest pieces of sculpture in India. It is said that, in the world of sculpture, few works of art depicting a divinity are as balanced.[637] Other famous rock-cut temples in the Maharashtra region are the Dhumer Lena and Dashvatara cave temples in Ellora (famous for its sculptures of Vishnu and Shivaleela) and the Jogeshvari temple near Mumbai. In Karnataka their most famous temples are the *Kashivishvanatha* temple and the Jain Narayana temple at Pattadakal, a UNESCO World Heritage site.[638] Other well-known temples are the Paramesh-

Figure 53: *Dravidian style architecture. Top view of Navalinga Temples at Kuknur, Karnataka*

wara temple at Konnur, Brahmadeva temple at Savadi, the Settavva, Kontigudi II, Jadaragudi and Ambigeragudi temples at Aihole, Mallikarjuna temple at Ron, Andhakeshwara temple at Huli (Hooli), Someshwara temple at Sogal, Jain temples at Lokapura, Navalinga temple at Kuknur, Kumaraswamy temple at Sandur, numerous temples at Shirival in Gulbarga,[639] and the *Trikuteshwara* temple at Gadag which was later expanded by Kalyani Chalukyas. Archeological study of these temples show some have the stellar (multigonal) plan later to be used profusely by the Hoysalas at Belur and Halebidu.[640] One of the richest traditions in Indian architecture took shape in the Deccan during this time which Adam Hardy calls *Karnata dravida* style as opposed to traditional Dravida style.[641]

Language

With the ending of the Gupta Dynasty in northern India in the early 6th century, major changes began taking place in the Deccan south of the Vindyas and in the southern regions of India. These changes were not only political but also linguistic and cultural. The royal courts of peninsular India (outside of Tamilakam) interfaced between the increasing use of the local Kannada language and the expanding Sanskritic culture. Inscriptions, including those that were bilingual, demonstrate the use of Kannada as the primary administrative language in conjunction with Sanskrit. Government archives used Kannada for recording pragmatic information relating to grants of land.[642] The

Figure 54: *9th century Old Kannada inscription at Navalinga temple in Kuknur, Karnataka*

local language formed the *desi* (popular) literature while literature in Sanskrit was more *marga* (formal). Educational institutions and places of higher learning (*ghatikas*) taught in Sanskrit, the language of the learned Brahmins, while Kannada increasingly became the speech of personal expression of devotional closeness of a worshipper to a private deity. The patronage Kannada received from rich and literate Jains eventually led to its use in the devotional movements of later centuries.[643]

Contemporaneous literature and inscriptions show that Kannada was not only popular in the modern Karnataka region but had spread further north into present day southern Maharashtra and to the northern Deccan by the 8th century.[644] Kavirajamarga, the work on poetics, refers to the entire region between the Kaveri River and the Godavari River as "Kannada country".[645,646,647] Higher education in Sanskrit included the subjects of Veda, *Vyakarana* (grammar), *Jyotisha* (astronomy and astrology), *Sahitya* (literature), *Mimansa* (Exegesis), *Dharmashastra* (law), *Puranas* (ritual), and *Nyaya* (logic). An examination of inscriptions from this period shows that the *Kavya* (classical) style of writing was popular. The awareness of the merits and defects in inscriptions by the archivists indicates that even they, though mediocre poets, had studied standard classical literature in Sanskrit.[648] An inscription in Kannada by King Krishna III, written in a poetic Kanda metre, has been found as far away as Jabalpur in modern Madhya Pradesh. Kavirajamarga, a work on poetics in Kannada by Amoghavarsha I, shows that the study of poetry was popular in the Deccan during this time. Trivikrama's Sanskrit writing, *Nalachampu*, is perhaps the earliest in the *champu* style from the Deccan.[649]

References

Books <templatestyles src="Template:Refbegin/styles.css" />

- Altekar, Anant Sadashiv (1934) [1934]. *The Rashtrakutas And Their Times; being a political, administrative, religious, social, economic and literary history of the Deccan during C. 750 A.D. to C. 1000 A.D*. Poona: Oriental Book Agency. OCLC 3793499[650].
- Chopra, P.N.; Ravindran, T.K.; Subrahmanian, N (2003) [2003]. *History of South India (Ancient, Medieval and Modern) Part 1*. New Delhi: Chand Publications. ISBN 81-219-0153-7.
- De Bruyne, J.L. (1968) [1968]. *Rudrakavis Great Poem of the Dynasty of Rastraudha*. EJ Brill.
- Dalby, Andrew (2004) [1998]. *Dictionary of Languages: The Definitive Reference to More Than 400 Languages*. New York: Columbia University Press. ISBN 0-231-11569-5.
- Hardy, Adam (1995) [1995]. *Indian Temple Architecture: Form and Transformation-The Karnata Dravida Tradition 7th to 13th Centuries*. Abhinav Publications. ISBN 81-7017-312-4.
- Houben, Jan E.M. (1996) [1996]. *Ideology and Status of Sanskrit: Contributions to the History of the Sanskrit language*. Brill. ISBN 90-04-10613-8.
- Jain, K.C. (2001) [2001]. *Bharatiya Digambar Jain Abhilekh*. Madhya Pradesh: Digambar Jain Sahitya Samrakshan Samiti.
- Kamath, Suryanath U. (2001) [1980]. *A concise history of Karnataka : from pre-historic times to the present*. Bangalore: Jupiter books. LCCN 80905179[651]. OCLC 7796041[652].
- Karmarkar, A.P. (1947) [1947]. *Cultural history of Karnataka : ancient and medieval*. Dharwar: Karnataka Vidyavardhaka Sangha. OCLC 8221605[653].
- Keay, John (2000) [2000]. *India: A History*. New York: Grove Publications. ISBN 0-8021-3797-0.
- Majumdar, R.C. (1966) [1966]. *The Struggle for Empire*. Bharatiya Vidya Bhavan.
- Masica, Colin P. (1991) [1991]. *The Indo-Aryan Languages*. Cambridge: Cambridge University Press. ISBN 0-521-29944-6.

- Narasimhacharya, R (1988) [1988]. *History of Kannada Literature*. New Delhi, Madras: Asian Educational Services. ISBN 81-206-0303-6.
- Reu, Pandit Bisheshwar Nath (1997) [1933]. *History of the Rashtrakutas (Rathodas)*. Jaipur: Publication Scheme. ISBN 81-86782-12-5.
- Pollock, Sheldon (2006) [2006]. *The Language of the Gods in the World of Men: Sanskrit, Culture, and Power in Premodern India*. Berkeley: University of California Press. ISBN 0-520-24500-8.
- Rao, Seshagiri, L.S (1988) [1988]. "Epic (Kannada)". In Amaresh Datta. *Encyclopaedia of Indian literature – vol 2*. Sahitya Akademi. ISBN 81-260-1194-7.
- Rice, E.P. (1982) [1921]. *Kannada Literature*. New Delhi: Asian Educational Services. ISBN 81-206-0063-0.
- Rice, B.L. (2001) [1897]. *Mysore Gazetteer Compiled for Government-vol 1*. New Delhi, Madras: Asian Educational Services. ISBN 81-206-0977-8.
- Sastri, Nilakanta K.A. (2002) [1955]. *A history of South India from prehistoric times to the fall of Vijayanagar*. New Delhi: Indian Branch, Oxford University Press. ISBN 0-19-560686-8.
- Sen, Sailendra Nath (1999) [1999]. *Ancient Indian History and Civilization*. New Age Publishers. ISBN 81-224-1198-3.
- Thapar, Romila (2003) [2003]. *Penguin History of Early India: From origins to AD 1300*. New Delhi: Penguin. ISBN 0-14-302989-4.
- Vaidya, C.V. (1979) [1924]. *History of Mediaeval Hindu India (Being a History of India from 600 to 1200 A.D.)*. Poona: Oriental Book Supply Agency. OCLC 6814734[654].
- Warder, A.K. (1988) [1988]. *Indian Kavya Literature*. Motilal Banarsidass. ISBN 81-208-0450-3.

Web <templatestyles src="Template:Refbegin/styles.css" />

- Arthikaje. "The Rashtrakutas"[655]. *History of karnataka*. OurKarnataka.Com. Archived from the original[656] on 2006-11-04. Retrieved 2006-12-31.
- Kamat, Jyotsna. "The Rashtrakutas"[657]. *Dynasties of the Deccan*. Retrieved 2007-02-03.
- Sastri & Rao, Shama & Lakshminarayan. "South Indian Inscriptions-Miscellaneous Inscriptions in Kannada"[658]. *Rashtrakutas*. Retrieved 2007-02-03.

External links

 Wikimedia Commons has media related to *Rashtrakuta Dynasty*.

 Wikisourcehas the text of the 1911 *Encyclopædia Britannica*article *Rashtrakuta*.

- Archaeological Survey of India[659]

<indicator name="featured-star"> ⭐ </indicator>

Pala Empire

Pala Empire	
8th century–12th century	
The Pala Empire in Asia in 800 CE	
Capital	
Languages	Sanskrit, Prakrit (including proto-Bengali), Pali
Religion	Mahayana Buddhism, Tantric Buddhism, and supported Shaivite Hinduism
Government	Monarchy
Emperor	
• 8th century	Gopala
• 12th century	Madanapala
Historical era	Classical India
• Established	8th century
• Disestablished	12th century
Preceded by	**Succeeded by**
Gauda Kingdom	Sena dynasty

Today part of	Bangladesh
	India
	Nepal
	Pakistan

The **Pala Empire** was an imperial power during the Late Classical period on the Indian subcontinent, which originated in the region of Bengal. It is named after its ruling dynasty, whose rulers bore names ending with the suffix of *Pala* ("protector" in Sanskrit). They were followers of the Mahayana and Tantric schools of Buddhism. The empire was founded with the election of Gopala as the emperor of Gauda in 750 CE. The Pala stronghold was located in Bengal and Bihar, which included the major cities of Vikrampura, Pataliputra, Gauda, Monghyr, Somapura, Ramvati (Varendra), Tamralipta and Jaggadala.

The Palas were astute diplomats and military conquerors. Their army was noted for its vast war elephant corps. Their navy performed both mercantile and defensive roles in the Bay of Bengal. The Palas were important promoters of classical Indian philosophy, literature, painting and sculpture. They built grand temples and monasteries, including the Somapura Mahavihara, and patronised the great universities of Nalanda and Vikramashila. The Proto-Bengali language developed under Pala rule. The empire enjoyed relations with the Srivijaya Empire, the Tibetan Empire and the Arab Abbasid Caliphate. Islam first appeared in Bengal during Pala rule, as a result of increased trade between Bengal and the Middle East. Abbasid coinage found in Pala archaeological sites, as well as records of Arab historians, point to flourishing mercantile and intellectual contacts. The House of Wisdom in Baghdad absorbed the mathematical and astronomical achievements of Indian civilisation during this period.

At its height in the early 9th century, the Pala Empire was the dominant power in the northern subcontinent, with its territory stretching across parts of modern-day eastern Pakistan, northern and northeastern India, Nepal and Bangladesh. The empire reached its peak under Emperors Dharmapala and Devapala. The Palas also exerted a strong cultural influence under Atisa in Tibet, as well as in Southeast Asia. Pala control of North India was ultimately ephemeral, as they struggled with the Gurjara-Pratiharas and the Rashtrakutas for the control of Kannauj and were defeated. After a short lived decline, Emperor Mahipala I defended imperial bastions in Bengal and Bihar against South Indian Chola invasions. Emperor Ramapala was the last strong Pala ruler, who gained control of Kamarupa and Kalinga. The empire was considerably weakened by the 11th century, with many areas engulfed in rebellion.

The resurgent Hindu Sena dynasty dethroned the Pala Empire in the 12th century, ending the reign of the last major Buddhist imperial power in the subcontinent. The Pala period is considered one of the golden eras of Bengali history.[661] The Palas brought stability and prosperity to Bengal after centuries of civil war between warring divisions. They advanced the achievements of previous Bengali civilisations and created outstanding works of art and architecture. They laid the basis for the Bengali language, including its first literary work, the *Charyapada*. The Pala legacy is still reflected in Tibetan Buddhism.

History

Origins

According to the Khalimpur copper plate inscription, the first Pala king Gopala was the son of a warrior named Vapyata. The *Ramacharitam* attests that Varendra (North Bengal) was the fatherland (*Janakabhu*) of the Palas. The ethnic origins of the dynasty are unknown, although the later records claim that Gopala was a Kshatriya belonging to the legendary Solar dynasty. The *Ballala-Carita* states that the Palas were Kshatriyas, a claim reiterated by Taranatha in his *History of Buddhism in India* as well as Ghanaram Chakrabarty in his *Dharmamangala* (both written in the 16th century CE). The *Ramacharitam* also attests the fifteenth Pala emperor, Ramapala, as a Kshatriya. Claims of belonging to the legendary Solar dynasty are unreliable and clearly appear to be an attempt to cover up the humble origins of the dynasty.[661] The Pala dynasty has also been branded as Śudra in some sources such as *Manjushri-Mulakalpa*; this might be because of their Buddhist leanings.[662,663] According to Abu'l-Fazl ibn Mubarak (in Ain-i-Akbari), the Palas were Kayasthas. There are even accounts that claim Gopala may have been from a Brahmin lineage.

Establishment

After the fall of Shashanka's kingdom, the Bengal region was in a state of anarchy. There was no central authority, and there was constant struggle between petty chieftains. The contemporary writings describe this situation as *matsya nyaya* ("fish justice" i.e. a situation where the big fish eat the small fish). Gopala ascended the throne as the first Pala king during these times. The Khalimpur copper plate suggests that the *prakriti* (people) of the region made him the king.[661] Taranatha, writing nearly 800 years later, also writes that he was democratically elected by the people of Bengal. However, his account is in form of a legend, and is considered historically unreliable. The legend mentions that after a period of anarchy, the people elected several kings in succession, all of whom were consumed by the Naga queen of an earlier king on the night following their election. Gopal, however managed to kill the queen and remained on the throne. The historical evidence indicates that Gopala was not elected directly by his citizens, but by a group of feudal chieftains. Such elections were quite common in contemporary societies of the region.[661]

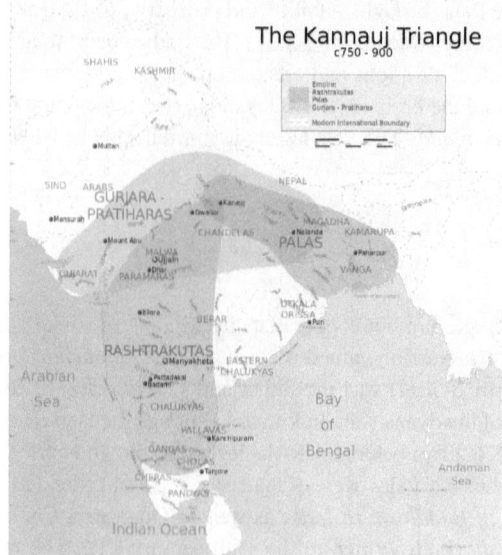

Figure 55: *An illustration of the Kannauj triangle*

Gopala's ascension was a significant political event as the several independent chiefs recognised his political authority without any struggle.

Expansion under Dharmapala and Devapala

Gopala's empire was greatly expanded by his son Dharmapala and his grandson Devapala. Dharmapala was initially defeated by the Pratihara ruler Vatsaraja. Later, the Rashtrakuta king Dhruva defeated both Dharmapala and Vatsaraja. After Dhruva left for the Deccan region, Dharmapala built a mighty empire in the northern India. He defeated Indrayudha of Kannauj, and installed his own nominee Chakrayudha on the throne of Kannauj. Several other smaller states in North India also acknowledged his suzerainty. Soon, his expansion was checked by Vatsaraja's son Nagabhata II, who conquered Kannauj and drove away Chakrayudha. Nagabhata II then advanced up to Munger and defeated Dharmapala in a pitched battle. Dharmapala was forced to surrender and to seek alliance with the Rashtrakuta emperor Govinda III, who then intervened by invading northern India and defeating Nagabhata II. The Rashtrakuta records show that both Chakrayudha and Dharmapala recognised the Rashtrakuta suzerainty. In practice, Dharmapala gained control over North India after Govinda III left for the Deccan. He adopted the title *Paramesvara Paramabhattaraka Maharajadhiraja*.

Dharmapala was succeeded by his son Devapala, who is regarded as the most powerful Pala ruler. His expeditions resulted in the invasion of Pragjyotisha (present-day Assam) where the king submitted without giving a fight and the Utkala (present-day Orissa) whose king fled from his capital city.[664] The inscriptions of his successors also claim several other territorial conquests by him, but these are highly exaggerated (see the Geography section below).[661]

First period of decline

Following the death of Devapala, the Pala empire gradually started disintegrating. Vigrahapala, who was Devapala's nephew, abdicated the throne after a brief rule, and became an ascetic. Vigrahapala's son and successor Narayanapala proved to be a weak ruler. During his reign, the Rashtrakuta king Amoghavarsha defeated the Palas. Encouraged by the Pala decline, the King Harjara of Assam assumed imperial titles and the Sailodbhavas established their power in Orissa.

Naryanapala's son Rajyapala ruled for at least 12 years, and constructed several public utilities and lofty temples. His son Gopala II lost Bengal after a few years of rule, and then ruled only Bihar. The next king, Vigrahapala II, had to bear the invasions from the Chandelas and the Kalachuris. During his reign, the Pala empire disintegrated into smaller kingdoms like Gauda, Radha, Anga and Vanga. Kantideva of Harikela (eastern and southern Bengal) also assumed the title *Maharajadhiraja*, and established a separate kingdom, later ruled by the Chandra dynasty. The Gauda state (West and North Bengal) was ruled by the Kamboja Pala dynasty. The rulers of this dynasty also bore names ending in the suffix -pala (e.g. Rajyapala, Narayanapala and Nayapala). However, their origin is uncertain, and the most plausible view is that they originated from a Pala official who usurped a major part of the Pala kingdom along with its capital.[661]

Revival under Mahipala I

Mahipala I recovered northern and eastern Bengal within three years of ascending the throne in 988 CE. He also recovered the northern part of the present-day Burdwan division. During his reign, Rajendra Chola I of the Chola Empire frequently invaded Bengal from 1021 to 1023 CE to get Ganges water and in the process, succeeded to humble the rulers, acquiring considerable booty. The rulers of Bengal who were defeated by Rajendra Chola were Dharmapal, Ranasur and Govindachandra, who might have been feudatories under Mahipala I of the Pala Dynasty.[665] Rajendra Chola I also defeated Mahipala, and obtained from the Pala king "elephants of rare strength, women and treasure". Mahipala also gained control of north and south Bihar, probably aided by the invasions of Mahmud of Ghazni, which exhausted the strength of other rulers of North India. He may have also conquered Varanasi and surrounding area, as his brothers Sthirapala and Vasantapala undertook construction and repairs of several sacred structures at Varanasi. Later, the Kalachuri king Gangeyadeva annexed Varanasi after defeating the ruler of Anga, which could have been Mahipala I.

Second period of decline

Nayapala, the son of Mahipala I, defeated the Kalachuri king Karna (son of Ganggeyadeva) after a long struggle. The two later signed a peace treaty at the mediation of the Buddhist scholar Atiśa. During the reign of Nayapala's son Vigrahapala III, Karna once again invaded Bengal but was defeated. The conflict ended with a peace treaty, and Vigrahapala III married Karna's daughter Yauvanasri. Vigrahapala III was later defeated by the invading Chalukya king Vikramaditya VI. The invasion of Vikramaditya VI saw several soldiers from South India into Bengal, which explains the southern origin of the Sena Dynasty. Vigrahapala III also faced another invasion led by the Somavamsi king Mahasivagupta Yayati of Orissa. Subsequently, a series of invasions considerably reduced the power of the Palas. The Varmans occupied eastern Bengal during his reign.[661]

Mahipala II, the successor of Vigrahapala III, brought a short-lived reign of military glory. His reign is well-documented by Sandhyakar Nandi in *Ramacharitam*. Mahipala II imprisoned his brothers Ramapala and Surapala II, on the suspicion that they were conspiring against him. Soon afterwards, he faced a rebellion of vassal chiefs from the Kaibarta (fishermen). A chief named Divya (or Divvoka) killed him and occupied the Varendra region. The region remained under the control of his successors Rudak and Bhima. Surapala II escaped to Magadha and died after a short reign. He was succeeded by his brother Ramapala, who launched a major offensive against Divya's grandson Bhima. He was supported by his maternal uncle Mathana of the Rashtrakuta dynasty, as well as several feudatory chiefs of south Bihar and south-west Bengal. Ramapala conclusively defeated Bhima, and killing him and his family in a cruel manner.[661]

Revival under Ramapala

After gaining control of Varendra, Ramapala tried to revive the Pala empire with limited success. He ruled from a new capital at Ramavati, which remained the Pala capital until the dynasty's end. He reduced taxation, promoted cultivation and constructed public utilities. He brought Kamarupa and Rar under his control, and forced the Varman king of east Bengal to accept his suzerainty. He also struggled with the Ganga king for control of present-day Orissa; the Gangas managed to annexe the region only after his death. Ramapala maintained friendly relations with the Chola king Kulottunga to secure support against the common enemies: the Ganas and the Chalukyas. He kept the Senas in check, but lost Mithila to a Karnataka chief named Nanyuadeva. He also held back the aggressive design of the Gahadavala ruler Govindacharndra through a matrimonial alliance.[661]

Final decline

Ramapala was the last strong Pala ruler. After his death, a rebellion broke out in Kamarupa during his son Kumarapala's reign. The rebellion was crushed by Vaidyadeva, but after Kumarapala's death, Vaidyadeva practically created a separate kingdom. According to *Ramacharitam*, Kumarapala's son Gopala III was murdered by his uncle Mandapala. During Madanapala's rule, the Varmans in east Bengal declared independence, and the Eastern Gangas renewed the conflict in Orissa. Madanapala captured Munger from the Gahadavalas, but was defeated by Vijayasena, who gained control of southern and eastern Bengal. A ruler named Govindapala ruled over the Gaya district around 1162 CE, but there is no concrete evidence about his relationship to the imperial Palas. The Pala dynasty was replaced by the Sena dynasty.[661]

Geography

The borders of the Pala Empire kept fluctuating throughout its existence. Though the Palas conquered a vast region in North India at one time, they could not retain it for long due to constant hostility from the Gurjara-Pratiharas, the Rashtrakutas and other less powerful kings.[666]

No records are available about the exact boundaries of original kingdom established by Gopala, but it might have included almost all of the Bengal region. The Pala empire extended substantially under Dharmapala's rule. Apart from Bengal, he directly ruled the present-day Bihar. The kingdom of Kannauj (present-day Uttar Pradesh) was a Pala dependency at times, ruled by his nominee Chakrayudha. While installing his nominee on the Kannauj throne, Dharmapala organised an imperial court. According to the Khalimpur copper plate issued by Dharmapala, this court was attended by the rulers of Bhoja (possibly Vidarbha), Matsya (Jaipur region), Madra (East Punjab), Kuru (Delhi region), Yadu (possibly Mathura, Dwarka or Simhapura in the Punjab), Yavana, Avanti, Gandhara and Kira (Kangra Valley).[661] These kings accepted the installation of Chakrayudha on the Kannauj throne, while "bowing down respectfully with their diadems trembling".[667] This indicates that his position as a sovereign was accepted by most rulers, although this was a loose arrangement unlike the empire of the Mauryas or the Guptas. The other rulers acknowledged the military and political supremacy of Dharmapala, but maintained their own territories.[661] The poet Soddhala of Gujarat calls Dharmapala an *Uttarapathasvamin* ("Lord of the North") for his suzerainty over North India.[668]

The epigraphic records credit Devapala with extensive conquests in hyperbolic language. The Badal pillar inscription of his successor Narayana Pala states that by the wise counsel and policy of his Brahmin minister Darbhapani, Devapala became the suzerain monarch or Chakravarti of the whole tract of Northern India bounded by the Vindhyas and the Himalayas. It also states that his empire extended up to the two oceans (presumably the Arabian Sea and the Bay of Bengal). It also claims that Devpala defeated Utkala (present-day Orissa), the Hunas, the Kambojas, the Dravidas, the Kamarupa (present-day Assam), and the Gurjaras:

- The Gurjara adversary may have been Mihira Bhoja, whose eastward expansion was checked by Devapala
- The identity of the Huna king is uncertain.
- The identity of the Kamboja prince is also uncertain. While an ancient country with the name Kamboja was located in what is now Afghanistan, there is no evidence that Devapala's empire extended that far. Kamboja, in this inscription, could refer to the Kamboja tribe that had entered North India (see Kamboja Pala dynasty).
- The Dravida king is usually identified with the Rashtrakuta king Amoghavarsha. Some scholars believe that the Dravida king could have been the Pandya ruler Shri Mara Shri Vallabha, since "Dravida" usually refers to the territory south of the Krishna river. According to this theory, Devapala could have been helped in his southern expedition by the Chandela king Vijaya. In any case, Devapala's gains in the south, if any, were temporary.

The claims about Devapala's victories are exaggerated, but cannot be dismissed entirely: there is no reason to doubt his conquest of Utkala and Kamarupa. Besides, the neighbouring kingdoms of Rashtrakutas and the Gurjara-Pratiharas were weak at the time, which might have helped him extend his empire. Devapala is also believed to have led an army up to the Indus river in Punjab.

The empire started disintegrated after the death of Devapala, and his successor Narayanapala lost control of Assam and Orissa. He also briefly lost control over Magadha and north Bengal. Gopala II lost control of Bengal, and ruled only from a part of Bihar. The Pala empire disintegrated into smaller kingdoms during the reign of Vigrahapala II. Mahipala recovered parts of Bengal and Bihar. His successors lost Bengal again. The last strong Pala ruler, Ramapala, gained control of Bengal, Bihar, Assam and parts of Orissa. By the time of

Madanapala's death, the Pala kingdom was confined to parts of central and east Bihar along with northern Bengal.

Administration

The Pala rule was monarchial. The king was the centre of all power. Pala kings would adopt imperial titles like *Parameshwara*, *Paramvattaraka*, *Maharajadhiraja*. Pala kings appointed Prime Ministers. The **Line of Garga** served as the Prime Ministers of the Palas for 100 years.

- Garga
- Darvapani (or Darbhapani)
- Someshwar
- Kedarmisra
- Bhatta Guravmisra

Pala Empire was divided into separate *Bhukti*s (Provinces). Bhuktis were divided into *Vishaya*s (Divisions) and *Mandala*s (Districts). Smaller units were *Khandala*, *Bhaga*, *Avritti*, *Chaturaka*, and Pattaka. Administration covered widespread area from the grass root level to the imperial court.[669]

The Pala copperplates mention following administrative posts:[670]

- *Raja*
- *Rajanyaka*
- *Ranaka* (possibly subordinate chiefs)
- *Samanta* and *Mahasamanta* (Vassal kings)
- *Mahasandhi-vigrahika* (Foreign minister)
- *Duta* (Head Ambassador)
- *Rajasthaniya* (Deputy)
- *Aggaraksa* (Chief guard)
- *Sasthadhikrta* (Tax collector)
- *Chauroddharanika* (Police tax)
- *Shaulkaka* (Trade tax)
- *Dashaparadhika* (Collector of penalties)
- *Tarika* (Toll collector for river crossings)
- *Mahaksapatalika* (Accountant)
- *Jyesthakayastha* (Dealing documents)
- *Ksetrapa* (Head of land use division) and *Pramatr* (Head of land measurements)
- *Mahadandanayaka* or *Dharmadhikara* (Chief justice)
- *Mahapratihara*
- *Dandika*
- *Dandapashika*

Figure 56: *Nalanda is considered one of the first great universities in recorded history. It reached its height under the Palas.*

- *Dandashakti* (Police forces)
- *Khola* (Secret service). Agricultural posts like *Gavadhakshya* (Head of dairy farms)
- *Chhagadhyakshya* (Head of goat farms)
- *Meshadyakshya* (Head of sheep farms)
- *Mahishadyakshya* (Head of Buffalo farms) and many other like *Vogpati*
- *Vishayapati*
- *Shashtadhikruta*
- *Dauhshashadhanika*
- *Nakadhyakshya*

Culture

Religion

The Palas were patrons of Mahayana Buddhism. A few sources written much after Gopala's death mention him as a Buddhist, but it is not known if this is true.[671] The subsequent Pala kings were definitely Buddhists. Taranatha states that Gopala was a staunch Buddhist, who had built the famous monastery at Odantapuri.Wikipedia:Verifiability Dharmapala made the Buddhist philosopher Haribhadra his spiritual preceptor. He established the Vikramashila

Figure 57: *Atisha was a Buddhist teacher, who helped establish the Sarma lineages of Tibetan Buddhism.*

monastery and the Somapura Mahavihara. Taranatha also credits him with establishing 50 religious institutions and patronising the Buddhist author Hari- ibhadra. Devapala restored and enlarged the structures at Somapura Mahav- ihara, which also features several themes from the epics *Ramayana* and *Ma- habharata*. Mahipala I also ordered construction and repairs of several sacred structures at Saranath, Nalanda and Bodh Gaya. The *Mahipala geet* ("songs of Mahipala"), a set of folk songs about him, are still popular in the rural areas of Bengal.

The Palas developed the Buddhist centres of learnings, such as the Vikra- mashila and the Nalanda universities. Nalanda, considered one of the first great universities in recorded history, reached its height under the patronage of the Palas. Noted Buddhist scholars from the Pala period include Atisha, San- taraksita, Saraha, Tilopa, Bimalamitra, Dansheel, Dansree, Jinamitra, Jnanas- rimitra, Manjughosh, Muktimitra, Padmanava, Sambhogabajra, Shantarakshit, Silabhadra, Sugatasree and Virachan.

As the rulers of Gautama Buddha's land, the Palas acquired great reputation in the Buddhist world. Balaputradeva, the Sailendra king of Java, sent an ambassador to him, asking for a grant of five villages for the construction of a monastery at Nalanda. The request was granted by Devapala. He ap- pointed the Brahmin Viradeva (of Nagarahara, present-day Jalalabad) as the head of the Nalanda monastery. The Budhdist poet Vajradatta (the author of Lokesvarashataka), was in his court. The Buddhist scholars from the Pala empire travelled from Bengal to other regions to propagate Buddhism. Atisha, for example, preached in Tibet and Sumatra, and is seen as one of the major figures in the spread of 11th-century Mahayana Buddhism.

The Palas also supported the Saiva ascetics, typically the ones associated with the Golagi-Math.[672] Narayana Pala himself established a temple of Shiva, and was present at the place of sacrifice by his Brahmin minister.[673] Queen of King Madanapaladeva, namely Chitramatika, made a gift of land to a Brahmin named Bateswara Swami as his remuneration for chanting the Mahabharata at her request, according to the principle of the Bhumichhidranyaya.Wikipedia:Citation needed Besides the images of the Buddhist deities, the images of Vishnu, Siva and Sarasvati were also constructed during the Pala dynasty rule.

Literature

The Palas patronised several Sanskrit scholars, some of whom were their officials. The *Gauda riti* style of composition was developed during the Pala rule. Many Buddhist Tantric works were authored and translated during the Pala rule. Besides the Buddhist scholars mentioned in the Religion section above, Jimutavahana, Sandhyakar Nandi, Madhava-kara, Suresvara and Chakrapani Datta are some of the other notable scholars from the Pala period.

The notable Pala texts on philosophy include *Agama Shastra* by Gaudapada, *Nyaya Kundali* by Sridhar Bhatta and *Karmanushthan Paddhati* by Bhatta Bhavadeva. The texts on medicine include

- *Chikitsa Samgraha, Ayurveda Dipika, Bhanumati, Shabda Chandrika* and *Dravya Gunasangraha* by Chakrapani Datta
- *Shabda-Pradipa, Vrikkhayurveda* and *Lohpaddhati* by Sureshwara
- *Chikitsa Sarsamgraha* by Vangasena
- *Sushrata* by Gadadhara Vaidya
- *Dayabhaga, Vyavohara Matrika* and *Kalaviveka* by Jimutavahana

Sandhyakar Nandi's semi-fictional epic *Ramacharitam* (12th century) is an important source of Pala history.

A form of the proto-Bengali language can be seen in the *Charyapada*s composed during the Pala rule.

Art and architecture

The Pala school of sculptural art is recognised as a distinct phase of the Indian art, and is noted for the artistic genius of the Bengal sculptors. It is influenced by the Gupta art.

Figure 58: *A basalt statue of Lalita flanked by Gaṇeśa and Kārttikeya*

Figure 59: *Carved shankhas*

Figure 60: *Sculpture of Khasarpana Lokesvara from Nalanda*

Figure 61: *Sculpture of Varaha avatar of Lord Vishnu*

As noted earlier, the Palas built a number of monasteries and other sacred structures. The Somapura Mahavihara in present-day Bangladesh is a World Heritage Site. It is a monastery with 21 acre (85,000 m²) complex has 177 cells, numerous stupas, temples and a number of other ancillary buildings. The gigantic structures of other Viharas, including Vikramashila, Odantapuri, and Jagaddala are the other masterpieces of the Palas. These mammoth structures were mistaken by the forces of Bakhtiyar Khalji as fortified castles and were demolished.Wikipedia:Citation needed The art of Bihar and Bengal during the Pala and Sena dynasties influenced the art of Nepal, Burma, Sri Lanka and Java.

Figure 62: *Somapura Mahavihara, a World Heritage Site, was built by Dharmapala*

Figure 63: *Central shrine decor at Somapura*

Figure 64: *A model of the Somapura Mahavihara by Ali Naqi*

Figure 65: *Ruins of Vikramashila*

List of Pala rulers

Most of the Pala inscriptions mention only the regnal year as the date of issue, without any well-known calendar era. Because of this, the chronology of the Pala kings is hard to determine. Based on their different interpretations of the various epigraphs and historical records, different historians estimate the Pala chronology as follows:

	RC Majumdar (1971)	AM Chowdhury (1967)	BP Sinha (1977)	DC Sircar (1975–76)	D. K. Ganguly (1994)
Gopala I	750–770	756–781	755–783	750–775	750–774
Dharmapala	770–810	781–821	783–820	775–812	774–806
Devapala	810–c. 850	821–861	820–860	812–850	806–845
Mahendrapala	NA (Mahendrapala's existence was conclusively established through a copper-plate charter discovered later.)				845–860
Shurapala I	850–853	861–866	860–865	850–858	860–872
Vigrahapala I				858–60	872–873
Narayanapala	854–908	866–920	865–920	860–917	873–927
Rajyapala	908–940	920–952	920–952	917–952	927–959
Gopala II	940–957	952–969	952–967	952–972	959–976
Vigrahapala II	960–c. 986	969–995	967–980	972–977	976–977
Mahipala I	988–c. 1036	995–1043	980–1035	977–1027	977–1027
Nayapala	1038–1053	1043–1058	1035–1050	1027–1043	1027–1043
Vigrahapala III	1054–1072	1058–1075	1050–1076	1043–1070	1043–1070
Mahipala II	1072–1075	1075–1080	1076–1078/9	1070–1071	1070–1071
Shurapala	1075–1077	1080–1082		1071–1072	1071–1072
Ramapala	1077–1130	1082–1124	1078/9–1132	1072–1126	1072–1126
Kumarapala	1130–1125	1124–1129	1132–1136	1126–1128	1126–1128
Gopala III	1140–1144	1129–1143	1136–1144	1128–1143	1128–1143
Madanapala	1144–1162	1143–1162	1144–1161/62	1143–1161	1143–1161
Govindapala	1155–1159	NA	1162–1176 or 1158–1162	1161–1165	1161–1165
Palapala	NA	NA	NA	1165–1199	1165–1200

Note:

- Earlier historians believed that Vigrahapala I and Shurapala I were the two names of the same person. Now, it is known that these two were cousins; they either ruled simultaneously (perhaps over different territories) or in rapid succession.
- AM Chowdhury rejects Govindapala and his successor Palapala as the members of the imperial Pala dynasty.
- According to BP Sinha, the Gaya inscription can be read as either the "14th year of Govindapala's reign" or "14th year after Govindapala's reign". Thus, two sets of dates are possible.

Military

The highest military officer in the Pala empire was the *Mahasenapati* (commander-in-chief). The Palas recruited mercenary soldiers from a number of kingdoms, including Malava, Khasa, Huna, Kulika, Kanrata, Lata, Odra and Manahali. According to the contemporary accounts, the Rashtrakutas had the best infantry, the Gurjara-Pratiharas had the finest cavalry and the Palas had the largest elephant force. The Arab merchant Sulaiman states that the Palas had an army bigger than those of the Balhara (possibly the Rashtrakutas) and the king of Jurz (possibly the Gurjara-Pratiharas). He also states that the Pala army employed 10,000–15,000 men for fuelling and washing clothes. He further claims that during the battles, the Pala king would lead 50,000 war elephants. Sulaiman's accounts seem to be based on exaggerated reports; Ibn Khaldun mentions the number of elephants as 5,000.[674]

Since Bengal did not have a good native breed of horses, the Palas imported their cavalry horses from the foreigners, including the Kambojas. They also had a navy, used for both mercantile and defence purposes.[675]

Sources

The main sources of information about the Pala empire include:[676]

Pala accounts

- Various epigraphs, coins, sculptures and architecture
- *Ramacharita*, a Sanskrit work by Abhinanda (9th century)
- *Ramacharitam*, a Sanskrit epic by Sandhyakar Nandi (12th century)
- *Subhasita Ratnakosa*, a Sanskrit compilation by Vidyakara (towards the end of the Pala rule)

Other accounts

- *Silsiltut-Tauarikh* by the Arab merchant Suleiman (951 CE), who referred to the Pala kingdom as *Ruhmi* or *Rahma*
- *Dpal dus khyi 'khor lo'i chos bskor gyi byung khungs nyer mkh* (History of Buddhism in India) by Taranatha (1608), contains a few traditional legends and hearsays about the Pala rule
- *Ain-i-Akbari* by Abu'l-Fazl (16th-century)

References

Bibliography

- Bagchi, Jhunu (1993). *The History and Culture of the Pālas of Bengal and Bihar, Cir. 750 A.D.-cir. 1200 A.D.*[677] Abhinav Publications. ISBN 978-81-7017-301-4.
- Huntington, Susan L. (1984). *The "Pāala-Sena" Schools of Sculpture*[678]. Brill Archive. ISBN 90-04-06856-2.
- Paul, Pramode Lal (1939). *The Early History of Bengal*[679]. Indian History. **1**. Indian Research Institute. Archived from the original[680] on 17 August 2016. Retrieved 28 March 2014.
- Sengupta, Nitish K. (2011). *Land of Two Rivers: A History of Bengal from the Mahabharata to Mujib*[681]. Penguin Books India. pp. 39–49. ISBN 978-0-14-341678-4.

Medieval Cholas

Medieval Cholas	
848 CE–1070 CE	
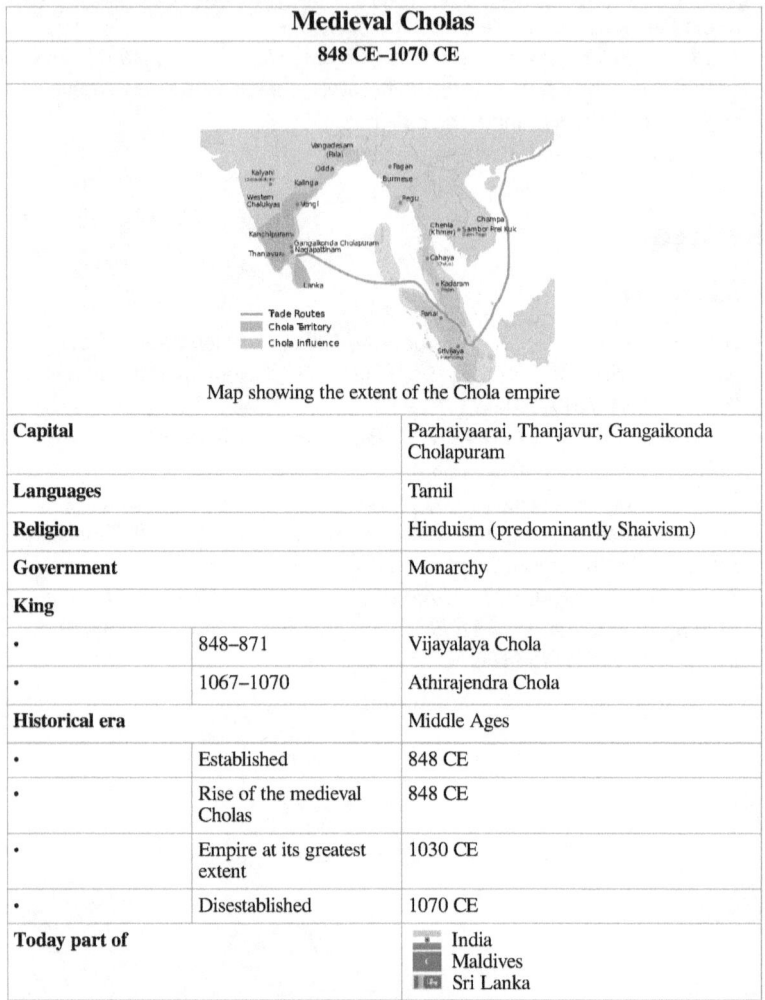 Map showing the extent of the Chola empire	
Capital	Pazhaiyaarai, Thanjavur, Gangaikonda Cholapuram
Languages	Tamil
Religion	Hinduism (predominantly Shaivism)
Government	Monarchy
King	
• 848–871	Vijayalaya Chola
• 1067–1070	Athirajendra Chola
Historical era	Middle Ages
• Established	848 CE
• Rise of the medieval Cholas	848 CE
• Empire at its greatest extent	1030 CE
• Disestablished	1070 CE
Today part of	India Maldives Sri Lanka

Medieval Cholas rose to prominence during the middle of the 9th century CE and established one of the greatest empires in South India. They successfully united South India under their rule and through their naval strength extended their influence in Southeast Asia and Sri Lanka. They had trade contacts with the Arabs in the west and with the Chinese in the east.

Medieval Cholas and Chalukyas were continuously in conflict over the control of Vengi and the conflict eventually exhausted both the empires and led to their decline. The Chola dynasty merged into the Eastern Chalukyan dynasty of Vengi through decades of alliances and later united under the Later Cholas.

List of Chola kings and emperors

Early Cholas

- Ellalan
- Kulakkottan
- Ilamchetchenni
- Karikala
- Nedunkilli
- Nalankilli
- Killivalavan
- Kopperuncholan
- Kochchenganan
- Perunarkilli

Interregnum (c. 200 – c. 848)

Medieval Cholas

Vijayalaya	848–891(?)
Aditya I	891–907
Parantaka I	907–950
Gandaraditya	950–957
Arinjaya	956–957
Sundara (Parantaka II)	957–970
Aditya II	(co-regent)
Uttama	970–985
Rajaraja I	985–1014
Rajendra I	1012–1044
Rajadhiraja	1044–1054
Rajendra II	1054–1063
Virarajendra	1063–1070
Athirajendra	1070–1070

Later Cholas

Kulothunga I	1070–1120
Vikrama	1118–1135
Kulothunga II	1133–1150
Rajaraja II	1146–1173
Rajadhiraja II	1166–1178
Kulothunga III	1178–1218
Rajaraja III	1216–1256
Rajendra III	1246–1279

Related dynasties

Telugu Cholas of Andhra
Chodagangas of Kalinga
Rajahnate of Cebu

Chola society

- Chola government
- Chola military
- Chola Navy
- Chola art
- Chola literature
- Flag of Chola
- Great Living Chola Temples
- Solesvara Temples
- Poompuhar
- Uraiyur
- Melakadambur
- Gangaikonda Cholapuram
- Thanjavur
- Tiruvarur

- v
- t
- e[682]

Part of **a series** on the
History of India

Early history

Vijayalaya Chola was probably a Pallava vassal. Vijayalaya captured Thanjavur in 848, making use of the opportunity during a war between Pandyas and Pallavas. The Cholas under Aditya I captured the Pallavas in the north (c. 869) and subdued the Pandayas and Cheras in the south (c. 903). Parantaka I drove the Pandayas out of their territories and captured Sri Lanka in 910. Rashtrakutas and Gangas in the north posed the biggest threat to the nascent Chola Empire and the Chola prince Rajaditya was killed in the battle of Thakkolam in 949. Parantaka had a long reign, and when he died in 950 his second son Gandaraditya became king. The Chola throne went to Gandaraditya's younger brother Arinjaya briefly before Arinjaya's son Sundara Chola took the reins of the kingdom overlooking the claims of Uttama Chola, son of Gandaraditya.

The Chola power recovered during Sundara Chola's reign. The Chola army under the command of the crown prince Aditya Karikala defeated the Pandyas and invaded up to Tondaimandalam in the north. Aditya Karikala was assassinated in a political plot suspected to be enacted by Uttama Chola. Uttama forced Sundara Chola to declare him as heir apparent and took over the reins in 970.

Golden Era

Raja Raja, the son of Sundara Chola, succeeded Uttama in 985. During the reign of Raja Raja and his son Rajendra Chola, the Chola influence spread across South East Asia. Rajaraja consolidated the Chola defences in the north by eliminating the last remnants of the Rashtrakutas. The Rashtrakutas were replaced by the Chalukyas, who were in constant conflict with the Cholas. Rajaraja soon extended his kingdom overseas to Lanka and the Chola army occupied northern portion of the island in 993. Rajaraja also invaded Vengi to restore the throne to his nephew Saktivarman. Rajendra Chola extended the empire by completing the conquest of Sri Lanka in 1018.

Rajendra marched up to the river Ganges in 1019, defeating the Pala king Mahipala. Rajendra also fought the Western Chalukyas in 1021 and invaded Vengi to sustain the Chola influence in 1031. The Chola navy attacked and conquered the kingdom of Srivijaya to secure Chola strategic interests. There was no permanent territorial gain and the kingdom was returned to the Srivijaya king for recognition of Chola superiority and the payment of periodic tributes.

Chola Chalukya Wars

The history of Cholas from the period of Rajaraja was tinged with a series of conflicts with the Western Chalukyas. The Old Chalukya dynasty had split into two sibling dynasties of the Western and Eastern Chalukyas. Rajaraja's daughter Kundavai was married to the Eastern Chalukya prince Vimaladitya, who ruled from Vengi. Western Chalukyas felt that the Vengi kingdom was under their natural sphere of influence. Cholas inflicted several defeats on the Western Chalukyas. For the most part, the frontier remained at the Tungabhadra River for both kingdoms and resulted in the death of king Rajadhiraja Chola.

Decline and fall

Rajendra's reign was followed by three of his sons in succession: Rajadhiraja Chola I, Rajendra Chola II and Virarajendra Chola. After Rajadhiraja died in 1054, Rajendra Chola II crowned himself on the battlefield. Later, Virarajendra succeeded in 1063 and managed to split the Western Chalukya kingdom by convincing Vikramaditya IV to an alliance. Vikramaditya tried to prevent Rajendra Chalukya, an Eastern Chalukyan prince of Chola descent, from ascending the throne of Vengi. However, when Virarajendra died in 1070, Rajendra Chalukya assassinated the Chola king Athirajendra and crowned himself Kulothunga Chola I, thereby starting the Later Chola dynasty.

Society and culture

The medieval Cholas under Rajaraja and his successors developed a highly organized administrative structure with central control and autonomous village assemblies. The system of government was a hereditary monarchy and the coronation of the king was an impressive ceremony. The royal household had numerous servants of varied descriptions. For the purpose of administration the empire was divided into convenient areas such as *valanadu*, *mandalam*, *nadu*, etc. Land revenue was the mainstay of public finance and great care was undertaken to recording land rights and revenue dues. Justice was administered by regularly constituted royal courts in addition to village courts. Crimes of the state, such as treason, were dealt with the king himself. The most striking feature of the Chola period was the unusual vigour and efficiency of the autonomous rural institutions.

This period of the Chola rule saw the maturity of the Tamil Temple architecture. Rajaraja built the great Brihadisvara Temple in Thanjavur. His son Rajendra imitated this effort by building the temple at his new capital Gangaikonda Cholapuram. This age also saw the Hindu religious revival in both Saiva and Vaishnava traditions. The Saiva and Vishnava canons were collected and categorized during this period.

Medieval Cholas			
	Vijayalaya 848-871		
	Aditya I 871-907		
	Parantaka I 907-950		
Rajaditya	Gandaraditya 950-957	Arinjaya 956-957	
	Uththama 970-985	Parantaka II 957-970	
	Aditya Karikala	Raja Raja I 985-1014	Kundavai
		Rajendra I 1012-1044	
	Rajadhiraja I 1018-1054	Rajendra II 1051-1063	Virarajendra 1063-1070
		Athirajendra 1067-1070	

References

<templatestyles src="Template:Refbegin/styles.css" />

- Nilakanta Sastri, K.A. (1955). *A History of South India*, OUP, New Delhi (Reprinted 2002).

| Preceded by
Early Cholas | **Chola empire:**
Medieval Cholas | Succeeded by
Later Cholas |

Western Chalukya Empire

Western Chalukya Empire	
Empire (Subordinate to Rashtrakuta until 973)	
973–1189	
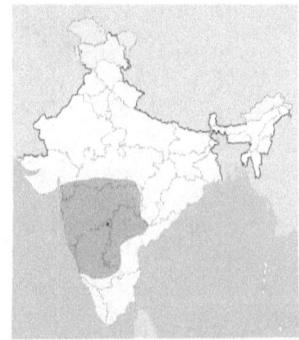 Extent of Western Chalukya Empire, 1121 CE	
Capital	Manyakheta, Basavakalyan
Languages	Kannada, Sanskrit
Religion	Hinduism Jainism
Government	Monarchy
King	
•	957 – 997	Tailapa II
•	1184 – 1189	Someshvara IV
History	
•	Earliest records	957
•	Established	973
•	Disestablished	1189
Preceded by	**Succeeded by**
Rashtrakuta dynasty	Hoysala Empire Kakatiya dynasty Seuna (Yadava) dynasty

The **Western Chalukya Empire** ruled most of the western Deccan, South India, between the 10th and 12th centuries. This Kannadiga dynasty is sometimes called the *Kalyani Chalukya* after its regal capital at Kalyani, today's Basavakalyan in the modern Bidar District of Karnataka state, and alternatively the *Later Chalukya* from its theoretical relationship to the 6th-century Chalukya dynasty of Badami. The dynasty is called Western Chalukyas to differentiate from the contemporaneous Eastern Chalukyas of Vengi, a separate dynasty. Prior to the rise of these Chalukyas, the Rashtrakuta empire of Manyakheta controlled most of Deccan and Central India for over two centuries. In 973, seeing confusion in the Rashtrakuta empire after a successful invasion of their capital by the ruler of the Paramara dynasty of Malwa, Tailapa II, a feudatory of the Rashtrakuta Dynasty ruling from Bijapur region defeated his overlords and made Manyakheta his capital. The dynasty quickly rose to power and grew into an empire under Someshvara I who moved the capital to Kalyani.

For over a century, the two empires of Southern India, the Western Chalukyas and the Chola dynasty of Tanjore fought many fierce wars to control the fertile region of Vengi. During these conflicts, the Eastern Chalukyas of Vengi, distant cousins of the Western Chalukyas but related to the Cholas by marriage took sides with the Cholas further complicating the situation. During the rule of Vikramaditya VI, in the late 11th and early 12th centuries, the Western Chalukyas convincingly contended with the Cholas and reached a peak ruling territories that spread over most of the Deccan, between the Narmada River in the north and Kaveri River in the south. His exploits were not limited to the south for even as a prince, during the rule of Someshvara I, he had led successful military campaigns as far east as modern Bihar and Bengal. During this period the other major ruling families of the Deccan, the Hoysalas, the Seuna Yadavas of Devagiri, the Kakatiya dynasty and the Southern Kalachuris of Kalyani, were subordinates of the Western Chalukyas and gained their independence only when the power of the Chalukya waned during the later half of the 12th century.

The Western Chalukyas developed an architectural style known today as a transitional style, an architectural link between the style of the early Chalukya dynasty and that of the later Hoysala empire. Most of its monuments are in the districts bordering the Tungabhadra River in central Karnataka. Well known examples are the Kasivisvesvara Temple at Lakkundi, the Mallikarjuna Temple at Kuruvatti, the Kallesvara Temple at Bagali and the Mahadeva Temple at Itagi. This was an important period in the development of fine arts in Southern India, especially in literature as the Western Chalukya kings encouraged writers in the native language Kannada, and Sanskrit.

Figure 66: *Old Kannada inscription dated 1028 AD from the rule of King Jayasimha II at the Praneshvara temple in Talagunda, Shivamogga district*

History

Knowledge of Western Chalukya history has come through examination of the numerous Kannada language inscriptions left by the kings (scholars Sheldon Pollock and Jan Houben have claimed 90 percent of the Chalukyan royal inscriptions are in Kannada),[684,685] and from the study of important contemporary literary documents in Western Chalukya literature such as *Gada Yuddha* (982) in Kannada by Ranna and *Vikramankadeva Charitam* (1120) in Sanskrit by Bilhana.[686] The earliest record is dated 957, during the rule of Tailapa II when the Western Chalukyas were still a feudatory of the Rashtrakutas and Tailapa II governed from Tardavadi in present-day Bijapur district, Karnataka.[687,688] The genealogy of the kings of this empire is still debated. One theory, based on contemporary literary and inscriptional evidence plus the finding that the Western Chalukyas employed titles and names commonly used by the early Chalukyas, suggests that the Western Chalukya kings belonged to the same family line as the illustrious Badami Chalukya dynasty of 6th-century,[689,690] while other Western Chalukya inscriptional evidence indicates they were a distinct line unrelated to the early Chalukyas.[691]

The records suggests a possible rebellion by a local Chalukya King, Chattigadeva of Banavasi-12000 province (c. 967), in alliance with local Kadamba

Figure 67: *Old Kannada inscription dated 1057 AD of King Someshvara I at Kalleshwara Temple, Hire Hadagali in Bellary district*

Figure 68: *Mahadeva Temple at Itagi in Koppal district, Karnataka*

chieftains. This rebellion however was unfruitful but paved the way for his successor Tailapa II.[692] A few years later, Tailapa II re-established Chalukya rule and defeated the Rashtrakutas during the reign of Karka II by timing his rebellion to coincide with the confusion caused in the Rashtrakuta capital of Manyakheta by the invading Paramaras of Central India in 973.[693,694] After overpowering the Rashtrakutas, Tailapa II moved his capital to Manyakheta and consolidated the Chalukya empire in the western Deccan by subjugating the Paramara and other aggressive rivals and extending his control over the land between the Narmada River and Tungabhadra River.[695] However, some inscriptions indicate that Balagamve in Mysore territory may have been a power centre up to the rule of Someshvara I in 1042.[696]

The intense competition between the kingdom of the western Deccan and those of the Tamil country came to the fore in the 11th century over the acutely contested fertile river valleys in the doab region of the Krishna and Godavari River called Vengi (modern coastal Andhra Pradesh). The Western Chalukyas and the Chola Dynasty fought many bitter wars over control of this strategic resource. The imperial Cholas gained power during the time of the famous king Rajaraja Chola I and the crown prince Rajendra Chola I.[697] The Eastern Chalukyas of Vengi were cousins of the Western Chalukyas but became increasingly influenced by the Cholas through their marital ties with the Tamil kingdom. As this was against the interests of the Western Chalukyas, they wasted no time in involving themselves politically and militarily in Vengi. When King Satyashraya succeeded Tailapa II to the throne, he was able to protect his kingdom from Chola aggression as well as his northern territories in Konkan and Gujarat although his control over Vengi was shaky.[698,699] His successor, Jayasimha II, fought many battles with the Cholas in the south around c. 1020–21 when both these powerful kingdoms struggled to choose the Vengi king.[700] Shortly thereafter in c. 1024, Jayasimha II subdued the Paramara of central India and the rebellious Yadava King Bhillama.

Chalukya dynasties

- v
- t
- e[701]

It is known from records that Jayasimha's son Someshvara I, whose rule historian Sen considers a brilliant period in the Western Chalukya rule, moved the Chalukya capital to Kalyani in c. 1042.[702,703] Hostilities with the Cholas continued while both sides won and lost battles, though neither lost significant territory[704,705] during the ongoing struggle to install a puppet on the Vengi throne.[703,706,707] In 1068 Someshvara I, suffering from an incurable illness, drowned himself in the Tungabhadra River (*Paramayoga*).[708,709,710] Despite many conflicts with the Cholas in the south, Someshvara I had managed to maintain control over the northern territories in Konkan, Gujarat, Malwa and Kalinga during his rule. His successor, his eldest son Someshvara II, feuded with his younger brother, Vikramaditya VI, an ambitious warrior who had initially been governor of Gangavadi in the southern Deccan when Someshvara II was the king. Before 1068, even as a prince, Vikramaditya VI had invaded Bengal, weakening the ruling Pala Empire. These incursions led to the establishment of *Karnata* dynasties such as the Sena dynasty and Varman dynasty in Bengal, and the Nayanadeva dynasty in Bihar.,[711,712,713] Married to a Chola princess (a daughter of Vira Rajendra Chola), Vikramaditya VI maintained a friendly alliance with them. After the death of the Chola king in 1070, Vikramaditya VI invaded the Tamil kingdom and installed his brother-in-law, Adhirajendra, on the throne creating conflict with Kulothunga Chola I, the powerful ruler of Vengi who sought the Chola throne for himself.[714] At the same time Vikramaditya VI undermined his brother, Someshvara II, by winning the loyalty of the Chalukya feudatories: the Hoysala, the Seuna and the Kadambas of Hangal. Anticipating a civil war, Someshvara II sought help from Vikramaditya VI's enemies, Kulothunga Chola I and the Kadambas of Goa. In the ensuing conflict of 1076, Vikramaditya VI emerged victorious and proclaimed himself king of the Chalukya empire.[715,716]

The fifty-year reign of Vikramaditya VI, the most successful of the later Chalukya rulers, was an important period in Karnataka's history and is referred to by historians as the "Chalukya Vikrama era".[717,718,719] Not only was he successful in controlling his powerful feudatories in the north (Kadamba Jayakesi II of Goa, Silhara Bhoja and the Yadava King) and south (Hoysala Vishnuvardhana), he successfully dealt with the imperial Cholas whom he defeated in the battle of Vengi in 1093 and again in 1118. He retained this territory for many years despite ongoing hostilities with the Cholas.[720,721,722,723] This victory in Vengi reduced the Chola influence in the eastern Deccan and made him emperor of territories stretching from the Kaveri River in the south to the Narmada River in the north, earning him the titles *Permadideva* and *Tribhuvanamalla* (lord of three worlds). The scholars of his time paid him glowing tributes for his military leadership, interest in fine arts and religious tolerance.[724,725] Literature proliferated and scholars in Kannada and Sanskrit adorned his court. Poet Bilhana, who immigrated from far away Kashmir, eulogised the king in his well-known work *Vikramankadeva Charita*.[726,727] Vikramaditya VI was not only an able warrior but also a devout king as indicated by his numerous inscriptions that record grants made to scholars and centers of religion.[728,729]

Figure 69: *Western Chalukyas of Kalyana, coin of King Somesvara I Trailokyamalla (1043-1068). Temple façade / Ornate floral ornament.*[730]

Figure 70: *Coin of the Chalukyas of Kalyana (Western Chalukyas). King Somesvara IV (1181-4/1189). Garuda, with prominent beak, running right / "Dapaga dapasa Murari(?)" in Kannada in three lines divided by pelleted lines.*[731]

The continual warring with the Cholas exhausted both empires, giving their subordinates the opportunity to rebel.[732] In the decades after Vikramaditya VI's death in 1126, the empire steadily decreased in size as their powerful feudatories expanded in autonomy and territorial command.[733] The time period between 1150 and 1200 saw many hard fought battles between the Chalukyas and their feudatories who were also at war with each other. By the time of Jagadhekamalla II, the Chalukyas had lost control of Vengi and his successor, Tailapa III, was defeated by the Kakatiya king Prola in 1149. Tailapa III was taken captive and later released bringing down the prestige of the Western Chalukyas. Seeing decadence and uncertainty seeping into Chalukya rule, the

Hoysalas and Seunas also encroached upon the empire. Hoysala Narasimha I defeated and killed Tailapa III but was unable to overcome the Kalachuris who were vying for control of the same region. In 1157 the Kalachuris of Kalyanis under Bijjala II captured Kalyani and occupied it for the next twenty years, forcing the Chalukyas to move their capital to Annigeri in the present day Dharwad district.[734]

The Kalachuris were originally immigrants into the southern Deccan from central India and called themselves *Kalanjarapuravaradhisavaras*.[735] Bijjala II and his ancestors had governed as Chalukya commanders (*Mahamandaleshwar*) over the Karhad-4000 and Tardavadi-1000 provinces (overlapping region in present-day Karnataka and Maharashtra) with Mangalavada or Annigeri[736] as their capital. Bijjala II's Chikkalagi record of 1157 calls him *Mahabhujabala Chakravarti* ("emperor with powerful shoulders and arms") indicating he no longer was a subordinate of the Chalukyas.[737] However the successors of Bijjala II were unable to hold on to Kalyani and their rule ended in 1183 when the last Chalukya scion, Someshvara IV made a final bid to regain the empire by recapturing Kalyani. Kalachuri King Sankama was killed by Chalukya general Narasimha in this conflict.[738,739] During this time, Hoysala Veera Ballala II was growing ambitious and clashed on several occasions with the Chalukyas and the other claimants over their empire. He defeated Chalukya Someshvara IV and Seuna Bhillama V bringing large regions in the Krishna River valley under the Hoysala domains, but was unsuccessful against Kalachuris.[740] The Seunas under Bhillama V were on an imperialistic expansion too when the Chalukyas regained Kalyani. Their ambitions were temporarily stemmed by their defeat against Chalukya general Barma in 1183 but they later had their vengeance in 1189.[741]

The overall effort by Someshvara IV to rebuild the Chalukya empire failed and the dynasty was ended by the Seuna rulers who drove Someshvara IV into exile in Banavasi 1189. After the fall of the Chalukyas, the Seunas and Hoysalas continued warring over the Krishna River region in 1191, each inflicting a defeat on the other at various points in time.[742] This period saw the fall of two great empires, the Chalukyas of the western Deccan and the Cholas of Tamilakam. On the ruins of these two empires were built the Kingdoms of their feudatories whose mutual antagonisms filled the annals of Deccan history for over a hundred years, the Pandyas taking control over some regions of the erstwhile Chola empire.[743]

Figure 71: *Mallikarjuna group of temples at Badami in Bagalkot district, Karnataka*

Administration

The Western Chalukya kingship was hereditary, passing to the king's brother if the king did not have a male heir. The administration was highly decentralised and feudatory clans such as the Alupas, the Hoysalas, the Kakatiya, the Seuna, the southern Kalachuri and others were allowed to rule their autonomous provinces, paying an annual tribute to the Chalukya emperor.[744] Excavated inscriptions record titles such as *Mahapradhana* (Chief minister), *Sandhivigrahika*, and *Dharmadhikari* (chief justice). Some positions such as *Tadeyadandanayaka* (commander of reserve army) were specialised in function while all ministerial positions included the role of *Dandanayaka* (commander), showing that cabinet members were trained as army commanders as well as in general administrative skills.[745]

The kingdom was divided into provinces such as *Banavasi-12000*, *Nolambavadi-32000*, *Gangavadi-96000*, each name including the number of villages under its jurisdiction. The large provinces were divided into smaller provinces containing a lesser number of villages, as in *Belavola-300*. The big provinces were called *Mandala* and under them were *Nadu* further divided into *Kampanas* (groups of villages) and finally a *Bada* (village). A *Mandala* was under a member of the royal family, a trusted feudatory or a senior official. Tailapa II himself was in charge of Tardavadi province during the Rashtrakuta rule. Chiefs of *Mandalas* were transferable based on political developments. For example, an official named Bammanayya administered Banavasi-12000 under King Someshvara III but was later transferred to Halasige-12000.

Figure 72: *Ornate mantapa at Kalleshvara Temple (987 CE) in Bagali, Davanagere district*

Women from the royal family also administered *Nadus* and *Kampanas*. Army commanders were titled *Mahamandaleshwaras* and those who headed a *Nadu* were entitled *Nadugouvnda*.[746]

The Western Chalukyas minted punch-marked gold pagodas with Kannada and Nagari legends[747] which were large, thin gold coins with several varying punch marks on the obverse side. They usually carried multiple punches of symbols such as a stylised lion, *Sri* in Kannada, a spearhead, the king's title, a lotus and others. Jayasimha II used the legend *Sri Jaya*, Someshvara I issued coins with *Sri Tre lo ka malla*, Someshvara II used *Bhuvaneka malla*, Lakshmideva's coin carried *Sri Lasha*, and Jagadhekamalla II coinage had the legend *Sri Jagade*. The Alupas, a feudatory, minted coins with the Kannada and *Nagari* legend *Sri Pandya Dhanamjaya*. Lakkundi in Gadag district and Sudi in Dharwad district were the main mints (*Tankhashaley*). Their heaviest gold coin was Gadyanaka weighting 96 grains, Dramma weighted 65 grains, Kalanju 48 grains, Kasu 15 grains, Manjadi 2.5 grains, Akkam 1.25 grains and Pana 9.6 grain.[748]

Economy

Agriculture was the empire's main source of income through taxes on land and produce. The majority of the people lived in villages and worked farming the staple crops of rice, pulses, and cotton in the dry areas and sugarcane in areas having sufficient rainfall, with areca and betel being the chief cash crops. The living conditions of the labourers who farmed the land must have been bearable as there are no records of revolts by the landless against wealthy landlords. If peasants were disgruntled the common practice was to migrate in large numbers out of the jurisdiction of the ruler who was mistreating them, thereby depriving him of revenue from their labor.[749]

Taxes were levied on mining and forest products, and additional income was raised through tolls for the use of transportation facilities. The state also collected fees from customs, professional licenses, and judicial fines.[750] Records show horses and salt were taxed as well as commodities (gold, textiles, perfumes) and agricultural produce (black pepper, paddy, spices, betel leaves, palm leaves, coconuts and sugar). Land tax assessment was based on frequent surveys evaluating the quality of land and the type of produce. Chalukya records specifically mention black soil and red soil lands in addition to wetland, dry land and wasteland in determining taxation rates.[751]

Part of a series on the
History of Karnataka

- Political history of medieval Karnataka
- Origin of Karnataka's name
- Kadambas and Gangas
- Chalukya Empire
- Rashtrakuta Empire
- Western Chalukya Empire
- Southern Kalachuri
- Hoysala Empire
- Vijayanagara Empire
- Bahmani Sultanate
- Bijapur Sultanate
- Kingdom of Mysore
- Nayakas of Keladi
- Nayakas of Chitradurga
- Haleri Kingdom
- Unification of Karnataka

Categories

- Architecture
- Forts
- Economies
- Societies

- v̱
- ṯ
- ḵ[752]

Key figures mentioned in inscriptions from rural areas were the Gavundas (officials) or Goudas. The Gavundas belonged to two levels of economic strata, the *Praja Gavunda* (people's Gavunda) and the *Prabhu Gavunda* (lord of Gavundas). They served the dual purpose of representing the people before the rulers as well as functioning as state appointees for tax collection and the raising of militias. They are mentioned in inscriptions related to land transactions, irrigation maintenance, village tax collection and village council duties.[753]

The organisation of corporate enterprises became common in the 11th century.[754] Almost all arts and crafts were organised into guilds and work was done on a corporate basis; records do not mention individual artists, sculptors and craftsman. Only in the regions ruled by the Hoysala did individual sculptors etched their names below their creations.[755] Merchants organised themselves into powerful guilds that transcended political divisions, allowing their operations to be largely unaffected by wars and revolutions. Their only threat was the possibility of theft from brigands when their ships and caravans traveled to distant lands. Powerful South Indian merchant guilds included the *Manigramam*, the *Nagarattar* and the *Anjuvannam*. Local guilds were called *nagaram*, while the *Nanadesis* were traders from neighbouring kingdoms who perhaps mixed business with pleasure. The wealthiest and most influential and celebrated of all South Indian merchant guilds was the self-styled *Ainnurruvar*, also known as the 500 *Svamis* of Ayyavolepura (Brahmins and *Mahajanas* of present-day Aihole),[756,757] who conducted extensive land and sea trade and thereby contributed significantly to the total foreign trade of the empire. It fiercely protected its trade obligations (*Vira Bananjudharma* or law of the noble merchants) and its members often recorded their achievements in inscriptions (*prasasti*). Five hundred such excavated *Prasasti* inscriptions, with their own flag and emblem, the bull, record their pride in their business.

Rich traders contributed significantly to the king's treasury through paying import and export taxes. The edicts of the Aihole *Svamis* mention trade ties with foreign kingdoms such as Chera, Pandya, Maleya (Malaysia), Magadh, Kaushal, Saurashtra, Kurumba, Kambhoja (Cambodia), Lata (Gujarat), Parasa (Persia) and Nepal. Travelling both land and sea routes, these merchants traded mostly in precious stones, spices and perfumes, and other specialty items such as camphor. Business flourished in precious stones such as diamonds, lapis lazuli, onyx, topaz, carbuncles and emeralds. Commonly traded spices were cardamom, saffron, and cloves, while perfumes included the by-products of sandalwood, bdellium, musk, civet and rose. These items were sold either in bulk or hawked on streets by local merchants in towns.[758] The Western Chalukyas controlled most of South India's west coast and by the 10th century they had established extensive trade ties with the Tang Empire of China, the empires of Southeast Asia and the Abbasid Caliphate in Bhagdad, and by the 12th century Chinese fleets were frequenting Indian ports. Exports to Song Dynasty China included textiles, spices, medicinal plants, jewels, ivory, rhino horn, ebony and camphor. The same products also reached ports in the west such as Dhofar and Aden. The final destinations for those trading with the west were Persia, Arabia and Egypt.[759] The thriving trade center of Siraf, a port on the eastern coast of the Persian Gulf, served an international clientele of merchants including those from the Chalukya empire who were feasted by wealthy local merchants during business visits. An indicator of the Indian merchants' importance in Siraf comes from records describing dining plates reserved for them.[760] In addition to this, Siraf received aloe wood, perfumes, sandalwood and condiments. The most expensive import to South India were Arabian horse shipments, this trade being monopolised by Arabs and local Brahmin merchants. Traveller Marco Polo, in the 13th century, recorded that the breeding of horses never succeeded in India due to differing climatic, soil and grassland conditions.

Culture

Religion

The fall of the Rashtrakuta empire to the Western Chalukyas in the 10th century, coinciding with the defeat of the Western Ganga Dynasty by the Cholas in Gangavadi, was a setback to Jainism. The growth of Virashaivism in the Chalukya territory and Vaishnava Hinduism in the Hoysala region paralleled a general decreased interest in Jainism, although the succeeding kingdoms continued to be religiously tolerant.[761] Two locations of Jain worship in the Hoysala territory continued to be patronaged, Shravanabelagola and Kambadahalli. The decline of Buddhism in South India had begun in the 8th century with the spread of Adi Shankara's Advaita philosophy.[762] The only places of Buddhist worship that remained during the Western Chalukya rule were at Dambal and Balligavi.[763] There is no mention of religious conflict in the writings and inscriptions of the time which suggest the religious transition was smooth.

Although the origin of the Virashaiva faith has been debated, the movement grew through its association with Basavanna in the 12th century.[764,765] Basavanna and other Virashaiva saints preached of a faith without a caste system.

Figure 73: *Basavanna Statue*

Figure 74: *A Hero stone with old Kannada inscription (1115 AD) during the rule of Vikarmaditya VI at the Kedareshvara temple in Balligavi*

In his Vachanas (a form of poetry), Basavanna appealed to the masses in simple Kannada and wrote "work is worship" (Kayakave Kailasa). Also known as the Lingayats (worshipers of the *Linga*, the universal symbol of Shiva), these Virashaivas questioned many of the established norms of society such as the belief in rituals and the theory of rebirth and supported the remarriage of widows and the marriage of unwed older women.[766] This gave more social freedom to women but they were not accepted into the priesthood. Ramanujacharya, the head of the Vaishnava monastery in Srirangam, traveled to the Hoysala territory and preached the way of devotion (bhakti marga). He later wrote *Sribhashya*, a commentary on Badarayana Brahmasutra, a critique on the Advaita philosophy of Adi Shankara.[767] Ramanujacharya's stay in Melkote resulted in the Hoysala King Vishnuvardhana converting to Vaishnavism, a faith that his successors also followed.

The impact of these religious developments on the culture, literature, and architecture in South India was profound. Important works of metaphysics and poetry based on the teachings of these philosophers were written over the next centuries. Akka Mahadevi, Allama Prabhu, and a host of Basavanna's followers, including Chenna Basava, Prabhudeva, Siddharama, and Kondaguli Kesiraja wrote hundreds of poems called Vachanas in praise of Lord Shiva.[768] The esteemed scholars in the Hoysala court, Harihara and Raghavanka, were Virashaivas.[769] This tradition continued into the Vijayanagar empire with such well-known scholars as Singiraja, Mallanarya, Lakkana Dandesa and other prolific writers of Virashaiva literature.[770,771] The Saluva, Tuluva and Aravidu dynasties of the Vijayanagar empire were followers of Vaishnavism and a Vaishnava temple with an image of Ramanujacharya exists today in the Vitthalapura area of Vijayanagara.[772] Scholars in the succeeding Mysore Kingdom wrote Vaishnavite works supporting the teachings of Ramanujacharya.[773] King Vishnuvardhana built many temples after his conversion from Jainism to Vaishnavism.

Society

The rise of Veerashaivaism was revolutionary and challenged the prevailing Hindu caste system which retained royal support. The social role of women largely depended on their economic status and level of education in this relatively liberal period. Freedom was more available to women in the royal and affluent urban families. Records describe the participation of women in the fine arts, such as Chalukya queen Chandala Devi's and Kalachuris of Kalyani queen Sovala Devi's skill in dance and music. The compositions of thirty Vachana women poets included the work of the 12th-century Virashaiva mystic Akka Mahadevi whose devotion to the *bhakti* movement is well known.[774]

Figure 75: *Kirtimukha relief at Kedareswara Temple in Balligavi, Shimoga district*

Contemporary records indicate some royal women were involved in administrative and martial affairs such as princess Akkadevi, (sister of King Jayasimha II) who fought and defeated rebellious feudals.[775,776] Inscriptions emphasise public acceptance of widowhood indicating that Sati (a custom in which a dead man's widow used to immolate herself on her husband's funeral pyre) though present was on a voluntary basis.[777] Ritual deaths to achieve salvation were seen among the Jains who preferred to fast to death (Sallekhana), while people of some other communities chose to jump on spikes (*Shoolabrahma*) or walking into fire on an eclipse.

In a Hindu caste system that was conspicuously present, Brahmins enjoyed a privileged position as providers of knowledge and local justice. These Brahmins were normally involved in careers that revolved around religion and learning with the exception of a few who achieved success in martial affairs. They were patronised by kings, nobles and wealthy aristocrats who persuaded learned Brahmins to settle in specific towns and villages by making them grants of land and houses. The relocation of Brahmin scholars was calculated to be in the interest of the kingdom as they were viewed as persons detached from wealth and power and their knowledge was a useful tool to educate and teach ethical conduct and discipline in local communities. Brahmins were also actively involved in solving local problems by functioning as neutral arbiters (*Panchayat*).[778]

Regarding eating habits, Brahmins, Jains, Buddhists and Shaivas were strictly vegetarian while the partaking of different kinds of meat was popular among other communities. Marketplace vendors sold meat from domesticated animals such as goats, sheep, pigs and fowl as well as exotic meat including partridge, hare, wild fowl and boar.[779] People found indoor amusement by attending wrestling matches (*Kusti*) or watching animals fight such as cock fights and ram fights or by gambling. Horse racing was a popular outdoor past time.[780] In addition to these leisurely activities, festivals and fairs were frequent and entertainment by traveling troupes of acrobats, dancers, dramatists and musicians was often provided.[781]

Schools and hospitals are mentioned in records and these were built in the vicinity of temples. Marketplaces served as open air town halls where people gathered to discuss and ponder local issues. Choirs, whose main function was to sing devotional hymns, were maintained at temple expense. Young men were trained to sing in choirs in schools attached to monasteries such as Hindu *Matha*, Jain *Palli* and Buddhist *Vihara*.[782] These institutions provided advanced education in religion and ethics and were well equipped with libraries (*Saraswati Bhandara*). Learning was imparted in the local language and in Sanskrit. Schools of higher learning were called *Brahmapuri* (or *Ghatika* or *Agrahara*). Teaching Sanskrit was a near monopoly of Brahmins who received royal endowments for their cause. Inscriptions record that the number of subjects taught varied from four to eighteen.[783] The four most popular subjects with royal students were Economics (*Vartta*), Political Science (*Dandaniti*), Veda (*trayi*) and Philosophy (*Anvikshiki*), subjects that are mentioned as early as Kautilyas Arthashastra.

Literature

The Western Chalukya era was one of substantial literary activity in the native Kannada, and Sanskrit.[784] In a golden age of Kannada literature,[785] Jain scholars wrote about the life of Tirthankaras and Virashaiva poets expressed their closeness to God through pithy poems called Vachanas. Nearly three hundred contemporary *Vachanakaras* (*Vachana* poets) including thirty women poets have been recorded.[786,787] Early works by Brahmin writers were on the epics, Ramayana, Mahabharata, Bhagavata, Puranas and Vedas. In the field of secular literature, subjects such as romance, erotics, medicine, lexicon, mathematics, astrology, encyclopedia etc. were written for the first time.[788]

Most notable among Kannada scholars were Ranna, grammarian Nagavarma II, minister Durgasimha and the Virashaiva saint and social reformer Basavanna. Ranna who was patronised by king Tailapa II and Satyashraya is one among the "three gems of Kannada literature".[789] He was bestowed the title "Emperor among poets" (*Kavi Chakravathi*) by King Tailapa II and has

Figure 76: *Grill work at Tripurantkesvara temple in Balligavi, Shimoga district*

five major works to his credit. Of these, *Saahasabheema Vijayam* (or *Gada yuddha*) of 982 in *Champu* style is a eulogy of his patron King Satyashraya whom he compares to Bhima in valour and achievements and narrates the duel between Bhima and Duryodhana using clubs on the eighteenth day of the Mahabharata war.[790] He wrote *Ajitha purana* in 993 describing the life of the second Tirthankara, Ajitanatha.[791,792]

Nagavarma II, poet laureate (*Katakacharya*) of King Jagadhekamalla II made contributions to Kannada literature in various subjects.[793,794] His works in poetry, prosody, grammar and vocabulary are standard authorities and their importance to the study of Kannada language is well acknowledged. *Kavyavalokana* in poetics, *Karnataka-Bhashabhushana* on grammar and *Vastukosa* a lexicon (with Kannada equivalents for Sanskrit words) are some of his comprehensive contributions.[795] Several works on medicine were produced during this period. Notable among them were Jagaddala Somanatha's *Karnataka Kalyana Karaka*.[796]

A unique and native form of poetic literature in Kannada called Vachanas developed during this time. They were written by mystics, who expressed their devotion to God in simple poems that could appeal to the masses. Basavanna, Akka Mahadevi, Allama Prabhu, Channabasavanna and Siddharama are the best known among them.[797]

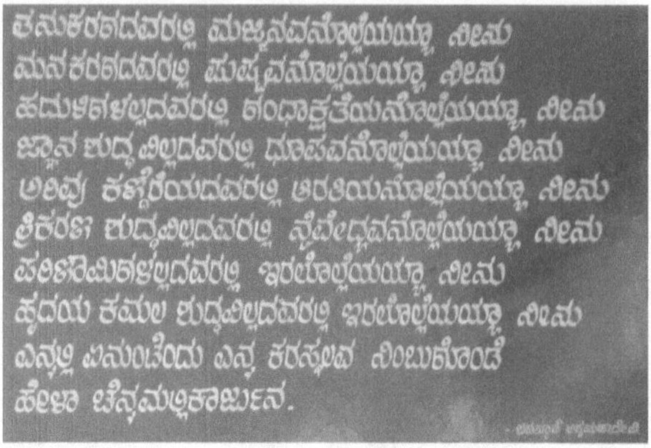

Figure 77: *A popular Vachana poem in the Kannada language by Akka Mahadevi*

In Sanskrit, a well-known poem (*Mahakavya*) in 18 cantos called *Vikramankadeva Charita* by Kashmiri poet Bilhana recounts in epic style the life and achievements of his patron king Vikramaditya VI. The work narrates the episode of Vikramaditya VI's accession to the Chalukya throne after overthrowing his elder brother Someshvara II.[798] The great Indian mathematician Bhāskara II (born c.1114) flourished during this time. From his own account in his famous work *Siddhanta Siromani* (c. 1150, comprising the *Lilavati*, *Bijaganita* on algebra, *Goladhaya* on the celestial globe and *Grahaganita* on planets) Bijjada Bida (modern Bijapur) was his native place.[799]

Manasollasa or *Abhilashitartha Chintamani* by king Someshvara III (1129) was a Sanskrit work intended for all sections of society. This is an example of an early encyclopedia in Sanskrit covering many subjects including medicine, magic, veterinary science, valuing of precious stones and pearls, fortifications, painting, music, games, amusements etc.[800] While the book does not give any of dealt topics particular hierarchy of importance, it serves as a landmark in understanding the state of knowledge in those subjects at that time.[801] Someshwara III also authored a biography of his famous father Vikramaditya VI called Vikraman-Kabhyudaya. The text is a historical prose narrative which also includes a graphic description of the geography and people of Karnataka.[802]

A Sanskrit scholar Vijnaneshwara became famous in the field of legal literature for his *Mitakshara*, in the court of Vikramaditya VI. Perhaps the most acknowledged work in that field, Mitakshara is a treatise on law (commentary on *Yajnavalkya*) based on earlier writings and has found acceptance in most parts of modern India. An Englishman Colebrooke later translated into English the section on inheritance giving it currency in the British Indian court

Figure 78: *Typical Western Chalukya dravida Vimana at Siddesvara temple in Haveri, Karnataka*

system.[803] Some important literary works of the time related to music and musical instruments were *Sangita Chudamani*, *Sangita Samayasara* and *Sangita Ratnakara*.[804]

Architecture

The reign of Western Chalukya dynasty was an important period in the development of Deccan architecture. The architecture designed during this time served as a conceptual link between the Badami Chalukya Architecture of the 8th century and the Hoysala architecture popularised in the 13th century.[805,806] The art of the Western Chalukyas is sometimes called the "Gadag style" after the number of ornate temples they built in the Tungabhadra River-Krishna River doab region of present-day Gadag district in Karnataka. The dynasty's temple building activity reached its maturity and culmination in the 12th century with over a hundred temples built across the Deccan, more than half of them in present-day central Karnataka.[807,808] Apart from temples, the dynasty's architecture is well known for the ornate stepped wells (*Pushkarni*) which served as ritual bathing places, a few of which are well preserved in Lakkundi. These stepped well designs were later incorporated by the Hoysalas and the Vijayanagara empire in the coming centuries.[809]

Figure 79: *Ornate pillars at Saraswati temple in Gadag city, Karnataka*

The Kasivisvesvara Temple at Lakkundi (Gadag district),[810,811] the Dodda Basappa Temple at Dambal (Gadag district),[812,813] the Mallikarjuna Temple at Kuruvatti (Bellary district),[814] the Kallesvara Temple at Bagali (Davangere district),[815] the Siddhesvara Temple at Haveri (Haveri district),[816,817] the Amrtesvara Temple at Annigeri (Dharwad district),[818] the Mahadeva Temple at Itagi (Koppal district),[819,820] the Kaitabheshvara Temple at Kubatur,[821] and the Kedareshvara Temple at Balligavi are the finest examples produced by the later Chalukya architects.[822] The 12th-century Mahadeva Temple with its well executed sculptures is an exquisite example of decorative detail. The intricate, finely crafted carvings on walls, pillars and towers speak volumes about Chalukya taste and culture. An inscription outside the temple calls it "Emperor of Temples" (*devalaya chakravarti*) and relates that it was built by Mahadeva, a commander in the army of king Vikramaditya VI.[823] The Kedareswara Temple (1060) at Balligavi is an example of a transitional Chalukya-Hoysala architectural style.[824] The Western Chalukyas built temples in Badami and Aihole during their early phase of temple building activity, such as Mallikarjuna Temple, the Yellamma Temple and the Bhutanatha group of Temples.[825]

The *vimana* of their temples (tower over the shrine) is a compromise in detail between the plain stepped style of the early Chalukyas and the decorative finish of the Hoysalas. To the credit of the Western Chalukya architects is the development of the lathe turned (tuned) pillars and use of Soapstone (Chloritic

Figure 80: *Brahma Jinalaya at Lakkundi dates to the mid-late 11th century*

Schist) as basic building and sculptural material, a very popular idiom in later Hoysala temples. They popularised the use of decorative *Kirtimukha* (demon faces) in their sculptures. Famous architects in the Hoysala kingdom included Chalukyan architects who were natives of places such as Balligavi.[826] The artistic wall decor and the general sculptural idiom was dravidian architecture. This style is sometimes called *Karnata dravida*, one of the notable traditions in Indian architecture.[827]

Language

The local language Kannada was mostly used in Western (Kalyani) Chalukya inscriptions and epigraphs. Some historians assert that ninety percent of their inscriptions are in the Kannada language while the remaining are in Sanskrit language.[828,829] More inscriptions in Kannada are attributed to Vikramaditya VI than any other king prior to the 12th century,[830] many of which have been deciphered and translated by historians of the Archaeological Survey of India. Inscriptions were generally either on stone (*Shilashasana*) or copper plates (*Tamarashasana*). This period saw the growth of Kannada as a language of literature and poetry, impetus to which came from the devotional movement of the Virashaivas (called Lingayatism) who expressed their closeness to their deity in the form of simple lyrics called Vachanas.[831] At an administrative level, the regional language was used to record locations and rights related to land

Figure 81: *Old Kannada inscription ascribed to King Vikramaditya VI, dated 1112 CE at Mahadeva Temple in Itagi, Karnataka*

grants. When bilingual inscriptions were written, the section stating the title, genealogy, origin myths of the king and benedictions were generally done in Sanskrit. Kannada was used to state terms of the grants, including information on the land, its boundaries, the participation of local authorities, rights and obligations of the grantee, taxes and dues, and witnesses. This ensured the content was clearly understood by the local people without any ambiguity.[832]

In addition to inscriptions, chronicles called *Vamshavalis* were written to provide historical details of dynasties. Writings in Sanskrit included poetry, grammar, lexicon, manuals, rhetoric, commentaries on older works, prose fiction and drama. In Kannada, writings on secular subjects became popular. Some well-known works are *Chandombudhi*, a prosody, and *Karnataka Kadambari*, a romance, both written by Nagavarma I, a lexicon called *Rannakanda* by Ranna (993), a book on medicine called *Karnataka-Kalyanakaraka* by Jagaddala Somanatha, the earliest writing on astrology called *Jatakatilaka* by Sridharacharya (1049), a writing on erotics called *Madanakatilaka* by Chandraraja, and an encyclopedia called *Lokapakara* by Chavundaraya II (1025).[833,834]

References

Book <templatestyles src="Template:Refbegin/styles.css" />

- Chopra, P.N.; Ravindran, T.K.; Subrahmanian, N (2003) [2003]. *History of South India (Ancient, Medieval and Modern) Part 1*. New Delhi: Chand Publications. ISBN 81-219-0153-7.
- Cousens, Henry (1996) [1926]. *The Chalukyan Architecture of Kanarese Districts*. New Delhi: Archaeological Survey of India. OCLC 37526233[835].
- Davison-Jenkins, Dominic J. (2001). "Hydraulic works". In John M. Fritz and George Michell (editors). *New Light on Hampi : Recent Research at Vijayanagara*. Mumbai: MARG. ISBN 81-85026-53-X.
- Foekema, Gerard (1996). *A Complete Guide To Hoysala Temples*. New Delhi: Abhinav. ISBN 81-7017-345-0.
- Hardy, Adam (1995) [1995]. *Indian Temple Architecture: Form and Transformation-The Karnata Dravida Tradition 7th to 13th Centuries*. Abhinav Publications. ISBN 81-7017-312-4.
- Houben, Jan E.M. (1996) [1996]. *Ideology and Status of Sanskrit: Contributions to the History of the Sanskrit language*. Brill. ISBN 90-04-10613-8.
- Kamath, Suryanath U. (2001) [1980]. *A concise history of Karnataka : from pre-historic times to the present*. Bangalore: Jupiter books. LCCN 80905179[836]. OCLC 7796041[837].
- Mack, Alexandra (2001). "The temple district of Vitthalapura". In John M. Fritz and George Michell (editors). *New Light on Hampi : Recent Research at Vijayanagara*. Mumbai: MARG. ISBN 81-85026-53-X.
- Moraes, George M. (1990) [1931]. *The Kadamba Kula, A History of Ancient and Medieval Karnataka*. New Delhi, Madras: Asian Educational Services. ISBN 81-206-0595-0.
- Narasimhacharya, R (1988) [1988]. *History of Kannada Literature*. New Delhi: Penguin Books. ISBN 81-206-0303-6.
- Pollock, Sheldon (2006) [2006]. *The Language of the Gods in the World of Men: Sanskrit, Culture, and Power in Premodern India*. Berkeley: University of California Press. ISBN 0-520-24500-8.
- Puranik, Siddya (1992). "Vachana literature (Kannada)". In Mohal Lal. *Encyclopaedia of Indian Literature: sasay to zorgot*. New Delhi: Sahitya Akademi. ISBN 81-260-1221-8.
- Rice, E.P. (1982) [1921]. *Kannada Literature*. New Delhi: Asian Educational Services. ISBN 81-206-0063-0.
- Sastri, Nilakanta K.A. (2002) [1955]. *A history of South India from prehistoric times to the fall of Vijayanagar*. New Delhi: Indian Branch, Oxford University Press. ISBN 0-19-560686-8.

- Sen, Sailendra Nath (1999) [1999]. *Ancient Indian History and Civilization*. New Age Publishers. ISBN 81-224-1198-3.
- Thapar, Romila (2003) [2003]. *The Penguin History of Early India*. New Delhi: Penguin Books. ISBN 0-14-302989-4.

Web

 Wikimedia Commons has media related to *Western Chalukya Empire*.

<templatestyles src="Template:Refbegin/styles.css" />

- Kamiya, Takeyo. "Architecture of Indian subcontinent"[838]. *Indian Architecture*. Gerard da Cunha. Retrieved 2006-12-31.
- Kamat, Jyotsna. "The Chalukyas of Kalyani"[839]. *Dynasties of Deccan*. Kamat's Potpourri. Retrieved 2006-12-31.
- "Indian Inscriptions, Vol 9,11,15,17,18,20"[840]. *Archaeological Survey of India*. What Is India Publishers (P) Ltd. Retrieved 2006-11-10.
- Githa U.B. "Balligavi - An important seat of learning"[841]. *History of Indian Art*. Chitralakshana.com 2002. Archived from the original[842] on 2006-10-06. Retrieved 2006-12-31.
- Gunther, Michael D. "Index IV, Late Chalukya"[843]. *Monuments of India*. Retrieved 2006-11-10.
- Kannikeswaran, K. "Kalyani Chalukyan temples"[844]. *TempleNet*. webmaster@templenet.com. Retrieved 2006-11-10.
- Prabhu, Govindaraya S. "Alupa Dynasty-catalogue"[845]. *Prabhu's web page on Indian Coins*. Archived from the original[846] on 2006-08-15. Retrieved 2006-11-10.
- Prabhu, Govindaraya S. "Chalukya Dynasty-catalogue"[847]. *Prabhu's web page on Indian Coins*. Retrieved 2006-11-10.
- Rao, Kishan. "Emperor among Temples crying for attention"[848]. *Southern States - Karnataka*. The Hindu. Retrieved 2006-11-10.

<indicator name="featured-star"> ★ </indicator>

Pallava dynasty

Pallava Empire	
Dynasty	
275 CE–897 CE	
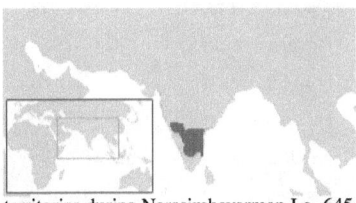 Pallava territories during Narasimhavarman I c. 645. This includes the Chalukya territories occupied by the Pallavas.	
Capital	Kanchipuram
Languages	Prakrit, Sanskrit, Tamil, Telugu
Religion	Hinduism
Government	Monarchy
King	
• 275–300	Simhavarman I
• 882–897	Aparajitavarman
Historical era	Classical India
• Established	275 CE
• Disestablished	897 CE
Preceded by	Succeeded by
Andhra Ikshvaku Kalabhra dynasty	Chola dynasty Eastern Chalukyas
Today part of	India Sri Lanka[849]

Pallava Kings (200s–800s)	
Vishnugopa II	
Simhavarman III	
Simhavishnu	
Mahendravarman I	(600-630)
Narasimhavarman I	(630–668)
Mahendravarman II	(668–670)
Paramesvaravarman I	(670–695)
Narasimhavarman II	(700-728)
Paramesvaravarman II	(728–731)
Nandivarman II	(731–795)
Dantivarman	(795–846)
Nandivarman III	(846-869)
Aparajitavarman	(880-897)
Aditya I (*Chola Empire*)	(870-907)

The **Pallava dynasty** was a South Indian dynasty that existed from 275 CE to 897 CE, ruling a portion of southern India. They gained prominence after the eclipse of the Satavahana dynasty, whom the Pallavas served as feudatories.[850,851]

Pallavas became a major power during the reign of Mahendravarman I (571 – 630 CE) and Narasimhavarman I (630 – 668 CE) and dominated the Telugu and northern parts of the Tamil region for about 600 years until the end of the 9th century. Throughout their reign they were in constant conflict with both Chalukyas of Badami in the north and the Tamil kingdoms of Chola and Pandyas in the south and were finally defeated by the Chola kings in the 9th century CE.Wikipedia:Citation needed

Pallavas are most noted for their patronage of architecture, the finest example being the Shore Temple, a UNESCO World Heritage Site in Mahabalipuram. The Pallavas, who left behind magnificent sculptures and temples, established the foundations of medieval South Indian architecture. They developed the Pallava script from which Grantha ultimately descended. The Pallava script gave rise to several other southeast Asian scripts. Chinese traveller Xuanzang visited Kanchipuram during Pallava rule and extolled their benign rule.

Pallava dynasty

Figure 82: *Kailasanathar Temple, Kanchipuram, Tamil Nadu, 685-705*

Origins

Inner court or the circumambulatory passage with 58 subshrines. Kailasanathar Temple, Kanchipuram

Pillar with multi-headed lions. Kailasanathar Temple, Kanchipuram

Kailasanathar Temple, Kanchipuram

A Sangam Period classic, *Manimekalai*, attributes the origin of the first Pallava King from a liaison between the daughter of a Naga king of Manipallava named Pilli Valai (Pilivalai) with a Chola king, Killivalavan, out of which union was born a prince, who was lost in ship wreck and found with a twig (*pallava*) of Cephalandra Indica (*Tondai*) around his ankle and hence named *Tondai-man*. Another version states that "Pallava" was born from the union of the Brahmin Ashvatthama with a Naga Princess also supposedly supported in the sixth verse of the Bahur plates which states "From Ashvatthama was born the king named Pallava". The Pallavas themselves claimed to descend from Brahma and Ashvatthama.

Though *Manimekalai* posits Ilam Tiriyan as a Chola, not a Pallava, the Velurpalaiyam plates dated to 852, do not mention the Cholas. Instead, they credit the Naga liaison episode, and creation of the Pallava line, to a different Pallava king named Virakurcha, while preserving its legitimising significance:

> *...from him (Aśvatthāman) in order (came) Pallava, the lord of the whole earth, whose fame was bewildering. Thence, came into existence the race of Pallavas... [including the son of Chūtapallava] Vīrakūrcha, of celebrated name, who simultaneously with (the hand of) the daughter of the chief of serpents grasped also the complete insignia of royalty and became famous.*

Historically, early relations between Nagas and Pallavas became well-established before the myth of Pallava's birth to Ashvatthama took root. A *prashasti* (literally "praise"), composed in 753 on the dynastic eulogy in the Kasakadi (Kasakudi) plates, by the Pallava Trivikrama, traces the Pallava lineage from creation through a series of mythic progenitors, and then praises the dynasty in terms of two similes hinged together by triple use of the word avatara ("descent"), as below:

> *From [them] descended the powerful, spotless Pallava dynasty [vaṁśāvatāra], which resembled a partial incarnation [aṁśāvatāra] of Visnu, as it displayed unbroken courage in conquering the circle of the world...and which resembled the descent of the Ganges [gaṅgāvatāra] as it purified the whole world.*

The *Proceedings of the First Annual Conference* of South Indian History Congress also notes: The word *Tondai* means a creeper and the term *Pallava* conveys a similar meaning. Since the Pallavas ruled in the territory extending from Bellary to Bezwada, it led to the theory that they were a northern dynasty who contracted marriages with princesses of the Andhra Dynasty and so inherited a portion of southern Andhra Pradesh.

Historian K. R. Subramanian says the Pallavas were originally a Telugu power rather than a Tamil one. Telugu sources know of a Trilochana Pallava as the earliest Telugu king and they are confirmed by later inscriptions.[852] The first Chalukya king is said to have been met, repulsed and killed by the same Trilochana near Mudivemu (Cuddappah district). A Buddhist story describes Kala the Nagaraja, resembling the Pallava Kalabhartar as a king of the region near Krishna district. The Pallava Bogga may be identified with the kingdom of Kala in Andhra which had close and early maritime and cultural relations with Ceylon.

K. A. Nilakanta Sastri postulated that Pallavas were descendants of a North Indian dynasty who moved southwards, adopted local traditions to their own use, and named themselves as Tondaiyar after the land called Tondai. K. P. Jayaswal also proposed a North Indian origin, putting forward the theory that the Pallavas were a branch of the Vakatakas.

The earliest inscriptions of the Pallavas were found in the districts of Bellary, Guntur and Nellore and all the inscriptions of the dynasty till the rise of Simhavishnu were found in the latter two of those.[853]

Rivalries

With Cholas

The Pallavas captured Kanchi from the Cholas as recorded in the Velurpalaiyam Plates, around the reign of the fifth king of the Pallava line Kumaravishnu I. Thereafter Kanchi figures in inscriptions as the capital of the Pallavas. The Cholas drove the Pallavas away from Kanchi in the mid-4th century, in the reign of Vishugopa, the tenth king of the Pallava line. The Pallavas re-captured Kanchi in the mid-6th century, possibly in the reign of Simhavishnu, the fourteenth king of the Pallava line, whom the Kasakudi plates state as "the lion of the earth". Thereafter the Pallavas held on to Kanchi until the 9th century, until the reign of their last king, Vijaya-Nripatungavarman.[854]

With Kadambas

The Pallavas were in conflict with major kingdoms at various periods of time. A contest for political supremacy existed between the early Pallavas and the Kadambas. Numerous Kadamba inscriptions provide details of Pallava-Kadamba hostilities.[855]

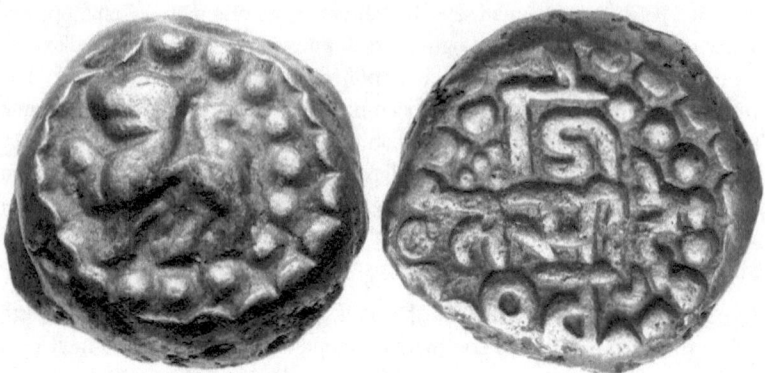

Figure 83: *Coin of the Pallavas of Coromandel, king Narasimhavarman I. (630-668 AD).Obv Lion left Rev Name of Narasimhavarman with solar and lunar symbols around.*

With Kalabhras

During the reign of Vishnugopavarman II (approx. 500-525), political convulsion engulfed the Pallavas due to the Kalabhra invasion of the Tamil country. Towards the close of the 6th century, the Pallava Simhavishnu stuck a blow against the Kalabhras. The Pandyas followed suit. Thereafter the Tamil country was divided between the Pallavas in the north with Kanchipuram as their capital, and Pandyas in the south with Madurai as their capital.

Birudas

The royal custom of using a series of descriptive honorific titles, *Birudas*, was particularly prevalent among the Pallavas. The birudas of Mahendravarman I are in Sanskrit, Tamil and Telugu. The Telugu birudas show Mahendravarman's involvement with the Andhra region continued to be strong at the time he was creating his cave-temples in the Tamil region. The suffix "Malla" was used by the Pallava rulers.[856] Mahendravarman I used the biruda, *Satrumalla*, "a warrior who overthrows his enemies", and his grandson Paramesvara I was called *Ekamalla* "the sole warrior or wrestler". Pallava kings, presumably exalted ones, were known by the title *Mahamalla* ("great wrestler").

Languages used

All the early Pallava royal inscriptions are either in Sanskrit or in Prakrit language, considered the official languages of the dynasty while the official scripts were Pallava script and later Grantha. Similarly, inscriptions found in Andhra Pradesh and Karnataka State are in Sanskrit and Prakrit.[857] The phenomenon of using Prakrit as official languages in which rulers left their inscriptions and epigraphies continued till the 6th century. It would have been in the interest of the ruling elite to protect their privileges by perpetuating their hegemony of Prakrit in order to exclude the common people from sharing power (Mahadevan 1995a: 173–188). The Pallavas in their Tamil country used Tamil and Sanskrit in their inscriptions.[858]

Tamil came to be the main language used by the Pallavas in their inscriptions, though a few records continued to be in Sanskrit. This language was first adopted by Mahendravarman I himself in a few records of his; but from the time of Paramesvaravarman I, the practice came into vogue of inscribing a part of the record in Sanskrit and the rest in Tamil. Almost all the copper plate records, viz., Kasakudi, Tandantottam, Pattattalmangalm, Udayendiram and Velurpalaiyam are composed both in Sanskrit and Tamil.

Writing system

Under the Pallava dynasty, a unique form of Grantha script, a descendant of Pallava script which is a type of Brahmic script, was used. Around the 6th century, it was exported eastwards and influenced the genesis of almost all Southeast Asian scripts.

Religion

Pallavas were followers of Hinduism and made gifts of land to gods and Brahmins. In line with the prevalent customs, some of the rulers performed the *Aswamedha* and other Vedic sacrifices. They were, however, tolerant of other faiths. The Chinese monk Xuanzang who visited Kanchipuram during the reign of Narasimhavarman I reported that there were 100 Buddhist monasteries, and 80 temples in Kanchipuram.[859]

Pallava architecture

The Pallavas were instrumental in the transition from rock-cut architecture to stone temples. The earliest examples of Pallava constructions are rock-cut temples dating from 610–690 and structural temples between 690–900. A number of rock-cut cave temples bear the inscription of the Pallava king, Mahendravarman I and his successors.[860]

Among the accomplishments of the Pallava architecture are the rock-cut temples at Mahabalipuram. There are excavated pillared halls and monolithic

Figure 84: *The Shore Temple at Mahabalipuram built by Narasimhavarman II*

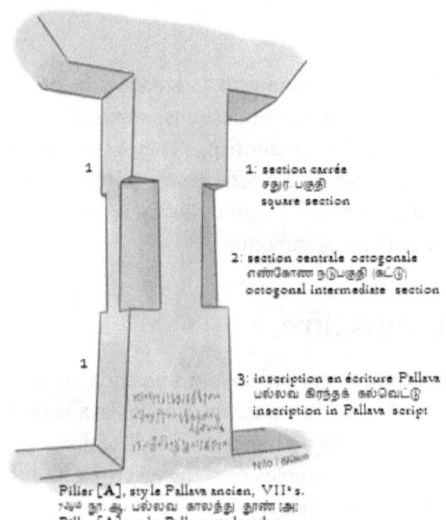

Pillar [A], style Pallava ancien, VII° s.
Pillar [A], early Pallava style, 7th c.

shrines known as *Rathas* in Mahabalipuram. Early temples were mostly dedicated to Shiva. The Kailasanatha temple in Kanchipuram and the Shore Temple built by Narasimhavarman II, rock cut temple in Mahendravadi by Mahendravarman are fine examples of the Pallava style temples.[861] The temple of Nalanda Gedige in Kandy, Sri Lanka is another. The famous Tondeswaram temple of Tenavarai and the ancient Koneswaram temple of Trincomalee were patronized and structurally developed by the Pallavas in the 7th century.Wikipedia:Citation needed

Pallava society

The Pallava period beginning with Simhavishnu (575 AD – 900 AD) was a transitional stage in southern Indian society with monument building, foundation of devotional (bhakti) sects of Alvars and Nayanars, the flowering of rural brahmanical institutions of Sanskrit learning, and the establishment of *chakravartin* model of kingship over a territory of diverse people; which ended the pre-Pallavan era of territorially segmented people, each with their culture, under a tribal chieftain. While a system of ranked relationship among groups existed in the classical period, the Pallava period extolled ranked relationships based on ritual purity as enjoined by the *shastras*. Burton distinguishes between the *chakravatin* model and the *kshatriya* model, and likens kshatriyas to locally based warriors with ritual status sufficiently high enough to share with Brahmins; and states that in south India the kshatriya model did not emerge. As per Burton, south India was aware of the Indo-Aryan *varna* organized society in which decisive secular authority was vested in the *kshatriyas*; but apart from the Pallava, Chola and Vijayanagar line of warriors which claimed *chakravartin* status, only few locality warrior families achieved the prestigious kin-linked organization of northern warrior groups.

Chronology

Sastri chronology

The earliest documentation on the Pallavas is the three copper-plate grants, now referred to as the *Mayidavolu*, *Hirahadagalli* and the *British Museum* plates (Durga Prasad, 1988) belonging to Skandavarman I and written in Prakrit.[862] Skandavarman appears to have been the first great ruler of the early Pallavas, though there are references to other early Pallavas who were probably predecessors of Skandavarman.[863] Skandavarman extended his dominions from the Krishna in the north to the Pennar in the south and to the Bellary district in the West. He performed the *Aswamedha* and other Vedic sacrifices and bore the title of "Supreme King of Kings devoted to dharma".

In the reign of Simhavarman IV, who ascended the throne in 436, the territories lost to the Vishnukundins in the north up to the mouth of the Krishna were recovered.Wikipedia:Citation needed The early Pallava history from this period onwards is furnished by a dozen or so copper-plate grants in Sanskrit. They are all dated in the regnal years of the kings.[864]

The following chronology was composed from these charters by Nilakanta Sastri in his *A History of South India*:

Early Pallavas

- Simhavarman I (275–300)
- Skandavarman (unknown)
- Visnugopa (350–355)
- Kumaravishnu I (350–370)
- Skandavarman II (370–385)
- Viravarman (385–400)
- Skandavarman III (400–436)
- Simhavarman II (436–460)
- Skandavarman IV (460–480)
- Nandivarman I (480–510)
- Kumaravishnu II (510–530)
- Buddhavarman (530–540)
- Kumaravishnu III (540–550)
- Simhavarman III (550–560)

Later Pallavas

The incursion of the Kalabhras and the confusion in the Tamil country was broken by the Pandya Kadungon and the Pallava Simhavishnu.[865] Mahendravarman I extended the Pallava Kingdom and was one of the greatest sovereigns. Some of the most ornate monuments and temples in southern India, carved out of solid rock, were introduced under his rule. He also wrote the play *Mattavilasa Prahasana*.

The Pallava kingdom began to gain both in territory and influence and were a regional power by the end of the 6th century, defeating kings of Ceylon and mainland Tamilakkam.[866] Narasimhavarman I and Paramesvaravarman I stand out for their achievements in both military and architectural spheres. Narasimhavarman II built the Shore Temple.

- Simhavishnu (575–600)
- Mahendravarman I (600–630)
- Narasimhavarman I (Mamalla) (630–668)
- Mahendravarman II (668–672)
- Paramesvaravarman I (670–695)

Figure 85: *The rock-cut temples at Mamallapuram constructed during the reign of Narasimhavarman I*

Figure 86: *Elephant carved out of a single-stone*

- Narasimhavarman II (Raja Simha) (695–722)
- Paramesvaravarman II (705–710)
- Nandivarman II (Pallavamalla) (730–795)
- Dantivarman (795–846)
- Nandivarman III (846–869)
- Aparajitavarman (879–897)

Aiyangar chronology

According to the available inscriptions of the Pallavas, historian S. Krishnaswami Aiyangar proposes the Pallavas could be divided into four separate families or dynasties; some of whose connections are known and some unknown.[867] Aiyangar states

> We have a certain number of charters in Prakrit of which three are important ones. Then follows a dynasty which issued their charters in Sanskrit; following this came the family of the great Pallavas beginning with Simha Vishnu; this was followed by a dynasty of the usurper Nandi Varman, another great Pallava. We are overlooking for the present the dynasty of the Ganga-Pallavas postulated by the Epigraphists. The earliest of these Pallava charters is the one known as the Mayidavolu 1 (Guntur district) copper-plates.

Based on a combination of dynastic plates and grants from the period, Aiyangar proposed their rule thus:

Early Pallavas

- Bappadevan (250-275) – married a Naga of Mavilanga (Kanchi) - *The Great Founder of a Pallava lineage*
- Shivaskandavarman I (275–300)
- Simhavarman (300-320)
- Bhuddavarman (320-335)
- Bhuddyankuran (335-340)

Middle Pallavas

- Visnugopa (340–355) (*Yuvamaharaja Vishnugopa*)
- Kumaravisnu I (355–370)
- Skanda Varman II (370–385)
- Vira Varman (385–400)
- Skanda Varman III (400–435)
- Simha Varman II (435–460)
- Skanda Varman IV (460–480)
- Nandi Varman I (480–500)

- Kumaravisnu II (c. 500–510)
- Buddha Varman (c. 510–520)
- Kumaravisnu III (c. 520–530)
- Simha Varman III (c. 530–537)

Later Pallavas

- Simhavishnu (537-570)
- Mahendravarman I (571–630)
- Narasimhavarman I (Mamalla) (630–668)
- Mahendravarman II (668–672)
- Paramesvaravarman I (672–700)
- Narasimhavarman II (Raja Simha) (700–727)
- Paramesvaravarman II (705–710)
- Nandivarman II (Pallavamalla) (732–796)
- Dantivarman (775–825)
- Nandivarman III (825–869)
- Nirupathungan (869–882)
- Aparajitavarman (882–896)

Genealogy

The genealogy of Pallavas mentioned in the *Māmallapuram Praśasti* is as follows:

- Vishnu
- Brahma
- Unknown / undecipherable
- Unknown / undecipherable
- Bharadvaja
- Drona
- Ashvatthaman
- Pallava
- Unknown / undecipherable
- Unknown / undecipherable
- Simhavarman I (c. 275)
- Unknown / undecipherable
- Unknown / undecipherable
- Simhavarman IV (436 — c. 460)
- Unknown / undecipherable
- Unknown / undecipherable
- Skandashishya
- Unknown / undecipherable

- Unknown / undecipherable
- Simhavisnu (c. 550-585)
- Mahendravarman I (c. 571-630)
- Maha-malla Narasimhavarman I (630-668)
- Unknown / undecipherable
- Paramesvaravarman I (669-690)
- Rajasimha Narasimhavaram II (690-728)
- Unknown / undecipherable
- Pallavamalla Nandivarman II (731-796)
- Unknown / undecipherable
- Nandivarman III (846-69)

Other relationships

Pallava royal lineages were influential in the old kingdom of Kedah of the Malay Peninsula under Rudravarman I, Champa under Bhadravarman I and the Kingdom of the Funan in Cambodia.

References

<templatestyles src="Template:Refbegin/styles.css" />

- Avari, Burjor (2007). *India: The Ancient Past*. New York: Routledge.
- Hermann, Kulke; Rothermund D (2001) [2000]. *A History of India*. Routledge. ISBN 0-415-32920-5.
- Minakshi, Cadambi (1938). *Administration and Social Life Under the Pallavas*. Madras: University of Madras.
- Prasad, Durga (1988). *History of the Andhras up to 1565 A.D.* Guntur, India: P.G. Publishers.
- Raghava Iyengar, R (1949). *Perumbanarruppatai, a commentary*. Chidambaram, India: Annamalai University Press.

External links

- Media related to Pallava at Wikimedia Commons

Chola dynasty

<indicator name="pp-default"> 🔒 </indicator>

Chola dynasty	
300s BCE–1279 CE	
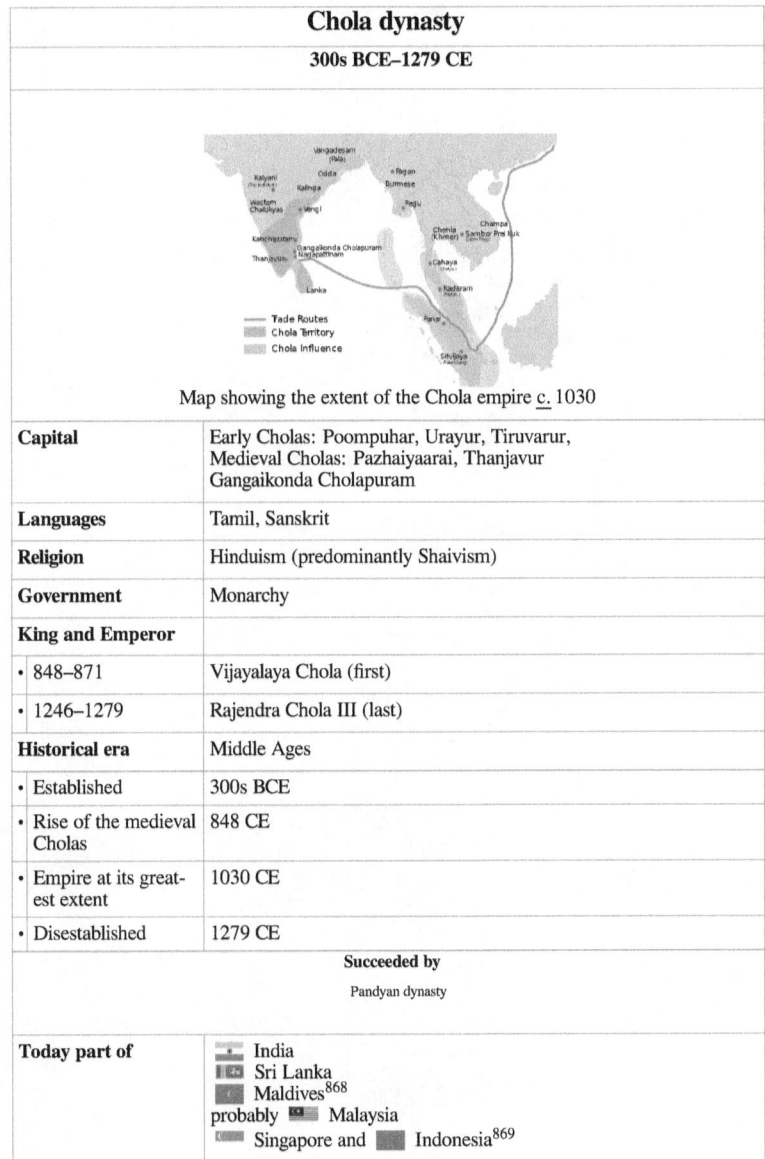 Map showing the extent of the Chola empire c. 1030	
Capital	Early Cholas: Poompuhar, Urayur, Tiruvarur, Medieval Cholas: Pazhaiyaarai, Thanjavur Gangaikonda Cholapuram
Languages	Tamil, Sanskrit
Religion	Hinduism (predominantly Shaivism)
Government	Monarchy
King and Emperor	
• 848–871	Vijayalaya Chola (first)
• 1246–1279	Rajendra Chola III (last)
Historical era	Middle Ages
• Established	300s BCE
• Rise of the medieval Cholas	848 CE
• Empire at its greatest extent	1030 CE
• Disestablished	1279 CE
Succeeded by	
Pandyan dynasty	
Today part of	India Sri Lanka Maldives[868] probably Malaysia Singapore and Indonesia[869]

List of Chola kings and emperors

Early Cholas

- Ellalan
- Kulakkottan
- Ilamchetchenni
- Karikala
- Nedunkilli
- Nalankilli
- Killivalavan
- Kopperuncholan
- Kochchenganan
- Perunarkilli

Interregnum (c. 200 – c. 848)

Medieval Cholas

Vijayalaya	848–891(?)
Aditya I	891–907
Parantaka I	907–950
Gandaraditya	950–957
Arinjaya	956–957
Sundara (Parantaka II)	957–970
Aditya II	(co-regent)
Uttama	970–985
Rajaraja I	985–1014
Rajendra I	1012–1044
Rajadhiraja	1044–1054
Rajendra II	1054–1063
Virarajendra	1063–1070
Athirajendra	1070–1070

Later Cholas

Kulothunga I	1070–1120
Vikrama	1118–1135
Kulothunga II	1133–1150
Rajaraja II	1146–1173
Rajadhiraja II	1166–1178
Kulothunga III	1178–1218
Rajaraja III	1216–1256
Rajendra III	1246–1279

Related dynasties

Telugu Cholas of Andhra
Chodagangas of Kalinga
Rajahnate of Cebu
Chola society
<ul><li>Chola government</li><li>Chola military</li><li>Chola Navy</li><li>Chola art</li><li>Chola literature</li><li>Flag of Chola</li><li>Great Living Chola Temples</li><li>Solesvara Temples</li><li>Poompuhar</li><li>Uraiyur</li><li>Melakadambur</li><li>Gangaikonda Cholapuram</li><li>Thanjavur</li><li>Tiruvarur</li></ul>
<ul><li>v</li><li>t</li><li>e[870]</li></ul>

Part of a series on
History of Tamil Nadu

<ul><li>v</li><li>t</li><li>e[871]</li></ul>

The **Chola dynasty** was one of the longest-ruling dynasties in the history of southern India. The earliest datable references to this Tamil dynasty are in inscriptions from the 3rd century BCE left by Ashoka, of the Maurya Empire (Ashoka Major Rock Edict No.13). As one of the Three Crowned Kings of Tamilakam, the dynasty continued to govern over varying territory until the 13th century CE.

The heartland of the Cholas was the fertile valley of the Kaveri River, but they ruled a significantly larger area at the height of their power from the later half of the 9th century till the beginning of the 13th century. The whole country south of the Tungabhadra was united and held as one state for a period of two centuries and more.[872] Under Rajaraja Chola I and his successors Rajendra Chola I, Rajadhiraja Chola, Virarajendra Chola and Kulothunga Chola I the dynasty became a military, economic and cultural power in South Asia and South-East Asia.[873] The power of the new empire was proclaimed to the eastern world by the expedition to the Ganges which Rajendra Chola I undertook and by the naval raids on cities of the maritime empire of Srivijaya, as well as by the repeated embassies to China.[874] The Chola fleet represented the zenith of ancient Indian sea power.

During the period 1010–1153, the Chola territories stretched from the islands of the Maldives in the south to as far north as the banks of the Godavari River in Andhra Pradesh.[875] Rajaraja Chola conquered peninsular South India, annexed parts of which is now Sri Lanka and occupied the islands of the Maldives. Rajendra Chola sent a victorious expedition to North India that touched the river Ganges and defeated the Pala ruler of Pataliputra, Mahipala. He also successfully invaded cities of Srivijaya of Malaysia and Indonesia.[876] The Chola dynasty went into decline at the beginning of the 13th century with the rise of the Pandyan Dynasty, which ultimately caused their downfall.[877,878]

The Cholas left a lasting legacy. Their patronage of Tamil literature and their zeal in the building of temples has resulted in some great works of Tamil literature and architecture. The Chola kings were avid builders and envisioned the temples in their kingdoms not only as places of worship but also as centres of economic activity.[879,880] They pioneered a centralised form of government and established a disciplined bureaucracy. The Chola school of art spread to Southeast Asia and influenced the architecture and art of Southeast Asia.[881,882]

Origins

The Cholas are also known as the *Choda*.[883] There is very little information available in regarding their origin. Its antiquity is evident from the mentions in ancient Tamil literature and in inscriptions. Later medieval Cholas also claimed a long and ancient lineage. Mentions in the early Sangam literature (c. 150 CE)[884] indicate that the earliest kings of the dynasty antedated 100 CE. Cholas were mentioned in Ashokan Edicts of 3rd Century BCE as one of the neighboring countries existing in the South.Wikipedia:Citation needed

A commonly held view is that *Chola* is, like *Chera* and *Pandya*, the name of the ruling family or clan of immemorial antiquity. The annotator Parimelazhagar said: "The charity of people with ancient lineage (such as the Cholas, the Pandyas and the Cheras) are forever generous in spite of their reduced means". Other names in common use for the Cholas are *Killi* (கிள்ளி), *Valavan* (வளவன்) and *Sembiyan* (செம்பியன்). *Killi* perhaps comes from the Tamil *kil* (கிள்) meaning dig or cleave and conveys the idea of a digger or a worker of the land. This word often forms an integral part of early Chola names like Nedunkilli, Nalankilli and so on, but almost drops out of use in later times. *Valavan* is most probably connected with "*valam*" (வளம்) – fertility and means owner or ruler of a fertile country. *Sembiyan* is generally taken to mean a descendant of Shibi – a legendary hero whose self-sacrifice in saving a dove from the pursuit of a falcon figures among the early Chola legends and forms the subject matter of the Sibi Jataka among the Jataka stories of Buddhism.[885] In Tamil lexicon *Chola* means *Soazhi* or *Saei* denoting a newly formed kingdom, in the lines of *Pandya* or the old country.[886]

There is very little written evidence available of the Cholas prior to the 7th century. Historic records exist thereafter, including inscriptions on temples. During the past 150 years, historians have gleaned significant knowledge on the subject from a variety of sources such as ancient Tamil Sangam literature, oral traditions, religious texts, temple and copperplate inscriptions. The main source for the available information of the early Cholas is the early Tamil literature of the Sangam Period.[887]</ref> There are also brief notices on the Chola country and its towns, ports and commerce furnished by the *Periplus of the Erythraean Sea* (*Periplus Maris Erythraei*), and in the slightly later work of the geographer Ptolemy. *Mahavamsa*, a Buddhist text written down during the 5th century CE, recounts a number of conflicts between the inhabitants of Ceylon and Cholas in the 1st century BCE.[888] Cholas are mentioned in the Pillars of Ashoka (inscribed 273 BCE–232 BCE) inscriptions, where they are mentioned among the kingdoms which, though not subject to Ashoka, were on friendly terms with him.[889]</ref>

History

The history of the Cholas falls into four periods: the Early Cholas of the Sangam literature, the interregnum between the fall of the Sangam Cholas and the rise of the Imperial medieval Cholas under Vijayalaya (c. 848), the dynasty of Vijayalaya, and finally the Later Chola dynasty of Kulothunga Chola I from the third quarter of the 11th century.[890]</ref>

Early Cholas

The earliest Chola kings for whom there is tangible evidence are mentioned in the Sangam literature. Scholars generally agree that this literature belongs to the second or first few centuries of the common era. The internal chronology of this literature is still far from settled, and at present a connected account of the history of the period cannot be derived. It records the names of the kings and the princes, and of the poets who extolled them.[891]

The Sangam literature also records legends about mythical Chola kings.[892] These myths speak of the Chola king Kantaman, a supposed contemporary of the sage Agastya, whose devotion brought the river Kaveri into existence.Wikipedia:Citation needed Two names are prominent among those Chola kings known to have existed who feature in Sangam literature: Karikala Chola and Kocengannan.[893,894,895,896] There are no sure means of settling the order of succession, of fixing their relations with one another and with many other princelings of around the same period.[897,898] Urayur (now a part of Thiruchirapalli) was their oldest capital.[892] Kaveripattinam also served as an early Chola capital.[899] The *Mahavamsa* mentions that an ethnic Tamil adventurer, a Chola prince known as Ellalan, invaded the island Sri Lanka and conquered it around 235 BCE with the help of a Mysore army.[892]

Interregnum

There is not much information about the transition period of around three centuries from the end of the Sangam age (c. 300) to that in which the Pandyas and Pallavas dominated the Tamil country. An obscure dynasty, the Kalabhras invaded Tamil country, displaced the existing kingdoms and ruled during that time.[900,901,902] They were displaced by the Pallava dynasty and the Pandyan dynasty in the 6th century.[894,903] Little is known of the fate of the Cholas during the succeeding three centuries until the accession of Vijayalaya in the second quarter of the 9th century.[904] As per inscriptions found in and around Thanjavur shows that the kingdom was ruled by Mutharaiyars for three centuries which was ended by Vijayalaya chola by Capturing Thanjavur from Ilango Mutharaiyar somewhere between 848-851.

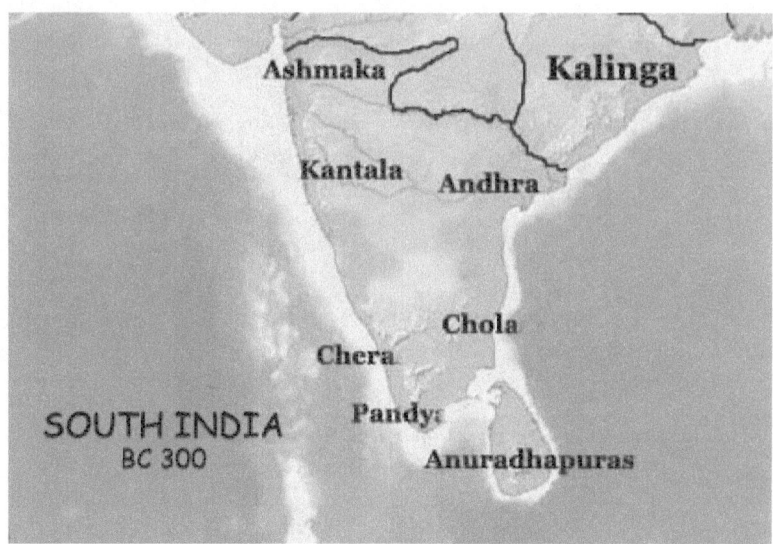

Figure 87: *South India in BC 300, showing the Chera, Pandya and Chola Kingdoms*

Epigraphy and literature provide few glimpses of the transformations that came over this line of kings during this long interval. It is certain that when the power of the Cholas fell to its lowest ebb and that of the Pandyas and Pallavas rose to the north and south of them,[895,905] this dynasty was compelled to seek refuge and patronage under their more successful rivals.[906,907]</ref> The Cholas continued to rule over a diminished territory in the neighbourhood of Uraiyur, but only in a minor capacity. In spite of their reduced powers, the Pandayas and Pallavas accepted Chola princesses in marriage, possibly out of regard for their reputation.[908]</ref> Numerous Pallava inscriptions of this period mention their having fought rulers of the Chola country.[909] Simhavishnu (575–600) is also stated to have seized the Chola country. Mahendravarman I was called the "crown of the Chola country" in his inscriptions.Wikipedia:Citation needed</ref> Despite this loss in influence and power, it is unlikely that the Cholas lost total grip of the territory around Uraiyur, their old capital, as Vijayalaya, when he rose to prominence hailed from that area.[910,911]

Around the 7th century, a Chola kingdom flourished in present-day Andhra Pradesh.[910] These Telugu Cholas traced their descent to the early Sangam Cholas. However, it is not known if they had any relation to the early Cholas.[913] It is possible that a branch of the Tamil Cholas migrated north during the time of the Pallavas to establish a kingdom of their own, away from the dominating influences of the Pandyas and Pallavas.[914]</ref> The Chinese

Figure 88: *An early silver coin of Uttama Chola found in Sri Lanka showing the tiger emblem of the Chola and in Nagari script.*[912]

pilgrim Xuanzang, who spent several months in Kanchipuram during 639–640 writes about the "kingdom of Culi-ya", in an apparent reference to these Telugu Cholas.[904,915]

Imperial Cholas

Vijayalaya was the founder of the Imperial Chola dynasty which was the beginning of one of the most splendid empires in Indian history.[916] Vijayalaya, possibly a feudatory of the Pallava dynasty, took an opportunity arising out of a conflict between the Pandya dynasty and Pallava dynasty in c. 850, captured Thanjavur from Muttarayar, and established the imperial line of the medieval Chola Dynasty.[917,918] Thanjavur became the capital of the Imperial Chola Dynasty.[919]

The Chola dynasty was at the peak of its influence and power during the medieval period.[920] Through their leadership and vision, Chola kings expanded their territory and influence. The second Chola King, Aditya I, caused the demise of the Pallava dynasty and defeated the Pandyan dynasty of Madurai in 885, occupied large parts of the Kannada country, and had marital ties with the Western Ganga dynasty. In 925, his son Parantaka I conquered Sri Lanka (known as Ilangai). Parantaka I also defeated the Rashtrakuta dynasty under Krishna II in the battle of Vallala.[921]

Rajaraja Chola I and Rajendra Chola I were the greatest rulers of the Chola dynasty, extending it beyond the traditional limits of a Tamil kingdom.[906] At its peak, the Chola Empire stretched from the island of Sri Lanka in the south to the Godavari-Krishna river basin in the north, up to the Konkan coast in

Figure 89: *Detail of the statue of Rajaraja Chola at Brihadisvara Temple at Thanjavur.*

Bhatkal, the entire Malabar Coast in addition to Lakshadweep, Maldives, and vast areas of Chera country. Rajaraja Chola I was a ruler with inexhaustible energy, and he applied himself to the task of governance with the same zeal that he had shown in waging wars. He integrated his empire into a tight administrative grid under royal control, and at the same time strengthened local self-government. Therefore, he conducted a land survey in 1000 CE to effectively marshall the resources of his empire.[922] He also built the Brihadeeswarar Temple in 1010 CE.

Rajendra Chola I conquered Odisha and his armies continued to march further north and defeated the forces of the Pala Dynasty of Bengal and reached the Ganges river in north India.[923] Rajendra Chola I built a new capital called Gangaikonda Cholapuram to celebrate his victories in northern India.[924] Rajendra Chola I successfully invaded the Srivijaya kingdom in Southeast Asia which led to the decline of the empire there.[925] This expedition had such a great impression to the Malay people of the medieval period that his name was mentioned in the corrupted form as Raja Chulan in the medieval Malay chronicle *Sejarah Melayu*.[926,927,928] He also completed the conquest of the island of Sri Lanka and took the Sinhala king Mahinda V as a prisoner, in addition to his conquests of Rattapadi (territories of the Rashtrakutas, Chalukya

Figure 90: *Gopuram Corner View of Thanjavur Brihadeeswara Temple.*

country, Talakkad, and Kolar, where the Kolaramma temple still has his portrait statue) in Kannada country.[929] Rajendra's territories included the area falling on the Ganges-Hooghly-Damodar basin,[930] as well as Sri Lanka and Maldives.[917] The kingdoms along the east coast of India up to the river Ganges acknowledged Chola suzerainty.[931] Three diplomatic missions were sent to China in 1016, 1033, and 1077.[917]

The Western Chalukya Empire under Satyashraya and Someshvara I tried to wriggle out of Chola domination from time to time, primarily due to the Chola influence in the Vengi kingdom.[932] The Western Chalukyas mounted several unsuccessful attempts to engage the Chola emperors in war, and except for a brief occupation of Vengi territories between 1118–1126, all their other attempts ended in failure with successive Chola emperors routing the armies of the Chalukyas at various places in many wars. Virarajendra Chola defeated Someshvara II of the Western Chalukya Empire and made an alliance with Prince Vikramaditya VI.[933] Cholas always successfully controlled the Chalukyas in the western Deccan by defeating them in war and levying tribute on them.[934] Even under the emperors of the Cholas like Kulothunga I and Vikrama Chola, the wars against the Chalukyas were mainly fought in Chalukya territories in Karnataka or in the Telugu country like Vengi, Kakinada, Anantapur, or Gutti. Then the former feudatories like the Hoysalas, Yadvas, and Kakatiyas steadily increased their power and finally replaced the

Figure 91: *Brihadeeswara Temple Entrance Gopurams, Thanjavur*

Figure 92: *Model of a Chola's ship's hull (200—848 CE), built by the ASI, based on a wreck 19 miles off the coast of Poombuhar, displayed in a Museum in Tirunelveli.*

Figure 93: *Airavateswara Temple, Darasuram in Thanjavur District.*

Chalukyas.[935] With the occupation of Dharwar in North Central Karnataka by the Hoysalas under Vishnuvardhana, where he based himself with his son Narasimha I in-charge at the Hoysala capital Dwarasamudra around 1149, and with the Kalachuris occupying the Chalukyan capital for over 35 years from around 1150–1151, the Chalukya kingdom was already starting to dissolve.[936]

The Cholas under Kulothunga Chola III collaborated to the herald the dissolution of the Chalukyas by aiding Hoysalas under Veera Ballala II, the son-in-law of the Chola monarch, and defeated the Western Chalukyas in a series of wars with Someshvara IV between 1185–1190. The last Chalukya king's territories did not even include the erstwhile Chalukyan capitals Badami, Manyakheta or Kalyani. That was the final dissolution of Chalukyan power though the Chalukyas existed only in name since 1135–1140. But the Cholas remained stable until 1215, were absorbed by the Pandyan empire and ceased to exist by 1279.[937]

On the other hand, throughout the period from 1150–1280, the staunchest opponents of the Cholas were Pandya princes who tried to win independence for their traditional territories. This period saw constant warfare between the Cholas and the Pandyas. The Cholas also fought regular wars with the Eastern Gangas of Kalinga, protected Vengi though it remained largely independent under Chola control, and had domination of the entire eastern coast with their feudatories the Telugu Cholas, Velananti Cholas, Renandu Cholas etc. who also always aided the Cholas in their successful campaigns against the

Chalukyas and levying tribute on the Kannada kingdoms and fought constantly with the Sinhalas, who attempted to overthrow the Chola occupation of Lanka, but until the time of the Later Chola king Kulottunga I the Cholas had firm control over Lanka. A Later Chola king, Rajadhiraja Chola II, was strong enough to prevail over a confederation of five Pandya princes who were aided by their traditional friend, the king of Lanka, this once again gave control of Lanka to the Cholas despite the fact that they were not strong under the resolute Rajadhiraja Chola II. However, his successor, the last great Chola monarch Kulottunga Chola III reinforced the hold of the Cholas by quelling rebellion and disturbances in Lanka and Madurai, defeated Hoysala generals under Veera Ballala II in Karuvur, in addition to holding on to his traditional territories in Tamil country, Eastern Gangavadi, Draksharama, Vengi and Kalinga. After this, he entered into a marital alliance with Veera Ballala II (with Ballala's marriage to a Chola princess) and his relationship with Hoysalas seems to have become friendlier.[934,938]</ref>

Overseas conquests

During the reign of Rajaraja Chola I and his successors Rajendra Chola I, Virarajendra Chola and Kulothunga Chola I the Chola armies invaded Sri Lanka, the Maldives and parts of Southeast Asia like Malaysia, Indonesia and Southern Thailand[939] of the Srivijaya Empire in the 11th century. Rajaraja Chola I launched several naval campaigns that resulted in the capture of Sri Lanka, Maldives and the Malabar Coast.[940] In 1025, Rajendra Chola launched naval raids on ports of Srivijaya and against the Burmese kingdom of Pegu.[941] A Chola inscription states that he captured or plundered 14 places, which have been identified with Palembang, Tambralinga and Kedah among others.[942] A second invasion was led by Virarajendra Chola, who conquered Kedah in Malaysia of Srivijaya in the late 11th century.[943]

Later Cholas (1070–1279)

Marital and political alliances between the Eastern Chalukyas began during the reign of Rajaraja following his invasion of Vengi. Rajaraja Chola's daughter married Chalukya prince Vimaladitya[944] and Rajendra Chola's daughter Ammanga Devi was married to the Eastern Chalukya prince Rajaraja Narendra.[945] Virarajendra Chola's son, Athirajendra Chola, was assassinated in a civil disturbance in 1070, and Kulothunga Chola I, the son of Ammanga Devi and Rajaraja Narendra, ascended the Chola throne. Thus began the Later Chola dynasty.[946]

The Later Chola dynasty was led by capable rulers such as Kulothunga Chola I, his son Vikrama Chola, other successors like Rajaraja Chola II, Rajadhiraja Chola II, and Kulothunga Chola III, who conquered Kalinga, Ilam, and

Figure 94: *Portrait of Rajaraja Chola and his guru Karuvurar at Brihadeeswarar Temple*

Kataha. However, the rule of the later Cholas between 1218, starting with Rajaraja Chola II, to the last emperor Rajendra Chola III was not as strong as those of the emperors between 850–1215. Around 1118, they lost control of Vengi to the Western Chalukya and Gangavadi (southern Mysore districts) to the Hoysala Empire. However, these were only temporary setbacks, because immediately following the accession of king Vikrama Chola, the son and successor of Kulothunga Chola I, the Cholas lost no time in recovering the province of Vengi by defeating Chalukya Someshvara III and also recovering Gangavadi from the Hoysalas. The Chola Empire, though not as strong as between 850–1150, was still largely territorially intact under Rajaraja Chola II (1146–1175) a fact attested by the construction and completion of the third grand Chola architectural marvel, the chariot-shaped Airavatesvara Temple at Dharasuram on the outskirts of modern Kumbakonam. Chola administration and territorial integrity until the rule of Kulothunga Chola III was stable and very prosperous up to 1215, but during his rule itself, the decline of the Chola power started following his defeat by Maravarman Sundara Pandiyan II in 1215–16.[947] Subsequently, the Cholas also lost control of the island of Lanka and were driven out by the revival of Sinhala power.Wikipedia:Citation needed

In continuation of the decline, also marked by the resurgence of the Pandyan dynasty as the most powerful rulers in South India, a lack of a controlling central administration in its erstwhile-Pandyan territories prompted a number of claimants to the Pandya throne to cause a civil war in which the Sinhalas and the Cholas were involved by proxy. Details of the Pandyan civil war and the role played by the Cholas and Sinhalas, are present in the *Mahavamsa* as well as the Pallavarayanpettai Inscriptions.[948,949]

The Cholas, under Rajaraja Chola III and later, his successor Rajendra Chola III, were quite weak and therefore, experienced continuous trouble. One feudatory, the Kadava chieftain Kopperunchinga I, even held Rajaraja Chola III as hostage for sometime.[950,951] At the close of the 12th century, the growing influence of the Hoysalas replaced the declining Chalukyas as the main player in the Kannada country, but they too faced constant trouble from the Seunas and the Kalachuris, who were occupying Chalukya capital because those empires were their new rivals. So naturally, the Hoysalas found it convenient to have friendly relations with the Cholas from the time of Kulothunga Chola III, who had defeated Hoysala Veera Ballala II, who had subsequent marital relations with the Chola monarch. This continued during the time of Rajaraja Chola III the son and successor of Kulothunga Chola III[947,952]

The Pandyas in the south had risen to the rank of a great power who ultimately banished the Hoysalas from Malanadu or Kannada country, who were allies of the Cholas from Tamil country and the demise of the Cholas themselves ultimately was caused by the Pandyas in 1279. The Pandyas first steadily gained control of the Tamil country as well as territories in Sri Lanka, Chera country, Telugu country under Maravarman Sundara Pandiyan II and his able successor Jatavarman Sundara Pandyan before inflicting several defeats on the joint forces of the Cholas under Rajaraja Chola III, his successor Rajendra Chola III and the Hoysalas under Someshwara, his son Ramanatha[947] Rajendra III tried to survive by aligning with the Kadava Pallavas and the Hoysalas in turn in order to counter the constantly rising power of the Pandyans who were the major players in the Tamil country from 1215 and had intelligently consolidated their position in Madurai-Rameswaram-Ilam-Cheranadu and Kanyakumari belt, and had been steadily increasing their territories in the Kaveri belt between Dindigul-Tiruchy-Karur-Satyamangalam as well as in the Kaveri Delta i.e., Thanjavur-Mayuram-Chidambaram-Vriddhachalam-Kanchi, finally marching all the way up to Arcot—Tirumalai-Nellore-Visayawadai-Vengi-Kalingam belt by 1250.[953]

The Pandyas steadily routed both the Hoysalas and the Cholas.[954] They also dispossessed the Hoysalas, by defeating them under Jatavarman Sundara Pandiyan at Kannanur Kuppam.[955] At the close of Rajendra's reign, the Pandyan empire was at the height of prosperity and had taken the place of the Chola empire in the eyes of the foreign observers.[956] The last recorded date of Rajendra III is 1279. There is no evidence that Rajendra was followed immediately by another Chola prince.[957,958] The Hoysalas were routed from Kannanur Kuppam around 1279 by Kulasekhara Pandiyan and in the same war the last Chola emperor Rajendra III was routed and the Chola empire ceased to exist thereafter. Thus the Chola empire was completely overshadowed by the Pandyan empire and sank into obscurity and ceased to exist by the end of the 13th century.[951,958]

Administration and society

Chola territory

According to Tamil tradition, the Chola country comprised the region that includes the modern-day Tiruchirapalli District, Tiruvarur District, Nagapattinam District, Ariyalur District, Perambalur district, Pudukkottai district, Thanjavur District in Tamil Nadu and Karaikal District. The river Kaveri and its tributaries dominate this landscape of generally flat country that gradually slopes towards the sea, unbroken by major hills or valleys. The river, which is also known as the *Ponni* (*Golden*) river, had a special place in the culture of Cholas. The annual floods in the Kaveri marked an occasion for celebration, known as *Adiperukku*, in which the whole nation took part.Wikipedia:Citation needed

Kaveripoompattinam on the coast near the Kaveri delta was a major port town.[892] Ptolemy knew of this, which he called Khaberis, and the other port town of Nagappattinam as the most important centres of Cholas.[959] These two towns became hubs of trade and commerce and attracted many religious faiths, including Buddhism.[960]</ref> Roman ships found their way into these ports. Roman coins dating from the early centuries of the common era have been found near the Kaveri delta.[961] Wikipedia:Citing sources[962]

The other major towns were Thanjavur, Uraiyur and Kudanthai, now known as Kumbakonam.[892] After Rajendra Chola moved his capital to Gangaikonda Cholapuram, Thanjavur lost its importance.[963]

Government

In the age of the Cholas, the whole of South India was for the first time brought under a single government.[965]

The Cholas' system of government was monarchical, as in the Sangam age.[894] However, there was little in common between the local chiefdoms of the earlier period and the imperial-like states of Rajaraja Chola and his successors.[966] Aside from the early capital at Thanjavur and the later on at Gangaikonda

Figure 95: *The mandalams of the Chola empire, c. 11th century.*[964]

Cholapuram, Kanchipuram and Madurai were considered to be regional capitals in which occasional courts were held. The king was the supreme leader and a benevolent authoritarian. His administrative role consisted of issuing oral commands to responsible officers when representations were made to him. Due to the lack of a legislature or a legislative system in the modern sense, the fairness of king's orders dependent on his morality and belief in *Dharma*. The Chola kings built temples and endowed them with great wealth. The temples acted not only as places of worship but also as centres of economic activity, benefiting the community as a whole.[967] Some of the output of villages throughout the kingdom was given to temples that reinvested some of the wealth accumulated as loans to the settlements.[968] The Chola Dynasty was divided into several provinces called Mandalams which were further divided into Valanadus and these Valanadus were sub-divided into units called Kottams or Kutrams.[969] According to Kathleen Gough, during the Chola period the Vellalar were the "dominant secular aristocratic caste ... providing the courtiers, most of the army officers, the lower ranks of the kingdom's bureaucracy, and the upper layer of the peasantry".[970]

Before the reign of Rajaraja Chola I huge parts of the Chola territory were ruled by hereditary lords and local princes who were in a loose alliance with the Chola rulers. Thereafter, until the reign of Vikrama Chola in 1133 CE when the Chola power was at its peak, these hereditary lords and local princes virtually vanished from the Chola records and were either replaced or turned into dependent officials. Through these dependent officials the administration was improved and the Chola kings were able to exercise a closer control over the different parts of the empire.[971] There was an expansion of the administrative structure, particularly from the reign of Rajaraja Chola I onwards. The government at this time had a large land revenue department, consisting of several tiers, which was largely concerned with maintaining accounts. The assessment and collection of revenue were undertaken by corporate bodies such as the ur, nadu, sabha, nagaram and sometimes by local chieftains who passed the revenue to the centre. During the reign of Rajaraja Chola I, the state initiated a massive project of land survey and assessment and there was a reorganisation of the empire into units known as valanadus.[972]

The order of the King was first communicated by the executive officer to the local authorities. Afterwards the records of the transaction was drawn up and attested by a number of witnesses who were either local magnates or government officers.[973]

At local government level, every village was a self-governing unit. A number of villages constituted a larger entity known as a *Kurram, Nadu* or *Kottam*, depending on the area.[974,975,976] A number of *Kurrams* constituted a *valanadu*.[977] These structures underwent constant change and refinement throughout the Chola period.[978]

Justice was mostly a local matter in the Chola Empire; minor disputes were settled at the village level.[976] Punishment for minor crimes were in the form of fines or a direction for the offender to donate to some charitable endowment. Even crimes such as manslaughter or murder were punished with fines. Crimes of the state, such as treason, were heard and decided by the king himself; the typical punishment in these cases was either execution or confiscation of property.[979]

Military

The Chola dynasty had a professional military, of which the king was the supreme commander. It had four elements, comprising the cavalry, the elephant corps, several divisions of infantry and a navy.[980] There were regiments of bowmen and swordsmen while the swordsmen were the most permanent and dependable troops. The Chola army was spread all over the country and was stationed in local garrisons or military camps known as *Kodagams*. The elephants played a major role in the army and the dynasty had numerous war elephants. These carried houses or huge Howdahs on their backs, full of soldiers who shot arrows at long range and who fought with spears at close quarters.[981]

The Chola rulers built several palaces and fortifications to protect their cities. The fortifications were mostly made up of bricks but other materials like stone, wood and mud were also used.[982,983] According to the ancient Tamil text *Silappadikaram*, the Tamil kings defended their forts with catapults that threw stones, huge cauldrons of boiling water or molten lead, and hooks, chains and traps.[984,985] Wikipedia:Verifiability

The soldiers of the Chola dynasty used weapons such as swords, bows, javelins, spears and shields which were made up of steel.[986] Particularly the famous Wootz steel, which has a long history in south India dating back to the period before the Christian era, seems also be used to produce weapons.[987] The army consisted of people from different castes but the warriors of the Kaikolar and Vellalar castes played a prominent role.[988,989]

The Chola navy was the zenith of ancient India sea power.[981] It played a vital role in the expansion of the empire, including the conquest of the Ceylon islands and naval raids on Srivijaya.[990] The navy grew both in size and status during the medieval Cholas reign. The Chola admirals commanded much respect and prestige. The navy commanders also acted as diplomats in some instances. From 900 to 1100, the navy had grown from a small backwater entity to that of a potent power projection and diplomatic symbol in all of Asia, but was gradually reduced in significance when the Cholas fought land battles subjugating the Chalukyas of the Andhra-Kannada area in South India.[991]

A martial art called *Silambam* was patronised by the Chola rulers. Ancient and medieval Tamil texts mention different forms of martial traditions but the ultimate expression of the loyalty of the warrior to his commander was a form of martial suicide called *Navakandam*. The medieval *Kalingathu Parani* text, which celebrates the victory of Kulothunga Chola I and his general in the battle for Kalinga, describes the practice in detail.

Economy

Land revenue and trade tax were the main source of income.[992] The Chola rulers issued their coins in gold, silver and copper.[993] The Chola economy was based on three tiers—at the local level, agricultural settlements formed the foundation to commercial towns nagaram, which acted as redistribution centres for externally produced items bound for consumption in the local economy and as sources of products made by nagaram artisans for the international trade. At the top of this economic pyramid were the elite merchant groups (*samayam*) who organised and dominated the regions international maritime trade.[994] Wikipedia:Please clarify

One of the main articles which were exported to foreign countries were cotton cloth.[995] Uraiyur, the capital of the early Chola rulers, was a famous centre for cotton textiles which were praised by Tamil poets.[996,997] The Chola rulers actively encouraged the weaving industry and derived revenue from it.[998] During this period the weavers started to organise themselves into guilds.[999] The weavers had their own residential sector in all towns. The most important weaving communities in early medieval times were the Saliyar and Kaikolar.[998] During the Chola period silk weaving attained a high degree and Kanchipuram became one of the main centres for silk.[1000,1001]

Metal crafts reached its zenith during the 10th to 11th centuries because the Chola rulers like Chembian Maadevi extended their patronage to metal craftsmen.[1002] Wootz steel was a major export item.[1003]

The farmers occupied one of the highest positions in society.[1004] These were the Vellalar community who formed the nobility or the landed aristocracy of the country and who were economically a powerful group.[1005] Agriculture was the principal occupation for many people. Besides the landowners, there were others dependent on agriculture.[1006] The Vellalar community was the dominant secular aristocratic caste under the Chola rulers, providing the courtiers, most of the army officers, the lower ranks of the bureaucracy and the upper layer of the peasantry.[970]

In almost all villages the distinction between persons paying the land-tax (iraikudigal) and those who did not was clearly established. There was a class of hired day-labourers who assisted in agricultural operations on the estates of other people and received a daily wage. All cultivable land was held in one of the three broad classes of tenure which can be distinguished as peasant proprietorship called vellan-vagai, service tenure and eleemosynary tenure resulting from charitable gifts.[1007] The vellan-vagai was the ordinary ryotwari village of modern times, having direct relations with the government and paying a land-tax liable to revision from time to time.[994] The vellan-vagai villages fell into two broad classes- one directly remitting a variable annual revenue to the state and the other paying dues of a more or less fixed character to the public institutions like temples to which they were assigned.[1008] The prosperity of an agricultural country depends to a large extent on the facilities provided for irrigation. Apart from sinking wells and excavating tanks, the Chola rulers threw mighty stone dams across the Kaveri and other rivers, and cut out channels to distribute water over large tracts of land.[1009] Rajendra Chola I dug near his capital an artificial lake, which was filled with water from the Kolerun and the Vellar rivers.[1008]

There existed a brisk internal trade in several articles carried on by the organised mercantile corporations in various parts of the country. The metal industries and the jewellers art had reached a high degree of excellence. The manufacture of sea-salt was carried on under government supervision and control. Trade was carried on by merchants organised in guilds. The guilds described sometimes by the terms nanadesis were a powerful autonomous corporation of merchants which visited different countries in the course of their trade. They had their own mercenary army for the protection of their merchandise. There were also local organisations of merchants called *"nagaram"* in big centres of trade like Kanchipuram and Mamallapuram.[1010,1008]

Hospitals

Hospitals were maintained by the Chola kings, whose government gave lands for that purpose. The Tirumukkudal inscription shows that a hospital was named after Vira Chola. Many diseases were cured by the doctors of the hospital, which was under the control of a chief physician who was paid annually 80 Kalams of paddy, 8 Kasus and a grant of land. Apart from the doctors, other remunerated staff included a nurse, barber (who performed minor operations) and a waterman.[1011]

The Chola queen Kundavai also established a hospital at Tanjavur and gave land for the perpetual maintenance of it.[1012,1013]

Society

During the Chola period several guilds, communities and castes emerged. The guild was one of the most significant institutions of south India and merchants organised themselves into guilds. The best known of these were the Manigramam and Ayyavole guilds though other guilds such as Anjuvannam and Valanjiyar were also in existence.[1014] The farmers occupied one of the highest positions in society. These were the Vellalar community who formed the nobility or the landed aristocracy of the country and who were economically a powerful group.[1005] The Vellalar community was the dominant secular aristocratic caste under the Chola rulers, providing the courtiers, most of the army officers, the lower ranks of the bureaucracy and the upper layer of the peasantry.[970] The Vellalar were also sent to northern Sri Lanka by the Chola rulers as settlers.[1015] The Ulavar community were working in the field which was associated with agriculture and the peasants were known as Kalamar.

The Kaikolar community were weavers and merchants but they also maintained armies. During the Chola period they had predominant trading and military roles.[1016] During the reign of the Imperial Chola rulers (10th-13th century) there were major changes in the temple administration and land ownership. There was more involvement of non-Brahmin elements in the temple administration. This can be attributed to the shift in money power. Skilled classes like the weavers and the merchant-class had become prosperous. Land ownership was no longer a privilege of the Brahmins (priest caste) and the Vellalar land owners.[1017]

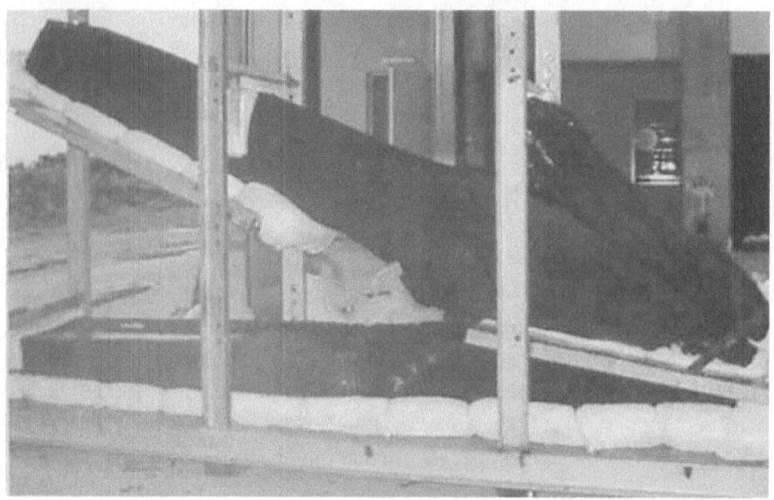

Figure 96: *This is the Anchor of an Unknown LOLA class Chola ship, excavated by the Indian Navy divers off the coast of Poombuhar.*

There is little information on the size and the density of the population during the Chola reign[1018] The stability in the core Chola region enabled the people to lead a productive and contented life. However, there were reports of widespread famine caused by natural calamities.[1019]

The quality of the inscriptions of the regime indicates a high level of literacy and education. The text in these inscriptions was written by court poets and engraved by talented artisans. Education in the contemporary sense was not considered important; there is circumstantial evidence to suggest that some village councils organised schools to teach the basics of reading and writing to children,[1020] although there is no evidence of systematic educational system for the masses.[1021] Vocational education was through hereditary training in which the father passed on his skills to his sons. Tamil was the medium of education for the masses; Religious monasteries (*matha* or *gatika*) were centres of learning and received government support.[1022]

Foreign trade

The Cholas excelled in foreign trade and maritime activity, extending their influence overseas to China and Southeast Asia.[1023] Towards the end of the 9th century, southern India had developed extensive maritime and commercial activity.[1024] The south Indian guilds played a major role in interregional and overseas trade. The best known of these were the Manigramam and Ayyavole guilds who followed the conquering Chola armies.[1014] The encouragement by the Chola court furthered the expansion of Tamil merchant associations such as the Ayyavole and Manigramam guilds into Southeast Asia and China.[1025] The Cholas, being in possession of parts of both the west and the east coasts of peninsular India, were at the forefront of these ventures.[1026,1027] The Tang dynasty of China, the Srivijaya empire under the Sailendras, and the Abbasid Kalifat at Baghdad were the main trading partners.[1028]

Some credit for the emergence of a world market must also go to the dynasty. It played a significant role in linking the markets of China to the rest of the world. The market structure and economic policies of the Chola dynasty were more conducive to a large-scale, cross-regional market trade than those enacted by the Chinese Song Dynasty. A Chola record gives their rationale for engagement in foreign trade: "Make the merchants of distant foreign countries who import elephants and good horses attach to yourself by providing them with villages and decent dwellings in the city, by affording them daily audience, presents and allowing them profits. Then those articles will never go to your enemies."[1029]

Song dynasty reports record that an embassy from *Chulian* (Chola) reached the Chinese court in 1077,[1030,1031] and that the king of the Chulian at the time, Kulothunga I, was called *Ti-hua-kia-lo*. This embassy was a trading venture and was highly profitable to the visitors, who returned with copper coins in exchange for articles of tribute, including glass and spices.[1032] Probably, the motive behind Rajendra's expedition to Srivijaya was the protection of the merchants' interests.[1033]

Canals and water tanks

There was tremendous agrarian expansion during the rule of the imperial Chola Dynasty (c. 900-1270 AD) all over Tamil Nadu and particularly in the Kaveri Basin. Most of the canals of the Kaveri River belongs to this period e.g., Uyyakondan canal, Rajendran vaykkal, Sembian Mahadegvi vaykkal. There was a well-developed and highly efficient system of water management from the village level upwards. The increase in the royal patronage and also the number of devadana and bramadeya lands which increased the role of the temples and village assemblies in the field. Committees like eri-variyam(tank-committee) and totta-variam(garden committees) were active as also the temples with their vast resources in land, men and money. The water tanks that came up during the Chola period are too many to be listed here. But a few most outstanding may be briefly mentioned. Rajendra Chola built a huge tank named Solagangam in his capital city Gangaikonda Solapuram and was described as the liquid pillar of victory. About 16 miles long, it was provided with sluices and canals for irrigating the lands in the neighbouring areas. Another very large lake of this period, which even today seems an important source

Figure 97: *Detail of the main vimanam (tower) of the Thanjavur Temple*

of irrigation was the Viranameri near Kattumannarkoil in South Arcot district founded by Parantaka Chola. Other famous lakes of this period are Madurantakam, Sundra-cholapereri, Kundavai-Pereri (after a Chola queen).[1034]

Cultural contributions

Under the Cholas, the Tamil country reached new heights of excellence in art, religion, music and literature.[1035] In all of these spheres, the Chola period marked the culmination of movements that had begun in an earlier age under the Pallavas.[1036] Monumental architecture in the form of majestic temples and sculpture in stone and bronze reached a finesse never before achieved in India.[1037]

The Chola conquest of Kadaram (Kedah) and Srivijaya, and their continued commercial contacts with the Chinese Empire, enabled them to influence the local cultures.[1038] Examples of the Hindu cultural influence found today throughout the Southeast Asia owe much to the legacy of the Cholas. For example, the great temple complex at Prambanan in Indonesia exhibit a number of similarities with the South Indian architecture.[1039,1040]

According to the Malay chronicle *Sejarah Melayu*, the rulers of the Malacca sultanate claimed to be descendants of the kings of the Chola

Figure 98: *With heavily ornamented pillars accurate in detail and richly sculpted walls, the Airavateswara temple at Darasuram is a classic example of Chola art and architecture*

Empire.[1041]Wikipedia:Citing sources#What information to include Chola rule is remembered in Malaysia today as many princes there have names ending with Cholan or Chulan, one such being Raja Chulan, the Raja of Perak.[1042]Wikipedia:Citing sources#What information to include[1043]Wikipedia:Citing sources#What information to include

Art

The Cholas continued the temple-building traditions of the Pallava dynasty and contributed significantly to the Dravidian temple design.[1044] They built a number of Shiva temples along the banks of the river Kaveri. The template for these and future temples was formulated by Aditya I and Parantaka.[1045,1046,1047] The Chola temple architecture has been appreciated for its magnificence as well as delicate workmanship, ostensibly following the rich traditions of the past bequeathed to them by the Pallava Dynasty.[1048] Architectural historian James Fergusson says that "the Chola artists conceived like giants and finished like jewelers". A new development in Chola art that characterised the Dravidian architecture in later times was the addition of a huge gateway called gopuram to the enclosure of the temple, which had gradually taken its form and attained maturity under the Pandya Dynasty. The Chola school of art also spread to Southeast Asia and influenced the architecture and art of Southeast Asia.[1049,1050]

Temple building received great impetus from the conquests and the genius of Rajaraja Chola and his son Rajendra Chola I.[1051] The maturity and grandeur to which the Chola architecture had evolved found expression in the two temples of Thanjavur and Gangaikondacholapuram. The magnificent Shiva temple of Thanjavur, completed around 1009, is a fitting memorial to the material achievements of the time of Rajaraja. The largest and tallest of all Indian temples of its time, it is at the apex of South Indian architecture. The temple of Gangaikondacholisvaram at Gangaikondacholapuram, the creation of Rajendra Chola, was intended to excel its predecessor. Completed around 1030, only two decades after the temple at Thanjavur and in the same style, the greater elaboration in its appearance attests the more affluent state of the Chola Empire under Rajendra.[1044,1052] Wikipedia:Citing sources The Brihadisvara Temple, the temple of Gangaikondacholisvaram and the Airavatesvara Temple at Darasuram were declared as World Heritage Sites by the UNESCO and are referred to as the Great living Chola temples.

The Chola period is also remarkable for its sculptures and bronzes.[1053,1054,1055] Among the existing specimens in museums around the world and in the temples of South India may be seen many fine figures of Shiva in various forms, such as Vishnu and his consort Lakshmi, and the Shaivite saints.[1044] Though conforming generally to the iconographic conventions established by long tradition, the sculptors worked with great freedom in the 11th and the 12th centuries to achieve a classic grace and grandeur. The best example of this can be seen in the form of Nataraja the Divine Dancer.[1056,1057]</ref>

Literature

The Imperial Chola era was the golden age of Tamil culture, marked by the importance of literature. Chola records cite many works, including the *Rajarajesvara Natakam*, *Viranukkaviyam* and *Kannivana Puranam*.[1058]

The revival of Hinduism from its nadir during the Kalabhras spurred the construction of numerous temples and these in turn generated Shaiva and Vaishnava devotional literature.[1059] Jain and Buddhist authors flourished as well, although in fewer numbers than in previous centuries.[1060] *Jivaka-chintamani* by Tirutakkatevar and *Sulamani* by Tolamoli are among notable works by non-Hindu authors.[1061,1062,1063] The grammarian Buddhamitra wrote a text on Tamil grammar called *Virasoliyam*.[1064] Commentaries were written on the great text *Tolkāppiyam* which deals with grammar but which also mentions ethics of warfare.[1065,1066,1067] *Periapuranam* was another remarkable literary

Figure 99: *Chola bronze from the Ulster Museum*

piece of this period. This work is in a sense a national epic of the Tamil people because it treats of the lives of the saints who lived in all parts of Tamil Nadu and belonged to all classes of society, men and women, high and low, educated and uneducated.[1068]

Kamban flourished during the reign of Kulothunga Chola III. His *Ramavataram* (also referred to as *Kambaramayanam*) is an epic of Tamil literature, and although the author states that he followed Valmiki's *Ramayana*, it is generally accepted that his work is not a simple translation or adaptation of the Sanskrit epic.[1069]Wikipedia:Citing sources He imports into his narration the colour and landscape of his own time; his description of Kosala is an idealised account of the features of the Chola country.[1063,1070]Wikipedia:Citing sources[1071]

Jayamkondar's masterpiece, *Kalingattuparani*, is an example of narrative poetry that draws a clear boundary between history and fictitious conventions. This describes the events during Kulothunga Chola I's war in Kalinga and depicts not only the pomp and circumstance of war, but the gruesome details of the field.[1071,1072] The Tamil poet Ottakuttan was a contemporary of Kulothunga Chola I and served at the courts of three of Kulothunga's successors.[1073,1074] Ottakuttan wrote *Kulothunga Cholan Ula*, a poem extolling the virtues of the Chola king.[1075]

Nannul is a Chola era work on Tamil grammar. It discusses all five branches of grammar and, according to Berthold Spuler, is still relevant today and is one of the most distinguished normative grammars of literary Tamil.[1076]

Of the devotional literature, the arrangement of the Shaivite canon into eleven books was the work of Nambi Andar Nambi, who lived close to the end of the 10th century.[1077,1078] However, relatively few Vaishnavite works were composed during the Later Chola period, possibly because of the rulers' apparent animosity towards them.[1079]

Cultural centres

Chola rulers took an active interest in the development of temple centres and used the temples to widen the sphere of their royal authority. They established educational institutions and hospitals around the temple, enhanced the beneficial aspects of the role of the temple, and projected the royalty as a very powerful and genial presence.[1080] A record of Virarajendra Chola's reign relates to the maintenance of a school in the Jananamandapa within the temple for the study of the Vedas, Sastras, Grammar, and Rupavatara, as well as a hostel for students. The students were provided with food, bathing oil on Saturdays, and oil for pups.Wikipedia:Please clarify A hospital named Virasolan was provided with fifteen beds for sick people. The items of expense set apart for their comforts are rice, a doctor, a surgeon, two maid servants for nursing the patients, and a general servant for the hospital.[1081]

Religion

In general, Cholas were followers of Hinduism. They were not swayed by the rise of Buddhism and Jainism as were the kings of the Pallava and Pandya dynasties. Kocengannan, an Early Chola, was celebrated in both Sangam literature and in the Shaivite canon as a Hindu saint.[896]

While the Cholas did build their largest and most important temple dedicated to Shiva, it can be by no means concluded that either they were followers of Shaivism only or that they were not favourably disposed to other faiths. This is borne out by the fact that the second Chola king, Aditya I (871–903 CE), built temples for Shiva and also for Vishnu. Inscriptions of 890 refer to his contributions to the construction of the Ranganatha Temple at Srirangapatnam in the country of the Western Gangas, who were both his feudatories and had connections by marriage with him. He also pronounced that the great temples of Shiva and the Ranganatha temple were to be the *Kuladhanam* of the Chola emperors.[1082]

Parantaka II was a devotee of the reclining Vishnu (Vadivu Azhagiya Nambi) at Anbil, on the banks of the Kaveri river on the outskirts of Tiruchy, to whom

Figure 100: *Bronze Chola Statue of Nataraja at the Metropolitan Museum of Art, New York City*

he gave numerous gifts and embellishments. He also prayed before him before his embarking on war to regain the territories in and around Kanchi and Arcot from the waning Rashtrakutas and while leading expeditions against both Madurai and Ilam (Sri Lanka).[1083] Parantaka I and Parantaka Chola II endowed and built temples for Shiva and Vishnu.[1084] Rajaraja Chola I patronised Buddhists and provided for the construction of the Chudamani Vihara, a Buddhist monastery in Nagapattinam, at the request of Sri Chulamanivarman, the Srivijaya Sailendra king.[1085,1086]

During the period of the Later Cholas, there are alleged to have been instances of intolerance towards Vaishnavites[1087] especially towards their acharya, Ramanuja.[1088] Kulothunga Chola II, a staunch Shaivite, is said to have removed a statue of Vishnu from the Shiva temple at Chidambaram, though there are no epigraphical evidences to support this theory. There is an inscription from 1160 that the custodians of Shiva temples who had social intercourses with Vaishnavites would forfeit their property. However, this is more of a direction to the Shaivite community by its religious heads than any kind of dictat by a Chola emperor. While Chola kings built their largest temples for Shiva and even while emperors like Rajaraja Chola I held titles like *Sivapadasekharan*, in none of their inscriptions did the Chola emperors proclaim that their clan only

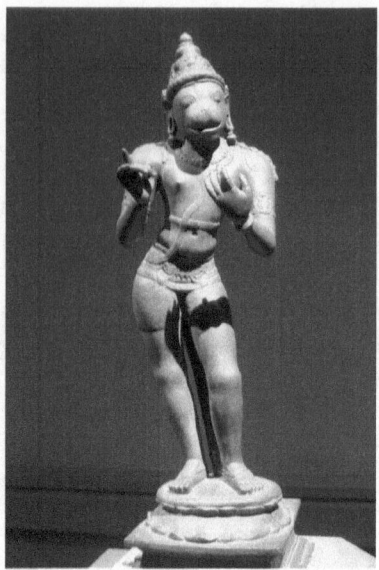

Figure 101: *Standing Hanuman, Chola Dynasty, 11th century.*

and solely followed Shaivism or that Shaivism was the state religion during their rule.[1089,1090,1091]

In popular culture

The Chola dynasty has inspired many Tamil authors.[1092] The most important work of this genre is the popular *Ponniyin Selvan* (The son of *Ponni*), a historical novel in Tamil written by Kalki Krishnamurthy. Written in five volumes, this narrates the story of Rajaraja Chola, dealing with the events leading up to the ascension of Uttama Chola to the Chola throne. Kalki had used the confusion in the succession to the Chola throne after the demise of Parantaka Chola II.[1093] The book was serialised in the Tamil periodical *Kalki* during the mid-1950s. The serialisation lasted for nearly five years and every week its publication was awaited with great interest.

Kalki's earlier historical romance, *Parthiban Kanavu*, deals with the fortunes of the imaginary Chola prince Vikraman, who was supposed to have lived as a feudatory of the Pallava king Narasimhavarman I during the 7th century. The period of the story lies within the interregnum during which the Cholas were in decline before Vijayalaya Chola revived their fortunes.[1094] *Parthiban Kanavu* was also serialised in the *Kalki* weekly during the early 1950s.Wikipedia:Citation needed

Sandilyan, another popular Tamil novelist, wrote *Kadal Pura* in the 1960s. It was serialised in the Tamil weekly *Kumudam*. *Kadal Pura* is set during the period when Kulothunga Chola I was in exile from the Vengi kingdom after he was denied the throne. It speculates the whereabouts of Kulothunga during this period. Sandilyan's earlier work, *Yavana Rani*, written in the early 1960s, is based on the life of Karikala Chola.[1095] More recently, Balakumaran wrote the novel *Udaiyar*, which is based on the circumstances surrounding Rajaraja Chola's construction of the Brihadisvara Temple in Thanjavur.

There were stage productions based on the life of Rajaraja Chola during the 1950s and in 1973 Sivaji Ganesan acted in a screen adaptation of a play titled *Rajaraja Cholan*. The Cholas are featured in the History of the World board game, produced by Avalon Hill.Wikipedia:Citation needed

The Cholas were the subject of the 2010 Tamil-language movie *Aayirathil Oruvan*.

References

Notes

Citations

Bibliography <templatestyles src="Template:Refbegin/styles.css" />

- Barua, Pradeep (2005), *The State at War in South Asia*, University of Nebraska Press, ISBN 978-0-80321-344-9
- Chopra, P. N.; Ravindran, T. K.; Subrahmanian, N. (2003), *History of South India: Ancient, Medieval and Modern*, S. Chand & Company Ltd, ISBN 81-219-0153-7
- Das, Sisir Kumar (1995), *History of Indian Literature (1911–1956): Struggle for Freedom – Triumph and Tragedy*, Sahitya Akademi, ISBN 81-7201-798-7
- Dehejia, Vidya (1990), *The Art of the Imperial Cholas*, Columbia University Press
- Devare, Hema (2009), "Cultural Implications of the Chola Maritime Fabric Trade with Southeast Asia", in Kulke, Hermann; Kesavapany, K.; Sakhuja, Vijay, *Nagapattinam to Suvarnadwipa: Reflections on the Chola Naval Expeditions to Southeast Asia*, Institute of Southeast Asian Studies, ISBN 978-9-81230-937-2
- Eraly, Abraham (2011), *The First Spring: The Golden Age of India*, Penguin Books, ISBN 978-0-67008-478-4
- Gough, Kathleen (2008), *Rural Society in Southeast India*, Cambridge University Press, ISBN 978-0-52104-019-8

- Harle, J. C. (1994), *The art and architecture of the Indian Subcontinent*, Yale University Press, ISBN 0-300-06217-6
- Hellmann-Rajanayagam, Dagmar (2004), "From Differences to Ethnic Solidarity Among the Tamils", in Hasbullah, S. H.; Morrison, Barrie M., *Sri Lankan Society in an Era of Globalization: Struggling To Create A New Social Order*, SAGE, ISBN 978-8-13210-320-2
- Jermsawatdi, Promsak (1979), *Thai Art with Indian Influences*, Abhinav Publications, ISBN 978-8-17017-090-7
- Kulke, Hermann; Rothermund, Dietmar (2001), *A History of India*, Routledge, ISBN 0-415-32920-5
- Lucassen, Jan; Lucassen, Leo (2014), *Globalising Migration History: The Eurasian Experience*, BRILL, ISBN 978-9-00427-136-4
- Majumdar, R. C. (1987) [1952], *Ancient India*, Motilal Banarsidass Publications, ISBN 81-208-0436-8
- John N. Miksic (2013). *Singapore and the Silk Road of the Sea, 1300_1800*[1096]. NUS Press. ISBN 978-9971-69-558-3.
- Mitter, Partha (2001), *Indian art*, Oxford University Press, ISBN 0-19-284221-8
- Mukherjee, Rila (2011), *Pelagic Passageways: The Northern Bay of Bengal Before Colonialism*, Primus Books, ISBN 978-9-38060-720-7
- Mukund, Kanakalatha (1999), *The Trading World of the Tamil Merchant: Evolution of Merchant Capitalism in the Coromandel*, Orient Blackswan, ISBN 978-8-12501-661-8
- Mukund, Kanakalatha (2012), *Merchants of Tamilakam: Pioneers of International Trade*, Penguin Books India, ISBN 978-0-67008-521-7
- Nagasamy, R. (1970), *Gangaikondacholapuram*, State Department of Archaeology, Government of Tamil Nadu
- Nagasamy, R. (1981), *Tamil Coins – A study*, Institute of Epigraphy, Tamil Nadu State Dept. of Archaeology
- Paine, Lincoln (2014), *The Sea and Civilization: A Maritime History of the World*, Atlantic Books, ISBN 978-1-78239-357-3
- Prasad, G. Durga (1988), *History of the Andhras up to 1565 A. D.*, P. G. Publishers
- Rajasuriar, G. K. (1998), *The history of the Tamils and the Sinhalese of Sri Lanka*
- Ramaswamy, Vijaya (2007), *Historical Dictionary of the Tamils*, Scarecrow Press, ISBN 978-0-81086-445-0
- Rothermund, Dietmar (1993), *An Economic History of India: From Pre-colonial Times to 1991* (Reprinted ed.), Routledge, ISBN 978-0-41508-871-8
- Sadarangani, Neeti M. (2004), *Bhakti Poetry in Medieval India: Its Inception, Cultural Encounter and Impact*, Sarup & Sons, ISBN 978-8-

17625-436-6
- Sakhuja, Vijay; Sakhuja, Sangeeta (2009), "Rajendra Chola I's Naval Expedition to South-East Asia: A Nautical Perspective", in Kulke, Hermann; Kesavapany, K.; Sakhuja, Vijay, *Nagapattinam to Suvarnadwipa: Reflections on the Chola Naval Expeditions to Southeast Asia*, Institute of Southeast Asian Studies, ISBN 978-9-81230-937-2
- Sastri, K. A. N. (1984) [1935], *The Cōḷas*, University of Madras
- Sastri, K. A. N. (2002) [1955], *A History of South India: From Prehistoric Times to the Fall of Vijayanagar*, Oxford University Press
- Scharfe, Hartmut (2002), *Education in Ancient India*, Brill Academic Publishers, ISBN 90-04-12556-6
- Schmidt, Karl J. (1995), *An Atlas and Survey of South Asian History*, M.E. Sharpe, ISBN 978-0-76563-757-4
- Sen, Sailendra Nath (1999), *Ancient Indian History and Civilization*, New Age International, ISBN 978-8-12241-198-0
- Sen, Tansen (2009), "The Military Campaigns of Rajendra Chola and the Chola-Srivija-China Triangle", in Kulke, Hermann; Kesavapany, K.; Sakhuja, Vijay, *Nagapattinam to Suvarnadwipa: Reflections on the Chola Naval Expeditions to Southeast Asia*, Institute of Southeast Asian Studies, ISBN 978-9-81230-937-2
- Singh, Upinder (2008), *A History of Ancient and Early Medieval India: From the Stone Age to the 12th Century*, Pearson Education India, ISBN 978-8-13171-120-0
- "South Indian Inscriptions"[1097], *Archaeological Survey of India*, What Is India Publishers (P) Ltd, retrieved 2008-05-30
- Spuler, Bertold (1975), *Handbook of Oriental Studies, Part 2*, BRILL, ISBN 978-9-00404-190-5
- Stein, Burton (1980), *Peasant state and society in medieval South India*, Oxford University Press
- Stein, Burton (1998), *A history of India*, Blackwell Publishers, ISBN 0-631-20546-2
- Subbarayalu, Y. (2009), "A Note on the Navy of the Chola State", in Kulke, Hermann; Kesavapany, K.; Sakhuja, Vijay, *Nagapattinam to Suvarnadwipa: Reflections on the Chola Naval Expeditions to Southeast Asia*, Institute of Southeast Asian Studies, ISBN 978-9-81230-937-2
- Thapar, Romila (1995), *Recent Perspectives of Early Indian History*, South Asia Books, ISBN 81-7154-556-4
- Tripathi, Rama Sankar (1967), *History of Ancient India*, Motilal Banarsidass, ISBN 81-208-0018-4
- Talbot, Austin Cynthia (2001), *Pre-colonial India in Practice: Society, Region, and Identity in Medieval Andhra*, Oxford University Press, ISBN 978-0-19803-123-9

- Vasudevan, Geeta (2003), *Royal Temple of Rajaraja: An Instrument of Imperial Cola Power*, Abhinav Publications, ISBN 81-7017-383-3
- Wolpert, Stanley A (1999), *India*, University of California Press, ISBN 0-520-22172-9

External links

 Wikimedia Commons has media related to *Chola dynasty*.

- UNESCO World Heritage sites – Chola temples[1098]
- Art of Cholas[1099]
- Chola coins of Sri Lanka[1100]

Western Ganga dynasty

Western Ganga dynasty	
Kingdom (Subordinate to Pallava until 350)	
350–1000	
Core Western Ganga Territory	
Capital	Kolar Talakad
Languages	Kannada Sanskrit
Religion	Jainism Hinduism
Government	Monarchy
Maharaja	
•	350–370	Konganivarma Madhava
•	986–999	Rachamalla V
History	
•	Earliest Ganga records	400
•	Established	350
•	Disestablished	1000
Preceded by	**Succeeded by**
Pallava dynasty	Chola dynasty
Today part of	India

Western Ganga kings

(350–999)

Konganivarman Madhava	(350–370)
Madhava	(370–390)
Harivarman	(390–410)
Vishnugopa	(410–430)
Madhava III Tandangala	(430–469)
Avinita	(469–529)
Durvinita	(529–579)
Mushkara	(579–604)
Polavira	(604–629)
Srivikrama	(629–654)
Bhuvikarma	(654–679)
Shivamara I	(679–726)
Sripurusha	(726–788)
Shivamara II	(788–816)
Rachamalla I	(816–843)
Ereganga Neetimarga	(843–870)
Rachamalla II	(870–907)
Ereganga Neetimarga II	(907–921)
Narasimha	(921–933)
Rachamalla III	(933–938)
Butuga II	(938–961)
Marulaganga Neetimarga	(961–963)
Marasimha II Satyavakya	(963–975)
Rachamalla IV Satyavakya	(975–986)
Rachamalla V (Rakkasaganga)	(986–999)
Neetimarga Permanadi	(999)

- v
- t
- e[1101]

Western Ganga was an important ruling dynasty of ancient Karnataka in India which lasted from about 350 to 1000 CE. They are known as 'Western Gangas' to distinguish them from the Eastern Gangas who in later centuries ruled over Kalinga (modern Odisha). The general belief is that the Western Gangas began their rule during a time when multiple native clans asserted their freedom due to the weakening of the Pallava empire in South India, a geo-political

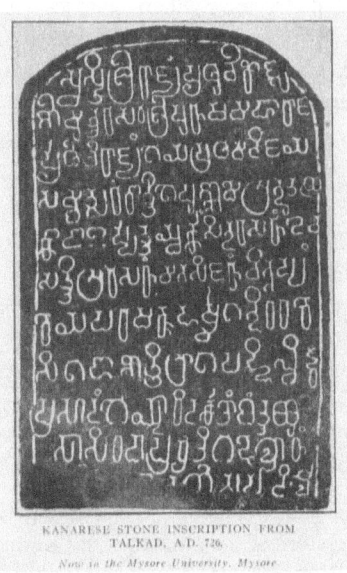

Figure 102: *Old Kannada inscription of c. 726 CE, discovered in Talakad, from the rule of King Shivamara I or Sripurusha*

Figure 103: *Ganga Dynasty emblem on a 10th-century copper plate*

event sometimes attributed to the southern conquests of Samudra Gupta. The Western Ganga sovereignty lasted from about 350 to 550 CE, initially ruling from Kolar and later, moving their capital to Talakadu on the banks of the Kaveri River in modern Mysore district.

After the rise of the imperial Chalukyas of Badami, the Gangas accepted Chalukya overlordship and fought for the cause of their overlords against the Pallavas of Kanchi. The Chalukyas were replaced by the Rashtrakutas of Manyakheta in 753 CE as the dominant power in the Deccan. After a century of struggle for autonomy, the Western Gangas finally accepted Rashtrakuta overlordship and successfully fought alongside them against their foes, the Chola Dynasty of Tanjavur. In the late 10th century, north of Tungabhadra river, the Rashtrakutas were replaced by the emerging Western Chalukya Empire and the Chola Dynasty saw renewed power south of the Kaveri river. The defeat of the Western Gangas by Cholas around 1000 resulted in the end of the Ganga influence over the region.

Though territorially a small kingdom, the Western Ganga contribution to polity, culture and literature of the modern south Karnataka region is considered important. The Western Ganga kings showed benevolent tolerance to all faiths but are most famous for their patronage toward Jainism resulting in the construction of monuments in places such as Shravanabelagola and Kambadahalli. The kings of this dynasty encouraged the fine arts due to which literature in Kannada and Sanskrit flourished. Chavundaraya's writing, *Chavundaraya Purana* of 978 CE, is an important work in Kannada prose. Many classics were written on various subjects ranging from religion to elephant management.

History

Multiple theories have been proposed regarding the ancestry of the founders of the Western Ganga dynasty (prior to the 4th century). Some mythical accounts point to a northern origin,[1102] while theories based on epigraphy suggest a southern origin. Historians who propose the southern origin have further debated whether the early petty chieftains of the clan (prior to their rise to power) were natives of the southern districts of modern Karnataka,[1103,1104,1105] the Kongu region in modern Tamil Nadu[1106] or of the southern districts of modern Andhra Pradesh.[1107,1108] These regions encompass an area of the southern Deccan where the three modern states merge geographically. It is theorised that the Gangas may have taken advantage of the confusion caused by the invasion of southern India by the northern king Samudra Gupta prior to 350, and carved out a kingdom for themselves. The area they controlled was called Gangavadi and included regions of the modern districts of Mysore, Hassan Chamarajanagar, Tumkur, Kolar, Mandya and Bangalore in Karnataka state.[1109] At times, they also controlled some areas in modern Tamil Nadu (Kongu region starting from the 6th century rule of King Avinita) and Andhra Pradesh (Ananthpur region starting from the middle of the 5th century). The founding king of the dynasty was Konganivarma Madhava who made Kolar his capital around 350 and ruled for about twenty years.

By the time of Harivarma in 390, the Gangas had consolidated their kingdom with Talakad as their capital. Their move from the early capital Kolar may have been a strategic one with the intention of containing the growing Kadamba power.[1110] By 430 they had consolidated their eastern territories comprising modern Bangalore, Kolar and Tumkur districts and by 470 they had gained control over Kongu region in modern Tamil Nadu, Sendraka (modern Chikkamagaluru and Belur), Punnata and Pannada regions (comprising modern Heggadadevanakote and Nanjangud) in modern Karnataka.[1111,1112] In 529, King Durvinita ascended the throne after waging a war with his younger brother who was favoured by his father, King Avinita.[1113] Some accounts suggest that in this power struggle, the Pallavas of Kanchi supported Avinita's choice of heir and the Badami Chalukya King Vijayaditya supported his father-in-law, Durvinita.[1114] From the inscriptions it is known that these battles were fought in Tondaimandalam and Kongu regions (northern Tamil Nadu) prompting historians to suggest that Durvinita fought the Pallavas successfully.[1115] Considered the most successful of the Ganga kings, Durvinita was well versed in arts such as music, dance, ayurveda and taming wild elephants. Some inscriptions sing paeans to him by comparing him to Yudhishthira and Manu – figures from Hindu mythology known for their wisdom and fairness.[1116,1117]

Politically, the Gangas were feudatories and close allies who also shared matrimonial relations with the Chalukyas. This is attested by inscriptions which describe their joint campaigns against their arch enemy, the Pallavas of Kanchi.[1118] From the year 725 onwards, the Gangavadi territories came to be called as the "Gangavadi-96000" (*Shannavati Sahasra Vishaya*) comprising the eastern and western provinces of modern south Karnataka.[1119] King Sripurusha fought the Pallava King Nandivarman Pallavamalla successfully, bringing Penkulikottai in north Arcot under his control temporarily for which he earned the title *Permanadi*.[1120,1121] A contest with the Pandyas of Madurai over control of Kongu region ended in a Ganga defeat, but a matrimony between a Ganga princess and Rajasimha Pandya's son brought peace helping the Gangas retain control over the contested region.[1122,1123]

In 753, when the Rashtrakutas replaced the Badami Chalukyas as the dominant force in the Deccan, the Gangas offered stiff resistance for about a century.[1124,1125] King Shivamara II is mostly known for his wars with the Rashtrakuta Dhruva Dharavarsha, his subsequent defeat and imprisonment, his release from prison and eventually his death on the battle field. The Ganga re-

Figure 104: *Saint Bharatha at Shravanabelagola temple complex*

sistance continued through the reign of Rashtrakuta Govinda III and by 819, a Ganga resurgence gained them partial control over Gangavadi under King Rachamalla.[1126] Seeing the futility of waging war with the Western Ganga, Rashtrakuta Amoghavarsha I gave his daughter Chandrabbalabbe in marriage to Ganga prince Butuga I, son of King Ereganga Neetimarga. The Gangas thereafter became staunch allies of the Rashtrakutas, a position they maintained till the end of the Rashtrakuta dynasty of Manyakheta.[1127,1128,1129]

After an uneventful period, Butuga II ascended the throne in 938 with the help of Rashtrakuta Amoghavarsha III (whose daughter he married).[1130] He helped the Rashtrakutas win decisive victories in Tamilakam in the battle of Takkolam against the Chola Dynasty. With this victory, the Rashtrakutas took control of modern northern Tamil Nadu.[1131,1132,1133] In return for their valour, the Gangas were awarded extensive territories in the Tungabhadra river valley.[1134] King Marasimha II who came to power in 963 aided the Rashtrakutas in victories against the Gurjara Pratihara King Lalla and the Paramara kings of Malwa in Central India.[1135,1136] Chavundaraya, a minister in the Western Ganga court was a valiant commander, able administrator and an accomplished poet in Kannada and Sanskrit.[1137,1138] He served King Marasimha II and his successors ably and helped King Rachamalla IV suppress a civil war in 975. Towards the end of the 10th century, the Rashtrakutas had been supplanted by the Western Chalukya Empire in Manyakheta. In the south, the Chola Dynasty who were seeing a resurgence of power under Rajaraja Chola I conquered Gangavadi around the year 1000, bringing the Western Ganga dynasty to an end. Thereafter, large areas of south Karnataka region came under Chola control for about a century.[1139]

Administration

The Western Ganga administration was influenced by principles stated in the ancient text *arthashastra*. The *praje gavundas* mentioned in the Ganga records held responsibilities similar to those of the village elders (*gramavriddhas*) mentioned by Kautilya. Succession to the throne was hereditary but there were instances when this was overlooked.[1140] The kingdom was divided into *Rashtra* (district) and further into *Visaya* (consisting of possibly 1000 villages) and *Desa*. From the 8th century, the Sanskrit term *Visaya* was replaced by the Kannada term *Nadu*. Examples of this change are Sindanadu-8000 and Punnadu-6000,[1141] with scholars differing about the significance of the numerical suffix. They opine that it was either the revenue yield of the division computed in cash terms[1142] or the number of fighting men in that division or the number of revenue paying hamlets in that division[1143] or the number of villages included in that territory.

Inscriptions have revealed several important administrative designations such as prime minister (*sarvadhikari*), treasurer (*shribhandari*), foreign minister (*sandhivirgrahi*) and chief minister (*mahapradhana*). All of these positions came with an additional title of commander (*dandanayaka*). Other designations were royal steward (*manevergade*), master of robes (*mahapasayita*), commander of elephant corps (*gajasahani*), commander of cavalry (*thuragasahani*) etc.[1144] In the royal house, *Niyogis* oversaw palace administration, royal clothing and jewellery etc. and the *Padiyara* were responsible for court ceremonies including door keeping and protocol.[1145]

Officials at the local level were the *pergade, nadabova, nalagamiga, prabhu* and *gavunda*.[1146] The *pergades* were superintendents from all social classes such as artisans, gold smiths, black smiths etc. The *pergades* dealing with the royal household were called *manepergade* (house superintendent) and those who collected tolls were called *Sunka vergades*.[1147] The *nadabovas* were accountants and tax collectors at the *Nadu* level and sometimes functioned as scribes.[1148] The *nalagamigas* were officers who organized and maintained defence at the *Nadu* level.[1149] The *prabhu* constituted a group of elite people drawn together to witness land grants and demarcation of land boundaries.[1150] The *gavundas* who appear most often in inscriptions were the backbone of medieval polity of the southern Karnataka region. They were landlords and local elite whom the state utilized their services to collect taxes, maintain records of landownership, bear witness to grants and transactions and even raise militia when required.[1151]

Inscriptions that specify land grants, rights and ownership were descriptive of the boundaries of demarcation using natural features such as rivers, streams, water channels, hillocks, large boulders, layout of the village, location of forts

Figure 105: *The Panchakuta Basadi in Kambadahalli was an important center of Jainism during the Ganga period.*

(*kote*) if any in the proximity, irrigation canals, temples, tanks and even shrubs and large trees. Also included was the type of soil, the crops meant to be grown and tanks or wells to be excavated for irrigation.[1152,1153] Inscriptions mention wet land, cultivable land, forest and waste land.[1154] There are numerous references to hamlets (*palli*) belonging to the hunter communities who resided in them (*bedapalli*).[1155] From the 6th century onwards, the inscriptions refer to feudal lords by the title *arasa*. The *arasas* were either brahmins or from tribal background who controlled hereditary territories paying periodic tribute to the king.[1156] The *velavali* who were loyal bodyguards of the royalty were fierce warriors under oath (*vele*). They moved with the royal family and were expected to fight for the master and be willing to lay down their lives in the process. If the king died, the *velavali* were required to self immolate on the funeral pyre of the master.[1157]

Economy

The Gangavadi region consisted of the malnad region, the plains (Bayaluseemae) and the semi-malnad with lower elevation and rolling hills. The main crops of the malnad region were paddy, betel leaves, cardamom and pepper and the semi-malnad region with its lower altitude produced rice, millets

Figure 106: *The famous Begur inscription in old Kannada, dated to c. 908–938 CE, from the rule of Western Ganga dynasty King Ereyappa.*

such as ragi and corn, pulses, oilseeds and it was also the base for cattle farming.[1158] The plains to the east were the flat lands fed by Kaveri, Tungabhadra and Vedavati rivers where cultivations of sugarcane, paddy, coconut, areca nut (*adeka totta*), betel leaves, plantain and flowers (*vara vana*) were common.[1159] Sources of irrigation were excavated tanks, wells, natural ponds and water bodies in the catchment area of dams (*Katta*).[1160] Inscriptions attesting to irrigation of previously uncultivated lands seem to indicate an expanding agrarian community.[1161]

Soil types mentioned in records are black soil (*Karimaniya*) in the Sinda-8000 territory and to red soil (*Kebbayya mannu*)[1162,1163] Cultivated land was of three types; wet land, dry land and to a lesser extent garden land with paddy being the dominant crop of the region. Wet lands were called *kalani, galde, nir mannu* or *nir panya* and was specifically used to denote paddy land requiring standing water.[1164] The fact that pastoral economies were spread throughout Gangavadi region comes from references to cowherds in many inscriptions. The terms *gosahasra* (a thousand cows), *gasara* (owner of cows), *gosasi* (donor of cows), *goyiti* (cowherdess), *gosasa* (protector of cows) attest to this.[1165] Inscriptions indicate ownership of cows may have been as important as cultivable land and that there may have existed a social hierarchy based on this.[1166] Inscriptions mention cattle raids attesting to the importance of the pastoral economy, destructive raids, assaults on women (*pendir-udeyulcal*), abduction of women by *bedas* (hunter tribes); all of which indicate the existing militarism of the age.[1167]

Lands that were exempt from taxes were called *manya* and sometimes consisted of several villages. They were granted by local chieftains without any reference to the overlord, indicating a de-centralised economy. These lands, often given to heroes who perished in the line of duty were called *bilavritti* or *kalnad*.[1168] When such a grant was made for the maintenance of temples at the time of consecration, it was called *Talavritti*.[1169] Some types of taxes on income were *kara* or *anthakara* (internal taxes), *utkota* (gifts due to the king), *hiranya* (cash payments) and *sulika* (tolls and duties on imported items). Taxes were collected from those who held the right to cultivate land; even if the land was not actually cultivated.[1170,1171]

Siddhaya was a local tax levied on agriculture and *pottondi* was a tax levied on merchandise by the local feudal ruler. Based on context, *pottondi* also meant 1/10, *aydalavi* meant 1/5 and *elalavi* meant 1/7.[1172] *Mannadare* literally meant land tax and was levied together with shepherds tax (*Kurimbadere*) payable to the chief of shepherds. *Bhaga* meant a portion or share of the produce from land or the land area itself. Minor taxes such as *Kirudere* (due to the landlords) and *samathadere* (raised by the army officers or *samantha*) are mentioned. In addition to taxes for maintenance of the local officer's retinue, villages were obligated to feed armies on the march to and from battles.[1173] *Bittuvatta* or *niravari* taxes comprised usually of a percentage of the produce and was collected for constructing irrigation tanks.[1174]

Culture

Religion

The Western Gangas gave patronage to all the major religions of the time; Jainism and the Hindu sects of Shaivism, Vedic Brahminism and Vaishnavism. However scholars have argued that not all Gangas kings may have given equal priority to all the faiths. Some historians believe that the Gangas were ardent Jains.[1175] However, inscriptions contradict this by providing references to *kalamukhas* (staunch Shaiva ascetics), *pasupatas* and *lokayatas* (followers of *Pasupatha* doctrine) who flourished in Gangavadi, indicating that Shaivism was also popular. King Madhava and Harivarma were devoted to cows and brahmins, King Vishnugopa was a devout Vaishnava,[1176] Madhava III's and Avinita's inscriptions describe lavish endowments to Jain orders and temples[1177] and King Durvinita performed Vedic sacrifices prompting historians to claim he was a Hindu.[1178]

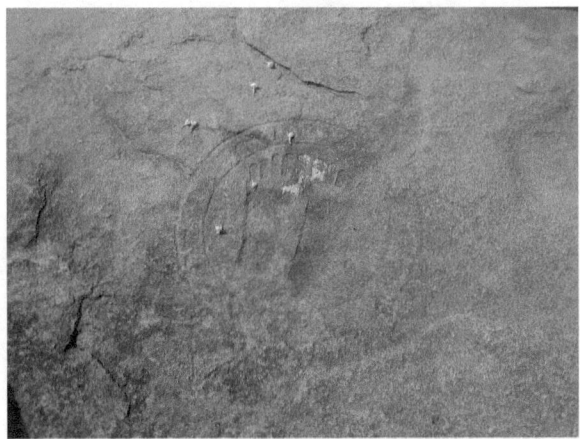

Figure 107: *Footprint worship at Shravanabelagola*

Figure 108: *A mantapa (hall) at the Jain Panchakuta basadi of 9th–10th century at Kambadahalli*

Figure 109: *Gommateshwara at Shravanabelagola (982–983) C.E.*

Jainism became popular in the dynasty in the 8th century when the ruler King Shivamara I constructed numerous Jain *basadis*.[1179] King Butuga II and minister Chavundaraya were staunch Jains which is evident from the construction of the Gommateshwara monolith.[1180] Jains worshipped the twenty four *tirthankars* (*Jinas*) whose images were consecrated in their temples. The worship of the footprint of spiritual leaders such as those of Bhadrabahu in Shravanabelagola from the 10th century is considered a parallel to Buddhism.[1181] Some brahminical influences are seen in the consecration of the Gomateshwara monolith which is the statue of Bahubali, the son of *Tirthankar Adinatha* (just as Hindus worshipped the sons of Shiva).[1182] The worship of subordinate deities such as *yaksa* and *yaksi*, earlier considered as mere attendants of the *tirthankars* was seen from the 7th century to the 12th century.[1183]

Vedic Brahminism was popular in the 6th and 7th centuries when inscriptions refer to grants made to *Srotriya* Brahmins.[1184] These inscriptions also describe the *gotra* (lineage) affiliation to royal families and their adherence of such Vedic rituals as *asvamedha* (horse sacrifice) and *hiranyagarbha*.[1185] Brahmins and kings enjoyed a mutually beneficial relationship; rituals performed by the brahmins gave legitimacy to kings and the land grants made by kings to brahmins elevated them in society to the level of wealthy landowners.[1186] Vaishnavism however maintained a low profile and not many inscriptions describe grants towards its cause.[1187] Some Vaishnava temples were built by the

Figure 110: *Kalleshwara Temple Complex, built in the 10th century by the Nolambas, a Western Ganga feudatory, at Aralaguppe in the Tumkur district*

Gangas such as the *Narayanaswami* temples at Nanjangud, Sattur and Hangala in modern Mysore district.[1188] The deity Vishnu was depicted with four arms holding a conch (*sanka*), discus (*cakra*), mace (*gada*) and lotus (*padma*).[1189]

From the beginning of the 8th century, patronage to Shaivism increased in every section of the society; the landed elite, landlords, assemblies (*samaya*), schools of learning (*aghraharas*)[1190] and minor ruling families such as the Bana, Nolamba and Chalukya clans.[1191,1192] The Shaiva temples contained a Shiva *linga* (phallus) in the sanctum sanctorum along with images of the mother goddess, Surya (Sun god)[1193] and Nandi (a bull and attendant of Shiva) which was normally enshrined in a separate pavilion facing the sanctum.[1194,1195] The *linga* was man made and in some cases had etchings of Ganapati (son of Shiva) and Parvati (consort and wife of Shiva) on it. Due to the vigorous efforts of priests and ascetics, Shaiva monastic orders flourished in many places such as Nandi Hills, Avani and Hebbata in modern Kolar district.[1196]

Society

The Western Ganga society in many ways reflected the emerging religious, political and cultural developments of those times. Women became active in local administration because Ganga kings distributed territorial responsibility to their queens such as the feudal queen Parabbaya-arasi of Kundattur[1197] and the queens of King Sripurusha, Butuga II and feudal king Permadi.[1198] Inheritance of fiscal and administrative responsibility by the son-in-law, the wife or

Figure 111: *Hero stone (870–906 A.D.) with old Kannada inscription at Kalleshvara temple in Aralaguppe*

by the daughter is evident. The position of prime minister of King Ereganga II and position of *nalgavunda* (local landlord) bestowed upon Jakkiabbe, the wife of a fallen hero are examples. When Jakkiabbe took to asceticism, her daughter inherited the position.[1199,1200]

The devadasi system (*sule* or courtesan) in temples was prevalent and was modelled after the structures in the royal palace.[1201] Contemporaneous literature such a *Vaddaradhane* makes a mention of the chief queen (*Dharani Mahadevi*) accompanied by lower ranking queens (*arasiyargal*) and courtesans of the women's royal quarter (*pendarasada suleyargal*). Some of the courtesans and concubines employed in the harem of the kings and chieftains were well respected, examples being Nandavva at whose instance a local chief made land grant to a Jain temple.[1202] Education in the royal family was closely supervised and included such subjects as political science, elephant and horse riding, archery, medicine, poetry, grammar, drama, literature, dance, singing and use of musical instruments. Brahmins enjoyed an influential position in society and were exempt from certain taxes and customs due on land. In turn they managed public affairs such as teaching, local judiciary, functioned as trustees and bankers, managed schools, temples, irrigation tanks, rest houses, collected taxes due from villages and raised money from public subscriptions.[1203]

By virtue of a Hindu belief that killing of a brahmin (*Bramhatya*) was a sin, capital punishment was not applicable to them.[1204] Upper caste kshatriyas (*satkshatriya*) were also exempt from capital punishment due to their higher position in the caste system. Severe crimes committed were punishable by the severing of a foot or hand.[1205] Contemporary literary sources reveal up to ten castes in the Hindu caste system; three among kshatriya, three among brahmin, two among vaishya and two among shudras.[1206] Family laws permitted a wife or daughter or surviving relatives of a deceased person to claim properties such as his home, land, grain, money etc. if there were no male heirs. If no claimants to the property existed, the state took possession of these properties as *Dharmadeya* (charitable asset).[1207] Intercaste marriage, child marriage, marriage of a boy to maternal uncles daughter, *Svayamvara* marriage (where the bride garlands her choice of a groom from among many aspirants) were all in vogue.[1208] Memorials containing hero stones (*virkal*) were erected for fallen heroes and the concerned family received monetary aid for maintenance of the memorial.[1209]

The presence of numerous *Mahasatikals* (or *Mastikal* – hero stones for a woman who accepted ritual death upon the demise of her husband) indicates the popularity of Sati among royalty.[1210] Ritual death by *sallekhana* and by *jalasamadhi* (drowning in water) were also practiced.[1211] Popular clothing among men was the use of two unrestricted garments, a Dhoti as a lower garment and a plain cloth as upper garment while women wore Saris with stitched petticoats. Turbans were popular with men of higher standing and people used umbrellas made with bamboo or reeds.[1212] Ornaments were popular among men and women and even elephants and horses were decorated. Men wore finger rings, necklaces (*honnasara* and *honnagala sara*), bracelets (*Kaduga*) and wristlets (*Kaftkina*). Women wore a nose jewel (*bottu*), nose ring (*mugutti*), bangles (*bale* or *kankana*) and various types of necklaces (*honna gante sara* and *kati sutra*). During leisure, men amused themselves with horse riding, watching wrestling bouts, cock fights and ram fights.[1213] There existed a large and well organised network of schools for imparting higher education and these schools were known by various names such as *agraharas*, *ghatikas*, *brahmapura* or *matha*.[1214] Inscriptions mention schools of higher education at Salotgi, Balligavi, Talagunda, Aihole, Arasikere and other places.

Literature

The Western Ganga rule was a period of brisk literary activity in Sanskrit and Kannada, though many of the writings are now considered extinct and are known only from references made to them. Chavundaraya's writing, *Chavundaraya Purana* (or *Trishashtilakshana mahapurana*) of 978 CE, is an early

Figure 112: *The famous Atakur inscription (949 C.E.), a classical Kannada composition pertaining to the Western Ganga-Rashtrakuta victory over the Chola dynasty of Tanjore in the famous battle of Takkolam*

existing work in prose style in Kannada and contains a summary of the Sanskrit writings, *Adipurana* and *Uttarapurana* which were written a century earlier by Jinasena and Gunabhadra during the rule of Rashtrakuta Amoghavarsha I.[1215] The prose, composed in lucid Kannada, was mainly meant for the common man and avoided any reference to complicated elements of Jain doctrines and philosophy. His writings seem to be influenced by the writings of his predecessor Adikavi Pampa and contemporary Ranna. The work narrates the legends of a total of 63 Jain proponents including twenty-four Jain *Tirthankar*, twelve *Chakravartis*, nine *Balabhadras*, nine *Narayanas* and nine *Pratinarayanas*.[1216,1217]

The earliest postulated Kannada writer from this dynasty is King Durvinita of the 6th century. Kavirajamarga of 850 CE, refers to a Durvinita as an early writer of Kannada prose.[1218,1219] Around 900 CE, Gunavarma I authored the Kannada works, *Shudraka* and *Harivamsha*. His writings are considered extinct but references to these writings are found in later years. He is known to have been patronised by King Ereganga Neetimarga II. In *Shudraka*, he has favourably compared his patron to King Shudraka of ancient times.[1220,1221] The great Kannada poet Ranna was patronised by Chavundaraya in his early

Figure 113: *Mahasthambha (pillar) and Chandragupta Basadi at Chandragiri Hill in Shravanabelagola*

literary days.[1222] Ranna's classic *Parashurama charite* is considered a eulogy of his patron who held such titles as *Samara Parashurama*.

Nagavarma I, a brahmin scholar who came from Vengi in modern Andhra Pradesh (late 10th century) was also patronised by Chavundaraya. He wrote *Chandombudhi* (ocean of prosody) addressed to his wife. This is considered the earliest available Kannada writing in prosody. He also wrote one of the earliest available romance classics in Kannada called *Karnataka Kadambari* in sweet and flowing *champu* (mixed verse and prose) style. It is based on an earlier romantic work in Sanskrit by poet Bana and is popular among critics. *Gajashtaka* (hundred verses on elephants), a rare Kannada work on elephant management was written by King Shivamara II around 800 CE but this work is now considered extinct.[1223] Other writers such as Manasiga and Chandrabhatta were known to be popular in the 10th century.[1224]

In an age of classical Sanskrit literature, Madhava II (brother of King Vishnugopa) wrote a treatise *Dattaka Sutravritti* which was based on an earlier work on erotics by a writer called Dattaka. A Sanskrit version of *Vaddakatha*, a commentary on Pāṇini's grammar called *Sabdavathara* and a commentary on the 15th chapter of a Sanskrit work called *Kiratarjunneya* by poet Bharavi (who was in Durvinita's court) are ascribed to Durvinita.[1225] King Shivamara II is known to have written *Gajamata Kalpana*. Hemasena, also known as Vidya Dhananjaya authored *Raghavapandaviya*, a narration of the stories of Rama and the Pandavas simultaneously through puns.[1226] *Gayachintamani* and *Kshatrachudamini* which were based on poet Bana's work *Kadambari* were written by Hemasena's pupil Vadeebhasimha in prose style. and Chavundaraya wrote *Charitarasara*.

Figure 114: *Chandragiri hill temple complex at Shravanabelagola*

Architecture

The Western Ganga style of architecture was influenced by the Pallava and Badami Chalukya architectural features, in addition to indigenous Jain features.[1227] The Ganga pillars with a conventional lion at the base and a circular shaft of the pillar on its head, the stepped *Vimana* of the shrine with horizontal mouldings and square pillars were features inherited from the Pallavas. These features are also found in structures built by their subordinates, the Banas and Nolambas.

The monolith of Gomateshwara commissioned by Chavundaraya is considered the high point of the Ganga sculptural contribution in ancient Karnataka. Carved from fine-grained white granite, the image stands on a lotus. It has no support up to the thighs and is 60 feet (18 m) tall with the face measuring 6.5 feet (2.0 m). With the serene expression on the face of the image, its curled hair with graceful locks, its proportional anatomy, the monolith size, and the combination of its artistry and craftsmanship have led it to be called the mightiest achievement in sculptural art in medieval Karnataka.[1228] It is the largest monolithic statue in the world. Their free standing pillars called *Mahasthambha* or *Bhrahmasthambha* are also considered unique, examples of which are the Brahmadeva pillar and Tyagada Brahmadeva Pillar.[1229,1230] At the top of the pillar whose shaft (cylindrical or octagonal) is decorated with creepers and other floral motifs is the seated *Brahma* and the base of the pillar normally has engravings of important Jain personalities and inscriptions.[1231]

Other important contributions are the Jain basadis' whose towers have gradually receding stories (*talas*) ornamented with small models of temples. These tiny shrines have in them engravings of tirthankars (Jain saints). Semicircular windows connect the shrines and decorative Kirtimukha (demon faces) are

Figure 115: *Ceiling sculpture, Panchakuta Basadi, Kambadahalli*

used at the top. The Chavundaraya basadi built in the 10th or 11th century, Chandragupta basadi built in the 6th century and the monolithic of Gomateshwara of 982 are the most important monuments at Shravanabelagola.[1232] Some features were added to the Chandragupta basadi by famous Hoysala sculptor Dasoja in the 12th century. The decorative doorjambs and perforated screen windows which depict scenes from the life of King Chandragupta Maurya are known to be his creation.[1233] The Panchakuta Basadi at Kambadahalli (five towered Jan temple) of about 900 with a Brahmadeva pillar is an excellent example of Dravidian art.[1234] The wall niches here are surmounted by *torana* (lintel) with carvings of floral motifs, flying divine creatures (*gandharva*) and imaginary monsters (*makara*) ridden by *Yaksas* (attendants of saints) while the niches are occupied by images of tirthankars themselves.[1235]

The Gangas built many Hindu temples with impressive Dravidian gopuras containing stucco figures from the Hindu pantheon, decorated pierced screen windows which are featured in the *mantapa* (hall) along with *saptamatrika* carvings (seven heavenly mothers).[1236] Some well known examples are the Arakeshvara Temple at Hole Alur,[1237] Kapileswara temple at Manne, Kolaramma temple at Kolar, Rameshvara temple at Narasamangala,[1238] Nagareshvara temple at Begur[1239] and the Kallesvara temple at Aralaguppe.[1240] At Talakad they built the Maralesvara temple, the Arakesvara temple and the Patalesvara temple. Unlike the Jain temples where floral frieze decoration is

Figure 116: *Chavundaraya basadi on Chandragiri hill in Shravanabelagola temple complex*

common, Hindu temples were distinguished by friezes (slab of stone with decorative sculptures) illustrating episodes from the epics and puranas. Another unique legacy of the Gangas are the number of *virgal* (hero stones) they have left behind; memorials containing sculptural details in relief of war scenes, Hindu deities, *saptamatrikas*, Jain tirthankars and ritual death (such as the Doddahundi hero stone).[1241]

Language

Part of a series on the
History of Karnataka
• Political history of medieval Karnataka • Origin of Karnataka's name • Kadambas and Gangas • Chalukya Empire • Rashtrakuta Empire • Western Chalukya Empire • Southern Kalachuri • Hoysala Empire

- Vijayanagara Empire
- Bahmani Sultanate
- Bijapur Sultanate
- Kingdom of Mysore
- Nayakas of Keladi
- Nayakas of Chitradurga
- Haleri Kingdom
- Unification of Karnataka

Categories

- Architecture
- Forts
- Economies
- Societies

- v
- t
- e[1242]

The Western Gangas used Kannada and Sanskrit extensively as their language of administration. Some of their inscriptions are also bilingual in these languages. In bilingual inscriptions the formulaic passages stating origin myths, genealogies, titles of Kings and benedictions tended to be in Sanskrit, while the actual terms of the grant such as information on the land or village granted, its boundaries, participation of local authorities, rights and obligations of the grantee, taxes and dues and other local concerns were in the local language.[1243] The usage of these two languages showed important changes over the centuries. During the first phase (350–725), Sanskrit copper plates dominated, indicating the initial ascendancy of the local language as a language of administration and the fact that majority of the records from this phase were *brahmadeya* grants (grants to Brahmin temples).[1244] In the second phase (725–1000), lithic inscriptions in Kannada outnumbered Sanskrit copper plates, consistent with the patronage Kannada received from rich and literate Jains who used Kannada as their medium to spread the Jain faith.[1245] Recent excavations at Tumbula near Mysore have revealed a set of early copper plate bilingual inscriptions dated 444. The genealogy of the kings of the dynasty is described in Sanskrit while Kannada was used to describe the boundary of the village. An interesting inscription discovered at Beguru near modern Bangalore that deserves mention is the epigraph dated 890 that refers to a *Bengaluru* war. This is in *Hale Kannada* (old Kannada) language and is the earliest mention of the name of Bangalore city. The Western Gangas minted coins with Kannada and Nagari legends,[1246] the most common feature on their coins was the image of an elephant on the obverse and floral petal symbols on the reverse. The Kannada legend *Bhadr*, a royal umbrella or a conch shell appeared on top of the elephant image. The denominations are the *pagoda* (weighing 52 grains), the

Figure 117: *Old Kannada inscription at the base of Gomateshwara monolith in Shravanabelagola (981 CE.)*

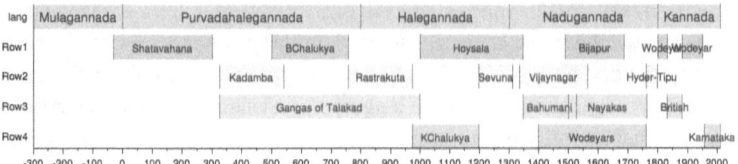

fanam weighting one tenth or one half of the *pagoda* and the quarter *fanams*.

Timeline

The template below shows the Timeline of Karnataka. Note the extent of time (around 700 years) the Ganga kingdom flourished.

Bibliography

 Wikimedia Commons has media related to ***Western Ganga Dynasty***.

Books <templatestyles src="Template:Refbegin/styles.css" />
- Adiga, Malini (2006) [2006]. *The Making of Southern Karnataka: Society, Polity and Culture in the early medieval period, AD 400–1030.* Chennai: Orient Longman. ISBN 81-250-2912-5.
- Altekar, Anant Sadashiv (1934) [1934]. *The Rashtrakutas And Their Times; being a political, administrative, religious, social, economic and literary history of the Deccan during C. 750 A.D. to C. 1000 A.D.* Poona: Oriental Book Agency. OCLC 3793499[1247].
- Chopra, Ravindran, Subrahmanian, P.N., T.K., N. (2003) [2003]. *History of South India (Ancient, Medieval and Modern) Part I.* New Delhi: Chand publications. ISBN 81-219-0153-7.
- Kamath, Suryanath U. (2001) [1980]. *A concise history of Karnataka : from pre-historic times to the present.* Bangalore: Jupiter books. LCCN 80905179[1248]. OCLC 7796041[1249].
- Karmarkar, A.P. (1947) [1947]. *Cultural history of Karnataka : ancient and medieval.* Dharwar: Karnataka Vidyavardhaka Sangha. OCLC 8221605[1250].
- Keay, John (2000) [2000]. *India: A History.* New York: Grove Publications. ISBN 0-8021-3797-0.
- Narasimhacharya, R (1988) [1988]. *History of Kannada Literature.* New Delhi, Madras: Asian Educational Services. ISBN 81-206-0303-6.
- Prabhu, Govindaraya S (2009). *The Nolambas Coinage and History.* Govindraya Prabhu S. ISBN 81-8465-141-4.
- Ramesh, K.V. (1984) [1984]. *Chalukyas of Vatapi.* Delhi: Agam Kala Prakashan. ASIN B0006EHSP0[1251]. LCCN 84900575[1252]. OCLC 13869730[1253]. OL 3007052M[1254].
- Sarma, I.K. (1992) [1992]. *Temples of the Gangas of Karnataka.* New Delhi: Archaeological Survey of India. ISBN 0-19-560686-8.
- Sastri, Nilakanta K.A. (2002) [1955]. *A history of South India from prehistoric times to the fall of Vijayanagar.* New Delhi: Indian Branch, Oxford University Press. ISBN 0-19-560686-8.
- Thapar, Romila (2003) [2003]. *Penguin History of Early India: From origins to AD 1300.* New Delhi: Penguin. ISBN 0-14-302989-4.

Web <templatestyles src="Template:Refbegin/styles.css" />
- "Gangas of Talakad" by [[S. Srikanta Sastri[1255]]]
- Arthikaje. "History of Karnataka: The Gangas of Talakad"[1256]. OurKarnataka.Com. Archived from the original[1257] on 15 December 2006. Retrieved 2006-12-31.
- Havalaiah, N (January 2004). "Ancient inscriptions"[1258]. *The Hindu.* Chennai, India. Retrieved 2007-05-30.

- Kamat, Jyotsna. "The Ganga Dynasty"[1259]. Kamat's Potpourri. Retrieved 2007-05-30.
- Khajane, Muralidhara (February 2006). "An ancient site connected with Jainism"[1260]. *The Hindu*. Chennai, India. Retrieved 2007-06-30.
- Prabhu, Govindaraya S. "Coins of Gangas"[1261]. *Indian Coins*. Prabhu's web page on Indian coinage. Archived from the original[1262] on 2007-07-10. Retrieved 2007-06-30.
- Staff Reporter (August 20, 2004). "Inscription reveals Bangalore is over 1,000 years old"[1263]. *The Hindu*. Chennai, India. Retrieved 2007-06-30.

<indicator name="featured-star"> </indicator>

Kakatiya dynasty

<indicator name="pp-default"> </indicator>

Kakatiya dynasty		
Empire (Subordinate to Western Chalukyas until 1163)		
1163[1264]–1323		
Capital		Orugallu (Warangal)
Languages		Telugu
Religion		Hinduism
Government		Monarchy
History		
•	Earliest rulers	c. 800
•	Established	1163[1264]
•	Disestablished	1323
Preceded by		**Succeeded by**
Western Chalukya Empire Eastern Chalukyas Velanati Chodas		Musunuri Nayaks Bahmani Sultanate Reddy dynasty Vijayanagara Empire
Today part of		India

Kakatiya dynasty

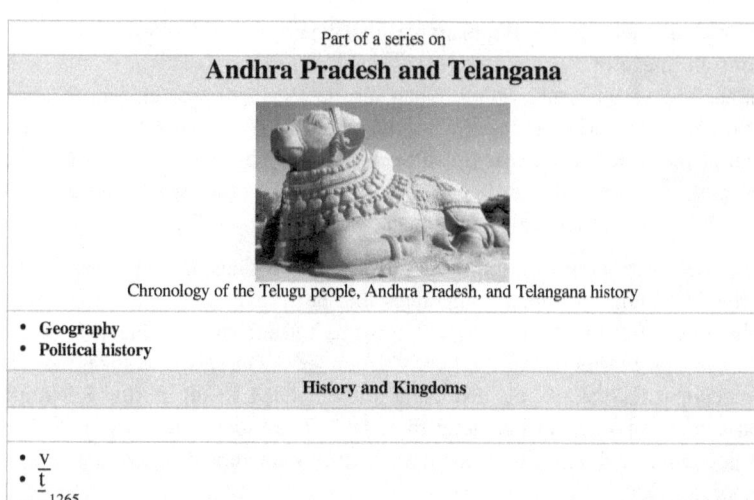

Part of a series on
Andhra Pradesh and Telangana
Chronology of the Telugu people, Andhra Pradesh, and Telangana history
• Geography • Political history
History and Kingdoms
• v • t • e[1265]

The **Kakatiya dynasty** was a South Indian dynasty whose capital was Orugallu, now known as Warangal. It was eventually conquered by the Delhi Sultanate.

The demise of Kakatiya dynasty resulted in confusion and anarchy under alien rulers for sometime, before the Musunuri Nayaks brought stability to the region.[1266]

Etymology and names

Studies of the inscriptions and coinage by the historian Dineshchandra Sircar reveal that there was no contemporary standard spelling of the family name. Variants include *Kakatiya*, *Kakatiyya*, *Kakita*, *Kakati* and *Kakatya*. The family name was often prefixed to the name of the monarch, giving constructs such as *Kakatiya-Prataparudra*. Some of the monarchs also had alternate names; for example, *Venkata* and *Venkataraya* may have been alternate names of Prataparuda I, with the former appearing on a coin in the form *Venkata-Kakatiya*.[1267,1268]

The dynasty's name derives from the word "Kakati", which is variously thought to be the name of a goddess or a place. It is possible that Kakati was the name of a deity worshipped by the early Kakatiya chiefs, and also the name of the place where they resided.[1269]

Kumarasvami Somapithin, a 15th-century writer who wrote a commentary on Vidyanatha's *Prataparudriya*, states that the dynasty was named after Kakati, a form of goddess Durga. Although the Hindu mythological texts do not mention any such form of Durga, the worship of a goddess named Kakati is attested by several other sources. For example, Vallabharaya's *Krida-bhiramamu* mentions an image of Kakatamma (Mother Kakati) in the Kakatiya capital Orugallu. the 16th century Shitap Khan inscription mentions the reinstallation of the image of goddess Jaganmatrika (mother of the universe) and the lotus seat of the Kakatirajya, which had been destroyed by the Turushkas (Turkic people).[1270] According to one theory, Kakati was originally a Jain goddess (possibly Padmavati), and later came to be regarded as a form of Durga.[1271]

The Bayyaram tank inscription from the reign of Ganapati-deva names the family's founder as Venna, and states that he resided at Kakati, because of which his descendants came to be known as Kakatishas.[1270] Ganapati-deva's Garavapadu charter names the family's founder as Durjaya, and states that his descendant Karikala Chola arrived at a town called Kakati during a hunting expedition, and set up his camp there.[1269] The modern identity of Kakati is uncertain: different historians have variously attempted to identify it with modern Kakati village in Karnataka and Kanker in Chhattisgarh. *Siddeshvara Charitra*, a later literary work, states that the ancestors of the Kakatiya family lived at Kandarapura (identified with modern Kandhar in Maharashtra). However, no other evidence supports this tradition.[1272]

Sources

Much of the information about the Kakatiya period comes from inscriptions, including around 1,000 stone inscriptions, and 12 copper-plate inscriptions.[1273] Most of these inscriptions document matters relating to religion, such as donations to Hindu temples. They are particularly abundant for the period 1175–1324 CE, which is the period when the dynasty most flourished and are a reflection of that. The probability is that many inscriptions have been lost due to buildings falling into disuse and also the ravages of subsequent rulers, most notably the Muslim Mughal Empire in the Telangana region. Inscriptions are still being discovered today but governmental agencies tend to concentrate on recording those that are already known rather than searching for new examples.[1274] According to a 1978 book, written bby P.V.P. Sastry's 1978 book on the history of the Kakatiyas, published by the Government of Andhra Pradesh

Information about the Kakatiya period also comes from Sanskrit and Telugu literary works written during Kakatiya and post-Kakatiya period. The most notable among these works include *Prataparudriyam*, *Krida-bhiramamu*, *Panditaradhya-charitamu*, *Sivayogasaramu*, *Nitisara*, *Niti-shastra-muktavali*, *Nritta-ratnavali*, *Pratapa-charita*, *Siddheshvara-charitra*, *Somadeva-rajiyamu*, *Palnativira-charitra*, *Velugotivari-vamsavali*, and *Velugotivari-vamsacharitra*.[1275] Chronicles by Muslim authors such as

Isami and Firishta describe Prataparudra's defeats against the Muslim armies. The Kannada text *Kumara-Ramana-charita* also provides information about Prataparudra's relations with the Kampili kingdom.[1276]

Besides epigraphs and literature, the forts, temples and tanks constructed during the Kakatiya period are an important source of information about the contemporary society, art and architecture.[1277]

Origin

The Kakatiya rulers traced their ancestry to a legendary chief or ruler named Durjaya. Many other ruling dynasties of Andhra also claimed descent from Durjaya. Nothing further is known about this chief.[1278]

Most of the Kakatiya records do not mention the varna (social class) of the family, but the majority of the ones that do, proudly describe them as Shudra.[1279] Examples include the Bothpur and Vaddamanu inscriptions of Ganapati's general Malyala Gunda *senani*. The Kakatiyas also maintained marital relations with other Shudra families, such as the Kotas and the Natavadi chiefs. All these evidences indicate that the Kakatiyas were of Shudra origin.[1280]

A few copper-plate inscriptions of the Kakatiya family describe them as belonging to the Kshatriya (warrior) varna. These inscriptions primarily document grants to brahmans, and appear to be inspired by the genealogies of the imperial Cholas.[1279] For example, the Motupalli inscription of Ganapati counts legendary solar dynasty kings such as Rama among the ancestors of Durjaya, the progenitor of the Kakatiya family. The Malkapuram inscription of Vishveshvara Shivacharya, the preceptor of Kakatiya rulers Ganapatideva and Rudrama-devi, also connects the Kakatiyas to the solar dynasty (Sūryavaṃsa).[1281] The term "Kshatriya" in these panegyric records appears to signify the family's warrior-like qualities rather than their actual varna.[1282]

Early feudatory chiefs

The regnal years of the early members of the Kakatiya family are not certain. Venna, said to have been born in the family of Durjaya, is the earliest known Kakatiya chief. The Bayyaram tank inscription names his successors as Gunda I, Gunda II, and Gunda III, comparing them to the three Ramas (Parashurama, Dasharatha-Rama, and Balarama). Gunda III was succeeded by Erra, who ruled Kurravadi and other regions. The inscription states that Erra's successor Gunda IV alias Pindi-Gunda (c. 955-995) beheaded all his enemies.[1283] Gunda IV is also mentioned in the Mangallu grant of the Eastern Chalukya ruler Dānārnava in 956 CE.[1284]

Gunda IV was succeeded by Beta I (c. 996-1051), who was succeeded by Prola I (c. 1052-1076), called *ari-gaja-kesari* ("lion to the elephant-like enemies") in the Bayyaram inscription.[1283] The succeeding chiefs included Beta II (c. 1076–1108), Tribhuvanamalla Durgaraja (c. 1108–1116) and then Prola II (c. 1116–1157).[1285]

The early Kakatiya rulers used the title "Reddi"[1286,1287] (derived from "Redu," meaning king in Telugu[1288]). However, after they became sovereigns they were addressed as "deva" (Lord or deity) and "devi" (Lady or deity). There appears to be a significant element of "sanskritisation" in this transition.

Relationship to the Rashtrakutas

Early members of Kakatiya family appear to have served as military generals of the Rashtrakutas, as indicated by a 956 inscription of the Vengi Chalukya prince Dānārnava.[1289] The inscription suggests that an attack by the Rashtrakuta king Krishna III forced the Vengi Chalukya king Amma II to flee his kingdom, after which Dānārnava (titled Vijayaditya) ruled the kingdom as a Rashtrakuta vassal. It records Dānārnava's grant of Mangallu village to a brahmana named Dommana, at the request of Kakatiya Gundyana. Dommana had performed a religious ceremony called *Karpati-vrata* for Gundyana, for which he received the village as an *agrahara*.[1290] The inscription names Gundyana's ancestors as Gundiya-Rashtrakuta and Eriya-Rashtrakuta.[1291] This suggests that Gundyana was a Rashtrakuta general, and not a Vengi Chalukya subordinate, as assumed by some earlier historians.[1291]

The Bayyaram tank inscription, which records the construction of *Dharma-kirti-samudra* tank by Ganapati's sister Mailama (or Mailamba), provides another genealogical list.[1283] The similarities of names mentioned in the Mangallu and Bayyaram inscriptions lists suggest that both of these refer to the same family:[1292]

Genealogical list of early Kakatiyas[1293]

Mangallu grant inscription	Bayyaram tank inscription
Kakatiya family	Durjaya family
	Venna-*nripa*
Gundiya Rashtrakuta	Gunda I
	Gunda II
	Gunda III
Eriya Rashtrakuta	Erra
Betiya (married Vandyanamba)	
Kakartya Gundyana	Pindi-Gunda (Gunda IV)

Historian P.V.P. Sastry theorizes that Betiya was the son of Eriya (alias Erra) and father of Gundyana (alias Pindi-Gunda), but may have become too insignificant to be mentioned by his descendants, because of a premature death or another reason.[1294]

The significance of the suffix "Rashtrakuta" in the names of the early Kakatiya chiefs is debated. According to one theory, the suffix implies that these chiefs were Rashtrakuta subordinates. This theory is based on the fact that the phrase *Rashtrakuta-kutumbinah* appears in several Rashtrakuta-era copper-plate inscriptions, and refers to the officers and subjects of the Rashtrakuta kingdom.[1295]

According to another theory, the suffix implies that the Kakatiyas were a branch of the Rashtrakuta family, because the term *Rashtrakuta-kutumbinah* was used for officers employed by the Rashtrakuta administration, not feudatory chiefs: the early records of the Kakatiya chiefs describe them as *samantas* (feudatory chiefs).[1296] The Kazipet Darga inscription of Tribhuvanamalla Durgaraja states that the Kakatiya chief Beta was born in the family of Samanta Visti.[1297] Historian P.V.P. Sastry theorises that "Visti" is a corruption of Vrishni, the name of a clan from which some Rashtrakutas claimed descent. He notes that some chiefs of Rashtrakuta origin adopted the title "Vitti-narayana", which means "as great as Narayana (Krishna) of the Vitti (Vrishni) family.[1298] Sastry further proposes that the term "Voddi", which appears in the phrase *Voddi-kula* ("Voddi family") in the Mangallu inscription may be same as "Visti".[1299] Sastry also believes that the early Kakatiya chiefs followed Jainism, which was also patronized by the Rashtrakutas, thus strengthening the view that the two dynasties were connected (see Religion section below).[1271]

The Kakatiyas seemed to have adopted the mythical bird Garuda as their royal insignia, as attested by the Ekamranatha temple inscription of Ganapatideva, the Palampet inscription of the Kakatiya general Recharla Rudra, and Vidyanatha's *Prataparudriya*.[1297] The Bayyaram tank inscription calls the Kakatiya chief Beta I (son of Gunda IV) *Garudamka*-Beta, and "Garuda" here appears to refer to the family's emblem.[1300] In Hindu mythology, Garuda is the vahana of god Vishnu. The Rashtrakutas and some other dynsaties of Deccan claimed descent from the Vrishni clan (associated with Vishnu's avatar Krishna), and had adopted Garuda as their royal insignia.[1296] According to Sastry, this corroborates the theory that the Kakatiyas were associated with the Rashtrakuta family.[1301] Sastry further speculates that the Kakatiyas may have adopted the Garuda symbol because of Jain influence: the yaksha of the Jain tirthankara Shantinatha is represented by the Garuda symbol.[1301]

Based on Ganapati-deva's Garavapadu inscription, which names Karikala Chola among the family's ancestors, epigraphist C.R.K. Charlu theorised that the Kakatiyas were a branch of the Telugu Cholas. However, no other Kakatiya record mentions Karikala, and unlike the Telugu Cholas, the Kakatiyas did not claim to belong to the Kashyapa-gotra. Therefore, Sastry dismisses Charlu's theory as untenable.[1299]

After the decline of the Rashtrakuta power, the Kakatiyas served as vassals of the Kalyani Chalukyas. After the decline of the Chalukya power in the 12th century, they assumed sovereignty by suppressing other Chalukya subordinates in the Telangana region.[1302]

As sovereigns

Prataparudra I

The 1149 Sanigaram inscription of Prola II is the last known record of the Kakatiyas as vassals. The 1163 Anumakonda inscription of Prataparudra I is the earliest known record that describes the Kakatiyas as a sovereign power.[1289]

According to Sastry, Prataparudra I reigned between around 1158 – 1195,[1285] while Sircar gives the dates 1163–1195. He was also known as Rudra Deva, Kakatiya Rudradeva, Venkata, and Venkataraya[1267,1303] He was the son of Prola II, who had made efforts to assert greater Kakatiya influence on territories in the western parts of the declining Western Chalukyan empire and who died in a battle fought against the Velanati Choda ruler Gonka II around 1157/1158 while doing so.[1304,1305] It was during Prataparudra's reign, in 1163, that the Kakatiyas declared an end to their status as feudatory chiefs of the Chalukyas.[1306] It is notable that inscriptions were henceforth written using the Kakatiya chiefs' vernacular Telugu rather than the Kannada language that had prevailed until that point.[1307]

Mahadeva succeeded Prataparudra I as king, reigning probably from 1195 to 1199.[1285]

Ganapati

Just as the Seuna and Hoysala dynasties took control of linguistically related areas during the 13th century, so too did the Kakatiyas under the rule of Ganapati.[1307] He is also known as Ganapathi Deva and, according to Sastry, reigned between 1199–1262; Sircar gives regnal dates of 1199–1260.[1285,1303] He significantly expanded Kakatiya lands during the 1230s when he launched a series of attacks outside the dynasty's traditional Telangana region and thus brought under Kakatiya control the Telugu-speaking lowland delta areas around the Godavari and Krishna rivers. The outcome in the case of all three dynasties, says historian Richard Eaton, was that they "catalysed processes of supralocal identity formation and community building".[1307]

Figure 118: *Ramappa Temple.*

The Kakatiya capital at Orugallu, established in 1195, was not forgotten while Ganapati expanded his territory. He organised the building of a massive granite wall around the city, complete with ramps designed for ease of access to its ramparts from within. A moat and numerous bastions were also constructed.[1308]

Ganapati was keen to bolster the dynasty's economy. He encouraged merchants to trade abroad, abolishing all taxes except for a fixed duty and supporting those who risked their lives to travel afar.[1309] He created the man-made Pakhal Lake.

Rudrama Devi

Rudrama Devi, also known as Rudramadevi, reigned around 1262–1289 CE (alternative dates: 1261–1295 CE) and is one of the few queens in Indian history.[1285,1310] Sources disagree regarding whether she was the widow of Ganapati or his daughter.[1311]

Marco Polo, who visited India probably some time around 1289–1293, made note of Rudrama Devi's rule and nature in flattering terms.[1312,1313] She continued the planned fortification of the capital, raising the height of Ganapati's wall as well as adding a second earthen curtain wall 1.5 miles (2.4 km) in diameter and with an additional 150 feet (46 m)-wide moat.[1308]

Figure 119: *Statue of Rudrama Devi.*

Rudrama was married to Virabhadra, an Eastern Chalukyan prince of Nidadavolu who had been selected for that purpose by her father.[1314] Having no son as an heir,[1308] Rudrama abdicated in favour of her grandson when it became apparent that the expansionist sultan Alauddin Khalji was encroaching on the Deccan and might in due course attack the Kakatiyas.[1311]

Prataparudra II

The earliest biography of Rudrama Devi's successor, Prataparudra II, is the *Prataparudra Caritramu*, dating from the 16th century.[1315] His reign began in 1289 (alternative date: 1295) and ended with the demise of the dynasty in 1323.[1285] It is described by Eaton as the "first chapter in a larger story" that saw the style of polity in the Deccan change from being regional kingdoms to transregional sultanates that survived until the arrival of the British East India Company in the 18th century.[1316]

Decline

The Kakatiya kingdom attracted the attention of the Delhi Sultanate ruler Alauddin Khalji because of the possibility for plunder.[1317] The first foray into the Kakatiya kingdom was made in 1303 and was a disaster due to the

Figure 120: *A replica of the Koh-i-Noor diamond. The diamond was originally owned by the Kakatiya dynasty.*

resistance of the Kakatiya army in the battle at Upparapalli.[1318,1319] In 1309 Alauddin sent a general, Malik Kafur, in an attempt to force Prataparudra into acceptance of a position subordinate to the sultanate at Delhi. Kafur organised a month-long siege of Orugallu that ended with success in February 1310. Prataparudra was forced to make various symbolic acts of obeisance designed to demonstrate his new position as a subordinate but, as was Alauddin's plan, he was not removed as ruler of the area but rather forced thereafter to pay annual tribute to Delhi.[1320] It was probably at this time that the Koh-i-Noor diamond passed from Kakatiya ownership to that of Alauddin, along with 20,000 horses and 100 elephants.[1317]

In 1311, Prataparudra formed a part of the sultanate forces that attacked the Pandyan empire in the south, and he took advantage of that situation to quell some of his vassals in Nellore who had seen his reduced status as an opportunity for independence. Later, though, in 1318, he failed to provide the annual tribute to Delhi, claiming that the potential for being attacked on the journey made it impossible. Alauddin's son Mubarak Shah responded by sending another of his generals, Khusrau Khan, to Orugallu with a force that bristled with technology previously unknown in the area, including trebuchet-like machines. Prataparudra had to submit once more, with his obeisance on this occasion being arranged by the sultanate to include a very public display whereby he bowed towards Delhi from the ramparts of Orugallu. The amount of his annual tribute was changed, becoming 100 elephants and 12,000 horses.[1321]

The new arrangements did not last long. Taking advantage of a revolution in Delhi that saw the Khalji dynasty removed and Ghiyasuddin Tughlaq installed as sultan, Prataparudra again asserted his independence in 1320. Tughlaq sent his son, Ulugh Khan, to defeat the defiant Kakatiya king in 1321. Khan's army was riven with internal dissension due to its containing factions from the Khalji and Tughluq camps. This caused the siege on this occasion to last much longer — six months, rather than the few weeks that had previously been the case. The attackers were initially repulsed and Khan's forces retreated to regroup in Devagiri. Prataparudra celebrated the apparent victory by opening up his grain stores for public feasting. Khan returned in 1323 with his revitalised and reinforced army and, with few supplies left, Prataparudra was forced into submission after a five-month siege. The unprepared and battle-weary army of Orugallu was finally defeated, and Orugallu was renamed as Sultanpur. It seems probable, from combining various contemporary and near-contemporary accounts, that Prataparudra committed suicide near to the Narmada River while being taken as a prisoner to Delhi.[1322,1323]

Characterization

Geography

The Kakatiya base was the city of Orugallu[1324] in the dry uplands of northern Telangana on the Deccan Plateau. From there they expanded their influence into Coastal Andhra, the delta between the Godavari and Krishna rivers that feed into the Bay of Bengal. According to Rao and Shulman, the latter contained a high proportion of Brahmins while the former was the haunt of "peasants, artisans and warriors".[1325] Under the Kakatiyas, cultural innovation often began in the uplands, was refined in the lowlands and then recycled back into the Deccan. This bi-directional flow of cultural influences brought into being a feeling of cultural affinity between those who spoke the Telugu language where nothing of that nature had previously existed.[1326] The unification of the distinct upland and lowland cultures was their most significant political achievement, achieved through a process of binding many locally powerful figures in allegiance to the empire.[1324]

The area of land under Kakatiya control reached its zenith around the 13th century CE during the rule of Ganapati Deva. By this time, South India and the Deccan was essentially under the aegis of four Hindu monarchies, of which the Kakatiyas were one.[1327] The four dynasties were in a constant state of warfare with each other, with the Kakatiyas eventually exercising control from close to Anagondi in the west to Kalyani in the north-east, and down to Kanei and Ganjam district in southern Orissa.[1328]

Architecture

A notable trend during the dynastic period was the construction of reservoirs for irrigation in the uplands, around 5000 of which were built by warrior families subordinate to the Kakatiyas. The dramatically altered the possibilities for development in the sparsely populated dry areas. Many of these edifices, often called "tanks", including the large examples at Pakala and Ramappa, are still used today.[1329]

Another notable architectural feature of the dynasty relates to temples. Even before the arrival of the dynasty, there were large, well-established and well-endowed Hindu places of worship in the relatively populous delta areas; however, the temples of the uplands, which were smaller and less cosmopolitan in origin and funding, did not exist until the Kakatiya period. In the lowlands, where Brahmins were numerous, the temples had long benefited from a desire to build social networks for the purposes of domestic and foreign trade, as well as for obtaining grazing rights in the face of competition; in the uplands, the endowment of the buildings was often associated with the construction and continued maintenance of reservoirs and enabled a different type of networking based on political hierarchies. The strengthening of those hierarchies, which was achieved in part by donating land for the temples and then attending worship, was necessary as the inland agrarian society grew rapidly in number and location.[1330]

Society

There is a disparity between analysis of inscriptions, of which the work of Cynthia Talbot has been in the vanguard, and the traditional works of Vedic Hinduism that described pre-colonial India in terms of a reverent and static society that was subject to the strictures of the caste system. Colonial British administrators found much that appealed to them in the latter works but the Kakatiya inscriptions of Andhra Pradesh, which depict a far wider range of society and events, suggest that the reality was far more fluid and very different from the idealised image.[1331]

Caste itself seems to have been of low importance as a social identifier.[1332] Even the Kakatiya kings, with one exception, considered themselves to be Shudras (in the ritual varna system).[1333] They were egalitarian in nature and promoted their subordinate warrior-chiefs who were similarly egalitarian and spurned the Kshatriya rank. Anyone, regardless of birth, could acquire the *nayaka* title to denote warrior status, and this they did. There is also little evidence that Kakatiya society paid much regard to caste identities, in the sense of *jāti*. Although occupation does appear to have been an important designator of social position, the inscriptions suggest that people were not bound to an occupation by birth.[1334,1335]

The population became more settled in geographic terms. The growth of an agricultural peasant class subsumed many tribal people who previously had been nomadic. The nexus of politics and military was a significant feature of the era, and the Kakatiya recruitment of peasants into the military did much to create a new warrior class, to develop social mobility and to extend the influence of the dynasty into areas of its kingdom that previously would have been untouched.[1336] The Kakatiya kings, and in particular the last two, encouraged an egalitarian ethos. The entrenched landed nobility that had existed prior to the dynasty found its power to be on the wane; the royal gifting of lands formerly in the possession of nobles to people of lesser status did much to effect this dilution.[1315]

Religion

Historian P.V.P. Sastry theorises that the early Kakatiya chiefs were followers of Jainism. A story in the *Siddheshvara-charita* states that Madhavavarman, an ancestor of the Kakatiyas, obtained military strength by the grace of goddess Padmakshi. The 1123 Govindapuram Jain inscription of Polavasa, another family of feudatory chiefs, contains a similar account of how their ancestor Madhavavarman obtained military strength by the grace of the Jain goddess Yaksheshvari.[1337]

According to tradition, Prola II was initiated into Shaivism by the Kalamukha preceptor Rameshvara Pandita, and established Shaivism as his family's religion. The Shaivism-affiliated personal names of the later Kakatiya kings (such as Rudra, Mahadeva, Harihara, and Ganapati) also indicate a shift towards Shaivism. This, according to Sastry, strengthens the theory that the early Kakatiya chiefs were Jains.[1301]

Genealogy

The following members of the Kakatiya family are known from epigraphic evidence. The rulers are children of their predecessors, unless otherwise specified.[1338]

Feudatory chiefs

- *Nripa* Venna, born in the family of Durjaya (r. c. 800-815)
- Gunda I (r. c. 815-?)
- Gunda II (r. c. ?-865)
- Gunda III (died before 900)
- *Nripati* Erra
- Betiya
- *Nripati* Gunda IV alias Pindi-Gunda (r. c. 955-995)
- *Nripati* Beta I alias Garuda Beta (r. c. 996-1051)
- Prola I (r. c. 1052-1076)
- Beta II alias Tribhuvanamalla (r. c. 1076-1108)
- Tribhuvanamalla Durgaraja (r. c. 1108-1116), son of Beta II
- Prola II (r. c. 1116-1157), son of Beta II, married Muppama
  - His children included Rudra, Mahadeva, Harihara, Ganapati and Repolla Durga

Sovereign rulers

- Rudra (r. c. 1158-1195), son of Prolla II, became a sovereign 1163
- Mahadeva (r. c. 1196-1199), son of Prolla II, married Bayyama
  - Had three children, including Ganapati-deva, Mailamba, and Kundamba
- Ganapati-deva (r. c. 1199-1262), married Somala-devi
  - Had two children, including Ganapamba (married Kota Beta) and Rudrama-devi
- Rudrama-devi (r. c. 1262-1289), married Chalukya Virabhadra
  - Had three children, including Mummadamba (married Kakati Mahadeva), Rudrama (married Yadava prince Ellana-deva), and Ruyyama (married Induluri Annaya-mantri)
- Prataparudra-deva (r. c. 1289-1323), son of Mummadamba, tributary to the Delhi Sultanate at times

Legacy

Tughlaq control of the area lasted only for around a decade.[1339] The fall of the Kakatiya dynasty resulted in both political and cultural disarray because of both disparate resistance to the sultanate and dissension within it.[1323] The structure of the Kakatiya polity disintegrated and their lands soon fell under the control of numerous families from communities such as the Reddies and Velamas.[1340] As early as 1330,[1341] Musunuri Nayaks who served as army chiefs for Kakatiya kingdom united the various Telugu clans and recovered Warangal from the Delhi Sultanate and ruled for half a century.[1342] Surrounded by more

Figure 121: *Ruins of the Kakatiya Kala Thoranam (Warangal Gate).*

significant states,[1340] by the 15th century these new entities had ceded to the Bahamani Sultanate and the Sangama dynasty, the latter of which evolved to become the Vijayanagara empire.[1343]

A brother of Prataparudra II, Annamaraja, has been associated with ruling what eventually became the princely state of Bastar during the British Raj period. This appears likely to be historical revisionism, dating from a genealogy published by the ruling family in 1703, because it records only eight generations spanning almost four centuries of rule. Such revisionism and tenuous claims of connection to the Kakatiyas was not uncommon because it was perceived as legitimising the right to rule and a warrior status. Talbot notes that there is a record of a brother called Annamadeva and that:

> *He is said to have left [Orugallu] for the northeast after anointing Prataparudra's son as king. Thus, the founder of the family fortunes in Bastar may very well have been a Telugu warrior from Telangana who was familiar with the prevalent legends about the Kakatiyas.*[1344]

According to Talbot and Eaton, a revisionist interpretation of Prataparudra II himself appeared much sooner, within a few years of his death, and for broadly similar reasons. A stone inscription dated 1330 mentions a Prolaya Nayaka, who was said to have restored order, as in Prataparudra days. He presented himself as a legitimate successor to Prataparudra, by portraying both of them as righteous monarchs, meanwhile reconstructing Prataparudra's life and career in a favorable way.[1345,1346] By 1420, Muslim rulers had become accommodated to the Deccan society, and strong dichotomies between Hindus and Muslims were no longer useful. Muslim rulers were no longer conceived as diametrically opposed to the figure of Prataparudra, but rather as rulers of equal status.[1347]

This type of revisionism, which Talbot describes as "social memories" and which persist to the present day,[1348] reappeared in the 16th century with the *Prataparudra Caritramu* hagiography, which claimed him to be the founder of the *padmanayaka* class of Telugu warrior and provided the elite of the Vijayanagara empire with what Talbot has described as a "charter of legitimacy". This work claimed, contrary to all reasonable evidence, that he did not die after being taken prisoner but instead met with the sultan, was recognised as being an avatar of Shiva, and allowed to return to Orugallu. Once back home, the *Prataparudra Caritamu* says, he released the *padmanayakas* from their allegiance to him and told them to become independent kings. The work also claims Vijayanagara to be an ally of Prataparudra, which is clearly anachronistic but served the purpose of elevating the role of the *padmanayakas*, whom it claimed to be ultimately subordinate to Vijayanagara during his time.[1349]

References

Footnotes

Citations

Bibliography <templatestyles src="Template:Refbegin/styles.css" />

- Asher, Catherine B.; Talbot, Cynthia, eds. (2006), "The expansion of Turkic power, 1180–1350", *India before Europe*[1350], Cambridge University Press, ISBN 978-0-52180-904-7
- Chakravarti, Ranabir (1991), "Horse Trade and Piracy at Tana (Thana, Maharashtra, India): Gleanings from Marco Polo", *Journal of the Economic and Social History of the Orient*, **34** (3): 159–182, doi: 10.2307/3632243[1351], JSTOR 3632243[1352], (Subscription required (help))
- Chattopadhyaya, B. D. (1998), *Representing the Other? Sanskrit Sources and the Muslims*, New Delhi: Manohar, ISBN 8173042527
- Desai, V. R. M. (1962), "Savings in Ancient Hindu Polity", *The Indian Journal of Political Science*, **23** (1/4): 268–276, JSTOR 41853935[1353], (Subscription required (help))
- Eaton, Richard M. (2005), *A Social History of the Deccan: 1300–1761*[1354], Cambridge University Press, ISBN 978-0-52125-484-7
- Jackson, Peter (2003), *The Delhi Sultanate: A Political and Military History*[1355] (Reprinted ed.), Cambridge University Press, ISBN 978-0-52154-329-3

- Kalia, Ravi (1994), *Bhubaneswar: From a Temple Town to a Capital City*[1356], Southern Illinois University Press – via Questia, (Subscription required (help))
- Kulke, Hermann; Rothermund, Dietmar, eds. (2004) [1986], *A History of India* (4th ed.), Routledge, ISBN 978-0-41532-920-0
- Prasad, G. Durga (1988), *History of the Andhras up to 1565 A. D.*[1357] (PDF), Guntur: P. G. Publishers
- Rao, P. (1994), *History and Culture of Andhra Pradesh*, Sterling
- Rao, Velcheru Narayana (2003), "Court, Temple, and Public", in Pollock, Sheldon, *Literary Cultures in History: Reconstructions from South Asia*[1358], University of California Press – via Questia, (Subscription required (help))
- Rao, Velcheru Narayana; Shulman, David, eds. (2002), *Classical Telugu Poetry: An Anthology*[1359], University of California Press – via Questia, (Subscription required (help))
- Rao, Velcheru Narayana; Shulman, David (2012), *Srinatha: The Poet Who Made Gods and Kings*[1360], Oxford University Press – via Questia, (Subscription required (help))
- Rubiés, Joan-Pau (2000), *Travel and Ethnology in the Renaissance: South India through European Eyes, 1250–1625*[1361], Cambridge University Press – via Questia, (Subscription required (help))
- Sastry, P. V. Parabhrama (1978). N. Ramesan, ed. *The Kākatiyas of Warangal*[1362]. Hyderabad: Government of Andhra Pradesh. OCLC 252341228[1363].
- Sharma, R. S. (1992). *A Comprehensive History of India*[1364]. Orient Longmans. p. 234. ISBN 978-81-7007-121-1.
- Sircar, D. C. (1979), *Some Epigraphical Records of the Medieval Period from Eastern India*[1365], Abhinav Publications, ISBN 978-8-17017-096-9
- Sircar, D. C. (2008) [1968], *Studies in Indian Coins*[1366] (Reprinted ed.), Motilal Banarsidass, ISBN 978-8-12082-973-2
- Subrahmanyam, Sanjay (1998), "Hearing Voices: Vignettes of Early Modernity in South Asia, 1400–1750", *Daedalus*, **127** (3): 75–104, JSTOR 20027508[1367], (Subscription required (help))
- Suryanarayana, Kolluru (1986), *History of the Minor Chaḷukya Families in Medieval Andhradesa*[1368], B. R. Publishing, ISBN 978-8-17018-330-3
- Talbot, Austin Cynthia (2001), *Pre-colonial India in Practice: Society, Region, and Identity in Medieval Andhra*[1369], Oxford University Press, ISBN 978-0-19803-123-9
- Ventakaramanayya, N. (1942), *The Early Muslim Expansion in South India*, University of Madras

Further reading

 Wikimedia Commons has media related to *Kakatiya dynasty*.

- Talbot, Cynthia (May 1991). "Temples, Donors, and Gifts: Patterns of Patronage in Thirteenth-Century South India". *The Journal of Asian Studies*. **50** (2): 308–340. doi: 10.2307/2057210[1370]. JSTOR 2057210[1371]. (Subscription required (help)).

Sena dynasty

Sena Empire	
সেন সাম্রাজ্য *Shen Shamrajjo*	
CE 1070–CE 1230	
Capital	Nabadwip
Languages	Sanskrit
Religion	Hinduism Buddhism
Government	Monarchy
King	
• 1070–1096 AD	Hemanta Sena
• 1159–1179 AD	Ballala Sena
• 1225–1230 AD	Keshava Sena
Historical era	Classical India
• Established	CE 1070
• Disestablished	CE 1230
Preceded by	Succeeded by
Pala Empire	Deva dynasty

Part of a series on the
History of Bengal

- v
- t
- e[1372]

The **Sena Empire** (Bengali: সেন সাম্রাজ্য, *Shen Shamrajjo*) was a Hindu dynasty during the Late Classical period on the Indian subcontinent, that ruled from Bengal through the 11th and 12th centuries. The empire at its peak covered much of the north-eastern region of the Indian subcontinent. The rulers of the Sena Dynasty traced their origin to the south Indian region of Karnataka.[1373]

The dynasty's founder was Samanta Sena. After him came Hemanta Sena who usurped power and styled himself king in 1095 AD. His successor Vijaya Sena (ruled from 1096 AD to 1159 AD) helped lay the foundations of the dynasty, and had an unusually long reign of over 60 years. Ballala Sena conquered Gaur from the Pala, became the ruler of the Bengal Delta, and made Nabadwip the capital as well. Ballala Sena married Ramadevi a princess of the Western Chalukya Empire which indicates that the Sena rulers maintained close social contact with south India.[1374] Lakshmana Sena succeeded Ballala Sena in 1179, ruled Bengal for approximately 20 years, and expanded the Sena Empire to Assam, Odisha, Bihar and probably to Varanasi. In 1203–1204 AD, the Turkic general Bakhtiyar Khalji attacked Nabadwip. Khalji defeated Lakshman Sen and captured northwest Bengal – although Eastern Bengal remained under Sena control.

Origins

The political space after the decline of the Pala power in Bengal was occupied by the Senas whose king Vijayasena succeeded in conquering a large part of Pala territory. The Senas were the supporters of orthodox Hinduism. The dynasty traces its origin to the South, to the Western Chalukya Empire of southern India.[1375] Theres is a record of a Western Chalukya invasion during the reign of Someshvara I led by his son Vikramaditya VI who defeated the kings of Gauda and Kamarupa.[1376,1377] This invasion of the Kannada ruler brought bodies of his countrymen from Karnataka into Bengal which explains the origin of the Sena Dynasty.

The founder of the Sena rule was Samantasena who described himself as a Kshatriya of Karnata (Karnataka). He himself stated that he fought the outlaws of Karnata and later turned an ascetic.Wikipedia:Citation needed The inscriptions of the Sena kings mention them as Brahma-Kshatriyas or Kshatriyas. Otherwise, sources have identified them with the Vaidya as well as the Ambashtha caste or sub-caste, considered as a mixed caste, being born of Brahmin father and Vaishya mother, and they married with and were identified with the Bengali Vaidyas (commonly known as Baidyas in Bengal) in Vaidya *Kula-panjikas* (family-tree accounts).

Sena Dynasty had ruled Bengal for little over a century (c 1097–1225). The emergence of the dynasty, which supplanted the Palas in Bengal towards the close of 11th century A.D., had constituted a significant epoch in the history of ancient India. Taking advantage of the revolt of Samantachakra in Varendra during the reign of Mahipala II, Vijayasena, founder of the Sena dynasty, gradually consolidated his position in western Bengal and ultimately assumed an independent position during the reign of Madanapala. One important aspect of Sena rule in Bengal is that the whole territory of Bengal was brought under a single rule for the first time. It is likely impossible to provide definite information to the question as to how the family entered Bengal. The Sena records also are amazingly silent about this.

The Sena kings claim in their own inscriptions that they are Brahma-Kshatriyas. Their remote ancestor was one Virasena, whose name was supposed to have been mentioned in Puranas. The "Deopara Inscription" of the Senas also traces the Sena ancestry from Virasena. Since there are no authentic records available still, a keen controversy prevails among scholars regarding origin of the Senas.Wikipedia:Citation needed

Like the origin of the Senas, their early history or circumstances, which led them to concentrate in Bengal is also still unknown. It has been presumed by historians that the Senas came to Bengal on the eve of the invading army led by the Chalukya kings Vikramaditya VI and Someswara III. Some scholars

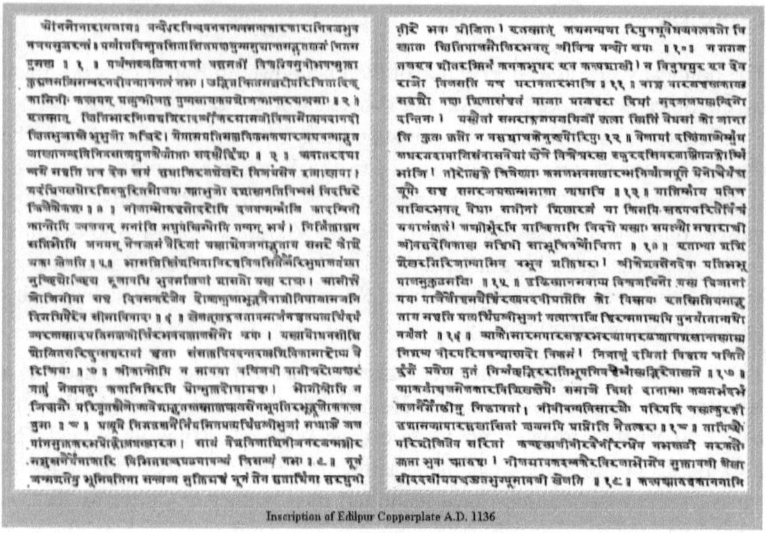

Figure 122: *Edilpur Copperplate*

have also suggested that when Rajendra Chola's army had invaded Bengal, the Senas had accompanied them. According to some other historians, a few Karnataka officials, who were subordinate to the Pala kings, had established their independent kingdom in the region of Radha, taking advantage of the weakness of the Pala powers. Those Karnataka chiefs might have arrived in Bengal in wake of the Chalukya invasion and had settled into a kingdom of their own. According to historians Samantasena was such a chief who had established his independent kingdom in the Radha region of Bengal.

Samantasena was a scion of the Sena family, who had distinguished himself through various warfares in South India. He had settled in Radha in Bengal, at an old age. He had also laid the foundation of the Sena family in Bengal. His son Hemantasena carved out an important kingdom in Radha, taking advantage of the decline of the Pala Empire. From their base in Radha, the Senas ultimately extended their powers over the whole of Bengal.

Inscriptions

Sena dynasty
1070 CE–1230 CE

Samanta Sena	–
Hemanta Sena	(1070 – 1096)
Vijaya Sena	(1095 – 1158)
Ballala Sena	(1158 – 1179)
Lakshmana Sena	(1179 – 1206)
Vishvarupa Sena	(1206 – 1225)
Keshava Sena	(1225 – 1230)

- v
- t
- e[1378]

A copperplate was found in the Adilpur or Edilpur pargana of Faridpur District in 1838 A.D. and was acquired by the Asiatic Society of Bengal, but now the copperplate is missing from collection. An account of the copperplate was published in the *Dacca Review* and *Epigraphic Indica*. The copperplate inscription is written in Sanskrit and in Ganda character, and dated 3rd jyaistha of 1136 samval, or 1079 A.D. In the Asiatic Society's proceeding for January 1838, an account of the copperplate states that three villages were given to a Brahman in the third year of Keshava Sena. The grant was given with the landlord rights, which include the power of punishing the chandrabhandas or Sundarbans, a race that lived in the forest. The land was granted in the village of Leliya in the Kumaratalaka mandala, which is situated in shatata-padamavati-visaya. The copperplate of Keshava Sena records that the king Vallala Sena carried away, from the enemies, the goddesses of fortune on palanquins (Shivaka), which elephant tusk staff supported; and also states that Vallala Sena's son, Lakshmana Sena (1179–1205), erected pillars of victory and sacrificial posts at Varanasi, Allahabad, and Adon Coast of the South Sea. The copperplate also describes the villages with smooth fields growing excellent paddy, the dancing and music in ancient Bengal, and ladies adorned with blooming flowers. The Edilpur copperplate of Keshava Sena records that the king made a grant in favour of Nitipathaka Isvaradeva Sarman for the inscae of the subhavarsha.

The Deopara Prashasti is a stone inscription eulogising the Sena kings, particularly Vijaya Sena, composed by the court poet Umapati Dhara.

Society

The Sena rulers consolidated the caste system in Bengal. Although Bengal borrowed from the caste system of Mithila, caste was not so strong in Bengal as in Mithila.[1379]

Architecture

The Sena dynasty is famous for building Hindu temples and monasteries, which include the renowned Dhakeshwari Temple in what is now Dhaka, Bangladesh.

In Kashmir, the dynasty also likely built a temple knows as Sankara Gaureshwara.

Literature

The Sena rulers were also great patrons of literature. During the Pala dynasty and the Sena dynasty, major growth in Bengali was witnessed. Some Bengali authors believe that Jayadeva, the famous Sanskrit poet and author of Gita Govinda, was one of the *Pancharatnas* (five gems) in the court of Lakshmana Sena. Dhoyin – himself an eminent court poet of Sena dynasty – mentions nine gems (ratna) in the court of Lakshmana Sena, among whom were:

- Govardhana
- Sarana
- Jayadeva
- Umapati
- Dhoyi/ Dhoyin Kaviraja

Legacy

After the Sena dynasty, the Deva dynasty ruled in eastern Bengal. The Deva dynasty was probably the last independent Hindu dynasty of Bengal.

References

Sources <templatestyles src="Template:Refbegin/styles.css" />

- Early History of India 3rd and revised edition by Vincent A Smith

External links

- Chowdhury, AM (2012). "Sena Dynasty"[1380]. In Islam, Sirajul; Jamal, Ahmed A. *Banglapedia: National Encyclopedia of Bangladesh* (Second ed.). Asiatic Society of Bangladesh.

| Preceded by **Pala dynasty** | **Bengal dynasty** | Succeeded by **Deva dynasty** |

Late medieval

Delhi Sultanate

Delhi Sultanate	
پادشاهی دهلی	
1206–1526	
Flag	
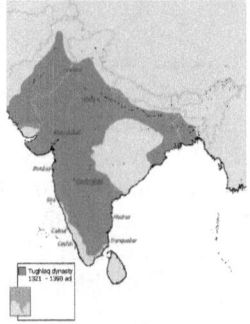 Delhi Sultanate reached its zenith under the Turko-Indian Tughlaq dynasty.	
Capital	• Lahore (1206–1210) • Badayun (1210–1214) • Delhi (1214–1327) • Daulatabad (1327–1334) • Delhi (1334–1506) • Agra (1506–1526)
Languages	Persian (official), Hindavi (1451–1526)
Religion	Sunni Islam
Government	Sultanate

Sultan	
• 1206–1210	Qutb al-Din Aibak (first)
• 1517–1526	Ibrahim Lodi (last)
Historical era	Middle Ages
• Independence	12 June 1206
• Battle of Amroha	20 December 1305
• Battle of Panipat	21 April 1526
	Preceded by **Succeeded by** Ghurid dynasty Gahadavala Chandela dynasty Paramara dynasty Deva dynasty Mughal Empire Seuna (Yadava) dynasty Bengal Sultanate Kakatiya dynasty Gujarat Sultanate Musunuri Nayaks Vaghela dynasty Yajvapala dynasty
Today part of	• Bangladesh • India • Nepal • Pakistan

The **Delhi Sultanate** (Persian: سلطان دهلی, Urdu: دہلی سلطنت) was a Muslim sultanate based mostly in Delhi that stretched over large parts of the Indian subcontinent for 320 years (1206–1526).[1381,1382] Five dynasties ruled over the Delhi Sultanate sequentially: the Mamluk dynasty (1206–90), the Khalji dynasty (1290–1320), the Tughlaq dynasty (1320–1414), the Sayyid dynasty (1414–51), and the Lodi dynasty (1451–1526). The sultanate is noted for being one of the few states to repel an attack by the Mongol Empire,[1383] and enthroned one of the few female rulers in Islamic history, Razia Sultana, who reigned from 1236 to 1240.[1384]

Qutb al-Din Aibak, a former Turkic Mamluk slave of Muhammad Ghori, was the first sultan of Delhi, and his Mamluk dynasty conquered large areas of northern India. Afterwards, the Khalji dynasty was also able to conquer most of central India, but both failed to conquer the whole of the Indian subcontinent. The sultanate reached the peak of its geographical reach during the Tughlaq dynasty, occupying most of the Indian subcontinent. This was followed by decline due to Hindu reconquests, states such as the Vijayanagara Empire asserting independence, and new Muslim sultanates such as the Bengal Sultanate breaking off.[1385,1386]

During and in the Delhi Sultanate, there was a synthesis of Indian civilization with that of Islamic civilization, and the further integration of the Indian subcontinent with a growing world system and wider international networks spanning large parts of Afro-Eurasia, which had a significant impact on Indian culture and society, as well as the wider world. The time of their rule included the earliest forms of Indo-Islamic architecture,[1387,1388] increased growth rates in India's population and economy, and the emergence of the Hindi-Urdu language. The Delhi Sultanate was also responsible for repelling the Mongol Empire's potentially devastating invasions of India in the 13th and 14th centuries. However, the Delhi Sultanate also caused large scale destruction and desecration of temples in the Indian subcontinent.[1389] In 1526, the Sultanate was conquered and succeeded by the Mughal Empire.

Background

The context behind the rise of the Delhi Sultanate in India was part of a wider trend affecting much of the Asian continent, including the whole of southern and western Asia: the influx of nomadic Turkic peoples from the Central Asian steppes. This can be traced back to the 9th century, when the Islamic Caliphate began fragmenting in the Middle East, where Muslim rulers in rival states began enslaving non-Muslim nomadic Turks from the Central Asian steppes, and raising many of them to become loyal military slaves called Mamluks. Soon, Turks were migrating to Muslim lands and becoming Islamicized. Many of the Turkic Mamluk slaves eventually rose up to become rulers, and conquered large parts of the Muslim world, establishing Mamluk Sultanates from Egypt to Afghanistan, before turning their attention to the Indian subcontinent.

It is also part of a longer trend predating the spread of Islam. Like other settled, agrarian societies in history, those in the Indian subcontinent have been attacked by nomadic tribes throughout its long history. In evaluating the impact of Islam on the subcontinent, one must note that the northwestern subcontinent was a frequent target of tribes raiding from Central Asia in the pre-Islamic era. In that sense, the Muslim intrusions and later Muslim invasions were not dissimilar to those of the earlier invasions during the 1st millennium.[1390]

By 962 AD, Hindu and Buddhist kingdoms in South Asia were under a wave of raids from Muslim armies from Central Asia.[1391] Among them was Mahmud of Ghazni, the son of a Turkic Mamluk military slave, who raided and plundered kingdoms in north India from east of the Indus river to west of Yamuna river seventeen times between 997 and 1030.[1392] Mahmud of Ghazni raided the treasuries but retracted each time, only extending Islamic rule into western Punjab.[1393,1394]

The wave of raids on north Indian and western Indian kingdoms by Muslim warlords continued after Mahmud of Ghazni.[1395] The raids did not establish or extend permanent boundaries of their Islamic kingdoms. The Ghurid sultan Mu'izz ad-Din Muhammad Ghori, commonly known as Muhammad of Ghor, began a systematic war of expansion into north India in 1173.[1396] He sought to carve out a principality for himself by expanding the Islamic world.[1392,1397] Muhammad of Ghor sought a Sunni Islamic kingdom of his own extending east of the Indus river, and he thus laid the foundation for the Muslim kingdom called the Delhi Sultanate.[1392] Some historians chronicle the Delhi Sultanate from 1192 due to the presence and geographical claims of Muhammad Ghori in South Asia by that time.[1398]

Ghori was assassinated in 1206, by Ismā'īlī Shia Muslims in some accounts or by Hindu Khokhars in others.[1399] After the assassination, one of Ghori's slaves (or mamluks, Arabic: مملوك), the Turkic Qutb al-Din Aibak, assumed power, becoming the first Sultan of Delhi.[1392]

Sultans of Delhi Sultanate

Delhi Sultanate
Ruling dynasties

- v
- t
- e[1400]

Sultans (Kings/Rulers)	King in	Death	Note
Qutb-ud-din Aibak	1206	1210	First Sultan
Aram Shah	1210	1211	
Iltutmish	1211	1236	
Rukn-ud-din Firuz	1236	1236	
Razia Sultan	1236	1240	Women Ruler
Muiz ud din Bahram	1240	1243	
Ala ud din Masud	1243	1249	
Nasir ud din Mahmud	1249	1266	

Ghiyas ud din Balban	1266	1287
Muiz ud din Qaiqabad	1287	1290
Jalaluddin Khalji	1290	1296
Alauddin Khalji	1296	1316
Shihabuddin Omar	1316	1316
Qutb-ud-din Mubarak	1316	1320
Khusrau Khan	1320	1321

Dynasties

Mamluk / Slave

Qutb al-Din Aibak, a former slave of Mu'izz ad-Din Muhammad Ghori (known more commonly as Muhammad of Ghor), was the first ruler of the Delhi Sultanate. Aibak was of Cuman-Kipchak (Turkic) origin, and due to his lineage, his dynasty is known as the Mamluk (Slave) dynasty (not to be confused with the Mamluk dynasty of Iraq or the Mamluk dynasty of Egypt).[1401] Aibak reigned as the Sultan of Delhi for four years, from 1206 to 1210.

After Aibak died, Aram Shah assumed power in 1210, but he was assassinated in 1211 by Shams ud-Din Iltutmish.[1402] Iltutmish's power was precarious, and a number of Muslim amirs (nobles) challenged his authority as they had been supporters of Qutb al-Din Aibak. After a series of conquests and brutal executions of opposition, Iltutmish consolidated his power.[1403] His rule was challenged a number of times, such as by Qubacha, and this led to a series of wars.[1404] Iltumish conquered Multan and Bengal from contesting Muslim rulers, as well as Ranthambore and Siwalik from the Hindu rulers. He also attacked, defeated, and executed Taj al-Din Yildiz, who asserted his rights as heir to Mu'izz ad-Din Muhammad Ghori.[1405] Iltutmish's rule lasted till 1236. Following his death, the Delhi Sultanate saw a succession of weak rulers, disputing Muslim nobility, assassinations, and short-lived tenures. Power shifted from Rukn ud-Din Firuz to Razia Sultana and others, until Ghiyas ud-Din Balban came to power and ruled from 1266 to 1287.[1404] He was succeeded by 17-year-old Muiz ud-Din Qaiqabad, who appointed Jalal ud-Din Firuz Khalji as the commander of the army. Khalji assassinated Qaiqabad and assumed power, thus ending the Mamluk dynasty and starting the Khalji dynasty.

Qutb al-Din Aibak initiated the construction of the Qutub Minar and the Quwwat-ul-Islam (Might of Islam) Mosque, now a UNESCO world heritage site. It was built from the remains of twenty seven demolished Hindu and Jain temples. The Qutub Minar Complex or Qutb Complex was expanded by Iltutmish, and later by Ala ud-Din Khalji (the second ruler of the Khalji dynasty)

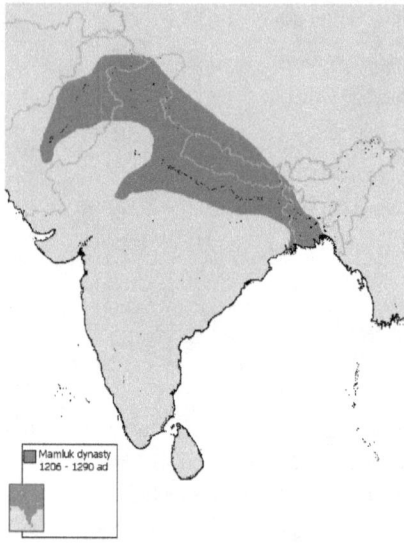

Figure 123: *Delhi Sultanate from 1206-1290 AD under the Mamluk dynasty.*

in the early 14th century.[1406,1407] During the Mamluk dynasty, many nobles from Afghanistan and Persia migrated and settled in India, as West Asia came under Mongol siege.

Khaljis

The Khalji dynasty was of Turko-Afghan heritage. They were originally of Turkic origin. They had long been settled in present-day Afghanistan before proceeding to Delhi in India. The name "Khalji" refers to an Afghan village or town known as Qalat-e Khalji (Fort of Ghilji). Sometimes they were treated by others as ethnic Afghans due to their intermarraiges with local Afghans, adoption of Afghan habits and customs. As a result of this, the dynasty is sometimes referred to as Turko-Afghan. The dynasty later also had Indian ancestry, through Jhatyapali (daughter of Ramachandra of Devagiri), wife of Alauddin Khalji and mother of Shihabuddin Omar.

The first ruler of the Khalji dynasty was Jalal ud-Din Firuz Khalji. Firuz Khalji had already gathered enough support among the Afghans for taking over the crown.[1408] He came to power in 1290 after killing the last ruler of the Mamluk dynasty, Muiz ud-Din Qaiqabad, with the support of Afghan and Turkic nobles. He was around 70 years old at the time of his ascension, and was known as a mild-mannered, humble and kind monarch to the general public. Jalal

Figure 124: *Alai Gate and Qutub Minar were built during the Mamluk and Khalji dynasties of the Delhi Sultanate.*

ud-Din Firuz was of Turko Afghan origin,[1409,1410,1411] and ruled for 6 years before he was murdered in 1296 by his nephew and son-in-law Juna Muhammad Khalji, who later came to be known as Ala ud-Din Khalji.

Ala ud-Din began his military career as governor of Kara province, from where he led two raids on Malwa (1292) and Devagiri (1294) for plunder and loot. His military campaigning returned to these lands as well other south Indian kingdoms after he assumed power. He conquered Gujarat, Ranthambore, Chittor, and Malwa.[1412] However, these victories were cut short because of Mongol attacks and plunder raids from the northwest. The Mongols withdrew after plundering and stopped raiding northwest parts of the Delhi Sultanate.[1413]

After the Mongols withdrew, Ala ud-Din Khalji continued expanding the Delhi Sultanate into southern India with the help of generals such as Malik Kafur and Khusro Khan. They collected lots of war booty (anwatan) from those they defeated.[1414] His commanders collected war spoils and paid ghanima (Arabic: الغَنيمَة, a tax on spoils of war), which helped strengthen the Khalji rule. Among the spoils was the Warangal loot that included the famous Koh-i-noor diamond.[1415]

Ala ud-Din Khalji changed tax policies, raising agriculture taxes from 20% to 50% (payable in grain and agricultural produce), eliminating payments and commissions on taxes collected by local chiefs, banned socialization among his officials as well as inter-marriage between noble families to help prevent any opposition forming against him, and he cut salaries of officials, poets, and scholars. These tax policies and spending controls strengthened his treasury to pay the keep of his growing army; he also introduced price controls on all agriculture produce and goods in the kingdom, as well as controls on where, how, and by whom these goods could be sold. Markets called "shahana-i-mandi" were created.[1416] Muslim merchants were granted exclusive permits and monopoly in these "mandis" to buy and resell at official prices. No one other than these merchants could buy from farmers or sell in cities. Those found violating these "mandi" rules were severely punished, often by mutilation. Taxes collected in the form of grain were stored in the kingdom's storage. During famines that followed, these granaries ensured sufficient food for the army.

Historians note Ala ud-Din Khalji as being a tyrant. Anyone Ala ud-Din suspected of being a threat to this power was killed along with the women and children of that family. In 1298, between 15,000 and 30,000 people near Delhi, who had recently converted to Islam, were slaughtered in a single day, due to fears of an uprising.[1417] He is also known for his cruelty against kingdoms he defeated in battle.

After Ala ud-Din's death in 1316, his eunuch general Malik Kafur, who was born in a Hindu family in India and had converted to Islam, tried to assume power. He lacked the support of Persian and Turkic nobility and was subsequently killed.[1418] The last Khalji ruler was Ala ud-Din Khalji's 18-year-old son Qutb ud-Din Mubarak Shah Khalji, who ruled for four years before he was killed by Khusro Khan, another of Ala ud-Din's generals. Khusro Khan's reign lasted only a few months, when Ghazi Malik, later to be called Ghiyath al-Din Tughlaq, killed him and assumed power in 1320, thus ending the Khalji dynasty and starting the Tughlaq dynasty.

Tughlaq

The Tughlaq dynasty lasted from 1320 to nearly the end of the 14th century. The first ruler Ghazi Malik rechristened himself as Ghiyath al-Din Tughlaq and is also referred to in scholarly works as Tughlak Shah. He was of Turko-Indian origins; his father was a Turkic slave and his mother was a Hindu. Ghiyath al-Din ruled for five years and built a town near Delhi named Tughlaqabad.Wikipedia:Citation needed According to some historians such as Vincent Smith,[1419] he was killed by his son Juna Khan, who then assumed power in 1325. Juna Khan rechristened himself as Muhammad bin Tughlaq and ruled for 26 years.[1420] During his rule, Delhi Sultanate reached its peak in terms of geographical reach, covering most of the Indian subcontinent.[1421]

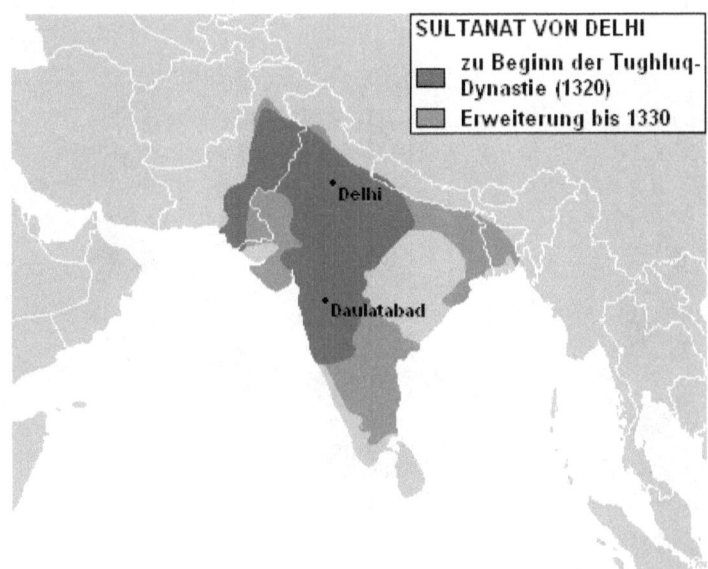

Figure 125: *Delhi Sultanate from 1321-1330 AD under the Tughlaq dynasty. After 1330, various regions rebelled against the Sultanate and the kingdom shrank.*

Muhammad bin Tughlaq was an intellectual, with extensive knowledge of the Quran, Fiqh, poetry and other fields. He was also deeply suspicious of his kinsmen and wazirs (ministers), extremely severe with his opponents, and took decisions that caused economic upheaval. For example, he ordered minting of coins from base metals with face value of silver coins - a decision that failed because ordinary people minted counterfeit coins from base metal they had in their houses and used them to pay taxes and jizya.

On another occasion, after becoming upset by some accounts, or to run the Sultanate from the center of India by other accounts, Muhammad bin Tughlaq ordered the transfer of his capital from Delhi to Devagiri in modern-day Maharashtra (renaming it to Daulatabad), by forcing the mass migration of Delhi's population. Those who refused were killed. One blind person who failed to move to Daulatabad was dragged for the entire journey of 40 days - the man died, his body fell apart, and only his tied leg reached Daulatabad. The capital move failed because Daulatabad was arid and did not have enough drinking water to support the new capital. The capital then returned to Delhi. Nevertheless, Muhammad bin Tughlaq's orders affected history as a large number of Delhi Muslims who came to the Deccan area did not return to Delhi to live near Muhammad bin Tughlaq. This influx of the then-Delhi residents into the Deccan region led to a growth of Muslim population in central and southern

Figure 126: *Muhammad bin Tughlaq moved his capital to the Deccan Plateau, and build a new capital called Daulatabad (shown). He later reversed his decision because Daulatabad lacked the fresh water supply that Delhi had.*

Figure 127: *A base metal coin of Muhammad bin Tughlaq that led to an economic collapse.*

India. Muhammad bin Tughlaq's adventures in the Deccan region also marked campaigns of destruction and desecration of Hindu and Jain temples, for example the Swayambhu Shiva Temple and the Thousand Pillar Temple.

Revolts against Muhammad bin Tughlaq began in 1327, continued over his reign, and over time the geographical reach of the Sultanate shrunk. The Vijayanagara Empire originated in southern India as a direct response to attacks from the Delhi Sultanate.,[1422] and liberated south India from the Delhi Sultanate's rule.[1423] In 1337, Muhammad bin Tughlaq ordered an attack on China,Wikipedia:Citation needed sending part of his forces over the Himalayas. Few survived the journey, and they were executed upon their return for failing. During his reign, state revenues collapsed from his policies such as the base metal coins from 1329-1332. To cover state expenses, he sharply raised taxes. Those who failed to pay taxes were hunted and executed. Famines, widespread poverty, and rebellion grew across the kingdom. In 1338 his own nephew rebelled in Malwa, whom he attacked, caught, and flayed alive.Wikipedia:Citation needed By 1339, the eastern regions under local Muslim governors and southern parts led by Hindu kings had revolted and declared independence from the Delhi Sultanate. Muhammad bin Tughlaq did not have the resources or support to respond to the shrinking kingdom.[1424] The historian Walford chronicled Delhi and most of India faced severe famines during Muhammad bin Tughlaq's rule in the years after the base metal coin experiment.[1425,1426] By 1347, the Bahmani Sultanate had become an independent and competing Muslim kingdom in Deccan region of South Asia.

The Tughlaq dynasty is remembered for its architectural patronage, particularly for ancient *lats* (pillars, left image), dated to be from the 3rd century BC, and of Buddhist and Hindu origins. The Sultanate initially wanted to use the pillars to make mosque minarets. Firuz Shah Tughlaq decided otherwise and had them installed near mosques. The meaning of Brahmi script on the pillar at right was unknown in Firuz Shah's time.[1427] The inscription was deciphered by James Prinsep in 1837; the pillar script of Emperor Ashoka asked people of his and future generations to seek a dharmic (virtuous) life, use persuasion in religion, grant freedom from religious persecution, stop all killing, and be compassionate to all living beings.

Muhammad bin Tughlaq died in 1351 while trying to chase and punish people in Gujarat who were rebelling against the Delhi Sultanate. He was succeeded by Firuz Shah Tughlaq (1351–1388), who tried to regain the old kingdom boundary by waging a war with Bengal for 11 months in 1359. However, Bengal did not fall. Firuz Shah ruled for 37 years. His reign attempted to stabilize the food supply and reduce famines by commissioning an irrigation canal from the Yamuna river. An educated sultan, Firuz Shah left a memoir.[1428] In it he wrote that he banned the practice of torture, such as amputations, tearing out of eyes, sawing people alive, crushing people's bones as punishment, pouring molten lead into throats, setting people on fire, driving nails into hands and feet, among others.[1429] He also wrote that he did not tolerate attempts by Rafawiz Shia Muslim and Mahdi sects from proselytizing people into their faith, nor did he tolerate Hindus who tried to rebuild temples that his armies had destroyed.[1430] As punishment for proselytizing, Firuz Shah put many Shias, Mahdi, and Hindus to death (siyasat). Firuz Shah Tughlaq also lists his accomplishments to include converting Hindus to Sunni Islam by announcing an exemption from taxes and jizya for those who convert, and by lavishing new converts with presents and honours. Simultaneously, he raised taxes and jizya, assessing it at three levels, and stopping the practice of his predecessors who had historically exempted all Hindu Brahmins from the jizya.[1431] He also vastly expanded the number of slaves in his service and those of Muslim nobles. The reign of Firuz Shah Tughlaq was marked by reduction in extreme forms of torture, eliminating favours to select parts of society, but also increased intolerance and persecution of targeted groups.

The death of Firuz Shah Tughlaq created anarchy and disintegration of the kingdom. The last rulers of this dynasty both called themselves Sultan from 1394 to 1397: Nasir ud-Din Mahmud Shah Tughlaq, the grandson of Firuz Shah Tughlaq who ruled from Delhi, and Nasir ud-Din Nusrat Shah Tughlaq, another relative of Firuz Shah Tughlaq who ruled from Firozabad, which was a few miles from Delhi.[1432] The battle between the two relatives continued till Timur's invasion in 1398. Timur, also known as Tamerlane in Western scholarly literature, was the Turkic ruler of the Timurid Empire. He became aware of the weakness and quarreling of the rulers of the Delhi Sultanate, so he marched with his army to Delhi, plundering and killing all the way.[1433] Estimates for the massacre by Timur in Dehli range from 100,000 to 200,000 people.[1434,1435] Timur had no intention of staying in or ruling India. He looted the lands he crossed, then plundered and burnt Delhi. Over five days, Timur and his army raged a massacre.Wikipedia:Citation needed Then he collected and carried the wealth, captured women and slaves (particularly skilled artisans), and returned to Samarkand. The people and lands within the Delhi Sultanate were left in a state of anarchy, chaos, and pestilence. Nasir ud-Din Mahmud Shah Tughlaq, who had fled to Gujarat during Timur's invasion, returned and nominally ruled as the last ruler of Tughlaq dynasty, as a puppet of various factions at the court.[1436]Wikipedia:Citation needed

Sayyid

The Sayyid dynasty was a Turkic dynasty[1437] that ruled the Delhi Sultanate from 1415 to 1451. The Timurid invasion and plunder had left the Delhi Sultanate in shambles, and little is known about the rule by the Sayyid dynasty. Annemarie Schimmel notes the first ruler of the dynasty as Khizr Khan, who assumed power by claiming to represent Timur. His authority was questioned even by those near Delhi. His successor was Mubarak Khan, who rechristened himself as Mubarak Shah and tried to regain lost territories in Punjab, unsuccessfully.

With the power of the Sayyid dynasty faltering, Islam's history on the Indian subcontinent underwent a profound change, according to Schimmel. The previously dominant Sunni sect of Islam became diluted, alternate Muslim sects such as Shia rose, and new competing centers of Islamic culture took roots beyond Delhi.

The Sayyid dynasty was displaced by the Lodi dynasty in 1451.

Lodi

The Lodi dynasty belonged to the Pashtun (Afghan) Lodi tribe. Bahlul Khan Lodi started the Lodi dynasty and was the first Pashtun, to rule the Delhi Sultanate.[1438] Bahlul Lodi began his reign by attacking the Muslim Jaunpur Sultanate to expand the influence of the Delhi Sultanate, and was partially successful through a treaty. Thereafter, the region from Delhi to Varanasi (then at the border of Bengal province), was back under influence of Delhi Sultanate.

After Bahlul Lodi died, his son Nizam Khan assumed power, rechristened himself as Sikandar Lodi and ruled from 1489 to 1517.[1439] One of the better known rulers of the dynasty, Sikandar Lodi expelled his brother Barbak Shah from Jaunpur, installed his son Jalal Khan as the ruler, then proceeded east to make claims on Bihar. The Muslim governors of Bihar agreed to pay tribute and taxes, but operated independent of the Delhi Sultanate. Sikandar Lodi led a campaign of destruction of temples, particularly around Mathura. He also moved his capital and court from Delhi to Agra,Wikipedia:Citation needed an

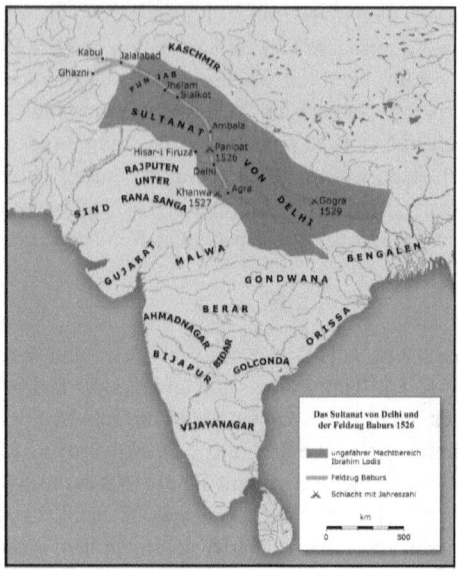

Figure 128: *Delhi Sultanate during Babur's invasion.*

ancient Hindu city that had been destroyed during the plunder and attacks of the early Delhi Sultanate period. Sikandar thus erected buildings with Indo-Islamic architecture in Agra during his rule, and the growth of Agra continued during the Mughal Empire, after the end of Delhi Sultanate.[1440]

Sikandar Lodi died a natural death in 1517, and his second son Ibrahim Lodi assumed power. Ibrahim did not enjoy the support of Afghan and Persian nobles or regional chiefs.[1441] Ibrahim attacked and killed his elder brother Jalal Khan, who was installed as the governor of Jaunpur by his father and had the support of the amirs and chiefs. Ibrahim Lodi was unable to consolidate his power, and after Jalal Khan's death, the governor of Punjab, Daulat Khan Lodi, reached out to the Mughal Babur and invited him to attack Delhi Sultanate.[1442] Babur defeated and killed Ibrahim Lodi in the Battle of Panipat in 1526. The death of Ibrahim Lodi ended the Delhi Sultanate, and the Mughal Empire replaced it.

Economy

Before and during the Delhi Sultanate, Islamic civilization was the most cosmopolitan civilization of the Middle Ages. It had a multicultural and pluralistic society, and wide-ranging international networks, including social and economic networks, spanning large parts of Afro-Eurasia, leading to escalating circulation of goods, peoples, technologies and ideas. While initially disruptive due to the passing of power from native Indian elites to Turkic Muslim elites, the Delhi Sultanate was responsible for integrating the Indian subcontinent into a growing world system, drawing India into a wider international network, which led to cultural and social enrichment in the Indian subcontinent.

Economist Angus Maddison has estimated that, during the Medieval Delhi Sultanate era, between 1000 and 1500, India's GDP grew nearly 80% up to $60.5 billion in 1500.

The worm gear roller cotton gin was invented in the Indian subcontinent during the early Delhi Sultanate era of the 13th–14th centuries,[1443] and is still used in India through to the present day. Another innovation, the incorporation of the crank handle in the cotton gin, first appeared in the Indian subcontinent some time during the late Delhi Sultanate or the early Mughal Empire.[1444] The production of cotton, which may have largely been spun in the villages and then taken to towns in the form of yarn to be woven into cloth textiles, was advanced by the diffusion of the spinning wheel across India during the Delhi Sultanate era, lowering the costs of yarn and helping to increase demand for cotton. The diffusion of the spinning wheel, and the incorporation of the worm gear and crank handle into the roller cotton gin, led to greatly expanded Indian cotton textile production.[1445]

Demographics

The Indian population had largely been stagnant at 75 million during the Middle Kingdoms era from 1 AD to 1000 AD. During the Medieval Delhi Sultanate era from 1000 to 1500, India experienced lasting population growth for the first time in a thousand years, with its population increasing nearly 50% to 110 million by 1500 AD.[1446,1447]

Culture

While the Indian subcontinent has had invaders from Central Asia since ancient times, what made the Muslim invasions different is that unlike the preceding invaders who assimilated into the prevalent social system, the successful Muslim conquerors retained their Islamic identity and created new legal and administrative systems that challenged and usually in many cases superseded the existing systems of social conduct and ethics, even influencing the non-Muslim rivals and common masses to a large extent, though the non-Muslim population was left to their own laws and customs. They also introduced new cultural codes that in some ways were very different from the existing cultural codes. This led to the rise of a new Indian culture which was mixed in nature, different from ancient Indian culture. The overwhelming majority of Muslims in India were Indian natives converted to Islam. This factor also played an important role in the synthesis of cultures.[1448]

The Hindustani language (Hindi-Urdu) began to emerge in the Delhi Sultanate period, developed from the Middle Indo-Aryan *apabhramsha* vernaculars of North India. Amir Khusro, who lived in the 13th century CE during the Delhi Sultanate period in North India, used a form of Hindustani, which was the *lingua franca* of the period, in his writings and referred to it as *Hindavi*.

Military

The bulk of Delhi Sultanate's army consisted of nomadic Turkic Mamluk military slaves, who were skilled in nomadic cavalry warfare. A major military contribution of the Delhi Sultanate was their successful campaigns in repelling the Mongol Empire's invasions of India, which could have been devastating for the Indian subcontinent, like the Mongol invasions of China, Persia and Europe. The Delhi Sultanate's Mamluk army were skilled in the same style of nomadic cavalry warfare used by the Mongols, making them successful in repelling the Mongol invasions, as was the case for the Mamluk Sultanate of Egypt. Were it not for the Delhi Sultanate, it is possible that the Mongol Empire may have been successful in invading India. The strength of the armies changes according to time. According to firishta during the battle of kili Alauddin led an army of 300,000 cavalry and 2,700 elephants. During the tughlaq period Muhammad bin tughlaq rose an army of 3 million. The soldiers used weapons such as swords, spears, shields etc. Armour such as steel helmet and chainmail was commonly used. Armored war elephants were effectively used against the enemies such as the Mongols.

Temple desecration

Iconoclasm under the Delhi Sultanate

The Somnath Temple in Gujarat was repeatedly destroyed by Islamic armies and rebuilt by Hindus. It was destroyed by Delhi Sultanate's army in 1299 CE.[1449]

The Kashi Vishwanath Temple was destroyed by the army of Qutb-ud-din Aibak.

Muhammad bin Bakhtiyar Khilji, the military general of Delhi Sultan Qutb al-Din Aibak, was responsible for the destruction of Nalanda university.[1450]

The armies of Delhi Sultanate led by Muslim Commander Malik Kafur plundered the Meenakshi Temple and looted it of its valuables.

Kakatiya Kala Thoranam (Warangal Gate) built by the Kakatiya dynasty in ruins; one of the many temple complexes destroyed by the Delhi Sultanate.[1389]

Artistic rendition of the Kirtistambh at Rudra Mahalaya Temple. The temple was destroyed by Alauddin Khalji.

Rani ki vav is a stepwell, built by the Chaulukya dynasty, located in Patan; the city was sacked by Sultan of Delhi Qutb-ud-din Aybak between 1200 and 1210, and it was destroyed by the Allauddin Khilji in 1298.

Pillar and ceiling carvings with a damaged *madanakai* at Hoysaleswara Temple. The temple was twice sacked and plundered by the Delhi Sultanate.

Historian Richard Eaton has tabulated a campaign of destruction of idols and temples by Delhi Sultans, intermixed with instances of years where the temples were protected from desecration.[1451,1452] In his paper, he has listed 37 instances of Hindu temples being desecrated or destroyed in India during the Delhi Sultanate, from 1234 to 1518, for which reasonable evidences are available.[1453,1454] He notes that this was not unusual in medieval India, as there were numerous recorded instances of temple desecration by Hindu and Buddhist kings against rival Indian kingdoms between 642 and 1520, involving conflict between devotees of different Hindu deities, as well as between Hindus, Buddhists and Jains. He also noted there were also many instances of Delhi sultans, who often had Hindu ministers, ordering the protection, maintenance and repairing of temples, according to both Muslim and Hindu sources. For example, a Sanskrit inscription notes that Sultan Muhammad bin Tughluq repaired a Siva temple in Bidar after his Deccan conquest. There was often a pattern of Delhi sultans plundering or damaging temples during conquest, and then patronizing or repairing temples after conquest. This pattern came to an end with the Mughal Empire, where Akbar the Great's chief minister Abu'l-Fazl criticized the excesses of earlier sultans such as Mahmud of Ghazni.

In many cases, the demolished remains, rocks and broken statue pieces of temples destroyed by Delhi sultans were reused to build mosques and other buildings. For example, the Qutb complex in Delhi was built from stones of 27 demolished Hindu and Jain temples by some accounts.[1455] Similarly, the Muslim mosque in Khanapur, Maharashtra was built from the looted parts and demolished remains of Hindu temples. Muhammad bin Bakhtiyar Khalji destroyed Buddhist and Hindu libraries and their manuscripts at Nalanda and Odantapuri Universities in 1193 AD at the beginning of the Delhi Sultanate.[1456]

The first historical record of a campaign of destruction of temples and defacement of faces or heads of Hindu idols lasted from 1193 through the early 13th century in Rajasthan, Punjab, Haryana and Uttar Pradesh under the command of Ghuri. Under the Khaljis, the campaign of temple desecration expanded to Bihar, Madhya Pradesh, Gujarat and Maharashtra, and continued through the late 13th century. The campaign extended to Telangana, Andhra Pradesh, Karnataka and Tamil Nadu under Malik Kafur and Ulugh Khan in the 14th century, and by the Bahmanis in 15th century.[1457] Orissa temples were destroyed in the 14th century under the Tughlaqs.

Beyond destruction and desecration, the sultans of the Delhi Sultanate in some cases had forbidden reconstruction of damaged Hindu, Jain and Buddhist temples, and they prohibited repairs of old temples or construction of any new temples.[1458,1459] In certain cases, the Sultanate would grant a permit for repairs and construction of temples if the patron or religious community paid jizya (fee, tax). For example, a proposal by the Chinese to repair Himalayan Buddhist temples destroyed by the Sultanate army was refused, on the grounds that such temple repairs were only allowed if the Chinese agreed to pay jizya tax to the treasury of the Sultanate.[1460,1461] In his memoirs, Firoz Shah Tughlaq describes how he destroyed temples and built mosques instead and killed those who dared build new temples.[1462] Other historical records from *wazirs, amirs* and the court historians of various Sultans of the Delhi Sultanate describe the grandeur of idols and temples they witnessed in their campaigns and how these were destroyed and desecrated.[1463]

Temple desecration during Delhi Sultanate period, a list prepared by Richard Eaton in *Temple Desecration and Indo-Muslim States*[1464]

Sultan / Agent	Dynasty	Years	Temple Sites Destroyed	States
Muhammad Ghori, Qutb al-Din Aibak	Mamluk	1193-1290	Ajmer, Samana, Kuhram, Delhi, Kol, Varanasi	Rajasthan, Punjab, Haryana, Uttar Pradesh
Muhammad bin Bakhtiyar Khalji, Shams ud-Din Iltumish, Jalal ud-Din Firuz Khalji, Ala ud-Din Khalji, Malik Kafur	Mamluk and Khalji	1290-1320	Nalanda, Odantapuri, Vikramashila, Bhilsa, Ujjain, Jhain, Vijapur, Devagiri, Somnath, Chidambaram, Madurai	Bihar, Madhya Pradesh, Rajasthan, Gujarat, Maharashtra, Tamil Nadu
Ulugh Khan, Firuz Shah Tughlaq, Raja Nahar Khan, Muzaffar Khan	Khalji and Tughlaq	1320-1395[1465]	Somnath, Warangal, Bodhan, Pillalamarri, Puri, Sainthali, Idar[1466]	Gujarat, Telangana, Orissa, Haryana
Sikandar, Muzaffar Shah, Ahmad Shah, Mahmud	Sayyid	1400-1442	Paraspur, Bijbehara, Tripuresvara, Idar, Diu, Manvi, Sidhpur, Delwara, Kumbhalmer	Gujarat, Rajasthan
Suhrab, Begdha, Bahmani, Khalil Shah, Khawwas Khan, Sikandar Lodi, Ibrahim Lodi	Lodi	1457-1518	Mandalgarh, Malan, Dwarka, Kondapalle, Kanchi, Amod, Nagarkot, Utgir, Narwar, Gwalior	Rajasthan, Gujarat, Himachal Pradesh, Madhya Pradesh

References

Bibliography

<templatestyles src="Template:Refbegin/styles.css" />

- Elliot, H. M. (Henry Miers), Sir; John Dowson. "15. Táríkh-i Fíroz Sháhí, of Ziauddin Barani"[1467]. *The History of India, as Told by Its Own Historians. The Muhammadan Period (Vol 3.).* London: Trübner & Co.
- Srivastava, Ashirvadi Lal (1929). *The Sultanate Of Delhi 711-1526 A D*[1468]. Shiva Lal Agarwala & Company.
- Khan, Mohd. Adul Wali (1974). *Gold and Silver Coins of Sultans of Delhi*[1469]. Government of Andhra Pradesh.
- Peter Jackson (2003). *The Delhi Sultanate: A Political and Military History*[1470]. Cambridge University Press. ISBN 978-0-521-54329-3.
- Majumdar, R. C., Raychaudhuri, H., & Datta, K. (1951). An advanced history of India: 2. London: Macmillan.
- Majumdar, R. C., & Munshi, K. M. (1990). The Delhi Sultanate. Bombay: Bharatiya Vidya Bhavan.

- Kumar, Sunil. (2007). The Emergence of the Delhi Sultanate. Delhi: Permanent Black.

External links

 Wikimedia Commons has media related to *Delhi Sultanate*.

 Wikiquote has quotations related to: *Delhi Sultanate*

Mamluk dynasty (Delhi)

<indicator name="pp-default"> </indicator>

Mamluk Dynasty	
1206–1290	
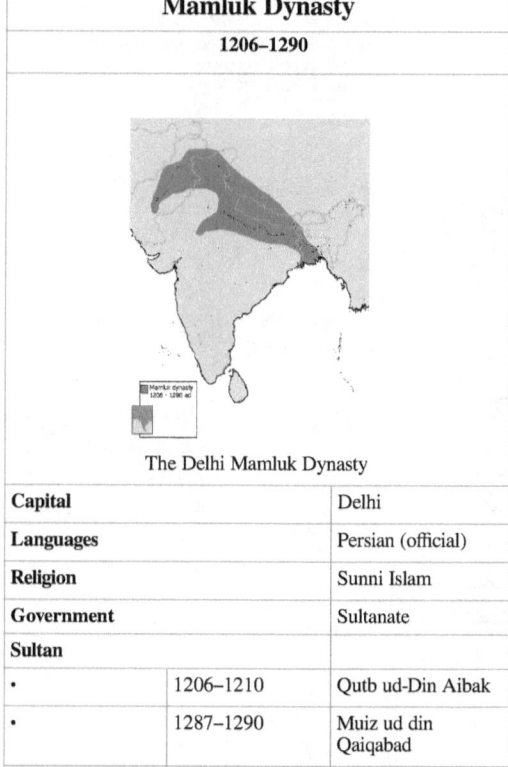 The Delhi Mamluk Dynasty	
Capital	Delhi
Languages	Persian (official)
Religion	Sunni Islam
Government	Sultanate
Sultan	
• 1206–1210	Qutb ud-Din Aibak
• 1287–1290	Muiz ud din Qaiqabad

History		
•	Established	1206
•	Disestablished	1290
Preceded by		Succeeded by
Chauhan Tomara dynasty Ghurid Sultanate Sena Empire		Khalji dynasty
Today part of		India

History of the Turkic peoples
Pre-14th century

Turkic Khaganate 552–744
Western Turkic
Eastern Turkic
Khazar Khaganate 618–1048
Xueyantuo 628–646
Great Bulgaria 632–668
Danube Bulgaria
Volga Bulgaria
Kangar union 659–750
Turk Shahi 665–850
Turgesh Khaganate 699–766
Uyghur Khaganate 744–840
Karluk Yabgu State 756–940
Kara-Khanid Khanate 840–1212
Western Kara-Khanid
Eastern Kara-Khanid
Ganzhou Uyghur Kingdom 848–1036
Qocho 856–1335

Pecheneg Khanates 860–1091	Kimek confederation 743–1035
Cumania 1067–1239	Oghuz Yabgu State 750–1055

Ghaznavid Empire 963–1186
Seljuk Empire 1037–1194
Sultanate of Rum
Kerait khanate 11th century–13th century
Khwarazmian Empire 1077–1231
Naiman Khanate –1204
Qarlughid Kingdom 1224–1266
Delhi Sultanate 1206–1526
Mamluk dynasty
Khalji dynasty
Tughlaq dynasty
Golden Horde 1240s–1502
Mamluk Sultanate (Cairo) 1250–1517
Bahri dynasty
Ottoman Empire 1299–1923

This box:
- view
- talk
- edit[1471]

The **Mamluk Dynasty** (sometimes referred as **Slave Dynasty** or **Ghulam Dynasty**) (Persian: سلطنت مملوک), (Urdu: غلام خاندان) was directed into Northern India by Qutb ud-Din Aibak, a Turkic Mamluk slave general from Central Asia. The Mamluk Dynasty ruled from 1206 to 1290; it was the first of five unrelated dynasties to rule as the Delhi Sultanate till 1526.[1472,1473] Aibak's tenure as a Ghurid dynasty administrator lasted from 1192 to 1206, a period during which he led invasions into the Gangetic heartland of India and established control over some of the new areas.Wikipedia:Citation needed

History

The Mamluk, literally meaning *owned*, was a soldier of slave origin who had converted to Islam. The phenomenon started in the 9th century and gradually the Mamluks became a powerful military caste in various Muslim societies.

Mamluks held political and military power most notably in Egypt, but also in the Levant, Iraq, and India.

In 1206, Muhammad of Ghor, Sultan of the Ghurid Empire was assassinated. Since he had no children, his empire split into minor sultanates led by his former mamluk generals. Taj-ud-Din Yildoz became the ruler of Ghazni. Muhammad bin Bakhtiyar Khilji got Bengal. Nasir-ud-Din Qabacha became the sultan of Multan. Qutb ud-Din Aibak became the sultan of Delhi, and that was the beginning of the Slave dynasty.

Aibak rose to power when a Ghorid superior was assassinated.[1474] However, his reign as the Sultan of Delhi was short lived as he died in 1210 and his son Aram Shah rose to the throne, only to be assassinated by Iltutmish in 1211.

The Sultanate under Iltutmish established cordial diplomatic contact with the Abbasid Caliphate between 1228–29 and had managed to keep India unaffected by the invasions of Genghis Khan and his successors. Following the death of Iltutmish in 1236 a series of weak rulers remained in power and a number of the noblemen gained autonomy over the provinces of the Sultanate. Power shifted hands from Rukn ud din Firuz to Razia Sultana until Ghiyas ud din Balban rose to the throne and successfully repelled both external threats to the Sultanate from the Chagatai Khanate invasions and internal threats from the rebellious sultanate nobles. The Khalji dynasty came into being when Jalal ud din Firuz Khalji overthrew the last of the Slave dynasty rulers, Muiz ud din Qaiqabad, the grandson of Balban, and assumed the throne at Delhi.[1475]

Sultans

The first Sultan of the Mamluk dynasty was Qutb ud-Din Aibak (قطب الدين ایبک), who had the titular name of *Sultan* (سلطان) and reigned from 1206 to 1210. He temporarily quelled the rebellions of Nasir-ud-Din Qabacha of Multan and Tajuddin Yildoz of Ghazni. Making Lahore his capital, he consolidated his control over North India through an administrative hold over Delhi. He also initiated the construction of Delhi's earliest Muslim monuments, the Quwwat-ul-Islam mosque and the Qutb Minar. In 1210, he died due to injuries received from an accident while playing a game of polo in Lahore; his horse fell and he was impaled on the pommel of his saddle. He was buried near the Anarkali Bazaar in Lahore.

The second Sultan was Aram Shah (آرام شاه), who had the titular name of *Sultan* and reigned from 1210 to 1211. An elite group of forty nobles named *Chihalgani* ("the Forty") conspired against Aram Shah and invited Shams-ud-din Iltutmish, then Governor of Badaun, to replace Aram. Iltutmish defeated Aram in the plain of Jud near Delhi in 1211. It is not quite certain what became of Aram.

Figure 129: *The Qutb Minar, an example of the Mamluk dynasty's works.*

The third Sultan was Shams-ud-din Iltutmish (شمس الدين التتمش), who had the titular name of *Nasir Amir-ul-Mu'minin* (ناصرامير المؤمنين) and reigned from 1211 to 1236. He shifted the capital from Lahore to Delhi and trebled the exchequer. He defeated Nasir-ud-Din Qabacha of Multan and Tajuddin Yildoz of Ghazni, who had declared themselves contenders of Delhi. Mongols invaded India in pursuit of Jalal-ud-din Mangabarni who was defeated at the Battle of Indus by Genghis Khan in 1221. After Genghis Khan's death, Iltutmish consolidated his hold on northern India by retaking many of the lost territories. In 1230, he built the Hauz-i-Shamsi reservoir in Mehrauli, and in 1231 he built Sultan Ghari, which was the first Islamic mausoleum in Delhi.

The fourth Sultan was Rukn-ud-din Feroze (ركن الدين فيروز), who had the titular name of *Sultan* and reigned from April 1236 to November 1236. He ruled for only seven months and his mother, Shah Turkan, for all practical purposes was running the government. He abandoned himself to the pursuit of personal pleasure and debauchery, to the considerable outrage of the citizenry. On 9 November 1236, both Rukn-ud-din Feroze and his mother Shah Turkan were assassinated by the Chihalgani.

The fifth Sultana was Razia al-Din (رضي☐ الدين), who had the titular name of *Jalâlat-ud-dîn Raziyâ Sultana* (جلال☐ الدين رضي☐ سلطان☐) and reigned from 1236 to 1240. As the first female Muslim ruler in Inda, she initial managed to impress the nobles and administratively handled the Sultanate well. However, she began associating with the African Jamal-ud-Din Yaqut, provoking racial antagonism amongst the nobles and clergy, who were primarily Central Asian Turkic and already resented the rule of a female monarch. She was defeated by the powerful nobleman Malik Altunia whom she agreed to marry. Her half-brother Muiz-ud-din Bahram, however, usurped the throne with the help of the Chihalgani and defeated the combined forces of the Sultana and her husband. The couple fled and reached Kaithal, where their remaining forces abandoned them. They both fell into the hands of Jats and were robbed and killed on 14 October 1240.

The sixth Sultan was Muiz-ud-din Bahram (معز الدين بهرام), who had the titular name of *Sultan* and reigned from 1240 to 15 May 1242. During his reign, the Chihalgani became disorderly and constantly bickered among each other. It was during this period of unrest that the Mongols invaded the Punjab and sacked Lahore. Muiz-ud-din Bahram was too weak to take any action against them, and the Chihalgani besieged him in the White Fort of Delhi and put him to death in 1242.

The seventh Sultan was Ala-ud-din Masud (علاءالدين مسعود), who had the titular name of *Sultan* and reigned from 1242 to 1246. He was effectively a puppet for the Chihalgani and did not actually have much power or influence in the government. Instead, he became infamous for his fondness of entertainment and wine. By 1246, the chiefs had become upset with Ala-ud-din Masud's increasing hunger for more power and replaced him with his cousin Nasir-ud-din Mahmud, who was another grandson of Iltutmish.

The eighth Sultan was Nasir-ud-din Mahmud (نصير الدين محمود), who had the titular name of *Nasir-ud-din Feroze Shah* (نصير الدين فيروز شاه) and reigned from 1246 to 1266. As a ruler, Mahmud was known to be very religious, spending most of his time in prayer and was renowned for aiding the poor and the distressed. It was his Deputy Sultan, Ghiyath-ud-din Balban, who primarily dealt with state affairs.

The ninth Sultan was Ghiyath-ud-din Balban (غياث الدين بلبن), who had the titular name of *Sultan* and reigned from 1266 to 1287. Balban ruled with an iron fist and broke up the Chihalgani group of noblemen. He tried to establish peace and order in India and built many outposts with garrisons of soldiers in areas where there had been disorder. Balban wanted to make sure everyone was loyal to the crown, so he established an efficient espionage system.

The tenth and final Sultan was Muiz-ud-din Muhammad Qaiqabad (معز الدين قيق آباد), who had the titular name of *Sultan* and reigned from 1287 to 1290. Being still young at the time, he ignored all state affairs. After four years, he suffered a paralytic stroke and was later murdered in 1290 by a Khalji chief. His three-year-old son Kayumars nominally succeeded him, but the Slave dynasty had ended with the rise of the Khaljis.

Architecture

The architectural legacy of the dynasty includes the Qutb Minar by Qutb ud-Din Aibak in Mehrauli, the Mausoleum of Prince Nasiru'd-Din Mahmud, eldest son of Iltumish, known as *Sultan Ghari* near Vasant Kunj, the first Islamic Mausoleum (tomb) built in 1231, and Balban's tomb, in the Mehrauli Archaeological Park.

References

- Anzalone, Christopher (2008). "Delhi Sultanate". In Ackermann, M. E. etc. *Encyclopedia of World History*. **2**. Facts on File. pp. 100–101. ISBN 978-0-8160-6386-4.
- Walsh, J. E. (2006). *A Brief History of India*. Facts on File. ISBN 0-8160-5658-7.
- Dynastic Chart[1476] The Imperial Gazetteer of India, v. 2, *p. 368*.

Further reading

- Srivastava, A. L. (1967). *The History of India, 1000-1707 A.D.*,[1477]. Shiva Lal Agarwala.

External links

- Encyclopædia Britannica (Online Edition) – Delhi sultanate[1478]

 Wikimedia Commons has media related to *Mamluk Sultanate (Delhi)*.

Khalji dynasty

<indicator name="pp-default"> 🔒 </indicator>

Khalji Sultanate	
1290–1320	
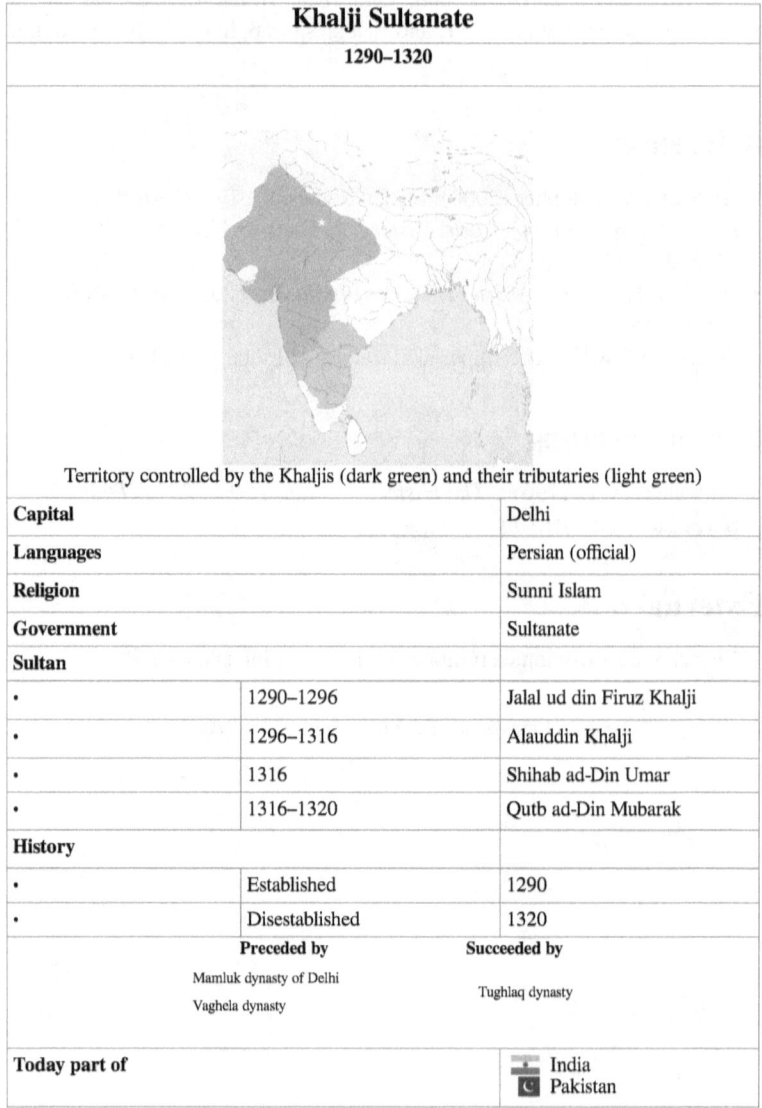	
Territory controlled by the Khaljis (dark green) and their tributaries (light green)	
Capital	Delhi
Languages	Persian (official)
Religion	Sunni Islam
Government	Sultanate
Sultan	
• 1290–1296	Jalal ud din Firuz Khalji
• 1296–1316	Alauddin Khalji
• 1316	Shihab ad-Din Umar
• 1316–1320	Qutb ad-Din Mubarak
History	
• Established	1290
• Disestablished	1320
Preceded by	Succeeded by
Mamluk dynasty of Delhi Vaghela dynasty	Tughlaq dynasty
Today part of	🇮🇳 India 🇵🇰 Pakistan

The **Khalji** or **Khilji** dynasty was a Muslim dynasty which ruled large parts of the Indian subcontinent between 1290 and 1320.[1479] It was founded by Jalal

Figure 130: *Copper coin of Alauddin Khalji*

ud din Firuz Khalji and became the second dynasty to rule the Delhi Sultanate of India. The dynasty is known for their faithlessness and ferocity, conquests into the Hindu south, and for successfully fending off the repeated Mongol invasions of India.

Origins

The Khaljis were of Turko-Afghan origin: they were a Turkic people, who had long been settled in Afghanistan before moving to Delhi. The ancestors of Jalaluddin Khalji had lived in the Helmand and Lamghan regions for over 200 years.[1480]

There is some debate about the ethnic group that the Khaljis belonged to, when the dynasty ruled. The Khalaj people in western Iran speak the Khalaj language, which is an archaic Turkic language.[1481] The modern Pashto-speaking Ghilzai Afghans are also descendants of Khalaj people; their transformation into an ethnic Afghan group can be dated to earlier than the 16th century. After a number of ethnic transformations, the Afghan Khalaj became the Ghilzay tribe of Afghans.[1482] Between 10th and 13th centuries, some sources refer to the Khalaj people as of Turkic, but some others do not.[1483] Ibn Khordadbeh (9th century) mentions the Khalaj people while describing the "land of the Turks". But the distance between the Amu Darya and the Talas is such as it would have been impossible for the tribes living beyond the Amu Darya to use the Talas pastures as winter quarters. Leading to the conclusion that the text is mutilated or still some Khalaj lived near the Khallukh. According to Minorsky the early history of the Khalaj tribe is obscure and adds the identity of the name Khalaj is still to be proved.[1484] Mahmud al-Kashgari (11th century) does not include the Khalaj among the Oghuz Turkic tribes, but includes them among the Oghuz-Turkman (where Turkman meant "Like the Turks") tribes. Kashgari felt the Khalaj did not belong to the original stock of Turkish tribes but had associated with them and therefore in language and dress often appeared 'like Turks'.[1483] The 11th century *Tarikh-i Sistan* and the Firdausi's *Shahnameh* also distinguish and differentiate the Khalaj from the Turks.[1485] Minhaj-i-Siraj Juzjani (13th century) never identified Khalaj as Turks, but was careful not to refer to them as Afghans. They were always a category apart from Turks, Tajiks and Afghans.[1483] Muhammad ibn Najib Bakran's *Jahannama* explicitly describes them as Turkic,[1486] although he notes that that their complexion had become darker (compared to the Turks) and their language had undergone alterations and become a different dialect. He notes acutely that the appearance and language of the Khalaj differ significantly from the Turks. The modern historian, Irfan Habib, has argued that the Khaljis were not related to the Turkic people, and were instead ethnic Afghans. Habib pointed out that in some 15th century Devanagari Sati inscriptions, the later Khaljis of Malwa have been referred to as "Khalchi" and "Khilchi", and that the 17th century chronicle *Padshahnama* an area near Boost in Afghanistan (where the Khalaj once resided) as "Khalich". Habib theorized that the earlier Persian chroniclers misread the name "Khalchi" as "Khalji", but this is unlikely, as this would mean that every Persian chronicler writing between 13th and 17th century made the same mistake. Habib also argued that no 13th century source refers to the Turkish background of the Khaljis, but this assertion is wrong, as Muhammad ibn Najib Bakran's *Jahan-nama* explicitly describes the Khalaj people as Turkic.[1486]

The accounts describing the Khaljis' rise to power in India indicate that they were regarded as a race quite distinct from the Turks in the late 13th century Delhi.[1487] Over the centuries in Afghanistan, the Khaljis had intermarried with the local Afghans, and had adopted their manners, culture, customs and practices.[1480,1488] They were looked down as non Turks by Turks. Therefore, the Turkish nobles wrongly looked upon them as Afghans. They were considered Afghans in the Delhi Court.[1489,1490,1491]

History

Delhi Sultanate
Ruling dynasties
• v • t • e[1492]

Jalal-ud-din Khalji

Khaljis were vassals of the Mamluk dynasty of Delhi and served the Sultan of Delhi, Ghiyas ud din Balban. Balban's successors were murdered over 1289-1290, and the Mamluk dynasty succumbed to the factional conflicts within the Mamluk dynasty and the Muslim nobility. As the struggle between the factions razed, Jalal ud din Firuz Khalji led a coup and murdered the 17-year-old Mamluk successor Muiz ud din Qaiqabad - the last ruler of Mamluk dynasty[1493]

Jalaluddin Firuz Khalji, who was around 70 years old at the time of his ascension, was known as a mild-mannered, humble and kind monarch to the general public.[1494]

Jalaluddin succeeded in overcoming the opposition of the Turkish nobles and ascended the throne of Delhi in January 1290.</ref> Jalal-ud-din was not universally accepted: During his six-year reign (1290–96), Balban's nephew revolted due to his assumption of power and the subsequent sidelining of nobility and commanders serving the Mamluk dynasty.[1495] Jalal-ud-din suppressed the revolt and executed some commanders, then led an unsuccessful expedition against Ranthambhor and repelled a Mongol force on the banks of the Sind River in central India with the help of his nephew Juna Khan.

Alauddin Khalji

Alauddin Khalji was the nephew and son-in-law of Jalal-ud-din, raided the Hindu Deccan peninsula and Deogiri - then the capital of the Hindu state of Maharashtra, looting their treasure.[1493,1496] He returned to Delhi in 1296, murdered his uncle who was also his father-in-law, then assumed power as Sultan.[1497]

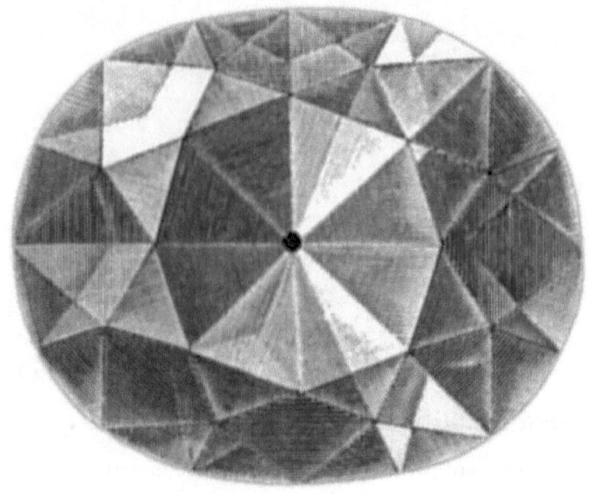

Figure 131: *The Koh-i-noor diamond was seized by Alauddin Khalji's army in 1310, from the Kakatiya dynasty in Warangal.*[1499]

Ala al-din Khalji continued expanding Delhi Sultanate into South India, with the help of generals such as Malik Kafur and Khusraw Khan, collecting large war booty (*Anwatan*) from those they defeated.[1498] His commanders collected war spoils from Hindu kingdoms, paid khums (one fifth) on *ghanima* (booty collected during war) to Sultan's treasury, which helped strengthen the Khalji rule.[1499]

Alauddin Khalji reigned for 20 years. He attacked and seized Hindu states of Ranthambhor (1301 AD), Chittorgarh (1303), Māndu (1305) and plundered the wealthy state of Devagiri,[1500] also withstood two Mongol raids. Ala al-din is also known for his cruelty against attacked kingdoms after wars. Historians note him as a tyrant and that anyone Ala al-din Khalji suspected of being a threat to this power was killed along with the women and children of that family. In 1298, between 15,000 and 30,000 people near Delhi, who had recently converted to Islam, were slaughtered in a single day, due to fears of an uprising.[1501] He also killed his own family members and nephews, in 1299-1300, after he suspected them of rebellion, by first gouging out their eyes and then beheading them.

In 1308, Alauddin's lieutenant, Malik Kafur captured Warangal, overthrew the Hoysala Empire south of the Krishna River and raided Madurai in Tamil

Nadu. He then looted the treasury in capitals and from the temples of south India. Among these loots was the Warangal loot that included one of the largest known diamond in human history, the Koh-i-noor.[1499] Malik Kafur returned to Delhi in 1311, laden with loot and war booty from Deccan peninsula which he submitted to Aladdin Khalji. This made Malik Kafur, born in a Hindu family and who had converted to Islam before becoming Delhi Sultanate's army commander, a favorite of Alauddin Khalji.

In 1311, Alauddin ordered a massacre of between 15,000 and 30,000 Mongol settlers, who had recently converted to Islam, after suspecting them of plotting an uprising against him.[1502]

The last Khalji sultans

Aladdin Khalji died in December 1315. Thereafter, the sultanate witnessed chaos, coup and succession of assassinations.[1493] Malik Kafur became the sultan but lacked support from the amirs and was killed within a few months.

Over the next three years, another three sultans assumed power violently and/ or were killed in coups. Following Malik Kafur's death, the amirs installed a six-year-old named Shihab-ud-din Omar as sultan and his teenage brother, Qutb ud din Mubarak Shah, as regent. Qutb killed his younger brother and appointed himself sultan. To win over the loyalty of the amirs and the Malik clan, Mubarak Shah offered Ghazi Malik the position of army commander in the Punjab. Others were given a choice between various offices and death. After ruling in his own name for less than four years, Mubarak Shah was murdered in 1320 by one of his generals, Khusraw Khan. Amirs persuaded Ghazi Malik – who was still army commander in the Punjab – to lead a coup. Ghazi Malik's forces marched on Delhi, captured Khusraw Khan and beheaded him. Upon becoming sultan, Ghazi Malik renamed himself Ghiyath al-Din Tughluq. He would become the first ruler of the Tughluq dynasty.

Economic policy and administration

Alauddin Khalji changed the tax policies to strengthen his treasury to help pay the keep of his growing army and fund his wars of expansion.[1503,1504] He raised agriculture taxes from 20% to 50% – payable in grain and agricultural produce (or cash),[1505] eliminating payments and commissions on taxes collected by local chiefs, banned socialization among his officials as well as inter-marriage between noble families to help prevent any opposition forming against him; he cut salaries of officials, poets and scholars in his kingdom.[1503,1504]

Alauddin Khalji enforced four taxes on non-Muslims in the Sultanate - *jizya* (poll tax), *kharaj* (land tax), *kari* (house tax) and *chari* (pasture tax).[1506,1507]

He also decreed that his Delhi-based revenue officers assisted by local Muslim *jagirdars*, *khuts*, *mukkadims*, *chaudharis* and *zamindars* seize by force half of all produce any farmer generates, as a tax on standing crop, so as to fill sultanate granaries.[1503,1508,1509] His officers enforced tax payment by beating up Hindu and Muslim middlemen responsible for rural tax collection.[1503] Furthermore, Alauddin Khalji demanded, state Kulke and Rothermund, from his "wise men in the court" to create "rules and regulations in order to grind down the Hindus, so as to reduce them to abject poverty and deprive them of wealth and any form of surplus property that could foster a rebellion; the Hindu was to be so reduced as to be left unable to keep a horse to ride on, to carry arms, to wear fine clothes, or to enjoy any of the luxuries of life".[1503] At the same time, he confiscated all landed property from his courtiers and officers. Revenue assignments to Muslim *jagirdars* were also cancelled and the revenue was collected by the central administration.[1510] Henceforth, state Kulke and Rothermund, "everybody was busy with earning a living so that nobody could even think of rebellion."

Alauddin Khalji taxation methods and increased taxes reduced agriculture output and the Sultanate witnessed massive inflation. In order to compensate for salaries that he had cut and fixed for Muslim officials and soldiers, Alauddin introduced price controls on all agriculture produce, goods, livestocks and slaves in kingdom, as well as controls on where, how and by whom these could be sold. Markets called *shahana-i-mandi* were created.[1511,1512] Muslim merchants were granted exclusive permits and monopoly in these *mandi* to buy and resell at official prices. No one other than these merchants could buy from farmers or sell in cities. Alauddin deployed an extensive network of *Munhiyans* (spies, secret police) who would monitor the *mandi* and had the power to seize anyone trying to buy or sell anything at a price different than the official controlled prices.[1503,1512,1513] Those found violating these *mandi* rules were severely punished, such as by cutting out their flesh. Taxes collected in form of seized crops and grains were stored in sultanate's granaries.[1514] Over time, farmers quit farming for income and shifted to subsistence farming, the general food supply worsened in north India, shortages increased and Delhi Sultanate witnessed increasingly worse and extended periods of famines.[1515] The Sultan banned private storage of food by anyone.[1503] Rationing system was introduced by Alauddin as shortages multiplied; however, the nobility and his army were exempt from the per family quota-based food rationing system.[1516] The shortages, price controls and rationing system caused starvation deaths of numerous rural people, mostly Hindus. However, during these famines, Khalji's sultanate granaries and wholesale *mandi* system with price controls ensured sufficient food for his army, court officials and the urban population in Delhi.[1504,1517] Price controls instituted by Khalji reduced prices, but also lowered wages to a point where ordinary people did not benefit from the low prices. The price control system collapsed shortly after the death of Alauddin Khalji, with prices of various agriculture products and wages doubling to quadrupling within a few years.[1518]

Historical impact

The tax system introduced during the Khalji dynasty had a long term influence on Indian taxation system and state administration,

> *Alauddin Khalji's taxation system was probably the one institution from his reign that lasted the longest, surviving indeed into the nineteenth or even the twentieth century. From now on, the land tax (kharaj or mal) became the principal form in which the peasant's surplus was expropriated by the ruling class.*
>
> *—The Cambridge Economic History of India: c.1200-c.1750,*[1519]

Slavery

Within Sultanate's capital city of Delhi, during Alauddin Khalji's reign, at least half of the population were slaves working as servants, concubines and guards for the Muslim nobles, amirs, court officials and commanders.[1520] Slavery in India during Khalji, and later Islamic dynasties, included two groups of people - persons seized during military campaigns, and people who failed to pay tax on time. The first group were people seized during military campaigns.[1521] The second group of people were revenue defaulters. If a family failed to pay the annual tax in full on time, their property was seized and even some cases all their family members seized then sold as slaves.[1522] The institution of slavery and bondage labor became pervasive during the Khalji dynasty; male slaves were referred to as *banda, qaid, ghulam,* or *burdah,* while female slaves were called *bandi, kaniz* or *laundi.*

Architecture

Ala-ud-din Khalji is credited with the early Indo-Mohammedan architecture, a style and construction campaign that flourished during Tughlaq dynasty. Among works completed during Khalji dynasty, are Alai Darwaza - the southern gateway of Qutb complex enclosure, the Idgah at Rapri, and the Jamat Khana (Khizri) Mosque in Delhi.[1523] The Alai Darwaza, completed in 1311, was included as part of Qutb Minar and its Monuments UNESCO World Heritage site in 1993.[1524]

Perso-Arabic inscriptions on monuments have been traced to the Khalji dynasty era.

Disputed historical sources

Historians have questioned the reliability of historical accounts about the Khalji dynasty. Genuine primary sources and historical records from 1260 to 1349 period have not been found.[1525] One exception is the short chapter on Delhi Sultanate from 1302-1303 AD by Wassaf in Persia, which is duplicated in *Jami al-Tawarikh*, and which covers the Balban rule, start of Jalal-ud-din Chili's rule and circumstances of succession of Alauddin Khalji. A semi-fictional poetry (*mathnawis*) by Yamin al-Din Abul Hasan, also known as Amir Khusraw Dihlawi, is full of adulation for his employer, the reigning Sultan. Abu Hasan's adulation-filled narrative poetry has been used as source of Khalji dynasty history, but this is a disputed source.[1525,1526] Three historical sources, composed 30 to 115 years after the end of Khalji dynasty, are considered more independent but also questioned given the gap in time. These are Isami's epic of 1349, Diya-yi Barani's work of 1357 and Sirhindi's account of 1434, which possibly relied on now lost text or memories of people in Khalji's court. Of these Barani's text is the most referred and cited in scholarly sources.[1525,1527]

List of rulers of Delhi (1290–1320)

Titular Name	Personal Name	Reign[1528]
Shāyista Khān (Jalal-ud-din) جلال الدين	Malik Fīroz ملک فيروز خلجى	1290–1296
Ala-ud-din علاءالدين	Ali Gurshasp على گرشاسپ خلجى	1296–1316
Shihab-ud-din شهاب الدين	Umar Khan عمر خان خلجى	1316
Qutb-ud-din قطب الدين	Mubarak Khan مبارک خان خلجى	1316–1320
Khusro Khan ended the Khalji dynasty in 1320.		

Notes

References

Bibliography

<templatestyles src="Template:Refbegin/styles.css" />

- Abraham Eraly (2015). *The Age of Wrath: A History of the Delhi Sultanate*[1529]. Penguin Books. p. 178. ISBN 978-93-5118-658-8.

- Ahmad Hasan Dani (1999). *History of Civilizations of Central Asia: The crossroads of civilizations: A.D. 250 to 750*[1530]. Motilal Banarsidass. ISBN 978-81-208-1540-7.
- Ashirbadi Lal Srivastava (1966). *The History of India, 1000 A.D.-1707 A.D.*[1531] (Second ed.). Shiva Lal Agarwala. OCLC 575452554[1532].
- Ashirbadi Lal Srivastava (1953). *The Sultanate of Delhi*[1533]. S. L. Agarwala. OCLC 555201052[1534].
- Hermann Kulke; Dietmar Rothermund (2004). *A History of India*[1535]. Psychology Press. ISBN 978-0-415-32919-4.
- Irfan Habib (1982). "Northern India under the Sultanate: Agrarian Economy". In Tapan Raychaudhuri; Irfan Habib. *The Cambridge Economic History of India*[1536]. 1, c.1200-c.1750. CUP Archive. ISBN 978-0-521-22692-9.
- Kishori Saran Lal (1950). *History of the Khaljis (1290-1320)*[1537]. Allahabad: The Indian Press. OCLC 685167335[1538].
- Marshall Cavendish (2006). *World and Its Peoples: The Middle East, Western Asia, and Northern Africa*[1539]. Marshall Cavendish. ISBN 0-7614-7571-0.
- Peter Malcolm Holt; Ann K. S. Lambton; Bernard Lewis, eds. (1977). *The Cambridge History of Islam*[1540]. Cambridge University Press. ISBN 978-0-521-29138-5.
- Peter Jackson (2003). *The Delhi Sultanate: A Political and Military History*[1541]. Cambridge University Press. ISBN 978-0-521-54329-3.
- Radhey Shyam Chaurasia (2002). *History of medieval India: from 1000 A.D. to 1707 A.D.*[1542] Atlantic. ISBN 81-269-0123-3.
- Sunil Kumar (1994). "When Slaves were Nobles: The Shamsi Bandagan in the Early Delhi Sultanate"[1543]. *Studies in History*. **10** (1): 23–52. doi: 10.1177/025764309401000102[1544].

External links

 Wikiquote has quotations related to: *Khalji dynasty*

- Media related to Khalji dynasty at Wikimedia Commons
- Khilji - A Short History of Muslim Rule in India[1545] I. Prasad, University of Allahabad
- The Role of Ulema in Indo-Muslim History[1546], Aziz Ahmad, Studia Islamica, No. 31 (1970), pp. 1–13

Tughlaq dynasty

<indicator name="pp-default"> 🔒 </indicator>

Tughlaq Dynasty	
1320–1413[1547]	
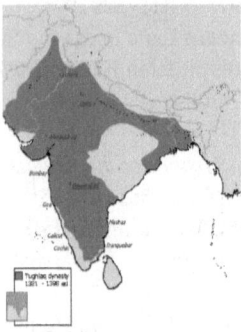 Territory under Tughlaq dynasty of Delhi Sultanate, 1330-1335 AD. The empire shrank after 1335 AD.	
Capital	Delhi
Languages	Persian (official)
Religion	Official: Sunni Islam Subjects: Hinduism,[1548] Shia, Others
Government	Sultanate
Sultan	
• 1321–1325	Ghiyath al-Din Tughluq
• 1325–1351	Muhammad bin Tughluq
• 1351–1388	Firuz Shah Tughlaq
• 1388–1413	Ghiyath-ud-din Tughluq Shah / Abu Bakr Shah / Muhammad Shah / Mahmud Tughlaq / Nusrat Shah
Historical era	Medieval
• Established	1320
• Disestablished	1413[1547]
Area	3,200,000 km² (1,200,000 sq mi)

	Preceded by	Succeeded by
	Khalji dynasty	Sayyid dynasty Vijayanagara Empire Bahmani Sultanate Bengal Sultanate Gujarat Sultanate
Today part of		India Nepal Pakistan Bangladesh

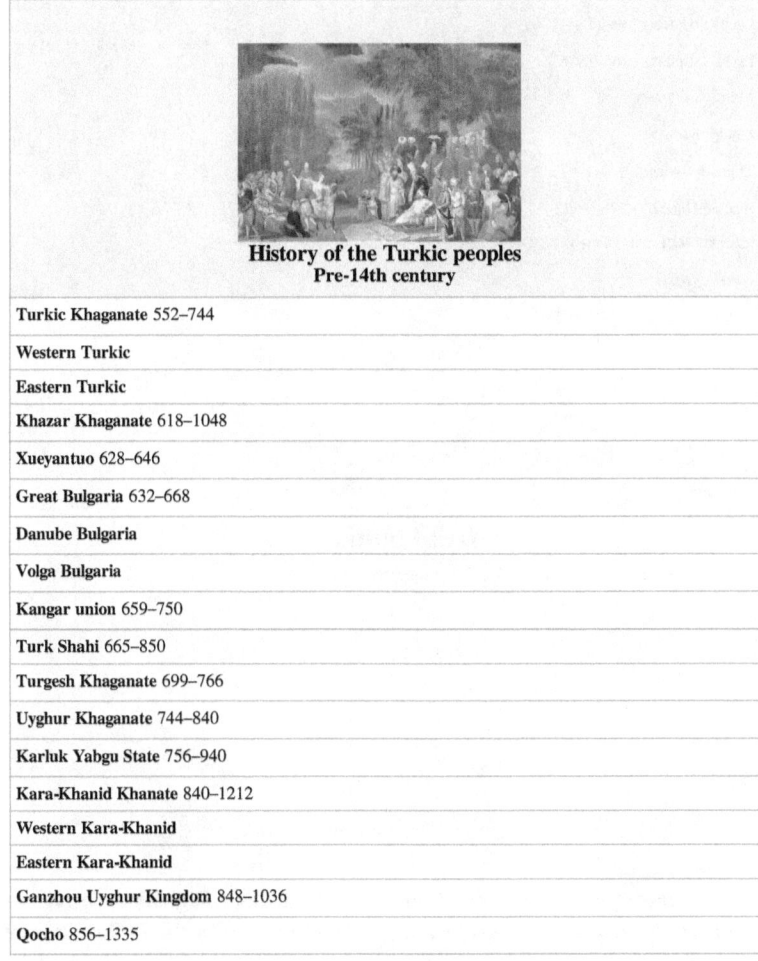

History of the Turkic peoples
Pre-14th century

Turkic Khaganate 552–744
Western Turkic
Eastern Turkic
Khazar Khaganate 618–1048
Xueyantuo 628–646
Great Bulgaria 632–668
Danube Bulgaria
Volga Bulgaria
Kangar union 659–750
Turk Shahi 665–850
Turgesh Khaganate 699–766
Uyghur Khaganate 744–840
Karluk Yabgu State 756–940
Kara-Khanid Khanate 840–1212
Western Kara-Khanid
Eastern Kara-Khanid
Ganzhou Uyghur Kingdom 848–1036
Qocho 856–1335

Pecheneg Khanates 860–1091	Kimek confederation 743–1035
Cumania 1067–1239	Oghuz Yabgu State 750–1055

Ghaznavid Empire 963–1186
Seljuk Empire 1037–1194
Sultanate of Rum
Kerait khanate 11th century–13th century
Khwarazmian Empire 1077–1231
Naiman Khanate –1204
Qarlughid Kingdom 1224–1266
Delhi Sultanate 1206–1526
Mamluk dynasty
Khalji dynasty
Tughlaq dynasty
Golden Horde 1240s–1502
Mamluk Sultanate (Cairo) 1250–1517
Bahri dynasty
Ottoman Empire 1299–1923

This box:
- view
- talk
- edit[1549]

Delhi Sultanate
Ruling dynasties
• v • t • e[1550]

The **Tughlaq dynasty**[1551] also referred to as Tughluq or Tughluk dynasty, was a Muslim dynasty of Turko-Indian origin which ruled over the Delhi sultanate in medieval India.[1552] Its reign started in 1320 in Delhi when Ghazi Malik assumed the throne under the title of Ghiyath al-Din Tughluq. The dynasty ended in 1413.

The dynasty expanded its territorial reach through a military campaign led by Muhammad bin Tughluq, and reached its zenith between 1330 and 1335. Its rule was marked with torture, cruelty and rebellions, resulting in the rapid disintegration of the dynasty's territorial reach after 1335 AD.[1553]

Origin

The etymology of the word "Tughluq" is not certain. The 16th century writer Firishta claims that it is a corruption of the Turkic term "Qutlugh", but this is doubtful.[1554] Literary, numismatic and epigraphic evidence makes it clear that Tughluq was the personal name of the dynasty's founder Ghiyath al-Din, and not an ancestral designation. Historians use the designation "Tughluq" to describe the entire dynasty as a matter of convenience, but the dynasty's kings did not use "Tughluq" as a surname: only Ghiyath al-Din's son Muhammad bin Tughluq called himself the son of Tughluq Shah ("bin Tughluq").[1554]

The ancestry of dynasty is debated among modern historians, because the earlier sources provide different information regarding it. Tughluq's court poet Badr-i Chach attempted to find a royal genealogy for the dynasty, but this can be dismissed as flattery. Another court poet Amir Khusrau, in his *Tughluq Nama*, states that Ghiyath al-Din Tughluq described himself as an unimportant man ("*awara mard*") in his early career.[1555] The contemporary Moroccan traveler Ibn Battuta states that Ghiyath al-Din Tughluq belonged to the "Qarauna tribe of the Turks", who lived in the hilly region between Turkestan and Sindh. Ibn Battuta's source for this claim was the Sufi saint Rukn-ud-Din Abul Fateh, but the claim is not corroborated by any other contemporary source.[1554] Firishta, bsaed on the inquiries made at Lahore, wrote that Tughluq was a Turkic slave of the earlier emperor Balban, and that his mother came from a Jat family of India. No contemporary sources corroborate this claim.[1555]

Rise to power

The Khalji dynasty ruled the Delhi Sultanate before 1320. Its last ruler, Khusro Khan, was a Hindu who had converted to Islam and then served Delhi Sultanate as the general of its army.[1556] Khusro Khan, along with Malik Kafur, had led numerous military campaigns on behalf of Alauddin Khalji, to expand the Sultanate and plunder non-Muslim kingdoms in India.[1557,1558]

After Alauddin Khalji's death from illness in 1316, a series of palace arrests and assassinations followed,[1559] with Khusro Khan coming to power in June 1320 after killing licentious son of Alauddin Khalji, Mubarak Khalji.[1560] However,

Figure 132: *Ghiyasuddin Tughlaq ordered the construction of Tughlakabad, a city near Delhi with fort to protect Delhi Sultanate from Mongol attacks. Above is the Tughlaq fort, now in ruins.*

he lacked the support of the nobels and aristocrats of the Khalji dynasty in Delhi. Delhi's aristocracy invited Ghazi Malik, then the governor in Punjab under the Khaljis, to lead a coup in Delhi and remove Khusro Khan. In 1320, Ghazi Malik launched an attack and killed Khusro Khan to assume power.[1561]

Chronology

Ghiyasuddin Tughlaq

After assuming power, Ghazi Malik renamed himself as Ghiyasuddin Tughlaq - thus starting and naming the Tughlaq dynasty.[1562] Ghiyasuddin Tughlaq is also referred in scholarly works as Tughlak Shah. He was of Turko-Indian origins; his father was a Turkic slave and his mother was a Hindu.[1563]

Ghiyasuddin Tughlaq rewarded all those *maliks*, *amirs* and officials of Khalji dynasty who had rendered him a service and helped him come to power. He punished those who had rendered service to Khusro Khan, his predecessor. He lowered the tax rate on Muslims that was prevalent during Khalji dynasty, but raised the taxes on Hindus, wrote his court historian Ziauddin Barani, so that they might not be blinded by wealth or afford to become rebellious.

He built a city six kilometers east of Delhi, with a fort considered more defensible against the Mongol attacks, and called it Tughlakabad.

In 1321, he sent his eldest son Ulugh Khan, later known as Muhammad bin Tughlaq, to Deogir to plunder the Hindu kingdoms of Arangal and Tilang (now part of Telangana). His first attempt was a failure.[1564] Four months later, Ghiyasuddin Tughlaq sent large army reinforcements for his son asking him to attempt plundering Arangal and Tilang again.[1565] This time Ulugh Khan succeeded. Arangal fell, was renamed to Sultanpur, and all plundered wealth, state treasury and captives were transferred from the captured kingdom to Delhi Sultanate.

The Muslim aristocracy in Lukhnauti (Bengal) invited Ghiyasuddin Tughlaq to extend his coup and expand eastwards into Bengal by attacking Shamsuddin Firoz Shah, which he did over 1324–1325 AD, after placing Delhi under control of his son Ulugh Khan, and then leading his army to Lukhnauti. Ghiyasuddin Tughlaq succeeded in this campaign. As he and his favorite son Mahmud Khan were returning from Lakhnauti to Delhi, Ghiyasuddin Tughlaq's eldest son Ulugh Khan schemed with Muslim preacher Nizamuddin Auliya to kill him inside a wooden structure (*kushk*) built without foundation and designed to collapse, making it appear as an accident. Historic documents state that the Sufi preacher and Ulugh Khan had learnt through messengers that Ghiyasuddin Tughlaq had resolved to remove them from Delhi upon his return.[1566] Ghiyasuddin Tughlaq along with his favorite son Mahmud Khan died inside the collapsed *kushk* in 1325 AD, while his eldest son watched.[1567] One official historian of Tughlaq court gives an alternate fleeting account of his death, as caused by a lightning bolt strike on the *kushk*.[1568] Another official historian, Al-Badā'unī 'Abd al-Kadir ibn Mulūk-Shāh, makes no mention of lightning bolt or weather, but explains the cause of structural collapse to be the running of elephants; Al-Badaoni includes a note of the rumor that the accident was pre-planned.

Patricide

According to many historians such as Ibn Battuta, al-Safadi, Isami, and Vincent Smith,[1569] Ghiyasuddin was killed by his son Ulugh Juna Khanr in 1325 AD. Juna Khan ascended to power as Muhammad bin Tughlaq, and ruled for 26 years.[1570]

Muhammad bin Tughluq

During Muhammad bin Tughluq's rule, Delhi Sultanate temporarily expanded to most of the Indian subcontinent, its peak in terms of geographical reach.[1571] He attacked and plundered Malwa, Gujarat, Mahratta, Tilang, Kampila, Dhursamundar, Mabar, Lakhnauti, Chittagong, Sunarganw and Tirhut.[1572] His distant campaigns were expensive, although each raid and attack on non-Muslim kingdoms brought new looted wealth and ransom payments from captured

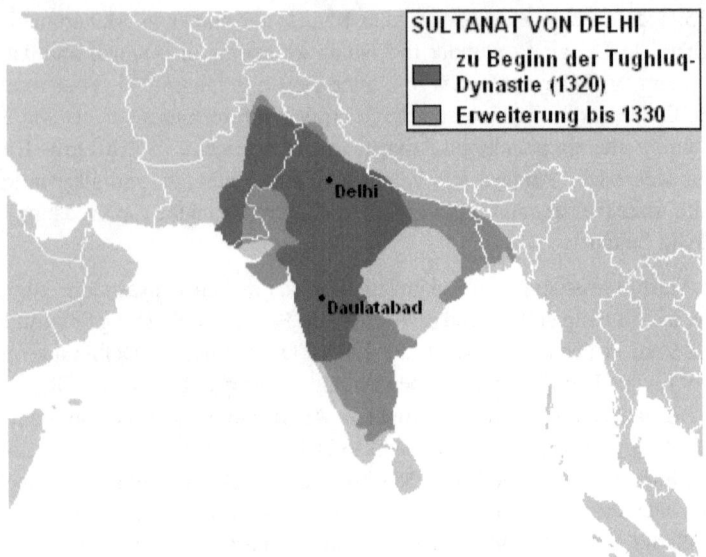

Figure 133: *A map showing the expansion of Delhi Sultanate from 1320 (dark green) to 1330. The map also shows the location of the new temporary capital under Muhammad bin Tughlaq.*

people. The extended empire was difficult to retain, and rebellions all over Indian subcontinent became routine.

He raised taxes to levels where people refused to pay any. In India's fertile lands between Ganges and Yamuna rivers, the Sultan increased the land tax rate on non-Muslims by tenfold in some districts, and twentyfold in others. Along with land taxes, dhimmis (non-Muslims) were required to pay crop taxes by giving up half or more of their harvested crop. These sharply higher crop and land tax led entire villages of Hindu farmers to quit farming and escape into jungles; they refused to grow anything or work at all. Many became robber clans. Famines followed. The Sultan responded with bitterness by expanding arrests, torture and mass punishments, killing people as if he was "cutting down weeds".[1573] Historical documents note that Muhammad bin Tughluq was cruel and severe not only with non-Muslims, but also with certain sects of Musalmans. He routinely executed *Sayyids* (Shia), *Sufis*, *Qalandars*, and other Muslim officials. His court historian Ziauddin Barni noted,

Not a day or week passed without spilling of much Musalman blood, (...)

—*Ziauddin Barni, Tarikh-I Firoz Shahi*[1574]

Muhammad bin Tughlaq founded a new city, called Jahanpannah (meaning, "Protection of the World"), which connected older Delhi with Siri.[1575] Later, he ordered that the capital of his Sultanate be moved from Delhi to Deogiri in present-day Indian state of Maharashtra (renaming it to Daulatabad). He ordered a forced mass migration of Delhi's population. Those who refused were killed. One blind person who failed to move to Deogir, was dragged for the entire journey of 40 days - the man died, his body fell apart, and only his tied leg reached Daulatabad. The capital move failed because Daulatabad was arid and did not have enough drinking water to support the new capital. The capital then returned to Delhi. Nevertheless, Muhammad bin Tughlaq orders affected history as large number of Delhi Muslims who came to Deccan area, did not return to Delhi to live near Muhammad bin Tughlaq. This influx of the then Delhi residents into Deccan region led to a growth of Muslim population in central and southern India.

Revolts against Muhammad bin Tughlaq began in 1327, continued over his reign, and over time the geographical reach of the Sultanate shrunk particularly after 1335. The Vijayanagara Empire originated in southern India as a direct response to attacks from the Delhi Sultanate.[1576] The Vijayanagara Empire liberated southern India from the Delhi Sultanate.[1577] In 1336 Kapaya Nayak of the Musunuri Nayak defeated the Tughlaq army and reconquered Warangal from the Delhi Sultanate.[1578] In 1338 his own nephew rebelled in Malwa, whom he attacked, caught and flayed alive. By 1339, the eastern regions under local Muslim governors and southern parts led by Hindu kings had revolted and declared independence from Delhi Sultanate. Muhammad bin Tughlaq did not have the resources or support to respond to the shrinking kingdom.[1579] By 1347, Bahmanid Sultanate had become an independent and competing Muslim kingdom in Deccan region of South Asia.[1580]

Muhammad bin Tughlaq was an intellectual, with extensive knowledge of Quran, Fiqh, poetry and other fields. He was deeply suspicious of his kinsmen and *wazirs* (ministers), extremely severe with his opponents, and took decisions that caused economic upheaval. For example, after his expensive campaigns to expand Islamic empire, the state treasury was empty of precious metal coins. So he ordered minting of coins from base metals with face value of silver coins - a decision that failed because ordinary people minted counterfeit coins from base metal they had in their houses.

Ziauddin Barni, a historian in Muhammad bin Tughlaq's court, wrote that the houses of Hindus became a coin mint and people in Hindustan provinces produced fake copper coins worth crores to pay the tribute, taxes and jizya imposed on them.[1581] The economic experiments of Muhammad bin Tughlaq resulted in a collapsed economy, and nearly a decade long famine followed that killed numerous people in the countryside. The historian Walford chronicled

Figure 134: *A base metal coin of Muhammad bin Tughlaq that led to an economic collapse.*

Delhi and most of India faced severe famines during Muhammad bin Tughlaq's rule, in the years after the base metal coin experiment.[1582,1583] Tughlaq introduced token coinage of brass and copper to augment the silver coinage which only led to increasing ease of forgery and loss to the treasury. Also, the people were not willing to trade their gold and silver for the new brass and copper coins.[1584] Consequently, the sultan had to withdraw the lot, "buying back both the real and the counterfeit at great expense until mountains of coins had accumulated within the walls of Tughluqabad."[1585]

Muhammad bin Tughlaq planned an attack on Khurasan and Irak (Babylon and Persia) as well as China to bring these regions under Sunni Islam. For Khurasan attack, a cavalry of over 300,000 horses were gathered near Delhi, for a year at state treasury's expense, while spies claiming to be from Khurasan collected rewards for information on how to attack and subdue these lands. However, before he could begin the attack on Persian lands in the second year of preparations, the plunder he had collected from Indian subcontinent had emptied, provinces were too poor to support the large army, and the soldiers refused to remain in his service without pay. For the attack on China, Muhammad bin Tughlaq sent 100,000 soldiers, a part of his army, over the Himalayas. However, Hindus closed the passes through the Himalayas and blocked the passage for retreat. The high mountain weather and lack of retreat destroyed that army in the Himalayas.[1586] The few soldiers who returned with bad news were executed under orders of the Sultan.[1587]

During his reign, state revenues collapsed from his policies. To cover state expenses, Muhammad bin Tughlaq sharply raised taxes on his ever-shrinking empire. Except in times of war, he did not pay his staff from his treasury.

Ibn Battuta noted in his memoir that Muhammad bin Tughlaq paid his army, judges (*qadi*), court advisors, wazirs, governors, district officials and others in his service by awarding them the right to force collect taxes on Hindu villages, keep a portion and transfer rest to his treasury. Those who failed to pay taxes were hunted and executed. Muhammad bin Tughlaq died in March 1351 while trying to chase and punish people for rebellion and their refusal to pay taxes in Sindh (now in Pakistan) and Gujarat (now in India).

Historians have attempted to determine the motivations behind Muhammad bin Tughlaq's behavior and his actions. Some state Tughlaq tried to enforce orthodox Islamic observance and practice, promote jihad in South Asia as *al-Mujahid fi sabilillah* ('Warrior for the Path of God') under the influence of Ibn Taymiyyah of Syria. Others[1588] suggest insanity.

At the time of Muhammad bin Tughlaq's death, the geographic control of Delhi Sultanate had shrunk to Vindhya range (now in central India).

Feroz Shah Tughluq

After Muhammad bin Tughluq died, a collateral relative, Mahmud Ibn Muhammad, ruled for less than a month. Thereafter, Muhammad bin Tughluq's 45-year-old nephew Firuz Shah Tughlaq replaced him and assumed the throne. His rule lasted 37 years. Firuz Shah was, like his grandfather, of Turko-Indian origins. His Turkic father Sipah Rajab became infatuated with a Hindu princess named Naila. She initially refused to marry him. Her father refused the marriage proposal as well. Sultan Muhammad bin Tughlaq and Sipah Rajab then sent in an army with a demand for one year taxes in advance and a threat of seizure of all property of her family and Dipalpur people. The kingdom was suffering from famines, and could not meet the ransom demand. The princess, after learning about ransom demands against her family and people, offered herself in sacrifice if the army would stop the misery to her people. Sipah Rajab and the Sultan accepted the proposal. Sipah Rajab and Naila were married and Firoz Shah was their first son.[1589]

The court historian Ziauddin Barni, who served both Muhammad Tughlaq and first 6 years of Firoz Shah Tughlaq, noted that all those who were in service of Muhammad were dismissed and executed by Firoz Shah. In his second book, Barni states that Firuz Shah was the mildest sovereign since the rule of Islam came to Delhi. Muslim soldiers enjoyed the taxes they collected from Hindu villages they had rights over, without having to constantly go to war as in previous regimes. Other court historians such as 'Afif record a number of conspiracies and assassination attempts on Firoz Shah Tughlaq, such as by his first cousin and the daughter of Muhammad bin Tughlaq.[1590]

Firoz Shah Tughlaq tried to regain the old kingdom boundary by waging a war with Bengal for 11 months in 1359. However, Bengal did not fall, and

Figure 135: *A painting of west gate of Firozabad fort, near Delhi. This fort was built by Feroz Shah Tughlaq in the 1350s, but destroyed by later dynasties.*

remained outside of Delhi Sultanate. Firuz Shah Tughlaq was somewhat weak militarily, mainly because of inept leadership in the army.

An educated sultan, Firoz Shah left a memoir.[1591] In it he wrote that he banned torture in practice in Delhi Sultanate by his predecessors, tortures such as amputations, tearing out of eyes, sawing people alive, crushing people's bones as punishment, pouring molten lead into throats, putting people on fire, driving nails into hands and feet, among others.[1592] The Sunni Sultan also wrote that he did not tolerate attempts by Rafawiz Shia Muslim and Mahdi sects from proselytizing people into their faith, nor did he tolerate Hindus who tried to rebuild their temples after his armies had destroyed those temples.[1593] As punishment, wrote the Sultan, he put many Shias, Mahdi and Hindus to death (*siyasat*). Shams-i Siraj 'Afif, his court historian, also recorded Firoz Shah Tughlaq burning Hindus alive for secretly following their religion and for refusing to convert to Islam.[1594] In his memoirs, Firoz Shah Tughlaq lists his accomplishments to include converting Hindus to Sunni Islam by announcing an exemption from taxes and jizya for those who convert, and by lavishing new converts with presents and honours. Simultaneously, he raised taxes and jizya, assessing it at three levels, and stopping the practice of his predecessors who had historically exempted all Hindu Brahmins from *jizya* tax.[1595] He also vastly expanded the number of slaves in his service and those of amirs (Muslim

Figure 136: *Wazirabad mosque, near Delhi, was built during Firoz Shah Tughlaq reign.*

nobles). Firoz Shah Tughlaq reign was marked by reduction in extreme forms of torture, eliminating favours to select parts of society, but an increased intolerance and persecution of targeted groups. After the death of his heir in 1376 AD, Firuz Shah started strict implementation of Sharia throughout his dominions.

Firuz Shah suffered from bodily infirmities, and his rule was considered by his court historians as more merciful than that of Muhammad bin Tughlaq.[1596] When Firuz Shah came to power, India was suffering from a collapsed economy, abandoned villages and towns, and frequent famines. He undertook many infrastructure projects including an irrigation canals connecting Yamuna-Ghaggar and Yamuna-Sutlej rivers, bridges, madrasas (religious schools), mosques and other Islamic buildings. He also undertook destruction of Hindu temples, suppressed non-Sunni sects by demolishing their structures. Firuz Shah Tughlaq is credited with patronizing Indo-Islamic architecture, including the installation of lats (ancient Hindu and Buddhist pillars) near mosques. The irrigation canals continued to be in use through the 19th century. After Feroz died in 1388, the Tughlaq dynasty's power continued to fade, and no more able leaders came to the throne. Firoz Shah Tughlaq's death created anarchy and disintegration of kingdom. In the years preceding his death, internecine strife among his descendants had already erupted.

Civil wars

The first civil war broke out in 1384 AD four years before the death of aging Firoz Shah Tughlaq, while the second civil war started in 1394 AD six years after Firoz Shah was dead. The Islamic historians Sirhindi and Bihamadkhani provide the detailed account of this period. These civil wars were primarily between different factions of Sunni Islam aristocracy, each seeking sovereignty and land to tax dhimmis and extract income from resident peasants.[1597]

Firuz Shah Tughluq's favorite grandson died in 1376. Thereafter, Firuz Shah sought and followed Sharia more than ever, with the help of his wazirs. He himself fell ill in 1384. By then, Muslim nobility who had installed Firuz Shah Tughluq to power in 1351 had died out, and their descendants had inherited the wealth and rights to extract taxes from non-Muslim peasants. Khan Jahan II, a wazir in Delhi, was the son of Firuz Shah Tughluq's favorite wazir Khan Jahan I, and rose in power after his father died in 1368 AD.[1598] The young wazir was in open rivalry with Muhammad Shah, the son of Firuz Shah Tughluq. The wazir's power grew as he appointed more amirs and granted favors. He persuaded the Sultan to name his great grandson as his heir. Then Khan Jahan II tried to convince Firuz Shah Tughlaq to dismiss his only surviving son. Instead of dismissing his son, the Sultan dismissed the wazir. The crisis that followed led to first civil war, arrest and execution of the wazir, followed by a rebellion and civil war in and around Delhi. Muhammad Shah too was expelled in 1387 AD. The Sultan Firuz Shah Tughlaq died in 1388 AD. Tughluq Khan assumed power, but died in conflict. In 1389, Abu Bakr Shah assumed power, but he too died within a year. The civil war continued under Sultan Muhammad Shah, and by 1390 AD, it had led to the seizure and execution of all Muslim nobility who were aligned, or suspected to be aligned to Khan Jahan II.

While the civil war was in progress, predominantly Hindu populations of Himalayan foothills of north India had rebelled, stopped paying Jizya and Kharaj taxes to Sultan's officials. Hindus of southern Doab region of India (now Etawah) joined the rebellion in 1390 AD. Sultan Muhammad Shah attacked Hindus rebelling near Delhi and southern Doab in 1392, with mass executions of peasants, and razing Etawah to the ground.[1599] However, by then, most of India had transitioned to a patchwork of smaller Muslim Sultanates and Hindu kingdoms. In 1394, Hindus in Lahore region and northwest South Asia (now Pakistan) had re-asserted self-rule. Muhammad Shah amassed an army to attack them, with his son Humayun Khan as the commander-in-chief. While preparations were in progress in Delhi in January 1394, Sultan Muhammad Shah died. His son, Humayun Khan assumed power, but was murdered within two months. The brother of Humayun Khan, Nasir-al-din Mahmud Shah assumed power - but he enjoyed little support from Muslim nobility, the wazirs and amirs. The Sultanate had lost command over almost all eastern and western provinces of already shrunken Sultanate. Within Delhi, factions of Muslim nobility formed by October 1394 AD, triggering the second civil war.

Tartar Khan installed a second Sultan, Nasir-al-din Nusrat Shah in Ferozabad, few kilometers from the first Sultan seat of power in late 1394. The two Sultans claimed to be rightful ruler of South Asia, each with a small army, controlled by a coterie of Muslim nobility. Battles occurred every month, duplicity and switching of sides by amirs became common place, and the civil war between the two Sultan factions continued through 1398, till the invasion by Timur.

Timur's Invasion

The lowest point for the dynasty came in 1398, when Turco-Mongol[1600,1601] invader, Timur (Tamerlane) defeated four armies of the Sultanate. During the invasion, Sultan Mahmud Khan fled before Tamerlane entered Delhi. For eight days Delhi was plundered, its population massacred, and over 100,000 prisoners were killed as well.

Ibn Battuta's memoir on Tughlaq dynasty

Ibn Battuta, the Moroccan Muslim traveller, left extensive notes on Tughlaq dynasty in his travel memoirs. Ibn Battuta arrived in India through the mountains of Afghanistan, in 1334, at the height of Tughlaq dynasty's geographic empire.[1602] On his way, he learnt that Sultan Muhammad Tughluq liked gifts from his visitors, and gave to his visitors gifts of far greater value in return. Ibn Battuta met Muhammad bin Tughluq, presenting him with gifts of arrows, camels, thirty horses, slaves and other goods. Muhammad bin Tughlaq responded by giving Ibn Battuta with a welcoming gift of 2,000 silver dinars, a furnished house and the job of a judge with an annual salary of 5,000 silver dinars that Ibn Battuta had the right to keep by collecting taxes from two and a half Hindu villages near Delhi.[1603]

In his memoirs about Tughlaq dynasty, Ibn Batutta recorded the history of Qutb complex which included Quwat al-Islam Mosque and the Qutb Minar.[1604] He noted the 7 year famine from 1335 AD, which killed thousands upon thousands of people near Delhi, while the Sultan was busy attacking rebellions. He was tough both against non-Muslims and Muslims. For example,

> *Not a week passed without the spilling of much Muslim blood and the running of streams of gore before the entrance of his palace. This included cutting people in half, skinning them alive, chopping off heads and displaying them on poles as a warning to others, or having prisoners tossed about by elephants with swords attached to their tusks.*

—*Ibn Battuta, Travel Memoirs (1334-1341, Delhi)*

The Sultan was far too ready to shed blood. He punished small faults and great, without respect of persons, whether men of learning, piety or high station. Every day hundreds of people, chained, pinioned, and fettered, are brought to this hall, and those who are for execution are executed, for torture tortured, and those for beating beaten.

—*Ibn Battuta, Chapter XV Rihla (Delhi)*[1605]

In Tughlaq dynasty, the punishments were extended even to Muslim religious figures who were suspected rebellion. For example, Ibn Battuta mentions Sheikh Shinab al-Din, who was imprisoned and tortured as follows:

On the fourteen day, the Sultan sent him food, but he (Sheikh Shinab al-Din) refused to eat it. When the Sultan heard this he ordered that the sheikh should be fed human excrement [dissolved in water]. [His officials] spread out the sheikh on his back, opened his mouth and made him drink it (the excrement). On the following day, he was beheaded.

—*Ibn Battuta, Travel Memoirs (1334-1341, Delhi)*

Ibn Batutta wrote that Sultan's officials demanded bribes from him while he was in Delhi, as well as deducted 10% of any sums that Sultan gave to him.[1606] Towards the end of his stay in Tughluq dynasty court, Ibn Battuta came under suspicion for his friendship with a Sufi Muslim holy man. Both Ibn Battuta and the Sufi Muslim were arrested. While Ibn Battuta was allowed to leave India, the Sufi Muslim was killed as follows according to Ibn Battuta during the period he was under arrest:

(The Sultan) had the holy man's beard plucked out hair by hair, then banished him from Delhi. Later the Sultan ordered him to return to court, which the holy man refused to do. The man was arrested, tortured in the most horrible way, then beheaded.

—*Ibn Battuta, Travel Memoirs (1334-1341, Delhi)*

Slavery under Tughlaq dynasty

Each military campaign and raid on non-Muslim kingdoms yielded loot and seizure of slaves. Additionally, the Sultans patronized a market (*al-nakhkhās*[1607]) for trade of both foreign and Indian slaves.[1608] This market flourished under the reign of all Sultans of Tughlaq dynasty, particularly Ghiyasuddin Tughlaq, Muhammad Tughlaq and Firoz Tughlaq.[1609]

Ibn Battuta's memoir record that he fathered a child each with two slave girls, one from Greece and one he purchased during his stay in Delhi Sultanate. This was in addition to the daughter he fathered by marrying a Muslim woman in India.[1610] Ibn Battuta also records that Muhammad Tughlaq sent along with his emissaries, both slave boys and slave girls as gifts to other countries such as China.[1611]

Muslim nobility and revolts

The Tughlaq dynasty experienced many revolts by Muslim nobility, particularly during Muhammad bin Tughlaq but also during other rulers such as Firoz Shah Tughlaq.[1612]

The Tughlaq's had attempted to manage their expanded empire by appointing family members and Muslim aristocracy as na'ib (نائب) of Iqta' (farming provinces, اقطاع) under contract. The contract would require that the na'ib shall have the right to force collect taxes from non-Muslim peasants and local economy, deposit a fixed sum of tribute and taxes to Sultan's treasury on a periodic basis. The contract allowed the na'ib to keep a certain amount of taxes they collected from peasants as their income, but the contract required any excess tax and seized property collected from non-Muslims to be split between na'ib and Sultan in a 20:80 ratio (Firuz Shah changed this to 80:20 ratio). The na'ib had the right to keep soldiers and officials to help extract taxes. After contracting with Sultan, the na'ib would enter into subcontracts with Muslim amirs and army commanders, each granted the right over certain villages to force collect or seize produce and property from dhimmis.[1613]

This system of tax extraction from peasants and sharing among Muslim nobility led to rampant corruption, arrests, execution and rebellion. For example, in the reign of Firoz Shah Tughlaq, a Muslim noble named Shamsaldin Damghani entered into a contract over the iqta' of Gujarat, promising an enormous sums of annual tribute while entering the contract in 1377 AD. He then attempted to force collect the amount deploying his cotorie of Muslim amirs, but failed. Even the amount he did manage to collect, he paid nothing to Delhi. Shamsaldin Damghani and Muslim nobility of Gujarat then declared rebellion and

Figure 137: *The Tomb of Shah Rukn-e-Alam in Multan, Pakistan, is considered to be the earliest example of Tughluq architecture.*

separation from Delhi Sultanate. However, the soldiers and peasants of Gujarat refused to fight the war for the Muslim nobility. Shamsaldin Damghani was killed. During the reign of Muhammad Shah Tughlaq, similar rebellions were very common. His own nephew rebelled in Malwa in 1338 AD; Muhammad Shah Tughlaq attacked Malwa, seized his nephew, and then flayed him alive in public.

Indo-Islamic Architecture

The Sultans of Tughlaq dynasty, particularly Firoz Shah Tughlaq, patronized many construction projects and are credited with the development of Indo-Islamic architecture.[1614]

Rulers

Titular Name	Personal Name Wikipedia:Citation needed	Reign
Sultan Ghiyath-ud-din Tughluq Shah سلطان غیاث الدین تغلق شاہ	Ghazi Malik غازی ملک	1321–1325
Sultan Muhammad Adil bin Tughluq Shah سلطان محمد عادل بن تغلق شاہ Ulugh Khan الغ خان Juna Khan جنا خان	Malik Fakhr-ud-din ملک فخر الدین	1325–1351
Sultan Feroze Shah Tughluq سلطان فیروز شاہ تغلق	Malik Feroze ibn Malik Rajab ملک فیروز ابن ملک رجب	1351–1388
Sultan Ghiyath-ud-din Tughluq Shah سلطان غیاث الدین تغلق شاہ	Tughluq Khan ibn Fateh Khan ibn Feroze Shah تغلق خان ابن فتح خان ابن فیروز شاہ	1388–1389
Sultan Abu Bakr Shah سلطان ابو بکر شاہ	Abu Bakr Khan ibn Zafar Khan ibn Fateh Khan ibn Feroze Shah ابو بکر خان ابن ظفر خان ابن فتح خان ابن فیروز شاہ	1389–1390
Sultan Muhammad Shah سلطان محمد شاہ	Muhammad Shah ibn Feroze Shah محمد شاہ ابن فیروز شاہ	1390–1394
Sultan Ala-ud-din Sikandar Shah سلطان علاءالدین سکندر شاہ	Humayun Khan ہمایوں خان	1394
Sultan Nasir-ud-din Mahmud Shah Tughluq سلطان ناصر الدین محمود شاہ تغلق	Mahmud Shah ibn Muhammad Shah محمود شاہ ابن محمد شاہ	1394–1412/-1413
Sultan Nasir-ud-din Nusrat Shah Tughluq سلطان ناصر الدین نصرت شاہ تغلق	Nusrat Khan ibn Fateh Khan ibn Feroze Shah نصرت خان ابن فتح خان ابن فیروز شاہ	1394–1398

- *The colored rows signify the splitting of Delhi Sultanate under two Sultans; one in the east (Orange) at Firozabad & the other in the west (Yellow) at Delhi.*

Figure 138: *Tughlaqabad Fort, Tughlaqabad, Delhi.*

Figure 139: *Sultan Ghiyath-ud-din Tughluq Shah's Mausoleum in Tughlaqabad Fort, Tughlaqabad, Delhi.*

Figure 140: *Tughlaqabad fort wall*

Figure 141: *Tughlaqabad Fort*

Figure 142: *Sultan Feroze Shah Tughlaq's tomb with adjoining Madrassa, in Hauz Khas Complex, Delhi.*

Figure 143: *Feroze Shah Kotla ruins, painted in 1802.*

Figure 144: *West Gate of Firozabad (present Feroz Shah Kotla), painted in 1802.*

Figure 145: *Feroz Shah Kotla remains next to the Feroz Shah Kotla Cricket Stadium.*

Figure 146: *Timur defeats the Sultan of Delhi, Nasir-ud-Din Mahmud Shah yesha in the winter of 1397-1398*

References

Bibliography

<templatestyles src="Template:Refbegin/styles.css" />

- Banarsi Prasad Saksena (1970). "The Tughluqs: Sultan Ghiyasuddin Tughluq". In Mohammad Habib and Khaliq Ahmad Nizami. *A Comprehensive History of India: The Delhi Sultanat (A.D. 1206-1526)*[1615]. 5. The Indian History Congress / People's Publishing House. OCLC 31870180[1616].

 Wikiquote has quotations related to: *Tughlaq dynasty*

Wikimedia Commons has media related to *Tughlaq Dynasty*.

Sayyid dynasty

Sayyid dynasty	
1414–1451	
 The tomb of Muhammad Shah at Lodi Gardens, New Delhi.	
Capital	Delhi
Languages	Persian (official)
Religion	Islam
Government	Sultanate
Sultan	
• 1414–1421	Khizr Khan
• 1421-1434	Mubarak Shah
• 1434-1445	Muhammad Shah
• 1445-1451	Ala-ud-Din Shah
History	
• Established	28 May 1414
• Disestablished	19 April 1451
Preceded by Tughlaq dynasty	**Succeeded by** Lodi dynasty
Today part of	India Pakistan

Delhi Sultanate
Ruling dynasties
• v • t • e[1617]

The **Sayyid dynasty** was the fourth dynasty of the Delhi Sultanate, with four rulers ruling from 1414 to 1451. Founded by a former governor of Multan, they succeeded the Tughlaq dynasty and ruled the sultanate until they were displaced by the Lodi dynasty. Members of the dynasty derived their title, Sayyid, or the descendants of the Prophet Muhammad, based on the claim that they belonged to the Prophet's lineage through his daughter Fatima, and son-in-law and cousin Ali.

History

Following the 1398 Sack of Delhi, Amir Timur appointed the Sayyids as the governors of Delhi. Their dynasty was established by Sayyid Khizr Khan, deputised by Timur to be the governor of Multan (Punjab). Khizr Khan captured Delhi on May 28, 1414 thereby establishing the Sayyid dynasty. Khizr Khan did not take up the title of Sultan and nominally, continued to be a *Rayat-i-Ala* (vassal) of the Timurids - initially that of Timur, and later his grandson Shah Rukh.[1618]

Khizr Khan was succeeded by his son Sayyid Mubarak Shah after his death on May 20, 1421. Mubarak Shah referred to himself as *Muizz-ud-Din Mubarak Shah* on his coins. A detailed account of his reign is available in the *Tarikh-i-Mubarak Shahi* written by Yahya-bin-Ahmad Sirhindi. After the death of Mubarak Shah, his nephew, Muhammad Shah ascended the throne and styled himself as Sultan Muhammad Shah. Just before his death, he called his son Sayyid Ala-ud-Din Shah from Badaun, and nominated him as successor.

The last ruler of the Sayyids, Ala-ud-Din, voluntarily abdicated the throne of the Delhi Sultanate in favour of Bahlul Khan Lodi on April 19, 1451, and left for Badaun, where he died in 1478.[1619]

Figure 147: *Billon Tanka of Khizr Khan INO Firoz Shah Tughlaq*

Kings

Khizr Khan

Khizr Khan was the governor of Multan under Firuz Shah Tughlaq. When Timur invaded India, Khizr Khan a sayyid from Multan joined him. Timur appointed him the governor of Multan and Lahore. He then conquered the city of Delhi and started the rule of the Sayyids in 1414. He was ruling in name of Timur. He could not assume an independent position in all respects. As a mark of recognition of the suzerainty of the Mongols, the name of the Mongol ruler (Shah Rukh) was recited in the khutba but as an interesting innovation, the name of Khizr Khan was also attached to it. But strangely enough the name of Mongol ruler was not inscribed on the coins and the name of old Tughlaq sultan continued on the currency. No coins are known in the name of Khizr Khan.[1620]

Mubarak Shah

Mubarak Shah was the son of Khizr Khan. He came to the throne in 1421. He was a man of great vision, but the nobles were against him and kept revolting.

Muhammad Shah

Muhammad Shah was a nephew of Mubarak Shah. He ruled from 1434-1445.

Figure 148: *Double falus of Mubarak Shah*

Figure 149: *Billon Tanka of 80 rati of Alam Shah*

Ala-ud-din Alam Shah

Alam Shah was a weak ruler. In 1451 he surrendered Delhi to Bahlul Lodi and went to Budaun where he spent rest of his life.

External links

- Encyclopædia Britannica - Sayyid Dynasty[1621]
- Coin Gallery - Sayyid Dynasty[1622]

Lodi dynasty

Lodi dynasty	
1451–1526	
Map showing the territory under the Lodi dynasty, marked as **Afghan Empire**.	
Capital	Delhi
Languages	Persian
Religion	Sunni Islam
Government	Monarchy
History	
• Established	1451
• Disestablished	1526
Preceded by	Succeeded by
Sayyid dynasty	Mughal Empire

Delhi Sultanate
Ruling dynasties
• v • t • e[1623]

The **Lodi dynasty** (or Lodhi) was an Afghan[1624] dynasty that ruled the Delhi Sultanate from 1451 to 1526. It was the last dynasty of the Delhi Sultanate, and was founded by Bahlul Khan Lodi when he replaced the Sayyid dynasty.

Bahlul Lodi

Bahlul Khan Lodi (r. 1451–1489) was the nephew and son-in-law of Malik Sultan Shah Lodi, the governor of Sirhind in (Punjab), India and succeeded him as the governor of Sirhind during the reign of Sayyid dynasty ruler Muhammad Shah. Muhammad Shah raised him to the status of an emir. He was the most powerful of the Punjab chiefs and a vigorous leader, holding together a loose confederacy of Afghan and Turkish chiefs with his strong personality.[25] He reduced the turbulent chiefs of the provinces to submission and infused some vigour into the government.Wikipedia:Citation needed After the last Sayyid ruler of Delhi, Ala-ud-Din Aalm Shah voluntarily abdicated in favour of him, Bahlul Khan Lodi ascended the throne of the Delhi sultanate on 19 April 1451.[1625] The most important event of his reign was the conquest of Jaunpur.Wikipedia:Citation needed Bahlul spent most of his time in fighting against the Sharqi dynasty and ultimately annexed it. He placed his eldest surviving son Barbak on the throne of Jaunpur in 1486.Wikipedia:Citation needed

Sikandar Lodi

Sikandar Lodi (r. 1489–1517) (born Nizam Khan), the second son of Bahlul, succeeded him after his death on 17 July 1489 and took up the title *Sikandar Shah*. He was nominated by his father to succeed him and was crowned sultan on 15 July 1489. He founded Agra in 1504 and built mosques. He shifted the capital from Delhi to Agra.[1626] He abolished corn duties and patronized trade and commerce. He was a poet of repute, composing under the penname of Gulruk. He was also patron of learning and ordered Sanskrit work in medicine to be translated into Persian and Afghani.[1627] He curbed the individualistic tendencies of his Pashtun nobles and compelled them to submit their accounts to state audit. He was, thus, able to infuse vigor and discipline in the administration. His greatest achievement was the conquest and annexation of Bihar.[1628]

Sultan Ibrahim Loudi (1517)
Figure 150: *Ibrahim Lodi.*

Ibrahim Lodi

Ibrahim Lodi (r. 1517–1526), the youngest son of Sikandar, was the last Lodi Sultan of Delhi. He had the qualities of an excellent warrior, but he was rash and impolitic in his decisions and actions. His attempt at royal absolutism was premature and his policy of sheer repression unaccompanied by measures to strengthen the administration and increase the military resources was sure to prove a failure.Wikipedia:Citation needed Ibrahim faced numerous rebellions and kept out the opposition for almost a decade. He was engaged in warfare with the Afghans and the Mughal Empire for most of his reign and died trying to keep the Lodi Dynasty from annihilation. Ibrahim was defeated in 1526 at the Battle of Panipat. This marked the end of the Lodi Dynasty and the rise of the Mughal Empire in India led by Babur (r. 1526–1530).

Fall of the empire

By the time Ibrahim ascended the throne, the political structure in the Lodi Dynasty had dissolved due to abandoned trade routes and the depleted treasury. The Deccan was a coastal trade route, but in the late fifteenth century the supply lines had collapsed. The decline and eventual failure of this specific trade route resulted in cutting off supplies from the coast to the interior, where the Lodi empire resided. The Lodi Dynasty was not able to protect itself if warfare were to break out on the trade route roads; therefore, they didn't use those trade routes, thus their trade declined and so did their treasury leaving them vulnerable to internal political problems. In order to take revenge of the insults done by Ibrahim, the governor of Lahore, Daulat Khan Lodi asked the ruler of Kabul, Babur to invade his kingdom. Ibrahim Lodi was thus killed in a battle with Babur. With the death of Ibrahim Lodi, the Lodi dynasty also came to an end.Wikipedia:Citation needed

Afghan factionalism

Another problem Ibrahim faced when he ascended the throne in 1517 were the Pashtun nobles, some of whom supported Ibrahim's older brother, Jalaluddin, in taking up arms against his brother in the area in the east at Jaunpur. Ibrahim gathered military support and defeated his brother by the end of the year. After this incident, he arrested those Pashtun nobles who opposed him and appointed his own men as the new administrators. Other Pashtun nobles supported the governor of Bihar, Dariya Khan, against Ibrahim.

Another factor that caused uprisings against Ibrahim was his lack of an apparent successor. His own uncle, Alam Khan, betrayed Ibrahim by supporting the Mughal invader Babur.

Battle of Panipat, 1526

After being assured of the cooperation of Alam Khan and Daulat Khan, Governor of the Punjab, Babur gathered his army. Upon entering the Punjab plains, Babur's chief allies, namely Langar Khan Niazi advised Babur to engage the powerful Janjua Rajputs to join his conquest. The tribe's rebellious stance to the throne of Delhi was well known. Upon meeting their chiefs, Malik Hast (Asad) and Raja Sanghar Khan, Babur made mention of the Janjua's popularity as traditional rulers of their kingdom and their ancestral support for his patriarch Emir Timur during his conquest of Hind. Babur aided them in defeating their enemies, the Gakhars in 1521, thus cementing their alliance. Babur employed them as Generals in his campaign for Delhi, the conquest of Rana Sanga and the conquest of India.Wikipedia:Citation needed

The new usage of guns allowed small armies to make large gains on enemy territory. Small parties of skirmishers who had been dispatched simply to test enemy positions and tactics, were making inroads into India. Babur, however, had survived two revolts, one in Kandahar and another in Kabul, and was careful to pacify the local population after victories, following local traditions and aiding widows and orphans.Wikipedia:Citation needed

Despite both being Sunni Muslims, Babur wanted Ibrahim's power and territory. Babur and his army of 24,000 men marched to the battlefield at Panipat armed with muskets and artillery. Ibrahim prepared for battle by gathering 100,000 men (well-armed but with no guns) and 1,000 elephants. Ibrahim was at a disadvantage because of his outmoded infantry and internecine rivalries. Even though he had more men, he had never fought in a war against gunpowder weapons and he did not know what to do strategically. Babur pressed his advantage from the start and Ibrahim perished on the battlefield in April 1526, along with 20,000 of his men.

Accession of Babur and the Mughals

After Ibrahim's death, Babur named himself emperor over Ibrahim's territory, instead of placing Alam Khan (Ibrahim's uncle) on the throne. Ibrahim's death marked the end of the Lodi dynasty and led to the establishment of the Mughal Empire in India. The remaining Lodi territories were absorbed into the new Mughal Empire. Babur continued to engage in more military campaigns.

Mahmud Lodi

Ibrahim Lodi's brother, Mahmud Lodi, declared himself Sultan and continued to resist Mughal forces. He provided 10,000 Afghan soldiers to Rana Sanga in battle of Khanwa. After the defeat, Mahmud Lodi fled eastwards and again posed a challenge to Babur two years later at the Battle of Ghaghra.[1629]

Further reading

- Desoulieres, Alain. "Mughal Diplomacy in Gujarat (1533–1534) in Correia's 'Lendas da India'". *Modern Asian Studies*. **22** (3): 454. doi: 10.1017/s0026749x00009616[1630]. JSTOR 312590[1631]. (Subscription required (help)).
- Haider, Najaf (1996). "Precious Metal Flows and Currency Circulation in the Mughal Empire". *Journal of the Economic and Social History of the Orient*. **39** (3): 298–364. doi: 10.1163/1568520962601180[1632]. JSTOR 3632649[1633]. (Subscription required (help)).
- Subrahmanyam, Sanjay (2000). "A Note on the Rise of Surat in the Sixteenth Century". *Journal of the Economic and Social History of the Orient*. **43** (1): 23–33. doi: 10.1163/156852000511222[1634]. JSTOR 3632771[1635]. (Subscription required (help)).
- Ud-Din, Hameed (January–March 1962). "Historians of Afghan Rule in India". *Journal of the American Oriental Society*. **82** (1): 44–51. JSTOR 595978[1636]. (Subscription required (help)).

External links

Wikiquote has quotations related to: *Lodi dynasty*

Wikimedia Commons has media related to *Lodi dynasty*.

- A History of Sind, Volume II, Translated from Persian Books by Mirza Kalichbeg Fredunbeg, chpt. 68[1637]
- Coin Gallery - Lodhi Dynasty[1638]

Pandyan dynasty

Pandyan Empire	
300 BCE–1650 CE	
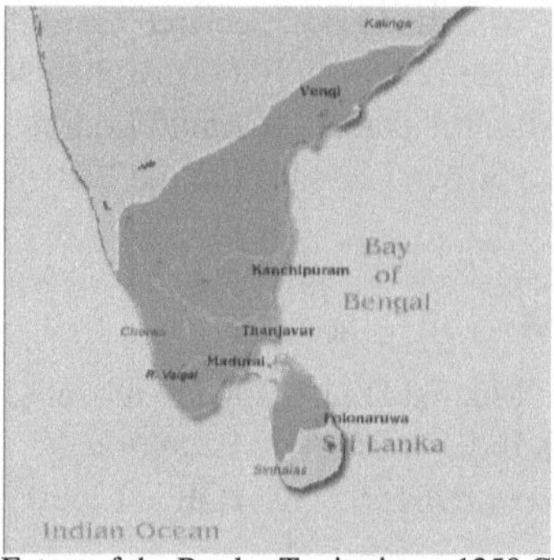 Extent of the Pandya Territories c. 1250 CE	
Capital	Korkai Madurai (3rd century BCE – 1345 CE) Tenkasi (1345 – 1630 CE), Tirunelveli (1345 – 1650 CE), Vizhinjam (Thiruvananthapuram) (Earlier Ay kingdom)Wikipedia:Citation needed
Languages	Tamil, Sanskrit
Religion	Jainism, Hinduism, Buddhism
Government	Monarchy
King	
• 560–590 CE	Kadungon

• 1309–1345 CE	Vira Pandyan IV
• 1422–1463 CE	Jatavarman Parakrama Pandyan
Historical era	Iron Age to Renaissance
• Established	300 BCE
• Disestablished	1650 CE
Succeeded by	
Delhi Sultanate	
Madurai Nayak dynasty	
Jaffna kingdom	
Sambuvaraya	
Today part of	India Sri Lanka

Part of a series on
History of Tamil Nadu

- v
- t
- e[1639]

The **Pandyan dynasty** was an ancient Tamil dynasty, one of the three Tamil dynasties, the other two being the Chola and the Chera. The kings of the three dynasties were referred to as the Three Crowned Kings of Tamilakam.

The Early Pandyans ruled parts of Southern India from at least 4th century BCE. Pandyan rule ended in the first half of the 16th century CE. They initially ruled their country *Pandya Nadu* from Korkai, a seaport on the southernmost tip of the Indian Peninsula, and in later times moved to Madurai. Fish being their flag, Pandyas were experts in water management, agriculture(mostly near river banks) and fisheries and they were eminent sailors and sea traders too. *Pandyan* was well known since ancient times, with contacts, even diplomatic, reaching the Roman Empire. The Pandyan empire was home to temples including Meenakshi Amman Temple in Madurai, and Nellaiappar Temple built on the bank of the river Thamirabarani in Tirunelveli.

The Pandya kings were called either Jatavarman or Maravarman. They were Jains in their early ages but later became Shaivaites. Strabo states that an Indian king called Pandion sent Augustus Caesar "presents and gifts of honour".[1640] The country of the Pandyans was described as *Pandyas* by Megasthenes, *Pandi Mandala* in the Periplus of the Erythraean Sea and described as *Pandyan Mediterranea* and *Modura Regia Pandionis* by Ptolemy.

Traditionally, the legendary Sangams were held in Madurai under their patronage, and some of the Pandya Kings were poets themselves. The early Pandyan Dynasty of the Sangam Literature faded into obscurity upon the invasion of the Kalabhras. The dynasty revived under Kadungon in the early 6th century, pushed the Kalabhras out of the Tamil country and ruled from Madurai. They again went into decline with the rise of the Cholas in the 9th century and were in constant conflict with them. The Pandyas allied themselves with the Sinhalese and the Cheras in harassing the Chola empire until they found an opportunity for reviving their fortunes during the late 13th century. The Later Pandyas (1216–1345) entered their golden age under Maravarman Sundara Pandyan and Jatavarman Sundara Pandyan (c. 1251), who expanded the empire into Telugu country, conquered Kalinga (Orissa) and invaded and conquered Sri Lanka. They also had extensive trade links with the Southeast Asian maritime empires of Srivijaya and their successors. The Pandyas excelled in both trade and literature. They controlled the pearl fisheries along the South Indian coast between Sri Lanka and India which produced some of the finest pearls in the known ancient world.

During their history, the Pandyas were repeatedly in conflict with the Pallavas, Cholas, Hoysalas and finally the Muslim invaders from the Delhi Sultanate. The Islamic invasion led to the end of Pandyan supremacy in South India and in 1323, the Jaffna Kingdom of Sri Lanka declared its independence from the crumbling Pandyan Empire.[1641,1642] The Pandyans lost their capital city Madurai to Madurai Sultanate in 1335. However, they shifted their capital to Tenkasi and continued to rule the Tirulnelveli, Tuticorin, Ramanad, Sivagangai regions. Meanwhile, Madurai sultanate was replaced by Nayaka governors of Vijayanagara in 1378. In 1529 Nayaka governors declared independence and established Madurai Nayak dynasty.

Etymology

The word Pandya is derived from the Tamil word "Pandu" meaning very old. Another theory is that the word "Pandya" is derived from the Tamil word "Pandi" meaning bull. Ancient Tamils, considered the bull as a sign of masculinity and valor. Robert Caldwell derives the word *Pandya* from Pandu, the father of the Pandavas from Mahabharata, whose descendants Pandyans claim.

Another theory suggests that in Sangam Tamil lexicon the word Pandya means *old country* in contrast with Chola meaning *new country*, Chera meaning *hill country* and Pallava meaning *branch* in Sanskrit. The Chera, Chola and Pandya are the traditional Tamil siblings and together with the Pallavas are the major Kings that ruled ancient Tamilakam.

Historians have used several sources to identify the origins of the early Pandyan dynasty with the pre-Christian Era and also to piece together the names of the Pandyan kings. The Pandyans were one of the longest ruling dynasty of Indian history.

Mythology

According to the Epic Mahabharatha the legendary Malayadwaja Pandya, who sided with the Pandavas and took part in the Kurukshetra War of the Mahabharata, is described as follows in Karna Parva (verse 20.25):[1643,1644]

"Although knowing that the shafts (arrows) of the high souled son of Drona employed in shooting were really inexhaustible, yet Pandya, that bull among men, cut them all into pieces".

Malayadwaja Pandya and his queen Kanchanamala had one daughter Thataathagai alias Meenakshi who succeeded her father and reigned the kingdom successfully. The Madurai Meenakshi Amman Temple was built after her. The city of Madurai was built around this temple. It is also notable that the etymology of the name Meenakshi or *Meenatchi*, is derived from either the Tamil *Meen* (fish) and Sanskrit *akshi* (eyes) which collectively means the one with "Fish-shaped eyes", or the Tamil words *Meen* (fish) and *aatchi* (rule), literally meaning "Rule of the Fish".

Figure 151: *Four-armed Vishnu, Pandya Dynasty, 8th–9th century CE.*

Sources

Sangam literature

Pandya kings find mention in a number of poems in the Sangam Literature. Among them Nedunjeliyan, 'the victor of Talaiyalanganam', and Mudukudimi Peruvaludi 'of several sacrifices' deserve special mention. Beside several short poems found in the *Akananuru* and the *Purananuru* collections, there are two major works – *Mathuraikkanci* and the *Netunalvatai* (in the collection of *Pattupattu*) – which give a glimpse into the society and commercial activities in the Pandyan kingdom during the Sangam age.

It is difficult to estimate the exact dates of these Sangam age Pandyas. The period covered by the extant literature of the Sangam is unfortunately not easy to determine with any measure of certainty. Except the longer epics *Silapathikaram* and *Manimekalai*, which by common consent belong to an age later than the Sangam age, the poems have reached us in the forms of systematic anthologies. Each individual poem has generally attached to it a colophon on the authorship and subject matter of the poem. The name of the king or chieftain to whom the poem relates and the occasion which called forth the eulogy are also found.Wikipedia:Citation needed

It is from these colophons, and rarely from the texts of the poems themselves, that we gather the names of many kings and chieftains and the poets patronised by them. The task of reducing these names to an ordered scheme in which the different generations of contemporaries can be marked off one another has not been easy. To add to the confusions, some historians have even denounced these colophons as later additions and untrustworthy as historical documents.Wikipedia:Citation needed

Any attempt at extracting a systematic chronology from these poems should take into consideration the casual nature of these poems and the wide differences between the purposes of the anthologist who collected these poems and the historian's attempts to arrive at a continuous history.

Pandyas are also mentioned by Greek Megesthenes where he writes about southern kingdom being ruled by women.

Epigraphy

The earliest Pandyan king to be found in epigraph is Nedunjeliyan, figuring in the Tamil-Brahmi Mangulam inscription assigned from the 2nd to the 1st centuries BCE.The record documents a gift of rock-cut beds, to a Jain ascetic. Silver Punch-marked coins with the fish symbol in the Pandya country dating from around the same time have also been found.

Pandyas are also mentioned in the Pillars of Ashoka (inscribed 273 – 232 BCE). In his inscriptions Ashoka refers to the peoples of south India – the Cholas, Cheras, Pandyas and Satiyaputras – as recipients of his Buddhist proselytism.[1645,1646] These kingdoms, although not part of the Mauryan Empire, were on friendly terms with Ashoka:

> The conquest by Dharma has been won here, on the borders, and even six hundred yojanas (5,400–9,600 km) away, where the Greek king Antiochos rules, beyond there where the four kings named Ptolemy, Antigonos, Magas and Alexander rule, likewise in the south among the Cholas, the Pandyas, and as far as Tamraparni river.[1647]

Kharavela, the Kalinga king who ruled during the 2nd century BCE, in his Hathigumpha inscription, claims to have destroyed a confederacy of Tamil states (*Tamiradesasanghatam*) which had lasted 132 years, and to have acquired a large quantity of pearls from the Pandyas.

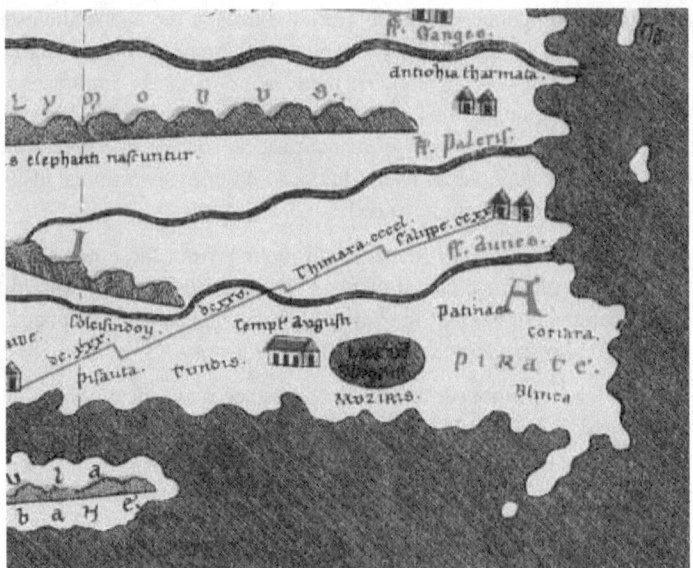

Figure 152: *Muziris, as shown in the Tabula Peutingeriana, with a "Templum Augusti".*

Foreign sources

Megasthenes knew of the Pandyan kingdom around 300 BCE. He described it in *Indika* as *occupying the portion of India which lies southward and extends to the sea*. According to his account, it had 365 villages, each of which was expected to meet the needs of the royal household for one day in the year. He described the Pandyan queen at the time, *Pandaia* as a daughter of Heracles.[1648]

The Periplus of the Erythraean Sea (c. 60 – c. 100 CE) describes the riches of a 'Pandian Kingdom':

> *...Nelcynda is distant from Muziris by river and sea about five hundred stadia, and is of another Kingdom, the Pandian. This place also is situated on a river, about one hundred and twenty stadia from the sea....*[1649]

The Chinese historian Yu Huan in his 3rd-century text, the *Weilüe*, mentions the Panyue kingdom: *...The kingdom of Panyue is also called* Hanyuewang. *It is several thousand li to the southeast of Tianzhu (Northern India)...The inhabitants are small; they are the same height as the Chinese....* John E. Hill identified Panyue as Pandya kingdom.[1650] However, others have identified it with an ancient state located in modern Burma or Assam.

The Roman emperor Julian received an embassy from a Pandya about 361. A Roman trading centre was located on the Pandyan coast at the mouth of the Vaigai river, southeast of Madurai.

Pandyas also had trade contacts with Ptolemaic Egypt and, through Egypt, with Rome by the 1st century, and with China by the 3rd century. The 1st-century Greek historian Nicolaus of Damascus met, at Antioch, the ambassador sent by a king from India "named Pandion or, according to others, Porus" to Caesar Augustus around 13 CE (Strabo XV.4 and 73).[1651,1652]

The Chinese traveler Xuanzang mentions a kingdom further south from Kanchipuram, a kingdom named *Malakutta*, identified with Madurai described by his Buddhist friends at Kanchipuram.

In the later part of the 13th century Venetian traveller Marco Polo visited the Pandyan kingdom and left a vivid description of the land and its people.[1653,1654] Polo exclaimed that:

The darkest man is here the most highly esteemed and considered better than the others who are not so dark. Let me add that in very truth these people portray and depict their gods and their idols black and their devils white as snow. For they say that God and all the saints are black and the devils are all white. That is why they portray them as I have described.[1655]

History

Literary sources

Although there are many instances of the Pandyas being referred to in surviving ancient Hindu texts including the Mahabharata, we currently have no way of determining a cogent genealogy of these ancient kings. We have a connected history of the Pandyas from the fall of Kalabhras during the middle of the 6th century.

Tamil literary sources

Several Tamil literary works, such as Iraiyanar Agapporul, mention the legend of three separate Tamil Sangams lasting several centuries before the Christian Era and ascribe their patronage to the Pandyas.

The Sangam poem *Maduraikkanci* by Mankudi Maruthanaar contains a full-length description of Madurai and the Pandyan country under the rule of Nedun cheliyan III. The *Nedunalvadai* by Nakkirar contains a description of the king's palace. The *Purananuru* and *Agananuru* collections of the 3rd century BCE contain poems sung in praise of various Pandyan kings and also poems that were composed by the kings themselves.

Figure 153: *Sculpture of Lord Rama*

Sanskrit literary sources

The *Ramayana* makes a few references to the Pandyas. For instance, when Sugriva sends his monkey warriors to search Sita, he mentions Chera, Chola and Pandya of the Southern region.[1656] Kalidasa's *Raghuvamsha*, an epic poem about Rama's dynasty, states that Ravana signed a peace treaty with a Pandya king.

The *Mahabharata* mentions the Pandyas a number of times. It states that the Pandya country was located on the sea shore, and supplied troops to the Pandava king Yudhishthira during the war (5:19). The Pandya king Sarangadhwaja commanded 140,000 warriors (7.23). Pandya warrior Malayadhwaja had a one-to-one fight with Drona's son Ashwatthama (8:20). *Mahabharata* mentions that *tirtha*s (sacred places) of Agastya, Varuna and Kumari were located in the Pandya country.

Early Pandyas (3rd century BCE – 3rd century CE)

The following is a partial list of Pandyan emperors who ruled during the Sangam age:

- Koon Pandyan
- Nedunjeliyan I (Aariyap Padai Kadantha Nedunj Cheliyan)

Figure 154: *Manikkavacakar, Minister of Pandya king Varagunavarman II (c. 862 – 885)*

- Pudappandyan
- Mudukudumi Peruvaludhi
- Nedunjeliyan II
- Nan Maran
- Nedunj Cheliyan III (Talaiyaalanganathu Seruvendra Nedunj Cheliyan)
- Maran Valudi
- Kadalan valuthi
- Musiri Mutriya Cheliyan
- Ukkirap Peruvaludi

First Pandyan Empire (6th – 10th centuries CE)

After the close of the Sangam age, the first Pandyan empire was established by Kadungon in the 6th century by defeating the Kalabhras. The following chronological list of the Pandya emperors is based on an inscription found on the Vaigai riverbeds. Succeeding kings assumed the titles of "Maravarman" and "Sadayavarman" alternately, where Sadayavarman denotes themselves as followers of Lord Sadaiyan ("The one with Jata", referring to Siva).

Figure 155: *Jatavarman Veera Pandyan II's double fish carp black granite bas-relief of the Koneswaram temple in Trincomalee, reminiscent of the dynasty's coinage symbols found on the island from the pre-modern era, installed after defeating the usurper Chandrabhanu of Tambralinga. Pandyan affairs in Northern Sri Lanka grew stronger following the intervention of Srimara Srivallabha in 815*

After the defeat of the Kalabhras, the Pandya kingdom grew steadily in power and territory. With the Cholas in obscurity, the Tamil country was divided between the Pallavas and the Pandyas, the river Kaveri being the frontier between them.

After Vijayalaya Chola conquered Thanjavur by defeating the Muttarayar chieftains who were part of Pandya family tree around 850, the Pandyas went into a period of decline. They were constantly harassing their Chola overlords by occupying their territories. Parantaka I invaded the Pandya territories and defeated Rajasimha III. However, the Pandyas did not wholly submit to the Cholas despite loss of power, territory and prestige. They tried to forge various alliances with the Cheras and the Kings of Lanka and tried to engage the Cholas in war to free themselves from Chola supremacy. But right from the times of Parantaka I to the early 12th century up to the times of Kulottunga Chola I the Pandyas could not overpower the Cholas who right from 880–1215 remained the most powerful empire spread over South India, Deccan and the Eastern and Western Coast of India during this period.

List of kings with dates as estimated by K. A. Nilakanta Sastri:[1657]

- Kadungon (r. c. 590–620 CE)
- Maravarman Avani Sulamani (r. c. 620-645 CE)
- Jayantavarman alias Seliyan Sendan (r. c. 645-670 CE)
- Arikesari Maravarman (r. c. 670–700 CE)
- Kochadaiyan Ranadhiran (r. c. 700–730 CE)
- Maravarman Rajasimha I (r. c. 735–765 CE)
- Jatila Parantaka Nedunjadayan (r. c. 765–815 CE)
- Maravarman Rajasimha II (r. c. 815-817 CE)
- Varaguna I (r. c. 817–835 CE)
- Srimara Srivallabha (r. c. 815–862 CE)
- Varaguna II (r. c. 862–885 CE)
- Parantaka Viranarayanan (r. c. 880–905 CE)
- Maravarman Rajasimha II (r. c. 905–920 CE)

Under Chola Influence (10th – 13th centuries)

The Chola domination of the Tamil country began in earnest during the reign of Parantaka Chola II. Chola armies led by Aditya Karikala, son of Parantaka Chola II defeated Vira Pandya in battle. The Pandyas were assisted by the Sinhalese forces of Mahinda IV. Pandyas were driven out of their territories and had to seek refuge on the island of Sri Lanka. This was the start of the long exile of the Pandyas. They were replaced by a series of Chola viceroys with the title *Chola Pandyas* who ruled from Madurai from c. 1020. Rajadhiraja III aided the Kulesekhara III by defeating the Sinhalese army and crowning him as king of Madurai. The "Chola yoke" started from about 920 and lasted until the start of the 13th century. The following list gives the names of the Pandya kings who were active during the 10th century and the first half of 11th century.

- Sundara Pandya I
- Vira Pandya I
- Vira Pandya II
- Amarabhujanga Tivrakopa
- Jatavarman Sundara Chola Pandya
- Maravarman Vikrama Chola Pandya
- Maravarman Parakrama Chola Pandya
- Jatavarman Chola Pandya
- Seervallabha Manakulachala (1101–1124)
- Maaravarman Seervallaban (1132–1161)
- Parakrama Pandyan I (1161–1162)
- Kulasekara Pandyan III
- Vira Pandyan III
- Jatavarman Srivallaban (1175–1180)
- Jatavarman Kulasekaran I (1190–1216)

Figure 156: *A Pandya Style Wikipedia:Citation needed sculpture*

Second Pandyan Empire (13th and 14th centuries)

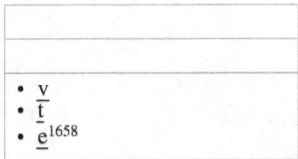

The 13th century is the greatest period in the history of the Pandyan Empire. This period saw the rise of seven prime Lord Emperors (*Ellarkku Nayanar – Lord of All*) of Pandyan, who ruled the kingdom alongside Pandyan princes. Their power reached its zenith under Jatavarman Sundara Pandyan in the middle of the 13th century. The foundation for such a great empire was laid by Maravarman Sundara Pandyan early in the 13th century.

- Parakrama Pandyan II (king of Polonnaruwa) (1212–1215)
- Maravarman Sundara Pandyan(1216–1238)
- Sundaravarman Kulasekaran II (1238–1240)
- Maravarman Sundara Pandyan II (1238–1251)
- Jatavarman Sundara Pandyan (1251–1268)
- Maravarman Kulasekara Pandyan I (1268–1310)
- Sundara Pandyan IV (1309–1327)
- Vira Pandyan IV (1309–1345)

The Pandyan kingdom was replaced by the Chola princes who assumed the title as Chola Pandyas in the 11th century. After being overshadowed by the Pallavas and Cholas for centuries, Pandyan glory was briefly revived by the much celebrated Jatavarman Sundara Pandyan I in 1251 AD.

Pandyan power extended from the Telugu countries on banks of the Godavari river to Sri Lanka, which was invaded by Jatavarman Sundara Pandyan I in 1258 and on his behalf by his younger brother Jatavarman Vira Pandyan II from 1262 to 1264. They ruled the whole peninsula and reduced the power of the Cholas and the Hoysala, also making Chera Nadu and Sri Lanka Pandyan provinces. Later Jatavarman Sundara Pandyan appointed his brother to rule Kongu country, Chola country and Hoysala country.

The marital alliance of Kulothunga Chola III and one of his successors, Rajaraja Chola III, with the Hoysalas did not yield any advantage in countering the Pandyan resurgence, who got defeated by Maravarman Sundara Pandyan I, who after the victory burnt down Uraiyur and Thanjavur. The Cholas renewed their control with the help of the Hoysalas under Hoysala king Vira Someshwara. The later successor of Maravarman Sundara Pandyan I, Maravarman Sundara Pandyan II got defeated by Rajendra Chola III around 1250.

Jatavarman Sundara Pandyan I subdued Rajendra Chola III in around 1258–1260 and was an equal antagonist of the Hoysalas whose presence he absolutely disliked in the Tamil country. He first vanquished the Kadava Pallavas

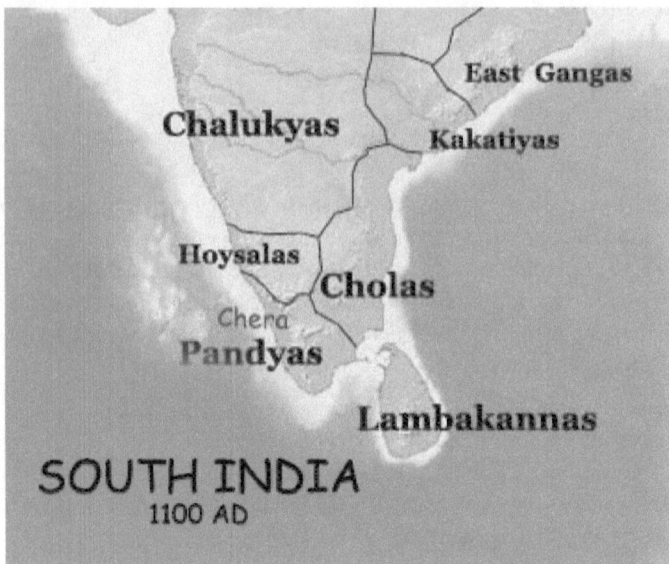

Figure 157: *Pandya power in South India*

under Kopperunchinga II, who had challenged the Hoysala army stationed in and around Kanchipuram and killed a few of their commanders.

Around 1260 dragged Jatavarman I first the Hoysalas into war by routing Vira Someshwara's son Ramanatha out of Tiruchirappalli. Vira Someshwara Hoysala, who had given the control of the empire to his sons tried to challenge Jatavarman. Between Samayapuram and Tiruchy, the armies of Vira Someshwara were routed with Vira Someshwara losing his life in this battle to Jatavarman Sundara Pandyan I in Kannanur.

Next concentrated Jatavarman I on completely wiping out the Chola empire. Rajendra Chola III had been counting on Hoysala assistance in case he was challenged by the Pandyans, keeping in mind the earlier marital alliance of the Cholas with the Hoysalas. Initially, Jatavarman consolidated the Pandyan hold on Tiruchirappalli and Thiruvarangam and marched towards Thanjavur and Kumbakonam. The Hoysala king Narasimha III joined hands with the Pandyans, opposing alliance with the Cholas. When challenged by Jatavarman Sundara Pandyan, Rajendra III marched against the Pandyans between Tanjore and Tiruchy, hoping for assistance and participation in war from the Hoysalas. However, the already vanquished Hoysalas were in a defensive position. They did not want to go to war and risk yet another defeat by the resurgent Pandyans. Jatavarman Sundara Pandyan who defeated the Kadava Pallavas, Hoysalas and also the Telugu Choda, forced Rajendra III to become his tributary vassal.

Jatavarman Sundara Pandiyan invaded Sri Lanka in 1258 and took control over Jaffna Kingdom by defeating the Javaka king Chandrabhanu, making the Javaka king paying tribute to him. Chandrabhanu and two Sinhalese princes revolted against the Pandyans in 1270, and got his final defeat in 1270 by the brother of Jatavarman Sundara Pandyan I, Jatavarman Vira Pandyan II.

Around 1279 was the combined force of Hoysala Ramanatha and Rajendra Chola III defeated by Maravarman Kulasekara Pandyan I, giving an ultimate end on the Chola dynasty.

Pandyan Civil War (AD 1308 to 1311)

After the death of the king Maravarman Kulashekhara, his sons Vira and Sundara fought a war of succession for control of the kingdom. Taking advantage of this situation, the neighbouring Hoysala king Ballala III invaded the Pandya territory. However, Ballala had to retreat to his capital, when Malik Kafur, a general of the Muslim Delhi Sultanate, invaded his kingdom at the same time.[1659] After subjugating Ballala, Malik Kafur marched to the Pandya territory in March 1311.[1660] His army raided a number of places in the kingdom, massacring people and destroying temples. The Pandya brothers fled their headquarters, and Kafur pursued them unsuccessfully, hoping to make one of them a tributary to the Delhi Sultan Alauddin Khalji. Nevertheless, the invaders obtained a large number of treasures, elephants and horses.[1661,1662]

According to the 14th century Sanskrit treatise *Lilatilakam*, a general named Vikrama Pandya defeated the Muslims. Some historians have identified Vikrama as an uncle of Vira and Sundara, and believe that he defeated Malik Kafur. However, this identification is not supported by historical evidence: Vikrama Pandya mentioned in *Leelathilakam* appears to have defeated a later Muslim army during 1365-70.[1663] By late April 1311, the rains had obstructed the operations of the Delhi forces, and the invading generals received the news that the defenders had assembled a large army against them.[1664] Kafur gave up his plans to pursue the Pandya brothers, and returned to Delhi with the plunder.[1665]

After Kafur's departure, Vira and Sundara resumed their conflict. Sundara Pandya was defeated, and sought help from the Delhi Sultanate. With their help, he regained control of the South Arcot region by 1314.[1664]

Decline and fall

Subsequently, this there were two other expeditions from the Khalji Sultanate in 1314 led by Khusro Khan (later Sultan Nasir-ud-din) and in 1323 by Ulugh Khan (Muhammad bin Tughluq) under Sultan Ghiyath al-Din Tughluq. These invasions shattered the Pandyan empire beyond revival. While the previous invasions were content with plunder, Ulugh Khan annexed the former Pandyan

Figure 158: *An aerial view of Madurai city from atop the Meenakshi Amman temple*

dominions to the Delhi Sultanate as the province of Ma'bar. Most of South India came under the Delhi's rule and was divided into five provinces – Devagiri, Tiling, Kampili, Dorasamudra and Ma'bar.[1666] Jalaluddin Ahsan Khan was appointed governor of the newly created southern-most Ma'bar province of the Delhi Sultanate by Muhammad bin Tughluq. In 1333, Sayyid Jalaluddin Ahsan Khan declared his independence and created Madurai Sultanate, a short lived independent Muslim kingdom based in the city of Madurai. Hoysala king Veera Ballala III, from his capital in Tiruvannamalai, challenged the Madurai Sultans at Kannanur Kuppam near Srirangam and died fighting them in 1343. Bukkaraya I of Vijayanagara Empire conquered the city of Madurai in 1371, imprisoned the Sultan, released and restored Arcot's Tamil prince Sambuva Raya to the throne. Bukka I appointed his son Veera Kumara Kampana as the viceroy of the Tamil region. Later, Nayaka governors were appointed.Wikipedia:Identifying reliable sources who would continue ruling till 1736.

Architecture

Rock cut and structural temples are significant part of pandyan architecture. The Vimana and mandapa are some of the features of the early Pandyan temples.

Groups of small temples are seen at Tiruchirappalli district of Tamil Nadu. The Shiva temples have a Nandi bull sculpture in front of the *maha mandapa*. In the later stages of Pandyas rule, finely sculptured idols, gopurams on the vimanas were developed. Gopurams are the rectangular entrance and portals of the temples.

Meenakshi Amman Temple in Madurai and Nellaiappar Temple in Tirunelveli were built during the reign of the Pandyas.

Figure 159: *The Gopuram of Nellaiappar Temple*

Figure 160: *One of the early coins of the Pandyans showing their emblem of the two fishes.*

Figure 161: *Temple between hill symbols and elephant coin of the Pandyas Sri Lanka 1st century CE.*

Coinage

The early coins of Tamilakam bore the symbols of the Three Crowned Kings, the tiger, the fish and the bow, representing the symbols of the Cholas, Pandyas and Cheras. Coins of Pandyas bear the legend of different Pandya ruler in different times. The Pandyas had issued silver punch-marked and die struck copper coins in the early period. A few gold coins were attributed to the Pandya rulers of this period. These coins bore the image of fish, singly or in pairs, which where their emblem.

Some of the coins had the names Sundara, Sundara Pandya or merely the letter 'Su' were etched. Some of the coins bore a boar with the legend of 'Vira-Pandya. It had been said that those coins were issued by the Pandyas and the feudatories of the Cholas but could not be attributed to any particular king.

The coins of Pandyas were basically square. Those coins were etched with elephant on one side and the other side remained blank. The inscription on the silver and gold coins during the Pandyas, were in Tamil-Brahmi and the copper coins bore the Tamil legends.

The coins of the Pandyas, which bore the fish symbols, were termed as 'Kodandaraman' and 'Kanchi' Valangum Perumal'. Apart from these, 'Ellamthalaiyanam' was seen on coins which had the standing king on one side and the

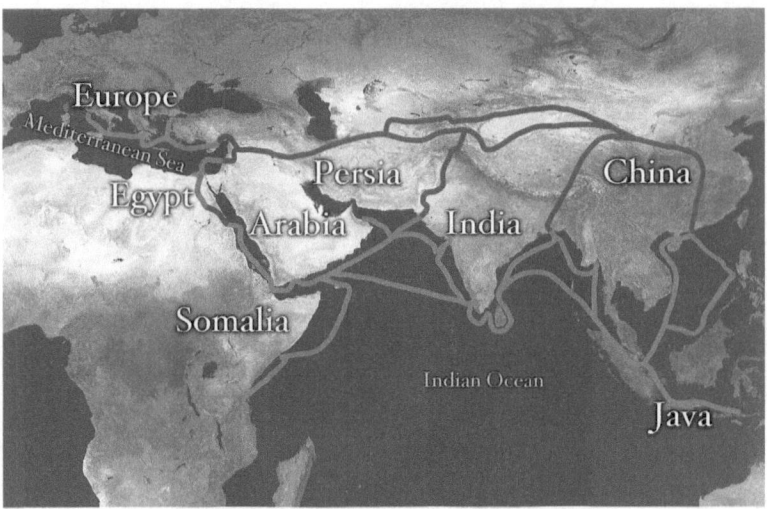

Figure 162: *Silk Road map showing ancient trade routes.*

fish on the other. 'Samarakolahalam' and 'Bhuvanekaviram' were found on the coins having a Garuda, 'Konerirayan' on coins having a bull and 'Kaliyugaraman' on coins that depict a pair of feet.

Government and Society

Trade

Roman and Greek traders frequented the ancient Tamil country, present day Southern India and Sri Lanka, securing trade with the seafaring Tamil states of the Pandyan, Chola and Chera dynasties and establishing trading settlements which secured trade with South Asia by the Greco-Roman world since the time of the Ptolemaic dynasty[1667] a few decades before the start of the Common Era and remained long after the fall of the Western Roman Empire.[1668] As recorded by Strabo, Emperor Augustus of Rome received at Antioch an ambassador from a South Indian King called **Pandyan**. The country of the Pandyas, Pandi Mandala, was described as *Pandyan Mediterranea* in the *Periplus* and *Modura Regia Pandyan* by Ptolemy.[1669] They also outlasted Byzantium's loss of the ports of Egypt and the Red Sea[1670] (c. 639-645) under the pressure of the Muslim conquests. Sometime after the sundering of communications between the Axum and Eastern Roman Empire in the 7th century, the Christian kingdom of Axum fell into a slow decline, fading into obscurity in western sources. It survived, despite pressure from Islamic forces, until the 11th century, when it was reconfigured in a dynastic squabble.

Figure 163: *Pearl fishing was an important industry in ancient Tamilakam*

Pearl fishing

Pearl fishing was another industry that flourished during the Sangam age. The Pandyan port city of Korkai was the center of pearl trade. Written records from Greek and Egyptian voyagers give details about the pearl fisheries off the Pandyan coast. The Periplus of the Erythraean Sea mentions that "Pearls inferior to the Indian sort are exported in great quantity from the marts of Apologas and Omana". The inferior variety of pearls that the Tamils did not require for their use was in very great demand in the foreign markets. Pearls were woven along with nice muslin cloth, before being exported. The most expensive animal product that was imported from India by the Roman Empire was the pearl from the Gulf of Mannar.[1671]

The pearls from the Pandyan Kingdom were also in demand in the kingdoms of north India. Several Vedic mantras refer to the wide use of the pearls. The royal chariots were decked with pearls, as were the horses that dragged them. The use of pearls was so high that the supply of pearls from the Ganges could not meet the demand. Literary references of the pearl fishing mention how the fishermen, who dive into the sea, avoid attacks from sharks, bring up the right-whorled chank and blow on the sounding shell. Convicts were according to the Periplus of the Erythraean Sea used as pearl divers in Korkai.

Megasthenes reported about the pearl fisheries of the Pandyas, indicating that the Pandyas derived great wealth from the pearl trade.[1672]

Religion

Historical Madurai was a stronghold of Shaivism. Following the invasion of Kalabhras, Jainism gained a foothold in the Pandyan kingdom. With the advent of Bhakti movements, Shaivism and Vaishnavism resurfaced. The latter-day Pandyas after 600 CE were Saivites who claimed to descend from Lord Shiva and Goddess Parvati. Pandyan Nedumchadayan was a staunch Vaishnavite.

References

 Wikimedia Commons has media related to *Pandyan Dynasty*.

<templatestyles src="Template:Refbegin/styles.css" />

- Balambal, V. (1998). *Studies in the History of the Sangam Age*. Kalinga Publications. ISBN 978-81-85163-87-1.
- Carswell, John. 1991. "The Port of Mantai, Sri Lanka." *RAI*, pp. 197–203.
- Curtin, Philip D. (1984). *Cross-Cultural Trade in World History*. Cambridge University Press. ISBN 978-0-521-26931-5.
- Hill, John E. 2004. *The Peoples of the West from the Weiliie 魏略 by Yu Huan 魚豢 : A Third Century Chinese Account Composed between 239 and 265 CE*. Draft annotated English translation.[1673]
- Holl, Augustin (2003). *Ethnoarchaeology of Shuwa-Arab Settlements*. Lexington Books. ISBN 978-0-7391-0407-1.
- Husaini, A.Q. (1972). *History of The Pandya Country*.
- Keay, John (2000) [2001]. *India: A history*. India: Grove Press. ISBN 0-8021-3797-0.
- Kulke, Hermann; Dietmar Rothermund (2004). *A History of India* (4 ed.).
- Lindsay, W S (2006). *History of Merchant Shipping and Ancient Commerce*. Adamant Media Corporation. ISBN 0-543-94253-8.
- Nagasamy, R (1981). *Tamil Coins – A study*. Institute of Epigraphy, Tamil Nadu State Dept. of Archaeology.
- Purushottam, Vi. Pi. (1989). *Cankakala Mannar Kalanilai Varalaru*.

- Ray, Himanshu Prabha, ed. 1996. *Tradition and Archaeology: Early Maritime Contacts in the Indian Ocean*. Proceedings of the International Seminar Techno-Archaeological Perspectives of Seafaring in the Indian Ocean 4th cent. BC – 15th cent. AD New Delhi, 28 February – 4 March 1994. New Delhi, and Jean-François SALLES, Lyon. First published 1996. Reprinted 1998. Manohar Publishers & Distributors, New Delhi.
- Reddy, P. Krishna Mohan. 2001. "Maritime Trade of Early South India: New Archaeological Evidences from Motupalli, Andhra Pradesh." *East and West* Vol. 51 – Nos. 1–2 (June 2001), pp. 143–156.
- Tripathi, Rama Sankar (1967). *History of Ancient India*. India: Motilal Banarsidass Publications. ISBN 81-208-0018-4.
- Sastri, K. A. Nilakanta. *The Pandyan Kingdom: From the Earliest Times to the Sixteenth Century*.
- Shaffer, Lynda (1996). *Maritime Southeast Asia to 1500 (Sources and Studies in World History)*. Armonk, N.Y: M.E. Sharpe. ISBN 1-56324-144-7.
- N. Subrahmanian (1962). *History of Tamilnad (To A. D. 1336)*[1674]. Madurai: Koodal. OCLC 43502446[1675]. Archived from the original[1676] on 23 November 2016.
- Venkata Subramanian, T. K. (1988). *Environment and Urbanisation in Early Tamilakam*[1677]. *Issue 92 of Tamil_p Palkalaik Kal_aka ve?iyi?u*. Tamil University. p. 55. ISBN 978-81-7090-110-5.
- Banarsi Prasad Saksena (1992). "The Khaljis: Alauddin Khalji". In Mohammad Habib and Khaliq Ahmad Nizami. *A Comprehensive History of India: The Delhi Sultanat (A.D. 1206-1526)*[1678]. **5** (Second ed.). The Indian History Congress / People's Publishing House. OCLC 31870180[1679].
- K.K.R. Nair (1987). "Venad: Its Early History"[1680]. *Journal of Kerala Studies*. University of Kerala. **14** (1): 1–34. ISSN 0377-0443[1681].
- Kishori Saran Lal (1950). *History of the Khaljis (1290-1320)*[1682]. Allahabad: The Indian Press. OCLC 685167335[1683].
- Peter Jackson (2003). *The Delhi Sultanate: A Political and Military History*[1684]. Cambridge University Press. ISBN 978-0-521-54329-3.

Vijayanagara Empire

Vijayanagara Empire	
1336–1646	
Extent of Vijayanagara Empire, 1446, 1520 CE	
Capital	Vijayanagara, Penukonda, Chandragiri
Languages	Kannada, Telugu, Sanskrit
Religion	Hinduism
Government	Monarchy
King	
•	1336–1356	Harihara Raya I
•	1642–1646	Sriranga III
History	
•	Established	1336
•	Earliest records	1343
•	Disestablished	1646
Currency	Varaha
Preceded by	Succeeded by
Hoysala Empire Kakatiya dynasty Madurai Sultanate Pandyan dynasty Musunuri Nayaks Reddy dynasty	Kingdom of Mysore Nayakas of Keladi Thanjavur Nayak kingdom Madurai Nayak dynasty Nayakas of Chitradurga Adil Shahi dynasty Qutb Shahi dynasty Nayakas of Gingee
Today part of	India

Vijayanagara Empire

Sangama dynasty	
Harihara I	1336–1356
Bukka Raya I	1356–1377
Harihara Raya II	1377–1404
Virupaksha Raya	1404–1405
Bukka Raya II	1405–1406
Deva Raya I	1406–1422
Ramachandra Raya	1422
Vira Vijaya Bukka Raya	1422–1424
Deva Raya II	1424–1446
Mallikarjuna Raya	1446–1465
Virupaksha Raya II	1465–1485
Praudha Raya	1485
Saluva dynasty	
Saluva Narasimha Deva Raya	1485–1491
Thimma Bhupala	1491
Narasimha Raya II	1491–1505
Tuluva dynasty	
Tuluva Narasa Nayaka	1491–1503
Vira Narasimha Raya	1503–1509
Krishna Deva Raya	1509–1529
Achyuta Deva Raya	1529–1542
Venkata I	1542

Sadasiva Raya	1542–1570
Aravidu dynasty	
Aliya Rama Raya	1542–1565
Tirumala Deva Raya	1565–1572
Sriranga I	1572–1586
Venkata II	1586–1614
Sriranga II	1614
Rama Deva Raya	1617–1632
Venkata III	1632–1642
Sriranga III	1642–1646

Part of **a series** on the
History of India

- v
- t
- e[1685]

The **Vijayanagara Empire** (also called **Karnata Empire**,[1686] and the **Kingdom of Bisnegar** by the Portuguese) was based in the Deccan Plateau region in South India. It was established in 1336 by Harihara I and his brother Bukka Raya I of Sangama Dynasty.[1687,1688] The empire rose to prominence as a culmination of attempts by the southern powers to ward off Islamic invasions by the end of the 13th century. It lasted until 1646, although its power declined after a major military defeat in 1565 by the combined armies of the Deccan sultanates. The empire is named after its capital city of Vijayanagara, whose ruins surround present day Hampi, now a World Heritage Site in Karnataka, India. The writings of medieval European travelers such as Domingo Paes, Fernão Nunes, and Niccolò Da Conti, and the literature in local languages provide crucial information about its history. Archaeological excavations at Vijayanagara have revealed the empire's power and wealth.

The empire's legacy includes many monuments spread over South India, the best known of which is the group at Hampi. Different temple building traditions in South and Central India came together in the Vijayanagara Architecture style. This synthesis inspired architectural innovation in Hindu temples' construction. Efficient administration and vigorous overseas trade brought new technologies such as water management systems for irrigation. The empire's patronage enabled fine arts and literature to reach new heights in Kannada, Telugu, Tamil, and Sanskrit, while Carnatic music evolved into its current form. The Vijayanagara Empire created an epoch in South Indian history that transcended regionalism by promoting Hinduism as a unifying factor.

Alternative name

Karnata Rajya (Karnata Empire) was another name for the Vijayanagara Empire, used in some inscriptions and literary works of the Vijayanagara times including the Sanskrit work *Jambavati Kalyanam* by King Krishnadevaraya and Telugu work *Vasu Charitamu*.[1689]

History

Differing theories have been proposed regarding the origins of the Vijayanagara empire. Many historians propose that Harihara I and Bukka I, the founders of the empire, were Kannadigas and commanders in the army of the Hoysala Empire stationed in the Tungabhadra region to ward off Muslim invasions from the Northern India.[1690,1691,1692,1693] Others claim that they were

Telugu people, first associated with the Kakatiya Kingdom, who took control of the northern parts of the Hoysala Empire during its decline.[1694] Irrespective of their origin, historians agree the founders were supported and inspired by Vidyaranya, a saint at the Sringeri monastery to fight the Muslim invasion of South India. Writings by foreign travelers during the late medieval era combined with recent excavations in the Vijayanagara principality have uncovered much-needed information about the empire's history, fortifications, scientific developments and architectural innovations.[1695,1696]

Before the early 14th-century rise of the Vijayanagara Empire, the Hindu states of the Deccan — the Yadava Empire of Devagiri, the Kakatiya dynasty of Warangal, the Pandyan Empire of Madurai had been repeatedly raided and attacked by Muslims from the north, and by 1336 these upper Deccan region (modern day Maharashtra, Telangana) had all been defeated by armies of Sultan Alauddin Khalji and Muhammad bin Tughluq of the Delhi Sultanate.

Further south in the Deccan region, a Hoysala commander, Singeya Nayaka-III (1280–1300 AD) declared independence after the Muslim forces of the Delhi Sultanate defeated and captured the territories of the Seuna Yadavas of Devagiri in 1294 CE. He created the Kampili kingdom, but this was a short lived kingdom during this period of wars. Kampili existed near Gulbarga and Tungabhadra river in northeastern parts of the present-day Karnataka state. It ended after a defeat by the armies of Delhi Sultanate. The triumphant army led by Malik Zada sent the news of its victory, over Kampili kingdom, to Muhammad bin Tughluq in Delhi by sending a straw-stuffed severed head of the dead Hindu king. Within Kampili, on the day of certain defeat, the populace committed a *jauhar* (ritual mass suicide) in 1327/28 CE. Eight years later, from the ruins of the Kampili kingdom emerged the Vijayanagara Kingdom in 1336 CE.

In the first two decades after the founding of the empire, Harihara I gained control over most of the area south of the Tungabhadra river and earned the title of *Purvapaschima Samudradhishavara* ("master of the eastern and western seas"). By 1374 Bukka Raya I, successor to Harihara I, had defeated the chiefdom of Arcot, the Reddys of Kondavidu, and the Sultan of Madurai and had gained control over Goa in the west and the Tungabhadra-Krishna River doab in the north.[1697] The original capital was in the principality of Anegondi on the northern banks of the Tungabhadra River in today's Karnataka. It was later moved to nearby Vijayanagara on the river's southern banks during the reign of Bukka Raya I, because it was easier to defend against the Muslim armies persistently attacking it from the northern lands.

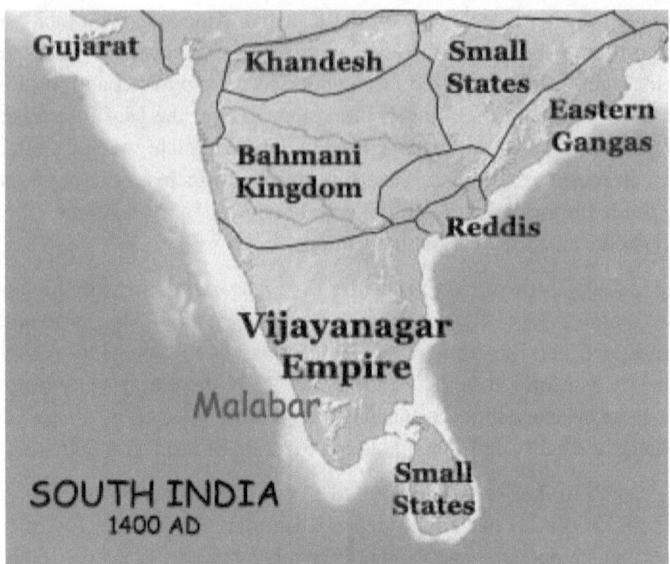

Figure 164: *Map of South India, 1400 AD*

With the Vijayanagara Kingdom now imperial in stature, Harihara II, the second son of Bukka Raya I, further consolidated the kingdom beyond the Krishna River and brought the whole of South India under the Vijayanagara umbrella.[1698] The next ruler, Deva Raya I, emerged successful against the Gajapatis of Odisha and undertook important works of fortification and irrigation.[1699] Italian traveler Niccolo de Conti wrote of him as the most powerful ruler of India.[1700] Deva Raya II (called *Gajabetekara*)[1701] succeeded to the throne in 1424 and was possibly the most capable of the Sangama dynasty rulers. He quelled rebelling feudal lords as well as the Zamorin of Calicut and Quilon in the south. He invaded the island of Sri Lanka and became overlord of the kings of Burma at Pegu and Tanasserim.[1702,1703,1704]

Firuz Bahmani of Bahmani Sultanate entered into a treaty with Deva Raya I of Vijayanagara in 1407 that required the latter to pay Bahmani an annual tribute of "100,000 huns, five maunds of pearls and fifty elephants". The Sultanate invaded Vijayanagara in 1417 when the latter defaulted in paying the tribute. Such wars for tribute payment by Vijayanagara repeated in the 15th century, such as in 1436 when Sultan Ahmad I launched a war to collect the unpaid tribute.[1705]

The ensuing Sultanates-Vijayanagara wars expanded the Vijayanagara military, its power and disputes between its military commanders. In 1485, Saluva

Figure 165: *Natural fortress at Vijayanagara*

Narasimha led a coup and ended the dynastic rule, while continuing to defend the Empire from raids by the Sultanates created from the continuing disintegration of the Bahmani Sultanate in its north.[1706] In 1505, another commander Tuluva Narasa Nayaka took over the Vijayanagara rule from the Sulava descendant in a coup. The empire came under the rule of Krishna Deva Raya in 1509, the son of Tuluva Narasa Nayaka. He strengthened and consolidated the reach of the empire, by hiring both Hindus and Muslims into his army.[1707] In the following decades, it covered Southern India and successfully defeated invasions from the five established Deccan Sultanates to its north.[1708]

The empire reached its peak during the rule of Krishna Deva Raya when Vijayanagara armies were consistently victorious.[1709,1710] The empire gained territory formerly under the Sultanates in the northern Deccan and the territories in the eastern Deccan, including Kalinga, in addition to the already established presence in the south.[1711] Many important monuments were either completed or commissioned during the time of Krishna Deva Raya.[1712]

Krishna Deva Raya was followed by his younger half-brother Achyuta Deva Raya in 1529. When Achyuta Deva Raya died in 1542, Sadashiva Raya, the teenage nephew of Achyuta Raya was appointed king with the caretaker being Aliya Rama Raya, Krishna Deva Raya's son-in-law and someone who had previously served Sultan Quli Qutb al-Mulk from 1512 when al-Mulk was assigned to Golkonda sultanate.[1713] Aliya Rama Raya left the Golconda Sultanate, married Deva Raya's daughter, and thus rose to power. When Sadashiva

Figure 166: *Royal Insignia: boar, sun, moon and dagger*

Raya – Deva Raya's son – was old enough, Aliya Rama Raya imprisoned him and allowed his uncle Achyuta Raya to publicly appear once a year.[1714] Further Aliya Rama Raya hired Muslim generals in his army from his previous Sultanate connections, and called himself "Sultan of the World".[1715]

The Sultanates to the north of Vijayanagara united and attacked Aliya Rama Raya's army, in January 1565, in a war known as the Battle of Talikota.[1716] The Vijayanagara side was winning the war, state Hermann Kulke and Dietmar Rothermund, but suddenly two Muslim generals of the Vijayanagara army switched sides and turned their loyalty to the Sultanates. The generals captured Aliya Rama Raya and beheaded him on the spot, with Sultan Hussain on the Sultanates side joining them for the execution and stuffing of severed head with straw for display.[1717,1718] The beheading of Aliya Rama Raya created confusion and havoc in the still loyal portions of the Vijayanagara army, which were then completely routed. The Sultanates' army plundered Hampi and reduced it to the ruinous state in which it remains; it was never re-occupied.[1719]

After the death of Aliya Rama Raya in the Battle of Talikota, Tirumala Deva Raya started the Aravidu dynasty, moved and founded a new capital of Penukonda to replace the destroyed Hampi, and attempted to reconstitute the remains of Vijayanagara Empire.[1720] Tirumala abdicated in 1572, dividing the remains of his kingdom to his three sons, and pursued a religious life until his death in 1578. The Aravidu dynasty successors ruled the region but the empire collapsed in 1614, and the final remains ended in 1646, from continued wars with the Bijapur sultanate and others.[1721,1722] During this period, more kingdoms in South India became independent and separate from Vijayanagara. These include the Mysore Kingdom, Keladi Nayaka, Nayaks of Madurai, Nayaks of Tanjore, Nayakas of Chitradurga and Nayak Kingdom of Gingee – all of which declared independence and went on to have a significant impact on the history of South India in the coming centuries.[1723]

Governance

The rulers of the Vijayanagara empire maintained the well-functioning administrative methods developed by their predecessors, the Hoysala, Kakatiya and Pandya kingdoms, to govern their territories and made changes only where necessary.[1724] The King was the ultimate authority, assisted by a cabinet of ministers (*Pradhana*) headed by the prime minister (*Mahapradhana*). Other important titles recorded were the chief secretary (*Karyakartha* or *Rayaswami*) and the imperial officers (*Adhikari*). All high-ranking ministers and officers were required to have military training.[1725] A secretariat near the king's palace employed scribes and officers to maintain records made official by using a wax seal imprinted with the ring of the king.[1726] At the lower administrative levels, wealthy feudal landlords (*Goudas*) supervised accountants (*Karanikas* or *Karnam*) and guards (*Kavalu*). The palace administration was divided into 72 departments (*Niyogas*), each having several female attendants chosen for their youth and beauty (some imported or captured in victorious battles) who were trained to handle minor administrative matters and to serve men of nobility as courtesans or concubines.

The empire was divided into five main provinces (*Rajya*), each under a commander (*Dandanayaka* or *Dandanatha*) and headed by a governor, often from the royal family, who used the native language for administrative purposes.[1727] A *Rajya* was divided into regions (*Vishaya Vente* or *Kottam*) and further divided into counties (*Sime* or *Nadu*), themselves subdivided into municipalities (*Kampana* or *Sthala*). Hereditary families ruled their respective territories and paid tribute to the empire, while some areas, such as Keladi and Madurai, came under the direct supervision of a commander.

On the battlefield, the king's commanders led the troops. The empire's war strategy rarely involved massive invasions; more often it employed small scale methods such as attacking and destroying individual forts. The empire was among the first in India to use long range artillery commonly manned by foreign gunners (those from present day Turkmenistan were considered the best). Army troops were of two types: The king's personal army directly recruited

Figure 167: *Kannada inscription of King Krishnadeva Raya, dated 1509, at the Virupaksha temple in Hampi, describing his coronation and the construction of the large open mantapa*

by the empire and the feudal army under each feudatory. King Krishnadevaraya's personal army consisted of 100,000 infantry, 20,000 cavalrymen and over 900 elephants. This number was only a part of the army numbering over 1.1 million soldiers, a figure that varied as an army of two million has also been recorded along with the existence of a navy as evidenced by the use of the term *Navigadaprabhu* (commander of the navy).[1728] The army recruited from all classes of society (supported by the collection of additional feudal tributes from feudatory rulers), and consisted of archers and musketeers wearing quilted tunics, shieldmen with swords and poignards in their girdles, and soldiers carrying shields so large that no armour was necessary. The horses and elephants were fully armoured and the elephants had knives fastened to their tusks to do maximum damage in battle.[1729]

The capital city was completely dependent on the water supply systems constructed to channel and store water, ensuring a consistent supply throughout the year. The remains of these hydraulic systems have given historians a picture of the prevailing surface water distribution methods in use at that time in the semiarid regions of South India.[1730] Contemporary records and notes of foreign travelers describe how huge tanks were constructed by labourers.[1731]

Figure 168: *Ancient market place and plantation at Hampi*

Excavations have uncovered the remains of a well-connected water distribution system existing solely within the royal enclosure and the large temple complexes (suggesting it was for the exclusive use of royalty, and for special ceremonies) with sophisticated channels using gravity and siphons to transport water through pipelines.[1732] The only structures resembling public waterworks are the remains of large water tanks that collected the seasonal monsoon water and then dried up in summer except for the few fed by springs. In the fertile agricultural areas near the Tungabhadra River, canals were dug to guide the river water into irrigation tanks. These canals had sluices that were opened and closed to control the water flow. In other areas the administration encouraged the digging of wells monitored by administrative authorities. Large tanks in the capital city were constructed with royal patronage while smaller tanks were funded by wealthy individuals to gain social and religious merit.

Economy

The economy of the empire was largely dependent on agriculture. Sorghum (*jowar*), cotton, and pulse legumes grew in semi-arid regions, while sugarcane, rice, and wheat thrived in rainy areas. Betel leaves, areca (for chewing), and coconut were the principal cash crops, and large scale cotton production supplied the weaving centers of the empire's vibrant textile industry. Spices such as turmeric, pepper, cardamom, and ginger grew in the remote Malnad hill region and were transported to the city for trade. The empire's capital city was a thriving business centre that included a burgeoning market in large quantities of precious gems and gold.[1733] Prolific temple-building provided employment to thousands of masons, sculptors, and other skilled artisans.

Land ownership was important. Most of the growers were tenant farmers and were given the right of part ownership of the land over time. Tax policies encouraging needed produce made distinctions between land use to determine tax levies. For example, the daily market availability of rose petals was important for perfumers, so cultivation of roses received a lower tax assessment.[1734] Salt production and the manufacture of salt pans were controlled by similar means. The making of ghee (clarified butter), which was sold as an oil for human consumption and as a fuel for lighting lamps, was profitable.[1735] Exports to China intensified and included cotton, spices, jewels, semi-precious stones, ivory, rhino horn, ebony, amber, coral, and aromatic products such as perfumes. Large vessels from China made frequent visits, some captained by the Chinese Admiral Zheng He, and brought Chinese products to the empire's 300 ports, large and small, on the Arabian Sea and the Bay of Bengal. The ports of Mangalore, Honavar, Bhatkal, Barkur, Cochin, Cannanore, Machilipatnam, and Dharmadam were the most important.[1736]

When merchant ships docked, the merchandise was taken into official custody and taxes levied on all items sold. The security of the merchandise was guaranteed by the administration officials. Traders of many nationalities (Arabs, Persians, Guzerates, Khorassanians) settled in Calicut, drawn by the thriving trade business. Ship building prospered and keeled ships of 1000–1200 *bahares* (burden) were built without decks by sewing the entire hull with ropes rather than fastening them with nails. Ships sailed to the Red Sea ports of Aden and Mecca with Vijayanagara goods sold as far away as Venice. The empire's principal exports were pepper, ginger, cinnamon, cardamom, myrobalan, tamarind timber, anafistula, precious and semi-precious stones, pearls, musk, ambergris, rhubarb, aloe, cotton cloth and porcelain. Cotton yarn was shipped to Burma and indigo to Persia. Chief imports from Palestine were copper, quicksilver (mercury), vermilion, coral, saffron, coloured velvets, rose water, knives, coloured camlets, gold and silver. Persian horses were imported to Cannanore before a two-week land trip to the capital. Silk arrived from China and sugar from Bengal.

East coast trade hummed, with goods arriving from Golkonda where rice, millet, pulses and tobacco were grown on a large scale. Dye crops of indigo and chay root were produced for the weaving industry. A mineral rich region, Machilipatnam was the gateway for high quality iron and steel exports. Diamond mining was active in the Kollur region. The cotton weaving industry produced two types of cottons, plain calico and muslin (brown, bleached or dyed). Cloth printed with coloured patterns crafted by native techniques were

Figure 169: *Horizontal friezes in relief on the outer wall enclosure of Hazara Rama temple, depicting life in the kingdom*

exported to Java and the Far East. Golkonda specialised in plain cotton and Pulicat in printed. The main imports on the east coast were non-ferrous metals, camphor, porcelain, silk and luxury goods.

Culture

Social life

Most information on the social life in Vijayanagara empire comes from the writings of foreign visitors and evidence that research teams in the Vijayanagara area have uncovered. The Hindu caste system was prevalent and rigidly followed, with each caste represented by a local body of elders who represented the community. These elders set the rules and regulations that were implemented with the help of royal decrees. Untouchability was part of the caste system and these communities were represented by leaders (*Kaivadadavaru*). The Muslim communities were represented by their own group in coastal Karnataka.[1737] The caste system did not, however, prevent distinguished persons from all castes from being promoted to high-ranking cadre in the army and administration. In civil life, by virtue of the caste system, Brahmins enjoyed a high level of respect. With the exception of a few who took to military careers, most Brahmins concentrated on religious and literary matters. Their separation from material wealth and power made them ideal arbiters in local judicial matters, and their presence in every town and village was a calculated investment made by the nobility and aristocracy to maintain order.[1738] However,

Figure 170: *Nāga (snake) stone worship at Hampi*

the popularity of low-caste scholars (such as Molla and Kanakadasa) and their works (including those of Vemana and Sarvajna) is an indication of the degree of social fluidity in the society.

Sati, the practice where a widow would immolate herself with her dead husband's body, is evidenced in Vijayanagara ruins. About fifty inscriptions have been discovered in Vijayanagara which are called *Satikal* (Sati stone) or *Sativirakal* (Sati hero stone).[1739] According to Ashis Nandy, the Vijayanagara practice was an example of an "epidemic" of sati practice just like Rajput kingdoms under attack by Mughal armies, attributing the practice to foreign intrusions from the persistent wars between Muslim sultanates and the Hindu kingdom, in contrast to others who question the evidence. According to scholars such as John Hawley, "the evidence about the extent of the custom and about the classes that practiced it is far from clear, since most accounts come from Muslim chroniclers or European travelers" who did not have means and objectivity to report about the practice or its circumstances accurately.

The socio-religious movements of the previous centuries, such as Lingayatism, provided momentum for flexible social norms to which women were expected to abide. By this time South Indian women had crossed most barriers and were actively involved in matters hitherto considered the monopoly of men, such as administration, business and trade, and involvement in the fine arts.[1740] Tirumalamba Devi who wrote *Varadambika Parinayam* and Gangadevi who wrote

Figure 171: *Vijaynagar period temple plates at the Dharmeshwara Temple, Kondarahalli, Hoskote, recorded by BL Rice*

Madhuravijayam were among the notable women poets of the era. Early Telugu women poets like Tallapaka Timmakka and Atukuri Molla became popular during this period. The court of the Nayaks of Tanjore is known to have patronised several women poets. The Devadasi system existed, as well as legalised prostitution relegated to a few streets in each city.[1741] The popularity of harems amongst men of the royalty is well known from records.

Well-to-do men wore the *Petha* or *Kulavi*, a tall turban made of silk and decorated with gold. As in most Indian societies, jewellery was used by men and women and records describe the use of anklets, bracelets, finger-rings, necklaces and ear rings of various types. During celebrations, men and women adorned themselves with flower garlands and used perfumes made of rose water, civet musk, musk or sandalwood.[1742] In stark contrast to the commoners whose lives were modest, the lives of the empire's kings and queens were full of ceremonial pomp in the court. Queens and princesses had numerous attendants who were lavishly dressed and adorned with fine jewellery, their daily duties being light.[1743]

Physical exercises were popular with men and wrestling was an important male preoccupation for sport and entertainment. Even women wrestlers are mentioned in records. Gymnasiums have been discovered inside royal quarters and records speak of regular physical training for commanders and their

Figure 172: *Painted ceiling from the Virupaksha temple depicting Hindu mythology, 14th century.*

armies during peace time. Royal palaces and market places had special arenas where royalty and common people alike amused themselves by watching matches such as cock fights, ram fights and wrestling between women. Excavations within the Vijayanagara city limits have revealed the existence of various types of community-based activities in the form of engravings on boulders, rock platforms and temple floors, implying these were places of casual social interaction. Some of these games are in use today and others are yet to be identified.[1744]

Religion

The Vijayanagara kings were tolerant of all religions and sects, as writings by foreign visitors show.[1745] The kings used titles such as *Gobrahamana Pratipalanacharya* (*literally*, "protector of cows and Brahmins") and *Hindurayasuratrana* (*lit*, "upholder of Hindu faith") that testified to their intention of protecting Hinduism and yet were at the same time staunchly Islamicate in their court ceremonials and dress. The empire's founders, Harihara I and Bukka Raya I, were devout Shaivas (worshippers of Shiva), but made grants to the Vaishnava order of Sringeri with Vidyaranya as their patron saint, and designated *Varaha* (the boar, an Avatar of Vishnu) as their emblem.[1746] Over one-fourth of the archaeological dig found an "Islamic Quarter" not far from the "Royal Quarter". Nobles from Central Asia's Timurid kingdoms also came to Vijayanagara. The later Saluva and Tuluva kings were Vaishnava by faith, but worshipped at the feet of Lord Virupaksha (Shiva) at Hampi as well as Lord Venkateshwara (Vishnu) at Tirupati. A Sanskrit work, *Jambavati Kalyanam* by King Krishnadevaraya, called Lord Virupaksha *Karnata Rajya*

Figure 173: *Virupaksha Temple, Hampi*

Figure 174: *Lakshmi Narasimha (Avatar of Vishnu) at Hampi*

Figure 175: *Ornate pillars, Virupaksha temple Hampi*

Figure 176: *Wall panel relief in Hazare Rama Temple at Hampi*

Raksha Mani ("protective jewel of Karnata Empire").[1747] The kings patronised the saints of the dvaita order (philosophy of dualism) of Madhvacharya at Udupi.[1748]

The Bhakti (devotional) movement was active during this time, and involved well known Haridasas (devotee saints) of that time. Like the Virashaiva movement of the 12th century, this movement presented another strong current of devotion, pervading the lives of millions. The haridasas represented two groups, the *Vyasakuta* and *Dasakuta*, the former being required to be proficient in the Vedas, Upanishads and other Darshanas, while the *Dasakuta* merely conveyed the message of Madhvacharya through the Kannada language to the people in the form of devotional songs (*Devaranamas* and *Kirthanas*). The philosophy of Madhvacharya was spread by eminent disciples such as Naraharitirtha, Jayatirtha, Sripadaraya, Vyasatirtha, Vadirajatirtha and others.[1749] Vyasatirtha, the *guru* (teacher) of Vadirajatirtha, Purandaradasa (Father of Carnatic music[1750,1751]) and Kanakadasa[1752] earned the devotion of King Krishnadevaraya.[1753,1754] The king considered the saint his *Kuladevata* (family deity) and honoured him in his writings. During this time, another great composer of early carnatic music, Annamacharya composed hundreds of *Kirthanas* in Telugu at Tirupati in present-day Andhra Pradesh.[1755]

The defeat of the Jain Western Ganga Dynasty by the Cholas in the early 11th century and the rising numbers of followers of Vaishnava Hinduism and Virashaivism in the 12th century was mirrored by a decreased interest in Jainism.[1756] Two notable locations of Jain worship in the Vijayanagara territory were Shravanabelagola and Kambadahalli.

Islamic contact with South India began as early as the 7th century, a result of trade between the Southern kingdoms and Arab lands. Jumma Masjids existed in the Rashtrakuta empire by the 10th century[1757] and many mosques flourished on the Malabar coast by the early 14th century.[1758] Muslim settlers married local women; their children were known as Mappillas (*Moplahs*) and were actively involved in horse trading and manning shipping fleets. The interactions between the Vijayanagara empire and the Bahamani Sultanates to the north increased the presence of Muslims in the south. The introduction of Christianity began as early as the 8th century as shown by the finding of copper plates inscribed with land grants to Malabar Christians. Christian travelers wrote of the scarcity of Christians in South India in the Middle Ages, promoting its attractiveness to missionaries.[1759] The arrival of the Portuguese in the 15th century and their connections through trade with the empire, the propagation of the faith by Saint Xavier (1545) and later the presence of Dutch settlements fostered the growth of Christianity in the south.

Language

Kannada, Telugu and Tamil were used in their respective regions of the empire. Over 7000 inscriptions (*Shilashasana*) including 300 copper plate inscriptions (*Tamarashasana*) have been recovered, almost half of which are in Kannada, the remaining in Telugu, Tamil and Sanskrit.[1760] Bilingual inscriptions had lost favour by the 14th century.[1761] The empire minted coins at Hampi, Penugonda and Tirupati with Nagari, Kannada and Telugu legends usually carrying the name of the ruler. Gold, silver and copper were used to issue coins called *Gadyana, Varaha, Pon, Pagoda, Pratapa, Pana, Kasu* and *Jital*. The coins contained the images of various gods including Balakrishna (infant Krishna), Venkateshwara (the presiding deity of the temple at Tirupati), goddesses such as Bhudevi and Sridevi, divine couples, animals such as bulls and elephants and birds. The earliest coins feature Hanuman and Garuda (divine eagle), the vehicle of Lord Vishnu. Kannada and Telugu inscriptions have been deciphered and recorded by historians of the Archaeological Survey of India.

Literature

During the rule of the Vijayanagara Empire, poets, scholars and philosophers wrote primarily in Kannada, Telugu and Sanskrit, and also in other regional languages such as Tamil and covered such subjects as religion, biography, *Prabandha* (fiction), music, grammar, poetry, medicine and mathematics. The administrative and court languages of the Empire were Kannada and Telugu—the latter was the court language and gained even more cultural prominence during the reign of the last Vijayanagara kings.[1762,1763] Telugu was a popular literary medium, reaching its peak under the patronage of Krishnadevaraya.

Most Sanskrit works were commentaries either on the Vedas or on the Ramayana and Mahabharata epics, written by well known figures such as Sayana and Vidyaranya that extolled the superiority of the Advaita philosophy over other rival Hindu philosophies. Other writers were famous Dvaita saints of the Udupi order such as Jayatirtha (earning the title *Tikacharya* for his polemicial writings), Vyasatirtha who wrote rebuttals to the Advaita philosophy and of the conclusions of earlier logicians, and Vadirajatirtha and Sripadaraya both of whom criticised the beliefs of Adi Sankara. Apart from these saints, noted Sanskrit scholars adorned the courts of the Vijayanagara kings and their feudal chiefs. Some members of the royal family were writers of merit and authored important works such as *Jambavati Kalyana* by King Krishnadevaraya, and *Madura Vijayam* by Princess Gangadevi, a daughter-in-law of King Bukka I. Also known as *Veerakamparaya Charita*, the book dwells on the conquest of the Madurai Sultanate by the Vijayanagara empire.

Figure 177: *Poetic inscription in Kannada by Vijayanagara poet Manjaraja (1398 CE)*

The Kannada poets and scholars of the empire produced important writings supporting the Vaishnava Bhakti movement heralded by the Haridasas (devotees of Vishnu), Brahminical and Veerashaiva (Lingayatism) literature. The *Haridasa* poets celebrated their devotion through songs called *Devaranama* (lyrical poems) in the native meters of *Sangatya* (quatrain), *Suladi* (beat based), *Ugabhoga* (melody based) and *Mundige* (cryptic).[1764] Their inspirations were the teachings of Madhvacharya and Vyasatirtha. Purandaradasa and Kanakadasa are considered the foremost among many *Dasas* (devotees) by virtue of their immense contribution. Kumara Vyasa, the most notable of Brahmin scholars wrote *Gadugina Bharata*, a translation of the epic *Mahabharata*. This work marks a transition of Kannada literature from old Kannada to modern Kannada. Chamarasa was a famous Veerashaiva scholar and poet who had many debates with Vaishnava scholars in the court of Devaraya II. His *Prabhulinga Leele*, later translated into Telugu and Tamil, was a eulogy of Saint Allama Prabhu (the saint was considered an incarnation of Lord Ganapathi while Parvati took the form of a princess of Banavasi).[1765]

At this peak of Telugu literature, the most famous writing in the *Prabandha* style was *Manucharitamu*. King Krishnadevaraya was an accomplished Telugu scholar and wrote the celebrated Amuktamalyada.[1766] *Amuktamalyada* ("One who wears and gives away garlands") narrates the story of the wedding of the god Vishnu to Andal, the Tamil Alvar saint poet and the daughter of Periyalvar at Srirangam. In his court were eight famous scholars regarded as the pillars (*Ashtadiggajas*) of the literary assembly. The most famous among them were Allasani Peddana who held the honorific *Andhrakavitapitamaha* (*lit*, "father of Telugu poetry") and Tenali Ramakrishna, the court jester who authored several notable works.[1767] The other six poets were Nandi Thimmana (Mukku Timmana), Ayyalaraju Ramabhadra, Madayyagari Mallana, Bhattu Murthi (Ramaraja Bhushana), Pingali Surana, and Dhurjati. This was the age of Srinatha, the greatest of all Telugu poets of the time. He wrote books such as *Marutratcharitamu* and *Salivahana-sapta-sati*. He was patronised by King Devaraya II and enjoyed the same status as important ministers in the court.

Though much of the Tamil literature from this period came from Tamil speaking regions ruled by the feudatory Pandya who gave particular attention on the cultivation of Tamil literature, some poets were patronised by the Vijayanagara kings. Svarupananda Desikar wrote an anthology of 2824 verses, *Sivaprakasap-perundirattu*, on the Advaita philosophy. His pupil the ascetic, Tattuvarayar, wrote a shorter anthology, *Kurundirattu*, that contained about half the number of verses. Krishnadevaraya patronised the Tamil Vaishnava poet Haridasa whose *Irusamaya Vilakkam* was an exposition of the two Hindu systems, Vaishnava and Shaiva, with a preference for the former.

Notable among secular writings on music and medicine were Vidyaranya's *Sangitsara*, Praudha Raya's *Ratiratnapradipika*, Sayana's *Ayurveda Sudhanidhi* and Lakshmana Pandita's *Vaidyarajavallabham*.[1768] The Kerala school of astronomy and mathematics flourished during this period under such well known scholars as Madhava (c. 1340–1425) who made important contributions to Trigonometery and Calculus, and Nilakantha Somayaji (c. 1444–1545) who postulated on the orbitals of planets.[1769]

Architecture

Vijayanagara architecture is a vibrant combination of the Chalukya, Hoysala, Pandya and Chola styles, idioms that prospered in previous centuries.[1770,1771] Its legacy of sculpture, architecture and painting influenced the development of the arts long after the empire came to an end. Its stylistic hallmark is the ornate pillared *Kalyanamantapa* (marriage hall), *Vasanthamantapa* (open pillared halls) and the *Rayagopura* (tower). Artisans used the locally available hard granite because of its durability since the kingdom was under constant threat of invasion. While the empire's monuments are spread over the whole of Southern India, nothing surpasses the vast open-air theatre of monuments at its capital at Vijayanagara, a UNESCO World Heritage Site.[1772]

In the 14th century the kings continued to build vesara or Deccan-style monuments but later incorporated Dravida-style gopuras to meet their ritualistic

Figure 178: *Yali pillars in Aghoreshwara Temple at Ikkeri in Shimoga District.*

needs. The Prasanna Virupaksha temple (underground temple) of Bukka and the Hazare Rama temple of Deva Raya are examples of Deccan architecture.[1773] The varied and intricate ornamentation of the pillars is a mark of their work.[1774] At Hampi, though the *Vitthala* temple is the best example of their pillared *Kalyanamantapa* style, the *Hazara Ramaswamy* temple is a modest but perfectly finished example.[1775] A visible aspect of their style is their return to the simplistic and serene art developed by the Chalukya dynasty.[1776] A grand specimen of Vijayanagara art, the *Vitthala* temple, took several decades to complete during the reign of the Tuluva kings.[1777]

Market place at Hampi and the sacred tank located near the Krishna temple.

Stone temple car in the Vitthala Temple at Hampi.

Another element of the Vijayanagara style is the carving and consecration of large monoliths such as the *Sasivekaalu* (mustard) Ganesha and *Kadalekaalu* (ground nut) Ganesha at Hampi, the Gommateshwara (Bahubali) monoliths in Karkala and Venur, and the Nandi bull in Lepakshi. The Vijayanagara temples of Kolar, Kanakagiri, Sringeri and other towns of Karnataka; the temples of Tadpatri, Lepakshi, Ahobilam, Tirumala Venkateswara Temple and Srikalahasti in Andhra Pradesh; and the temples of Vellore, Kumbakonam, Kanchi and Srirangam in Tamil Nadu are examples of this style. Vijayanagara art includes wall-paintings such as the Dashavatara and *Girijakalyana* (marriage of Parvati, Shiva's consort) in the Virupaksha Temple at Hampi, the *Shivapurana* murals (tales of Shiva) at the Virabhadra temple at Lepakshi, and those at the Kamaakshi and Varadaraja temples at Kanchi.[1778] This mingling of the South Indian styles resulted in a richness not seen in earlier centuries, a focus on reliefs in addition to sculpture that surpasses that previously in India.[1779]

An aspect of Vijayanagara architecture that shows the cosmopolitanism of the great city is the presence of many secular structures bearing Islamic features. While political history concentrates on the ongoing conflict between the Vijayanagara empire and the Deccan Sultanates, the architectural record reflects a more creative interaction. There are many arches, domes and vaults that show these influences. The concentration of structures like pavilions, stables and towers suggests they were for use by royalty.[1780] The decorative details of these structures may have been absorbed into Vijayanagara architecture during the early 15th century, coinciding with the rule of Deva Raya I and Deva Raya II. These kings are known to have employed many Muslims in their army and court, some of whom may have been Muslim architects. This harmonious exchange of architectural ideas must have happened during rare periods of peace between the Hindu and Muslim kingdoms.[1781] The "Great Platform" (*Mahanavami Dibba*) has relief carvings in which the figures seem to have the facial features of central Asian Turks who were known to have been employed as royal attendants.[1782]

References

<templatestyles src="Template:Refbegin/styles.css" />

- Arthikaje. "Literary Activity, Art and Architecture"[1783]. *History of karnataka*. OurKarnataka.Com. Archived from the original[1784] on 12 October 2008. Retrieved 2006-12-31.
- Dallapiccola, Anna L. (2001). "Relief carvings on the great platform". In John M. Fritz and George Michell (editors). *New Light on Hampi: Recent Research at Vijayanagara*. Mumbai: MARG. ISBN 81-85026-53-X.

Figure 179: *An aerial view of the Meenakshi Temple from the top of the southern gopuram, looking north. The temple was rebuilt by the Vijayanagar Empire.*

- Davison-Jenkins, Dominic J. (2001). "Hydraulic works". In John M. Fritz and George Michell (editors). *New Light on Hampi: Recent Research at Vijayanagara*. Mumbai: MARG. ISBN 81-85026-53-X.
- Durga Prasad, J. (1988). *History of the Andhras up to 1565 A. D.*[1785] (PDF). Guntur: P.G. Publisher. Archived from the original[1786] (PDF) on 22 April 2006. Retrieved 2007-01-27.
- Eaton, Richard M. (2006). *A social history of the Deccan, 1300–1761: eight Indian lives*. Cambridge: Cambridge University Press. ISBN 978-0-521-71627-7.
- *Hampi travel guide* (2003). New Delhi: Good Earth publication & Department of Tourism, India. ISBN 81-87780-17-7, LCCN 2003-334582[1787].
- Fritz, John M. and George Michell (editors) (2001). *New Light on Hampi: Recent Research at Vijayanagar*. Mumbai: MARG. ISBN 81-85026-53-X.
- Kamath, Suryanath U. (2001) [1980]. *A concise history of Karnataka: from pre-historic times to the present*. Bangalore: Jupiter books. LCCN 80905179[1788]. OCLC 7796041[1789].
- Karmarkar, A.P. (1947) [1947]. *Cultural history of Karnataka: ancient and medieval*. Dharwad: Karnataka Vidyavardhaka Sangha. OCLC 8221605[1790].
- Kulke and Rothermund, Hermann and Dietmar (2004) [2004]. *A History of India*. Routledge (4th edition). ISBN 0-415-32919-1.
- Mack, Alexandra (2001). "The temple district of Vitthalapura". In John M. Fritz and George Michell (editors). *New Light on Hampi: Recent Research at Vijayanagara*. Mumbai: MARG. ISBN 81-85026-53-X.
- Nilakanta Sastri, K. A. (1955) [reissued 2002]. *A history of South India from prehistoric times to the fall of Vijayanagar*. New Delhi: Indian Branch, Oxford University Press. ISBN 0-19-560686-8.

- Iyer, Panchapakesa A.S. (2006) [2006]. *Karnataka Sangeeta Sastra*. Chennai: Zion Printers.
- Philon, Helen (2001). "Plaster decoration on Sultanate-styled courtly buildings". In John M. Fritz and George Michell (editors). *New Light on Hampi: Recent Research at Vijayanagara*. Mumbai: MARG. ISBN 81-85026-53-X.
- Pujar, Narahari S.; Shrisha Rao; H.P. Raghunandan. "Sri Vyâsa Tîrtha (1460–1539) – a short sketch"[1791]. Dvaita Home Page. Retrieved 2006-12-31.
- Ramesh, K. V. "Introduction"[1792]. *South Indian Inscription, Volume 16: Telugu Inscriptions from Vijayanagar Dynasty*. New Delhi: Archaeological Survey of India. Retrieved 2006-12-31.Wikipedia:Link rot
- Shiva Prakash, H.S. (1997). "Kannada". In Ayyappapanicker. *Medieval Indian Literature:An Anthology*. Sahitya Akademi. ISBN 81-260-0365-0.
- Rice, B.L. (2001) [1897]. *Mysore Gazetteer Compiled for Government-vol 1*. New Delhi, Madras: Asian Educational Services. ISBN 81-206-0977-8.
- Verghese, Anila (2001). "Memorial stones". In John M. Fritz and George Michell (editors). *New Light on Hampi: Recent Research at Vijayanagara*. Mumbai: MARG. ISBN 81-85026-53-X.
- Thapar, Romila (2003) [2003]. *The Penguin History of Early India*. New Delhi: Penguin Books. ISBN 0-14-302989-4.
- Michell, George (editor) (2008). *Vijayanagara: Splendour in Ruins*. Ahmedabad: Mapin Publishing and The Alkazi Collection of Photography. ISBN 978-81-89995-03-4.
- Nagaraj, D.R. (2003). "Tensions in Kannada Literary Culture". In Sheldon Pollock. *Literary Cultures in History: Reconstructions from South Asia*. Berkeley and Los Angeles: University of California. ISBN 0-520-22821-9.
- Asher & Talbot, Catherine & Cynthia (2006). "Creation of Pan South Indian Culture". *India Before Europe*. Cambridge: Cambridge University Press. ISBN 978-0-521-00539-5.
- Rice, E.P. (1982) [1921]. *A History of Kanarese Literature*. New Delhi: Asian Educational Services. ISBN 81-206-0063-0.

Further reading

<templatestyles src="Template:Refbegin/styles.css" />

- Bang, Peter Fibiger; Kolodziejczyk, Dariusz, eds. (2012). "Ideologies of state building in Vijayanagara India". *Universal Empire: A Comparative Approach to Imperial Culture and Representation in Eurasian History*. Cambridge University Press. ISBN 978-1-107-02267-6.

- Stein, Burton (1989). *The New Cambridge History of India: Vijayanagara*[1793]. Cambridge University Press. ISBN 978-0-521-26693-2.

External links

Wikiquote has quotations related to: *Vijayanagara Empire*

Wikimedia Commons has media related to *Vijayanagara Empire*.

Wikisourcehas the text of the 1911 *Encyclopædia Britannica*article *Vijayanagar*.

- Hampi – History and Tourism[1794]
- www.Hampi.in[1795] – Photos, descriptions & maps of the Hampi Ruins.
- Archaeos Mapping Project at Vijayanagara – Seasons 1[1796]
- Archaeos Mapping Project at Vijayanagara – Seasons 2–3[1797]
- Archaeos Mapping Project at Vijayanagara – Seasons 1–4 Summary[1798]
- Coins of Vijayanagar[1799]
- Indian Inscriptions - Archaeological Survey Of India[1800]
- Hazararama Temple Photographs, 2013[1801]
- Mahanavami Dibba Photographs, 2013[1802]

<indicator name="featured-star"> ⭐ </indicator>

Bengal Sultanate

	Bangalah Bengala
	শাহী বাংলা شاهی بنگاله
	Sultanate
	1352–1576
	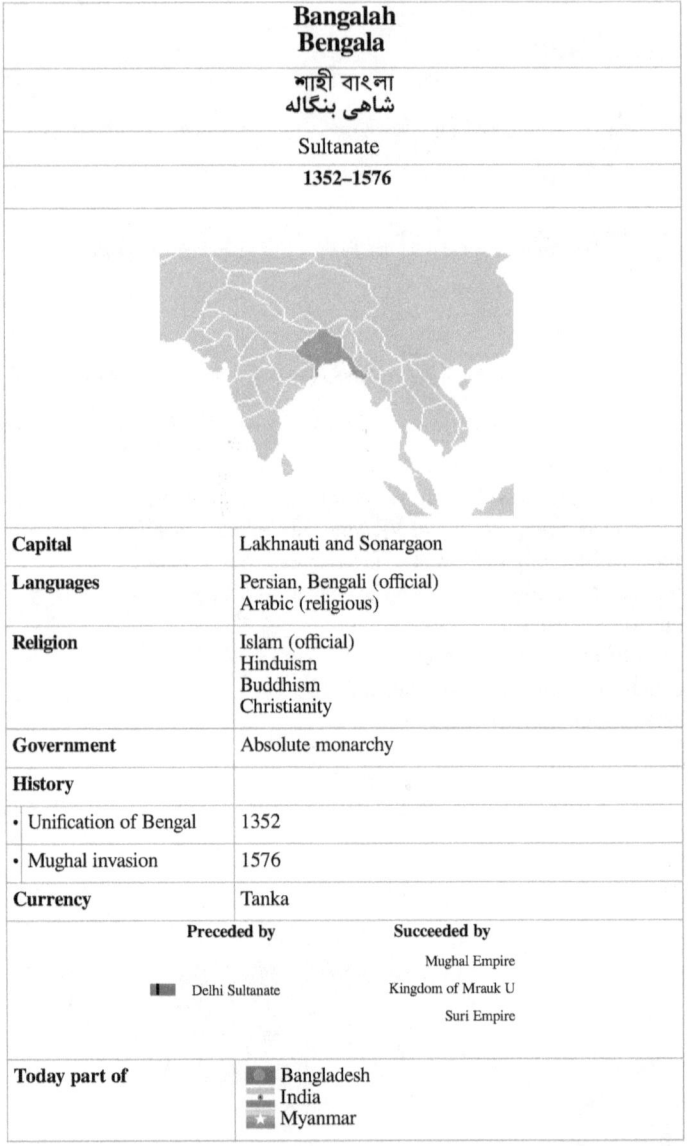
Capital	Lakhnauti and Sonargaon
Languages	Persian, Bengali (official) Arabic (religious)
Religion	Islam (official) Hinduism Buddhism Christianity
Government	Absolute monarchy
History	
• Unification of Bengal	1352
• Mughal invasion	1576
Currency	Tanka
Preceded by	Succeeded by
Delhi Sultanate	Mughal Empire Kingdom of Mrauk U Suri Empire
Today part of	Bangladesh India Myanmar

The **Sultanate of Bengal** (also known as the **Bengal Sultanate**; **Bangalah** (Persian: بنگاله *Bangālah*, Bengali: বাঙ্গালা/বঙ্গালা) and **Shahi Bangalah** (Persian:

شاهى بنگاله *Shāhī Bangālah*, Bengali: শাহী বাঙলা)) was a Muslim state, established in Bengal during the 14th century, as part of the Muslim conquest of the Indian subcontinent. It was the first independent unified Bengali kingdom under Muslim rule. The region became widely known as *Bangalah* and *Bengala* under this kingdom. The two terms are precursors to the modern terms *Bangla* and *Bengal*.

The kingdom was formed after governors of the Delhi Sultanate declared independence in the region. Shamsuddin Ilyas Shah united the region's states into a single government headed by an imperial Sultan. The kingdom was ruled by five dynasties. At the height of its territorial empire, the kingdom ruled over areas in Eastern South Asia and Southeast Asia. It re-established diplomatic relations between China and the Indian subcontinent. It permitted the creation of the Portuguese settlement in Chittagong, the first European enclave in Bengal. The kingdom looked west for cultural inspiration, particularly from Persianate cultures. Its rulers sponsored the construction of colleges in Mecca and Medina, which host the holiest sites of Islam. Literature was fostered in Persian and Bengali, with strong Sufi influences. Bengali architecture evolved significantly during this period, with several external influences. The kingdom had an influential Hindu minority, which included aristocrats, military officers and bureaucrats. It assisted the Buddhist king of Arakan to regain control of his country from the Burmese.

The kingdom began to disintegrate in the 16th century, in the aftermath of Sher Shah Suri's conquests. The Mughal Empire began to absorb Bengal under its first emperor, Babur. The second Mughal emperor Humayun occupied the Bengali capital of Gaurh. In 1576, the armed forces of emperor Akbar defeated the last reigning Sultan, Daud Khan Karrani. The region later became Mughal Bengal.

History

The Delhi Sultanate lost its hold over Bengal in 1338 when separatist states were established by governors, including Fakhruddin Mubarak Shah in Sonargaon, Alauddin Ali Shah in Lakhnauti and Shamsuddin Ilyas Shah in Satgaon. In 1352, Ilyas Shah defeated the rulers of Sonargaon and Lakhnauti and united the Bengal region into an independent kingdom. He founded the Turkic Ilyas Shahi dynasty which ruled Bengal until 1490. During this time, much of the agricultural land was controlled by Hindu zamindars, which caused tensions with Muslim Taluqdars. The Ilyas Shahi rule was challenged by Raja Ganesha, a powerful Hindu landowner, who briefly managed to place his son, Jalaluddin Muhammad Shah, on the throne in the early 15th century, before the Ilyas Shahi dynasty was restored in 1432. The late 1480s saw four usurper sultans

Figure 180: *The Adina Mosque was built by Sikandar Shah*

from the mercenary corps. Tensions between different Muslim communities often affected the kingdom.

After a period of instability, Alauddin Hussain Shah gained control of Bengal in 1494 when he was prime minister. As Sultan, Hussain Shah ruled till 1519. The dynasty he founded reigned till 1538. Muslims and Hindus jointly served in the royal administration during the Hussain Shahi dynasty. This era is often regarded as a golden age of the Bengal Sultanate, in which Bengali territory included areas of Arakan, Orissa, Tripura and Assam. The sultanate gave permission for establishing the Portuguese settlement in Chittagong. Sher Shah Suri conquered Bengal in the 16th century, during which he renovated the Grand Trunk Road. After conquering Bengal, Sher Shah Suri proceeded to Agra.

The absorption of Bengal into the Mughal Empire was a gradual process beginning with the defeat of Bengali forces under Sultan Nasiruddin Nasrat Shah by Babur at the Battle of Ghaghra and ending with the Battle of Raj Mahal where the Pashtun Karrani dynasty, the last reigning Sultans of Bengal, were defeated.

Figure 181: *Babur began absorbing Bengal in the early 16th century*

Governance

The Bengal Sultanate was an absolute monarchy. The Ilyas Shahi dynasty promoted a Persianate society. It copied the pre-Muslim Persian tradition of monarchy and statecraft. The courts of the capital cities sanctified the sultan, used Persianized royal paraphernalia, adopted an elaborate court ceremony modeled on the Sasanian imperial paradigm, employed a hierarchical bureaucracy, and promoted Islam as the state religion. The rise of Jalaluddin Muhammad Shah saw more native elements inducted in the courts. The Hussain Shahi dynasty employed many Hindus in the government and promoted a form of religious pluralism.[1803]

Military

Military strength was the existential basis of medieval kingdoms in Bengal and other parts of India. The sultans had a well-organised army, including cavalry, artillery, infantry and war elephants; and a navy. Due to the riverine geography and climate, it was not feasible to use cavalry throughout the year in Bengal. The cavalry was probably the weakest component of the Bengal Sultanate's army, as the horses had to be imported from foreign countries. The artillery was an important section. Portuguese historian João de Barros opined that the military supremacy of Bengal over Arakan and Tripura was due to its efficient artillery. The artillery used cannons and guns of various sizes.

The *paiks* formed the vital part of the Bengal infantry during this period. There were occasions when the paiks also tackled political situations. The particular battle array of the foot-soldiers who used bows, arrows and guns attracted the attention of Babur.

War elephants played an important part in the Bengal army. Apart from carrying war materials, elephants were also used for the movement of the armed personnel. In riverine Bengal the usefulness of elephants, though very slow, could not be minimised. The navy was of prime necessity in riverine Bengal. In fact, the cavalry could ensure the hold over this country for a period of six months whereas the boats backed by the paiks could command supremacy over the other half of the year. Since the time of Iwaz Khalji, who first organised a naval force in Islamic Bengal, the war boats played an important role in the political affairs of the country. The chief of the admiralty had various responsibilities, including shipbuilding, river transport, to fit out strong boats for transporting war elephants; to recruit seamen; to patrol the rivers and to collect tolls at ghats. The efficiency of the navy eroded during the Hussain Shahi dynasty. The sultans also built forts, including temporary mud walled forts.

Name of Conflict	Belligerents		Outcome
	Allies	*Opponent(s)*	
Bengal Sultanate-Delhi Sultanate War (1353–1359)	Velanati Chodas	Delhi Sultanate	Victory • Delhi recognizes Bengal Sultanate
Bengal Sultanate-Jaunpur Sultanate War (1415-1420)	Timurid Empire Ming China	Jaunpur Sultanate	Victory • Jaunpur halts raids on Bengal
Reconquest of Arakan (1429-1430)	Launggyet	Burmese Kingdoms • Hanthawaddy Kingdom • Kingdom of Ava	Victory • Kingdom of Mrauk U established as protectorate of Bengal
Bengal Sultanate–Kamata Kingdom War (1498)		Kamata Kingdom	Victory • Khen dynasty overthrown
Bengal Sultanate-Kingdom of Mrauk U War of 1512-1516		Kingdom of Mrauk U	Victory • Chittagong and North Arakan return to Bengal Sultanate rule
Battle of Ghaghra (1529)	Eastern Afghan Confederates	Mughal Empire	Defeat • Bengal signs peace treaty with Mughals

Battle of Raj Mahal (1576)	Mughal Empire	Defeat • Last Bengal Sultan captured

Economy

When Muslim rule was established, Bengal was rich in gold and silver from the pre-Islamic period. A new political economy was established by the Sultans. The taka was introduced as the standard currency of Bengal. The new currency consolidated the legitimacy of the sultanate. A salaried bureaucracy was established. Provincial autonomy manifested in governors and zamindars being allowed to retain shares of land revenue to maintain their own armed forces.

During his two visits to the sultanate, Ibn Battuta described Bengal as a vibrant fertile land overflowing with agricultural commodities. Most of its people were agricultural labourers and textile weavers. The Chinese traveler Ma Huan noted its large shipbuilding industry. Bengali traders were found in Malacca at the time of the sultanate. Shell currency was widely used in the sultanate and imported from the Sultanate of the Maldives in the Indian Ocean. The Maldives received abundant rice supplies in exchange for its cowry shells.[23] During the early part of its reign, the sultanate had a strong trade network with the Horn of Africa, including the Ajuraan sultanate and Ethiopia. Abyssinians were imported through the port of Chittagong. An African giraffe imported by the Bengali Sultan was gifted to the Chinese emperor.

The Grand Trunk Road connected the Bengali heartland with Kabul. Besides its handlooms in silk and cotton muslin, the region exported grain, salt, fruit, liquors and wines, precious metals and ornaments.Du ring the reopening of European trade with the East Indies following the Portuguese conquests of Malacca and Goa, Bengal was identified by European traders as "the richest country to trade with".[1804]

Currency and mint towns

The Taka was the currency of the Bengal Sultanate. Locations hosting a mint also served as provincial capitals, known as mint towns. The following includes a partial listing of mint towns in the Bengal Sultanate.

1. Lakhnauti
2. Sonargaon
3. Ghiaspur (Mymensingh)
4. Satgaon
5. Firuzabad (Pandua)

Figure 182: *Silver taka with a lion symbol, 15th century*

6. Shahr-i-Naw (Pandua)
7. Muzzamabad (Sonargaon)
8. Jannatabad (Lakhnauti)
9. Fathabad (Faridpur)
10. Chatgaon (Chittagong)
11. Rotaspur (Bihar)
12. Mahmudabad (Jessore and Nadia)
13. Barbakaabad (Dinajpur)
14. Muzaffarabad (Pandua)
15. Muahmmadabad
16. Husaynabad (24 Parganas)
17. Chandrabad (Murshidabad)
18. Nusratabad (Bogra and Rangpur)
19. Khalifatabad (Bagerhat)
20. Badarpur (Bagerhat)
21. Sharifabad (Birbhum)
22. Tandah (Malda)

Trade

The only eastern political and economic pole of Islamic India was Bengal. Like the Gujarat Sultanate, it was open to the sea and accumulated profits from trade with agricultural incomes. Traders from around the world were present in the Bay of Bengal area, which included the Ganges-Brahmaputra delta and the Irrawaddy delta. Bengal's position as a major cotton textile exporter was unique in Islamic India.

Figure 183: *The Bengal Sultanate, shown as the Ganges Delta, in the Portuguese Miller Atlas map from 1519*

Immigration

Bengal was a melting pot under the sultanate. It received settlers from North India, the Middle East and Central Asia. They included Turks, Afghans, Persians and Arabs. An important migrant community were Persians. Many Persians in Bengal were teachers, lawyers, scholars and clerics. Mercenaries were widely imported for domestic, military and political service.

Diplomatic relations

China

Political relations between China and the Indian subcontinent became nonexistent after the decline of Buddhism in India. In the 15th century, the Bengal Sultanate revived the subcontinent's relations with China for the first time in centuries. Sultan Ghiyasuddin Azam Shah began sending envoys to the Ming dynasty. He sent ambassadors in 1405, 1408 and 1409. Emperor Yongle of China responded by sending ambassadors to Bengal between 1405 and 1433, including members of the Treasure voyages fleet led by Admiral Zheng He.[1805] The exchange of embassies included the gift of an East African giraffe by Sultan Shihabuddin Bayazid Shah to the Chinese emperor in 1414. China

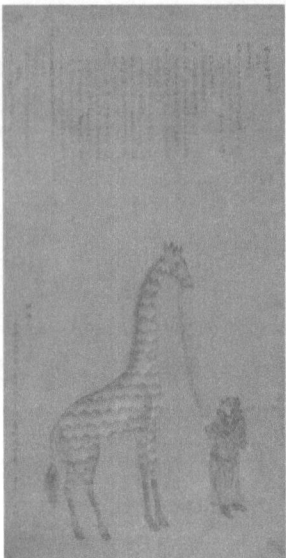

Figure 184: *The giraffe gifted by Bengal to China in 1414*

also mediated an end to the Bengal-Jaunpur War after a request from Sultan Jalaluddin Muhammad Shah.

Portugal

Following Vasco Da Gama's landing in southern India, Portuguese traders from Malacca, Ceylon and Bombay began traversing the sea routes of the Bay of Bengal. In the early 16th century, Bengal received official Portuguese envoys. Permission was given for the establishment of the Portuguese settlement in Chittagong.

Egypt

There are records of diplomatic relations between Sultan Jalaluddin Muhammad Shah and Sultan Ashraf Barsbay of Mamluk Egypt. The latter sent the Bengali sultan a robe of honor and a letter of recognition.

Africa

There are records of envoys from the East African city state of Malindi being hosted in the Bengali court. Animals constituted a significant part of tributes in medieval courts. The East African envoys brought giraffes, which were noticed by Chinese envoys.

Herat

There are records of contacts between Sultan Jalaluddin Muhammad Shah and Sultan Shahrukh Mirza, the Timurid ruler of Herat.

Jaunpur

Sultan Ghiyasuddin Azam began sending envoys to the neighboring Jaunpur Sultanate. He sent elephants as gifts to Sultan Khawja Jahan. The two kingdoms fought a war between 1415 and 1420. The end of the war brought a long period of peace between the neighboring states. In 1494, Sultan Husayn Shah Sharqi of Jaunpur took refuge in Bengal.[1806]

Contribution to Mecca and Medina

Sultan Ghiyasuddin Azam sponsored the construction of madrasas (Islamic theological schools) in Mecca and Medina. The schools became known as the Ghiyasia Madrasa and Banjaliah Madrasa. Taqiuddin Fasi, a contemporary Arab historian, was a teacher at the madrasa in Mecca. The madrasa in Medina was built at a place called Husn al-Atiq near the Prophet's Mosque. Several other Bengali sultans also sponsored madrasas in Mecca and Medina, including Sultan Jalaluddin Muhammad Shah.

Travelers

The kingdom was visited by noblemen from city states such as the Venetian Republic, including Niccolo De Conti, Caeser Frederick and Ludovico di Varthema.

Figure 185: *Tomb of Hafez in Shiraz. The Iranian poet wrote a poem for the Sultan of Bengal*

Literature

Muslim poets were writing in the Bengali language by the 15th century. By the turn of the 16th century, a vernacular literature based on concepts of Sufism and Islamic cosmology flourished in the region. Bengali Muslim mystic literature was one of the most original in Islamic India.

> *And with the three washers [cups of wine], this dispute is going on.*
>
> *All the parrots [poets] of India have fallen into a sugar shattering situation (become excited)*
>
> *That this Persian candy [ode], to Bangalah [Bengal] is going on.*
> *-An excerpt of a poem jointly penned by Hafez and Sultan Ghiyasuddin Azam Shah in the 14th century.*

With Persian as an official language, Bengal witnessed an influx of Persian scholars, lawyers, teachers and clerics. It was the preferred language of the aristocracy and the Sufis. Thousands of Persian books and manuscripts were published in Bengal. The earliest Persian work compiled in Bengal was a translation of Amrtakunda from Sanskrit by Qadi Ruknu'd-Din Abu Hamid Muhammad bin Muhammad al-'Amidi of Samarqand, a famous Hanafi jurist and Sufi. During the reign of Ghiyasuddin Azam Shah, the city of Sonargaon became an important centre of Persian literature, with many publications of prose and poetry. The period is described as the "golden age of Persian literature in Bengal". Its stature is illustrated by the Sultan's own correspondence with the Persian poet Hafez. When the Sultan invited Hafez to complete an incomplete ghazal by the ruler, the renowned poet responded by acknowledging the grandeur of the king's court and the literary quality of Bengali-Persian poetry.

In the 15th century, the Sufi poet Nur Qutb Alam pioneered Bengali Muslim poetry by establishing the Rikhta tradition, which saw poems written half in Persian and half in colloquial Bengali. The invocation tradition saw Islamic figures replacing the invocation of Hindu gods and goddesses in Bengali texts. The literary romantic tradition saw poems by Shah Muhammad Sagir on Yusuf and Zulaikha, as well as works of Bahram Khan and Sabirid Khan. The *Dobhashi* culture featured the use of Arabic and Persian words in Bengali texts to illustrate Muslim conquests. Epic poetry included *Nabibangsha* by Syed Sultan, *Janganama* by Abdul Hakim and *Rasul Bijay* by Shah Barid. Sufi literature flourished with a dominant theme of cosmology. Bengali Muslim writers produced translations of numerous Arabic and Persian works, including the Thousand and One Nights and the Shahnameh.

Architecture

The large number of mosques built during the Bengal Sultanate indicates the rapidity with which the local population converted to Islam. The period between 1450 and 1550 was an intensive mosque building era. These mosques dotted the countryside, ranged from small to medium sizes and were used for daily devotion. Most mosques were either of rectangular or square shape. The rectangular building without an enclosed courtyard became a popular type for both large and medium sized mosques. Bengali mosques would be covered several small domes. Other features of Bengali mosques would include corner towers, curved roofs, multiple mihrabs, pointed arches and in some cases, a dome in the shape of a hut's roof. Bengali mosques had a conspicuous absence of minarets. Ponds were often located beside a mosque. Arabic inscriptions in the mosques often include the name of the patron or builder. The most commonly cited verse from the Quran in inscriptions was Surah 72, Al-Jinn. A glimpse of houses in the Bengal Sultanate can be seen in the *Iskandar Nama* (Tale of Alexander) published by Sultan Nasiruddin Nasrat Shah.

The buildings were made of brick. The brick mosque with terracotta decoration represented a grand structure in the Bengal Sultanate. They were often the gift of a wealthy patron and the fruit of extraordinary effort, which would not be found in every Muslim neighborhood.

An exceptional building was the Adina Mosque, the imperial mosque of Bengal and the largest mosque ever built in the Indian subcontinent. The monumental structure was designed in the hypostyle of early of Islam with a plan similar to the Umayyad Mosque. The style is associated with the introduction of Islam in new areas.

List of Sultans
Ilyas Shahi dynasty (1342-1414)

Name	Reign	Notes
Shamsuddin Ilyas Shah	1342–1358	Became the first sole ruler of whole Bengal comprising Sonargaon, Satgaon and Lakhnauti.
Sikandar Shah	1358–1390	Assassinated by his son and successor, Ghiyasuddin Azam Shah
Ghiyasuddin Azam Shah	1390–1411	
Saifuddin Hamza Shah	1411–1413	
Muhammad Shah bin Hamza Shah	1413	Assassinated by his father's slave Shihabuddin Bayazid Shah on the orders of the landlord of Dinajpur, Raja Ganesha
Shihabuddin Bayazid Shah	1413–1414	
Alauddin Firuz Shah I	1414	Son of Shihabuddin Bayazid Shah. Assassinated by Raja Ganesha

House of Raja Ganesha (1414-1435)

Name	Reign	Notes
Raja Ganesha	1414–1415	
Jalaluddin Muhammad Shah	1415–1416	Son of Raja Ganesha and converted into Islam
Raja Ganesha	1416–1418	Second Phase
Jalaluddin Muhammad Shah	1418–1433	Second Phase
Shamsuddin Ahmad Shah	1433–1435	

Restored Ilyas Shahi dynasty (1435-1487)

Name	Reign	Notes
Nasiruddin Mahmud Shah I	1435–1459	
Rukunuddin Barbak Shah	1459–1474	
Shamsuddin Yusuf Shah	1474–1481	
Sikandar Shah II	1481	
Jalaluddin Fateh Shah	1481–1487	

Habshi rule (1487-1494)

Name	Reign	Notes
Shahzada Barbak	1487	
Saifuddin Firuz Shah	1487–1489	
Mahmud Shah II	1489–1490	
Shamsuddin Muzaffar Shah	1490–1494	

Hussain Shahi dynasty (1494-1538)

Name	Reign	Notes
Alauddin Hussain Shah	1494–1518	
Nasiruddin Nasrat Shah	1518–1533	
Alauddin Firuz Shah II	1533	
Ghiyasuddin Mahmud Shah	1533–1538	

Governors under Suri rule (1539-1554)

Name	Reign	Notes
Khidr Khan	1539–1541	Declared independence in 1541 and was replaced
Qazi Fazilat	1541–1545	
Muhammad Khan Sur	1545–1554	Declared independence upon the death of Islam Shah Suri

Figure 186: *An illustration of the conqueror Sher Shah Suri*

Muhammad Shah dynasty (1554-1564)

Name	Reign	Notes
Muhammad Khan Sur	1554–1555	Declared independence and styled himself as *Shamsuddin Muhammad Shah*
Ghiyasuddin Bahadur Shah I	1555–1561	
Ghiyasuddin Jalal Shah	1561–1563	
Ghiyasuddin Bahadur Shah II	1563-1564	

Karrani dynasty (1564-1576)

Name	Reign	Notes
Taj Khan Karrani	1564–1566	
Sulaiman Khan Karrani	1566–1572	
Bayazid Khan Karrani	1572	
Daud Khan Karrani	1572–1576	

Further reading

- Yegar, Moshe (2002). *Between Integration and Secession: The Muslim Communities of the Southern Philippines, Southern Thailand, and Western Burma/Myanmar*. Lanham, MD: Lexington Books. p. 23–24. ISBN 978-0-7391-0356-2.
- Hussain, Syed Ejaz (2003). The Bengal Sultanate: Politics, Economy and Coins, A.D. 1205–1576. Manohar. ISBN 978-81-7304-482-3.
- *The Grammar of Sultanate Mosque in Bengal Architecture*, Nujaba Binte Kabir (2012)

Coordinates: 24°52′0″N 88°8′0″E[1807]

Ahom kingdom

<indicator name="pp-default"> 🔒 </indicator>

Ahom kingdom

আহোম ৰাজ্য

1228–1826

Coat of arms

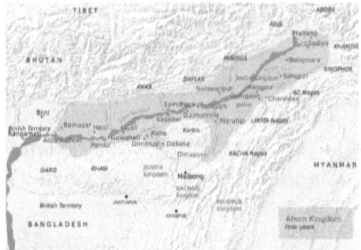

The Ahom kingdom. *Circa* 1826. The kingdom was founded by Sukaphaa between the Dikhau and the Dihing rivers in the 13th century, and by the end of the 19th century, the western outpost was the Assam Choki, or Hadira Choki, contiguous with British territories. The southern boundaries was defined by Doboka and Dimapur. The eastern portion around Bengmara, the Matak regions, was under the autonomous control of the Barsenapati. Jorhat became the capital of the kingdom after the Moamoria rebellion.

Capital		Charaideo, Garhgaon, Rangpur, Jorhat
Languages		Assamese Tai-Ahom
Religion		Tai folk religion and Hinduism
Government		Absolute monarchy with Unitary state
Sri Srimat Swargadeo Maharaja		
•	1228–1268	Sukaphaa
•	1648–1663	Sutamla
•	1811–1818, 1819–1821	Sudingphaa
History		
•	Established	1228
•	Disestablished	1826
	Preceded by Kamarupa	Succeeded by India
Today part of		Burma Assam, Nagaland, Tripura, Manipur, Arunachal Pradesh part of India

Ahom dynasty

1	Sukaphaa	1228–1268
2	Suteuphaa	1268–1281
3	Subinphaa	1281–1293
4	Sukhaangphaa	1293–1332
5	Sukhrangpha	1332–1364
	Interregnum	1364–1369
6	Sutuphaa	1369–1376
	Interregnum	1376–1380
7	Tyao Khamti	1380–1389
	Interregnum	1389–1397
8	Sudangphaa	1397–1407
9	Sujangphaa	1407–1422
10	Suphakphaa	1422–1439
11	Susenphaa	1439–1488
12	Suhenphaa	1488–1493
13	Supimphaa	1493–1497
14	Suhungmung	1497–1539
15	Suklenmung	1539–1552
16	Sukhaamphaa	1552–1603
17	Susenghphaa	1603–1641
18	Suramphaa	1641–1644
19	Sutingphaa	1644–1648
20	Sutamla	1648–1663
21	Supangmung	1663–1670
22	Sunyatphaa	1670–1672
23	Suklamphaa	1672–1674
24	Suhung	1674–1675
25	Gobar Roja	1675–1675
26	Sujinphaa	1675–1677
27	Sudoiphaa	1677–1679
28	Sulikphaa	1679–1681
29	Gadadhar Singha	1681–1696
30	Sukhrungphaa	1696–1714
31	Sutanphaa	1714–1744
32	Sunenphaa	1744–1751

33	Suremphaa	1751–1769
34	Sunyeophaa	1769–1780
35	Suhitpangphaa	1780–1795
36	Suklingphaa	1795–1811
37	Sudingphaa	1811–1818
38	Purandar Singha	1818–1819
39	Sudingphaa	1819–1821
40	Jogeswar Singha	1821–1822
41	Purandar Singha	1833–1838

- $\underline{v}$
- $\underline{t}$
- $\underline{e}^{1808}$

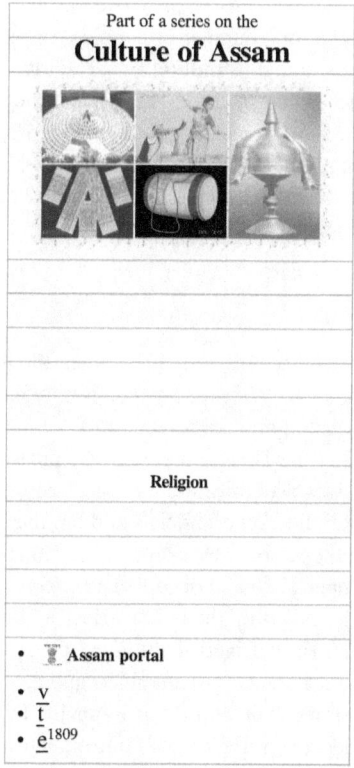

Part of a series on the
Culture of Assam

Religion

- Assam portal
- $\underline{v}$
- $\underline{t}$
- $\underline{e}^{1809}$

The **Ahom kingdom** (/'ɑːhɑːm, <wbr />'ɑːhəm/, 1228–1826, also called *Kingdom of Assam*[1810]) was a kingdom in the Brahmaputra Valley in Assam,

India. It is well known for maintaining its sovereignty for nearly 600 years and successfully resisting Mughal expansion in Northeast India. Established by Sukaphaa, a Tai prince from Mong Mao, it began as a mong in the upper reaches of the Brahmaputra based on wet rice agriculture. It expanded suddenly under Suhungmung in the 16th century and became multi-ethnic in character, casting a profound effect on the political and social life of the entire Brahmaputra valley. The kingdom became weaker with the rise of the Moamoria rebellion, and subsequently fell to repeated Burmese invasions of Assam. With the defeat of the Burmese after the First Anglo-Burmese War and the Treaty of Yandabo in 1826, control of the kingdom passed into East India Company hands.

Though it came to be called the Ahom kingdom in the colonial and subsequent times, it was largely multi-ethnic, with the ethnic Ahom people constituting less than 10% of the population toward the end.[1811] The 1901 census of India enumerated approximately 179,000 people identifying as Ahom. The latest available census records slightly over 2 million Ahom individuals however, estimates of the total number of people descended from the original Tai-Ahom settlers are as high as 8 million.[1812] The total population of Assam being at 31 million according to the 2011 census, they presently constitute slightly over 25%. The Ahoms called their kingdom *Mong Dun Shun Kham*, (Assamese: xunor-xophura; English: casket of gold) while others called it *Assam*. The British-controlled province after 1838 and later the Indian state of Assam came to be known by this name.

History

The Ahom kingdom was established in 1228 when the first Ahom king Chao Lung Siu-Ka-Pha came from *Mong Mao* which is now included within the Dehong Dai and Jingpo Autonomous Prefecture of Yunnan in People's Republic of China and entered the Brahmaputra valley, crossing the rugged Patkai mountain range. He was accompanied by his three queens, two sons, several nobles and their families, other officials and families, and soldiers totaling more than nine thousand persons. He crossed the Patkai and reached Namruk (Namrup) on 2 December 1228 and occupied a region on the south bank with the Burhidihing river in the north, the Dikhau river in the south and the Patkai mountains in the east. He befriended the local groups, the Barahi and the Marans, finally settled his capital at Charaideo and established the offices of the Dangarias—the Burhagohain and the Borgohain. In the 1280s, these two offices were given independent regions of control, and the check and balance that these three main offices accorded each other was established. The Ahoms brought with them the technology of wet rice cultivation that they shared with other groups. The people that took to the Ahom way of life and polity were incorporated into their fold in a process of Ahomization.[1813] As a result of this process the Barahi people, for instance, were completely subsumed, and some of other groups like some Nagas and the Maran peoples became Ahoms, thus enhancing the Ahom numbers significantly. This process of Ahomization was particularly significant till the 16th century, when under Suhungmung, the kingdom made large territorial expansions at the cost of the Chutiya and the Kachari kingdoms.

Ahom architecture

Kareng Ghar is a seven-storied royal palace built by Rajeswar Singha.

Rang Ghar, built by Pramatta Singha in Ahom Kingdom's capital Rongpur, is one of the earliest pavilions of outdoor stadia in the Indian subcontinent.

Talatal Ghar is a royal palace by Rudra Singha.

The expansion was so large and so rapid that the Ahomization process could not keep pace and the Ahoms became a minority in their kingdom. This resulted in a change in the character of the kingdom and it became multi-ethnic and inclusive. Hindu influences, which were first felt under Bamuni Konwar at the end of the 14th century, became significant. The Assamese language entered the Ahom court and co-existed with the Tai language for some time in the 17th century before finally replacing it.[1814] The rapid expansion of the state was accompanied by the installation of a new high office, the Borpatrogohain, at par with the other two high offices and not without opposition from them. Two special offices, the Sadiakhowa Gohain and the Marangikowa Gohain were created to oversee the regions won over from the Chutiya and the Kachari kingdoms respectively. The subjects of the kingdom were organized under the Paik system, initially based on the *phoid* or kinship relations, which formed the militia. The kingdom came under attack from Turkic and Afghan rulers of Bengal, but it withstood them. On one occasion, the Ahoms under Ton Kham Borgohain[1815] pursued the invaders and reached the Karatoya river,[1816] and the Ahoms began to see themselves as the rightful heir of the erstwhile Kamarupa kingdom.[1817]

The Ahom kingdom took many features of its mature form under Pratap Singha (1603–1641). The Paik system was reorganized under the professional *khel* system, replacing the kinship based *phoid* system. Under the same king, the offices of the Borphukan, and the Borbarua were established along with other smaller offices. No more major restructuring of the state structure was attempted till the end of the kingdom. The kingdom came under repeated Mughal attacks in the 17th century, and on one occasion in 1662, the Mughals under Mir Jumla occupied the capital, Garhgaon. The Mughals were unable to keep it, and in at the end of the Battle of Saraighat, the Ahoms not only fended off a major Mughal invasion, but extended their boundaries west, up to the Manas river. Following a period of confusion, the kingdom got itself the last set of kings, the Tungkhungia kings, established by Gadadhar Singha.

The rule of Tungkhungia kings was marked by peace and achievements in the Arts and engineering constructions. The later phase of the rule was also marked by increasing social conflicts, leading to the Moamoria rebellion. The rebels were able to capture and maintain power at the capital Rangpur for some years, but were finally removed with the help of the British under Captain Welsh. The following repression led to a large depopulation due to emigration as well as execution, but the conflicts were never resolved. A much weakened kingdom fell to repeated Burmese attacks and finally after the Treaty of Yandabo in 1826, the control of the kingdom passed into British hands.

Ahom economic system

The Ahom kingdom was based on the Paik system, a type of corvee labor that is neither feudal nor Asiatic. The first coins were introduced by Suklenmung in the 16th century, though the system of personal service under the Paik system persisted. In the 17th century when the Ahom kingdom expanded to include erstwhile Koch and Mughal areas, it came into contact with their revenue systems and adapted accordingly.

Ahom administration

Swargadeo and Patra Mantris

The Ahom kingdom was ruled by a king, called *Swargadeo* (Ahom language: *Chao-Pha*), who had to be a descendant of the first king Sukaphaa. Succession was generally by primogeniture but occasionally the great Gohains (*Dangarias*) could elect another descendant of Sukaphaa from a different line or even depose an enthroned one.

Dangarias: Sukaphaa had two great Gohains to aid him in administration: Burhagohain and the Borgohain. In the 1280s, they were given independent territories, they were veritable sovereigns in their given territories called *bilat* or *rajya*. The Burhagohain's territory was between Sadiya and Gerelua river in the north bank of the Brahmaputra river and the Borgohain's territory was to the west up to the Burai river. They were given total command over the *paiks* that they controlled. These positions were generally filled from specific families. Princes who were eligible for the position of Swargadeo were not considered for these positions and vice versa. In the 16th century Suhungmung added a third Gohain, Borpatrogohain. The Borpatrogohain's territory was located between the territories of the other two Gohains.

Royal officers: Pratap Singha added two offices, Borbarua and Borphukan, that were directly under the king. The Borbarua, who acted as the military as well as the judicial head, was in command of the region east of Kaliabor not under the command of the *Dangarias*. He could use only a section of the paiks at his command for his personal use (as opposed to the Dangariyas), the rest rendering service to the Ahom state. The Borphukan was in military and civil command over the region west of Kaliabor, and acted as the *Swargadeo's* viceroy in the west. Borbaruas were mostly from different Kachari communities, while Borphukans were from the Chutia community.

Patra Mantris: The five positions constituted the *patra mantris* (council of ministers). From the time of Supimphaa (1492–1497), one of the *patra mantris* was made the *Rajmantri* (prime minister, also *Borpatro*; Ahom language: *Shenglung*) who enjoyed additional powers and the service of a thousand additional paiks from the Jakaichuk village.

Other officials

The Borbarua and the Borphukan had military and judicial responsibilities, and they were aided by two separate councils (*sora*) of *Phukans*. The Borphukan's *sora* sat at Guwahati and the Borbarua's *sora* at the capital. Superintending officers were called *Baruas*. Among the officers the highest in rank were the Phukans. Six of them formed the council of the Borbarua, but each had also his separate duties. The Naubaicha Phukan, who had an allotment of thousand men managed the royal boats, the Bhitarual Phukan, the Na Phukan, the Dihingia Phukan, the Deka Phukan and the Neog Phukan formed the council of Phukan. The Borphukan also had a similar council of six subordinate Phukans whom he was bound to consult in all matters of importance, this council included Pani Phukan, who commanded six thousand *paiks*, Deka Phukan who commanded four thousand *paiks*, the Dihingia Phukan, Nek Phukan and two Chutiya Phukans.

The Baruas of whom there were twenty or more included Bhandari Barua or treasurer; the Duliya Barua, who was in charge of the royal palanquins; the Chaudang Barua who superintended executions; Khanikar Barua was the chief artificer; Sonadar Barua was the mint master and chief jeweler; the Bez Barua was the physician to the Royal family, Hati Barua, Ghora Barua, etc. Other official included twelve Rajkhowas, and a number of Katakis, Kakatis and Dolais. The Rajkhowas were governors of given territories and commanders of three thousand *paiks*. They were arbitrator who settled local disputes and supervised public works. The Katakis were envoys who dealt with foreign countries and hill tribes. The Kakatis were writers of official documents, and the Dolais expounded astrology and determined auspicious time and dates for any important event and undertaking.

Governors

Members of the royal families ruled certain areas, and they were called *Raja*.

- *Charing Raja*, the heir apparent to the *Swargadeo*, administered the tracts around Joypur on the right bank of the Burhidihing river.
- *Tipam Raja* is the second in line.
- *Namrup Raja* is the third in line

Members of the royal families who occupy lower positions are given regions called *mel*s, and were called *meldangia* or *melkhowa raja*. Meldangia *gohain*s were princes of an even lesser grade, of which there were two: *Majumelia gohain* and *Sarumelia gohain*.

Royal ladies were given individual *mel*s, and by the time of Rajeshwar Singha, there were twelve of them. The most important of these was the *Raidangia mel* given to the chief queen.

Forward governors, who were military commanders, ruled and administered forward territories. The officers were usually filled from the families that were eligible for the three great Gohains.

- *Sadiya Khowa Gohain* based in Sadiya, administered the regions that were acquired after the conquest of the Chutiya kingdom in 1523.

- *Marangi khowa Gohain* administered the region that were contiguous to the Naga groups west of the Dhansiri river.
- *Solal Gohain* administered a great part of Nagaon and a portion of Chariduar after the headquarters of the Borphukan was transferred to Gauhati.
- *Kajalimukhiya Gohain* served under the Borphukan, administered Kajalimukh and maintained relations with Jaintia and Dimarua.
- *Jagiyal Gohain* served under Borbarua, administered Jagi at Nagaon and maintained relations with seven tribal chiefs, called *Sat Raja*.

Lesser governors were called Rajkhowas, and some of them were:

- Bacha
- Darrang
- Solaguri
- Abhaypur

The dependent kings or vassals were also called *Raja*. Except for the Raja of Rani, all paid an annual tribute. These Rajas were required to meet the needs for resources and paiks when the need arose, as during the time of war.

- Darrang Raja ruled the later-day Darrang district, and were the descendants of Sundar Narayan, a great-grandson of Chilarai of the Koch dynasty
- Rani
- Beltola ruled the tracts southwest of Guwahati, and were the descendants of Gaj Narayan, a grandson of Chilarai of the Koch dynasty
- Luki
- Barduar
- Dimarua
- Tapakuchi

Paik officials

The Ahom kingdom was dependent on the Paik system, a form of corvee labor. Every common subject was a *paik*, and four *paiks* formed a *got*. At any time of the year, one of the *paiks* in the *got* rendered direct service to the king, as the others in his *got* tended to his fields. The Paik system was administered by the Paik officials: Bora was in charge of 20 *paiks*, a Saikia of 100 and a Hazarika of 1000.

Land survey

Gadadhar Singha became acquainted with the land measurement system of Mughals during the time he was hiding in Kamrup, before he succeeded to the throne. As soon as the wars with Mughals were over he issued orders for the introduction of a similar system throughout his dominions. Surveyors were imported from Koch Behar and Bengal for the work. It was commenced in Sibsagar and was pushed on vigorously, but it was not completed until after his death. Nowgaon was next surveyed; and the settlement which followed was supervised by Rudra Singha himself. According to historians, the method of survey included measuring the four sides of each field with a *nal*, or bamboo pole of 12 feet (3.7 m) length and calculating the area, the unit was the "lucha" or 144 square feet (13.4 m^2) and 14,400 sq ft (1,340 m^2). is one "Bigha". Four 'bigha' makes one 'Pura'. A similar land measurement system is still being followed in modern Assam.

Classes of people

Subinphaa (1281–1293), the third Ahom king, dilineated the *Satgharia Ahom* ("Ahom of the seven houses") aristocracy: the *Chaophaa*, the Burhagohain and the Borgohain families (the *Gohains*), and four priestly lineages—the *Deodhai*, the *Mohan*, the *Bailung* and the *Chiring* (the *Gogois*). These lines maintained exogamous marital relationships. The number of lineages increased in later times as either other lineages were incorporated, or existing lineages divided. The king could belong to only the first family whereas the Burhagohain and the Borgohain only to the second and the third families. Most of the Borphukans belonged to the Chutiya ethnic group, whereas the Borbaruas belonged to the Moran, Kachari, Chiring and Khamti groups. Later on Naga, Mising and Nara (Mogaung) oracles became a part of the *Bailung* group. The extended nobility consisted of the landed aristocracy and the spiritual class that did not pay any form of tax.

The *apaikan chamua* was the gentry that were freed from the *khels* and paid only money-tax. The *paikan chamua* consisted of artisans, the literati and skilled people that did non-manual work and rendered service as tax. The *kanri paik* rendered manual labor. The lowest were the *licchous*, *bandi-beti* and other serfs and bondsmen. There was some degree of movement between the classes. Momai Tamuli Borbarua rose from a bondsman through the ranks to become the first Borbarua under Prataap Singha.

References

<templatestyles src="Template:Refbegin/styles.css" />

- Gogoi, Jahnabi (2002), *Agrarian system of medieval Assam*, Concept Publishing Company, New Delhi
- Gogoi, Lila (1991), *The History of the system of Ahom administration*, Punthi Pustak, Calcutta
- Gogoi, Nitul Kumar (2006), *Continuity and Change among the Ahoms*, Concept Publishing Company, Delhi
- Gogoi, Padmeshwar (1968), *The Tai and the Tai kingdoms*, Gauhati University, Guwahati
- Guha, Amalendu (1991), *Medieval and Early Colonial Assam: Society, Polity and Economy*, K.P. Bagchi & Co, Calcutta
- Guha, Amalendu (December 1983), "The Ahom Political System: An Enquiry into the State Formation Process in Medieval Assam (1228-1714)", *Social Scientist*, **11** (12): 3–34, doi: 10.2307/3516963[1818], JSTOR 3516963[1819]
- Kakoty, Sanjeeb (2003), *Technology, Production and Social Formation in the Evolution of the Ahom State*, Regency Publications, New Delhi
- Sharma, Benudhar, ed. (1972), *An Account of Assam*, Gauhati: Assam Jyoti

Coordinates: 26°55′59″N 94°44′53″E[1820]

Reddy dynasty

Reddy dynasty	
1325–1448	
Capital	Addanki (initial) Kondavidu Rajahmundry
Languages	Telugu
Religion	ॐ Hinduism
Government	Monarchy
Historical era	Medieval India
• Established	1325
• Disestablished	1448

Preceded by	Succeeded by
Kakatiya dynasty	Vijayanagara Empire Gajapati Kingdom

Part of a series on
Andhra Pradesh and Telangana

Chronology of the Telugu people, Andhra Pradesh, and Telangana history

- Geography
- Political history

History and Kingdoms

- v
- t
- e[1821]

Reddy Kings (1325-1448)	
Prolaya Vema Reddy	(1325 - 1335)
Anavota Reddy	(1335 - 1364)
Anavema Reddy	(1364 - 1386)
Kumaragiri Reddy	(1386 - 1402)
Kataya Vema Reddy	(1395 - 1414)
Allada Reddy	(1414 - 1423)
Veerabhadra Reddy	(1423 - 1448)

The **Reddy dynasty** (1325–1448 CE) was established in southern India by Prolaya Vema Reddy. The region that was ruled by the Reddy dynasty is now part of modern-day coastal and central Andhra Pradesh. Prolaya Vema Reddy was part of the confederation that started a movement against the invading Turkic armies of the Delhi Sultanate in 1323 and succeeded in repulsing them from Warangal.

Origin

The first of the Reddy clans came into prominence during the period Rashtrakuta dynasty. Later, the Reddy chiefs were appointed as generals under the Kakatiyas. During this time, the Reddys carved out feudal principalities for themselves. After the Delhi Sultanate conquered Warangal annexed the Kakatiya empire, the Reddy chiefs became independent. Prolaya Vema Reddy proclaimed independence and established the Reddy Kingdom in Addanki.Wikipedia:Verifiability

Extent of rule

They ruled coastal and central Andhra for over a hundred years from 1325 to 1448.Wikipedia:Verifiability At its maximum extent, the Reddy kingdom stretched from Cuttack, Orissa to the north, Kanchi to the south and Srisailam to the west.[1822] The initial capital of the kingdom was Addanki. Later, it was moved to Kondavidu and subsequently to Rajahmundry.Wikipedia:Verifiability The Reddys were known for their fortifications. Two major hill forts, one at Kondapalli, 20 km north west of Vijayawada and another at Kondavidu about 30 km west of Guntur stand testimony to

Figure 187: *Water colour painting - Kondavidu fort, Reddy Kingdom.*

the fort building skill of the Reddy kings.[1823] The forts of Bellamkonda, Vinukonda and Nagarjunakonda in the Palnadu region were also part of the Reddy kingdom.[1823] The dynasty remained in power till the middle of the 15th century and was supplanted by the Gajapatis of Odisha, who gained control of coastal Andhra.[1824] The Gajapatis eventually lost control of coastal Andhra after Gajapati Prataprudra Deva was defeated by Krishna Deva Raya of Vijaynagar. The territories of the Reddy kingdom eventually came under the control of the Vijayanagara Empire.

Prolaya Vema Reddy

Prolaya Vema Reddy, the first king of the Reddy dynasty. Vema assembled a large army of peasants and herdsmen, and adopted guerrilla warfare. It is said that when he attacked Muslims, Vema Reddy had their water supply lines contaminated with sewage leading to dysentery in their ranks. Veera Ballala III of Dwarasamudra helped the coalition leader Kapaya Nayaka. Vema Reddy was part of the coalition. Vema then led a blitzkrieg on the Kondavidu fort and hacked off the head of Maliq Gurjar, the Muslim commander there after pitched battles. Vema then defeated an army of Jalaluddin Shah in a raid on Tondaimandalam, while Vira Ballala engaged the Sultan himself. Vira Ballala was finally defeated and skinned alive, and his dry skin was hung from the

Figure 188: *Sanskrit-Telugu on copper plates, 1358, Anavota Reddy.*

walls of Madurai where Ibn Battuta reportedly saw it later. Undaunted, Vema continued his lightning raids on the Muslim-occupied forts of Bellamkonda, Vinukonda and Nagarjunakonda and captured them all. He then declared himself a *raja* (king) with Kondavidu as his capital. Prolaya Vema reddy's sister's daughter got married to Basthar land lord Gandla potu Narsimha reddy's brother's son.He built the fortress at Kondapalle.

His famous inscriptions from this period state: "I restored all the agraharas of Brahmins, which had been taken away by the evil Muslim kings. I am indeed an Agastya to the ocean which was made of the Muslim".

Prolaya Vema Reddy commissioned major repairs to the Srisailam Mallikarjuna Swami temple, and had a flight of steps built from the Krishna river to the temple. He also had the Sri Maha Vishnu temple at Ahobilam repaired. The restoration of peace starting with his reign brought about a revival of literature and the arts. Errana, the translator of the Mahabharata, lived during his period. He built 108 temples for Lord Siva.

Later kings

Anavota Reddy (1353-1364 CE) was the successor of Prolaya Vema Reddy.

Anavema Reddy (1364-1386 CE) was the brother of Anavota Reddy. He also conquered the Simhachalam fort and parts of the Kalinga kingdom. He built the Vira Siromandapam at the Srisailam temple. His inscription from Srisailam states that their family belongs to the 'Vellacheri' gotram. His inscription states: "I the valiant member of the fourth Varna destroyed the throngs of Muslims and gathered learned Brahmanas at this court". He extended the dominion of the kingdom to Rajahmundry on the north, Kanchi on the south and Srisailam on the west.

Kumaragiri (Komaragiri) Reddy (1386-1402 CE) was the son of Anavota Reddy. Kataya Vema Reddy, the Senapathi of Anavota Reddy and the brother-in-law of Kumaragiri Reddy, and Pedakomati Vema Reddy always indulged in internal squabbles. Many parts of the kingdom announced their independence and did not pay taxes. Kumaragiri Reddy had only one son named Anavotha Reddy 2. He was made in charge of Rajamaendravaram. He died in 1295.[1825].

Pedakomati Vemareddi (1403-1420 CE) was a great patron of literature.

Kataya Vema Reddy (1395-1414 CE) suppressed the revolt in Rajamahendravaram and ruled it for 19 years. Harihara Rayalu, the ruler of Vijayanagara empire, married his daughter Vijayalakshmi to Kataya Vema Reddy's son Kataya after his defeat to Kataya Vema Reddy at Tripurantakam Battle in 1385. Hariharamba was their daughter, married to Vema Reddy, son of Allada Reddy. He fought many wars with Pedakomati Vema Reddy. He had two sons Kataya and Komaragiri named after his brother-in-law. Kataya died during the lifetime of Kataya Vema. Anitalli was the daughter of Kataya Vema was Married to Veerabhadra Reddy of Rajamahendravaram.

Allada Reddy (1414-1423 CE) ruled on behalf of the young Komaragiri Reddy who was only 10 years old at the time. Allada Reddy managed to fend off Pedakomati Reddy twice, and made peace treaties with Vijayanagar and Kalinga.

Veerabhadra Reddy (1423-1448 CE) succeeded to the kingdom of Rajamahendravaram. Devaraya II of Vijayanagara came to the support of the Reddy kings against the Gajapathis of Orissa. The Reddys could not get the support from Mallikarjuna of Vijayanagar, the successor of Devaraya II, in time and lost to Hamvira, the son of Kapilendra Gajapathi. The Reddy kingdom started to decline because of internecine warfare with the Recherla Velamas and the Gajapathis. By 1448 CE, Rajamahendravaram and the surrounding places were taken by Kapilendra Gajapathi. By 1454 CE, the Kondavidu region also came under the control of the Gajapathis. Srinathudu, the greatest Telugu poet of the time was his court poet.

Figure 189: *Mallikarjuna Swamy Temple, Srisailam*

Religion

The Reddy rulers played a prominent part in post-Kakatiyas of Telangana. The Kakatiya empire came to an end in 1323 after the army of the Delhi sultanate invaded Warangal and captured Kakatiya ruler Pratapa Rudra. Warangal fell to the invaders and Ulugh Khan commanded Warangal and Telangana. During this time of foreign invasion and chaos in Telugu country, seeds of revolt were sown by two princes, Annaya Mantri and Kolani Rudradeva. They united the Telugu nobles with the purpose of reclaiming the kingdom. Musunuri Prolaya Nayaka, Prolaya Vema Reddy, Recharla Singama Nayaka, Koppula Prolaya Nayaka and Manchikonda Ganapatinayaka were the prominent nobles. Musunuri Prolaya Nayaka was the chosen leader of this confederation of Telugu nobles who united and vowed to put an end to the Sultanate's rule. They succeeded in repulsing those forces from Warangal and then established independent Kingdoms of their own.Wikipedia:Verifiability

It was during this chaotic period in Andhra history that Prolaya Vema Reddy established the Reddy kingdom in 1325. The Reddy rulers patronised and protected Hinduism and its institutions. The Brahmins were given liberal grants by the Reddy kings and the agraharas of Brahmins were restored. Vedic studies were encouraged. The Hindu temples of Srisailam and Ahobilam were provided with more facilities. Prolaya Vema Reddy bestowed a number of

Figure 190: *Lord Narasimha, Narasimha Swamy Temple, Ahobilam*

agraharas on the Brahmins. He was revered by the title of *Apratima-Bhudana-Parasurama*. He commissioned major repairs to the Srisailam Mallikarjuna Swami temple, and had a flight of steps built from the Krishna river to the temple. The Narasimha Swamy temple at Ahobilam was built during his reign. He built 108 temples for Shiva.[1826]

Literature

Telugu literature blossomed under the Reddy kings. The Reddy kings also patronized Sanskrit. Several of the Reddy kings themselves were distinguished scholars and authors. Kumaragiri Reddy, Kataya Vema Reddy and Pedakomati Vema Reddy were the most outstanding among them. Errapragada (Errana), Srinatha and Potana were the remarkable poets of this period. Errapragada, the last of the Kavitraya (Trinity of Poets) was the court poet of Prolaya Vema Reddy. He completed the Telugu translation of the Mahabharata. He completed the rendition of the Aranya Parva of Mahabharata left incomplete by Nannaya Bhattu (Aadi Kavi who started the translation of Mahabharata into Telugu). He wrote Hari Vamsa and Narasimha Purana. Errana's translation of the Ramayana in *Chapu* form (a style of poetry) has been lost.[1823]

Srinatha was considered the most distinguished writer of the Reddy period. He was the court poet of Pedakomati Vema Reddy. He wrote 'Palnadu Viracharitra' in 'Dwipada' meter. This story chronicles the 12th century war between two branches of Kalachuri family that ruled from Gurazala and Macherla. This battle changed the course of Andhra history, with political control passing into Kakateeya hands. Other works of Srinatha, include 'Pandita-radhya Charita', 'Sivaratrimahatmya,' 'Haravilasa', 'Bhimakhanda' and 'Kasikhanda'.

Administration

The administration was carried according to the "Dharmasutras". One sixth of agriculture surplus was levied as tax. Under the reign of Anavota Reddy custom duties and taxes on trade were lifted. As a result, trade flourished. Sea trade was carried through the port Motupalli. Large number of merchants settled down near it. Celebrating 'Vasantotsavalu' was revived during the rule of Anavema Reddy. The Brahmins were given liberal grants by the Reddy kings. Caste system was observed. Heavy taxes by Racha Vema Reddy made him highly unpopular.[1827]

Notes and references

 Wikimedia Commons has media related to *Reddy dynasty*.

Book sources

- Rao (1994), *History And Culture Of Andhra Pradesh: From The Earliest Times To The Present Day*, Sterling Publishers, ISBN 81-207-1719-8

Reddy dynasty	
1325–1448	
Capital	Addanki (initial) Kondavidu Rajahmundry
Languages	Telugu
Religion	ॐ Hinduism
Government	Monarchy
Historical era	Medieval India
• Established	1325
• Disestablished	1448
Preceded by	Succeeded by
Kakatiya dynasty	Vijayanagara Empire Gajapati Kingdom

Part of a series on

Andhra Pradesh and Telangana

Chronology of the Telugu people, Andhra Pradesh, and Telangana history

- Geography
- Political history

History and Kingdoms

- v
- t
- e[1821]

Reddy Kings (1325-1448)	
Prolaya Vema Reddy	(1325 - 1335)
Anavota Reddy	(1335 - 1364)
Anavema Reddy	(1364 - 1386)

Kumaragiri Reddy	(1386 - 1402)
Kataya Vema Reddy	(1395 - 1414)
Allada Reddy	(1414 - 1423)
Veerabhadra Reddy	(1423 - 1448)

The **Reddy dynasty** (1325–1448 CE) was established in southern India by Prolaya Vema Reddy. The region that was ruled by the Reddy dynasty is now part of modern-day coastal and central Andhra Pradesh. Prolaya Vema Reddy was part of the confederation that started a movement against the invading Turkic armies of the Delhi Sultanate in 1323 and succeeded in repulsing them from Warangal.

Andhra historians often state that Reddy kings belong to the Reddy caste group. However, the modern castes of Andhra region did not originate until the late stages of the Vijayanagara Empire.[1828]

Origin

The first of the Reddy clans came into prominence during the period Rashtrakuta dynasty. Later, the Reddy chiefs were appointed as generals under the Kakatiyas. During this time, the Reddys carved out feudal principalities for themselves. After the Delhi Sultanate conquered Warangal annexed the Kakatiya empire, the Reddy chiefs became independent. Prolaya Vema Reddy proclaimed independence and established the Reddy Kingdom in Addanki.Wikipedia:Verifiability

Extent of rule

They ruled coastal and central Andhra for over a hundred years from 1325 to 1448.Wikipedia:Verifiability At its maximum extent, the Reddy kingdom stretched from Cuttack, Orissa to the north, Kanchi to the south and Srisailam to the west.[1822] The initial capital of the kingdom was Addanki. Later, it was moved to Kondavidu and subsequently to Rajahmundry.Wikipedia:Verifiability The Reddys were known for their fortifications. Two major hill forts, one at Kondapalli, 20 km north west of Vijayawada and another at Kondavidu about 30 km west of Guntur stand testimony to the fort building skill of the Reddy kings.[1823] The forts of Bellamkonda, Vinukonda and Nagarjunakonda in the Palnadu region were also part of the Reddy kingdom.[1823] The dynasty remained in power till the middle of the

Figure 191: *Water colour painting - Kondavidu fort, Reddy Kingdom.*

15th century and was supplanted by the Gajapatis of Odisha, who gained control of coastal Andhra.[1824] The Gajapatis eventually lost control of coastal Andhra after Gajapati Prataprudra Deva was defeated by Krishna Deva Raya of Vijaynagar. The territories of the Reddy kingdom eventually came under the control of the Vijayanagara Empire.

Prolaya Vema Reddy

Prolaya Vema Reddy, the first king of the Reddy dynasty. Vema assembled a large army of peasants and herdsmen, and adopted guerrilla warfare. It is said that when he attacked Muslims, Vema Reddy had their water supply lines contaminated with sewage leading to dysentery in their ranks. Veera Ballala III of Dwarasamudra helped the coalition leader Kapaya Nayaka. Vema Reddy was part of the coalition. Vema then led a blitzkrieg on the Kondavidu fort and hacked off the head of Maliq Gurjar, the Muslim commander there after pitched battles. Vema then defeated an army of Jalaluddin Shah in a raid on Tondaimandalam, while Vira Ballala engaged the Sultan himself. Vira Ballala was finally defeated and skinned alive, and his dry skin was hung from the walls of Madurai where Ibn Battuta reportedly saw it later. Undaunted, Vema continued his lightning raids on the Muslim-occupied forts of Bellamkonda,

Figure 192: *Sanskrit-Telugu on copper plates, 1358, Anavota Reddy.*

Vinukonda and Nagarjunakonda and captured them all. He then declared himself a *raja* (king) with Kondavidu as his capital. Prolaya Vema reddy's sister's daughter got married to Basthar land lord Gandla potu Narsimha reddy's brother's son. He built the fortress at Kondapalle.

His famous inscriptions from this period state: "I restored all the agraharas of Brahmins, which had been taken away by the evil Muslim kings. I am indeed an Agastya to the ocean which was made of the Muslim".

Prolaya Vema Reddy commissioned major repairs to the Srisailam Mallikarjuna Swami temple, and had a flight of steps built from the Krishna river to the temple. He also had the Sri Maha Vishnu temple at Ahobilam repaired. The restoration of peace starting with his reign brought about a revival of literature and the arts. Errana, the translator of the Mahabharata, lived during his period. He built 108 temples for Lord Siva.

Later kings

Anavota Reddy (1353-1364 CE) was the successor of Prolaya Vema Reddy.

Anavema Reddy (1364-1386 CE) was the brother of Anavota Reddy. He also conquered the Simhachalam fort and parts of the Kalinga kingdom. He built the Vira Siromandapam at the Srisailam temple. His inscription from Srisailam states that their family belongs to the 'Vellacheri' gotram. His inscription states: "I the valiant member of the fourth Varna destroyed the throngs of Muslims and gathered learned Brahmanas at this court". He extended the dominion of the kingdom to Rajahmundry on the north, Kanchi on the south and Srisailam on the west.

Kumaragiri (Komaragiri) Reddy (1386-1402 CE) was the son of Anavota Reddy. Kataya Vema Reddy, the Senapathi of Anavota Reddy and the brother-in-law of Kumaragiri Reddy, and Pedakomati Vema Reddy always indulged in internal squabbles. Many parts of the kingdom announced their independence and did not pay taxes. Kumaragiri Reddy had only one son named Anavotha Reddy 2. He was made in charge of Rajamaendravaram. He died in 1295.[1829].

Pedakomati Vemareddi (1403-1420 CE) was a great patron of literature.

Kataya Vema Reddy (1395-1414 CE) suppressed the revolt in Rajamahendravaram and ruled it for 19 years. Harihara Rayalu, the ruler of Vijayanagara empire, married his daughter Vijayalakshmi to Kataya Vema Reddy's son Kataya after his defeat to Kataya Vema Reddy at Tripurantakam Battle in 1385. Hariharamba was their daughter, married to Vema Reddy, son of Allada Reddy. He fought many wars with Pedakomati Vema Reddy. He had two sons Kataya and Komaragiri named after his brother-in-law. Kataya died during the lifetime of Kataya Vema. Anitalli was the daughter of Kataya Vema was Married to Veerabhadra Reddy of Rajamahendravaram.

Allada Reddy (1414-1423 CE) ruled on behalf of the young Komaragiri Reddy who was only 10 years old at the time. Allada Reddy managed to fend off Pedakomati Reddy twice, and made peace treaties with Vijayanagar and Kalinga.

Veerabhadra Reddy (1423-1448 CE) succeeded to the kingdom of Rajamahendravaram. Devaraya II of Vijayanagara came to the support of the Reddy kings against the Gajapathis of Orissa. The Reddys could not get the support from Mallikarjuna of Vijayanagar, the successor of Devaraya II, in time and lost to Hamvira, the son of Kapilendra Gajapathi. The Reddy kingdom started to decline because of internecine warfare with the Recherla Velamas and the Gajapathis. By 1448 CE, Rajamahendravaram and the surrounding places were taken by Kapilendra Gajapathi. By 1454 CE, the Kondavidu region also came under the control of the Gajapathis. Srinathudu, the greatest Telugu poet of the time was his court poet.

Figure 193: *Mallikarjuna Swamy Temple, Srisailam*

Religion

The Reddy rulers played a prominent part in post-Kakatiyas of Telangana. The Kakatiya empire came to an end in 1323 after the army of the Delhi sultanate invaded Warangal and captured Kakatiya ruler Pratapa Rudra. Warangal fell to the invaders and Ulugh Khan commanded Warangal and Telangana. During this time of foreign invasion and chaos in Telugu country, seeds of revolt were sown by two princes, Annaya Mantri and Kolani Rudradeva. They united the Telugu nobles with the purpose of reclaiming the kingdom. Musunuri Prolaya Nayaka, Prolaya Vema Reddy, Recharla Singama Nayaka, Koppula Prolaya Nayaka and Manchikonda Ganapatinayaka were the prominent nobles. Musunuri Prolaya Nayaka was the chosen leader of this confederation of Telugu nobles who united and vowed to put an end to the Sultanate's rule. They succeeded in repulsing those forces from Warangal and then established independent Kingdoms of their own.Wikipedia:Verifiability

It was during this chaotic period in Andhra history that Prolaya Vema Reddy established the Reddy kingdom in 1325. The Reddy rulers patronised and protected Hinduism and its institutions. The Brahmins were given liberal grants by the Reddy kings and the agraharas of Brahmins were restored. Vedic studies were encouraged. The Hindu temples of Srisailam and Ahobilam were provided with more facilities. Prolaya Vema Reddy bestowed a number of

Figure 194: *Lord Narasimha, Narasimha Swamy Temple, Ahobilam*

agraharas on the Brahmins. He was revered by the title of *Apratima-Bhudana-Parasurama*. He commissioned major repairs to the Srisailam Mallikarjuna Swami temple, and had a flight of steps built from the Krishna river to the temple. The Narasimha Swamy temple at Ahobilam was built during his reign. He built 108 temples for Shiva.[1826]

Literature

Telugu literature blossomed under the Reddy kings. The Reddy kings also patronized Sanskrit. Several of the Reddy kings themselves were distinguished scholars and authors. Kumaragiri Reddy, Kataya Vema Reddy and Pedakomati Vema Reddy were the most outstanding among them. Errapragada (Errana), Srinatha and Potana were the remarkable poets of this period. Errapragada, the last of the Kavitraya (Trinity of Poets) was the court poet of Prolaya Vema Reddy. He completed the Telugu translation of the Mahabharata. He completed the rendition of the Aranya Parva of Mahabharata left incomplete by Nannaya Bhattu (Aadi Kavi who started the translation of Mahabharata into Telugu). He wrote Hari Vamsa and Narasimha Purana. Errana's translation of the Ramayana in *Chapu* form (a style of poetry) has been lost.[1823]

Srinatha was considered the most distinguished writer of the Reddy period. He was the court poet of Pedakomati Vema Reddy. He wrote 'Palnadu Viracharitra' in 'Dwipada' meter. This story chronicles the 12th century war between two branches of Kalachuri family that ruled from Gurazala and Macherla. This battle changed the course of Andhra history, with political control passing into Kakateeya hands. Other works of Srinatha, include 'Pandita-radhya Charita', 'Sivaratrimahatmya,' 'Haravilasa,' 'Bhimakhanda' and 'Kasikhanda'.

Administration

The administration was carried according to the "Dharmasutras". One sixth of agriculture surplus was levied as tax. Under the reign of Anavota Reddy custom duties and taxes on trade were lifted. As a result, trade flourished. Sea trade was carried through the port Motupalli. Large number of merchants settled down near it. Celebrating 'Vasantotsavalu' was revived during the rule of Anavema Reddy. The Brahmins were given liberal grants by the Reddy kings. Caste system was observed. Heavy taxes by Racha Vema Reddy made him highly unpopular.[1827]

Notes and references

 Wikimedia Commons has media related to *Reddy dynasty*.

Book sources

- Rao (1994), *History And Culture Of Andhra Pradesh: From The Earliest Times To The Present Day*, Sterling Publishers, ISBN 81-207-1719-8

Gajapati Kingdom

Gajapati Kingdom	
1434–1541	
Capital	Cuttack
Languages	Odia[1830]
Religion	Hinduism
Government	Monarchy
Sri Sri Gajapati Gaudesvara Navakoti Karnata Utkala Kalavargeshvara	
• 1434–66	Kapilendra Deva
• 1466–97	Purushottama Deva
• 1497–1540	Prataprudra Deva
• 1540–1541	Kalua Deva
• 1541	Kakharua Deva
Historical era	Medieval India
• Established	1434
• Disestablished	1541
Preceded by: Eastern Ganga dynasty	Succeeded by: Bhoi dynasty

The **Gajapatis** were a medieval Hindu dynasty from the Indian subcontinent, which originated in the region of Kalinga (most of present-day Odisha and Northern coastal Andhra) from 1434 to 1541 CE. Under Kapilendra Deva, Gajapatis became an empire stretching from the lower Ganga in the north to the Kaveri in the south.

The Gajapati dynasty was established by Emperor Kapilendra Deva (1434–66 CE) in 1434. During the reign of Kapilendra Deva, the borders of the empire were expanded immensely; from large parts of Andhra Pradesh and West Bengal, and the eastern and central parts of Madhya Pradesh and Jharkhand. The king took the title of *Sri Sri ... (108 times) Gajapati Gaudesvara Nava Koti Karnata Kalvargesvara*. This title is still used by the kings of Puri during the Ratha Yatra. The significant rulers of this dynasty were Purushottama Deva (1466–1497) and Prataparudra Deva (1497–1540). The last ruler Kakharua Deva was killed by Govinda Vidyadhara in 1541, who founded the Bhoi dynasty.

Etymology

In Sanskrit, "Gaja" means elephant and "Pati" means *master* or *husband*. As such, Gajapati etymologically means *a king with an army of elephants*.

History

The region known as Kalinga (present-day Odisha) was controlled by the Odia rulers Eastern Gangas of the Vasistha gotra. The early Eastern Gangas ruled from Kalinga-nagara (Mukhalingam near Srikakulam, Andhra Pradesh). They shifted their capital to Puri in the 12th century. Religious leader Ramanujacharya had a great influence on the Raja Choda Ganga Deva, who renovated the temple at Puri. Narasimha Deva built the Sun Temple at Konark. The Gangas were succeeded by the Gajapati rulers. Two copper plates of the early Pallava dynasty have been found in the Kolleru Lake, traced to Gajapati Langula Narasimha Deva, an Oriya ruler(Odiya Raju). According to legend, the Gajapati fort was located at Kolleti Kota on one of the eastern islands of the lake, which protected the Odia forces. The enemy general encamped at Chiguru Kota located on the shores and tried to excavate a channel in the modern-day Upputeru, so that the water of the lake would empty into the sea and allow an attack on the Gajapathi fort.

The Suryavansi Gajapatis of Odisha, at the height of their power in the 15th century, ruled over an empire extending from the Ganges in the north near Hoogly to the Cauvery in the south under Gajapati Kapilendra Deva. But by the early 16th century, the Gajapatis lost great portions of their southern dominion to Vijayanagar and Golconda. This period was marked by the influence of Chaitanya Mahaprabhu and by the expansion of Jaganatha temple across the length and breadth of the empire. One of the causes of the reduction in militarism of the population has been attested to the Bhakti movement initiated by Sri Chaitanya Mahaprabhu, who arrived in the empire at the time of Emperor Prataparudra and stayed for 18 long years at Puri. Emperor Prataparudra was highly influenced by the works of Chaitanya and gave up the military tradition of the Odia emperors. He retired himself into the life of an ascetic leaving the future of the empire uncertain. The traitor Govinda Vidyadhara took the opportunity to murder the sons of the emperor and usurped the throne himself and carved out the destruction of the once mighty empire.

Cultural contributions

Their rule in eastern India is associated with a high point in the growth of regional culture and architecture. Sarala Mahabharata by Sarala Dasa, a transcreation of the original Sanskrit one was written during this period. Similarly transcreation of the Ramayana and Bhagvata Purana were written. They constitute the best examples of ancient Odia literature.

Rulers

1. Kapilendra Deva (1434–70)
2. Purushottama Deva (1470–97)
3. Prataparudra Deva (1497–1540)
4. Kalua Deva (1540–41)
5. Kakharua Deva (1541)

References

- Majumdar, Ramesh Chandra; Pusalker, A. D.; Majumdar, A. K., eds. (1960). *The History and Culture of the Indian People*. VI: The Delhi Sultanate. Bombay: Bharatiya Vidya Bhavan. pp. 365–372.

Appendix

References

[1] //en.wikipedia.org/w/index.php?title=Template:Human_history&action=edit
[2] Cunningham, (1888) p. 33.
[3] Cunningham (1888), p. 33.
[4] Barstow (1928), reprint 1985, pp. 105-135, 63, 155, 152, 145.
[5] Latif (1984), p. 56.
[6] Mortimer Wheeler *Flames over Persepolis* (London, 1968). Pp. 112 *ff.* It is unclear whether the Hellenistic street plan found by John Marshall's excavations dates from the Indo-Greeks or from the Kushans, who would have encountered it in Bactria; Tarn (1951, pp. 137, 179) ascribes the initial move of Taxila to the hill of Sirkap to Demetrius I, but sees this as "not a Greek city but an Indian one"; not a *polis* or with a Hippodamian plan.
[7] "Menander had his capital in Sagala" Bopearachchi, "Monnaies", p.83. McEvilley supports Tarn on both points, citing Woodcock: "Menander was a Bactrian Greek king of the Euthydemid dynasty. His capital (was) at Sagala (Sialkot) in the Punjab, "in the country of the Yonakas (Greeks)"." McEvilley, p.377. However, "Even if Sagala proves to be Sialkot, it does not seem to be Menander's capital for the Milindapanha states that Menander came down to Sagala to meet Nagasena, just as the Ganges flows to the sea."
[8] 11.34 http://www.perseus.tufts.edu/cgi-bin/ptext?lookup=Plb.+11.34
[9] Polybius 11.34 http://www.perseus.tufts.edu/cgi-bin/ptext?lookup=Plb.+11.34
[10] "Notes on Hellenism in Bactria and India". https://www.jstor.org/stable/623931 W. W. Tarn. *Journal of Hellenic Studies*, Vol. 22 (1902), pages 268–293
[11] "A vast hoard of coins, with a mixture of Greek profiles and Indian symbols, along with interesting sculptures and some monumental remains from Taxila, Sirkap and Sirsukh, point to a rich fusion of Indian and Hellenistic influences", *India, the Ancient Past*, Burjor Avari, p.130
[12] "When the Greeks of Bactria and India lost their kingdom they were not all killed, nor did they return to Greece. They merged with the people of the area and worked for the new masters; contributing considerably to the culture and civilization in southern and central Asia." Narain, "The Indo-Greeks" 2003, p. 278.
[13] See: Notes on the Races, Tribes, and Castes inhabiting the Province of Oudh, Lucknow, Oudh Government Press 1868, p 4; The Geographical Data in Early Puranas, a Critical Studies, 1972, p 135, Dr M. R. Singh; Sacred Books of the East, XXV, Intr. p cxv, Rapson, Coins of Ancient India, p 37, n.2.
[14] The Geographical Data in Early Puranas, a Critical Studies, 1972, p 135, M. R. Singh; Sacred Books of the East, XXV, Intr. p cxv; Rapson, Coins of Ancient India, p 37, n.2.
[15] Agarwala (1954), p. 444.
[16] Kharapallana and Vanaspara are known from an inscription discovered in Sarnath, and dated to the 3rd year of Kanishka, in which they were paying allegiance to the Kushanas. Source: "A Catalogue of the Indian Coins in the British Museum. Andhras etc..." Rapson, p ciii
[17] Ptolemy, *Geographia*, Chap 7
[18] Hill (2009), pp. 29, 31.
[19] Hill (2004)
[20] Chadurah, 1991 & 45.
[21] Hasan 1959, pp. 54.
[22] Singh 2008, p. 571.
[23] Majumdar 1977, pp. 260–3.
[24] Wink, 1991 & 72-74.
[25] Shahi Family. Encyclopædia Britannica. 2006. Encyclopædia Britannica Online. 16 October 2006 http://www.britannica.com/eb/article-9067075.
[26] Sehrai, Fidaullah (1979). Hund: *The Forgotten City of Gandhara*, p. 2. Peshawar Museum Publications New Series, Peshawar.
[27] Darius used titles like "Kshayathiya, Kshayathiya Kshayathiyanam" etc.

435

[28] The Shahi Afghanistan and Punjab, 1973, pp 1, 45-46, 48, 80, Dr D. B. Pandey; The Úakas in India and Their Impact on Indian Life and Culture, 1976, p 80, Vishwa Mitra Mohan - Indo-Scythians; Country, Culture and Political life in early and medieval India, 2004, p 34, Daud Ali.
[29] Journal of the Royal Asiatic Society, 1954, pp 112 ff; The Shahis of Afghanistan and Punjab, 1973, p 46, Dr D. B. Pandey; The Úakas in India and Their Impact on Indian Life and Culture, 1976, p 80, Vishwa Mitra Mohan - Indo-Scythians.
[30] India, A History, 2001, p 203, John Keay.
[31] Agrawal, Sadananda (2000): Śrī Khāravela, Sri Digambar Jain Samaj, Cuttack, Odisha
[32] Keling_English Version http://www.visvacomplex.com/Keling_English_Version.html . Visvacomplex.com. Retrieved on 2013-07-12.
[33] Shashi Kant (2000): The Hathigumpha Inscription of Kharavela and the Bhabru Edict of Ashoka, D K Printworld Pvt. Ltd.
[34] A Panorama of Indian Culture: Professor A. Sreedhara Menon Felicitation Volume edited by K. K. Kusuman, Page no 153
[35] India - Historical Setting - The Classical Age - Gupta and Harsha http://historymedren.about.com/library/text/bltxtindia7.htm
[36] The Age of the Guptas and After http://www.wsu.edu:8001/~dee/ANCINDIA/GUPTA.HTM
[37] Gupta dynasty (Indian dynasty) - Britannica Online Encyclopedia http://www.britannica.com/EBchecked/topic/249590/Gupta-dynasty
[38] Encyclopedia - Britannica Online Encyclopedia http://www.britannica.com/EBchecked/topic-art/285248/1960/The-Gupta-empire-at-the-end-of-the-4th-century
[39] The Gupta Empire of India | Chandragupta I | Samudragupta http://www.historybits.com/gupta.htm
[40] Trade | The Story of India - Photo Gallery | PBS https://www.pbs.org/thestoryofindia/gallery/photos/8.html
[41] The Gurjaras of Rajputana and Kannauj, Vincent A. Smith, The Journal of the Royal Asiatic Society of Great Britain and Ireland, (Jan., 1909), pp. 53-75
[42] Roychaudhuri, H.C. (1972). *Political History of Ancient India*, University of Calcutta, Calcutta, pp.553-4
[43] Mahajan V.D. (1960, reprint 2007). *Ancient India*, S. Chand & Company, New Delhi, , pp. 594-6
[44] Gurjara-Pratihara dynasty definition of Gurjara-Pratihara dynasty in the Free Online Encyclopedia http://encyclopedia2.thefreedictionary.com/Gurjara-Pratihara+dynasty
[45] Dharam Prakash Gupta, "Seminar on Katoch dynasty trail". *Himachal Plus*. On line. http://www.tribuneindia.com/2009/20091104/himplus.htm#8
[46] Medieval India: From Sultanat to the Mughals (1206-1526) - I By Satish Chandra https//books.google.com
[47] *A History of India* by August Friedrich Rudolf Hoernle, Herbert Alick Stark
[48] Stella Snead - Guardian Lion http://www.archipelago.org/vol3-4/snead3.htm
[49] Agnivansha: Paramara Dynasty http://agnivanshi.blogspot.com/2008/05/paramara-dynasty.html
[50] Upinder Singh 2008, p. 571.
[51] D. C. Ganguly 1981, p. 704.
[52] Sailendra Nath Sen 1999, p. 339.
[53] Dilip Kumar Ganguly 1984, p. 117.
[54] Ganga Dynasty http://www.britannica.com/eb/topic-225335/Ganga-dynasty www.britannica.com.
[55] Suresh Kant Sharma, Usha Sharma - 2005,"Discovery of North-East India: Geography, History, Culture, ... - Volume 3", Page 248, Davaka (Nowgong) and Kamarupa as separate and submissive friendly kingdoms.
[56] Arun Bhattacharjee (1993), *Assam in Indian Independence*, Page 143 While Pushyavarman was the contemporary of the Gupta Emperor Samudra Gupta, Bhaskaravarman was the contemporary of Harshavardhana of Kanauj.

[57] "Three thousand years after these mythical ancestors (Naraka, Bhagadatta and Vajradatta) there occurred Pushyavarman as the first historical king, after whom we have an uninterrupted line of rulers up to Bhaskarvarman."
[58] "According to him (D C Sircar) Narayanavarma, the father of Bhutivarman, was the first Kamarupa king to perform horse-sacrifices and thus for the first time since the days of Pusyavarman freedom from the Gupta political supremacy was declared by Narayanavarma. But a careful study or even a casual perusal of the seal attached to the Dubi C.P. and of the nalanda seals should show that it is Sri Mahendra, the father of Narayanavarma himself, who is described as the performer of two horse-sacrifices."
[59] N. Laxminarayana Rao and S. C. Nandinath in Kamath 2001, p57
[60] Keay (2000), p168
[61] Jayasimha and Ranaraga, ancestors of Pulakeshin I, were administrative officers in the Badami province under the Kadambas (Fleet in Kanarese Dynasties, p343), (Moraes 1931, p51)
[62] Thapar (2003), p328
[63] Quote:"They belonged to the Karnataka country and their mother tongue was Kannada" (Sen 1999, p360); Kamath (2001), p58,
[64] Considerable number of their records are in Kannada (Kamath 2001, p67)
[65] 7th century Chalukya inscriptions call Kannada the natural language (Thapar 2003, p345)
[66] Sen (1999), p360
[67] In this composition, the poet deems himself an equal to Sanskrit scholars of lore like Bharavi and Kalidasa (Sastri 1955, p312
[68] Kamath (2001), p59
[69] Keay (2000), p169
[70] Sen (1999), pp361–362
[71] Kamath (2001), pp59–60
[72] Some of these kingdoms may have submitted out of fear of Harshavardhana of Kannauj (Majumdar in Kamat 2001, p59)
[73] The rulers of Kosala were the Panduvamshis of South Kosala (Sircar in Kamath 2001, pp59)
[74] Keay (2000), p170
[75] Kamath (2001), pp58
[76] Ramesh 1984, p76
[77] From the notes of Arab traveller Tabari (Kamath 2001, p60)
[78] Sen (1999), p362
[79] Thapar (2003), p331, p345
[80] Sastri (1955) p140
[81] Ramesh (1984), pp159–160
[82] Sen (1999), p364
[83] Ramesh (1984), p159
[84] Hardy (1995), p65–66
[85] Over 125 temples exist in Aihole alone,
[86] The Badami Chalukya introduced in the western Deccan a glorious chapter alike in heroism in battle and cultural magnificence in peace (K.V. Sounderrajan in Kamath 2001, p68
[87] Kamath (2001), p68
[88] K.A.N. Sastri, *A History of South India* pp 91–92
[89] Durga Prasad, *History of the Andhras up to 1565 A. D.*, pp 68
[90] Kamil V. Zvelebil (1987). "The Sound of the One Hand", *Journal of the American Oriental Society*, Vol. 107, No. 1, p. 125-126.
[91] 'Advanced History of India', K.A. Nilakanta Sastri (1970)p. 181-182, Allied Publishers Pvt. Ltd., New Delhi
[92] http://www.whatsindia.org
[93] From the Rashtrakuta inscriptions (Kamath 2001, p57, p64)
[94] The Samangadh copper plate grant (753) confirms that feudatory Dantidurga defeated the Chalukyas and humbled their great *Karnatik* army (referring to the army of the Badami Chalukyas) (Reu 1933, p54)
[95] A capital which could put to shame even the capital of gods-From Karda plates (Altekar 1934, p47)

[96] A capital city built to excel that of Indra (Sastri, 1955, p4, p132, p146)
[97] Altekar (1934), pp411–413
[98] Chopra (2003), p87, part1; Literature in Kannada and Sanskrit flowered during the Rashtrakuta rule (Kamath 2001, p73, pp 88–89)
[99] Even royalty of the empire took part in poetic and literary activities (Thapar 2003, p334)
[100] Reu (1933), pp37–38
[101] Chopra (2003), p89, part1; His victories were a "digvijaya" gaining only fame and booty in that region (Altekar in Kamath 2001, p75)
[102] Chopra (2003), p90, part1
[103] Keay (2000), p199)
[104] Kamath 2001, p76
[105] Kavirajamarga in Kannada and *Prashnottara Ratnamalika* in Sanskrit (Reu 1933, p38)
[106] Kamath (2001), p90
[107]
[108] Panchamukhi in Kamath (2001), p80
[109] Chopra (2003), p92, part1; Altekar in Kamath 2001, p81
[110] Chopra (2003), p92–93, part1
[111] Reu (1933), p39
[112] *Murujul Zahab* by Al Masudi (944), *Kitabul Akalim* by Al Istakhri (951), *Ashkal-ul-Bilad* by Ibn Haukal (976) (Reu 1933, p41–42)
[113] From the Sanjan inscriptions,
[114] Keay (2000), p200
[115] Chopra (2003), p137, part1
[116] Fleet, Bhandarkar and Altekar and Gopal B.R. in (Kamath 2001, p100)
[117]
[118] Sen (1999), p. 393
[119] Sastri (1955), pp356–358; Kamath (2001), p114
[120] More inscriptions in Kannada are attributed to the Chalukya King Vikramaditya VI than to any other king prior to the 12th century,
[121] From the 957 and 965 records (Kamath 2001, p101)
[122] Sastri 1955, p162
[123] Tailapa II was helped in this campaign by the Kadambas of Hanagal (Moraes 1931, pp 93–94)
[124] Ganguli in Kamath 2001, p103
[125] Sastri (1955), p167–168
[126] Kamath (2001), p104
[127] Sastri (1955), p164, p174; The Cholas occupied Gangavadi from 1004–1114 (Kamath 2001, p118)
[128] Chopra (2003), p139, part1
[129] Thapar, 2003, pp 468–469
[130] Chopra (2003), p139, part 1
[131] Poet Bilhana in his Sanskrit work wrote "Rama Rajya" regarding his rule, poet Vijnaneshwara called him "A king like none other" (Kamath 2001, p106)
[132] Sastri (1955), p6
[133] Sastri (1955), pp 427–428; Quote:"Their creations have the pride of place in Indian art tradition" (Kamath 2001, p115)
[134] Quote:"Of the city of Kalyana, situated in the north of Karnataka nothing is left, but a fabulous revival in temple building during the 11th century in central Karnataka testifies to the wealth during Kalyan Chalukya rule"(Foekema (1996), p14)
[135] Kamath (2001), p107
[136] From the 1142 and 1147 records, Kamath (2001), p108
[137] Chopra (2003), p139, part1; From the Chikkalagi records (Kamath 2001, p108)
[138] Chopra (2003), p140, part1; Kamath (2001) p109
[139] Students' Britannica India By Dale Hoiberg, Indu Ramchandani.
[140] Sen (1999), p498
[141] Sen (1999), p499

[142] Vishnuvardhana made many military conquests later to be further expanded by his successors into one of the most powerful empires of South India—William Coelho. He was the true maker of the Hoysala kingdom—B.S.K. Iyengar in Kamath (2001), p124–126

[143] B.L. Rice in Kamath (2001), p123

[144] Keay (2000), p251

[145] Thapar (2003), p367

[146] Kamath (2001), p123

[147] Natives of south Karnataka (Chopra, 2003, p150 Part1)

[148] Shiva Prakash in Ayyappapanicker (1997), pp164, 203; Rice E. P. (1921), p59

[149] Kamath (2001), pp132–134

[150] Sastri (1955), p359, p361

[151] Sastri (1955), p427

[152] Sen (1999), pp500–501

[153] Foekema (1996), p14

[154] Kamath (2001), p124

[155] The most outstanding of the Hoysala kings according to Barrett and William Coelho in Kamath (2001), p126

[156] B.S.K. Iyengar in Kamath (2001), p126

[157] Keay (2000), p252

[158] Sen (1999), p500

[159] Two theories exist about the origin of Harihara I and his brother Bukka Raya I. One states that they were Kannadiga commanders of the Hoysala army and another that they were Telugu speakers and commanders of the earlier Kakatiya Kingdom (Kamath 2001, pp 159–160)

[160] Great Living Chola Temples http://whc.unesco.org/en/list/250.

[161] https://books.google.com/books?id=kXtDAAAAYAAJ

[162] https://books.google.com/books?id=7v76i0eF9tQC&pg=PA117

[163] http://depts.washington.edu/silkroad/texts/weilue/weilue.html#section7

[164] https://books.google.com/books?id=nTFuAAAAMAAJ

[165] https://books.google.com/?id=EUlwmXjE9DQC&pg=PA2

[166] https://books.google.com/books?id=Wk4_ICH_g1EC&pg=PA172

[167] https://books.google.com/books?id=H3lUIIYxWkEC&pg=PA383

[168] http://lcweb2.loc.gov/frd/cs/

[169] http://lcweb2.loc.gov/frd/cs/intoc.html

[170] Keay, 155 "... the history of what used to be called 'medieval' India ..."; Harle, 9 "I have eschewed the term 'medieval', meaningless in the Indian context, for the years from c. 950 to c. 1300 ..."

[171] Ahmed, xviii

[172] Keay, 155 "... the history of what used to be called 'medieval' India ..."

[173] Rowland, 273

[174] Examples: Farooqui; Radhey Shyam Chaurasia, *History of Medieval India: From 1000 A.D. to 1707 A.D.*, 2002, google books https://books.google.co.uk/books?isbn=8126901233; Satish Chandra, *Medieval India: From Sultanat to the Mughals*, 2004 (2 vols), google books https://books.google.co.uk/books?isbn=8124110646; Upinder Singh, *A History of Ancient and Early Medieval India: From the Stone Age to the 12th century*, 2008, google books https://books.google.co.uk/books?isbn=813171120X

[175] A Textbook of Historiography, 500 B.C. to A.D. 2000 By E. Sreedharan, p. 457, referencing Peter Hardy

[176] Rowland, 273; Stein, 105

[177] Not for Burjor Avari, who ends "ancient India" at 1200. Avari, 2

[178] For architecture, see Michell, 87-88. For "classical hinduism", see the note at Outline of ancient India.

[179] Keay, xxii-xxiii

[180] Keay, xx-xxi

[181] https://books.google.co.uk/books?id=WTaTDAAAQBAJ&printsec=frontcover

[182] https://books.google.co.uk/books?id=sxhAtCflwOMC&printsec=frontcover

[183] https://web.archive.org/web/20070929125948/http://persian.packhum.org/persian/index.jsp?serv=pf&file=80201010&ct=0
[184] https://web.archive.org/web/20070929132016/http://persian.packhum.org/persian/index.jsp
[185] https://books.google.com/books?id=nyYslywJUE8C&printsec=frontcover&source=gbs_ge_summary_r&cad=0#v=onepage&q&f=false
[186] An inscription dated 1095 CE of Vikramaditya VI mentions grants to a *Vihara* of Buddha and Arya-Taradevi (Cousens 1926, p11)
[187] N. Laxminarayana Rao and Dr. S. C. Nandinath have claimed the Chalukyas were *Kannadigas* (Kannada speakers) and very much the natives of Karnataka (Kamath 2001, p. 57)
[188] The Chalukyas were Kannadigas (D.C. Sircar in Mahajan V.D., 1960, Reprint 2007, Ancient India, Chand and Company, New Delhi, p. 690,)
[189] Natives of Karnataka (Hans Raj, 2007, Advanced history of India: From earliest times to present times, Part-1, Surgeet publications, New Delhi, p. 339
[190] The Chalukyas hailed from Karnataka (John Keay, 2000, p. 168)
[191] Quote:"They belonged to Karnataka country and their mother tongue was Kannada" (Sen 1999, 360)
[192] The Chalukyas of Badami seem to be of indigenous origin (Kamath 2001, p. 58)
[193] Jayasimha and Ranaraga, the first members of the Chalukya family were possibly employees of the Kadambas in the northern part of the Kadamba Kingdom (Fleet [in *Kanarese Dynasties*, p. 343] in Moraes, 1931, pp. 51–52)
[194] Pulakesi I must have been an administrative official of the northern Kadamba territory centered in Badami (Moraes 1931, pp. 51–52)
[195] The Chalukya base was Badami and Aihole (Thapar 2003, p. 328)
[196] Inscriptional evidence proves the Chalukyas were native Kannadigas (Karmarkar, 1947, p. 26)
[197] Pulakesi I of Badami who was a feudatory of the Kadamba king Krishna Varman II, overpowered his overlord in c. 540 and took control of the Kadamba Kingdom (Kamath 2001, p. 35)
[198] Jayasimha (Pulakesi I's grandfather) is known from the Kaira inscription of 472–473 CE. Both Jayasimha and Ranaraga (Pulakesi I's father) are known from Mahakuta inscription of 599 CE and Aihole record of 634 CE (Ramesh 1984, pp. 26–27, p. 30)
[199] From the Badami Cliff inscription of Pulakesi I and from the Hyderabad record of Pulakesi II which states their family ancestry (Kamath 2001, pp. 56–58)
[200] Sastri (1955), p. 154
[201] Chopra (2003), p. 73, part 1
[202] Kamath (2001), p. 56
[203] Moraes (1931). pp. 10–11
[204] Ramesh (1984), p. 19
[205]
[206] Bilhana, in his Sanskrit work *Vikramanakadevacharitam* claims the Early Chalukya family were born from the feet of Hindu God Brahma, implying they were Shudras by caste, while other sources claim they were born in the arms of Brahma, and hence were Kshatriyas (Ramesh 1984, p. 15)
[207] Sircar D.C. (1965), p. 48, *Indian Epigraphy*, Motilal Banarsidass Publishers, Delhi,
[208] Kamath (2001), p. 57
[209] Houben (1996), p. 215
[210] Professor N.L. Rao has pointed out that some of their family records in Sanskrit have also named the princes with "arasa", such as Kattiyarasa (Kirtivarman I), Bittarasa (Kubja Vishnuvardhana) and Mangalarasa (Mangalesha, Kamath 2001, pp. 57–60)
[211] Historians Shafaat Ahmad Khan and S. Krishnasvami Aiyangar clarify that **Arasa** is Kannada word, equivalent to Sanskrit word **Raja** – *Journal of Indian History* p. 102, Published by Department of Modern Indian History, University of Allahabad
[212] Dr. Hoernle suggests a non-Sanskrit origin of the dynastic name. Dr. S.C. Nandinath feels the Chalukyas were of agricultural background and of Kannada origin who later took up a martial career. He feels the word *Chalki* found in some of their records must have originated from *salki*, an agricultural implement (Kamath 2001, p. 57)
[213] The word *Chalukya* is derived from a Dravidian root (Kittel in Karmarkar 1947, p. 26)
[214] Kamath (2001), p. 6, p. 10, p. 57, p. 59, p. 67

[215] Ramesh (1984), p. 76, p. 159, pp. 161–162
[216] Kamath (2001), p. 59
[217] Thapar, (2003), p. 326
[218] Kamath (2001), pp. 12, 57, 67
[219] Pulakesi II's *Maharashtra* extended from Nerbudda (Narmada river) in the north to Tungabhadra in the south (Vaidya 1924, p. 171)
[220] Kamath (2001), p. 60
[221] From the notes of Arab traveller Tabari (Kamath 2001, p. 60)
[222] Chopra (2003), p. 75, part 1
[223] The Buddhist Caves at Aurangabad: Transformations in Art and Religion, Pia Brancaccio, BRILL, 2010 p.82 https://books.google.com/books?id=m_4pXm7dD78C&pg=PA82
[224] Ramesh (1984), p. 14
[225] Kamath 2001, pp. 56
[226] Quote:"Another unhistorical trend met with in the epigraphical records of the 11th and subsequent centuries is the attempt, on the part of the court poets, no doubt, again, with the consent of their masters, to invent mythical genealogies which seek to carry back the antiquity of the royal families not merely to the periods of the epics and the Vedas but to the very moment of their creation in the heavens. As far as the Chalukyas of Vatapi are concerned, the blame of engineering such travesties attaches, once again, to the Western Chalukyas of Kalyani and their Eastern Chalukya contemporaries. The Eastern Chalukyas, for instance, have concocted the following long list of fifty-two names commencing with no less a personage than the divine preserver"(Ramesh 1984, p. 16)
[227] Dr. Lewis's theory has not found acceptance because the Pallavas were in constant conflict with the Kadambas, prior to the rise of Chalukyas (Kamath 2001, p. 57)
[228] //en.wikipedia.org/w/index.php?title=Template:Chalukyas&action=edit
[229] Thapar (2003), p. 326
[230] Popular theories regarding the name are: *Puli* – "tiger" in Kannada and *Kesin* – "haried" in Sanskrit; *Pole* – "lustrous" in Kannada, from his earliest Badami cliff inscription that literally spells *Polekesi*; *Pole* – from Tamil word *Punai* (to tie a knot; Ramesh 1984, pp. 31–32)
[231] The name probably meant "the great lion" (Sastri 1955, p. 134)
[232] The name probably meant "One endowed with the strength of a great lion" (Chopra 2003, p. 73, part 1)
[233] Kamath (2001), pp. 58–59
[234] Ramesh (1984), p. 76
[235] Chopra 2003, p. 74, part 1
[236] Quote:"His fame spread far and wide even beyond India" (Chopra 2003, p. 75 part 1)
[237] Quote:"One of the great kings of India". He successfully defied the expansion of king Harshavardhana of Northern India into the deccan. The Aihole inscription by Ravikirti describes how King Harsha lost his *Harsha* or cheerful disposition after his defeat. The Chinese traveller Hiuen Tsiang also confirms Pulakesi II's victory over King Harsha in his travelogue. Pulakesi II took titles such as *Prithvivallabha* and *Dakshinapatha Prithviswamy* (Kamath 2001, pp. 58–60)
[238] Quote:"Thus began one of the most colourful careers in Indian History" (Ramesh 1984, p. 76)
[239] Vikramaditya I, who later revived the Chalukya fortunes was born to Pulakesi II and the daughter of Western Ganga monarch Durvinita (Chopra 2003, p. 74, part 1)
[240] His other queen, an Alupa princess called Kadamba was the daughter of Aluka Maharaja (G.S. Gai in Kamath 2001, p. 94)
[241] Quote:"The Aihole record gives an impressive list of his military conquests and other achievements. According to the record, he conquered the Kadambas, the Western Gangas, the north Konkan by naval victory, Harsha of Thanesar, the Latas, the Malwas, the Gurjaras (thereby obtaining sovereignty over the Maharashtras), Berar, Maharashtra and Kuntala (with their nine and ninety thousand villages), the Kalingas and the Kosalas, Pishtapura (Pishtapuram in eastern Andhra) and Kanchipuram, whose king had opposed the rise of his power" (Chopra 2003, p. 74 part 1)
[242] Ramesh (1984), pp. 79–80, pp. 86–87

[243] According to Dr. R. C. Majumdar, some principalities may have submitted to Pulakesi II out of fear of Harsha of Kanauj (Kamath 2001, p. 59)
[244] Sastri (1955), pp. 135–136
[245] Sastri (1955), p. 136
[246] This is attested to by an inscription behind the Mallikarjuna temple in Badami (Sastri 1955, p. 136)
[247] Chopra (2003), pp. 75–76, part 1
[248] From the Gadval plates dated c. 674 of Vikramaditya I (Chopra 2003, p. 76, part 1)
[249] Chopra (2003), p. 76, part 1
[250] Sastri (1955), p. 138
[251] From the Kannada inscription at the Kailasanatha temple in Kanchipuram (Sastri 1955, p. 140)
[252] Kamath (2001), p. 63
[253] Thapar (2003), p. 331
[254] Ramesh (1984), pp. 159–160
[255] Dikshit, Durga Prasad (1980), p. 166–167, *Political History of the Chālukyas of Badami*, Abhinav Publications, New Delhi, OCLC 831387906
[256] Ramesh (1984), p. 159
[257] Ramesh (1984), pp. 173–174
[258] Poet Bilhanas 12th century Sanskrit work *Vikramadeva Charitam* and Ranna's Kannada work *Gadayuddha* (982) and inscriptions from Nilagunda, Yevvur, Kauthem and Miraj claim Tailapa II was son of Vikramaditya IV, seventh in descent from Bhima, brother of Badami Chalukya Vikramaditya II (Kamath 2001, p. 100)
[259] Kings of the Chalukya line of Vemulavada, who were certainly from the Badami Chalukya family line used the title "Malla" which is often used by the Western Chalukyas. Names such as "Satyashraya" which were used by the Badami Chalukya are also names of a Western Chalukya king, (Gopal B.R. in Kamath 2001, p. 100)
[260] Unlike the Badami Chalukyas, the Kalyani Chalukyas did not claim to be *Harithiputhras* of *Manavysya gotra* in lineage. The use of titles like *Tribhuvanamalla* marked them as of a distinct line (Fleet, Bhandarkar and Altekar in Kamath 2001, p. 100)
[261] Later legends and tradition hailed Tailapa as an incarnation of the God Krishna who fought 108 battles against the race of Ratta (Rashtrakuta) and captured 88 fortresses from them (Sastri 1955, p. 162)
[262] From his c. 957 and c.965 records (Kamath 2001, p. 101
[263] Vijnyaneshavara, the Sanskrit scholar in his court, eulogised him as "a king like none other" (Kamath 2001, p. 106)
[264] The writing *Vikramankadevacharita* by Bilhana is a eulogy of the achievements of the king in 18 cantos (Sastri, 1955 p. 315)
[265] Cousens 1926, p. 11
[266] Vikrama–Chalukya era of 1075 CE (Thapar 2003, p. 469)
[267] Chopra (2003), p. 139, part 1
[268] Sastri (1955), p. 175
[269] Kamath (2001), pp. 114–115
[270] Narasimhacharya (1988), pp. 18–20
[271] Sastri (1955), p. 192
[272] Pulakesi II made Vishnuvardhana the *Yuvaraja* or crown prince. Later Vishnuvardhana become the founder of the Eastern Chalukya empire (Sastri 1955, pp. 134–136, p. 312)
[273] Chopra (2003), p. 132, part 1
[274] Kamath (2001), p. 8
[275] Kamath 2001, p. 60
[276] Chopra (2003), p. 133
[277] Sastri (1955), pp. 164–165
[278] Sastri (1955), p. 165
[279] Narasimhacharya (1988), p. 68
[280] The Eastern Chalukya inscriptions show a gradual shift towards Telugu with the appearance of Telugu stanzas from the time of king Gunaga Vijayaditya (Vijayaditya III) in the middle of the 9th century,

[281] The first work of Telugu literature is a translation of *Mahabharata* by Nannaya during the rule of Eastern Chalukya king Rajaraja Narendra (1019–1061; Sastri 1955, p. 367)
[282] by Tartakov, Gary Michael (1997), *The Durga Temple at Aihole: A Historiographical Study*, Oxford University Press,
[283] Hardy (1995), p. 5
[284] Quote:"The Badami Chalukyas had introduced a glorious chapter, alike in heroism in battle and cultural magnificence in peace, in the western Deccan" (K.V. Sounder Rajan in Kamath 2001, p. 68)
[285] Kamath 2001, p. 68
[286] Tarr, Gary (1970), p.156, *Chronology and Development of the Chāḷukya Cave Temples*, Ars Orientalis, Vol. 8, pp. 155–184
[287] Hardy (1995), p. 65
[288] Sastri (1955), p. 406
[289] Quote:"The Chalukyas cut rock like titans but finished like jewellers"(Sheshadri in Kamath 2001, pp. 68–69)
[290] Percy Brown in Kamath (2001), p. 68
[291] Sastri (1955), p. 407
[292] Hardy (1995), p. 67
[293] Foekema (2003), p. 11
[294] Sastri (1955), pp. 407–408
[295] Carol Radcliffe Bolon, (1980) pp. 303–326, *The Pārvatī Temple, Sandur and Early Images of Agastya*, Artibus Asiae Vol. 42, No. 4
[296] Hardy (1995), p.342, p.278
[297] Sastri (1955), p. 408
[298] Kamath (2001), p. 69
[299] Quote:"Their creations have the pride of place in Indian art tradition" (Kamath 2001, p. 115)
[300] Sastri (1955), p. 427
[301] Cousens (1926, p 17
[302] Foekema (1996), p. 14
[303] Hardy (1995), p. 156
[304] Hardy (1995), pp. 6–7
[305] Cousens (1926), pp. 100–102
[306] Hardy (1995), p. 333
[307] Cousens (1926), pp. 79–82
[308] Hardy (1995), p. 336
[309] Hardy (1995), p. 323
[310] The Mahadeva Temple at Itagi has been called the finest in Kannada country after the Hoysaleswara temple at Halebidu (Cousens in Kamath 2001, p 117)
[311] Cousens (1926), pp. 114–115
[312] Hardy (1995), p. 326
[313] Cousens (1926), pp. 85–87
[314] Hardy (1995), p. 330
[315] Foekema (2003), p. 52
[316] Hardy (1995), p. 321
[317]
[318] The Badami Chalukyas influenced the art of the rulers of Vengi and those of Gujarat (Kamath 2001, pp. 68, 69)
[319] Quote:"He deemed himself the peer of Bharavi and Kalidasa". An earlier inscription in Mahakuta, in prose is comparable to the works of Bana (Sastri, 1955, p. 312)
[320] Sastri, 1955, p. 312
[321] The writing is on various topics including traditional medicine, music, precious stones, dance etc. (Kamath 2001, p. 106)
[322] Sen (1999), p. 366
[323] Thapar (2003), p. 345
[324] Sahitya Akademi (1988), p. 1717
[325]

[326] Such as Indranandi's *Srutavatara*, Devachandra's *Rajavalikathe* (Narasimhacharya, 1934, pp. 4–5); Bhattakalanka's *Sabdanusasana* of 1604 (Sastri 1955, p. 355)
[327] Sastri (1955), p. 355
[328] Mugali (1975), p. 13
[329] Narasimhacharya (1988), p. 4
[330] Sastri 1955, p. 356
[331] Chopra (2003), p. 196, part 1
[332] Sastri (1955), p. 367
[333] Chopra (2003), p. 77, part1
[334] Kamath (2001), p. 64
[335] Kamath 2001, pp. 57, 65
[336] The breakup of land into *mandalas*, *vishaya* existed in the Kadamba administrative machinery (Kamath 2001, pp. 36, 65, 66)
[337] Kamath (2001), p. 65
[338] However, they issued gold coins that weighed 120 grams, in imitation of the Gupta dynasty (A.V. Narasimha Murthy in Kamath 2001, p. 65)
[339] //en.wikipedia.org/w/index.php?title=Template:Karnataka_History&action=edit
[340] Chopra (2003), p. 191, part 1
[341] Sastri (1955), p. 391
[342] Kamath 2001, p. 66
[343] Chopra (2003), p. 78, part 1
[344] Vinopoti, a concubine of King Vijayaditya is mentioned with due respect in an inscription (Kamath 2001, p. 67)
[345] One record mentions an artist called Achala who was well versed in *Natyashastra* (Kamath 2001, p. 67)
[346] From the Shiggaon plates of c. 707 and Gudigeri inscription dated 1076 (Ramesh 1984, pp. 142, 144)
[347] Cousens (1926), p. 59
[348] Sastri (1955), p. 309
[349] Sastri (1955), p. 324
[350] //doi.org/10.2307/3249519
[351] //www.jstor.org/stable/3249519
[352] //www.worldcat.org/oclc/37526233
[353] //lccn.loc.gov/80905179
[354] //www.worldcat.org/oclc/7796041
[355] //www.worldcat.org/oclc/8221605
[356] //www.worldcat.org/oclc/2492406
[357] //www.worldcat.org/oclc/567370037
[358] //www.worldcat.org/oclc/6814734
[359] https://web.archive.org/web/20061206081329/http://www.aponline.gov.in/Quick%20links/HIST-CULT/history_ancient.html#ChalukyasPart
[360] http://www.aponline.gov.in/quick%20links/hist-cult/history_ancient.html#ChalukyasPart
[361] http://www.indoarch.org/place.php?placelink=R%3D5%2BS%3D18%2BP%3D0%2BM%3D0
[362] https://web.archive.org/web/20070210222449/http://www.deccanherald.com/deccanherald/jul262005/spectrum1422512005725.asp
[363] http://www.deccanherald.com/deccanherald/jul262005/spectrum1422512005725.asp
[364] http://www.kamat.com/kalranga/deccan/chalukya/
[365] http://www.kamat.com/kalranga/kar/literature/history1.htm
[366] http://www.art-and-archaeology.com/india/aihole/aihplan.html
[367] http://www.art-and-archaeology.com/india/badami/baplan.html
[368] http://www.art-and-archaeology.com/india/pattadakal/pat0.html
[369] http://www.kamat.com/kalranga/deccan/chalukya/kalyani.htm
[370] https://web.archive.org/web/20060815095514/http://prabhu.50g.com/southind/alupa/south_alupacat.html
[371] http://prabhu.50g.com/southind/alupa/south_alupacat.html

[372] CNG Coins https://www.cngcoins.com/Coin.aspx?CoinID=261204
[373] India: History, Religion, Vision and Contribution to the World, by Alexander P. Varghese p.26
[374] International Dictionary of Historic Places: Asia and Oceania by Trudy Ring, Robert M. Salkin, Sharon La Boda p.507
[375] Ancient India by Ramesh Chandra Majumdar p.274
[376] Harsha Charitra by Banabhatt https://books.google.com/boo.../about/The_Harshacharita.html...
[377] *Legislative Elite in India: A Study in Political Socialization* by Prabhu Datta Sharma, Publ. Legislators 1984, p32
[378] *Revival of Buddhism in Modern India* by Deodas Liluji Ramteke, Publ Deep & Deep, 1983, p19
[379] *Some Aspects of Ancient Indian History and Culture* by Upendra Thakur, Publ. Abhinav Publications, 1974,
[380] https://books.google.com/books/about/Indian_History.html?id=X4j7Nf_MU24C
[381] http://www.uio.no/studier/emner/hf/iakh/HIS2172/h07/
[382] http://www.srikanta-sastri.org/conquests-siladitya-in-south/4584992949
[383] //en.wikipedia.org/w/index.php?title=Template:Part_of_History_of_India&action=edit
[384] Kalhana (1147-1149); Rajatarangini.
[385] Wink 2002, p. 243.
[386] Chadurah 1991, p. 45.
[387] Hasan 1959, p. 54.
[388] https://books.google.com/books?id=g2m7_R5P2oAC&pg=PA243
[389] https://books.google.com/books?id=nTFuAAAAMAAJ
[390] https://books.google.com/books?id=EUlwmXjE9DQC&&pg=PA2
[391] "India" in this page refers to the territory of present day India.
[392] Majumdar 1977, p. 279.
[393] Blankinship 1994, p. 29.
[394] Blankinship 1994, p. 30.
[395] Blankinship 1994, pp. 19, 41.
[396] Blankinship 1994, p. 19.
[397] : "And Al-Qasim wrote letters 'to the kings of Hind (*bi-mulūk-i-hind*) calling upon them all to surrender and accept the faith of Islam (*bi-muṭāwa'at-o-islām*)'. Ten-thousand cavalry were sent to Kanauj from Multan, with a decree of the caliph, inviting the people 'to share in the blessings of Islam, to submit and do homage and pay tribute'."
[398] Al-Baladhuri 1924, p. 223.
[399] Wink 2002, p. 206.
[400] Tripathi 1989, p. 218.
[401] Blankinship 1994, p. 132.
[402] Wink 2002, p. 207.
[403] ; ;
[404] Blankinship 1994, p. 133-134.
[405] Blankinship 1994, pp. 147–148.
[406] Blankinship 1994, p. 187.
[407] ; ;
[408] ; ; ; ; ;
[409] Blankinship 1994, p. 188.
[410] Sanjay Sharma 2006, p. 204.
[411] Sanjay Sharma 2006, p. 187.
[412] Bhandarkar 1929, p. 30.
[413] ; ; ;
[414] Puri 1986, p. 46.
[415] Blankinship 1994, pp. 189–190.
[416] Blankinship 1994, p. 189.
[417] Hem Chandra Ray 1931, pp. 9–10.
[418] Vaidya 1921, p. 73.
[419] Hem Chandra Ray 1931, p. 9.
[420] Hem Chandra Ray 1931, p. 10.

[421] Majumdar 1955, Vol. IV, pp. 98–99.
[422] Elliot 1869, Vol. 1, p. 446.
[423] Majumdar 1955, Vol. IV, pp. 24–25, 128.
[424] //www.jstor.org/stable/41682407
[425] https://books.google.com/books?id=Jz0Yy053WS4C
[426] https://books.google.co.uk/books?id=dMgNAAAAQAAJ
[427] https://books.google.com/books?id=kHEBAAAAMAAJ&q=Gurjar+parihar&dq=Gurjar+parihar&cd=1
[428] //doi.org/10.1177/025764300602200202
[429] https://books.google.com/books?id=2Tnh2QjGhMQC&pg=PA218
[430] https://books.google.co.uk/books?id=bCVyhH5VDjAC
[431] //openlibrary.org/books/OL1830998M
[432] Sen, S.N., 2013, A Textbook of Medieval Indian History, Delhi: Primus Books,
[433] //en.wikipedia.org/w/index.php?title=Template:Part_of_History_of_India&action=edit
[434] https://books.google.com/books?id=XNxiN5tzKOgC&pg=PA282
[435] //en.wikipedia.org/w/index.php?title=Template:Part_of_History_of_India&action=edit
[436] Avari 2007, pp. 204–205: Madhyadesha became the ambition of two particular clans among a tribal people in Rajasthan, known as Gurjara and Pratihara. They were both part of a larger federation of tribes, some of which later came to be known as the Rajputs
[437] Avari 2007, p. 303.
[438] Sircar 1971, p. 146.
[439] Partha Mitter, Indian art, Oxford University Press, 2001 pp.66
[440] Sanjay Sharma 2006, p. 188.
[441] Sanjay Sharma 2006, p. 190.
[442] Tripathi 1959, p. 223.
[443] Puri 1957, p. 7.
[444] Puri 1957, p. 9-13.
[445] Sanjay Sharma 2006, p. 189.
[446] Majumdar 1981, pp. 612-613.
[447] Puri 1957, p. 1-18.
[448] Tripathi 1959, p. 222.
[449] Ganguly 1935, p. 167.
[450] Ganguly 1935, pp. 167-168.
[451] Ganguly 1935, p. 168.
[452] Puri 1986, pp. 9-10.
[453] Mishra 1954, pp. 50-51.
[454] Shanta Rani Sharma 2012, p. 8.
[455] Shanta Rani Sharma 2012, p. 7.
[456] Puri 1957, p. 1-2.
[457] Puri 1957, p. 2.
[458] Puri 1957, pp. 4-6.
[459] Yadava 1982, p. 35.
[460] Singh 1964, pp. 17-18.
[461] {{cite web | url=https://m.hindustantimes.com/india-news/asi-to-resume-restoration-of-bateshwar-temple-complex-in-chambal/story-kBaxGfcRWVsrNbw3Vw8dLN.html
[462] https://books.google.com/books?id=DmB_AgAAQBAJ&pg=PT204
[463] https://books.google.com/books?id=AqKw1Mn8WcwC
[464] https://books.google.com/books?id=ahFuAAAAMAAJ
[465] //www.jstor.org/stable/41784918
[466] https://books.google.com/books?id=szkhAAAAMAAJ
[467] //doi.org/10.1177/025764300602200202
[468] //doi.org/10.1177/0376983612449525
[469] https://books.google.com/books?id=TKs9AAAAIAAJ
[470] https://books.google.com/books?id=U8GPENMw_psC&pg=PA231
[471] https://books.google.com/books?id=aY_I3zgxfpsC&pg=PA32

[472] The Rise and Decline of Buddhism in India, K.L. Hazara, Munshiram Manoharlal, 1995, pp288–294
[473] Reu (1933), p39
[474] Reu (1933), pp1–5
[475] Altekar (1934), pp1–32
[476] Reu (1933), pp6–9, pp47–53
[477] Reu (1933), p1
[478] Kamath (2001), p72
[479]
[480] Reu (1933), pp1–15
[481] J. F. Fleet in Reu (1933), p6
[482] A Kannada dynasty was created in Berar under the rule of Badami Chalukyas (Altekar 1934, p21–26)
[483] Kamath 2001, p72–3
[484] A.C. Burnell in Pandit Reu (1933), p4
[485] C.V. Vaidya (1924), p171
[486] D.R.Bhandarkar in Reu, (1933), p1, p7
[487] Hultzsch and Reu in Reu (1933), p2, p4
[488] Kamath (2001), p73
[489] Pollock 2006, p332
[490] Houben(1996), p215
[491] Altekar (1934), p411–3
[492] Dalby (1998), p300
[493] Sen (1999), pp380-381
[494] During the rule of the Rashtrakutas, literature in Kannada and Sanskrit flowered (Kamath 2001, pp 88–90)
[495] Even royalty of the empire took part in poetic and literary activities – Thapar (2003), p334
[496] Narasimhacharya (1988), pp17–18, p68
[497] Altekar (1934), pp21–24
[498] Possibly Dravidian Kannada origin (Karmarkar 1947 p26)
[499] Masica (1991), p45-46
[500] Rashtrakutas are described as Kannadigas from Lattaluru who encouraged the Kannada language (Chopra, Ravindran, Subrahmanian 2003, p87)
[501] Reu (1933), p54
[502] From Rashtrakuta inscriptions call the Badami Chalukya army *Karnatabala* (power of *Karnata*) (Kamath 2001, p57, p65)
[503] Altekar in Kamath (2001), p72
[504] Sastri (1955), p141
[505] Thapar (2003), p333
[506] Sastri (1955), p143
[507] Sen (1999), p368
[508] Desai and Aiyar in Kamath (2001), p75
[509] Reu (1933), p62
[510] Sen (1999), p370
[511] The Rashtrakutas interfered effectively in the politics of Kannauj (Thapar 2003), p333
[512] From the Karda inscription, a *digvijaya* (Altekar in Kamath 2001, p75)
[513] The ablest of the Rashtrakuta kings (Altekar in Kamath 2001, p77)
[514] Modern Morkhandi (Mayurkhandi in Bidar district (Kamath 2001, p76)
[515] modern Morkhand in Maharashtra (Reu 1933, p65)
[516] Sooloobunjun near Ellora (Couseris in Altekar 1934, p48). Perhaps Elichpur remained the capital until Amoghavarsha I built Manyakheta. From the Wani-Dmdori, Radhanpur and Kadba plates, Morkhand in Maharashtra was only a military encampment, from the Dhulia and Pimpen plates it seems Nasik was only a seat of a viceroy, and the Paithan plates of Govinda III indicate that neither Latur nor Paithan was the early capital.(Altekar, 1934, pp47–48)
[517] Kamath 2001, MCC, p76
[518] From the Sanjan inscriptions,

[519] Keay (2000), p199
[520] From the Nesari records (Kamath 2001, p76)
[521] Reu (1933), p65
[522] Sastri (1955), p144
[523] "The victorious march of his armies had literally embraced all the territory between the Himalayas and Cape Comorin" (Altekar in Kamath 2001, p77)
[524] Sen (1999), p371
[525] Which could put to shame even the capital of gods-From Karda plates (Altekar 1934, p47)
[526] A capital city built to excel that of Indra (Sastri, 1955, p4, p132, p146)
[527] Reu 1933, p71
[528] from the Cambay and Sangli records. The Bagumra record claims that Amoghavarsha saved the "Ratta" kingdom which was drowned in a "ocean of Chalukyas" (Kamath 2001, p78)
[529] Sastri (1955), p145
[530] Narasimhacharya (1988), p1
[531] Reu (1933), p38
[532] Panchamukhi in Kamath (2001), p80
[533] Sastri (1955), p161
[534] From the writings of Adikavi Pampa (Kamath 2001, p81)
[535] Sen (1999), pp373-374
[536] Kamath (2001), p82
[537] The Rashtrakutas of Manyakheta gained control over Kannauj for a brief period during the early 10th century (Thapar 2003, p333)
[538] From the Siddalingamadam record of 944 – Krishna III captured Kanchi and Tanjore as well and had full control over northern Tamil regions (Aiyer in Kamath 2001, pp82–83)
[539] From the Tirukkalukkunram inscription – Kanchi and Tanjore were annexed by Krishna III. From the Deoli inscription – Krishna III had feudatories from Himalayas to Ceylon. From the Laksmeshwar inscription – Krishna III was an incarnation of death for the Chola Dynasty (Reu 1933, p83)
[540] Conqueror of Kanchi, (Thapar 2003, p334)
[541] Conqueror of Kanchi and Tanjore (Sastri 1955, p162)
[542] Sen 1999), pp374-375
[543] The province of Tardavadi in the very heart of the Rashtrakuta empire was given to Tailapa II as a *fief* (provincial grant) by Rashtrakuta Krishna III for services rendered in war (Sastri 1955, p162)
[544] Kamath (2001), p101
[545] Kamath (2001), pp100–103
[546] Reu (1933), p39–41
[547] Keay (2000), p200
[548] Kamath (2001), p94
[549] Burjor Avari (2007), *India: The Ancient Past:* A History of the Indian Sub-Continent from c. 7000 BC to AD 1200, *pp.207–208,* Routledge, New York,
[550] Reu (1933), p93
[551] Reu (1933), p100
[552] Reu (1933), p113
[553] Reu (1933), p110
[554] Jain (2001), pp67–75
[555] Reu (1933), p112
[556] De Bruyne (1968)
[557] Majumdar (1966), pp50–51
[558] //en.wikipedia.org/w/index.php?title=Template:Karnataka_History&action=edit
[559] whose main responsibility was to draft and maintain inscriptions or *Shasanas* as would an archivist. (Altekar in Kamath (2001), p85
[560] Kamath (2001), p86
[561] From the notes of Al Masudi (Kamath 2001, p88)
[562] Kamath (2001), p88
[563] Altekar (1934), p356

[564] Altekar (1934), p355
[565] From notes of Periplus, Al Idrisi and Alberuni (Altekar 1934, p357)
[566]
[567] Altekar (1934), p358
[568] Altekar (1934), p358–359
[569] Altekar (1934), p368
[570] Altekar (1934), p370–371
[571] Altekar (1934), p223
[572] Altekar (1934), p213
[573] From the Davangere inscription of Santivarma of Banavasi-12000 province (Altekar 1934, p234
[574] From the writings of Chandesvara (Altekar 1934, p216)
[575] From the notes of Al Idrisi (Altekar (1934), p223
[576] From the Begumra plates of Krishna II (Altekar 1934, p227
[577]
[578]
[579] Altekar (1934), p242
[580] From the writings of Somadeva (Altekar 1934, p244)
[581] From the Hebbal inscriptions and Torkhede inscriptions of Govinda III (Altekar 1934, p232
[582] "Wide and sympathetic tolerance" in general characterised the Rashtrakuta rule (Altekar in Kamath 2001, p92)
[583] Kamath (2001), p92
[584] Altekar in Kamath (2001), p92
[585] Reu (1933), p36
[586] The Vaishnava Rashtrakutas patronised Jainism (Kamath 2001, p92)
[587] Kamath (2001), p91
[588] Reu (1933), p34
[589] Reu (1933, p34
[590] A 16th-century Buddhist work by Lama Taranatha speaks disparagingly of Shankaracharya as close parallels in some beliefs of Shankaracharya with Buddhist philosophy was not viewed favourably by Buddhist writers (Thapar 2003, pp 349–350, 397)
[591] From the notes of 10th-century Arab writer Al-Ishtakhri (Sastri 1955, p396)
[592] From the notes of Masudi (916) (Sastri 1955, p396)
[593] From the notes of Magasthenesis and Strabo from Greece and Ibn Khurdadba and Al Idrisi from Arabia (Altekar 1934, p317)
[594] From the notes of Alberuni (Altekar 1934, p317)
[595] Altekar (1934), p318
[596] From the notes of Alberuni (Altekar 1934, p324)
[597] From the notes of Alberuni (Altekar 1934, pp330–331)
[598] From the notes of Alberuni, Altekar (1934) p325
[599] From the notes of Abuzaid (Altekar 1934, p325)
[600] From the notes of Alberuni (Altekar 1934, p326)
[601] Altekar (1934), p329
[602] From the notes of Yuan Chwang, Altekar (1934), p331
[603] From the notes of Alberuni (Altekar 1934, p332, p334)
[604] From the notes of Ibn Khurdadba (Altekar 1934, p337)
[605] From the notes of Alberuni (Altekar 1934, p337)
[606] From the notes of Al Masudi and Al Idrisi (Altekar 1934, p339)
[607] From the Tarkhede inscription of Govinda III, (Altekar 1934, p339)
[608] Altekar (1934), p341
[609] From the notes of Alberuni (Altekar 1934, p342)
[610] From the notes of Sulaiman and Alberuni (Altekar 1934, p343)
[611] Altekar (1934), p345
[612] From the notes of Ibn Khurdadba (Altekar 1934, p346)
[613] Altekar (1934), p349
[614] Altekar (1934), p350
[615] Altekar (1934), p351

[616] From the notes of Ibn Kurdadba (Altekar 1934, p353)
[617] Warder A.K. (1988), p. 248
[618] Kamath (2001), p89
[619] "Mathematical Achievements of Pre-modern Indian Mathematicians", Putta Swamy T.K., 2012, chapter=Mahavira, p.231, Elsevier Publications, London,
[620]
[621] The *Bedande* and *Chattana* type of composition (Narasimhacharya 1988, p12)
[622] It is said *Kavirajamarga* may have been co-authored by Amoghavarsha I and court poet Sri Vijaya (Sastri 1955, pp355–356)
[623] Other early writers mentioned in *Kavirajamarga* are Vimala, Udaya, Nagarjuna, Jayabhandu for Kannada prose and Kavisvara, Pandita, Chandra and Lokapala in Kannada poetry (Narasimhacharya 1988, p2)
[624] Warder A.K. (1988), p240
[625] Sastri (1955), p356
[626] L.S. Seshagiri Rao in Amaresh Datta (1988), p1180
[627] Narasimhacharya (1988, p18
[628] Sastri (1955), p314
[629] S.K. Ramachandra Rao, (1985), Encyclopedia of Indian Medicine: Historical perspective, pp100-101, Popular Prakashan, Mumbai,
[630] Narasimhachar (1988), p11
[631] Hardy (1995), p111
[632] Hardy (1995), p327
[633] Vincent Smith in
[634] Percy Brown and James Fergusson in
[635] Kamath (2001), p93
[636] Arthikaje in
[637] Grousset in
[638] Hardy (1995), p.341
[639] Hardy (1995), p344-345
[640] Sundara and Rajashekar,
[641] Hardy (1995), p5 (introduction)
[642] Thapar (2002), pp393–4
[643] Thapar (2002), p396
[644] Vaidya (1924), p170
[645] Sastri (1955), p355
[646] Rice, E.P. (1921), p12
[647] Rice, B.L. (1897), p497
[648] Altekar (1934), p404
[649] Altekar (1934), p408
[650] //www.worldcat.org/oclc/3793499
[651] //lccn.loc.gov/80905179
[652] //www.worldcat.org/oclc/7796041
[653] //www.worldcat.org/oclc/8221605
[654] //www.worldcat.org/oclc/6814734
[655] https://web.archive.org/web/20061104123203/http://www.ourkarnataka.com/states/history/historyofkarnataka18.htm
[656] http://www.ourkarnataka.com/states/history/historyofkarnataka18.htm
[657] http://www.kamat.com/kalranga/deccan/deckings.htm
[658] http://www.whatisindia.com/inscriptions/south_indian_inscriptions/volume_9/rashtrakutas.html
[659] http://archive.wikiwix.com/cache/20110707080339/http://asi.nic.in/
[660] Huntington 1984, p. 56.
[661] Sengupta 2011, pp. 39–49.
[662] Bagchi 1993, p. 37.
[663] The Caste of the Palas, The Indian Culture, Vol IV, 1939, pp 113–14, B Chatterji
[664] Bhagalpur Charter of Narayanapala, year 17, verse 6, *The Indian Antiquary*, XV p 304.

[665] Sengupta 2011, p. 45.
[666] Bagchi 1993, p. 4.
[667] Paul 1939, p. 38.
[668] Bagchi 1993, p. 39–40.
[669] Paul 1939, p. 122–124.
[670] Paul 1939, p. 111–122.
[671] Huntington 1984, p. 39.
[672] Bagchi 1993, p. 19.
[673] Bagchi 1993, p. 100.
[674] Paul 1939, p. 139–143.
[675] Paul 1939, p. 143–144.
[676] Bagchi 1993, pp. 2–3.
[677] https://books.google.com/books?id=J7RKoMeAtpUC&pg=PA2
[678] https://books.google.com/books?id=xLA3AAAAIAAJ&pg=PA32
[679] https://web.archive.org/web/20160817073236/http://dli.ernet.in/handle/2015/503174
[680] http://dli.ernet.in/handle/2015/503174
[681] https://books.google.com/books?id=kVSh_TyJ0YoC&pg=PA40
[682] //en.wikipedia.org/w/index.php?title=Template:Chola_history&action=edit
[683] //en.wikipedia.org/w/index.php?title=Template:Part_of_History_of_India&action=edit
[684] Pollock (2006), pp. 288–289, 332
[685] Houben(1996), p. 215
[686] Kamath (2001), pp10–12, p100
[687] The province of Tardavadi, lying in the very heart of the Rashtrakuta empire, was given to Tailapa II as a *fief* (provincial grant) by Rashtrakuta Krishna III for services rendered in war (Sastri 1955, p162)
[688] Kamath (2001), p101
[689] poet Bilhana's 12th-century Sanskrit work *Vikramadeva Charitam* and Ranna's Kannada work *Gadayuddha* (982) and inscriptions from Nilagunda, Yevvur, Kauthem and Miraj claim Tailapa II was son of Vikramaditya IV, seventh in descent from Bhima, brother of Badami Chalukya Vikramaditya II (Kamath 2001, p100)
[690] Kings of the Chalukya line of Vemulavada, who were certainly from the Badami Chalukya family line used the title "Malla" which is often used by the Western Chalukyas. Names such as "Satyashraya" which were used by the Badami Chalukya are also name of a Western Chalukya king, (Gopal B.R. in Kamath 2001, p100)
[691] Unlike the Badami Chalukyas, the Kalyani Chalukyas did not claim to be *Harithiputhras* of *Manavysya gotra* in lineage. The use of titles like *Tribhuvanamalla* marked them of as a distinct line (Fleet, Bhandarkar and Altekar in Kamath 2001, p100)
[692] Moraes (1931), pp88-93
[693] Later legends and tradition hailed Tailapa as an incarnation of the God Krishna who fought 108 battles against the race of Ratta (Rashtrakuta) and captured 88 fortresses from them (Sastri 1955, p162)
[694] According to a 973 inscription, Tailapa II helped by Kadambas of Hangal, destroyed the Rattas (Rashtrakutas), killed the valiant Munja (of the Paramara kingdom), took the head of Panchala (Ganga dynasty) and restored the royal dignity of the Chalukyas (Moraes 1931, pp 93–94)
[695] Sastri (1955), p164
[696] A minor capital of Jayasimha II (Cousens 1926, p10, p105)
[697] King Rajaraja Chola conquered parts of Chalukya territory in present-day South Karnataka by subjugating the Western Ganga Dynasty of Gangavadi (Kamath 2001, p102)
[698] From the Hottur inscriptions dated 1007 – 1008, Satyashraya was able to defeat crown prince Rajendra Chola (Kamath 2001, p102)
[699] Sen (1999), p383
[700] Jayasimha's choice was Vijayaditya VII while the Cholas sought to place Rajaraja Narendra, son-in-law of Rajendra Chola I (Kamath 2001, p102
[701] //en.wikipedia.org/w/index.php?title=Template:Chalukyas&action=edit
[702] Quote:"Beautified it so that it surpassed all the other cities of the earth" (Cousens 1926, p10)
[703] Sen (1999), p384

[704] Ganguli in Kamath 2001, p103
[705] Sastri (1955), p166
[706] Someshvara I supported the cause of Shaktivarman II, son of Vijayaditya II while the Cholas preferred Rajendra, son of the previous king Rajaraja Narendra (Kamath 2001, p103)
[707] Sastri (1955), p169
[708] Kamath (2001), p104
[709] Sastri (1955), p170
[710] Cousens (1926), pp10–11
[711]
[712]
[713]
[714] Sastri (1955), p171
[715] Sastri 1955, p172
[716] Eulogising Vikramaditya VI, Kashmiri poet Bilhana wrote in his *Vikramanakadeva Charita* that lord Shiva himself advised Chalukya Vikramaditya VI to replace his elder brother from the throne (Thapar 2003, p468)
[717] Vikramaditya VI abolished the *saka* era and established the *Vikrama-varsha* (Vikrama era). Most Chalukya inscriptions thereafter are dated to this new era (Cousens 1926, p11)
[718] Vikramaditya's rule is mentioned as an era (*samvat*) along with Satavahana Vikrama era 58 BCE, Shaka era, of 78 CE, Harshavardhana era of 606 CE (Thapar, 2003, pp 468–469)
[719] Sen (1999), p386
[720]
[721]
[722]
[723]
[724] Vijnyaneshavara, his court scholar in Sanskrit, wrote of him as a king like none other (Kamath 2001, p106)
[725] Cousens (1926), p12
[726] Bilhana called the reign "Rama Rajya" in his writing that consisted of 18 cantos. The last canto of this work is about the life of author himself who writes that the work was composed by him in gratitude for the great honor bestowed upon him by the ruler of *Karnata* (Sastri 1955, p315)
[727] Bilhana was made *Vidyapati* (chief pandit) by the king (Cousens 1926, p12)
[728] No other king prior to the Vijayanagara rulers have left behind so many records as Vikramaditya VI (Kamath 2001, p105)
[729] Sen (1999), p387
[730] CNG Coins https://www.cngcoins.com/Coin.aspx?CoinID=302739
[731] CNG Coins https://www.cngcoins.com/Coin.aspx?CoinID=133198
[732] Their feudatories, Hoysalas of Mysore region, Kakatiyas of Warangal, Seunas of Devagiri and the Pandyas of Madurai wasted no time in seizing the opportunity, (Sastri 1955,p158)
[733] Sastri (1955), p176
[734] Sen (1999), p388
[735] Kamath (2001), p107
[736] Cousens (1926), p13
[737]
[738] From the Minajagi record of 1184 (Kamath 2001, p109)
[739] A Kalachuri commander called Barmideva or Brahma is known to have given support to the Chalukyas (Sastri 1955, p179–180)
[740] Kamath (2001), p127
[741] Sen (1999), pp388-389
[742] Sastri (1955), p180
[743] Sastri (1955), p192
[744] Kamath (2001), p110
[745] Kamath (2001), p109
[746] There was flexibility to the terms used to designate territorial division (Dikshit G.S. in Kamath 2001, p110)
[747] Coins of Western Chalukyas with Kannada legends have been found (Kamath 2001, p12)

[748] Kamath (2001), p111
[749] Thapar (2002), p373
[750] Thapar (2002), p378
[751] Sastri (1955), p298
[752] //en.wikipedia.org/w/index.php?title=Template:Karnataka_History&action=edit
[753] Thapar (2002), p379
[754] Thapar (2002), p382
[755] Sastri (1955), p299
[756] Sastri (1955), p300
[757] Thapar (2002), p384
[758] Sastri (1955), 301
[759] Thapar (2002), 383
[760] Sastri (1955), p302
[761] Kamath (2001), p112, p132
[762] A 16th-century Buddhist work by Lama Taranatha speaks disparagingly of Shankaracharya as close parallels in some beliefs of Shankaracharya with Buddhist philosophy was not viewed favourably by Buddhist writers (Thapar, 2003, pp 349–350, p397)
[763] An inscription dated 1095 CE of Vikramaditya VI mentions grants to a *Vihara* of Buddha and Arya-Taradevi (Cousens 1926, p11)
[764] It is said five earlier saints Renuka, Daruka, Ekorama, Panditharadhya and Vishwaradhya were the original founders of Virashaivism (Kamath 2001, p152)
[765] However it is argued that these saints were from the same period as Basavanna (Sastri 1955, p393)
[766] Thapar (2003), p299
[767] He criticised Adi Shankara as a "Buddhist in disguise" (Kamath 2001, p151)
[768] Narasimhacharya (1988), p20
[769] Sastri (1955), p361–362
[770] Kamath (2001), p182
[771] Narasimhacharya (1988), p22
[772] Mack (2001), pp35–36
[773] Kamath (2001), p152
[774] She was not only a pioneer in the era of Women's emancipation but also an example of a transcendental world-view (Thapar 2003, p392)
[775] Sastri (1955), p286
[776] This is in stark contrast to the literature of the time (like Vikramankadeva Charita of Bilhana) that portrayed women as retiring, overly romantic and unconcerned with affairs of the state (Thapar 2003, p392)
[777] The Belathur inscription of 1057 describes the end of a widow called Dekabbe who committed Sati despite the requests of her parents not to while some widows such as Chalukya queen Attimabbe long survived their deceased husbands (Kamath 2001, pp 112–113)
[778] The intellectual qualifications of the Brahmins made them apt to serve as ministers and advisers of Kings(*Rajguru*), (Charles Eliot in Sastri 1955, p289)
[779] Sastri (1955), p288
[780] Sastri (1955), p289
[781] The *Manasollasa* written by King Someshvara III contains significant information of the social life of Western Chalukyan times (Kamath 2001, p112)
[782] Orchestras were popularised by the Kalamukhas, a cult who worshipped Lord Shiva (Kamath 2001, p115)
[783] Sastri (1955), p292
[784] Kamath (2001), p114
[785] Sen (1999), p. 393
[786] S.S.Basavanal in Puranik, p4452, (1992)
[787] Sastri (1955), p361
[788] Narasimhacharya (1988), pp18–20
[789] The other two gems are Adikavi Pampa and Sri Ponna (Sastri 1955, p356)

[790] A composition written in a mixed prose-verse style is called Champu (Narasimhacharya 1988, p12)
[791] This also is in *Champu* style and was written at the request of Attimabbe, a pious widow of general Nagavarma who promoted the cause of Jainism (Sastri 1955, p356)
[792] E.P.Rice (1921), p32
[793] Narasimhacharya (1988), pp64–65,
[794] E.P.Rice (1921), p34
[795] Nagavarma II was the teacher (*guru*) of another noteworthy scholar Janna who later adorned the court of Hoysala Empire (Sastri 1955, p358)
[796] Narasimhachar (1988), p.63
[797] Vachanas are disconnected paragraphs ending with a name attributed to lord Shiva or one of his forms. The poems teach the valuelessness of riches, rituals and book learning and the spiritual privileges of worshipping Shiva, (B.L. Rice in Sastri 1955, p361)
[798] Thapar (2003), p394
[799] "Mathematical Achievements of Pre-modern Indian Mathematicians", Putta Swamy T.K., 2012, chapter=Bhaskara II, p331, Elsevier Publications, London,
[800] Thapar, (2003), p393
[801] Sastri (1955), p315
[802] A Textbook of Historiography, 500 B.C. to A.D. 2000 by E. Sreedharan p.328
[803] Sastri (1955), p324
[804] *Sangita Ratnakara* being written in the court of feudatory Seuna kingdom, (Kamath 2001, p115)
[805] An important period in the development of Indian art (Kamath 2001, p115)
[806] Sastri (1955), p427
[807] A fabulous revival of Chalukya temple building in central Karnataka in the 11th century (Foekema (1996), p14)
[808] Hardy (1995), pp156-157
[809] Davison-Jenkins (2001), p89
[810] Cousens (1926), pp79–82
[811] Hardy (1995), p336
[812] Cousens (1926), pp114–115
[813] Hardy (1995), p326
[814] Kamath (2001), p117
[815] Hardy (1995), p323
[816] Cousens (1926), pp85–87
[817] Hardy (1995), p330
[818] Hardy (1995), p321
[819] Cousens (1926), pp100–102
[820] Hardy (1995), p333
[821] Hardy (1995), p335
[822] Hardy (1995), p324
[823] Quote:"A title it fully deserves, for it is probably the finest temple in Kanarese districts, after Halebidu"(Cousens 1926, p101)
[824] Cousens (1926), pp105–106
[825] Hardy (1995), p 157
[826] Kamath (2001), pp116–118
[827] Hardy (1995), pp6–7
[828] Pollock (2006), p332
[829] Houben(1996), p215
[830] Thousands of Kannada language inscriptions are ascribed by Vikramaditya VI and pertain to his daily land and charitable grants (*Nityadana*),
[831] Kannada enjoyed patronage from royalty, influential Jains and the Lingayat movement of Virashaivas (Thapar 2003, p396)
[832] However by the 14th century, bilingual inscriptions lost favour and inscriptions became mostly in the local language (Thapar, 2003, pp393–95)
[833]

[834] E.P.Rice (1921), p33
[835] //www.worldcat.org/oclc/37526233
[836] //lccn.loc.gov/80905179
[837] //www.worldcat.org/oclc/7796041
[838] http://www.indoarch.org/place.php?placelink=R%3D5%2BS%3D18%2BP%3D0%2BM%3D0
[839] http://www.kamat.com/kalranga/deccan/deckings.htm
[840] http://www.whatisindia.com/inscriptions/
[841] https://web.archive.org/web/20061006025111/http://chitralakshana.com/articles/UB%20githa/balligavi.htm
[842] https://www.chitralakshana.com/articles/UB%20githa/balligavi.htm
[843] http://www.art-and-archaeology.com/india/india.html
[844] http://www.templenet.com/Karnataka/kalyani_chalukya.html
[845] https://web.archive.org/web/20060815095514/http://prabhu.50g.com/southind/alupa/south_alupacat.html
[846] http://prabhu.50g.com/southind/alupa/south_alupacat.html
[847] https://www.forumancientcoins.com/india/southind/chalukya/south_chalcat.html
[848] http://www.hinduonnet.com/2002/06/10/stories/2002061003760500.htm
[849] Ancient Jaffna: Being a Research Into the History of Jaffna from Very Early Times to the Portuguese Period, C. Rasanayagam, p.241, Asian Educational Services 1926
[850] The journal of the Numismatic Society of India, Volume 51, p.109
[851] Alī Jāvīd and Tabassum Javeed. (2008). World heritage monuments and related edifices in India, p.107 https://books.google.com/books?id=54XBlIF9LFgC&pg=PA107
[852] KR Subramanian. (1989). Buddhist remains in Āndhra and the history of Āndhra between 224 & 610 A.D, p.71: *The Pallavas were first a Telugu and not a Tamil power. Telugu traditions know a certain Trilochana Pallava as the earliest Telugu King and they are confirmed by later inscriptions.* https://books.google.com/books?id=vnO2BMPdYEoC&pg=PA71
[853]
[854] Rev. H Heras, SJ (1931) Pallava Genealogy: An attempt to unify the Pallava Pedigrees of the Inscriptions, Indian Historical Research Institute
[855] KR Subramanian. (1989). Buddhist remains in Āndhra and the history of Āndhra between 224 & 610 A.D, p.106-109
[856] Marilyn Hirsh (1987) Mahendravarman I Pallava: Artist and Patron of Māmallapuram, Artibus Asiae, Vol. 48, Number 1/2 (1987), pp. 109-130
[857] Rajan K. (Jan-Feb 2008). Situating the Beginning of Early Historic Times in Tamil Nadu: Some Issues and Reflections, Social Scientist, Vol. 36, Number 1/2, pp. 40-78
[858] Heras, p 38
[859] Kulke and Rothermund, pp121–122
[860] Nilakanta Sastri, pp412–413
[861] Nilakanta Sastri, p139
[862] Nilakanta Sastri, *A History of South India*, p.91
[863] Nilakanta Sastri, *A History of South India*, p.91–92
[864]
[865] Kulke and Rothermund, p.120
[866] Kulke and Rothermund, p111
[867] S.Krishnaswami Aiyangar. Some Contributions Of South India To Indian Culture. Early History of the Pallavas http://chestofbooks.com/history/india/South-India-Culture/Chapter-VIII-Early-History-Of-The-Pallavas.html
[868] A History of Ancient and Early Medieval India: From the Stone Age to the 12th Century (2008), Upinder Singh, p. 559.
[869] John N. Miksic 2013, p. 79"...the north end of the Straits, from Barus to Kedah and Takuapa, may have been under direct Chola administration; a crown prince of the Chola dynasty probably served as viceroy in Kedah."
[870] //en.wikipedia.org/w/index.php?title=Template:Chola_history&action=edit
[871] //en.wikipedia.org/w/index.php?title=Template:TNhistory&action=edit
[872] K.A. Nilakanta Sastri, *A History of South India*, p 157

[873] Keay, p 215
[874] K.A. Nilakanta Sastri, *A History of South India*, p 158
[875] Majumdar (contains no mention of Maldives)
[876] Meyer, p 73
[877] K.A. Nilakanta Sastri, *A History of South India*, p 195
[878] K.A. Nilakanta Sastri, *A History of South India*, p 196
[879] Vasudevan, pp 20–22
[880] Keay, pp 217–218
[881] Thai Art with Indian Influences by Promsak Jermsawatdi p.57
[882] Columbia Chronologies of Asian History and Culture by John Stewart Bowman p.335
[883] Prasad (1988), p. 120
[884] The age of Sangam is established through the correlation between the evidence on foreign trade found in the poems and the writings by ancient Greek and Romans such as *Periplus*. K.A. Nilakanta Sastri, *A History of Cyril and Lulu Charles*, p 106
[885] Sastri (1984), pp. 19-20
[886] Archaeological News A. L. Frothingham, Jr. *The American Journal of Archaeology and of the History of the Fine Arts*, Vol. 4, No. 1 (Mar., 1998), pp. 69–125
[887] The period covered by the Sangam poetry is likely to extend not longer than five or six generations.<ref name="FOOTNOTESastri19843">Sastri (1984), p. 3
[888] Columbia Chronologies of Asian History and Culture by John Bowman p.401
[889] The Ashokan inscriptions speak of the Cholas in plural, implying that, in his time, there were more than one Chola.<ref name="FOOTNOTESastri198420">Sastri (1984), p. 20
[890] The direct line of Cholas of the Vijayalaya dynasty came to an end with the death of Virarajendra Chola and the assassination of his son Athirajendra Chola. Kulothunga Chola I, ascended the throne in 1070.<ref name="FOOTNOTESastri2002170-172">Sastri (2002), pp. 170-172
[891] Sastri (2002), pp. 19-20, 104-106
[892] Tripathi (1967), p. 457
[893] Majumdar (1987), p. 137
[894] Kulke & Rothermund (2001), p. 104
[895] Tripathi (1967), p. 458
[896] Sastri (2002), p. 116
[897] Sastri (2002), pp. 105-106
[898] The only evidence for the approximate period of these early kings is the Sangam literature and the synchronisation with the history of Sri Lanka as given in the *Mahavamsa*. Gajabahu I who is said to be the contemporary of the Chera Senguttuvan, belonged to the 2nd century and this means the poems mentioning Senguttuvan and his contemporaries date to that period.Wikipedia:Citation needed
[899] Sastri (2002), p. 113
[900] Sastri (2002), pp. 130, 135, 137
[901] Majumdar (1987), p. 139
[902] Thapar (1995), p. 268
[903] Sastri (2002), p. 135
[904] Sastri (2002), pp. 130, 133Quote:"The Cholas disappeared from the Tamil land almost completely in this debacle, though a branch of them can be traced towards the close of the period in Rayalaseema – the Telugu-Chodas, whose kingdom is mentioned by Yuan Chwang in the seventh century A.D."
[905] Sastri (1984), p. 102
[906] Kulke & Rothermund (2001), p. 115
[907] Pandya Kadungon and Pallava Simhavishnu overthrew the Kalabhras. Acchchutakalaba is likely the last Kalabhra king.<ref name="FOOTNOTESastri1984102">Sastri (1984), p. 102
[908] *Periyapuranam*, a Shaivite religious work of 12th century tells us of the Pandya king Nindrasirnedumaran, who had for his queen a Chola princess.<ref name="FOOTNOTEChopraRavindranSubrahmanian200395">Chopra, Ravindran & Subrahmanian (2003), p. 95

[909] Copperplate grants of the Pallava Buddhavarman (late 4th century) mention that the king as the "underwater fire that destroyed the ocean of the Chola army".<ref name="FOOTNOTESastri1984104-105">Sastri (1984), pp. 104-105
[910] Chopra, Ravindran & Subrahmanian (2003), p. 95
[911] Tripathi (1967), p. 459
[912] Chopra, Ravindran & Subrahmanian (2003), p. 31
[913] Sastri (2002), p. 4Quote:"it is not known what relation, if any, the Telugu-Chodas of the Renadu country in the Ceded District, bore to their namesakes of the Tamil land, though they claimed descent from Karikala, the most celebrated of the early Chola monarchs of the Sangam age."
[914] K. A. Nilakanta Sastri postulates that there was a live connection between the early Cholas and the Renandu Cholas of the Andhra country. The northward migration probably took place during the Pallava domination of Simhavishnu. Sastri also categorically rejects the claims that these were the descendants of Karikala Chola.<ref name="FOOTNOTESastri1984107">Sastri (1984), p. 107
[915] Tripathi (1967), pp. 458-459
[916] Sen (1999), pp. 477-478
[917] Dehejia (1990), p. xiv
[918] Kulke & Rothermund (2001), pp. 122–123
[919] Eraly (2011), p. 67
[920] Sastri (2002), p. 157
[921] Sen (1999), pp. 373
[922] Eraly (2011), p. 68
[923] *The Dancing Girl: A History of Early India* by Balaji Sadasivan p.133
[924] *A Comprehensive History of Medieval India*, by Farooqui Salma Ahmed, Salma Ahmed Farooqui p.25
[925] *Power and Plenty: Trade, War, and the World Economy in the Second Millennium* by Ronald Findlay, Kevin H. O'Rourke p.67
[926] *History Without Borders: The Making of an Asian World Region, 1000-1800* by Geoffrey C. Gunn p.43
[927] Sen (2009), p. 91
[928] *Buddhism, Diplomacy, and Trade: The Realignment of Sino-Indian Relations* by Tansen Sen p. 226
[929] Kalā: The Journal of Indian Art History Congress, The Congress, 1995, p.31
[930] Sastri (1984), pp. 194-210
[931] Majumdar (1987), p. 407
[932] Sastri (2002), p. 158
[933] *Ancient India: Collected Essays on the Literary and Political History of Southern India* by Sakkottai Krishnaswami Aiyangar p.233
[934] Chopra, Ravindran & Subrahmanian (2003), pp. 107-109
[935] ndia: The Most Dangerous Decades by Selig S. Harrison p.31
[936] Sastri (2002), p. 184
[937] Mukund (2012), p. xlii
[938] "After the second Pandya War, Kulottunga undertook a campaign to check to the growth of Hoysala power in that quarter. He re-established Chola suzerainty over the Adigaimans of Tagadur, defeated a Chera ruler in battle and performed a *vijayabhisheka* in Karuvur (1193). His relations with the Hoysala Ballala II seem to have become friendly afterwards, for Ballala married a Chola princess".<ref name="FOOTNOTESastri2002178">Sastri (2002), p. 178
[939] Between 2 Oceans (2nd Edn): A Military History of Singapore from 1275 to 1971 by Malcolm H. Murfett, John Miksic, Brian Farell, Chiang Ming Shun p.16
[940] *South India* by Stuart Butler, Jealous p.38
[941] *Asia: A Concise History* by Arthur Cotterell p.190
[942] Paine (2014), p. 281
[943] *History of Asia* by B.V. Rao p.211
[944] Majumdar (1987), p. 405
[945] Chopra, Ravindran & Subrahmanian (2003), p. 120

[946] Majumdar (1987), p. 408
[947] Tripathi (1967), p. 471
[948] *South Indian Inscriptions*, Vol. 12
[949] Chopra, Ravindran & Subrahmanian (2003), pp. 128-129
[950] Sastri (2002), p. 194
[951] Tripathi (1967), p. 472
[952] Majumdar (1987), p. 410
[953] South India and Her Muhammadan Invaders by S. Krishnaswami Aiyangar p.40-41
[954] Sastri (2002), pp. 195-196
[955] Sastri (2002), p. 196
[956] Tripathi (1967), p. 485
[957] Sastri (2002), p. 197
[958] Chopra, Ravindran & Subrahmanian (2003), p. 130
[959] Proceedings, American Philosophical Society *(1978), vol. 122, No. 6, p 414*
[960] The Buddhist work *Milinda Panha* dated to the early Christian era, mentions Kolapttna among the best-known sea ports on the Chola coast.<ref name="FOOTNOTESastri198423">Sastri (1984), p. 23
[961] Nagasamy (1981)
[962] Sastri (2002), p. 107
[963] Chopra, Ravindran & Subrahmanian (2003), p. 106
[964] Karashima 2014, p. 132.
[965] The only other time when peninsular India would be brought under one umbrella before the independence of India was during the Vijayanagara Empire (1336–1614).Wikipedia:Citation needed
[966] Stein (1998), p. 26
[967] Vasudevan (2003), pp. 20-22
[968] A Global History of Architecture by Francis D. K. Ching, Mark M. Jarzombek, Vikramaditya Prakash p.338
[969] History of India by N. Jayapalan p.171
[970] Gough (2008), p. 29
[971] Talbot (2001), p. 172.
[972] Singh (2008), p. 590
[973] *Administrative System in India: Vedic Age to 1947* by U. B. Singh p.77
[974] Tripathi (1967), pp. 474-475
[975] Stein (1998), p. 20
[976] Sastri (2002), p. 185
[977] Sastri (2002), p. 150
[978] Sastri (1984), p. 465
[979] Sastri (1984), p. 477
[980] Sakhuja & Sakhuja (2009), p. 88
[981] Barua (2005), p. 18
[982] Dehejia (1990), p. 79
[983] Subbarayalu (2009), pp. 97-99
[984] Eraly (2011), p. 176
[985] Rajasuriar (1998), p. 15
[986] Sen (1999), p. 205
[987] Technology and Society by Menon R.V.G. p.15
[988] Stein (1980), p. 130
[989] Lucassen & Lucassen (2014), p. 120
[990] The State at War in South Asia by Pradeep Barua p.17
[991] Sastri (2002), p. 175
[992] *The Pearson General Studies Manual* 2009, 1/e by Showick Thorpe Edgar Thorpe p.59
[993] Singh (2008), p. 54
[994] Schmidt (1995), p. 32
[995] Devare (2009), p. 179
[996] Eraly (2011), p. 208

[997] Ramaswamy (2007), p. 20
[998] Singh (2008), p. 599
[999] *Trade and Politics on the Coromandel Coast: Seventeenth and Early Eighteenth centuries* by Radhika Seshan p.18
[1000] *Indian Textiles: Past and Present* by G. K. Ghosh, Shukla Ghosh p.123-124
[1001] *Kanchipuram: Land of Legends, Saints and Temples* by P. V. L. Narasimha Rao p.134
[1002] Ramaswamy (2007), p. 51
[1003] Mukherjee (2011), p. 105
[1004] *History of People and Their Environs: Essays in Honour of Prof. B.S. Chandrababu* by S.Ganeshram p.319
[1005] Singh (2008), p. 592
[1006] Sen (1999), pp. 490-492
[1007] Indian History by Reddy p.B57
[1008] Mukund (1999), pp. 30-32
[1009] Ramaswamy (2007), p. 86
[1010] Rothermund (1993), p. 9
[1011] *Economic History of India* by N. Jayapalan p.49
[1012] Temple art under the Chola queens by Balasubrahmanyam Venkataraman p.72
[1013] *Temple Art Under the Chola Queens* by Balasubrahmanyam Venkataraman p.72
[1014] Mukund (1999), p. 29-30
[1015] Hellmann-Rajanayagam (2004), p. 104
[1016] *The Political Economy of Craft Production: Crafting Empire in South India*, by Carla M. Sinopoli p.188
[1017] Sadarangani (2004), p. 16
[1018] Sastri (2002), p. 284
[1019] Chopra, Ravindran & Subrahmanian (2003), pp. 125, 129
[1020] Scharfe (2002), p. 180
[1021] 17th century Italian traveler Pietro Della Valle (1623) has given a vivid account of the village schools in South India. These accounts reflect the system of primary education in existence until the morder times in Tamil Nadu
[1022] Sastri (2002), p. 293
[1023] Kulke & Rothermund (2001), pp. 116-117
[1024] Kulke & Rothermund (2001), pp. 12, 118
[1025] Buddhism, Diplomacy, and Trade: The Realignment of Sino-Indian Relations by Tansen Sen p. 159
[1026] Kulke & Rothermund (2001), p. 124
[1027] Tripathi (1967), pp. 465, 477
[1028] Sastri (1984), p. 604
[1029] *Buddhism, Diplomacy, and Trade: The Realignment of Sino-Indian Relations* by Tansen Sen p. 156
[1030] Kulke & Rothermund (2001), p. 117
[1031] Thapar (1995), p. xv
[1032] Mukund (2012), p. 92
[1033] Mukund (2012), p. 95
[1034] *History of Agriculture in India, Up to c. 1200 A.D.* by Lallanji Gopal p.501
[1035] Mitter (2001), p. 2
[1036] Sastri (2002), p. 418
[1037] Thapar (1995), p. 403Quote: "It was, however, in bronze sculptures that the Chola craftsmen excelled, producing images rivalling the best anywhere."
[1038] Kulke & Rothermund (2001), p. 159
[1039] Sastri (1984), p. 789
[1040] Kulke & Rothermund (2001), pp. 159-160
[1041] A History of Early Southeast Asia: Maritime Trade and Societal Development by Kenneth R. Hall
[1042] Aryatarangini, the Saga of the Indo-Aryans, by A. Kalyanaraman p.158
[1043] India and Malaya Through the Ages: by S. Durai Raja Singam

[1044] Tripathi (1967), p. 479
[1045] Dehejia (1990), p. 10
[1046] Harle (1994), p. 295
[1047] Mitter (2001), p. 57
[1048] *Temples of South India* by V. V. Subba Reddy p.110
[1049] Jermsawatdi (1979), p. 57
[1050] *Columbia Chronologies of Asian History and Culture* by John Stewart Bowman p.335
[1051] Vasudevan (2003), pp. 21-24
[1052] Nagasamy (1970)
[1053] Chopra, Ravindran & Subrahmanian (2003), p. 186
[1054] Mitter (2001), p. 163
[1055] Thapar (1995), p. 309-310
[1056] Wolpert (1999), p. 174
[1057] By common consent, the finest Chola masterpieces are the bronze images of Siva Nataraja.<ref name="FOOTNOTEMitter200159">Mitter (2001), p. 59
[1058] Sastri (1984), pp. 663-664
[1059] Sastri (2002), p. 333
[1060] Sastri (2002), p. 339
[1061] Chopra, Ravindran & Subrahmanian (2003), p. 188
[1062] Sastri (2002), pp. 339-340
[1063] Ismail (1988), p. 1195
[1064] *Ancient India: Collected Essays on the Literary and Political History of southern India* by Sakkottai Krishnaswami Aiyangar p.127
[1065] *The Princeton Encyclopedia of Poetry and Poetics* by Roland Greene, Stephen Cushman, Clare Cavanagh, Jahan Ramazani, Paul F. Rouzer, Harris Feinsod, David Marno, Alexandra Slessarev p.1410
[1066] Singh (2008), p. 27
[1067] *Portraits of a Nation: History of Ancient India*, by Kamlesh Kapur p.617
[1068] *Concise Encyclopaedia Of India* by Kulwant Rai Gupta, Amita Gupta p.288
[1069] *Legend of Ram* By Sanujit Ghose
[1070] *Rays and Ways of Indian Culture* By D. P. Dubey
[1071] Chopra, Ravindran & Subrahmanian (2003), p. 116
[1072] Sastri (2002), pp. 20, 340-341
[1073] Sastri (2002), pp. 184, 340
[1074] Chopra, Ravindran & Subrahmanian (2003), p. 20
[1075] *Encyclopaedia of Indian literature, vol. 1*, p 307
[1076] Spuler (1975), p. 194
[1077] Sastri (2002), pp. 342-343
[1078] Chopra, Ravindran & Subrahmanian (2003), p. 115
[1079] Sastri (1984), p. 681
[1080] Sadarangani (2004), p. 15
[1081] *South Indian Shrines*, Illustrated by P. V. Jagadisa Ayyar p.23
[1082] Darasuram Temple Inscriptions @ http://www.whatisindia.com/inscriptions/south_indian_inscriptions/darasuram/kulottunga.html. Whatisindia.com (2007-01-29). Retrieved on 2013-07-12.
[1083] Tripathi (1967), p. 480
[1084] Vasudevan (2003), p. 102
[1085] Sastri (1984), p. 214
[1086] Majumdar (1987), p. 4067
[1087] Stein (1998), p. 134
[1088] Vasudevan (2003), p. 104
[1089] Sastri (2002), p. 176
[1090] Sastri (1984), p. 645
[1091] Chopra, Ravindran & Subrahmanian (2003), p. 126
[1092] Das (1995), p. 108
[1093] Das (1995), pp. 108-109

[1094] Das (1995), p. 109
[1095] *Encyclopaedia of Indian Literature, vol. 1*, pp 631–632
[1096] https://books.google.com/books?id=8NJ3BgAAQBAJ&pg=PA79
[1097] http://www.whatisindia.com/inscriptions/
[1098] http://whc.unesco.org/pg.cfm?cid=31&id_site=250
[1099] http://www.indianartcircle.com/arteducation/page_14_artofCholas.shtml
[1100] http://lakdiva.org/coins/medievalindian/rajaraja_chola.html
[1101] //en.wikipedia.org/w/index.php?title=Template:Western_Ganga_kings&action=edit
[1102] (Rice in Adiga 2006, p88)
[1103] Adiga and Sheik Ali in Adiga (2006), p89
[1104] Sarma (1992), pp1–3
[1105] Ramesh (1984), pp1–2
[1106] Baji and Arokiaswamy in Adiga (2006), p89
[1107] Kamath (2001), p39
[1108] Krishna Rao in Adiga (2006), p88
[1109] Kamath (2001), pp39–40
[1110]
[1111] Adiga 2006, p97, p100
[1112] From the Cakra-Kedara grant, Kodunjeruvu grant (Adiga 2006, p99)
[1113] Kamath (2001), p40
[1114] Sheik Ali and Ramesh in Adiga (2006), p100–101
[1115] Adiga (2006), p101
[1116] from the Nallala grant (Kamath 2001, p41)
[1117] Adiga (2006), p109
[1118] From the Aihole inscriptions and the Jangamarahalli inscription (Adiga 2006, 102)
[1119] (Adiga 2006, p103)
[1120] From the Shimoga records (N.L. Rao in Kamath 2001, p41)
[1121] The title was given to a later Ganga King Rachamalla I (Ramesh in Adiga p115), the Agali grant and Devarahalli inscription calls Sripurusha *Maharajadhiraja Paramamahesvara Bhatara* (Adiga 2006, pp115–116)
[1122] Sastri in Adiga 2006, p115
[1123] From Salem plates of Sripurusha dated 771 and the Koramangala grant (Ramesh in Adiga 2006, p116)
[1124] Kamath (2001), p42
[1125] From several Tumkur inscriptions (Adiga 2006, p117)
[1126] Adiga 2006, p118
[1127] from the Konnur inscriptions of 860 and Rajaramadu inscription (Adiga 2006, p119)
[1128] From the Keregodi Rangapura plates and Chikka Sarangi inscription of 903 (Adiga 2006, p119)
[1129] Kamath (2001), p43
[1130] Kamath (2001), p44
[1131] Tirukkalukkunram and Laksmeshwar inscriptions – Kanchi and Tanjore were annexed by Krishna III who was an incarnation of death for the Chola Dynasty (Reu 1933, p83)
[1132] Thapar 2003, p334
[1133] Sastri 1955, p162
[1134] From the Kudlur inscription of King Marasimha II (Adiga 2006, p120)
[1135] From the Kukkanur inscription (Adiga 2006, p122)
[1136] These victories were recorded in a Kannada inscription of 964 near Jabalpur (Kamath 2001, p83)
[1137] Kamath (2001), p45
[1138] Sastri (1955), pp356–357
[1139] Kamath (2001), p118
[1140] Kamath (2001), p46
[1141] Adiga (2006), p10
[1142] Rice in Adiga (2006), p15)
[1143] Sharma in Adiga (2006), p16
[1144] Kamath (2001), p47

[1145] Adiga (2006), p238
[1146] Adiga (2006), pp161–177
[1147] From the Kanatur inscription (Adiga 2006, p161)
[1148] From the Kanatur inscription (Adiga 2006, p164)
[1149] From the Mavali inscription of the 8th century and Indravalli inscription (Adiga 2006), p165
[1150] Doddakunce inscription, the Karagada and Maruru inscription (Adiga 2006, p167–68)
[1151] Bedirur inscriptions of 635 (Adiga 2006, p168)
[1152] From the Kumsi inscription of 931 and Doddahomma inscription of 977 (Adiga 2006, pp21–22, p27, p29)
[1153] From the Mavali inscription and Indivalli inscription (Adiga 2006, p31)
[1154] From the Devarahalli and Hosur copper plates (Adiga 2006, p33)
[1155] From inscriptions and literary writings such as *Vaddaradhane* (920) and *Pampa Bharata* (940) (Adiga 2006, p36–37)
[1156] Adiga (2006), p208
[1157] Adiga (2006), pp233–234
[1158] Adiga (2006), p6
[1159] from the Melkote copper plates and Mamballi inscriptions, Medutambihalli inscription of the 9th century (Adiga 2006, p53)
[1160] Adiga (2006), p42
[1161] Adiga (2006), p45
[1162] from the Narasimhapura plates (Adiga 2006, p46)
[1163] From the Doddahomma inscription of Rachaballa IV of 977 (Adiga 2006, p47)
[1164] Kittel in Adiga (2006), p48
[1165] Belagi inscription of 964, Sasarvalli inscription of 1001 (Krishna and Adiga 2006, p55/56)
[1166] Adiga (2006), p57
[1167] From the Kodagu inscription of the 11th century, Guduve inscription of 1032, Kambadahalli inscription of 979 (Adiga 2006, p59, p60, p63)
[1168] From the Narasimhapura inscription of the 9th century (Sircar and Ramesh in Adiga 2006, pp210–211)
[1169] Indian epigraphical glossary, Hecca inscription pF 939 for SriKanteshvara temple (Adiga 2006, p213)
[1170] From Nonamangala copper plates of the 5th century of King Avinita (Adiga 2006, p216)
[1171] From the Kuppepalya inscription of the 8th century (Adiga 2006, p218)
[1172] Kotutu inscription of the 9th century, Rampura inscription of 905 (Adiga 2006, p219)
[1173] Varuna inscription, (Adiga 2006, p223–224)
[1174] Adiga (2006), p230
[1175] Dr. Lewis Rice, S. R. Sharma and M. V. Krishna Rao
[1176] Srikantha Shastri in Kamath (2001), p49
[1177] Adiga (2006), p249
[1178] Srikanta Sastri in
[1179] From the Kulaganga and Narasimhapura copper plates (Adiga 2006, p255)
[1180] From the Kudlur plates of Butuga II (Adiga 2006, p256)
[1181] P.B. Desai and Jaiswal in Adiga (2006), pp263–264
[1182] Adiga (2006), p264
[1183] Adiga (2006), pp264–265
[1184] Adiga (2006), p253
[1185] From the Bendiganhalli and Bangalore copper plates, the Chaluvanahalli plates, Kutalur grant, Kadagattur and Nallala grants of King Durvinita, Kondunjeruvu grant of King Avinita (Adiga 2006, pp281–282)
[1186] Adiga (2006), p282
[1187] Adiga (2006), p313
[1188] From the Kalkunda inscription (Adiga 2006, pp314–316)
[1189] Adiga (2006), p317
[1190] Adiga (2006), p291
[1191] From the Nandi copper plates of Rashtrakuta Govinda III of 800, Koyattur-12000 grant of King Dodda Naradhipa Bana in 810, the Ganiganur inscription, Nolamba King Mahendradhirajas

grant of his house towards a Shaiva temple in 878, Baragur inscription of 914 of King Ayappadeva Nolamba, the Ninneshvaradeva temple built by King Dilipayya Nolamba in 942.

[1192] Among minor Chalukya kings, Narasinga Chalukya of Mysore constructed the Narasingeshwara temple and Kings Goggi and Durga build the Buteshvara temple at Varuna in modern Mysore region – From the Kukkarahalli, Manalevadi, Aragodupalli and Torevalli inscriptions, (Adiga 2006, 294)

[1193] This was popularised by the *kalamukha* monks (Adiga 2006, p292)

[1194] Adiga (2006), p301

[1195] H.V. Stietencron in Adiga 2006, p303

[1196] From Nandi copper plates of 800, Avani pillar inscription, Perbetta hero stones, 878 inscription of Nolamba Mahendradhiraja, Baragur inscription of 919, 942 Tumkur grant and Basavanahalli inscriptions (Adiga 2006, p304–305)

[1197] From the Kuntur inscription of the 10th century (Adiga 2006, p203)

[1198] Karmarkar (1947), p66

[1199] from the Bandalike inscription of 919 (Adiga 2006, p203)

[1200] From the Shravanabelagola inscription (Adiga 2006, p204)

[1201] Adiga (2006), p398

[1202] From the Perur plates (Adiga 2006, p398)

[1203] Karmarkar (1947), pp. 72, 74

[1204] Altekar (1934), p329

[1205] From the notes of Alberuni and Bouchet (Karmarkar 1947, p103)

[1206] From the notes of Yuan Chwang (Karmarkar 1947, p103)

[1207] From a modern Bijapur inscription of 1178 (Karmarkar, 1947, p104)

[1208] The *Svayamvara* marriage of Chalukya King Vikramaditya VI to Chandaladevi in the 11th century being an example (Karmarkar, 1947 p105)

[1209] Karmarkar (1947), p109

[1210] From the writings of Marco Polo, Ibn Batuta, Bernier and Tavernier (Karmarkar 1947, p110)

[1211] Karmarkar (1947), p110

[1212] Karmarkar (1947), p111

[1213] Karmarkar (1947), p112

[1214] Karmarkar (1947), p113

[1215]

[1216] Sastri (1955), p357

[1217] Kulkarni (1975) in Adiga (2006), p256

[1218] Sastri (1955), p355

[1219] Narasimhacharya (1988), p2

[1220] kamath (2001), p50

[1221] Narasimhacharya (1988), p18

[1222] One among the three gems of Kannada literature (Sastri 1955, p356)

[1223] Kamath (2001), p50

[1224] Narasimhacharya (1988), p19

[1225]

[1226] Venkatasubbiah in Kamath (2001), p50

[1227] Reddy, Sharma and Krishna Rao in Kamath (2001), pp 50–52

[1228] Seshadri in Kamath (2001), p51

[1229] If there is one aspect of Indian architecture which has its perfection and weakness, it is these free standing pillars (Fergusson in Kamath 2001, p52)

[1230] Sarma (1992), p153, p206, p208

[1231] In the whole of Indian art, nothing perhaps equals these pillars in good taste, Vincent Smith in Kamath (2001), p52

[1232] Some historians claim the Chavundaraya basadi was built by Chavundaraya himself while others argue it was the work of his on Jinadevana (Gopal et al. in Adiga 2006, p256). Another view holds that the original shrine was consecrated in the 11th century and built in memory of Chavundaraya (Settar in Adiga 2006, 256)

[1233] Adiga 2006, p269

[1234] Sarma (1992), pp153–167

[1235] Adiga 2006, p268
[1236] Kamath (2001), p51
[1237] Sarma (1992), pp.105–111
[1238] Sarma (1992), pp91–102
[1239] Sarma (1992), pp78–83
[1240] Sarma (1992), pp88–91
[1241] Sarma (1992), p17, p202, p204
[1242] //en.wikipedia.org/w/index.php?title=Template:Karnataka_History&action=edit
[1243] Thapar 2003, pp393–394
[1244] Adiga (2006), p110
[1245] Thapar 2003, p396
[1246] Kamath (2001), p12
[1247] //www.worldcat.org/oclc/3793499
[1248] //lccn.loc.gov/80905179
[1249] //www.worldcat.org/oclc/7796041
[1250] //www.worldcat.org/oclc/8221605
[1251] //www.amazon.com/dp/B0006EHSP0
[1252] //lccn.loc.gov/84900575
[1253] //www.worldcat.org/oclc/13869730
[1254] //openlibrary.org/books/OL3007052M
[1255] http://www.srikanta-sastri.org/#/gangas-of-talakad-article/4550857520
[1256] https://web.archive.org/web/20061215103823/http://www.ourkarnataka.com/states/history/historyofkarnataka11.htm
[1257] http://www.ourkarnataka.com/states/history/historyofkarnataka11.htm
[1258] http://www.hindu.com/2004/01/24/stories/2004012407180300.htm
[1259] http://www.kamat.com/kalranga/deccan/gangas.htm
[1260] http://www.hindu.com/2006/02/03/stories/2006020313510400.htm
[1261] https://web.archive.org/web/20070710231517/http://prabhu.50g.com/southind/ganga/south_gangacat.html
[1262] http://prabhu.50g.com/southind/ganga/south_gangacat.html
[1263] http://www.hindu.com/2004/08/20/stories/2004082016400300.htm
[1264] Talbot 2001, p. 26.
[1265] //en.wikipedia.org/w/index.php?title=Template:History_of_Andhra_Pradesh&action=edit
[1266] ˙,˙
[1267] Sircar 2008, p. 241.
[1268] Kakatiya coins bore the Nandinagari script.(Prasad 1988, p. 9)
[1269] Sastry 1978, pp. 22-23.
[1270] Sastry 1978, p. 22.
[1271] Sastry 1978, pp. 24-25.
[1272] Sastry 1978, p. 23.
[1273] Sastry 1978, pp. 3-6.
[1274] Talbot 2001, pp. 11, 17, 19.
[1275] Sastry 1978, pp. 8-12.
[1276] Sastry 1978, p. 12.
[1277] Sastry 1978, pp. 12-13.
[1278] Talbot 2001, p. 53.
[1279] Talbot 2001, p. 51.
[1280] Sastry 1978, p. 29.
[1281] Sastry 1978, p. 27.
[1282] Sastry 1978, pp. 27-29.
[1283] Sastry 1978, p. 30.
[1284] Quote: "Eriya was succeeded not by his son Beta but by his grandson Gunda IV who, according to the Mangallu grant, in his early career had been deputed by Rashtrakuta Krishna III in 956 to help the Chalukya prince Danarnava in his attempts to oust his step-brother..."
[1285] Sastry 1978, p. 36.

[1286] Quote: "poet named Balasarasvati author of an inscription dated S. 1136 had lived at the court of Prola Reddi, ruler of the same Kakatiya dynasty."
[1287] Quote: "Displacement was rapid as the Reddis with their superior technology swiftly spread over the entire Telangana... and were aided by a stronger political power of Kakatiya Reddi kingdom."
[1288] Quote: "Redu is a king. Reddi is supposed to be another form of Redu.:
[1289] Sastry 1978, p. 2.
[1290] Sastry 1978, p. 15.
[1291] Sastry 1978, p. 16.
[1292] Sastry 1978, pp. 17-18.
[1293] Sastry 1978, p. 17.
[1294] Sastry 1978, p. 18.
[1295] Sastry 1978, pp. 18-19.
[1296] Sastry 1978, p. 19.
[1297] Sastry 1978, p. 20.
[1298] Sastry 1978, pp. 20-21.
[1299] Sastry 1978, p. 21.
[1300] Sastry 1978, p. 19, 25.
[1301] Sastry 1978, p. 25.
[1302] Sastry 1978, p. 6.
[1303] Sircar 1979, p. 130.
[1304] Prasad 1988, pp. 119, 124.
[1305] Talbot 2001, p. 184.
[1306] Talbot (2001, p. 128): "Soon after he came to power, Rudradeva had the Thousand Pillared temple built in Hanumakonda, then the Kakatiya capital. The Sanskrit inscription recording its foundation in 1163 contains an elaborate genealogy of Rudradeva's ancestry... Since it was the earliest of Rudradeva's inscriptions to omit any mention of the Chalukya dynasty of Kalyani, we can assume that the construction of the temple was meant to mark Rudradeva's new status as an overlord in his own right."
[1307] Eaton 2005, p. 13.
[1308] Eaton 2005, p. 17.
[1309] Desai 1962.
[1310] Kalia 1994, p. 21.
[1311] Rubiés 2000, p. 73.
[1312] Rubiés 2000, pp. 50, 73.
[1313] Marco Polo referred to the kingdom as Mutfili, which was the name for the area around a major port of the dynasty, now known as Masulipatnam.(Chakravarti 1991)
[1314] Suryanarayana 1986, p. 163.
[1315] Eaton 2005, p. 16.
[1316] Eaton 2005, pp. 9-11.
[1317] Asher & Talbot 2006, p. 40.
[1318] Kulke & Rothermund 2004, p. 160 "An earlier attack on Warangal in 1304 had been unsuccessful.".
[1319] Sharma (1992, p. 234): "Vennama, the son of Dāma, led his troops in a defeat of the Turks very probably during Ala-ud-din Khalji's first invasion of Telangana in 1303. This success against the Turkish arms took place in the battle of Upparapalli, where Potuganti Maili is said to have put the enemies to flight."
[1320] Eaton 2005, pp. 17–18.
[1321] Eaton 2005, pp. 18–19.
[1322] Eaton 2005, pp. 20-21.
[1323] Talbot 2001, p. 176.
[1324] Rao & Shulman 2012, p. 17.
[1325] Rao & Shulman 2002, p. 4.

[1326] The term *andhra bhasa*, meaning *language of Andhra*, appeared as a synonym for the Telugu language at least as early as 1053 and suggests an emerging correlation of linguistics and geography. (Eaton 2005, p. 13) The linguistic mapping of regions of India continues to the present day and formed a part of the States Reorganisation Act, 1956.

[1327] Aside from the Kakatiyas, the dominant Hindu monarchies in South India and the Deccan around the 13th century CE were the Seunas, the Hoysalas and the Pandyas. The Seunas, Hoysalas and Kakatiyas had carved up what had been the area controlled by the Western Chalukya Empire, while the Pandyas controlled lands formerly under the Chola Empire. (Ventakaramanayya 1942, p. 1)

[1328] Ventakaramanayya 1942, pp. 1–2.
[1329] Eaton 2005, p. 14.
[1330] Eaton 2005, pp. 14–15.
[1331] Eaton 2005, p. 12.
[1332] Subrahmanyam 1998.
[1333] Talbot (2001, p. 51): "An inscription reads: 'The Kakatiya dynasty, praised by the entire world and belonging to the fourth *varna*, then came into existence. In it was born the king named Prola, who was renowned for being exceedingly judicious.'... [In a handful of inscriptions], the Kakatiyas are linked with the solar dynasty of the ancient *kshatriyas*, stemming from Ikshvaku through Dasharatha and Rama... The lack of consistency regarding the *varna* rank of the Kakatiya dynasty is noteworthy, as is the fact that their *kshatriya* claims were put forth primarily in documents associated with gifts to *brahmans*."
[1334] Eaton 2005, pp. 15–16.
[1335] Talbot 2001, pp. 50-52.
[1336] Talbot 2001, p. 174.
[1337] Sastry 1978, p. 24.
[1338] Sastry 1978, pp. 30-36.
[1339] Asher & Talbot 2006, p. 43.
[1340] Rao & Shulman 2012, p. 16.
[1341] Talbot 2001, p. 177.
[1342] Talbot 2001, pp. 177-182.
[1343] Eaton 2005, p. 22.
[1344] Talbot 2001, pp. 192–193.
[1345] Eaton 2005, pp. 26-27.
[1346] Chattopadhyaya (1998, pp. 57–58) quotes from the Vilasa grant of Prolaya Nayaka: "[W]hen Prataparudra of the Kakati family ruled, even such celebrated rulers of the past as *Yayati*, *Nabhaga* and *Bhagiratha* were completely forgotten."... "[W]hen the Sun, *viz.*, Prataparudra set, the world was enveloped in the *Turuska* darkness. The evil (*adharma*), which he had up to that time kept under check, flourished under them, as the conditions were very favourable for its growth."
[1347] Eaton 2005, pp. 27-28.
[1348] Talbot 2001, p. 175.
[1349] Eaton 2005, pp. 28-29.
[1350] https://books.google.com/books?id=ZvaGuaJIJgoC
[1351] //doi.org/10.2307/3632243
[1352] //www.jstor.org/stable/3632243
[1353] //www.jstor.org/stable/41853935
[1354] https://books.google.com/books?id=DNNgdBWoYKoC
[1355] https://books.google.com/books?id=lt2tqOpVRKgC
[1356] https://www.questia.com/read/55271807
[1357] http://www.katragadda.com/articles/HistoryOfTheAndhras.pdf
[1358] https://www.questia.com/read/108156994
[1359] https://www.questia.com/read/105967930
[1360] https://www.questia.com/read/121703743
[1361] https://www.questia.com/read/105026315
[1362] https://books.google.com/books?id=FiRuAAAAMAAJ
[1363] //www.worldcat.org/oclc/252341228

[1364] https://books.google.com/books?id=ucQKAQAAIAAJ
[1365] https://books.google.com/books?id=-O18xhA_BXUC
[1366] https://books.google.com/books?id=m1JYwP5tVQUC
[1367] //www.jstor.org/stable/20027508
[1368] https://books.google.com/books?id=f6seAAAAMAAJ
[1369] https://books.google.com/books?id=pfAKljlCJq0C
[1370] //doi.org/10.2307/2057210
[1371] //www.jstor.org/stable/2057210
[1372] //en.wikipedia.org/w/index.php?title=Template:History_of_Bengal&action=edit
[1373] The History of the Bengali Language by Bijay Chandra Mazumdar p.50
[1374] Land of Two Rivers: A History of Bengal from the Mahabharata to Mujib by Nitish K. Sengupta p.51
[1375] Ancient India by Ramesh Chandra Majumdar p.320
[1376] The Cambridge Shorter History of India p.10
[1377] B.P. Sinha in George E. Somers, Dynastic History of Magadha, p.214, Abhinav Publications, 1977, New Delhi,
[1378] //en.wikipedia.org/w/index.php?title=Template:Sena_dynasty&action=edit
[1379] Momtazur Rahman Tarafdar, "Itihas O Aitihasik", Bangla Academy Dhaka, 1995
[1380] http://en.banglapedia.org/index.php?title=Sena_Dynasty
[1381] Delhi Sultanate http://www.britannica.com/EBchecked/topic/156530/Delhi-sultanate, Encyclopædia Britannica
[1382] A. Schimmel, Islam in the Indian Subcontinent, Leiden, 1980
[1383] Pradeep Barua *The State at War in South Asia*, , p. 29-30
[1384] Bowering et al., The Princeton Encyclopedia of Islamic Political Thought, , Princeton University Press
[1385] Hermann Kulke and Dietmar Rothermund, A History of India, 3rd Edition, Routledge, 1998, , pp 187-190
[1386] Vincent A Smith, , Chapter 2, Oxford University Press
[1387] A. Welch, "Architectural Patronage and the Past: The Tughluq Sultans of India," Muqarnas 10, 1993, Brill Publishers, pp 311-322
[1388] J. A. Page, Guide to the Qutb https://archive.org/stream/guidetothequtbde031434mbp#page/n15/mode/2up/search/temple, Delhi, Calcutta, 1927, page 2-7
[1389] Richard Eaton (2000), Temple Desecration and Indo-Muslim States http://jis.oxfordjournals.org/content/11/3/283.extract, Journal of Islamic Studies, 11(3), pp 283-319
[1390] Richard M. Frye, "Pre-Islamic and Early Islamic Cultures in Central Asia", in *Turko-Persia in Historical Perspective*, ed. Robert L. Canfield (Cambridge U. Press c. 1991), 35–53.
[1391] See: • M. Reza Pirbha, Reconsidering Islam in a South Asian Context, , Brill • The Islamic frontier in the east: Expansion into South Asia, Journal of South Asian Studies, 4(1), pp. 91-109 • Sookoohy M., Bhadreswar - Oldest Islamic Monuments in India, , Brill Academic; see discussion of earliest raids in Gujarat
[1392] Peter Jackson 2003, pp. 3-30.
[1393] T. A. Heathcote, The Military in British India: The Development of British Forces in South Asia:1600-1947, (Manchester University Press, 1995), pp 5-7
[1394] Barnett, Lionel (1999), , Atlantic pp. 73–79
[1395] Richard Davis (1994), Three styles in looting India, History and Anthropology, 6(4), pp 293-317,
[1396] MUHAMMAD B. SAM Mu'izz AL-DIN, T.W. Haig, Encyclopaedia of Islam, Vol. VII, ed. C.E.Bosworth, E.van Donzel, W.P. Heinrichs and C. Pellat, (Brill, 1993)
[1397] C.E. Bosworth, Tidge History of Iran, Vol. 5, ed. J. A. Boyle, John Andrew Boyle, (Cambridge University Press, 1968), pp 161-170
[1398] History of South Asia: A Chronological Outline http://afe.easia.columbia.edu/timelines/southasia_timeline.htm Columbia University (2010)
[1399] Mu'izz al-Dīn Muḥammad ibn Sām http://www.britannica.com/EBchecked/topic/396618/Muizz-al-Din-Muhammad-ibn-Sam Encyclopædia Britannica (2011)
[1400] //en.wikipedia.org/w/index.php?title=Template:Delhi_Sultanate&action=edit

[1401] Jackson P. (1990), The Mamlūk institution in early Muslim India, Journal of the Royal Asiatic Society of Great Britain & Ireland (New Series), 122(02), pp 340-358
[1402] C.E. Bosworth, The New Islamic Dynasties, Columbia University Press (1996)
[1403] Barnett & Haig (1926), A review of History of Mediaeval India, from ad 647 to the Mughal Conquest - Ishwari Prasad, Journal of the Royal Asiatic Society of Great Britain & Ireland (New Series), 58(04), pp 780-783
[1404] Peter Jackson 2003, pp. 29-48.
[1405] Anzalone, Christopher (2008), "Delhi Sultanate", in Ackermann, M. E. etc. (Editors), Encyclopedia of World History 2,
[1406]
[1407] Welch and Crane note that the Quwwat-ul-Islam Mosque was built with the remains of demolished Hindu and Jain temples; See:
[1408] South Asia : A Historical Narrative by Mohammad Yunus, Aradhana Parmar, P. 97, https://books.google.co.in/books?redir_esc=y&id=opbtAAAAMAAJ&focus=searchwithinvolume&q=afghan, quote = Firuz Khalji had already gathered enough support among the Afghans for taking over the crown.
[1409] https//books.google.de
[1410] https://www.mapsofindia.com/history/khilji-dynasty.html
[1411] https//books.google.de
[1412] Alexander Mikaberidze, Conflict and Conquest in the Islamic World: A Historical Encyclopedia, , pp 62-63
[1413] Rene Grousset - Empire of steppes, Chagatai Khanate; Rutgers Univ Press, New Jersey, U.S.A, 1988
[1414] Frank Fanselow (1989), Muslim society in Tamil Nadu (India): an historical perspective, Journal Institute of Muslim Minority Affairs, 10(1), pp 264-289
[1415] Hermann Kulke and Dietmar Rothermund, A History of India, 3rd Edition, Routledge, 1998,
[1416] AL Srivastava, Delhi Sultanate https://archive.org/stream/sultanateofdelhi001929mbp#page/n189/mode/2up 5th Edition, , pp 156-158
[1417] Vincent A Smith, , Chapter 2, **pp 231-235**, Oxford University Press
[1418]
[1419] Vincent A Smith, , Chapter 2, **pp 236-242**, Oxford University Press
[1420] Elliot and Dowson, Tárīkh-i Fīroz Shāhī of Ziauddin Barani, The History of India as Told by Its Own Historians. The Muhammadan Period (Vol 3), London, Trübner & Co
[1421]
[1422] Hermann Kulke and Dietmar Rothermund, *A History of India*, (Routledge, 1986), 188.
[1423] Advanced Study in the History of Medieval India by Jl Mehta p.97
[1424] Vincent A Smith, , Chapter 2, **pp 242-248**, Oxford University Press
[1425] Cornelius Walford (1878), , **pp 9-10**
[1426] Judith Walsh, A Brief History of India, , pp 70-72; Quote: "In 1335-42, during a severe famine and death in the Delhi region, the Sultanate offered no help to the starving residents."
[1427] HM Elliot & John Dawson (1871), Tarikh I Firozi Shahi - Records of Court Historian Sams-i-Siraj https://archive.org/stream/cu31924073036737#page/n367/mode/2up The History of India as told by its own historians, Volume 3, Cornell University Archives, pp 352-353
[1428] Firoz Shah Tughlak, Futuhat-i Firoz Shahi - Memoirs of Firoz Shah Tughlak https://archive.org/stream/cu31924073036737#page/n389/mode/2up, Translated in 1871 by Elliot and Dawson, Volume 3 - The History of India, Cornell University Archives
[1429] Vincent A Smith, , Chapter 2, **pp 249-251**, Oxford University Press
[1430] Firoz Shah Tughlak, Futuhat-i Firoz Shahi - Autobiographical memoirs https://archive.org/stream/cu31924073036737#page/n393/mode/2up, Translated in 1871 by Elliot and Dawson, Volume 3 - The History of India, Cornell University Archives, pp 377-381
[1431] Annemarie Schimmel, Islam in the Indian Subcontinent, , Brill Academic, pp 20-23
[1432] Vincent A Smith, , Chapter 2, **pp 248-254**, Oxford University Press
[1433] Peter Jackson (1999), The Delhi Sultanate: A Political and Military History, Cambridge University Press, pp 312–317
[1434] Lionel Trotter (1906), History of India: From the Earliest Times to the Present Day, Gorham Publishers London/New York, pp 74

[1435] Annemarie Schimmel (1997), Islam in the Indian Subcontinent, Brill Academic, , pp 36-37; Also see: Elliot, Studies in Indian History, 2nd Edition, pp 98-101
[1436] Annemarie Schimmel, Islam in the Indian Subcontinent, , Brill Academic, Chapter 2
[1437] Judith Walsh, A Brief History of India,
[1438] Vincent A Smith, , Chapter 2, **pp 253-257**, Oxford University Press
[1439] Digby, S. (1975), The Tomb of Buhlūl Lōdī, Bulletin of the School of Oriental and African Studies, 38(03), pp 550-561
[1440] Andrew Petersen, Dictionary of Islamic Architecture, Routledge, , pp 7
[1441] Richards, John (1965), The Economic History of the Lodi Period: 1451-1526, Journal de l'histoire economique et sociale de l'Orient, Vol. 8, No. 1, pp 47-67
[1442]
[1443] Irfan Habib (2011), *Economic History of Medieval India, 1200-1500*, page 53 https://books.google.com/books?id=K8kO4J3mXUAC&pg=PA53, Pearson Education
[1444] Irfan Habib (2011), *Economic History of Medieval India, 1200-1500*, pages 53-54 https://books.google.com/books?id=K8kO4J3mXUAC&pg=PA53, Pearson Education
[1445] Irfan Habib (2011), *Economic History of Medieval India, 1200-1500*, page 54 https://books.google.com/books?id=K8kO4J3mXUAC&pg=PA54, Pearson Education
[1446] Angus Maddison (2001), *The World Economy: A Millennial Perspective*, pages 241-242 http://theunbrokenwindow.com/Development/MADDISON%20The%20World%20Economy--A%20Millennial.pdf#page=242, OECD Development Centre
[1447] Angus Maddison (2001), *The World Economy: A Millennial Perspective*, page 236 http://theunbrokenwindow.com/Development/MADDISON%20The%20World%20Economy--A%20Millennial.pdf#page=237, OECD Development Centre
[1448] Eaton, Richard M."The Rise of Islam and the Bengal Frontier, 1204–1760. Berkeley: University of California Press, c1993 1993, accessed on 1 May 2007
[1449] Eaton (2000), Temple desecration in pre-modern India http://www.columbia.edu/itc/mealac/pritchett/00islamlinks/txt_eaton_temples2.pdf Frontline, p. 73, item 16 of the Table, Archived by Columbia University
[1450] History of Ancient India: Earliest Times to 1000 A. D.; Radhey Shyam Chaurasia, Atlantic, 2009 [p191]
[1451] Richard M. Eaton, *Temple Desecration and Indo-Muslim States*, Part II, **Frontline**, January 5, 2001, 70-77.http://ftp.columbia.edu/itc/mealac/pritchett/00islamlinks/txt_eaton_temples2.pdf
[1452] Richard M. Eaton, *Temple Desecration and Indo-Muslim States*, Part I, **Frontline**, December 22, 2000, 62-70.http://www.columbia.edu/itc/mealac/pritchett/00islamlinks/txt_eaton_temples1.pdf
[1453] Annemarie Schimmel, Islam in the Indian Subcontinent, , Brill Academic, pp 7-50
[1454] James Brown (1949), The History of Islam in India, The Muslim World, 39(1), 11-25
[1455] Welch, Anthony (1993), Architectural patronage and the past: The Tughluq sultans of India, Muqarnas, Vol. 10, 311-322
[1456] Gul and Khan (2008), Growth and Development of Oriental Libraries in India http://digitalcommons.unl.edu/libphilprac/182, Library Philosophy and Practice, University of Nebrasaka-Lincoln
[1457]
[1458] Eva De Clercq (2010), ON JAINA APABHRAMŚA PRAŚASTIS, Acta Orientalia Academiae Scientiarum Hung. Volume 63 (3), pp 275–287
[1459] R Islam (1997), A Note on the Position of the non-Muslim Subjects in the Sultanate of Delhi under the Khaljis and the Tughluqs, Journal of the Pakistan Historical Society, 45, pp. 215–229; R Islam (2002), Theory and Practice of Jizyah in the Delhi Sultanate (14th Century), Journal of the Pakistan Historical Society, 50, pp. 7–18
[1460] A.L. Srivastava (1966), Delhi Sultanate https://archive.org/stream/sultanateofdelhi001929mbp#page/n345/mode/2up/, 5th Edition, Agra College
[1461] Peter Jackson (2003), The Delhi Sultanate: A Political and Military History, Cambridge University Press, , pp 287-295
[1462] Firoz Shah Tughlak, Futuhat-i Firoz Shahi - Memoirs of Firoz Shah Tughlaq https://archive.org/stream/cu31924073036737#page/n395/mode/2up, Translated in 1871 by Elliot and Dawson, Volume 3 - The History of India, Cornell University Archives, pp 377-381

[1463] Hasan Nizami et al, Taju-l Ma-asir & Appendix https://archive.org/stream/cu31924073036729#page/n233/mode/2up, Translated in 1871 by Elliot and Dawson, Volume 2 - The History of India, Cornell University Archives, pp 22, 219, 398, 471

[1464] Richard Eaton, Temple desecration and Indo-Muslim states, Frontline (January 5, 2001), pp 72-73

[1465] Ulugh Khan also known as Almas Beg was brother of Ala-al Din Khalji; his destruction campaign overlapped the two dynasties

[1466] Somnath temple went through cycles of destruction by Sultans and rebuilding by Hindus

[1467] https://archive.org/stream/cu31924073036737#page/n107/mode/2up

[1468] https://archive.org/stream/sultanateofdelhi001929mbp#page/n5/mode/2up

[1469] https://archive.org/stream/goldandsilvercoi019909mbp#page/n0/mode/2up

[1470] https://books.google.com/books?id=lt2tqOpVRKgC&pg=PA221

[1471] //en.wikipedia.org/w/index.php?title=Template:History_of_the_Turkic_peoples_pre-14th_century&action=edit

[1472] Walsh, pp. 68-70

[1473] Anzalone, p. 100

[1474] Walsh, p. 70

[1475] Anzalone, p. 101

[1476] http://dsal.uchicago.edu/reference/gazetteer/pager.html?objectid=DS405.1.I34_V02_403.gif

[1477] http://lccn.loc.gov/sa%2065000828

[1478] http://www.britannica.com/EBchecked/topic/156530/Delhi-sultanate

[1479] Dynastic Chart http://dsal.uchicago.edu/reference/gazetteer/pager.html?objectid=DS405.1.I34_V02_403.gif The Imperial Gazetteer of India, v. 2, *p. 368.*

[1480] Ashirbadi Lal Srivastava 1953, p. 150.

[1481] Ahmad Hasan Dani 1999, p. 181.

[1482] Ahmad Hasan Dani 1999, pp. 181-182.

[1483] Sunil Kumar 1994, p. 36.

[1484] Ahmad Hasan Dani 1999, pp. 180-181.

[1485] Ahmad Hasan Dani 1999, pp. 180.

[1486] Sunil Kumar 1994, p. 31.

[1487] Peter Jackson 2003, p. 82.

[1488] Marshall Cavendish 2006, p. 320:"The members of the new dynasty, although they were also Turkic, had settled in Afghanistan and brought a new set of customs and culture to Delhi."

[1489] Ashirbadi Lal Srivastava 1966, p. 98:"His ancestors, after having migrated from Turkistan, had lived for over 200 years in the Helmand valley and Lamghan, parts of Afghanistan called Garmasir or the hot region, and had adopted Afghan manners and customs. They were, therefore, wrongly looked upon as Afghans by the Turkish nobles in India as they had intermarried with local Afghans and adopted their customs and manners. They were looked down as non Turks by Turks"

[1490] Abraham Eraly 2015, p. 126:"The prejudice of Turks was however misplaced in this case, for Khaljis were actually ethnic Turks. But they had settled in Afghanistan long before the Turkish rule was established there, and had over the centuries adopted Afghan customs and practices, intermarried with the local people, and were therefore looked down on as non-Turks by pure-bred Turks."

[1491] Radhey Shyam Chaurasia 2002, p. 28:"The Khaljis were a Turkish tribe but having been long domiciled in Afghanistan, had adopted some Afghan habits and customs. They were treated as Afghans in Delhi Court. They were regarded as barbarians. The Turkish nobles had opposed the ascent of Jalal-ud-din to the throne of Delhi."

[1492] //en.wikipedia.org/w/index.php?title=Template:Delhi_Sultanate&action=edit

[1493] Peter Jackson 2003.

[1494] Ashirbadi Lal Srivastava 1966, p. 141.

[1495] Peter Jackson 2003, pp. 81-86.

[1496] William Wilson Hunter, , WH Allen & Co., London, pp 334-336

[1497] P. M. Holt et al. 1977, pp. 8-14.

[1498] Frank Fanselow (1989), Muslim society in Tamil Nadu (India): an historical perspective, Journal Institute of Muslim Minority Affairs, 10(1), pp 264-289

[1499] Hermann Kulke & Dietmar Rothermund 2004.

[1500] Sastri (1955), pp 206-208
[1501] Vincent A Smith, , Chapter 2, pp 231-235, Oxford University Press
[1502] The Life and Works of Sultan Alauddin Khalji- By Ghulam Sarwar Khan Niazi https://books.google.com/books?id=nbZgnqfXjnQC&pg=PA143&source=gbs_toc_r&cad=3#v=onepage&q&f=false
[1503] Hermann Kulke & Dietmar Rothermund 2004, p. 171-174.
[1504] P. M. Holt et al. 1977, pp. 9-13.
[1505] Irfan Habib 1982, pp. 61-62.
[1506] Hermann Kulke and Dietmar Rothermund (1998), A History of India, 3rd Edition, Routledge, , pp 161-162
[1507] Peter Jackson 2003, pp. 196-202.
[1508] Elliot and Dowson (1871), , Vol. 3, pp 182-188
[1509] N. Jayapalan (2008), Economic History of India: Ancient to Present Day, Atlantic Publishers, pp. 81-83,
[1510] Kenneth Kehrer (1963), The Economic Policies of Ala-ud-Din Khalji, Journal of the Punjab University Historical Society, vol. 16, pp. 55-66
[1511] Ashirbadi Lal Srivastava 1953, pp. 156-158.
[1512] Peter Jackson 2003, pp. 244-248.
[1513] M.A. Farooqi (1991), The economic policy of the Sultans of Delhi, Konark publishers,
[1514] Irfan Habib (1984), The price regulations of Alauddin Khalji - a defense of Zia Barani, Indian Economic and Social History Review, vol. 21, no. 4, pp. 393-414
[1515]
[1516]
[1517] Vincent A Smith (1983), The Oxford History of India, Oxford University Press, pp 245-247
[1518] Irfan Habib 1982, pp. 87-88.
[1519] Irfan Habib 1982, pp. 62-63.
[1520] Raychaudhuri et al (1982), The Cambridge Economic History of India: c. 1200-1750, Orient Longman, pp 89-93
[1521] Irfan Habib (1978), Economic history of the Delhi Sultanate: An essay in interpretation, Indian Council of Historical Research, Vol 4, No. 2, pp 90-98, 289-297
[1522] Scott Levi (2002), Hindu beyond Hindu Kush: Indians in Central Asian Slave Trade, Journal of the Royal Asiatic Society, Vol 12, Part 3, pp 281-293
[1523] Alexander Cunningham (1873), Archaeological Survey of India, Report for the year 1871-72, Volume 3, page 8
[1524] UNESCO, Qutb Minar and its Monuments, Delhi http://whc.unesco.org/en/list/233, World Heritage Site
[1525] Peter Jackson 2003, pp. 49-52.
[1526] Elliot and Dawson (1871), The History of India as told by its own Historians, Vol. 3, pp 94-98
[1527] Irfan Habib (1981), "Barani's theory of the history of the Delhi Sultanate", Indian Historical Review, Vol. 7, No. 1, pp 99-115
[1528] Kishori Saran Lal 1950, p. 385.
[1529] https://books.google.com/books?id=vyEoAwAAQBAJ&pg=PT178
[1530] https://books.google.com/books?id=FcKtIPVQ6REC&pg=PA179
[1531] https://books.google.com/books?id=Bdw9AAAAMAAJ
[1532] //www.worldcat.org/oclc/575452554
[1533] https://books.google.com/books?id=ht21AAAAIAAJ
[1534] //www.worldcat.org/oclc/555201052
[1535] https://books.google.com/books?id=TPVq3ykHyH4C&pg=PP1
[1536] https://books.google.com/books?id=L-s8AAAAIAAJ&pg=PA62
[1537] https://books.google.com/books?id=2XXqAQAACAAJ
[1538] //www.worldcat.org/oclc/685167335
[1539] https://books.google.com/?id=j894miuOqc4C
[1540] https://books.google.com/books?id=UfQWT_esc5cC
[1541] https://books.google.com/books?id=lt2tqOpVRKgC&pg=PA82
[1542] https://books.google.com/?id=8XnaL7zPXPUC

[1543] https://www.researchgate.net/publication/249767771_When_Slaves_were_Nobles_The_Shamsi_Bandagan_in_the_Early_Delhi_Sultanate
[1544] //doi.org/10.1177/025764309401000102
[1545] https://archive.org/stream/shorthistoryofmu035015mbp#page/n121/mode/2up
[1546] https://www.jstor.org/stable/1595059
[1547] Edmund Wright (2006), A Dictionary of World History, 2nd Edition, Oxford University Press,
[1548] Henry Sharp (1938), DELHI: A STORY IN STONE https://www.jstor.org/stable/41361236, Journal of the Royal Society of Arts, Vol. 86, No. 4448, pp 321-327
[1549] //en.wikipedia.org/w/index.php?title=Template:History_of_the_Turkic_peoples_pre-14th_century&action=edit
[1550] //en.wikipedia.org/w/index.php?title=Template:Delhi_Sultanate&action=edit
[1551] The historical spelling is Ṭughlāq (طغلاق).
[1552] Lombok, E.J. Brill's First Encyclopedia of Islam, Vol 5, , pp 30, 129-130
[1553] W. Haig (1958), The Cambridge History of India: Turks and Afghans, Volume 3, Cambridge University Press, pp 153-163
[1554] Banarsi Prasad Saksena 1970, p. 460.
[1555] Banarsi Prasad Saksena 1970, p. 461.
[1556] Vincent Smith, , Oxford University Press, pp 81-82
[1557] William Hunter (1903), , Frowde - Publisher to the Oxford University, London, 23rd Edition, pages 123-124
[1558] Elliot and Dowson (Translators), Tarikh-I Alai https://archive.org/stream/historyindiaast06elligoog#page/n102/mode/2up Amir Khusru, The History of India by its own Historians - The Muhammadan Period, Volume 3, Trubner London, pages 67-92; Quote - "The Rai again escaped him, and he ordered a general massacre at Kandur. He heard that in Brahmastpuri there was a golden idol. (He found it). He then determined on razing the beautiful temple to the ground. The roof was covered with rubies and emeralds, in short it was the holy place of the Hindus, which Malik dug up from its foundations with greatest care, while heads of idolaters fell to the ground and blood flowed in torrents. The Musulmans destroyed all the lings (idols). Much gold and valuable jewels fell into the hands of the Musulmans who returned to the royal canopy in April 1311 AD. Malik Kafur and the Musulmans destroyed all the temples at Birdhul, and placed in the plunder in the public treasury."
[1559] Tarikh-I Firoz Shahi https://archive.org/stream/historyindiaast06elligoog#page/n222/mode/2up Ziauddin Barni, The History of India by its own Historians - The Muhammadan Period, Volume 3, Trubner London, pages 214-218
[1560]
[1561] Mohammad Arshad (1967), An Advanced History of Muslim Rule in Indo-Pakistan, , pp 90-92
[1562] Tarikh-I Firoz Shahi https://archive.org/stream/historyindiaast06elligoog#page/n236/mode/2up Ziauddin Barni, The History of India by its own Historians - The Muhammadan Period, Volume 3, Trubner London, pages 229-231
[1563] William Hunter (1903), , 23rd Edition, pp. 124-127
[1564] William Lowe (Translator), , Volume 1, pages 296-301
[1565] Tarikh-I Firoz Shahi https://archive.org/stream/historyindiaast06elligoog#page/n240/mode/2up Ziauddin Barni, The History of India by its own Historians - The Muhammadan Period, Volume 3, Trubner London, pages 233-234
[1566] Elliot and Dowson (Translators), Travels of Ibn Battuta https://archive.org/stream/historyindiaast06elligoog#page/n610/mode/2up Ibn Battuta, The History of India by its own Historians - The Muhammadan Period, Volume 3, Trubner London, pages 609-611
[1567] Henry Sharp (1938), DELHI: A STORY IN STONE https://www.jstor.org/stable/41361236, Journal of the Royal Society of Arts, Vol. 86, No. 4448, pp 324-325
[1568] Elliot and Dowson (Translators), Táríkh-i Fíroz Sháh https://archive.org/stream/historyindiaast06elligoog#page/n242/mode/2up Ziauddin Barani, The History of India by its own Historians - The Muhammadan Period, Volume 3, Trubner London, pages 609-611
[1569] Vincent A Smith, , Chapter 2, pp 236-242, Oxford University Press
[1570] Elliot and Dowson, Táríkh-i Fíroz Sháhí of Ziauddin Barani, The History of India, as Told by Its Own Historians. The Muhammadan Period (Vol 3), London, Trübner & Co

[1571] Muḥammad ibn Tughluq http://www.britannica.com/EBchecked/topic/396460/Muhammad-ibn-Tughluq Encyclopædia Britannica
[1572] Tarikh-I Firoz Shahi https://archive.org/stream/historyindiaast06elligoog#page/n242/mode/2up Ziauddin Barni, The History of India by its own Historians - The Muhammadan Period, Volume 3, Trubner London, pages 236-237
[1573]
[1574]
[1575] Henry Sharp (1938), DELHI: A STORY IN STONE https://www.jstor.org/stable/41361236, Journal of the Royal Society of Arts, Vol. 86, No. 4448, pp 321-322, 325-326
[1576] Hermann Kulke and Dietmar Rothermund, *A History of India*, (Routledge, 1986), 188.
[1577] Advanced Study in the History of Medieval India by Jl Mehta p.97
[1578] A Social History of the Deccan, 1300-1761: Eight Indian Lives, by Richard M. Eaton p.50
[1579] Vincent A Smith, , Chapter 2, pp 242-248, Oxford University Press
[1580] See: • M. Reza Pirbha, Reconsidering Islam in a South Asian Context, , Brill • Richards J. F. (1974), The Islamic frontier in the east: Expansion into South Asia, Journal of South Asian Studies, 4(1), pp. 91-109
[1581] Tarikh-I Firoz Shahi https://archive.org/stream/historyindiaast06elligoog#page/n246/mode/2up Ziauddin Barni, The History of India by its own Historians - The Muhammadan Period, Volume 3, Trubner London, pages 239-242
[1582] Cornelius Walford (1878), , pp 9-10
[1583] Judith Walsh, A Brief History of India, , pp 70-72; Quote: "In 1335-42, during a severe famine and death in the Delhi region, the Sultanate offered no help to the starving residents."
[1584] Domenic Marbaniang, "The Corrosion of Gold in Light of Modern Christian Economics", *Journal of Contemporary Christian*, Vol.5, No.1 (Bangalore: CFCC), August 2013, p.66
[1585] John Keay, *India: A History* (New Delhi: Harper Perennial, 2000), p.269
[1586]
[1587] Vincent A Smith, The Oxford History of India: From the Earliest Times to the End of 1911, Oxford University Press, Chapter 2, pp 236-242
[1588] George Roy Badenoc (1901), , 3rd Series, Volume 9, Nos. 21-22, pages 13-15
[1589] Elliot and Dowson (Translators), Tarikh-i Firoz Shahi https://archive.org/stream/historyindiaast06elligoog#page/n278/mode/2up Shams-i Siraj 'Afif, The History of India by its own Historians - The Muhammadan Period, Volume 3, Trubner London, pages 271-273
[1590] Elliot and Dowson (Translators), Tarikh-i Firoz Shahi https://archive.org/stream/historyindiaast06elligoog#page/n296/mode/2up Shams-i Siraj 'Afif, The History of India by its own Historians - The Muhammadan Period, Volume 3, Trubner London, pages 290-292
[1591] Firoz Shah Tughlak, Futuhat-i Firoz Shahi - Memoirs of Firoz Shah Tughlak https://archive.org/stream/cu31924073036737#page/n389/mode/2up, Translated in 1871 by Elliot and Dawson, Volume 3 - The History of India, Cornell University Archives
[1592] Vincent A Smith, , Chapter 2, pp 249-251, Oxford University Press
[1593] Firoz Shah Tughlak, Futuhat-i Firoz Shahi - Autobiographical memoirs https://archive.org/stream/cu31924073036737#page/n393/mode/2up, Translated in 1871 by Elliot and Dawson, Volume 3 - The History of India, Cornell University Archives, pp 377-381
[1594] Elliot and Dowson (Translators), Tarikh-i Firoz Shahi https://archive.org/stream/historyindiaast06elligoog#page/n372/mode/2up Shams-i Siraj 'Afif, The History of India by its own Historians - The Muhammadan Period, Volume 3, Trubner London, pp 365-366
[1595] Annemarie Schimmel, Islam in the Indian Subcontinent, , Brill Academic, pp 20-23
[1596] William Hunter (1903), , Frowde - Publisher to the Oxford University, London, 23rd Edition, pages 126-127
[1597] Agha Mahdi Husain (1963), Tughluq Dynasty, Thacker Spink, Calcutta
[1598] Elliot and Dowson (Translators), Tarikh-i Firoz Shahi https://archive.org/stream/historyindiaast06elligoog#page/n374/mode/2up Shams-i Siraj 'Afif, The History of India by its own Historians - The Muhammadan Period, Volume 3, Trubner London, pages 367-371
[1599] Bihamadkhani, Muhammad (date unclear, estim. early 15th century) Ta'rikh-i Muhammadi, Translator: Muhammad Zaki, Aligarh Muslim University
[1600] B.F. Manz, *The rise and rule of Timur*, Cambridge University Press, Cambridge 1989, p. 28: "... We know definitely that the leading clan of the Barlas tribe traced its origin to Qarchar

Barlas, head of one of Chaghadai's regiments ... These then were the most prominent members of the Ulus Chaghadai: the old Mongolian tribes - Barlas, Arlat, Soldus and Jalayir ..."

[1601] M.S. Asimov & C. E. Bosworth, *History of Civilizations of Central Asia*, UNESCO Regional Office, 1998, , p. 320: "... *One of his followers was [...] Timur of the Barlas tribe. This Mongol tribe had settled [...] in the valley of Kashka Darya, intermingling with the Turkish population, adopting their religion (Islam) and gradually giving up its own nomadic ways, like a number of other Mongol tribes in Transoxania ..."*

[1602]

[1603]

[1604] H. Gibb (1956), The Travels of Ibn Battuta, Vols. I, II, III, Hakluyt Society, Cambridge University Press, London, pp 693-709

[1605] Ibn Batutta, Travels in Asia and Africa, 1325-1354, Translated by H Gibb, Routledge, , p. 203

[1606] Ibn Batutta, Travels in Asia and Africa, 1325-1354, Translated by H Gibb, Routledge, , pp. 208-209

[1607] "nakhkhās", Encyclopaedia of Islam, Second Edition, Editors: P.J. Bearmanet al, Brill, The Netherlands

[1608] I.H. Siddiqui (2012), Recording the Progress of Indian History: Symposia Papers of the Indian History Congress, Saiyid Jafri (Editor), , pp 443-448

[1609] Elliot and Dowson (Translators), Tarikh-i Firoz Shahi https://archive.org/stream/historyindiaast06elligoog#page/n346/mode/2up Shams-i Siraj 'Afif, The History of India by its own Historians - The Muhammadan Period, Volume 3, Trubner London, pages 340-341

[1610] Insights into Ibn Battuta's Ideas of Women and Sexuality http://ibnbattuta.berkeley.edu/sidetrips.html The Travels of Ibn Battuta, University of California, Berkeley

[1611] Samuel Lee (translator), Ibn Battuta - The Travels of Ibn Battuta: in the Near East, Asia and Africa, 2010, , pp 151-155

[1612] James Brown (1949), The History of Islam in India, The Muslim World, Volume 39, Issue 1, pages 11–25

[1613]

[1614] William McKibben (1994), The Monumental Pillars of Fīrūz Shāh Tughluq. Ars orientalis, Vol. 24, pp 105-118

[1615] https://books.google.com/books?id=_9cmAQAAMAAJ

[1616] //www.worldcat.org/oclc/31870180

[1617] //en.wikipedia.org/w/index.php?title=Template:Delhi_Sultanate&action=edit

[1618] Mahajan, V.D. (1991, reprint 2007). *History of Medieval India*, Part I, New Delhi: S. Chand, , p.237

[1619] Mahajan, V.D. (1991, reprint 2007). *History of Medieval India*, Part I, Now Delhi: S. Chand, , p.244

[1620] Nizami, K.A. (1970, reprint 2006) *A Comprehensive History of India*, Vol-V, Part-1, People Publishing House, , p.631

[1621] http://www.britannica.com/eb/article-9065995/Sayyid-Dynasty

[1622] http://www.zeno.ru/showgallery.php?cat=6708

[1623] //en.wikipedia.org/w/index.php?title=Template:Delhi_Sultanate&action=edit

[1624] Lodi Dynasty https://www.britannica.com/topic/Lodi-dynasty. Encyclopaedia Britannica. Retrieved 4 September 2017.

[1625] Mahajan, V.D. (1991, reprint 2007). *History of Medieval India*, Part I, New Delhi: S. Chand, , p.244

[1626] Mahajan, V.D. (1991, reprint 2007). *History of Medieval India*, Part I, New Delhi: S. Chand, , p.256

[1627] Prof K.Ali (1950, reprint 2006)"A new history of Indo-Pakistan" Part 1, p.311

[1628] Srivastava, A.L (1966). The Sultanate of Delhi (711 - 1526 A.D), Agra: Shiva Lal Agarwala and Company, p. 245

[1629] http://www.britannica.com/EBchecked/topic/358301/Mahmud-Lodi

[1630] //doi.org/10.1017/s0026749x00009616

[1631] //www.jstor.org/stable/312590

[1632] //doi.org/10.1163/156852096260 1180

[1633] //www.jstor.org/stable/3632649

[1634] //doi.org/10.1163/156852000511222
[1635] //www.jstor.org/stable/3632771
[1636] //www.jstor.org/stable/595978
[1637] http://persian.packhum.org/persian/search?q=Lodhi
[1638] http://www.zeno.ru/showgallery.php?cat=6709
[1639] //en.wikipedia.org/w/index.php?title=Template:TNhistory&action=edit
[1640] The First Spring: The Golden Age of India – Abraham Eraly – Google Books https://books.google.com/books?id=te1sqTzTxD8C&pg=PA72&lpg=PA72. Books.google.co.in. Retrieved on 12 July 2013.
[1641] Sri Lanka and South-East Asia: Political, Religious and Cultural Relations from A.D. C. 1000 to C. 1500, 1978 By W. M. Sirisena, 57 p.
[1642] Politics of Tamil Nationalism in Sri Lanka, South Asian Publishers, 1996 By Ambalavanar Sivarajah, 22 p.
[1643] Mahabharata Book Eight: Karna By Adam Bowles
[1644] The Mahabharata of Krishna-Dwaipayana Vyasa translated into ..., Volume 8 By Kisari Mohan Ganguli
[1645] Kulke and Rothermund, p104
[1646] Keay, p119
[1647] S. Dhammika, *The Edicts of King Ashoka: An English Rendering* http://www.cs.colostate.edu/~malaiya/ashoka.html Buddhist Publication Society, Kandy (1994)
[1648] India By John Keay
[1649] *Periplus* 54. Original Greek: "Ἡ δὲ Νέλκυνδα σταδίους μὲν ἀπὸ Μουζιρέως ἀπέχει σχεδὸν πεντακοσίους, ὁμοίως διά τε ποταμοῦ (καὶ πεζῇ) καὶ διὰ θαλάσσης, βασιλείας δέ ἐστιν ἑτέρας, τῆς Πανδίονος· κεῖται δὲ καὶ αὐτὴ παρὰ ποταμόν, ὡσεὶ ἀπὸ σταδίων ἑκατὸν εἴκοσι τῆς θαλάσσης."
[1650] Hill, John
[1651] Strabo, Geography, BOOK XV., CHAPTER I., section 73 http://www.perseus.tufts.edu/hopper/text?doc=Perseus%3Atext%3A1999.01.0239%3Abook%3D15%3Achapter%3D1%3Asection%3D73. Perseus.tufts.edu. Retrieved on 12 July 2013.
[1652] Keay, p121
[1653] Travel and ethnology in the Renaissance: South India through European eyes, Joan-Pau Rubiés https://books.google.com/books?id=adpkHQ9SCq0C&pg=PA5
[1654] Muslim identity, print culture, and the Dravidian factor in Tamil Nadu, J. B. Prashant More https://books.google.com/books?id=11FYACaVySoC&pg=PA9
[1655] Layers of blackness: colourism in the African diaspora, Deborah Gabriel https://books.google.com/books?id=0-yEfRP0RwgC&pg=PA110
[1656] The Ramayana, The Great Hindu Epic Translated by R C Dutt, RAMAYANA BOOK VII: KISHKINDHA (Part – VI THE QUEST FOR SITA)
[1657] N. Subrahmanian 1962, pp. 133-136.
[1658] //en.wikipedia.org/w/index.php?title=Template:Part_of_History_of_India&action=edit
[1659] Banarsi Prasad Saksena 1992, p. 412.
[1660] Banarsi Prasad Saksena 1992, p. 414.
[1661] Banarsi Prasad Saksena 1992, pp. 416-417.
[1662] Kishori Saran Lal 1950, pp. 208-213.
[1663] K.K.R. Nair 1987, p. 27.
[1664] Peter Jackson 2003, p. 207.
[1665] Kishori Saran Lal 1950, p. 212.
[1666] Nilakanta Sastri, P.213
[1667] Lindsay (2006) p. 101
[1668] Curtin 1984: 100
[1669] The cyclopædia of India and of Eastern and Southern Asia By Edward Balfour
[1670] Holl 2003: 9
[1671] Venkata Subramanian 1988, p. 55.
[1672] Kulke and Rothermund, p99, p107
[1673] http://depts.washington.edu/silkroad/texts/weilue/weilue.html
[1674] https://archive.is/20161123181101/http://www.dli.ernet.in/handle/2015/462306

[1675] //www.worldcat.org/oclc/43502446
[1676] http://www.dli.ernet.in/handle/2015/462306
[1677] https://books.google.com/books?id=NN4fAAAAIAAJ
[1678] https://books.google.com/books?id=_9cmAQAAMAAJ
[1679] //www.worldcat.org/oclc/31870180
[1680] https://books.google.com/books?id=EgSSAAAAIAAJ
[1681] //www.worldcat.org/issn/0377-0443
[1682] https://books.google.com/books?id=2XXqAQAACAAJ
[1683] //www.worldcat.org/oclc/685167335
[1684] https://books.google.com/books?id=lt2tqOpVRKgC&pg=PA174
[1685] //en.wikipedia.org/w/index.php?title=Template:Part_of_History_of_India&action=edit
[1686] Stein 1989, p. 1.
[1687] By James Mansel Longworth page 204
[1688] edited by J C morris page 261
[1689] New Light on Hampi, Recent research in Vijayanagara, edited by John M. Fritz and George Michell, MARG, 2001, p14
[1690] Historians such as P. B. Desai (*History of Vijayanagar Empire*, 1936), Henry Heras (*The Aravidu Dynasty of Vijayanagara*, 1927), B.A. Saletore (*Social and Political Life in the Vijayanagara Empire*, 1930), G.S. Gai (Archaeological Survey of India), William Coelho (*The Hoysala Vamsa*, 1955) and Kamath (Kamath 2001, pp157–160)
[1691] Karmarkar (1947), p30
[1692] Kulke and Rothermund (2004), p188
[1693] Rice (1897), p345
[1694] Robert Sewell (*A Forgotten Empire Vijayanagar: A Contribution to the History of India*, 1901), , N. Ventakaramanayya (*The Early Muslim expansion in South India*, 1942) and B. Surya Narayana Rao (*History of Vijayanagar*, 1993) in Kamath (2001) pp157–160.
[1695] Portuguese travelers Barbosa, Barradas and Italian Varthema and Caesar Fredericci in 1567, Persian Abdur Razzak in 1440, Barani, Isamy, Tabataba, Nizamuddin Bakshi, Ferishta and Shirazi and vernacular works from the 14th century to the 16th century. (Kamath 2001, pp157–158)
[1696] Fritz & Michell (2001) pp1–11
[1697] Kamath (2001), p162
[1698] The success was probably also due to the peaceful nature of Muhammad II Bahmani, according to
[1699] From the notes of Portuguese Nuniz. Robert Sewell notes that a big dam across was built the Tungabhadra and an aqueduct long was cut out of rock ().
[1700] Columbia Chronologies of Asian History and Culture, John Stewart Bowman p.271, (2013), Columbia University Press, New York,
[1701] Also deciphered as *Gajaventekara*, a metaphor for "great hunter of his enemies", or "hunter of elephants" (Kamath 2001, p163).
[1702] From the notes of Persian Abdur Razzak. Writings of Nuniz confirms that the kings of Burma paid tributes to Vijayanagara empire
[1703] Kamath (2001), p164
[1704] From the notes of Abdur Razzak about Vijayanagara: *a city like this had not been seen by the pupil of the eye nor had an ear heard of anything equal to it in the world* (*Hampi, A Travel Guide* 2003, p11)
[1705] Eaton 2006, pp. 89-90 with footnote 28.
[1706] Eaton 2006, pp. 86-87.
[1707] Eaton 2006, pp. 87-88.
[1708] Kamath (2001), p159
[1709] From the notes of Portuguese traveler Domingo Paes about Krishna Deva Raya: *A king who was perfect in all things* (*Hampi, A Travel Guide* 2003, p31)
[1710] Eaton 2006, pp. 88-89.
[1711] The notes of Portuguese Barbosa during the time of Krishna Deva Raya confirms a very rich and well provided Vijayanagara city (Kamath 2001, p186)

[1712] Most monuments including the royal platform (*Mahanavami Dibba*) were actually built over a period spanning several decades (Dallapiccola 2001, p66)
[1713] Eaton 2006, p. 79, Quote: "Rama Raya first appears in recorded history in 1512, when Sultan Quli Qutb al-Mulk enrolled this Telugu warrior as a military commander and holder of a land assignment in the newly emerged sultanate of Golkonda.".
[1714] Eaton 2006, p. 92.
[1715] Eaton 2006, pp. 93-101.
[1716] Eaton 2006, pp. 96-98.
[1717] , Quote: "When battle was joined in January 1565, it seemed to be turning in favor of Vijayanagara - suddenly, however, two Muslim generals of Vijayanagara changes sides. Rama Raya was taken prisoner and immediately beheaded."
[1718] Eaton 2006, pp. 98, Quote: "Husain (...) ordered him beheaded on the spot, and his head stuffed with straw (for display).".
[1719] Eaton 2006, pp. 98-101.
[1720] Eaton 2006, pp. 100-101.
[1721] Kamath (2001), p174
[1722] Eaton 2006, pp. 101-115.
[1723] Kamath (2001), p220, p226, p234
[1724] A war administration, (K.M. Panikkar in Kamath 2001, p174)
[1725] From the notes of Persian Abdur Razzak and research by B.A. Saletore (Kamath 2001, p175)
[1726] From the notes of Nuniz (Kamath 2001, p175)
[1727] From the notes of Duarte Barbosa (Kamath 2001, p176). However, the kingdom may have had nine provinces (T. V. Mahalingam in Kamath 2001, p176)
[1728] From the notes of Abdur Razzaq and Paes respectively (Kamath 2001, p176)
[1729] From the notes of Nuniz)
[1730] Davison-Jenkins (2001), p89
[1731] From the notes of Domingo Paes and Nuniz (Davison-Jenkins 2001, p98)
[1732] Davison-Jenkins (2001), p90
[1733] From the notes of Duarte Barbosa (Kamath 2001, p181).
[1734] From the notes of Abdur Razzak in
[1735] From the notes of Abdur Razzak in
[1736] From the notes of Abdur Razzak in
[1737] Kamath (2001), p179
[1738] According to Sir Charles Elliot, the intellectual superiority of Brahmins justified their high position in society ()
[1739] Verghese (2001), p 41
[1740] B.A. Saletore in Kamath (2001), p179
[1741] Kamath, p180
[1742] Kamath (2001), p. 180
[1743] From the writings of Portuguese Domingo Paes ()
[1744] Mack (2001), p39
[1745] From the notes of Duarte Barbosa (Kamath 2001, p. 178)
[1746] Kamath (2001), p. 177
[1747] Fritz & Michell, p. 14
[1748] Kamath (2001), p. 177–178
[1749] Shiva Prakash in Ayyappapanicker (1997), p192, pp194–196
[1750] Iyer (2006), p93
[1751] Owing to his contributions to carnatic music, Purandaradasa is known as *Karnataka Sangita Pitamaha*. (Kamat, *Saint Purandaradasa*)
[1752] Shiva Prakash (1997), p196
[1753] Shiva Prakash (1997), p195
[1754] Kamath (2001), p178
[1755] Kamath (2001), p185
[1756] Kamath (2001), pp.112, 132
[1757] From the notes of Arab writer Al-Ishtakhri ()
[1758] From the notes of Ibn Batuta ()

[1759] From the notes of Jordanus in 1320–21 ()
[1760] G.S. Gai in Kamath (2001), p10, 157.
[1761] Thapar (2003), pp 393–95
[1762], Nagaraj in Pollock (2003), p378
[1763] Quote:"Royal patronage was also directed to the support of literature in several languages: Sanskrit (the pan-Indian literary language), Kannada (the language of the Vijayanagara home base in Karnataka), and Telugu (the language of Andhra). Works in all three languages were produced by poets assembled at the courts of the Vijayanagara kings". Quote:"The Telugu language became particularly prominent in the ruling circles by the early 16th century, because of the large number of warrior lords who were either from Andhra or had served the kingdom there", Asher and Talbot (2006), pp 74–75
[1764] Shiva Prakash in Ayyappapanicker (1997), p164, pp 193–194, p203
[1765] Rice E.P. (1921), p.68
[1766] During the rule of Krishnadevaraya, encouragement was given to the creation of original *Prabandhas* (stories) from Puranic themes ()
[1767] Like the nine gems of King Vikramaditya's court, the *Ashtadiggajas* were famous during the 16th century.()
[1768] Prasad (1988), pp.268–270
[1769] "History of Science and Philosophy of Science: A Historical Perspective of the Evolution of Ideas in Science", editor: Pradip Kumar Sengupta, author: Subhash Kak, 2010, p91, vol XIII, part 6, Publisher: Pearson Longman,
[1770] Art critic Percy Brown calls Vijayanagara architecture a blossoming of Dravidian style (Kamath 2001, p182)
[1771] Arthikaje, *Literary Activity, Art and Architecture*, History of karnataka. OurKarnataka.Com
[1772] "So intimate are the rocks and the monuments they were used for make, it was sometimes impossible to say where nature ended and art began" (Art critic Percy Brown, quoted in *Hampi, A Travel Guide*, p64)
[1773] Fritz & Michell, p9
[1774] Nilakanta Sastri about the importance of pillars in the Vijayanagar style in Kamath (2001), p183
[1775] "Drama in stone" wrote art critic Percy Brown, much of the beauty of Vijayanagara architecture came from their pillars and piers and the styles of sculpting (*Hampi, A Travel Guide*, p77)
[1776] About the sculptures in Vijayanagara style, see Kamath (2001), p184
[1777] Several monuments are categorised as Tuluva art (Fritz & Michell 2001, p9)
[1778] Some of these paintings may have been redone in later centuries (Rajashekhar in Kamath 2001, p184)
[1779] Historians and art critics K.A. Nilakanta Sastri, A. L. Basham, James Fergusson and S. K. Saraswathi have commented about Vijayanagara architecture (Arthikaje *Literary Activity*).
[1780] Fritz & Michell (2001), p10
[1781] Philon (2001), p87
[1782] Dallapiccola (2001), p69
[1783] https://web.archive.org/web/20081012045138/http://www.ourkarnataka.com/states/history/historyofkarnataka47.htm
[1784] http://www.ourkarnataka.com/states/history/historyofkarnataka47.htm
[1785] https://web.archive.org/web/20060422120411/http://202.41.85.234:8000/gw_44_5/hi-res/hcu_images/G2.pdf
[1786] http://202.41.85.234:8000/gw_44_5/hi-res/hcu_images/G2.pdf
[1787] https://lccn.loc.gov/2003334582
[1788] //lccn.loc.gov/80905179
[1789] //www.worldcat.org/oclc/7796041
[1790] //www.worldcat.org/oclc/8221605
[1791] http://www.dvaita.org/scholars/vyasaraja/
[1792] http://www.whatisindia.com/inscriptions/south_indian_inscriptions/volume_16/introduction_2.html
[1793] https://books.google.com/books?id=OpxeaYQbGDMC&pg=PA1
[1794] http://www.hampionline.com/
[1795] http://www.hampi.in/

[1796] http://www.archaeos.org/vmp-season-1/
[1797] http://www.archaeos.org/vmp-season-2-3/
[1798] http://www.archaeos.org/vmp-summary.html
[1799] http://coinindia.com/galleries-vijayanagar.html
[1800] http://inscriptions.whatisindia.com
[1801] http://indiatourism.ws/hampi/hazararama_temple/
[1802] http://indiatourism.ws/hampi/mahanavami_dibba/
[1803] "He founded the Bengali Husayn Shahi dynasty, which ruled from 1493 to 1538, and was known to be tolerant to Hindus, employing many on them in his service and promoting a form of religious pluralism"
[1804] Nanda, J. N (2005).
[1805] http://journals.sagepub.com/doi/abs/10.1177/097194580400700101
[1806] Perween Hasan (15 August 2007). Sultans and Mosques: The Early Muslim Architecture of Bangladesh. I.B.Tauris. p. 16.
[1807] //tools.wmflabs.org/geohack/geohack.php?pagename=Bengal_Sultanate&params=24_52_0_N_88_8_0_E_region:IN_type:country
[1808] //en.wikipedia.org/w/index.php?title=Template:Ahom_Dynasty&action=edit
[1809] //en.wikipedia.org/w/index.php?title=Template:Culture_of_Assam&action=edit
[1810] "The Kingdom of Assam, where it is entered from Bengal, commences on the north of the Berhampooter, at the Khonder Chokey, nearly opposite to the picturesque estate of the late Mr Raush at Goalpara; and at the Nagrabaree Hill on the South", Wade, Dr John Peter, (1805) " A Geographical Sketch of Assam https://books.google.com/books?id=WItJAAAAMAAJ&pg=RA2-PA116" in Asiatic Annual Register, reprinted
[1811] "The Ahoms were never numerically dominant in the state they built and, at the time of 1872 and 1881 Censuses, they formed hardly one-tenth of the populations relevant to the erstwhile Ahom territory (i.e, by and large, the Brahmaputra Valley without the Goalpara district.)"
[1812] Ahom. Ethnologue (1999-02-19). Retrieved on 2013-07-12.
[1813] "(In Upper Assam), the Ahoms assimilated some of their Naga, Moran and Barahi neighbours and later, also large sections of the Chutiya and Kachari tribes. This Ahomisation process went on until the expanded Ahom society itself began to be Hinduised from the mid-16th century onward."
[1814] "In (the 17th) century of Ahom-Mughal conflicts, (the Tai) language first coexisted with and then was progressively replaced by Assamese (Asamiya) at and outside the Court."
[1815] Tom Kham was the son of Phrasengmong Borgohain and Mula Gabhoru, both warriors who were killed in battles against Turbak.
[1816] "The Ahom expeditionary force, led by General Ton Kham and aided by General Kan Seng and General Kham Peng, pursued the retreating enemies across Muslim domains of Kamarupa and Kamata receiving little resistance in them and reached Karatoya, the eastern boundary of Gaur proper, where the victors washed their swords."
[1817] :The Ahom statesmen and chroniclers wishfully looked forward to the Karatoya as their natural western frontier. They also looked upon themselves as the heirs of the glory that was ancient Kamarupa by right of conquest, and they long cherished infructuously their unfulfilled hopes of expanding up to that frontier." , and notes.
[1818] //doi.org/10.2307/3516963
[1819] //www.jstor.org/stable/3516963
[1820] //tools.wmflabs.org/geohack/geohack.php?pagename=Ahom_kingdom&params=26_55_59_N_94_44_53_E_source:kolossus-svwiki
[1821] //en.wikipedia.org/w/index.php?title=Template:History_of_Andhra_Pradesh&action=edit
[1822] Rao 1994, p. 82.
[1823] Rao 1994, p. 83.
[1824] Rao 1994, p. 87.
[1825] Reddy Kingdoms by M Somasekhara Sarma
[1826] Rao 1994, p. 89.
[1827] Rao 1994, pp. 87,88.
[1828] Talbot 2001, p. 86.
[1829] Reddy Kingdoms by M Somasekhara Sarma

1830 Classicism of Odia Language http://magazines.odisha.gov.in/Orissareview/2011/Feb-Mar/engpdf/55-59.pdf

Article Sources and Contributors

The sources listed for each article provide more detailed licensing information including the copyright status, the copyright owner, and the license conditions.

Middle kingdoms of India *Source:* https://en.wikipedia.org/w/index.php?oldid=847084253 *License:* Creative Commons Attribution-Share Alike 3.0 *Contributors:* 28bytes, Adamgerber80, Againme, Akram0101, Alan, AlanM1, Anadrev, Andres rojas22, Arnavmikel21, Arunsingh16, AtticusX, Aurorion, BD2412, Bender235, Bgwhite, Bhaskarbhagawati, Biscuittin, Blaylockjam10, Bongan, Capankajsmilyo, Cartakes, Chaipau, Charles Matthews, Chewings72, Chhora, Chris the speller, ChrisCork, ChrisGualtieri, Chuniyana, ClueBot NG, Colonies Chris, CommonsDelinker, Compfreak7, CouvGeek, Cpt.a.haddock, Crusoe8181, Cyberbot II, Dbkasar, Dewritech, EWikist, Eddie891, Esszet, Faizhaider, Filippof, Fixer88, FoCuSandLeArN, Fratrep, Frietjes, GDibyendu, Gaius Cornelius, Generalboss3, GermanJoe, Ghatus, Grafen, Greg Grahame, Hebrides, Hmains, HotWinters, Iitkgpatiitk, JLincoln, JaGa, Jayarathina, Jduperra, Jjtanwar, John Hill, John of Reading, Jonathanarpith, Jonesey95, Jonoikobangali, Josh3580, Joshua Jonathan, JzG, Kanashimi, Ketiltrout, Kwamikagami, Kwiki, Kww, Lateg, LilHelpa, Look2See1, LouisAragon, Maestro2016, Manjunath Doddamani Gajendragad, Marcocapelle, Marcus Cyron, Materialscientist, Mbartelsm, Merbabu, Mkrestin, Mogism, MohitSingh, Nayansatya, Nayvik, Neo-Jay, Nick Number, NickTheRipper, Nizamboy, Ogress, Onel5969, PhnomPencil, Pratyya Ghosh, R'n'B, Reahad, Reddi, Rich Farmbrough, Ricky81682, Rjwilmsi, Sanjoydey33, SchreiberBike, SchuminWeb, Seanwal111111, Shreevatsa, Sitush, Solomon7968, Sreenath sree103, Tassedethe, Thapa 75, Thomas.W, Tijfo098, ToonLucas22, Utcursch, Vanished user qwqwijr8hwrkjdnvkanfoh4, Vin09, Wbm1058, Welsh, Wiae, Wikid77, Woohookitty, Xezbeth, 133 anonymous edits 1

Medieval India *Source:* https://en.wikipedia.org/w/index.php?oldid=852724350 *License:* Creative Commons Attribution-Share Alike 3.0 *Contributors:* 10metreh, Acaiber, Adam9007, Adzz, Akshay0412, Antrocent, Arcade81, Arjayay, AtticTapestry, Ayman shariff, BD2412, Bentogoa, Capankajsmilyo, Chandra.shreya, ClueBot NG, Daiyusha, Dbachmann, Delusion23, Denisarona, Dthomsen8, ESP6502, Edward, Ekabhishek, Fez Cap 12, Fixer88, Flinders Petrie, Floatjon, FxdhMxdh, Gauravvaid0, Ginsuloft, Highpeaks35, I.am.viji, Imad bahadur, JaGa, JackintheBox, John of Reading, Johnbod, Jonesey95, Just4edit, Look2See1, Lor, Maestro2016, Malcolma, Marcocapelle, Marek69, Murgh Krahi, NewEnglandYankee, Oshwah, PRVVGP, PlyrStar93, Qefqef, QuartierLatin1968, Quinton Feldberg, SamanthaAnderson12, Seaphoto, Serols, Shyamsunder, Sideways713, Singhalkartik72, Skylark2008, Sunriseshore, Suparnawiki123, Tachs, Tarique012, Tinku Sinha, Tompop888, Tournesol, Ugog Nizdast, Utcursch, Viscious81, Widr, WikiDan61, Wikiuser13, Worldbruce, Xander009, Yintan, 135 anonymous edits 40

Chalukya dynasty *Source:* https://en.wikipedia.org/w/index.php?oldid=851744431 *License:* Creative Commons Attribution-Share Alike 3.0 *Contributors:* AManWithNoPlan, Alan, Anand.Hegde, Ansumang, Begoon, Bender235, Bisasam7, Bob1960evens, CambridgeBayWeather, Capankajsmilyo, CapitalR, Chackerian, Chalukya123, Chewings72, Chhora, Chris the speller, Citation bot 1, Civfanatic, Cpt.a.haddock, Crusoe8181, Dbkasar, DivermanAU, Donner60, DrKay, Dthomsen8, EdwardElric2016, Ekabhishek, Eric-Wester, Ermahgerd9, Fayenatic london, Fconaway, Feminist, Frietjes, Fyyer, GenQuest, Giraffedata, Gnanapiti, Good Olfactory, Gurjar singh, HaeB, Hind meri jaan, Hmains, Holenarasipura, Human3015, IM3847, Ivanpares, Jethwarp, Jim1138, John of Reading, Jonesey95, Kamal singh munda, Kansas Bear, Kautilya3, Khardamagh, Khazar2, Klisz, Kumarrao, Kwamikagami, Kww, Lachs1, Lanet303, Laszlo Panaflex, LilHelpa, MALLUS, MANGOSEEDSDATES, Manju24nath, Manjunath Doddamani Gajendragad, MatthewVanitas, Mayasandra, Mkrestin, Morinae, Mr Stephen, Mx. Granger, NERIUM, NQ, Niceguyedc, Nick Number, Nissar khan234, Nithin bolar k, Nittavinoda, Nizil Shah, O.Koslowski, Onel5969, Pebble101, Pi3.124, Pied Hornbill, Pratyk321, Priyadarshineeraj, Rajaashoka, Ricky81682, Rjwilmsi, RobertG, Roland zh, Rubbish computer, Satdeep Gill, Solomon7968, Sumitkachroo, Sushilkumarmishra, Sushilmishra, Takafumi1, Tangopaso, The Quixotic Potato, Thumperward, Timrollpickering, Tom.Reding, Trivialist, Utcursch, Utkarsh sawale, Vibhss, WOSlinker, Wavelength, Woohookitty, Worldciv2017 Chalukya Empire, पाटलिपुत्र, Ἀλέξανδρος ὁ Μέγας, 122 anonymous edits 47

Harsha *Source:* https://en.wikipedia.org/w/index.php?oldid=853533942 *License:* Creative Commons Attribution-Share Alike 3.0 *Contributors:* Aayush18, Abhishek0831996, Againme, Allens, Ambarishatluri, Amitrochates, Anir1uph, Aravind V R, Arunkumararun, AryamanA, Ashokachola, Bender235, Bgwhite, Bkrish68, CLCStudent, Caballero1967, Capankajsmilyo, Cartakes, Chewings72, Chris the speller, ClueBot NG, CommonsDelinker, Cpt.a.haddock, Crazynyancat, DVdm, Derek R Bullamore, Dewritech, Discospinster, DynamoDegsy, Ecsunil92, Ekabhishek, Frietjes, Gilabrand, Gilliam, Gurpreetsingh56, Harshacan, Hebrides, Highpeaks35, Hmains, Hmainsbot1, Jaideepnain123, Jairaj991, John K, Jonesmith4, Kagundu, Kautilya3, Klbrain, Kmg90, Kongugirl, Library Guy, Mahensingha, Materialscientist, MatthewVanitas, Mike Rosoft, Morinae, Mzilikazi1939, Naam Tamilar, Napoleon 100, Nick Number, Nimishv, Niteshgughane, Nizil Shah, NottNott, Ntrikha, Ohconfucius, Oshwah, Padmacharan123, Pinethicket, Pratyya Ghosh, Raghav Sharman, Raghuvanshidude, Ranaharra, Rani nurmai, Rao Ravindra, Reliable88, Roland zh, RoyalBharat, Rsrikanth05, SalariaRajput, Sandeyad, Serols, Shash, Shubhbilam, Sidlivestrong, Sitush, Skinsmoke, Sparta3, StarmanW, Stjohn1970, Strike Eagle, Sumone10154, Team VJ, Thakurjiofficial, TheDevMor, Tigerleapgorge, Timrollpickering, Titodutta, Uday.zaildar, Utcursch, Vijay bramhane, VishalB, Vishnukumar1974, War wizard90, WarriorRaj, Wbm1058, Wiki-uk, Wikiuser13, Woohookitty, Worldbruce, Xiaoxkzh, Yokeesh, पाटलिपुत्र, 221 anonymous edits 70

Karkoṭa Empire *Source:* https://en.wikipedia.org/w/index.php?oldid=852722338 *License:* Creative Commons Attribution-Share Alike 3.0 *Contributors:* Bender235, Capankajsmilyo, Cpt.a.haddock, Highpeaks35, Kautilya3, Kriteesh, KylieTastic, Magentic Manifestations, Mntzr, Pol098, Shivansh.ganjoo, UserNumber, Utcursch, Xz786, पाटलिपुत्र, 46 anonymous edits 75

Umayyad campaigns in India *Source:* https://en.wikipedia.org/w/index.php?oldid=851121574 *License:* Creative Commons Attribution-Share Alike 3.0 *Contributors:* Abecedare, Ahivarn, Akmal94, AnwarInsaan, AshLin, Atlantic306, Bananaw, Basist.abhishek, Bender235, Bob1960evens, Bodyman123, CactusWriter, CambridgeBayWeather, Capankajsmilyo, Capitals00, Chauhan1192, Chewings72, Choy4311, ClueBot NG, Count Count, Cplakidas, Dalveer85, Danski454, Devanampriya, Dewritech, Dhkstuopj, Dthomsen8, Edward321, Ekabhishek, Fafnir1, Faizhaider, Fowler&fowler, Fundamental metric tensor, Gaurav.p.chaturvedi, George Ponderevo, Ghatus, Giraffedata, GünniX, Helganoth mj, Hugo999, Iamasquid, Jim1138, Jonesey95, Jonesmith4, Josve05a, Justice007, Kansas Bear, Kautilya3, Krish5555, LilHelpa, MBlaze Lightning, Mar4d, Marcocapelle, Mogism, MonsterHunter32, Ms Sarah Welch, Mx. Granger, My Lord, Nakon, NearThatTown, Niceguyedc, Nizil Shah, OccultZone, Onel5969, Orientls, PassionApple, Ponyo, RA0808, RegentsPark, Rossen4, Shekhar.yaadav, Sitush, SuperJew, Takafumi1, Terrek, Tom.Reding, Utcursch, Vice regent, Vyom25, Winkelvi, Wxzapghy, Xtremedood, Ymblanter, 190 anonymous edits 77

Tripartite Struggle *Source:* https://en.wikipedia.org/w/index.php?oldid=853115453 *License:* Creative Commons Attribution-Share Alike 3.0 *Contributors:* Asad2723, Aspening, Bearcat, Bender235, Bgwhite, Biscuittin, Calaka, Capitals00, Catlemur, ChrisGualtieri, ClueBot NG, Cpt.a.haddock, Gahlot.amar, Hind meri jaan, Hmains, Hugo999, John Kroshan, MatthewVanitas, NTSE Worker, Petrb, Pi3.124, Rathfelder, Ricky81682, SchreiberBike, Shyamsunder, Sitush, Utcursch, 48 anonymous edits 87

Gurjara-Pratihara dynasty *Source:* https://en.wikipedia.org/w/index.php?oldid=853331323 *License:* Creative Commons Attribution-Share Alike 3.0 *Contributors:* Abhisheksingh2001a, Ajayrajposwal, Alpha3031, Arjayay, Axtramedium, Bender235, Biker1985, Bladesmulti, BrownHairedGirl, CAPTAIN RAJU, Capankajsmilyo, Cartakes, Chaudharys-3591, Chewings72, Chief Editor(Apoorv), ClueBot NG, Cpt.a.haddock, Deepaksinghchn, Dewritech, DpkKumar34, Frietjes, Ganganathlal, Gaurav Gurjar Sahab, Gewingewin, Grant65, Gujjar Han, Highpeaks35, Hmains, India culture, Iridescent, IronGargoyle, JediKnight20, Jitendra Singh Gurjar, Jonesey95, KartikMistry, Kautilya3, Kumar aaaditya, KylieTastic, Liz, Lokeshbhati45, Marek69, Mark Ironie, Matt7899, Mayank china, Mewla bhatti, Mohitnagar96, Morinae, Niceguyedc, Nizil Shah, Onel5969, Original thinker, Oshwah, Parthvipulpandya, Pi3.124, PolicyReformer, Prabhat1729, RT Gujar, Rajput Sirdar, Rajputtiger0, Ribena786, Ricky81682, Risto hot sir, Ronneythakur, Sandip tanwar, Saqib A. Gujjar, Sitush, SpacemanSpiff, Utcursch, Virender rakwal, Vishal0soni, WereSpielChequers, Winnan Tirunallur, Wxzapghy, Yadav1985, Yamaguchi先生 , 134 anonymous edits 89

Rashtrakuta dynasty *Source:* https://en.wikipedia.org/w/index.php?oldid=851162415 *License:* Creative Commons Attribution-Share Alike 3.0 *Contributors:* Adamgerber80, Altes, Anand.Hegde, Ashokachola, Ashvawiki, BD2412, Bappa3, Bender235, Bgwhite, Biscuittin, Brad101, BrainProgrammers, BudChrSch, Capankajsmilyo, Capitals00, Chewings72, Chris the speller, Classicwiki, ClueBot NG, Cpt.a.haddock, Crisco 1492, Daonguyen95, Discospinster, Donner60, DrKay, Dragonflame1738, Dthomsen8, EdwardElric2016, Ekabhishek, EncyclopediaUpdaticus, Fayenatic london, Feminist, Firebrace, Flegmon12, Frietjes, Gerda Arendt, Good Olfactory, Gryffindor, Holenarasipura, Human3015, I.am.viji, Inikac, John of Reading, Jonesey95, Jonesmith4, Kautilya3, Keith D, Kethrus, Khazar2, Knife-in-the-drawer, Koavf, Kogmaw, Kww, Languagehat, Lifebonzza, Look2See1, Maddiebb77, Magmar3, Malaiya, Manjunath Doddamani Gajendragad, Marcocapelle, Marcus Cyron, Mary Ria, Materialscientist, Mayasandra, Mr Stephen, Natg 19, Niceguyedc, Nick Number, NitinBhargava2016, Onel5969, Pied Hornbill, Pratyk321, R'n'B, Raguks, Redtigerxyz, Richard Keatinge, Ricky81682, Sanjoydey33, Shadowjams, Shhashhi, Shyamsunder, Solomon7968, Srikanth Aviator, Steamerrr, Sushilkumarmishra, Sushilmishra, Takafumi1, Tamilyomen, Thnidu, Thor Dockweiler, Thumperward, Titodutta, Tpbradbury, Ugog Nizdast, Utcursch, Veeresh1209, Vyom25, Wiae, Zcarstvnz, 한번영, 162 anonymous edits 100

Pala Empire *Source:* https://en.wikipedia.org/w/index.php?oldid=851661252 *License:* Creative Commons Attribution-Share Alike 3.0 *Contributors:* Abecedare, Againme, Akib.H, Altes, Arjayay, Ashish-Sharma-Dilli, Astynax, Avanendra psr, BD2412, Bazaan, Bender235, BirBikrom, BrightStarSky, Callanecc, Capankajsmilyo, Cartakes, Chaipau, Chewings72, ClueBot NG, Cpt.a.haddock, DaGizza, Dakinijones, Deepak D'Souza, Diya Titu, Editor2020, Farihashabnam, Fayenatic london, Fylindfotberserk, Gavia immer, GenQuest, Generalboss3, Gyrodoor33, Helpsome, Hibernian, Highpeaks35, Himanshu.raam, Ibrahim Husain Meraj, Iktus, Jagged 85, Jamesx12345, Jayjg, Jim1138, Jodosma, John of Reading, Johnbod, Jonesey95, Jonesmith4, JorisvS, Joy1963, Just4edit, K6ka, Kadamburvijay, Kamlesh4rmBhopal, Koavf, Kww, LilHelpa, Lonely Explorer, Malaiya, Mar4d, Markwiki, Mashupzone, Materialscientist, Mayasandra, Mayasutra, Mdmday, Melakavijay, Mimihitam, Morinae, Musabbir Islam, NadirAli, Niceguyedc, Nick Number, Nikhilmn2002, Nimetapoeg, Niteshgughane, Ohconfucius, Omnipaedista, Osprey39, PIL1987, PKT, Paulrajarshi, Petronis, Pied Hornbill, Proudtobeindian007, Raghuholkar, Rahulwiki1996, Rayaraya, Reahad, Redtigerxyz, Rickjpelleg, Ricky81682, Rjwilmsi, Rockin It Loud, RockyAlley, RockyMasum, Samudrakula,

Sanjoydey33, Serols, Shiggy1, Shivamtanwer, Shubh leo5, Shyamsunder, Skinsmoke, Sodabottle, Solomon7968, Tachs, Takafumi1, Titodutta, Utcursch, Vanished user ija0qfr2o3ijfi 4i4tijwci823irnf, Vanished user qwqwijr8hwrkjdnvkanfoh4, Vanished user zm34pq51mz, Vastu, Vikram singh06, WOSlinker, Wieralee, WikHead, Wikipapon, Woohookitty, Worldbruce, Worldciv pala, Xufanc, Zhongguoyingdu, רפז-ה, বিজয় চক্রবর্তী, 102 anonymous edits .. 123

Medieval Cholas *Source:* https://en.wikipedia.org/w/index.php?oldid=836556351 *License:* Creative Commons Attribution-Share Alike 3.0 *Contributors:* Balablitz, Bgwhite, BreakfastJr, Capankajsmilyo, Corlyon, Dan Koehl, Dbachmann, Dewan357, Dl2000, Eshwar.om, Fratrep, Frietjes, Giraffedata, Grafen, Hmainsbot1, Jagged 85, Jayarathina, John of Reading, Magentic Manifestations, Magioladitis, Mlpkr, Nmadhubala, Plastikspork, Polylerus, R'n'B, Robbiecda, Sarvagnya, Shyamsunder, Sodabottle, Srirangam99, Utcursch, Valfontis, Venu62, Wavelength, Woohookitty, 13 anonymous edits 142

Western Chalukya Empire *Source:* https://en.wikipedia.org/w/index.php?oldid=851162202 *License:* Creative Commons Attribution-Share Alike 3.0 *Contributors:* -revi, AManWithNoPlan, Adamgerber80, Adimovk5, Ankush 89, Astynax, BD2412, BDD, Ben Ben, Bender235, BrownHairedGirl, Calliopejen1, Capankajsmilyo, Catlemur, Chewings72, Chris the speller, Cpt.a.haddock, DashyGames, Dcirovic, Dewan357, Dewritech, Dineshkannambadi, Doug Weller, Dppowell, Dr.Radha Mohan Das Agrawal, DrKay, EdwardElric2016, Ermahgerd9, Fayenatic london, Frietjes, Gimmetrow, Good Olfactory, Green Mostaza, Gurjar singh, Holenarasipura, Hugo999, Human3015, J04n, Jonesey95, Jonesmith4, Just4edit, Kbdank71, Krishnachandranvn, Kwamikagami, Kww, LilHelpa, Magioladitis, Manjunath Doddamani Gajendragad, Marcus Cyron, Masterknower, Mayasandra, Mr Stephen, Neelix, Niceguyedc, Nick Number, Nvvchar, Onel5969, Oshwah, Ost316, Papa November, Pi3.124, Pied Hornbill, Pratyk321, Raghith, Rajaashoka, RekishiEJ, Rich Farmbrough, Ricky81682, Rjwilmsi, Roland zh, Sai18021993, SchreiberBike, ShelfSkewed, Shellwood, Shiggy1, Shreevatsa, Shyamsunder, Sitush, Srirangam99, Sun Creator, Sushilkumarmishra, Tabletop, Tahc, Tamilyomen, Thumperward, Tim!, Tiptoety, Titodutta, Topbanana, Ugog Nizdast, Utcursch, Vanished user vjhsduheuiui4t5hjri, Vin09, Vyom25, WOSlinker, Widr, Woohookitty, Worldciv2017 Chalukya Empire, YellowMonkey, पाटलिपुत्र, ಶಿವಕುಮಾರ, 90 anonymous edits 148

Pallava dynasty *Source:* https://en.wikipedia.org/w/index.php?oldid=853224060 *License:* Creative Commons Attribution-Share Alike 3.0 *Contributors:* Abbanadu, Aggi007, Alvinraj86, Amarprasad.v, Ambivaidy, ArunGYadhav, Arvind asia, Ashwinrajagopalan85, Awsmsp, Babushan, Balablitz, Banda.krishna, Bender235, Capankajsmilyo, Chewings72, ClueBot NG, Cpt.a.haddock, DMacks, Delan singh, Dewritech, Dharmaputhra, Doncram, Duraish, Eshwar.om, Feanor0, Good Olfactory, Highpeaks35, Hmains, Holenarasipura, Ira Leviton, Iyengar 1960, Javith akram, Jeff G., Joefromrandb, John of Reading, Johnbod, Kbssomnath, L Manju, Last edited by:, Luigi Boy, Mayasutra, Muvendar, Naveen Uppalapati, Navops47, Niceguyedc, Nick Number, Nilo.boss, Nittavinoda, Oshwah, Paul2520, Phanindrabn, Pi3.124, Premthanjavur, Prince raja emperor, Raja.m82, Reddyvx, Ricky81682, Robevans123, Rsrikanth05, Sahrudayan, Sai18021993, Saibala18, Sangitha rani111, Satheeshpukal, Shellwood, Sitush, Soumit ban, SpacemanSpiff, Srksamala, Ssriram mt, Steamerrr, Sundarelsa, Tachs, Takafumi1, Tlroche, Utcursch, Vatasura, Vermont, WikiArasu, Wikiname12345, पाटलिपुत्र, 189 anonymous edits .. 173

Chola dynasty *Source:* https://en.wikipedia.org/w/index.php?oldid=849951517 *License:* Creative Commons Attribution-Share Alike 3.0 *Contributors:* Abecedare, Abhishek0831996, Aggi007, Ajithnandhini, Amirthalingam ariyalur, Andyjsmith, AntanO, Arcadio Maxwell, BD2412, Babushan, Bender235, Bgwhite, Blackknight12, Capankajsmilyo, Chackerian, Chewings72, ClueBot NG, Cpt.a.haddock, Czeror, Dcirovic, Dharmaputhra, DragoniteLeopard, Drewmutt, Eggishorn, Ermahgerd9, Eshwar.om, Frosty, Furius, Giraffedata, Gunkarta, Gurjar singh, HaeB, Harithvh, Hessamnia, Hugo999, I dream of horses, I enjoy sandwiches, Jessica meena, Jim1138, John of Reading, Karnantamilking, Kbssomnath, KumaranMee86, Letters From Adi, Linguist111, LittleWink, M.K.Dan, Magentic Manifestations, Mark Ironie, Materialscientist, Mayavan murugan, Mish sta, Mx. Granger, Navops47, Neelyadi, Nidafatimashahi, NitinBhargava2016, Notthebestusername, Onel5969, Pearll's sun, Philostratus, Pi3.124, Rahulbigg, Ranjithsiji, Rubbish computer, S9971706h, Sakthiprasanna, Sarafvpz, Serols, Sipabacus, Sitush, Skabe24, Snori, SpacemanSpiff, Srednuas Lenoroc, SrivijayP, Sskmuhil, Stylez995, Tahc, Takafumi1, The Transhumanist, Utcursch, Vatasura, Vibhss, Vijay Kumar S, Waleed Baqeer, WinterVacation, WorldGov, Worldbruce, Worldciv2017 chola, पाटलिपुत्र, फ़िलप्री, 159 anonymous edits 187

Western Ganga dynasty *Source:* https://en.wikipedia.org/w/index.php?oldid=842609428 *License:* Creative Commons Attribution-Share Alike 3.0 *Contributors:* 52 Pickup, 777sms, 83d40m, Adimovk5, Aldo samulo, All Worlds, Altzinn, Amarrg, Anand.Hegde, Another Believer, Anwar saadat, Asenine, BD2412, Bender235, Bobblehead, Bongwarrior, Br'er Rabbit, Brant.merrell, Brederode∼enwiki, Bugs2beatles, Capankajsmilyo, Celebrategoodtimes, Chandru1234, Charlik, Chimino, Chris the speller, ClueBot NG, Colonies Chris, CommonsDelinker, Cor anglais 16, Courcelles, Cpt.a.haddock, DaGizza, Daonguyen95, DashyGames, Dcirovic, Deepak D'Souza, Demiurge1000, Dewan357, Dineshkannambadi, Dirkbb, DrKay, Dudley Miles, Dwaipayanc, Favonian, Fayenatic london, Flubeca, Fratrep, Frietjes, Gimmetrow, Gnanapiti, Gryffindor, Gyrodoor33, Harryboyles, Holenarasipura, Indian Chronicles, Ineck, Iohannes Animosus, Jayapal.hr, Jim1138, John of Reading, Jrsanthosh, Jugaari cross, KNM, Kbdank71, Ketiltrout, Khazar2, Kww, Leolaursen, Lightmouse, Lugia2453, Makyen, Marcus Cyron, Mathighat, Mayasandra, Mayesdan, Meredyth, MorelMWilliam, Mr Stephen, Nishkid64, NuclearWarfare, Onel5969, Paxsimius, PeterSymonds, PhnomPencil, Pied Hornbill, Piledhigheranddeeper, Pinecar, Primefac, Psubhashish, Raul654, Ravichandar84, Razimantv, Redtigerxyz, Rich Farmbrough, Rjwilmsi, Roland zh, Sardanaphalus, Sarvagnya, Shyamsunder, Skinsmoke, Sri Harsha Bhogi, Stemonitis, Sushilkumarmishra, Sushilmishra, Tahc, Tamilyomen, Teammm, Tellasitis, Theonlynitin, Thumperward, Timeshifter, Titodutta, Topbanana, Utcursch, Visor, VoABot II, Wilfredsimon, Woohookitty, World8115, YellowMonkey, Zanhe, आशीष भटनागर, जैन, ಶಿವಕುಮಾರ, Ἀλέξανδρος ὁ Μέγας, 100 anonymous edits 221

Kakatiya dynasty *Source:* https://en.wikipedia.org/w/index.php?oldid=852929702 *License:* Creative Commons Attribution-Share Alike 3.0 *Contributors:* 79spirit, Ahendra, Aldis90, Allamsanjeev, BAYYAPPANAHALLI, BD2412, Bender235, Bladesmulti, Capankajsmilyo, Civfanatic, Cpt.a.haddock, Devanampriya, DrNavid, Fastifex, Fauzan, Home Lander, I dream of horses, Iridescent, John of Reading, Joshua Jonathan, Kautilya3, Lakun.patra, Lateraldissonance, LilHelpa, Lillinan1, Madurai nayak vamsa, Marutheeraja, Memesfornoobs, MrBill3, Narky Blert, NeilN, Niceguyedc, Ohconfucius, Onel5969, Param Mudgal, Pi3.124, Plantdrew, Psuedocode, Rajal naikil, Randhirreddy, Rich Farmbrough, Rjwilmsi, Satishk01, ScitDei, Shashi.Arjula, Sitush, Stesmo, TeeVeeed, The Ajan, The Blade of the Northern Lights, Utcursch, Vijender.sriramoju1, WOSlinker, Warangalite, Weckkrum, Wikiuser13, Woodlot, 97 anonymous edits 244

Sena dynasty *Source:* https://en.wikipedia.org/w/index.php?oldid=851471839 *License:* Creative Commons Attribution-Share Alike 3.0 *Contributors:* Anionmission, Astynax, Avanendra, Avanendra psr, Balthazarduju, Bender235, Bongan, BrightStarSky, Cartakes, ClueBot NG, Colonies Chris, Cpt.a.haddock, Dangerous-Boy, Dewan357, Dewan753, Dineshkannambadi, Doug Weller, Dthomsen8, Dwaipayanc, Ekdalian, Frietjes, Garg92, Good Olfactory, Greenshed, Holenarasipura, InedibleHulk, Jacob.jose, Janmejaya09, Je regrette, Jonesmith4, Katharineamy, Kayastha Shiromani, Khoikhoi, Kiranmayi pal, Kww, Le Anh-Huy, Magioladitis, Malaiya, Mayasandra, Mimihitam, Mizan1947, Monster eagle, Nakula Kedar Valsan, Ohconfucius, Pearle, Pi3.124, PiCo, Pied Hornbill, Precision0203, R'n'B, Ragib, Rama's Arrow, Recurring dreams, Rkghadai, Rmky87, Rockin It Loud, RonBeeCNC, Rumpelstiltskin223, STK YATHU, Salilb, SameerKhan, Samudrakula, Shiggy1, Shyamsunder, Skinsmoke, Sminthopsis84, Solomon7968, SpacemanSpiff, Springnuts, Tahmidal Zami, Takafumi1, Tarikur, TheDragonFire300, Tinton5, Utcursch, Varadarajd, WTucker, Wavelength, Windrider24584, Wizardman, Woohookitty, Worldbruce, Xezbeth, ¥, 132 anonymous edits 261

Delhi Sultanate *Source:* https://en.wikipedia.org/w/index.php?oldid=853136865 *License:* Creative Commons Attribution-Share Alike 3.0 *Contributors:* 1989, Aaruru.varun, Adityavagarwal, Akman5599, Audacity, Avantiputra7, BD2412, Bgwhite, Bishonen, BrownHairedGirl, CAPTAIN RAJU, Capankajsmilyo, Chaipau, Chandan963, Chewings72, ClueBot NG, Cpt.a.haddock, CyanoTex, Dipendra2007, Dona-Hue, Donner60, EdenKZD, Edward321, Emir of Wikipedia, Eperoton, FawadAliKhan11, Fuortu, GB fan, GünniX, Hairy Dude, Hamtechperson, Haytham Morsy, Highpeaks35, I enjoy sandwiches, IM3847, Jim1138, Jn045, Johnbod, JzG, Kansas Bear, KapilMehta, Kautilya3, KylieTastic, LCalpurniusPiso, Laszlo Panaflex, LouisAragon, Maestro2016, Marcocapelle, Mark the train, Materialscientist, MelbourneStar, Muhammad Umair Mirza, Mz7, NUMWARZ, Narky Blert, NineTimes, Nizil Shah, Onel5969, Panam2014, Pauli133, Plantdrew, Polyenetian, Ponyo, Pranay.rocking, Preethisersh, Primefac, Promethean, Rajkumar 1 02, Rattans, Rich Farmbrough, Rishi tkd, Risto hot sir, Ronakshah1990, SAUNDARYA KESHARI, Serols, Shahrizal shahanshah, Spasage, Syednajmushshafi, Theinstantmatrix, TompaDompa, Trinity4156, TwoTwoHello, Utcursch, VSK1008, VibeScepter, Vishubdeep, WOSlinker, Worldbruce, Yinf, Zoraiz926, Zthewiki, 236 anonymous edits 269

Mamluk dynasty (Delhi) *Source:* https://en.wikipedia.org/w/index.php?oldid=845052582 *License:* Creative Commons Attribution-Share Alike 3.0 *Contributors:* Againme, Ahendra, Amitprabhakar, Anbu121, AroundTheGlobe, Awais141, BarryM9944, Bearly541, Beren Dersi, BrownHairedGirl, Capankajsmilyo, Chamal N, Chapultepec, Chris the speller, Colonies Chris, Cpt.a.haddock, Delhiunit, Dennis Brown, Dewan357, Dl2000, Ekabhishek, El C, Enerelt, Enric Naval, Erlik.khan, Eukesh, Faisalkhilji, Fconaway, FlieGerFaUstMe262, GLGerman∼enwiki, GeorgeofOrange, Good Olfactory, Grafen, Greenshed, Gyrodoor33, Hmains, Hmainsbot1, Hormuzgani1, Hugo999, ImpuMozhi, Irishpunktom, Ishvara7, Jaraalbe, John of Reading, Kansas Bear, Kapitop, Khan1982, Kww, Laszlo Panaflex, Leandrod, Look2See1, Lysozym, MER-C, Maestro2016, Marcocapelle, Matt Heard, Mayooranathan, Md.altaf.rahman, Michaeldsuarez, Muhends, NEWUSER, Nikkul, NineTimes, Nograpes, Noor Aalam, Nostradamus1, PJDF2367, Pahari Sahib, PhnomPencil, Pi3.124, Plotruly, Ptbotgourou, Qatarihistorian, QueenKordeilia, Raja-Hindoostani, Rayaraya, Rich Farmbrough, Ricky81682, Ronakshah1990, Rui Gabriel Correia, Shyamsunder, Siddiqui, Sidmegh, Signsamong29, Spasage, Spitecents6, Stevertigo, Supersaiyen312, TaBOT-zerem, Tbhotch, The Anomebot2, Tigercompanion25, Tigeroo, TimBentley, Titodutta, Tom Radulovich, Topbanana, Tree Biting Conspiracy, Udayiitm, Usmanreddy, Utcursch, VS Roy, Vanished user qwqwijr8hwrkjdnvkanfoh4, Wandering-teacher, Wario-Man, Wavelength, WikiTryHardDieHard, Woohookitty, Worlingham, Zhongguoyingdu, Ἀλέξανδρος ὁ Μέγας, 52 anonymous edits 289

Khalji dynasty *Source:* https://en.wikipedia.org/w/index.php?oldid=849634567 *License:* Creative Commons Attribution-Share Alike 3.0 *Contributors:* 22 Male Cali, Againme, Ahendra, AlphaGamma1991, Amakuru, Awais141, Awaisius, BD2412, Bagwoosh, BeachHome, Bender235, Beren Dersi, Blue Papa Boy, BrownHairedGirl, Capitals00, Carlossuarez46, ClueBot NG, Cpt.a.haddock, Delhiunit, Dennis Brown, Dewritech, Dl2000, Edward321, Ekabhishek, Faizhaider, FawadAliKhan11, Ghatus, GoingBatty, Grant65, Gulumeemee, Gyrodoor33, Harsimaja, Hayras123, HeratiPashtun, HgandVenus, Highpeaks35, HistoryofIran, Indian raja, Iridescent, Iroony, Jaggajat, Jawwad khan marwat, Kansas Bear, Kapitop, Ketabtoon, Khazar2, Khestwol, Kizznyc, Kww, LilHelpa, Look2See1, Lorstaking, Lotje, LouisAragon, Lysozym, M.Ibrahimkhel, MALLUS, Maestro2016, Magioladitis, Mar4d, MatthewVanitas, Michaeldsuarez, Mild Bill Hiccup, Miniapolis, N5iln, Nfr-Maat, Nikhilmn2002, NineTimes, Nizil Shah, Obaid Raza, Onel5969, Paknur, Permanlam, PhnomPencil, Pi3.124, PrasanthVRegy, Ptbotgourou, Qara xan, Qatarihistorian, Rich Farmbrough, Risto hot sir, Rjwilmsi, Saladin1987, Scythian1, Sheeraz07mba, Shxahxh, Signsamong29, Solomon7968, Steveodinkirk, Tabletop, Tajik, Takabeg, Tbhotch, Tigercompanion25,

Timtrent, Tkkkk, Tommy2010, TompaDompa, Tpbradbury, Trust Is All You Need, Ugog Nizdast, Utcursch, Wario-Man, WarriorsPride6565, Wavelength, Woohookitty, WorldCreaterFighter, Worldbruce, Zompist, Zppix, 七战功成 , 58 anonymous edits 296

Tughlaq dynasty *Source:* https://en.wikipedia.org/w/index.php?oldid=849671512 *License:* Creative Commons Attribution-Share Alike 3.0 *Contributors:* 468Shahi, Againme, Ahulandiy, AjaxSmack, Alren, Analytikone, Awais141, Awaisius, Babbage, Barthateslisa, BeachHome, Bejnar, Beren Dersi, Bhadani, Bless sins, CanadianLinuxUser, Capankajsmilyo, ClueBot NG, Colonies Chris, Cpt.a.haddock, Curryfranke, David Haberlah, Deeptrivia, Delhiunit, Dengesizz, Dennis Brown, Dewan357, Diannaa, DorisAntony, Ekabhishek, Everyking, Farvartish, Ghatus, Good Olfactory, Grant65, Greenshed, Gyrodoor33, Huon, Imc, ImpuMozhi, IndianGeneralist, Indira22, JogiAsad, John of Reading, Jonathansammy, Joy1963, KahnJohn27, Kbir1, Kwamikagami, Kww, Lillinan1, MALLUS, MER-C, Maestro2016, Malgudi Days, Marcocapelle, Marduking, Mevagiss, MonsterHunter32, Narson, New786678, Nick Number, Nikhilmn2002, NineTimes, Nizil Shah, Nostradamus1, OccultZone, Ohconfucius, PKT, Pi3.124, Qara xan, Qatarihistorian, QuartierLatin1968, Rayaraya, Rich Farmbrough, Risto hot sir, Salman 0902, Samee, Sasuke1346, SchreiberBike, Sharkslayer87, Siddiqui, Signsamong29, Sipabacus, Sitush, Solomon7968, Spasage, Stephen G. Brown, Sunquanliangxiuhao, Tajik, Takabeg, Takafumi1, Tbhotch, Theelf29, Thor Dockweiler, Topbanana, Tree Biting Conspiracy, Utcursch, Vanished user qwqwijr8hwrkjdnvkanfoh4, Velella, Wahabijaz, Wario-Man, Wavelength, Wbm1058, Whytecypress, Willard84, Worldkacitizen, Yazid97, YukioSanjo, Zppix, Ἀλέξανδρος ὁ Μέγας, 51 anonymous edits 306

Sayyid dynasty *Source:* https://en.wikipedia.org/w/index.php?oldid=845373238 *License:* Creative Commons Attribution-Share Alike 3.0 *Contributors:* 72, Aamer85, Aelfthrytha, Againme, AlphaGamma1991, Andy M. Wang, Armand Abian, Babajobu, Bgwhite, Bot-Schafter, BrownHairedGirl, Caerwine, Capankajsmilyo, Cartakes, ChrisGualtieri, ClueBot NG, Cpt.a.haddock, Darylgolden, Deeptrivia, Delhiunit, Dewan357, Ekabhishek, Gazkthul, Gyrodoor33, GünniX, Hongooi, ImpuMozhi, Iridescent, Island, Jacobolus, Joy1963, Kansas Bear, Ketabtoon, Kutchkutch, Kww, KylieTastic, MALLUS, MatthewVanitas, Michaeldsuarez, Miltonzs, Mogism, Monticores, MtDutchling, Nersy, Neutron Jack, Niceguyedc, Ongar the World-Weary, Optakeover, OrenBochman, Pi3.124, Ponyo, Prem Kishan Raj, Qatarihistorian, Rayaraya, Rbbloom, RegentsPark, Rich Farmbrough, Ricky81682, Rodw, Sankalpdravid, Signsamong29, Skr15081997, Spasage, Tariq353, Tbhotch, Tessarman, Texture, Utcursch, VihaanDoshi, VivaEmilyDavies, Vssun, Widr, Willard84, 79 anonymous edits 329

Lodi dynasty *Source:* https://en.wikipedia.org/w/index.php?oldid=851783554 *License:* Creative Commons Attribution-Share Alike 3.0 *Contributors:* A Fistful of Dollars, Afghan,pashtun,persian, Aibel john panicker, Akbar Khan89, AlimNaz, AlphaGamma1991, Alsikandar, Amitwikid, Anikeshkamath, Apuldram, Azgs, Barthateslisa, Bender235, Benramm, BlackCheck, Buzz-tardis, Chewings72, Chilum aw charrs, ClueBot NG, Coinmanj, ConnectedOnSunday, Cookiemohnsta, Cpt.a.haddock, Cricketaman13, Crown Prince, Dadamkhan, Delhiunit, Delljvc, Dig deeper, Divyraj, Donner60, ESkog, Excirial, Faizan, Gilliam, Gryffindor, Gyrodoor33, GünniX, HS201Team19, Hagoromo's Susanoo, Highpeaks35, HitroMilanese, Itish.mandhana, Jawwad khan marwat, Jnorton7558, Joy1963, Kansas Bear, Ketabtoon, Krzyhorse22, Kww, Lodhi1234, Lodhimuhammad, LouisAragon, MALLUS, MANGOSEEDSDATES, Magioladitis, Makhdoom Ali Ameen Lodhi, Mar4d, Marduking, Materialscientist, MatthewVanitas, Misarxist, Mjroots, Mooch025, Muhandes, Niceguyedc, NikNaks, Oluwa2Chainz, Onel5969, Paxtoon, Persianpashtun, Peterbruce01, Pi3.124, Pleasecreatemyaccount, Pratyya Ghosh, Qatarihistorian, R'n'B, Ranjeet Lodhi, Ranjit.gadgil, Risto hot sir, Rjwilmsi, Saladin1987, Samir javed, Shelley Christine, Shimlaites, Signsamong29, Sitush, Smalljim, Spasage, SpikeToronto, Supdiop, Tariq353, Tbhotch, Tessarman, The Herald, Thewritething123, Thomas.W, Thssn1234, TwoTwoHello, Ur-loki, UsmanPathanKhan, Varnitakaushik, VenomousConcept, Vssun, Wavelength, Wearelodi, Wikikanvas, Willard84, Woohookitty, ZxxZxxZ, \\'arrior 786, Ἀλέξανδρος ὁ Μέγας, 183 anonymous edits 333

Pandyan dynasty *Source:* https://en.wikipedia.org/w/index.php?oldid=853229246 *License:* Creative Commons Attribution-Share Alike 3.0 *Contributors:* 2016rewind, Abhishek0831996, Aggi007, Ahamed Adnan Bin Alim, Anup Ramakrishnan, ArunGYadhav, Arunnagammal, Azhaganvimalan, Azhaganvimalan96, BD2412, Bender235, CAPTAIN RAJU, Capankajsmilyo, Chewings72, Chris the speller, Classicwiki, ClueBot NG, Cocohead781, CommanderOzEvolved, CommonsDelinker, Cpt.a.haddock, Daniel0Wellby sch, Dewritech, Dharani Maran, Dirkbb, EdmundT, Euryalus, Fort5000, Gilliam, Gurjar singh, HaeB, Helwett, Highpeaks35, I dream of horses, Ira Leviton, JaconaFrere, Jennica, Jtrrs0, JudeBob123, Kansas Bear, Kongugirl, Lakun.patra, Let There Be Sunshine, LiamKasbar, Luigi Boy, Madhu siddharth, Magentic Manifestations, Materialscientist, Mccapra, Menaechmi, Muvendar, Mx. Granger, Natg 19, Navops47, NitinBhargava2016, Nittavinoda, PKT, Pratyk321, Ramanan KL, Ranjithsiji, Redtigerxyz, Rich Farmbrough, Ros1602, Rubbish computer, SA 13 Bro, Saibala18, Sakthisainath, Sandhyanathtiwari, Sarafvpz, Sbrighton, Shkarthikeyan, SirPigwig, SpacemanSpiff, Srirangam99, StanchevFPS, Takafumi1, Timmyshin, UY Scuti, Utcursch, Vatasura, Vijay Kumar S, Vijayakumar Kaushik, Winnan Tirunallur, Xenani, Աշոտ Տ Ն, தென்காசி சுப்பிரமணியன், 167 anonymous edits 338

Vijayanagara Empire *Source:* https://en.wikipedia.org/w/index.php?oldid=851024177 *License:* Creative Commons Attribution-Share Alike 3.0 *Contributors:* Aggi007, Akshayeashok, Alexf, Alphathon, Amarprasad.v, Ankit2, BD2412, Baddu676, Bender235, Bgwhite, Binggo666, Capankajsmilyo, Chewings72, Chris the speller, ClueBot NG, CommonsDelinker, Cpt.a.haddock, D4iNa4, DANABOENAVEERAVARAPRASAD, Deepak birva, Dona-Hue, DrKay, Dushanyk, El C, Epicgenius, Ermahgerd9, Finnusertop, Flyer22 Reborn, Google editor, Hairy Dude, Haploidavey, Highpeaks35, Holenarasipura, IronGargoyle, Ishitagupta, Jim1138, Jugaari cross, KARTHIK VINOD, Kautilya3, Kautuk1, Laszlo Panaflex, LeoFrank, Madhukarmohan, Materialscientist, Mayasandra, Mild Bill Hiccup, Mistresd, Mr Stephen, Ms Sarah Welch, Mx. Granger, Mywikicommons, Nahushavk, Natg 19, New786678, Niceguyedc, Nikhil Nayak, Northern Muriqui, Oshwah, Philg88, Pi3.124, Pied Hornbill, PiedPiperofAgra321, Polyenetian, Prabhav Goel, Pragsrao, Pranam.shetty55446, PseudoSkull, Raghu Naik NC, Rattans, Rhno0001, Rich Farmbrough, Risto hot sir, Rkkrajarajan, Samyakoften, Sangitharani111, Sbhushi, Serols, Sitush, SpacemanSpiff, Srinivasa247, Sriyerram, Sunnya343, Takafumi1, Theinstantmatrix, Utcursch, Vibhss, Vijaypatham, Vik1697, Vin09, WereSpielChequers, WestCoastMusketeer, Woodlot, Woodstop45, Worldciv 2017 kushan, Worldciv17 VN, Xaosflux, 165 anonymous edits 361

Bengal Sultanate *Source:* https://en.wikipedia.org/w/index.php?oldid=849635873 *License:* Creative Commons Attribution-Share Alike 3.0 *Contributors:* Adnandastagir, Ahmad dhaka, Akib.H, Arjayay, ArmanJ, Asm sultan, BD2412, Bazaan, Bruce Hall, Chewings72, CommonsDelinker, Courcelles, Cpt.a.haddock, Cuddly Visionary, DA1, Damien2016, Derek R Bullamore, Dl2000, F2416, Faizan, Fantastic mapper, Farabi1994, Fez Cap 12, Giraffedata, GrindtXX, H.Arian, HistoryofBangladesh, Ibrahim Husain Meraj, Intakhab, Ira Leviton, Iridescent, JJMC89, John of Reading, Johnsoniensis, Keith D, Kiarazuri, Lenticel, LittleWink, Look2See1, LouisAragon, Maestro2016, Magioladitis, Marcocapelle, Melaen, Messiaindarain, Mikeblas, Mild Bill Hiccup, Mywikimediaaccount, Natg 19, Nomian, Ohconfucius, Onel5969, Petrb, PhnomPencil, Pi3.124, Pooyaf, Popolon, R'n'B, Rattans, Reahad, RegentsPark, Risto hot sir, Roland zh, S.A.Farabi, SJ Defender, SheriffIsInTown, Sitush, SpacemanSpiff, Squids and Chips, The Anomebot2, Tiger Hafiz, Titodutta, Trip Tucker, Troyoleg, Vanished user indfoijwe3ty, Vanished user kjn lsr35kjhwertsek4, Vaza12, Vinegarymass911, Worldbruce, Xarhunter, Роман Курносенко, 136 anonymous edits 388

Ahom kingdom *Source:* https://en.wikipedia.org/w/index.php?oldid=851109632 *License:* Creative Commons Attribution-Share Alike 3.0 *Contributors:* 7VIES, Acroterion, Ahoerstemeier, Alistair1978, Arjayay, Baalmatlab, Bdebbarma, Bijay Dutta, Binit00gogoi, Chaipau, Chopstixx, Chris the speller, Chuniyana, Citation bot 1, ClaretAsh, ClueBot NG, Compfreak7, Cpt.a.haddock, Darklilac, Debasisbora, Dewan357, Dewritech, Dkonwar, Dl2000, ESkog, Eagleash, Egha95, Emeraude, Euchiasmus, FaisalAbbasid, FourViolas, Frietjes, Gherkinmad, Good Olfactory, Highpeaks35, Hongooi, Hrishikesh borgohain, Hybernator, JaGa, Jakichandan, Jalal567, Jim1138, John of Reading, John.kakoty, JzG, Kansas Bear, Karthikndr, Kelly Martin, Koavf, Kurmaa, Lachitbarphukan, Leandrod, Liberal Humanist, Lightmouse, MKar, Merchant of Meluha, Mimihitam, Msasag, Muhandes, Nafsadh, Nisankh, Ogress, Omnipaedista, Pawyilee, Penguinnumbers, Pericombubulat0r, Pravakar Borpatra Gohain, Quibitos, Ranjan Pratik, RenamedUser01302013, Rex86, Rjwilmsi, Roland zh, SchreiberBike, Scoobycentric, Serols, Shekhar Jyoti Das, Shyamsunder, Spandan28, Sreekanthv, Svetavaraha, The Anomebot2, Tkynerd, Toolen, Trappist the monk, Uragn borpatrogohain, VegaDark, Weegeeweeg, แอนเดอร์สัน, 76 anonymous edits 403

Reddy dynasty *Source:* https://en.wikipedia.org/w/index.php?oldid=851386345 *License:* Creative Commons Attribution-Share Alike 3.0 *Contributors:* Abdulmc, Againme, American55, Arjayay, Auric, BD2412, Ballkat, Bender235, Bndy206, BrownHairedGirl, Bsr465, CAPTAIN RAJU, Capankajsmilyo, Chincater, ClueBot NG, DadaNeem, Daderot, Devanampriya, Dewritech, Fastily, Firsfron, Foodie 377, Fylindfotberserk, Glassfisher, Harsh reddy, Highpeaks35, Hmains, Holenarasipura, Hugo999, Jagadishnayani, Jovianeye, Juru sreenivas, Just4edit, Kautilya3, Krish163, Kumarrao, Kww, Llywrch, Loopy30, MANGOSEEDSDATES, Mahveotm, Malcolma, Masioq, Mekala Harika, Mild Bill Hiccup, Moe Epsilon, Mogism, Muppavarapu Navya, My name is not dave, Narky Blert, PC-XT, Pip2andahalf, Pleiotrop3, Prasadreddyoln, R'n'B, Rajshekhar Reddy Arya, Ranjithreddych, Rayaraya, Rjwilmsi, Robert McClenon, Roland zh, Rushbugled13, Sai1312, Sau226, Shreewiki, Sitush, Skinsmoke, Sodabottle, Sonicyouth86, SpacemanSpiff, Sun Creator, Sushilkumarmishra, Svabhiman, Tabletop, Tahc, The Ajan, The Transhumanist, Thumperward, Townblight, Utcursch, Vinod999reddy, Vivek Ray, Vulvaro, Weckkrum, Wifione, Woohookitty, YVSREDDY, Yamaguchi先生 , 159 anonymous edits 416

Gajapati Kingdom *Source:* https://en.wikipedia.org/w/index.php?oldid=851547015 *License:* Creative Commons Attribution-Share Alike 3.0 *Contributors:* 4c27f8e656bb34703d936fc59ede9a, Ansumang, Anthony Bradbury, Arjayay, Basua, Bdmishrawiki, BrownHairedGirl, CanisRufus, Cindersblu, Cpt.a.haddock, Dineshkannambadi, Foodie 377, Fylbecatulous, Gabriel1907, GeorgeofOrange, Indianprithvi, JaGa, Janmejaya09, John of Reading, JohnCD, Johnpacklambert, Joy1963, Kenfyre, Kwamikagami, MatthewVanitas, Mvrr.bill, Nayansatya, Nick Number, Ninney, Pi3.124, Prabhu Prasad Tripathy, PrincessofLlyr, Priyanath, R'n'B, Rayaraya, Richard-of-Earth, Ricky81682, Sadaryohan, Shyamsunder, Sitush, Sodabottle, Sohantripathy, Sri Harsha Bhogi, The Anomebot2, Titodutta, Utcursch, WP MANIKHANTA, Woohookitty, Worldbruce, Zenpriyesh1, 55 anonymous edits 432

Image Sources, Licenses and Contributors

The sources listed for each image provide more detailed licensing information including the copyright status, the copyright owner, and the license conditions.

Figure 1 *Source:* https://en.wikipedia.org/w/index.php?title=File:DemetriusCoin.jpg *License:* Public Domain *Contributors:* ESnible 3
Figure 2 *Source:* https://en.wikipedia.org/w/index.php?title=File:Kushanmap.jpg *License:* Creative Commons Attribution-ShareAlike 3.0 Unported *Contributors:* PHGCOM 6
Figure 3 *Source:* https://en.wikipedia.org/w/index.php?title=File:HephthaliteCoin.jpg *License:* GNU Free Documentation License *Contributors:* Allforrous, File Upload Bot (Magnus Manske), Howchewg, Leobouvdv, MGA73, OgreBot 2, Roland zh, Zaccarias, पाटलिपुत्र 7
Figure 4 *Source:* https://en.wikipedia.org/w/index.php?title=File:Karkota_Empire,_India_(derived).jpg *License:* Creative Commons Attribution-Sharealike 3.0 *Contributors:* Amitrochates, Daderot, Utcursh 8
Figure 5 *Source:* https://en.wikipedia.org/w/index.php?title=File:Silver_Coin_of_Kumaragupta_I.jpg *License:* GNU Free Documentation License *Contributors:* Athaenara, Bodhisattwa, Chaoborus, File Upload Bot (Magnus Manske), MGA73bot2, Mhmrodrigues, OgreBot 2 10
Figure 6 *Source:* https://en.wikipedia.org/w/index.php?title=File:Ajanta_(63).jpg *License:* Creative Commons Attribution-ShareAlike 3.0 Unported *Contributors:* User:Soman 12
Figure 7 *Source:* https://en.wikipedia.org/w/index.php?title=File:Prithvi_Raj_Chauhan_(Edited).jpg *License:* GNU Free Documentation License *Contributors:* Prithvi_Raj_Chauhan.JPG: LRBurdak at en.wikipedia derivative work: original uploader was Dhiresh b at en.wikipedia 15
Figure 8 *Source:* https://en.wikipedia.org/w/index.php?title=File:Sun_Temple_Sabha_Mandap.JPG *License:* Creative Commons Attribution 2.5 *Contributors:* Uday Parmar / Parmar uday at en.wikipedia 16
Figure 9 *Source:* https://en.wikipedia.org/w/index.php?title=File:IndianBuddha11.JPG *License:* Public domain *Contributors:* BotMultichill, Ekabhishek, Farm, Gryffindor, Ismoon, Nagy, Podzemnik, Roland zh 17
Figure 10 *Source:* https://en.wikipedia.org/w/index.php?title=File:Konark_Sun_Temple_Front_view.jpg *License:* Public Domain *Contributors:* http://en.wikipedia.org/wiki/User_talk:Vinayreddym 19
Figure 11 *Source:* https://en.wikipedia.org/w/index.php?title=File:Assam_MK_Lion.JPG *License:* Creative Commons Attribution 3.0 *Contributors:* Porikolpok Oxom 21
Figure 12 *Source:* https://en.wikipedia.org/w/index.php?title=File:Doddagaddavalli_Lakshmidevi_temple1_retouched.JPG *License:* GNU Free Documentation License *Contributors:* OgreBot 2, Rcbutcher, Roland zh 25
Figure 13 *Source:* https://en.wikipedia.org/w/index.php?title=File:Gomateswara.jpg *License:* Attribution *Contributors:* FSII, Fontema, Guanaco, Hystrix, Jungpionier, Kilom691, MPF, Ranveig, Roland zh, Soerfm, Str4nd, Thuresson, Vssun, 8 anonymous edits 26
Figure 14 *Source:* https://en.wikipedia.org/w/index.php?title=File:Relief_of_seated_Vishnu_at_the_Badami_cave_temple_no.3.jpg *License:* Public domain *Contributors:* Original uploader was Dineshkannambadi at en.wikipedia 28
Figure 15 *Source:* https://en.wikipedia.org/w/index.php?title=File:Mamallapuram1a.jpg *License:* Creative Commons Attribution 2.0 *Contributors:* mckaysavage 29
Figure 16 *Source:* https://en.wikipedia.org/w/index.php?title=File:Indian_Rashtrakuta_Empire_map.svg *License:* Creative Commons Attribution-Sharealike 3.0 *Contributors:* AnonMoos, Aschroet, Io Herodotus, Nikotins, Planemad, Roland zh 31
Figure 17 *Source:* https://en.wikipedia.org/w/index.php?title=File:Kailasha_temple_at_ellora.JPG *License:* Creative Commons Attribution-Sharealike 2.5 *Contributors:* Pratheepps 31
Figure 18 *Source:* https://en.wikipedia.org/w/index.php?title=File:Ornate_pillars_in_the_Saraswati_temple_at_Gadag.jpg *License:* GNU Free Documentation License *Contributors:* AnRo0002, Dineshkannambadi, File Upload Bot (Magnus Manske), MGA73bot2, Marcus Cyron, Neithsabes, OgreBot 2, Papa November, Roland zh 34
Figure 19 *Source:* https://en.wikipedia.org/w/index.php?title=File:Kudalasangama.jpg *License:* Public domain *Contributors:* Denniss, File Upload Bot (Magnus Manske), OgreBot 2, Roland zh, Tine 35
Figure 20 *Source:* https://en.wikipedia.org/w/index.php?title=File:Shilabaalika_on_pillar_bracket_in_Chennakeshava_Temple_at_Belur3.jpg *License:* GNU Free Documentation License *Contributors:* Alan, Dineshkannambadi, File Upload Bot (Magnus Manske), MGA73bot2, OgreBot 2, Papa November, Roland zh, Vivek Sarje, Xufanc, 1 anonymous edits 36
Figure 21 *Source:* https://en.wikipedia.org/w/index.php?title=File:Rajendra_map_new.svg *License:* GNU Free Documentation License *Contributors:* Rajendra_map_new.png: derivative work: Gregors (talk) 38
Image *Source:* https://en.wikipedia.org/w/index.php?title=File:PD-icon.svg *License:* Public Domain *Contributors:* Alex.muller, Anomie, Anonymous Dissident, CBM, Jo-Jo Eumerus, MBisanz, PBS, Quadell, Rocket000, Strangerer, Timotheus Canens, 1 anonymous edits 39
Image *Source:* https://en.wikipedia.org/w/index.php?title=File:Badami-chalukya-empire-map.svg *License:* Creative Commons Attribution-ShareAlike 3.0 Unported *Contributors:* Mlpkr 47
Image *Source:* https://en.wikipedia.org/w/index.php?title=File:Blank.png *License:* Public Domain *Contributors:* Bastique, Chlewey, ChrisDHDR, Ghouston, It Is Me Here, Jed, Paradoctor, Patrick, Penubag, Perhelion, Rocket000, Roomba, Sarang, Timeroot, Tintazul 48
Image *Source:* https://en.wikipedia.org/w/index.php?title=File:Flag_of_India.svg *License:* Public Domain *Contributors:* Anomie, Jo-Jo Eumerus, Mifter 48
Figure 22 *Source:* https://en.wikipedia.org/w/index.php?title=File:6th_century_Kannada_inscription_in_cave_temple_number_3_at_Badami.jpg *License:* Creative Commons Attribution-Sharealike 3.0 *Contributors:* Dineshkannambadi (talk) 22:48, 30 July 2008 (UTC) 49
Figure 23 *Source:* https://en.wikipedia.org/w/index.php?title=File:8th_century_Kannada_inscription_on_victory_pillar_at_Pattadakal.jpg *License:* Creative Commons Attribution-Sharealike 3.0 *Contributors:* Dineshkannambadi (talk) 22:39, 30 July 2008 (UTC) 50
Figure 24 *Source:* https://en.wikipedia.org/w/index.php?title=File:Bhutanatha_temple_in_Badami,_Karnataka,_India.jpg *License:* Creative Commons Attribution-Sharealike 3.0 *Contributors:* User:Gs9here 53
Figure 25 *Source:* https://en.wikipedia.org/w/index.php?title=File:Virupaksha_temple_at_Pattadakal.jpg *License:* Creative Commons Attribution-Sharealike 3.0 *Contributors:* Dineshkannambadi (talk) 23:05, 1 August 2008 (UTC) 56
Figure 26 *Source:* https://en.wikipedia.org/w/index.php?title=File:Badami,_Höhle_4,_Bahubali_(1999).jpg *License:* Public domain *Contributors:* ArnoldBetten 58
Figure 27 *Source:* https://en.wikipedia.org/w/index.php?title=File:Vishnu_image_inside_cave_number_3_in_Badami.jpg *License:* Creative Commons Attribution-Sharealike 3.0 *Contributors:* Dineshkannambadi (talk) 03:35, 13 August 2008 (UTC) 59
Figure 28 *Source:* https://en.wikipedia.org/w/index.php?title=File:Bhutanatha_temple_complex_in_Badami.jpg *License:* Creative Commons Attribution-Sharealike 3.0 *Contributors:* Dineshkannambadi (talk) 22:33, 1 August 2008 (UTC) 59
Figure 29 *Source:* https://en.wikipedia.org/w/index.php?title=File:Parvati_temple_at_Krauncha_Giri_near_Sandur,_Ballary_district.jpg *License:* Creative Commons Attribution-Sharealike 3.0 *Contributors:* User:Shreyasu 59
Figure 30 *Source:* https://en.wikipedia.org/w/index.php?title=File:Durga_Temple.jpg *License:* Creative Commons Attribution-Sharealike 3.0 *Contributors:* User:Nag4pl 60
Figure 31 *Source:* https://en.wikipedia.org/w/index.php?title=File:Jain_basadi.JPG *License:* Creative Commons Attribution-Sharealike 3.0 *Contributors:* User:Shishir jain 60
Figure 32 *Source:* https://en.wikipedia.org/w/index.php?title=File:Mallikarjuna_and_Kasivisvanatha_temples_at_Pattadakal.jpg *License:* Creative Commons Attribution-Sharealike 3.0 *Contributors:* Dineshkannambadi (talk) 22:46, 1 August 2008 (UTC) 61
Figure 33 *Source:* https://en.wikipedia.org/w/index.php?title=File:Badami-shiva.JPG *License:* Public domain *Contributors:* Original uploader was Ashwatham at en.wikipedia 61
Figure 34 *Source:* https://en.wikipedia.org/w/index.php?title=File:Papanatha_temple_at_Pattadakal.jpg *License:* Creative Commons Attribution-Sharealike 3.0 *Contributors:* 23:09, 1 August 2008 (UTC 62
Figure 35 *Source:* https://en.wikipedia.org/w/index.php?title=File:Aihole_inscription_of_Ravi_Kirti.jpg *License:* Creative Commons Attribution-Sharealike 3.0 *Contributors:* Dineshkannambadi (talk) 12:36, 1 August 2008 (UTC) 63
Figure 36 *Source:* https://en.wikipedia.org/w/index.php?title=File:Cave_temple_number_3_at_Badami.jpg *License:* Creative Commons Attribution-Sharealike 3.0 *Contributors:* Dineshkannambadi (talk) 03:32, 13 August 2008 (UTC) 65
Image *Source:* https://en.wikipedia.org/w/index.php?title=File:GBerunda.JPG *License:* Creative Commons Attribution-ShareAlike 3.0 Unported *Contributors:* Sarvagnya 65
Image *Source:* https://en.wikipedia.org/w/index.php?title=File:Cscr-featured.svg *License:* GNU Lesser General Public License *Contributors:* Anomie 69
Image *Source:* https://en.wikipedia.org/w/index.php?title=File:Commons-logo.svg *License:* logo *Contributors:* Anomie, Callanecc, CambridgeBayWeather, Jo-Jo Eumerus, RHaworth 69

Image *Source:* https://en.wikipedia.org/w/index.php?title=File:Harshavardhana_Circa_AD_606-647.jpg *License:* GNU Free Documentation License *Contributors:* पाटलिपुत्र ... 70
Figure 37 *Source:* https://en.wikipedia.org/w/index.php?title=File:Palace_ruins_2.JPG *License:* Creative Commons Attribution-Sharealike 3.0 *Contributors:* User:Viraat2000 ... 71
Figure 38 *Source:* https://en.wikipedia.org/w/index.php?title=File:Harshabysumchung.jpg *Contributors:* Sum Chung ... 72
Image *Source:* https://en.wikipedia.org/w/index.php?title=File:Wikisource-logo.svg *License:* Creative Commons Attribution-Sharealike 3.0 *Contributors:* ChrisiPK, Guillom, INeverCry, Jarekt, JuTa, Leyo, Lokal Profil, MichaelMaggs, NielsF, Rei-artur, Rocket000, Romaine, Steinsplitter ... 74
Image *Source:* https://en.wikipedia.org/w/index.php?title=File:Flag_of_Afghanistan.svg *Contributors:* 5ko, Ahmad2099, Alex Great, Alkari, Amateur55, Andres gb.ldc, Ankry, Antonsusi, Avala, Bastique, BotMultichill, BotMultichillT, Cycn, Dancingwombatsrule, Dbenbenn, Denelson83, Denniss, Domhnall, Duduziq, Erlenmeyer, F l a n k e r, Farhod, Frigotoni, Fry1989, Gast32, Golden Bosnian Lily, GoldenRainbow, Happenstance, Henriquebachelor, Herbythyme, Homo lupus, Ilfga, Illegitimate Barrister, Jarekt, Jebulon, JoaoPedro10029, Khwahan, Klemen Kocjancic, Koefbac, Kookaburra, Lokal Profil, Ludger1961, Lumia1234, MPF, Mattes, MrPanyGoff, Myself488, Neq00, Nersy, Nightstallion, O, Orange Tuesday, Palosirkka, Prev, RainbowSilver, Rainforest tropicana, Reisio, Ricordisamoa, Rocket000, Sangjinhwa, Sarang, Sarilho1, SiBr4, Smaug the Golden, Smooth O, Sojah, Solar Police, Stasyan117, SteveGOLD, Stewi101015, Supreme Dragon, TFerenczy, Tabasco~commonswiki, Tcfc2349, Unma.af, Zscout370, \\'arrior 786, Şêr, ייהליושמר, 李焜泽 567, 33 anonymous edits ... 75
Image *Source:* https://en.wikipedia.org/w/index.php?title=File:Flag_of_Pakistan.svg *License:* Public Domain *Contributors:* User:Zscout370 ... 75
Image *Source:* https://en.wikipedia.org/w/index.php?title=File:Flag_of_Bangladesh.svg *License:* Public Domain *Contributors:* User:SKopp ... 75
Image *Source:* https://en.wikipedia.org/w/index.php?title=File:North_Gateway_-_Rear_Side_-_Stupa_1_-_Sanchi_Hill_2013-02-21_4480-4481.JPG *License:* Creative Commons Attribution 3.0 *Contributors:* Biswarup Ganguly ... 76
Image *Source:* https://en.wikipedia.org/w/index.php?title=File:Sindh_700ad.jpg *License:* Creative Commons Attribution 3.0 *Contributors:* Thomas Lessman (Contact!) ... 77
Image *Source:* https://en.wikipedia.org/w/index.php?title=File:Umayyad_Flag.svg *License:* Public Domain *Contributors:* Ch1902 ... 77
Figure 39 *Source:* https://en.wikipedia.org/w/index.php?title=File:Muhammad_bin_Qasim's_expedition_into_Sindh.png *License:* Creative Commons Attribution-Sharealike 3.0 *Contributors:* User:Khateeb88 ... 78
Figure 40 *Source:* https://en.wikipedia.org/w/index.php?title=File:QASIM.PNG *License:* GNU Free Documentation License *Contributors:* MODIFIED from IVC_Map.png. Disclaimer by en:User:Dbachmann and based off the referenced map ... 80
Figure 41 *Source:* https://en.wikipedia.org/w/index.php?title=File:Arabsumf.png *License:* Creative Commons Attribution 3.0 *Contributors:* Maglorbd ... 81
Figure 42 *Source:* https://en.wikipedia.org/w/index.php?title=File:Indian_Kanauj_triangle_map.svg *License:* Creative Commons Attribution-Sharealike 3.0 *Contributors:* Aschroet, Capankajsmilyo, Chhora, Io Herodotus, Nikotins, Pierpao, Planemad, Roland zh, Wieralee, Zykasaa, 1 anonymous edits ... 88
Figure 43 *Source:* https//en.wikipedia.org *Contributors:* Holenarasipura ... 92
Figure 44 *Source:* https://en.wikipedia.org/w/index.php?title=File:VarahaVishnuAvatarPratiharaKings850-900CE.jpg *License:* Creative Commons Attribution-ShareAlike 3.0 Unported *Contributors:* User:PHGCOM, User:PHGCOM ... 94
Image *Source:* https://en.wikipedia.org/w/index.php?title=File:Vishnu_Trivikrama_Delhi_National_Museum_ni02-24.jpg *Contributors:* User:G41rn8 ... 96
Image *Source:* https://en.wikipedia.org/w/index.php?title=File:Teli_ka_mandir_fort_Gwalior_-_panoramio_-_Gyanendrasinghchauha..._(1).jpg *License:* Creative Commons Attribution 3.0 *Contributors:* JiriMatejicek, Kalbbes ... 96
Image *Source:* https://en.wikipedia.org/w/index.php?title=File:Wikiquote-logo.svg *License:* Public Domain *Contributors:* Rei-artur ... 100
Figure 45 *Source:* https://en.wikipedia.org/w/index.php?title=File:Ellora_Kailash_temple_Shiva_panel.jpg *License:* Creative Commons Attribution 2.5 *Contributors:* User:QuartierLatin1968, User:QuartierLatin1968 ... 103
Figure 46 *Source:* https://en.wikipedia.org/w/index.php?title=File:Ellora-Jain-cave.jpg *License:* GNU Free Documentation License *Contributors:* KRS(talk). Original uploader was KRS at en.wikipedia ... 103
Figure 47 *Source:* https://en.wikipedia.org/w/index.php?title=File:Rashtrakuta-empire-map.svg *License:* Creative Commons Attribution-ShareAlike 3.0 Unported *Contributors:* Mlpkr ... 104
Figure 48 *Source:* https://en.wikipedia.org/w/index.php?title=File:Kasivisvanatha_temple_at_Pattadakal.jpg *License:* Creative Commons Attribution-Sharealike 3.0 *Contributors:* Dineshkannambadi (talk) 23:13, 30 July 2008 (UTC) ... 110
Figure 49 *Source:* https://en.wikipedia.org/w/index.php?title=File:Ellora-Kailasanatha-5.jpg *License:* GNU Free Documentation License *Contributors:* KRS(talk) ... 112
Figure 50 *Source:* https://en.wikipedia.org/w/index.php?title=File:Jain_Narayana_temple1_at_Pattadakal.jpg *License:* Creative Commons Attribution-Sharealike 3.0 *Contributors:* Dineshkannambadi (talk) 02:46, 13 August 2008 (UTC) ... 115
Figure 51 *Source:* https://en.wikipedia.org/w/index.php?title=File:Kavi_file2.jpg *License:* Creative Commons Attribution-Sharealike 3.0 *Contributors:* Jrsanthosh (talk) ... 116
Figure 52 *Source:* https://en.wikipedia.org/w/index.php?title=File:Kailasha_temple_at_ellora.JPG *License:* Creative Commons Attribution-Sharealike 2.5 *Contributors:* Pratheepps ... 118
Figure 53 *Source:* https://en.wikipedia.org/w/index.php?title=File:Kuknur_Navalinga_temples.JPG *License:* GNU Free Documentation License *Contributors:* en:User:Dineshkannambadi ... 119
Figure 54 *Source:* https://en.wikipedia.org/w/index.php?title=File:Old_Kannada_inscription_in_the_mantapa_of_Navalinga_temple_at_Kuknur.jpg *License:* GNU Free Documentation License *Contributors:* en:User:Dineshkannambadi ... 120
Image *Source:* https://en.wikipedia.org/w/index.php?title=File:Asia_800ad.jpg *License:* Creative Commons Attribution 3.0 *Contributors:* Artix Kreiger 2, BotMultichill, Denniss, File Upload Bot (Magnus Manske), Gecary, Grendill, Gryffindor, JuTa, Kaba, OgreBot 2, P199, Rocket000, Sreejithk2000, Takeaway, Tatmadav, Unserefahne, Verdy p ... 123
Image *Source:* https://en.wikipedia.org/w/index.php?title=File:Flag_of_Nepal.svg *License:* Public Domain *Contributors:* Drawn by User:Pumbaa80, User:Achim1999 ... 124
Figure 55 *Source:* https://en.wikipedia.org/w/index.php?title=File:Indian_Kanauj_triangle_map.svg *License:* Creative Commons Attribution-Sharealike 3.0 *Contributors:* Aschroet, Capankajsmilyo, Chhora, Io Herodotus, Nikotins, Pierpao, Planemad, Roland zh, Wieralee, Zykasaa, 1 anonymous edits ... 126
Figure 56 *Source:* https://en.wikipedia.org/w/index.php?title=File:Nalanda.jpg *License:* Creative Commons Attribution-Sharealike 2.5 *Contributors:* myself ... 132
Figure 57 *Source:* https://en.wikipedia.org/w/index.php?title=File:Atisha.jpg *License:* Public Domain *Contributors:* Unknown [Tibet (a Kadampa monastery)] ... 133
Figure 58 *Source:* https://en.wikipedia.org/w/index.php?title=File:Lalita_statue.jpg *License:* Creative Commons Attribution-Sharealike 3.0 *Contributors:* User:Fæ ... 135
Figure 59 *Source:* https://en.wikipedia.org/w/index.php?title=File:Carved_Conch.jpg *License:* Creative Commons Attribution-Sharealike 2.0 *Contributors:* Claire H. ... 135
Figure 60 *Source:* https://en.wikipedia.org/w/index.php?title=File:Khasarpana_Lokesvara.jpg *License:* Creative Commons Attribution-Sharealike 2.0 *Contributors:* Hyougushi ... 136
Figure 61 *Source:* https//en.wikipedia.org *License:* Creative Commons Attribution-ShareAlike 3.0 Unported *Contributors:* User:Sailko, user:sailko 136
Figure 62 *Source:* https://en.wikipedia.org/w/index.php?title=File:Naogaon_Paharpur_11Oct12_IMG_3656.jpg *Contributors:* User:Krabdallah 137
Figure 63 *Source:* https://en.wikipedia.org/w/index.php?title=File:Central_Sherine_deccor-Paharpur.jpg *License:* Public Domain *Contributors:* User:Ori~ ... 137
Figure 64 *Source:* https://en.wikipedia.org/w/index.php?title=File:Naqi_model.jpg *License:* Creative Commons Attribution 3.0 *Contributors:* Ali Naqi, modified by Hafizur Rahaman ... 138
Figure 65 *Source:* https://en.wikipedia.org/w/index.php?title=File:Vikramshila_2012-08-10-17.48.39.jpg *License:* Creative Commons Attribution-Sharealike 3.0 *Contributors:* User:Prataparya ... 138
Image *Source:* https://en.wikipedia.org/w/index.php?title=File:Flag_of_Maldives.svg *License:* Public Domain *Contributors:* user:Nightstallion 142
Image *Source:* https://en.wikipedia.org/w/index.php?title=File:Flag_of_Sri_Lanka.svg *License:* Public Domain *Contributors:* Zscout370 ... 142
Image *Source:* https://en.wikipedia.org/w/index.php?title=File:Western-chalukya-empire-map.svg *License:* Creative Commons Attribution-ShareAlike 3.0 Unported *Contributors:* Mlpkr ... 148
Figure 66 *Source:* https://en.wikipedia.org/w/index.php?title=File:Virgal_(hero_stone)_in_Praneshvara_temple_at_Talagunda.JPG *License:* Creative Commons Attribution-Sharealike 3.0 *Contributors:* User:Dineshkannambadi ... 150
Figure 67 *Source:* https://en.wikipedia.org/w/index.php?title=File:Old_Kannada_inscription_(c.1057)_in_Kalleshvara_temple_at_Hire_Hadagali.jpg *License:* Creative Commons Attribution-Sharealike 3.0 *Contributors:* User:Dineshkannambadi ... 151
Figure 68 *Source:* https://en.wikipedia.org/w/index.php?title=File:Itagi_Mahadeva_temple.JPG *License:* GNU Free Documentation License *Contributors:* Dinesh Kannambadi (User:Dineshkannambadi) ... 151
Figure 69 *Source:* https://en.wikipedia.org/w/index.php?title=File:Western_Chalukyas_of_Kalyana_King_Somesvara_I_Trailokyamalla_1043-1068.jpg *License:* GNU Free Documentation License *Contributors:* पाटलिपुत्र ... 154

Figure 70 *Source:* https://en.wikipedia.org/w/index.php?title=File:Chalukyas_of_Kalyana_(Western_Chalukyas)_Possibly_King_Somesvara_IV_Chalukya._1181-4_1189.jpg *License:* GNU Free Documentation License *Contributors:* पाटलिपुत्र ... 154

Figure 71 *Source:* https://en.wikipedia.org/w/index.php?title=File:Mallikarjuna_group_of_temples_at_Badami.jpg *License:* Creative Commons Attribution-Sharealike 3.0 *Contributors:* Dineshkannambadi (talk) 23:11, 7 August 2008 (UTC) ... 156

Figure 72 *Source:* https://en.wikipedia.org/w/index.php?title=File:Open_mantapa_(hall)_in_Kalleshvara_temple_at_Bagali_1.JPG *License:* Creative Commons Attribution-Sharealike 3.0 *Contributors:* User:Dineshkannambadi ... 157

Figure 73 *Source:* https://en.wikipedia.org/w/index.php?title=File:Basava_statue.jpg *License:* GNU Free Documentation License *Contributors:* Kajasudhakarababu∼commonswiki, MGA73bot2, OgreBot 2, Roland zh, TeleComNasSprVen ... 161

Figure 74 *Source:* https://en.wikipedia.org/w/index.php?title=File:Virgal_(hero_stone)_in_Kedareshvara_temple_at_Balligavi4.JPG *License:* Creative Commons Attribution-Sharealike 3.0 *Contributors:* User:Dineshkannambadi ... 161

Figure 75 *Source:* https://en.wikipedia.org/w/index.php?title=File:Kirtimukha_(gargoyle)_sculpture_on_vesara_tower_in_the_Kedareshvara_temple_at_Balligavi.jpg *License:* GNU Free Documentation License *Contributors:* -revi, Dineshkannambadi, File Upload Bot (Magnus Manske), MGA73bot2, MathewTownsend, OgreBot 2, Papa November, Roland zh, Xufanc ... 163

Figure 76 *Source:* https://en.wikipedia.org/w/index.php?title=File:Tripurantakesvara_Temple_Sculpture_and_Grill_work_at_Balligavi.jpg *License:* GNU Free Documentation License *Contributors:* File Upload Bot (Magnus Manske), MGA73bot2, OgreBot 2, Papa November, Roland zh ... 165

Figure 77 *Source:* https://en.wikipedia.org/w/index.php?title=File:Akkamahadevi_Vachana2.JPG *License:* GNU Free Documentation License *Contributors:* Amarrg ... 166

Figure 78 *Source:* https://en.wikipedia.org/w/index.php?title=File:Siddesvara_Temple_Shrine_at_Haveri.JPG *License:* GNU Free Documentation License *Contributors:* File Upload Bot (Magnus Manske), MGA73bot2, OgreBot 2, Papa November, Roland zh ... 167

Figure 79 *Source:* https://en.wikipedia.org/w/index.php?title=File:Ornate_pillars_in_the_Saraswati_temple_at_Gadag.jpg *License:* GNU Free Documentation License *Contributors:* AnRo0002, Dineshkannambadi, File Upload Bot (Magnus Manske), MGA73bot2, Marcus Cyron, Neithsabes, OgreBot 2, Papa November, Roland zh ... 168

Figure 80 *Source:* https://en.wikipedia.org/w/index.php?title=File:Jain_temple_at_Lakkundi.jpg *License:* Creative Commons Attribution-Sharealike 3.0 *Contributors:* User:Rkiran josh ... 169

Figure 81 *Source:* https://en.wikipedia.org/w/index.php?title=File:Old_Kannada_inscription_(1112_CE)_of_King_Vikramaditya_VI_in_the_Mahadeva_temple_at_Itagi.jpg *License:* GNU Free Documentation License *Contributors:* Abhishekjoshi, Cpt.a.haddock, Dineshkannambadi, File Upload Bot (Magnus Manske), Green Mostaza, MGA73bot2, Mhmrodrigues, OgreBot 2, Papa November, Roland zh ... 170

Image *Source:* https://en.wikipedia.org/w/index.php?title=File:Pallava_territories.png *License:* GNU Free Documentation License *Contributors:* BotMultichill, BotMultichillT, Discanto, Electionworld, Roland zh ... 173

Figure 82 *Source:* https://en.wikipedia.org/w/index.php?title=File:Kailasanathar_Temple.jpg *License:* Creative Commons Attribution 2.0 *Contributors:* Keshav Mukund Kandhadai ... 175

Image *Source:* https://en.wikipedia.org/w/index.php?title=File:Kailasawaathar_innercourt.jpg *License:* Public Domain *Contributors:* R. Mayooranathan ... 175

Image *Source:* https://en.wikipedia.org/w/index.php?title=File:01Kailasanathar_Temple_Rich_Architecture_in_Sculptures_Design.jpg *License:* Creative Commons Attribution 2.0 *Contributors:* FlickreviewR, INeverCry, Ismoon, Keyan20, Parabolooidal, Roland zh ... 175

Image *Source:* https://en.wikipedia.org/w/index.php?title=File:Kailayanathar2.jpg *License:* Creative Commons Attribution-Sharealike 3.0 *Contributors:* User:Ssriram mt ... 175

Figure 83 *Source:* https://en.wikipedia.org/w/index.php?title=File:Pallavas_of_Coromandel.jpg *License:* GNU Free Documentation License *Contributors:* Balajijagadesh, DenghiùComm, Jeff G., Nizil Shah, पाटलिपुत्र ... 178

Figure 84 *Source:* https://en.wikipedia.org/w/index.php?title=File:Shore_Temple_(Detail_of_North_Face,_2011-05-28).jpg *License:* Creative Commons Attribution-Sharealike 3.0 *Contributors:* User:Pratyeka ... 180

Image *Source:* https://en.wikipedia.org/w/index.php?title=File:Pallava_Pillar_Mandagappattu.png *Contributors:* User:Nilo.boss ... 180

Figure 85 *Source:* https://en.wikipedia.org/w/index.php?title=File:Mamallapuram_Five_Rathas.jpg *License:* GNU Free Documentation License *Contributors:* Venu62 ... 183

Figure 86 *Source:* https://en.wikipedia.org/w/index.php?title=File:Elephant_mpuram.jpg *License:* Public Domain *Contributors:* Vrraghy ... 183

Image *Source:* https://en.wikipedia.org/w/index.php?title=File:Padlock-silver.svg *Contributors:* AzaToth, BotMultichill, BotMultichillT, Gurch, Jarekt, Kallerna, Multichill, Perhelion, Rd232, Riana, Sarang, Siebrand, Steinsplitter, 4 anonymous edits ... 187

Image *Source:* https://en.wikipedia.org/w/index.php?title=File:Flag_of_Malaysia.svg *Contributors:* , and ... 187

Image *Source:* https://en.wikipedia.org/w/index.php?title=File:Flag_of_Singapore.svg *License:* Public Domain *Contributors:* Various ... 187

Image *Source:* https://en.wikipedia.org/w/index.php?title=File:Flag_of_Indonesia.svg *License:* Public Domain *Contributors:* Drawn by User:SKopp 187

Image *Source:* https://en.wikipedia.org/w/index.php?title=File:Thanjavur_temple.jpg *License:* Public Domain *Contributors:* AnRo0002, Bgag, Elcobbola, Fransvannes, Maximaximax, OgreBot 2, Roland zh, Woudloper ... 189

Figure 87 *Source:* https://en.wikipedia.org/w/index.php?title=File:South_India_in_BC_300.jpg *License:* Creative Commons Attribution-Sharealike 3.0 *Contributors:* User:Yon Man33 ... 193

Figure 88 *Source:* https://en.wikipedia.org/w/index.php?title=File:Uttama_coin.png *License:* Creative Commons Attribution-Sharealike 2.5 *Contributors:* Marcus334, Mhmrodrigues, Mindmatrix, Roland zh, Tetraktys, Venu62∼commonswiki, 3 anonymous edits ... 194

Figure 89 *Source:* https://en.wikipedia.org/w/index.php?title=File:Raraja_detail.png *License:* Public Domain *Contributors:* User:Venu62∼commonswiki ... 195

Figure 90 *Source:* https://en.wikipedia.org/w/index.php?title=File:Gopuram_Corner_View_of_Thanjavur_Brihadeeswara_Temple..JPG *Contributors:* User:KARTY JazZ ... 196

Figure 91 *Source:* https://en.wikipedia.org/w/index.php?title=File:Brihadeeswara_Temple_Entrance_Gopurams,_Thanjavur.JPG *Contributors:* User:KARTY JazZ ... 197

Figure 92 *Source:* https://en.wikipedia.org/w/index.php?title=File:Ship_compartments.jpg *License:* GNU Free Documentation License *Contributors:* AntanO, OgreBot 2, Speravir ... 197

Figure 93 *Source:* https://en.wikipedia.org/w/index.php?title=File:Airavateswara_Temple,Darasuram_in_Thanjavur_District..JPG *Contributors:* User:KARTY JazZ ... 198

Figure 94 *Source:* https://en.wikipedia.org/w/index.php?title=File:Rajaraja_mural-2.jpg *License:* Public Domain *Contributors:* Rajaraja_mural.jpg: Original uploader was Venu62 at en.wikipedia derivative work: Keyan20 (talk) ... 200

Figure 95 *Source:* https://en.wikipedia.org/w/index.php?title=File:Chera_kingdom,_chieftaincies,_and_Chola_mandalams_c._11th_century_(zoom).svg *Contributors:* User:Cpt.a.haddock ... 203

Figure 96 *Source:* https://en.wikipedia.org/w/index.php?title=File:Anchor_of_an_unknown_Lola(ship).jpg *License:* Creative Commons Attribution 3.0 *Contributors:* Everdawn, Onel5969 ... 208

Figure 97 *Source:* https://en.wikipedia.org/w/index.php?title=File:Thanjavur_temple.jpg *License:* Public Domain *Contributors:* AnRo0002, Bgag, Elcobbola, Fransvannes, Maximaximax, OgreBot 2, Roland zh, Woudloper ... 210

Figure 98 *Source:* https://en.wikipedia.org/w/index.php?title=File:Ornamented_pillar_Darasuram.jpg *License:* Creative Commons Attribution 3.0 *Contributors:* RavichandarMy coffee shop. Ravichandar84 at en.wikipedia ... 211

Figure 99 *Source:* https://en.wikipedia.org/w/index.php?title=File:Cholacrop.jpg *License:* Creative Commons Attribution-Sharealike 2.5 *Contributors:* Robert Nash ... 213

Figure 100 *Source:* https://en.wikipedia.org/w/index.php?title=File:NatarajaMET.JPG *License:* Creative Commons Attribution-Sharealike 2.5 *Contributors:* User Kaysov on en.wikipedia ... 215

Figure 101 *Source:* https://en.wikipedia.org/w/index.php?title=File:StandingHanumanCholaDynasty11thCentury.jpg *License:* Creative Commons Attribution-Sharealike 3.0,2.5,2.0,1.0 *Contributors:* PHGCOM ... 216

Image *Source:* https://en.wikipedia.org/w/index.php?title=File:Western-ganga-empire-map.svg *License:* Creative Commons Attribution-ShareAlike 3.0 Unported *Contributors:* Mlpkr ... 221

Figure 102 *Source:* https://en.wikipedia.org/w/index.php?title=File:TalakadInscription.jpg *License:* Public Domain *Contributors:* Edward P Rice 223

Figure 103 *Source:* https://en.wikipedia.org/w/index.php?title=File:Ganga_file.jpg *License:* Creative Commons Attribution-Sharealike 3.0 *Contributors:* Jrsanthosh ... 223

Figure 104 *Source:* https://en.wikipedia.org/w/index.php?title=File:Bharatha.jpg *License:* Creative Commons Attribution 2.5 *Contributors:* Nikhil Varma ... 226

Figure 105 *Source:* https://en.wikipedia.org/w/index.php?title=File:Panchakuta_Basadi_(10th_century_AD)_at_Kambadahalli.JPG *License:* Creative Commons Attribution-Sharealike 3.0 *Contributors:* User:Dineshkannambadi ... 228

Figure 106 *Source:* https://en.wikipedia.org/w/index.php?title=File:Old_Kannada_inscription_(908-938_AD)_of_Western_Ganga_dynasty_King_Ereyappa_on_hero_stone_at_Begur.jpg *Contributors:* Holenarasipura ... 229

Figure 107 *Source:* https://en.wikipedia.org/w/index.php?title=File:Rock_edit_-_inscription.jpg *License:* Creative Commons Attribution 2.5 *Contributors:* Nikhil Varma ... 231

Figure 108 *Source:* https://en.wikipedia.org/w/index.php?title=File:A_mantapa_(hall)_in_Panchakuta_Basadi_at_Kambadahalli.JPG *License:* Creative Commons Attribution-Sharealike 3.0 *Contributors:* User:Dineshkannambadi ... 231

Figure 109 *Source:* https://en.wikipedia.org/w/index.php?title=File:Gomateswara.jpg *License:* Attribution *Contributors:* FSII, Fontema, Guanaco, Hystrix, Jungpionier, Kilom691, MPF, Ranveig, Roland zh, Soerfm, Str4nd, Thuresson, Vssun, 8 anonymous edits 232

Figure 110 *Source:* https://en.wikipedia.org/w/index.php?title=File:Kalleshvara_Temple_at_Aralaguppe_(10th_century_AD).JPG *License:* Creative Commons Attribution-Sharealike 3.0 *Contributors:* User:Dineshkannambadi 233

Figure 111 *Source:* https://en.wikipedia.org/w/index.php?title=File:Old_Kannada_inscription_Hero_Stone_from_9th_century_AD_in_Kalleshvara_Temple_at_Aralaguppe.jpg *License:* Creative Commons Attribution-Sharealike 3.0 *Contributors:* User:Dineshkannambadi 234

Figure 112 *Source:* https://en.wikipedia.org/w/index.php?title=File:Atakur_memorial_stone_with_inscription_in_old_Kannada_(949_C.E.).jpg *License:* Creative Commons Attribution-Sharealike 3.0 *Contributors:* User:Holenarasipura 236

Figure 113 *Source:* https://en.wikipedia.org/w/index.php?title=File:View_of_Chandragupta_Basadi_at_Chandragiri_hill_in_Shravanabelagola.jpg *License:* Creative Commons Attribution-Sharealike 3.0 *Contributors:* Dineshkannambadi (talk) 01:06, 21 May 2008 (UTC) 237

Figure 114 *Source:* https://en.wikipedia.org/w/index.php?title=File:Chandragiri_hill_temple_complex_at_Shravanabelagola.jpg *License:* Creative Commons Attribution-Sharealike 3.0 *Contributors:* Dineshkannambadi (talk) 00:42, 21 May 2008 (UTC) 238

Figure 115 *Source:* https://en.wikipedia.org/w/index.php?title=File:Relief_of_Jain_tirthankara_in_the_Panchakuta_Basadi_at_Kambadahalli.jpg *License:* GNU Free Documentation License *Contributors:* en:User:Dineshkannambadi 239

Figure 116 *Source:* https://en.wikipedia.org/w/index.php?title=File:Chavundaraya_Basadi_on_Chandragiri_hill_at_Shravanabelagola.jpg *License:* Creative Commons Attribution-Sharealike 3.0 *Contributors:* Dineshkannambadi (talk) 00:48, 21 May 2008 (UTC) 240

Figure 117 *Source:* https://en.wikipedia.org/w/index.php?title=File:Old_Kannada_inscription_dated_981_CE_in_Vindyagiri_hill_at_Shravanabelagola.jpg *License:* GNU Free Documentation License *Contributors:* en:User:Dineshkannambadi 242

Image *Source:* https://en.wikipedia.org/w/index.php?title=File:Flag_of_vijaynagara.jpg *Contributors:* User:Vydya.areyur 244

Image *Source:* https://en.wikipedia.org/w/index.php?title=File:Lepakshi...jpg *License:* Creative Commons Attribution-Sharealike 3.0 *Contributors:* User:Vinay332211 245

Figure 118 *Source:* https://en.wikipedia.org/w/index.php?title=File:Ramappa1.jpg *License:* Creative Commons Attribution-Sharealike 3.0 *Contributors:* Ravichandrae 251

Figure 119 *Source:* https://en.wikipedia.org/w/index.php?title=File:Rudrama_devi_vigraham.JPG *License:* Creative Commons Attribution-Sharealike 3.0 *Contributors:* User:Bhaskaranaidu 252

Figure 120 *Source:* https://en.wikipedia.org/w/index.php?title=File:Koh-i-Noor_old_version_copy.jpg *License:* GNU Free Documentation License *Contributors:* Borvan53, Chris 73, Kluka, Ra'ike 253

Figure 121 *Source:* https://en.wikipedia.org/w/index.php?title=File:Kakatiya_Kala_Thoranam_(Warangal_Gate)_and_Ruins.jpg *License:* Creative Commons Attribution-Sharealike 3.0 *Contributors:* User:Sridhar Raju 258

Image *Source:* https://en.wikipedia.org/w/index.php?title=File:Royal_Peacock_Barge_LACMA_M.82.154.jpg *Contributors:* Fæ, JMCC1 262

Figure 122 *Source:* https://en.wikipedia.org/w/index.php?title=File:Edilpur_copperplate.jpg *License:* Creative Commons Attribution-Sharealike 3.0 *Contributors:* Mizan1947 264

Image *Source:* https://en.wikipedia.org/w/index.php?title=File:Delhi_Sultanate_Flag_(catalan_atlas).png *Contributors:* User:History of Persia 269

Image *Source:* https://en.wikipedia.org/w/index.php?title=File:Tughlaq_dynasty_1321_-_1398_ad.PNG *License:* Public domain *Contributors:* . Later version(s) were uploaded by 269

Figure 123 *Source:* https://en.wikipedia.org/w/index.php?title=File:Mamluk_dynasty_1206_-_1290_ad.GIF *License:* Public domain *Contributors:* Athaenara, Capankajsmilyo, File Upload Bot (Magnus Manske), Quadell, Roland zh, Sreejithk2000, Takabeg 274

Figure 124 *Source:* https://en.wikipedia.org/w/index.php?title=File:Alai_Gate_and_Qutub_Minar.jpg *License:* Creative Commons Attribution-Sharealike 2.0 *Contributors:* Dennis Jarvis from Halifax, Canada 275

Figure 125 *Source:* https://en.wikipedia.org/w/index.php?title=File:Sultanat_von_Delhi_Tughluq-Dynastie.png *License:* GNU Free Documentation License *Contributors:* Jungpionier 277

Figure 126 *Source:* https://en.wikipedia.org/w/index.php?title=File:A_View_from_Daulatabad_Fort.jpg *License:* Creative Commons Attribution-Sharealike 3.0 *Contributors:* User:Vu2sga 278

Figure 127 *Source:* https://en.wikipedia.org/w/index.php?title=File:Forced_token_currency_coin_of_Muhammad_bin_Tughlak.jpg *License:* Creative Commons Attribution-Sharealike 3.0 *Contributors:* Drnsreedhar1959 278

Image *Source:* https://en.wikipedia.org/w/index.php?title=File:The_Lat_of_Ferozeh_Shah_-Delhi-..jpg *License:* Public Domain *Contributors:* Bourne, Samuel 279

Image *Source:* https://en.wikipedia.org/w/index.php?title=File:Ashoka_Pillar_at_Feroze_Shah_Kotla,_Delhi_05.JPG *License:* Creative Commons Attribution-Sharealike 3.0 *Contributors:* User:Dhamijalok 279

Figure 128 *Source:* https://en.wikipedia.org/w/index.php?title=File:Baburs_Invasion_1526.gif *License:* Creative Commons Attribution 2.5 *Contributors:* Stefan Bollmann 282

Image *Source:* https://en.wikipedia.org/w/index.php?title=File:Somnath_temple_ruins_(1869).jpg *License:* Public Domain *Contributors:* Anhilwara, Hansmuller, Magog the Ogre, Ms Sarah Welch, P199, Razr Nation, Rosarino, 1 anonymous edits 284

Image *Source:* https://en.wikipedia.org/w/index.php?title=File:Benares-_The_Golden_Temple,_India,_ca._1915_(IMP-CSCNWW33-OS14-66).jpg *Contributors:* Auntof6, Fæ, OgreBot 2, Oo91, Redtigerxyz, Roland zh 285

Image *Source:* https://en.wikipedia.org/w/index.php?title=File:Nalanda_University_India_ruins.jpg *License:* Creative Commons Attribution 2.0 *Contributors:* A ri gi bod, Bpilgrim, FlickreviewR, G41rn8, Trijnstel, Vyzasatya, 2 anonymous edits 285

Image *Source:* https://en.wikipedia.org/w/index.php?title=File:Temple_de_Mînâkshî01.jpg *License:* Creative Commons Attribution-Sharealike 3.0,2.5,2.0,1.0 *Contributors:* Bernard Gagnon 285

Image *Source:* https://en.wikipedia.org/w/index.php?title=File:Warangal_fort.jpg *License:* Public domain *Contributors:* Andy Dingley, Hydrargyrum, Kajasudhakarababu∼commonswiki, Lomita, Materialscientist, O (bot), OgreBot 2, Roland zh, 1 anonymous edits 285

Image *Source:* https://en.wikipedia.org/w/index.php?title=File:Elevation_of_Kirtistambh_Rudramahalaya_Sidhpur_Gujarat_India.jpg *License:* Public Domain *Contributors:* Nizil Shah 286

Image *Source:* https://en.wikipedia.org/w/index.php?title=File:Rani_ki_vav1.jpg *Contributors:* User:Kshitij Charania 286

Image *Source:* https//en.wikipedia.org *Contributors:* User:Ms Sarah Welch 286

Image *Source:* https://en.wikipedia.org/w/index.php?title=File:Hunting_Party_with_the_Sultan_Jean_Baptiste_Vanmour_18th_century.JPG *License:* Public Domain *Contributors:* BotMultichill, Cretanforever, JMCC1, Leyo, Mercurywoodrose, Vincent Steenberg 290

Figure 129 *Source:* https://en.wikipedia.org/w/index.php?title=File:Qutab.jpg *License:* Creative Commons Attribution-Sharealike 2.0 *Contributors:* 444pixels, FlickreviewR, Jungpionier, Look2See1, Roland zh 293

Image *Source:* https://en.wikipedia.org/w/index.php?title=File:Delhi_Sultanate_under_Khalji_dynasty_-_based_on_A_Historical_Atlas_of_South_Asia.svg *Contributors:* User:Utcursch, User:Uwe Dedering 296

Figure 130 *Source:* https://en.wikipedia.org/w/index.php?title=File:Copper_coin_of_Alauddin_Khilji.jpg *License:* GNU Free Documentation License *Contributors:* Alfons Åberg, Ekabhishek, File Upload Bot (Magnus Manske), OgreBot 2, Utcursch 297

Figure 131 *Source:* https://en.wikipedia.org/w/index.php?title=File:Koh-i-noor_(after_1852)_black.png *License:* Public Domain *Contributors:* Ahnode 300

Image *Source:* https://en.wikipedia.org/w/index.php?title=File:Gujarat_Sultanate_Flag.gif *License:* Creative Commons Zero *Contributors:* User:Nizil Shah 307

Figure 132 *Source:* https://en.wikipedia.org/w/index.php?title=File:Bastions_at_the_Old_City_of_Tughlaqabad.JPG *License:* Creative Commons Attribution-Sharealike 3.0 *Contributors:* User:Sachi.caesar 310

Figure 133 *Source:* https://en.wikipedia.org/w/index.php?title=File:Sultanat_von_Delhi_Tughluq-Dynastie.png *License:* GNU Free Documentation License *Contributors:* Jungpionier 312

Figure 134 *Source:* https://en.wikipedia.org/w/index.php?title=File:Forced_token_currency_coin_of_Muhammad_bin_Tughlak.jpg *License:* Creative Commons Attribution-Sharealike 3.0 *Contributors:* Drnsreedhar1959 314

Figure 135 *Source:* https://en.wikipedia.org/w/index.php?title=File:West_Gate_of_Feruzabad_since_destroyed.jpg *License:* Public Domain *Contributors:* Orme, William (fl. 1794 - 1819) 316

Figure 136 *Source:* https://en.wikipedia.org/w/index.php?title=File:Wazirabad_mosque.jpg *License:* Creative Commons Attribution-Sharealike 3.0 *Contributors:* User:Mohitnarayanan 317

Figure 137 *Source:* https://en.wikipedia.org/w/index.php?title=File:Tome_of_Shah_Rukn-e-Alam.jpg *License:* Creative Commons Attribution-Sharealike 3.0 *Contributors:* User:ZainShahid117 322

Figure 138 *Source:* https://en.wikipedia.org/w/index.php?title=File:Tughlaqabad_Fort,_Tughlaqabad,_Delhi.jpg *License:* Creative Commons Attribution 2.0 *Contributors:* Saad.Akhtar 324

Figure 139 *Source:* https://en.wikipedia.org/w/index.php?title=File:Ghiyath_aldin_tughluq_tomb.JPG *License:* GNU Free Documentation License *Contributors:* Blademasterx, Johnbod, OgreBot 2 324

Figure 140 *Source:* https://en.wikipedia.org/w/index.php?title=File:Tughlaqabad_fort_wall.jpg *License:* Creative Commons Attribution-Sharealike 3.0 *Contributors:* Nvvchar 324

Figure 141 *Source:* https://en.wikipedia.org/w/index.php?title=File:Tughlaqabad_walls.jpg *License:* Creative Commons Attribution-ShareAlike 3.0 Unported *Contributors:* Ondřej Žváček 325

Figure 142 *Source:* https://en.wikipedia.org/w/index.php?title=File:Feroze_Sha's_tomb_with_adjoining_Madrasa.JPG *License:* Creative Commons Attribution-Sharealike 3.0 *Contributors:* Nvvchar (talk) 325

Figure 143 *Source:* https://en.wikipedia.org/w/index.php?title=File:Remains_of_buildings_at_Firoze_Shah_Kotla,_Delhi.jpg *License:* Public Domain *Contributors:* AnRo0002, Belasd, Ekabhishek, Revent, Wiki-uk, 2 anonymous edits ... 326

Figure 144 *Source:* https://en.wikipedia.org/w/index.php?title=File:West_Gate_of_Feruzabad_since_destroyed.jpg *License:* Public Domain *Contributors:* Orme, William (fl. 1794 - 1819) ... 326

Figure 145 *Source:* https://en.wikipedia.org/w/index.php?title=File:Feroz_shah_kotla02_by_ashish.jpg *License:* Public Domain *Contributors:* User:आशीष भटनागर ... 327

Figure 146 *Source:* https://en.wikipedia.org/w/index.php?title=File:Timur_defeats_the_sultan_of_Delhi.jpg *License:* Public Domain *Contributors:* Zafarnama of Sharaf Al-Din 'Ali Yazdi ... 327

Image *Source:* https://en.wikipedia.org/w/index.php?title=File:Lodhi_Garden,_New_Delhi._taken_by_Anita_Mishra.JPG *License:* Creative Commons Attribution-Sharealike 3.0 *Contributors:* User:Anita Mishra ... 329

Figure 147 *Source:* https://en.wikipedia.org/w/index.php?title=File:Sultans_of_Dehli,_D0651,_Khidr_Khan,_BI_80_Rati_Tanka_INO_Firoz_Shah_Tughlaq.jpg *Contributors:* User:Tariq353 ... 331

Figure 148 *Source:* https://en.wikipedia.org/w/index.php?title=File:Sultans_of_Dehli,_D0662,_Mubarak_Shah,_AE_Double_falus.jpg *Contributors:* User:Tariq353 ... 332

Figure 149 *Source:* https://en.wikipedia.org/w/index.php?title=File:Sultans_of_Dehli,_D0684,_Alam_Shah,_BI_Tanka.jpg *Contributors:* User:Tariq353 ... 332

Image *Source:* https://en.wikipedia.org/w/index.php?title=File:India_in_1525_Joppen.jpg *License:* Public Domain *Contributors:* Charles Joppen 333

Figure 150 *Source:* https://en.wikipedia.org/w/index.php?title=File:Sultan-Ibrahim-Lodhi.jpg *Contributors:* Beria, BotMultichill, Cpt.a.haddock, Officer, Tryphon, ابراهيمخلل-بياباني-نجيب-احمد ... 335

Image *Source:* https://en.wikipedia.org/w/index.php?title=File:Pandya_territories.png *License:* GNU Free Documentation License *Contributors:* Blackknight12, BotMultichill, BotMultichillT, Electionworld, Roland zh, 4 anonymous edits ... 338

Figure 151 *Source:* https://en.wikipedia.org/w/index.php?title=File:FourArmedVishnuPandyaDynasty8-9thCentury.jpg *License:* Creative Commons Attribution-Sharealike 3.0,2.5,2.0,1.0 *Contributors:* PHGCOM ... 342

Figure 152 *Source:* https://en.wikipedia.org/w/index.php?title=File:TabulaPeutingerianaMuziris.jpg *License:* Public Domain *Contributors:* Aschroet, Challiyan, Kilom691, Roland zh, World Imaging ... 344

Figure 153 *Source:* https://en.wikipedia.org/w/index.php?title=File:Rama_at_Srivaikundam.jpg *Contributors:* - ... 346

Figure 154 *Source:* https://en.wikipedia.org/w/index.php?title=File:The_Hindu_Saint_Manikkavacakar_LACMA_AC1997.16.1_(1_of_12).jpg *Contributors:* Fæ, Redtigerxyz ... 347

Figure 155 *Source:* https://en.wikipedia.org/w/index.php?title=File:Double_fish_Pandyan_relief,_Koneswaram.jpg *License:* Creative Commons Zero *Contributors:* User:RuperDoc ... 348

Figure 156 *Source:* https://en.wikipedia.org/w/index.php?title=File:Srivaikundam_Temple_Structure,_Thirunelveli4.jpg *License:* Creative Commons Attribution 2.0 *Contributors:* sowrirajan s ... 350

Figure 157 *Source:* https://en.wikipedia.org/w/index.php?title=File:South_India_in_AD_1100.jpg *License:* Creative Commons Attribution-Sharealike 3.0 *Contributors:* User:Yon Man33 ... 352

Figure 158 *Source:* https://en.wikipedia.org/w/index.php?title=File:An_aerial_view_of_Madurai_city_from_atop_of_Meenakshi_Amman_temple.jpg *License:* Creative Commons Attribution 3.0 *Contributors:* எஸ்ஸார் ... 354

Figure 159 *Source:* https://en.wikipedia.org/w/index.php?title=File:Tirunelveli_Nellaiappar_Temple_1.jpg *License:* Creative Commons Attribution 2.0 *Contributors:* arunpnair ... 355

Figure 160 *Source:* https://en.wikipedia.org/w/index.php?title=File:Coin_Pandya_Bull_Obv_2.jpg *License:* Public Domain *Contributors:* User:Jnumis, User:JnumisJnumis ... 355

Figure 161 *Source:* https://en.wikipedia.org/w/index.php?title=File:Temple_between_hill_symbols_and_elephant_coin_of_the_Pandyas_Sri_Lanka_1st_century_CE.jpg *License:* Creative Commons Attribution-Sharealike 3.0 *Contributors:* Uploadalt ... 356

Figure 162 *Source:* https://en.wikipedia.org/w/index.php?title=File:Silk_route.jpg *License:* Public Domain *Contributors:* User:HighInBC ... 357

Figure 163 *Source:* https://en.wikipedia.org/w/index.php?title=File:White_pearl_necklace.jpg *License:* Creative Commons Attribution 2.0 *Contributors:* Flickr.com user "tanakawho" ... 358

Image *Source:* https://en.wikipedia.org/w/index.php?title=File:Vijayanagara-empire-map.svg *License:* Creative Commons Attribution-ShareAlike 3.0 Unported *Contributors:* Mlpkr ... 361

Image *Source:* https://en.wikipedia.org/w/index.php?title=File:Flag_of_Mysore.svg *License:* Public Domain *Contributors:* Lucas Larson, based on work of MChew ... 361

Image *Source:* https://en.wikipedia.org/w/index.php?title=File:QutbshahiFlag.PNG *License:* Creative Commons Attribution-Sharealike 3.0 *Contributors:* User:Kaygtr ... 361

Figure 164 *Source:* https://en.wikipedia.org/w/index.php?title=File:South_India_in_AD_1400.jpg *License:* Creative Commons Attribution-Sharealike 3.0 *Contributors:* User:Yon Man33 ... 366

Figure 165 *Source:* https://en.wikipedia.org/w/index.php?title=File:Panaromic_view_of_the_natural_fortification_and_landscape_at_Hampi.jpg *License:* GNU Free Documentation License *Contributors:* en User:Dineshkannambadi ... 367

Figure 166 *Source:* https://en.wikipedia.org/w/index.php?title=File:Vijayanagara_royal_insignia.jpg *License:* Creative Commons Attribution-Sharealike 3.0 *Contributors:* Pratheepps ... 368

Figure 167 *Source:* https//en.wikipedia.org *License:* Creative Commons Attribution-Sharealike 3.0 *Contributors:* User:Dineshkannambadi ... 370

Figure 168 *Source:* https://en.wikipedia.org/w/index.php?title=File:Hampi_marketplace.jpg *License:* GNU Free Documentation License *Contributors:* Dineshkannambadi, Jianhui67, MGA73bot2, Roland zh ... 371

Figure 169 *Source:* https://en.wikipedia.org/w/index.php?title=File:Evidence_of_Vijaynagar_pomp.jpg *License:* Creative Commons Attribution 2.0 *Contributors:* Soham Banerjee ... 373

Figure 170 *Source:* https://en.wikipedia.org/w/index.php?title=File:Vijayanagar_snakestone.jpg *License:* GNU Free Documentation License *Contributors:* Adityamadhav83, MGA73bot2, Magog the Ogre, Roland zh ... 374

Figure 171 *Source:* https://en.wikipedia.org/w/index.php?title=File:Dharmeshwara_Temple_Plates.jpg *License:* Public Domain *Contributors:* 2know4power, WestCoastMusketeer ... 375

Figure 172 *Source:* https://en.wikipedia.org/w/index.php?title=File:Ceiling_paintings_depicting_scenes_from_Hindu_mythology_at_the_Virupaksha_temple_in_Hampi_3.JPG *License:* Creative Commons Attribution-Sharealike 3.0 *Contributors:* User:Dineshkannambadi ... 376

Figure 173 *Source:* https://en.wikipedia.org/w/index.php?title=File:Karnataka_Hampi_IMG_0730.jpg *License:* GNU Free Documentation License *Contributors:* Ajar ... 377

Figure 174 *Source:* https://en.wikipedia.org/w/index.php?title=File:Ugranarasimha_statue_at_Hampi.JPG *Contributors:* - ... 377

Figure 175 *Source:* https://en.wikipedia.org/w/index.php?title=File:Ornate_pillared_mantapa_at_the_Virupaksha_temple_in_Hampi.jpg *License:* GNU Free Documentation License *Contributors:* Dineshkannambadi, MGA73bot2, Magog the Ogre, Marcus Cyron, MathewTownsend, Quibik, Roland zh, Soranoch ... 378

Figure 176 *Source:* https://en.wikipedia.org/w/index.php?title=File:Hazara_Ramachandra_Temple-.JPG *License:* Creative Commons Attribution-Sharealike 3.0 *Contributors:* User:Rkiran josh ... 378

Figure 177 *Source:* https://en.wikipedia.org/w/index.php?title=File:Poetic_Kannada_inscription_of_Manjaraja_dated_1398_CE_at_Vindyagiri_hill_in_Shravanabelagola.jpg *License:* GNU Free Documentation License *Contributors:* en:User:Dineshkannambadi. Cropped (and slightly lightened) by Ali'i on 15:07, 16 June 2008 (UTC) ... 381

Figure 178 *Source:* https://en.wikipedia.org/w/index.php?title=File:Yali_pillars1_in_Aghoreshwara_Temple_in_Ikkeri.jpg *License:* Creative Commons Attribution-Sharealike 3.0 *Contributors:* Dineshkannambadi (talk) 16:19, 26 May 2008 (UTC) ... 383

Image *Source:* https://en.wikipedia.org/w/index.php?title=File:Krishna_Pushkarani_-_Hampi_Ruins.jpg *License:* Creative Commons Attribution-Sharealike 3.0 *Contributors:* User:Dey.sandip ... 383

Image *Source:* https://en.wikipedia.org/w/index.php?title=File:The_Stone_Chariot,Hampi.jpg *Contributors:* User:Hawinprinto ... 383

Figure 179 *Source:* https://en.wikipedia.org/w/index.php?title=File:An_aerial_view_of_Madurai_city_from_atop_of_Meenakshi_Amman_temple.jpg *License:* Creative Commons Attribution 3.0 *Contributors:* எஸ்ஸார் ... 385

Image *Source:* https://en.wikipedia.org/w/index.php?title=File:Bengal_Sultanate.png *License:* Creative Commons Attribution-Sharealike 3.0 *Contributors:* User:ArmanJ ... 388

Image *Source:* https://en.wikipedia.org/w/index.php?title=File:Flag_of_Myanmar.svg *License:* Public Domain *Contributors:* *drew∼commonswiki, AnonMoos, Artix Kreiger, Cathy Richards, CommonsDelinker, Cycn, Daphne Lantier, Dinsdagskind, Duduziq, Fry1989, Garam, Gunkarta, Homo lupus, INeverCry, Josegeographic, Klemen Kocjancic, Legnaw, Mason Decker, Mattes, Neq00, Nightstallion, Pixeltoo, Rfc1394, Rodejong, Sangjinhwa, Sarang, SeNeKa∼commonswiki, SiBr4, Sixflashphoto, Stevanb, TFerenczy, Takahara Osaka, Techman224, ThomasPusch, Túrelio, UnreifeKirsche, Vividuppers, WikipediaMaster, Winzipas, Xiengyod∼commonswiki, Zscout370, 白布飘扬 , 21 anonymous edits 388

Figure 180 *Source:* https://en.wikipedia.org/w/index.php?title=File:Malda_~_Adina_Mosque_5.JPG *License:* Creative Commons Attribution-Sharealike 3.0 *Contributors:* User:B.saptarshi1984 ... 390

Figure 181 *Source:* https://en.wikipedia.org/w/index.php?title=File:Babur.2.jpg *License:* Public Domain *Contributors:* Eugene a, Khorazmiy, Roland zh, Shxahxh 391
Figure 182 *Source:* https://en.wikipedia.org/w/index.php?title=File:Silver_Coin_of_Jalaluddin.jpg *License:* Creative Commons Attribution-Sharealike 3.0 *Contributors:* Rani nurmai 394
Figure 183 *Source:* https://en.wikipedia.org/w/index.php?title=File:AtlasMiller_BNF_Indian_Ganges.jpg *License:* Public Domain *Contributors:* Hispalois, Roland zh 395
Figure 184 *Source:* https://en.wikipedia.org/w/index.php?title=File:Tribute_Giraffe_with_Attendant.jpg *License:* Public Domain *Contributors:* ArmanJ, Bobisbob~commonswiki, BoringHistoryGuy, Choufanging, Cold Season, Courcelles, Deadstar, Frank C. Müller, Gryffindor, Jann, Louis le Grand~commonswiki, Mattes, Mjrmtg, PericlesofAthens, Roland zh, Sevilledade, Shakko, Soerfm, Sternoc, Vmenkov 396
Figure 185 *Source:* https://en.wikipedia.org/w/index.php?title=File:Hafez_880714_095.jpg *License:* Creative Commons Attribution-Sharealike 3.0 *Contributors:* en:User:Amirskip4life (original: I created this work entirely by myself.) 398
Figure 186 *Source:* https://en.wikipedia.org/w/index.php?title=File:Shershah.jpg *License:* Public Domain *Contributors:* Ustad Abdul Ghafur Breshna, a prominent Afghan artist from Kabul 402
Image *Source:* https://en.wikipedia.org/w/index.php?title=File:Ahom_insignia_plain.svg *License:* GNU Free Documentation License *Contributors:* Chaipau (talk) 404
Image *Source:* https://en.wikipedia.org/w/index.php?title=File:Ahom-kingdom-c1826p.png *License:* Creative Commons Attribution-Sharealike 3.0 *Contributors:* Chaipau 404
Image *Source:* https://en.wikipedia.org/w/index.php?title=File:Flag_of_the_British_East_India_Company_(1801).svg *License:* Public Domain *Contributors:* User:Yaddah 404
Image *Source:* https://en.wikipedia.org/w/index.php?title=File:Montage_of_Asamiya_Cultural_Symbols.png *Contributors:* User:Rex845 407
Image *Source:* https://en.wikipedia.org/w/index.php?title=File:Seal_of_Assam.png *License:* Public Domain *Contributors:* OgreBot 2, Roland zh, Shubhamkanodia, Urdangaray 407
Image *Source:* https://en.wikipedia.org/w/index.php?title=File:Gargaon'r_Kareng_Ghor.JPG *License:* Creative Commons Attribution-Sharealike 3.0 *Contributors:* User:Aniruddha Buragohain 409
Image *Source:* https://en.wikipedia.org/w/index.php?title=File:Rang_Ghar_Sibsagar.jpg *License:* Creative Commons Attribution-Sharealike 3.0 *Contributors:* Bishnu Saikia, MGA73bot2, Roland zh 409
Image *Source:* https://en.wikipedia.org/w/index.php?title=File:Talatal_Ghar.jpg *License:* Creative Commons Attribution-Sharealike 3.0 *Contributors:* User:Debasisbora 409
Image *Source:* https://en.wikipedia.org/w/index.php?title=File:Om.svg *Contributors:* Kashmiri 416
Figure 187 *Source:* https://en.wikipedia.org/w/index.php?title=File:Kondavid-drug._Signed_'W.R.'.jpg *License:* Public Domain *Contributors:* R., William (fl. 1784-1816) 418
Figure 188 *Source:* https://en.wikipedia.org/w/index.php?title=File:Copper_plates_NMND-10.JPG *License:* Public Domain *Contributors:* Daderot 419
Figure 189 *Source:* https://en.wikipedia.org/w/index.php?title=File:Srisailam-temple-entrance.jpg *License:* Public Domain *Contributors:* Chintohere 421
Figure 190 *Source:* https://en.wikipedia.org/w/index.php?title=File:Jwala_Narasimha_Ahobilam.JPG *License:* Creative Commons Attribution-Sharealike 3.0 *Contributors:* Ilya Mauter 422
Figure 191 *Source:* https://en.wikipedia.org/w/index.php?title=File:Kondavid-drug._Signed_'W.R.'.jpg *License:* Public Domain *Contributors:* R., William (fl. 1784-1816) 426
Figure 192 *Source:* https://en.wikipedia.org/w/index.php?title=File:Copper_plates_NMND-10.JPG *License:* Public Domain *Contributors:* Daderot 427
Figure 193 *Source:* https://en.wikipedia.org/w/index.php?title=File:Srisailam-temple-entrance.jpg *License:* Public Domain *Contributors:* Chintohere 429
Figure 194 *Source:* https://en.wikipedia.org/w/index.php?title=File:Jwala_Narasimha_Ahobilam.JPG *License:* Creative Commons Attribution-Sharealike 3.0 *Contributors:* Ilya Mauter 430

License

Creative Commons Attribution-Share Alike 3.0
//creativecommons.org/licenses/by-sa/3.0/

Index

Aalm Shah, 334
Aayirathil Oruvan (2010 film), 217
Abbasid, 160, 209
Abbasid Caliphate, 124, 292
Abdul Hakim (poet), 399
Abraham Eraly, 304
Absolute monarchy, 388, 391, 404
Abul-Fazl ibn Mubarak, 125, 141, 287
Achalpur, 101
Acharya, 112
Achyuta Deva Raya, 362, 367
Addanki, 416, 417, 424, 425
Aden, 160, 372
Adikavi Pampa, 63, 116, 236, 448, 453
Adil Shahi dynasty, 66, 108, 158, 241, 361
Adina Mosque, 390, 400
Adiperukku, 202
Adipurana, 116, 236
Adi Sankara, 380
Adi Shankara, 113, 160
Aditya I, 143, 145, 147, 174, 188
Aditya Karikala, 145, 147, 349
Aditya Karikalan, 143, 188
Aditya I, 194
Admiralty, 392
Admiral Zheng He, 395
Advaita, 113, 160, 162, 380
Afghan, 274, 334
Afghanistan, 3, 7, 18, 75, 76, 274, 297
Afghan people, 281
Afro-Eurasia, 271, 282
Agananuru, 345
Agastya, 192, 346
Agnivansha, 52, 93
Agra, 269, 281, 334, 390
Agrahara, 248
Agraharam, 422, 430
Agrarian society, 271
A Historical Atlas of South Asia, 75
A History of South India: From Prehistoric Times to the Fall of Vijayanagar, 182
Ahmadnagar, 109
Ahmedabad, 16
Ahobilam, 384, 419, 421, 427, 429

Ahom dynasty, 405, 414
Ahom Kingdom, 42, **403**, 409
Ahom language, 404, 411
Ahom people, 408
Aihole, 23, 27, 28, 51, 56, 60, 119, 159, 168, 235
Aihole inscriptions, 51
Ain-i-Akbari, 125, 141
Ainnurruvar, 159
Airavatesvara Temple, 200, 212
Ajanta Caves, 11, 12, 23, 28
Ajitha purana, 165
Ajmer, 14, 288
Akananuru, 342
Akbar the Great, 287, 389
Akka Mahadevi, 162, 165
A. K. Warder, 122
Alam Shah, 329, 330
Alauddin Ali Shah, 389
Alauddin Firuz Shah I, 400
Alauddin Firuz Shah II, 401
Alauddin Hussain Shah, 390, 401
Alauddin Khalji, 252, 273–275, 286, 296, 297, 299, 304, 309, 353, 365
Ala ud din Masud, 272, 294
Ala ud-din Sikandar Shah, 323
Al-Baladhuri, 80
Alchon Huns, 70
Alexander Cunningham, 39
Alexander II of Epirus, 343
Alexander Mikaberidze, 468
Alexander the Great, 4, 32, 105
Al Hakam ibn Awana, 77
Ali, 330
Aliya Rama Raya, 363
Al-Jinn, 399
Allama Prabhu, 162, 165, 381
Allasani Peddana, 382
Allauddin Khilji, 286
Al-Masudi, 107
Aloe, 160
Alupas, 27, 53, 156
Alvars, 181, 382
Al-Walid I, 79

Amaravathi village, Guntur district, 9
Amazon Standard Identification Number, 243
Ambashtha, 263
Amber, 14
Amir, 319
Amir Khusrau, 309
Amir Khusro, 284
Amoghavarsha, 101, 127
Amoghavarsha I, 32, 102, 105, 106, 108, 109, 116, 117, 121, 236
Amoghavarsha II, 101
Amoghavarsha III, 101, 226
Amravati district, 30
Amu Darya, 5
Amuktamalyada, 381
Anahilapataka, 82
Anantnag district, 76
Anant Sadashiv Altekar, 121
Anarkali Bazaar, 292
Ancient Greece, 345
Ancient history, 1
Ancient Near East, 1
Ancient Tamil country, 24, 33, 51, 53, 152, 174, 341, 357
Andal, 382
Andaman and Nicobar Islands, 38
Andhra dynasty, 176
Andhra Ikshvaku, 49, 173
Andhra in Indian epic literature, 5
Andhra Pradesh, 10, 18, 29, 30, 41, 42, 53, 55, 104, 152, 190, 224, 225, 245, 379, 384, 416, 417, 424, 425, 432
Anegondi, 365
Anga, 10
Anglo-Maratha Wars, 42
Anglo-Sikh wars, 43
Angus Maddison, 283, 469
Anhilwara, 16
Anjuvannam, 159
Annamacharya, 379
Annemarie Schimmel, 281, 468, 469, 473
Annigeri, 155
Antarala, 57
Antechamber, 57
Antigonus II Gonatas, 343
Antimony, 110
Antioch, 345, 357
Antiochus III the Great, 4
Antiochus II Theos, 343
Antiquity, 1
Anviksiki, 164
Apabhramsha, 112, 284
Apama, 4
Aparajitavarman, 173, 174, 184, 185
Arab, 22, 93, 113, 124, 379
Arabia, 109

Arabian Sea, 12, 130, 372
Arabic, 388, 399
Arabs, 7, 372
Arachosia, 2
Arakan, 389, 390, 392
Arakeshvara Temple, Hole Alur, 239
Aram Shah, 272, 273, 292
Aranya Parva, 422, 430
Arasikere, 235
Aravidu dynasty, 363
Arch, 384, 399
Archaeological Survey of India, 197, 380
Archery, 370
Architecture, 38
Arcot, 225, 365
Areca, 158, 229, 371
Ariaca, 5
Arikesari II, 117
Arikesari Maravarman, 349
Arinjaya, 143, 145, 147, 188
Ariyalur District, 202
Arjuna, 32, 105, 116
Aror, 7
Art, 210
Artemidoros Aniketos, 4
Arthashastra, 164, 227
Artillery, 369, 391
Arunachal Pradesh, 404
Aryabhata, 11

Āryāvarta, 91

Asaga, 115
Ashirbadi Lal Srivastava, 288
Ashoka, 32, 102, 106, 190, 280, 343
Ashoka Major Rock Edict No.13, 190
Ashtadiggajas, 382
Ashvamedha, 10, 20, 265
Ashvatthama, 176
Ashwamedha, 66
Ashwatthama, 346
Asia, 271
Asiatic mode of production, 410
Asiatic Society of Bangladesh, 266
Asiatic Society of Bengal, 265
Assam, 18, 20, 42, 95, 127, 262, 344, 390, 404, 407, 408
Assamese language, 404, 408, 409
Aswamedha, 179
Atakur inscription, 115, 236
Athirajendra Chola, 142, 143, 146, 147, 153, 188, 199, 456
Atisa, 124
Atiśa, 128
Atisha, 133
Attimabbe, 453, 454

August Friedrich Rudolf Hoernle, 436
Augustus, 340, 344
Avalon Hill, 217
Avani, 233
Avanijanashraya Pulakeshin, 82
Avani Sulamani, 349
Avanti (India), 81, 83, 85, 129
Avanti Varman (Utpala dynasty), 76
Avatar, 249, 259, 376, 377
Avinita, 222, 225
Ayodhya, 49, 52
Ayurveda, 225
Ayyalaraju Ramabhadrudu, 382

Babur, 42, 282, 335, 389–392
Bactria, 2, 3, 5
Badami, 23, 26–28, 30, 41, 47, 48, 51, 53, 59, 104, 149, 156, 168, 174
Badami Cave Temples, 28, 56
Badami Chalukya Architecture, 167
Badami Chalukyas, 33, 101, 104
Badaun, 292
Badayun, 269
Bagalkot, 53
Bagalkot district, 56, 112, 156
Bagerhat, 394
Baghdad, 209
Bahamani Sultanate, 258
Bahlikas, 3
Bahlul Khan Lodi, 281, 330, 332, 334
Bahmani Sultanate, 65, 108, 158, 241, 244, 307, 313, 366
Bahri dynasty, 291, 308
Bahubali, 26, 41, 58, 232, 384
Baidya, 263
Baij Nath Puri, 82, 86, 99
Bakhtiyar Khalji, 137
Balakumaran, 217
Balarama, 247
Balban, 309
Balbans tomb, 295
Bali, 10
Ballala Sena, 261, 262, 265
Ballal Sena, 20
Balligavi, 113, 160, 163, 168, 235
Baluch people, 83
Bamyan, 6
Bamyan City, 11
Banabhatta, 71
Bāṇabhaṭṭa, 73
Bana Kingdom, 64, 233
Banaras, 32, 105
Banarsi Prasad Saksena, 328, 360
Banavasi, 24, 48, 109, 150, 155
Bangalore, 241
Bangalore district, 224

Bangladesh, 20, 75, 124, 270, 307, 388
Bappa Rawal, 77, 83
Barkur, 372
Barsbay, 396
Basadi, 67, 231, 232
B.A. Saletore, 476
Basavakalyan, 33, 48, 148, 149, 255
Basavakalyana, 34
Basavanna, 67, 160, 161, 164
Bastar state, 258
Bastion, 251
Bateshwar Hindu temples, Madhya Pradesh, 96
Battle of Amroha, 270
Battle of Ghaghra, 390, 392
Battle of Indus, 293
Battle of Panipat (1526), 270, 282, 335
Battle of Raj Mahal, 390, 393
Battle of Saraighat, 410
Battle of Takkolam, 226, 236
Battle of Talikota, 368
Battle of Tarain, 15
Bayaluseemae, 228
Bayazid Khan Karrani, 403
Bay of Bengal, 27, 124, 130, 254, 372, 394, 396
Bdellium, 160
Bellamkonda, 419, 426
Bellary, 109, 176, 177, 181
Bellary district, 151, 168
Belur, 37, 41, 119, 225
Belur, Karnataka, 36
Bengal, 17, 20, 32, 38, 41, 72, 91, 94, 101, 124, 129, 149, 153, 195, 262, 273, 292, 372, 389, 400, 410
Bengali language, 17, 124, 125, 134, 262, 266, 388, 389, 398
Bengali Muslim, 399
Bengal Sultanate, 42, 270, 307, **388**
Bengal Sultanate-Delhi Sultanate War, 392
Bengal Sultanate–Kamata Kingdom War, 392
Bengal Sultanate-Jaunpur Sultanate War, 392, 397
Bengal Sultanate-Kingdom of Mrauk U War of 1512-1516, 392
Berar Province, 104
Berar Sultanate, 30, 447
Betel, 109, 158, 228, 371
Betel nut, 110
Bezwada, 176
Bhadrabahu, 232
Bhagavata, 164
Bhagdad, 160
Bhakti, 23, 67, 162, 379, 381
Bharata Muni, 67
Bharatanatyam, 67
Bharshiva Dynasty, 10

495

Bharuch, 12, 79, 81, 105, 109
Bhāskara II, 166
Bhatkal, 372
Bhattis, 81
Bhil, 16
Bhima, 165
Bhinmal, 12, 79, 81, 83, 85
Bhoi dynasty, 432
Bhoja I, 83
Bhoja II (Gurjara-Pratihara dynasty), 98
Bhoj II, 95
Bhubaneswar, 10
Bhudevi, 380
Bhutan, 18, 20
Bhutanatha group, 168
Bidar, 287
Bidar district, 447
Bigha, 414
Bihar, 12, 20, 95, 124, 149, 281, 334, 336, 394
Bijapur district, Karnataka, 33, 54, 106, 149, 150, 166
Bijjala II, 33, 155
Bijolia, 17
Bikaner, 52
Bikrampur, 124
Bilhana, 50, 150, 166, 438, 442, 451
Billon (alloy), 7
Bindeshwari Prasad Sinha, 139
Birbhum, 394
Bisheshwar Nath Reu, 447
Bishweshwar Nath Reu, 122
Black pepper, 228
B. Lewis Rice, 375, 386
Bodhidharma, 29
Bodhisattva, 17
Bodo-Kachari people, 411
Bogra, 394
Bombay, 23
Borbarua, 410, 411, 414
Borgohain, 408, 410, 411, 414
Borneo, 10
Borpatrogohain, 409, 411
Borphukan, 410–413
Brahma, 52, 176, 440
Brahmadeya, 241
Brahma Jinalaya, 169
Brahman, 265
Brahma Pala, 21
Brahmaputra, 42, 408
Brahmaputra River, 407
Brahmaputra Valley, 20
Brahmasutra, 162
Brahmic script, 179
Brahmin, 64, 113, 125, 163, 164, 176, 228, 247, 248, 254, 280, 316, 373, 381, 421, 429

Brahmins, 113, 159
Brihadeeswarar Temple, 38, 195, 200
Brihadisvara Temple, 147, 195, 212
British East India Company, 43, 252
British India, 40, 42, 93
British Museum, 94
British Raj, 258
Bronze, 210, 215
Budaun, 330, 332
Buddhamitra, 212
Buddhavarman, 182
Buddhism, 2, 6, 7, 9, 11, 22–24, 29, 47, 70, 73, 100, 113, 124, 177, 191, 232, 261, 338, 388, 447
Buddhist, 17, 18, 24, 41, 191, 286
Bukka, 383
Bukka I, 364, 380
Bukka Raya I, 362, 364
Bukka Raya II, 362
Bundelkhand, 95
Burdwan division, 127
Bureaucracy, 391
Burhagohain, 408, 411, 414
Burhanpur, 109
Burjor Avari, 99, 448
Burma, 10, 11, 42, 344, 366, 372, 404
Burmese invasions of Assam, 408
Burton Stein, 40, 219
Butuga II, 222, 226
Byzantium, 357

Caesar Augustus, 345
Calendar era, 139
Calico (fabric), 372
Calico (textile), 109
Caliph Al-Amin, 85
Caliph Al-Mahdi, 85
Caliphate, 79, 271
Caliphate campaigns in India, 90
Caliph Umar, 84
Cambodia, 10, 159
Cambridge University, 473
Camlet, 372
Campaign against the Tughlaq Dynasty, 280
Cannon, 392
Cape Comorin, 32, 102, 105
Carbuncle (gemstone), 159
Cardamom, 228, 371
Carnatic music, 364
Caste, 113
Caste system, 160
Caste system in India, 255
Category:Architecture of Karnataka, 66, 108, 159, 241
Category:Assam, 407
Category:Forts in Karnataka, 66, 108, 159, 241

496

Category:Historical economies of Karnataka, 66, 108, 159, 241
Category:Historical Societies of Karnataka, 66, 108, 159, 241
Category:History of Andhra Pradesh, 245, 416, 424
Category:History of Bengal, 262
Category:History of India, 76, 87, 90, 144, 350, 363
Category:History of Karnataka, 65, 107, 158, 240
Category:History of Tamil Nadu, 189, 339
Cauvery, 433
Cavalry, 284
Central Asia, 3, 42, 76, 271, 283, 291
Central Asian, 9
Central India, 48, 105, 149, 226
Ceylon, 182, 191
Chagatai Khanate, 292
Chahamanas of Shakambhari, 90, 95
Chainmail, 284
Chalukya, 9, 11–13, 22, 24, 36, 52, 54, 82, 150, 152, 233
Chalukya dynasty, 26, **47**, 65, 71, 77–79, 97, 101, 108, 149, 158, 177, 224, 240, 382
Chalukyas, 18, 30, 36, 142, 145, 174
Chalukyas of Kalyani, 250
Chalukyas of Vemulavada, 116
Chalukyas of Vengi, 248
Chamarajanagar district, 224
Chamarasa, 381
Chambal River, 15
Champu, 116
Chandela, 90, 95, 127
Chandela dynasty, 270
Chandrabhanu, 348, 353
Chandra dynasty, 127
Chandragiri, 361
Chandragiri Hill, 237
Chandragupta Basadi, 237
Chandragupta I, 11
Chandragupta II, 11
Chandragupta Maurya, 239
Chandravansha, 102
Chandravanshi, 127
Channabasavanna, 165
Charaideo, 404, 408
Charyapada, 125, 134
Chauhan, 97, 290
Chaulukya dynasty, 52, 286
Chavda, 82
Chavda dynasty, 90
Chavundaraya, 27, 224, 226, 232
Chay root, 372
Chedi Kingdom, 35
Chennakesava Temple, 37

Chera dynasty, 23, 24, 27, 54, 159, 191, 339, 341
Chera Empire, 357
Chera Nadu, 351
Cherry plum, 372
Chhatri, 384
Chhattisgarh, 18, 246
Chidambaram, 38
Chidambaram Temple, 38
Chief Minister of Karnataka, 67
Chikkamagaluru, 225
Chilarai, 413
China, 5, 27, 160, 193, 389, 395
Chittagong, 392, 394
Chittor, 81, 85, 275
Chittor Fort, 300
Chola, 30, 54, 55, 197, 215, 340, 341, 348, 349, 351, 352
Chola art, 144, 189
Chola dynasty, 23, 24, 26, 27, 143, 148, 149, 152, 173, 174, 176, 177, **187**, 188, 221, 224, 226, 339, 351, 353, 382
Chola Empire, 38, 41, 124, 127, 357, 466
Chola government, 144, 189, 190
Chola invasion of Srivijaya, 190
Chola literature, 144, 189, 190
Chola military, 144, 189
Chola Nadu, 351
Chola Navy, 144, 189, 205
Cholas, 30, 54, 142, 247, 340, 343, 348, 351
Christianity, 379, 388
Chudamani Vihara, 215
Chutiya kingdom, 409, 412
Chutiya people, 411, 414
Cilappatikaram, 23
CITEREFAbraham Eraly2015, 470
CITEREFAhmad Hasan Dani1999, 470
CITEREFAl-Baladhuri1924, 445
CITEREFAsherTalbot2006, 465, 466
CITEREFAshirbadi Lal Srivastava1953, 470, 471
CITEREFAshirbadi Lal Srivastava1966, 470
CITEREFAvari2007, 446
CITEREFBagchi1993, 450, 451
CITEREFBanarsi Prasad Saksena1970, 472
CITEREFBanarsi Prasad Saksena1992, 475
CITEREFBarua2005, 458
CITEREFBhandarkar1929, 445
CITEREFBlankinship1994, 445
CITEREFChadurah1991, 445
CITEREFChadurah199145, 435
CITEREFChakravarti1991, 465
CITEREFChattopadhyaya1998, 466
CITEREFChopraRavindranSubrahmanian2003, 456–460
CITEREFDas1995, 460, 461

CITEREFD. C. Ganguly1981, 436
CITEREFDehejia1990, 457, 458, 460
CITEREFDesai1962, 465
CITEREFDevare2009, 458
CITEREFDilip Kumar Ganguly1984, 436
CITEREFEaton2005, 465, 466
CITEREFEaton2006, 476, 477
CITEREFElliot1869, 446
CITEREFEraly2011, 457, 458
CITEREFGanguly1935, 446
CITEREFGough2008, 458
CITEREFHarle1994, 460
CITEREFHasan1959, 435, 445
CITEREFHellmann-Rajanayagam2004, 459
CITEREFHem Chandra Ray1931, 445
CITEREFHermann KulkeDietmar Rothermund2004, 470, 471
CITEREFHuntington1984, 450, 451
CITEREFIrfan Habib1982, 471
CITEREFIsmail1988, 460
CITEREFJermsawatdi1979, 460
CITEREFJohn N. Miksic2013, 455
CITEREFKalia1994, 465
CITEREFKarashima2014, 458
CITEREFKishori Saran Lal1950, 471, 475
CITEREFK.K.R. Nair1987, 475
CITEREFKulkeRothermund2001, 456, 457, 459
CITEREFKulkeRothermund2004, 465
CITEREFLucassenLucassen2014, 458
CITEREFMajumdar1955, 446
CITEREFMajumdar1977, 435, 445
CITEREFMajumdar1981, 446
CITEREFMajumdar1987, 456–458, 460
CITEREFMarshall Cavendish2006, 470
CITEREFMishra1954, 446
CITEREFMitter2001, 459, 460
CITEREFMukherjee2011, 459
CITEREFMukund1999, 459
CITEREFMukund2012, 457, 459
CITEREFNagasamy1970, 460
CITEREFNagasamy1981, 458
CITEREFN. Subrahmanian1962, 475
CITEREFPaine2014, 457
CITEREFPaul1939, 451
CITEREFPeter Jackson2003, 467, 468, 470, 471, 475
CITEREFP. M. Holt et al.1977, 470, 471
CITEREFPrasad1988, 456, 464, 465
CITEREFPuri1957, 446
CITEREFPuri1986, 445, 446
CITEREFRadhey Shyam Chaurasia2002, 470
CITEREFRajasuriar1998, 458
CITEREFRamaswamy2007, 459
CITEREFRao1994, 479
CITEREFRaoShulman2002, 465
CITEREFRaoShulman2012, 465, 466
CITEREFRothermund1993, 459
CITEREFRubiés2000, 465
CITEREFSadarangani2004, 459, 460
CITEREFSailendra Nath Sen1999, 436
CITEREFSakhujaSakhuja2009, 458
CITEREFSanjay Sharma2006, 445, 446
CITEREFSastri1984, 456–460
CITEREFSastri2002, 456–460
CITEREFSastry1978, 464–466
CITEREFScharfe2002, 459
CITEREFSchmidt1995, 458
CITEREFSen1999, 457–459
CITEREFSen2009, 457
CITEREFSengupta2011, 450, 451
CITEREFShanta Rani Sharma2012, 446
CITEREFSharma1992, 465
CITEREFSingh1964, 446
CITEREFSingh2008, 435, 458–460
CITEREFSircar1971, 446
CITEREFSircar1979, 465
CITEREFSircar2008, 464
CITEREFSpuler1975, 460
CITEREFStein1980, 458
CITEREFStein1989, 476
CITEREFStein1998, 458, 460
CITEREFSubbarayalu2009, 458
CITEREFSubrahmanyam1998, 466
CITEREFSunil Kumar1994, 470
CITEREFSuryanarayana1986, 465
CITEREFTalbot2001, 458, 464–466, 479
CITEREFThapar1995, 456, 459, 460
CITEREFTripathi1959, 446
CITEREFTripathi1967, 456–460
CITEREFTripathi1989, 445
CITEREFUpinder Singh2008, 436
CITEREFVaidya1921, 445
CITEREFVasudevan2003, 458, 460
CITEREFVenkata Subramanian1988, 475
CITEREFVentakaramanayya1942, 466
CITEREFWink199172-74, 435
CITEREFWink2002, 445
CITEREFWolpert1999, 460
CITEREFYadava1982, 446
Civet, 160
Civetone, 375
Classical antiquity, 1
Classical India, 75, 90, 123, 124, 173, 262
Clifford Edmund Bosworth, 474
C. Minakshi, 186
Coastal Andhra, 254, 417, 418, 425, 426
Coccinia grandis, 176
Cochin, 372
Cockfighting, 235
Coconut, 229
Colonial Assam, 408

Column, 382
Common Era, 2, 102, 192, 357
Commons:Category:Chalukya dynasty, 69
Commons:Category:Chola dynasty, 220
Commons:Category:Delhi Sultanate, 289
Commons:Category:Gurjara-Pratihara, 100
Commons:Category:Kakatiya dynasty, 261
Commons:Category:Khilji dynasty, 305
Commons:Category:Lodhi Empire, 338
Commons:Category:Mamluk Sultanate (Delhi), 295
Commons:Category:Pallava, 186
Commons:Category:Pandyan Dynasty, 359
Commons:Category:Rashtrakuta Dynasty, 123
Commons:Category:Reddy dynasty, 423, 431
Commons:Category:Tughlaq Dynasty, 329
Commons:Category:Vijayanagara Empire, 387
Commons:Category:Western Chalukya Empire, 172
Commons:Category:Western Ganga Dynasty, 242
Compassion, 280
Contemporary history, 1
Copper plate grant, 101, 113
Copper-plate grant, 191
Copyright status of work by the U.S. government, 39
Corvee, 410
Corvee labor, 413
Cosmology, 399
Cosmopolitanism, 73, 282
Cotton, 157, 283
Cotton gin, 283
Crank (mechanism), 283
Crore, 313
Crown land, 111
Cudappah, 109
Cuddappah district, 177
Cultural pluralism, 282
Culture of Assam, 407
Cuman, 273
Cumania, 291, 308
Curtain wall (fortification), 251
Cuttack, 432
Cuttack, Orissa, 417, 425

Damascus, 97
Dambal, 58, 113, 160, 168
Dantidurga, 30, 54, 82, 94, 100, 101, 104
Dantivarman, 174, 184, 185
Darasuram, 212
Dariya Khan, 336
Darshanas, 379
Dasakuta, 379
Dashavatara, 384
Daud Khan Karrani, 403

Daulatabad, Maharashtra, 34, 269, 277, 313
Daulat Khan, 336
Daulat Khan Lodi, 282, 336
Davaka, 20
Davanagere district, 157
Davangere district, 58, 168
Deccan, 335
Deccan Plateau, 9, 11, 13, 18, 23, 26, 29, 35, 42, 48, 52, 82, 94, 106, 149, 196, 224, 254, 278, 287, 299, 364
Deccan sultanates, 364, 367
Decimal, 11
Dehong Dai and Jingpo Autonomous Prefecture, 408
Delhi, 14–16, 42, 269, 270, 274, 276, 288, 289, 292, 293, 296, 306, 308, 323, 329, 330, 333, 334
Delhi Sultanate, 2, 40, 42, 245, 252, 257, **269**, 272, 289, 291, 297, 299, 306, 308, 323, 330, 333, 334, 339, 340, 353, 365, 388, 389, 392, 417, 421, 425, 429
Delhi Sultanate (1206–1526), 270
Demetrius I of Bactria, 3, 10
Democratic election, 17
Demographics of India, 271, 283
Demonym, 92
Deogiri, 299
Deopara Prashasti, 265
Devadasi, 67, 115
Devadasi system, 375
Deva dynasty, 261, 266, 267, 270
Devagiri, 42, 275, 288, 300
Devanagari, 64, 157, 380
Devapala (Pala dynasty), 18, 124, 126, 139
Devaraja (Gurjara-Pratihara dynasty), 98
Deva Raya, 383
Deva Raya I, 362, 366
Deva Raya II, 362, 366
Devi Kanya Kumari, 346
Devotional movements, 120
Dhaka, 266
Dhakeshwari Temple, 266
Dhar, 15
Dharma, 280, 343
Dharmadam, 372
Dharmamangalkavya, 125
Dharmapala, 94
Dharma Pala, 21
Dharmapala (emperor), 124, 126
Dharmapala of Bengal, 18, 105, 139
Dharwad district, 58, 155, 157, 168
Dharwar, 109
Dhimmi, 312
Dhimmis, 321
Dhofar, 160
Dhoti, 114, 235

499

Dhoyin, 266
Dhruva Dharavarsha, 32, 94, 101, 105, 126, 225
Dhurjati, 382
Dietmar Rothermund, 260
Digital object identifier, 68, 86, 99, 259, 261, 305, 337, 415
Dinajpur, 394, 400
Dineshchandra Sircar, 49, 139, 245, 260
Diu, India, 288
Doab, 32, 91, 102, 106, 152, 167, 365
Dodda Basappa Temple, 58, 168
Doddagaddavalli, 25
Doddahundi nishidhi inscription, 240
Dome, 384
Domestication and use, 27
Domingo Paes, 364
Dondra Head, 181
Drachma, 7
Dravida, 18
Dravidian architecture, 29, 58, 102, 169, 239, 478
Dravidian languages, 23, 67
Dravidian people, 67
Dravidian peoples, 130
D. R. Bhandarkar, 85
Dreadlocks, 347
Durga, 57, 67, 245
Durgasimha, 164
Durjaya, 21
Durvinita, 116, 222, 225, 441
Duryodhana, 165
Dutch (ethnic group), 379
Dvaita, 379, 380
Dwarka, 288
Dynasty, 17, 70, 101, 262

Early Cholas, 143, 148, 188, 192
Early historical era, 1
Early history of Kedah, 186
Early modern period, 1, 40
Early Pandyan Kingdom, 339
Eastern Chalukya, 13, 252
Eastern Chalukyas, 41, 48, 52, 54, 105, 146, 149, 173, 199, 244
Eastern Ganga Dynasty, 26, 41, 129, 144, 189, 222, 432, 433
Eastern Roman Empire, 357
Eastern South Asia, 389
Eastern Turkic Khaganate, 290, 307
East India Company, 408
Eclecticism, 73
Economic history of India, 2, 271
Eelam, 199
Egypt, 109, 292, 357
Elephant, 224

Elephanta Caves, 118
Elephanta Island, 23
Ellalan, 143, 188, 192
Ellora, 41, 117, 118
Ellora Caves, 9, 23, 31, 32, 102, 103
Ellora Kailasanathar Temple, 31, 102, 112, 117
Eluru, 30
Emblem, 376
Emeralds, 159
Emperor, 187
Emperor Augustus, 357
Emperor Kanishka, 6
Emperor Taizong of Tang, 73
Empire, 41, 90
Empire of Harsha, 12, 41, 70, 73, 90, 94
Encyclopaedia Britannica, 474
Encyclopædia Britannica Eleventh Edition, 74, 123, 387
Encyclopedia, 63
English, 407
English Bazar, 394
English language, 166
Englishman, 166
Epic poetry, 399
Epigraphy, 50, 150, 159, 193, 224, 227
Errana, 419, 427
Etawah, 318
Ethnologue:aho, 479
Etymology of Karnataka, 65, 107, 158, 240
Euthydemus I, 4
Exogamy, 414

Fakhruddin Mubarak Shah, 389
Fan Hu Ta, 186
Far East, 373
Faridpur District, 265, 394
Fatimah, 330
Ferishta, 476
Fernão Nunes, 364
Feroz Shah Kotla, 327
Fertility goddess, 66
Feudal, 410
Feudatories, 174
Feudatory, 101, 105, 250
Finger millet, 229
Fiqh, 277, 313
Firishta, 247, 309
Firozabad, 280, 323, 327
Firoz Shah Tughlaq, 315
First Anglo-Burmese War, 408
First Bulgarian Empire, 290, 307
Firuz Shah Tughlaq, 280, 306, 315, 326, 331
Flag of Chola, 144, 189
Flag of Pandya, 340
Flaying, 322
Foreign trade, 357

Fort, 392
Francis Xavier, 379
Future, 1
Futures studies, 1

Gadadhar Singha, 406, 410, 414
Gadag, 119, 167, 168
Gadag district, 58, 66, 157, 167
Gahadavala, 270
Gajabahu I, 456
Gajapati Kingdom, 42, 416, 418, 420, 424, 426, 428, **432**
Gajapatis, 366
Ganapathi, 66, 381
Ganapati, 233
Ganda language, 265
Gandaraditya, 143, 145, 147, 188
Gandhara, 2, 129
Gaṇeśa, 135
Ganesha, 384
Ganga, 432
Gangadevi, 374, 380
Gangaikondacholapuram, 212
Gangaikonda Cholapuram, 38, 142, 144, 147, 187, 189, 195
Gangas, 105, 109, 145, 198
Ganges, 5, 10, 12, 102, 105, 106, 145, 190, 291, 433
Ganges Basin, 312
Ganges-Brahmaputra delta, 394
Ganges River, 32, 74
Gangetic plains, 32
Gangeyadeva, 128
Ganjam district, 255
Ganzhou Uyghur Kingdom, 290, 307
Garhgaon, 404
Garuda, 154, 249, 357, 380
Gauda (city), 124, 389
Gauḍa (city), 311, 388, 393, 400
Gauda Kingdom, 123
Gauḍa (region), 7
Gauhati, 413
Gaur, West Bengal, 17, 124, 262
Gautama Buddha, 17, 74, 133
Genghis Khan, 292, 293
Geographic coordinate system, 403, 415
Geography, 127
Geography of Andhra Pradesh, 245, 416, 424
Geography (Ptolemy), 4
Getae, 3
Ghaggar-Hakra River, 12
Ghat, 392
Ghazal, 399
Ghaznavid campaigns in the Indian Subcontinent, 89
Ghaznavids, 271, 291, 308

Ghazni, 292
Ghee, 372
Ghilji, 274
Ghilzai, 297
Ghiyasia Madrasa, 397
Ghiyasuddin Azam Shah, 395, 398, 400
Ghiyasuddin Bahadur Shah II, 402
Ghiyas ud din Balban, 273, 292, 294, 299
Ghiyasuddin Jalal Shah, 402
Ghiyasuddin Mahmud Shah, 401
Ghiyasuddin Tughlaq, 254
Ghiyath al-Din Tughlaq, 276
Ghiyath al-Din Tughluq, 301, 306, 309, 323, 324, 353
Ghurid dynasty, 270, 272, 291
Ghurid Empire, 292
Ghurid Sultanate, 90, 290
Gilgit, 8
Giraffe, 395
Gita Govinda, 266
Goa, 24, 64, 153, 365
Gobar Roja, 406
Godavari River, 33, 106, 120, 152, 190, 254, 351
Golconda, 109, 433
Golden Age, 48, 390, 399
Golden Age of India, 11
Golden Horde, 291, 308
Golden Shower Tree, 372
Golkonda, 372
Gomateshwara, 238, 239
Gommateshwara, 232, 384
Gondophares, 4
Gonka II, 250
Gopala, 124
Gopala II, 127, 139
Gopala III, 139
Gopala (Pala king), 17, 123, 139
Gopura, 382
Gopuram, 239, 354, 355, 385
Gotra, 250
Government of Karnataka, 67
Govinda II, 101
Govinda III, 32, 87, 94, 101, 105, 126, 226, 462
Govinda IV, 101, 106, 113
Govindapala, 139
Govinda Vidyadhara, 432
Gowda (caste), 159
Grain (measure), 109, 157
Grand Trunk Road, 390
Granite, 251
Grantha alphabet, 174
Grantha script, 179
Greater Bengal, 18, 20
Greater Khorasan, 314, 372

Great Living Chola Temples, 38, 144, 189, 212
Great power, 190
Greco-Bactrian Kingdom, 3
Greco-Buddhist art, 4
Greco-Roman world, 357
Gross domestic product, 283
Guerrilla warfare, 418, 426
Guhilot, 83
Guhilots, 81
Guild, 159
Gujarat, 2, 5, 7, 13, 14, 16, 22, 42, 52, 77–79, 83, 84, 107, 152, 159, 275, 281, 315, 321
Gujarat Sultanate, 270, 307, 394
Gujar Khan, 372
Gulbarga, 101, 116, 119, 365
Gulbarga district, 30, 102
Gulf of Mannar, 358
Gun, 392
Gundan Anivaritachari, 58, 68
Guntur, 417, 425
Guntur district, 177
Gupta Dynasty, 25, 119
Gupta Empire, 2, 9–14, 20, 22, 40, 53, 71–73, 91, 129, 135, 444
Gurjar, 12, 92
Gurjara, 14, 18, 79
Gurjaradesa, 92
Gurjara Pratihara, 78
Gurjara-Pratihara, 77, 78, 83, 124, 126
Gurjara-Pratihara dynasty, **89**, 100
Gurjaras, 81
Gurjaras of Lata, 82
Gurjaratra, 79, 85
Guru, 117
Guwahati, 20
Gwalior, 93, 288

Hafez, 398, 399
Halebidu, 37, 41, 119, 354, 454
Haleri Kingdom, 66, 108, 158, 241
Hampi, 42, 364, 371, 377, 378, 383, 384
Hanagal, 24, 438
Hangal, 451
Hanthawaddy Kingdom, 392
Hanuman, 216, 380
Haribhadra (Buddhist philosopher), 132
Haridasa, 379, 381
Harihara, 57, 66
Harihara I, 37, 362, 364
Harihara II, 366
Harihara (poet), 162
Harihara Raya I, 361
Harihara Raya II, 362
Harikela, 127
Harsha, 9, 12, 13, 15, 41, 53, **70**, 74, 94

Harshacharita, 71
Harshavardhan, 76, 88
Harshavardhana, 78
Haryana, 16, 95
Hassan district, 224
Hathigumpha inscription, 10, 343
Hauz-i-Shamsi, 293
Haveri, 58, 167, 168
Haveri district, 58, 168
Heggadadevanakote, 225
Hellenistic period, 3
Helmand Province, 297
Help:IPA, 48
Hemanta Sena, 261, 265
Henry Heras, 476
Henry Miers Elliot, 85
Henry Thomas Colebrooke, 67
Hephthalite Empire, 6
Heracles, 344
Heras, 455
Herat, 397
Hermann Kulke, 217, 219, 260
Hero stone, 115, 161, 235, 374
Hill fort, 417, 425
Himachal Pradesh, 42, 80
Himalaya, 12, 279
Himalayas, 91
Hindi, 13
Hindi-Urdu, 271, 284
Hindu, 6, 16, 23, 42, 76, 124, 230, 246, 262, 270, 276, 286, 309, 345, 364, 389, 432
Hindu caste system, 66, 93, 162, 235, 373
Hindu culture, 11
Hinduism, 2, 20, 23, 47, 70, 75, 89, 100, 102, 113, 142, 148, 173, 187, 221, 244, 261, 306, 338, 361, 364, 388, 404, 416, 424, 432
Hinduism in Southeast Asia, 210
Hindu Kush, 3
Hindus, 391
Hindu Shahi, 79
Hindustan, 13, 90
Hindustani language, 269, 284
Hindu temple, 266, 286
Hippodamian plan, 435
Hisham, 80
Hisham ibn Abd al-Malik, 79
Historical Vedic religion, 179, 230, 255
Historiography of early Islam, 40
History of Andhra Pradesh, 245, 416, 424
History of Bengal, 262
History of Champa, 186
History of China, 40
History of East Asia, 1
History of India, 3, 76, 87, 90, 144, 350, 363
History of Karnataka, 65, 107, 158, 240

History of Kozhikode, 366
History of Oceania, 1
History of Sindh, 93
History of Sri Lanka, 456
History of Tamil Nadu, 189, 339
History of Telangana, 245, 416, 424
History of the Republic of India, 458
History of the taka, 388, 393
History of the world, 1
History of the World (board game), 217
History of writing, 1
Hiuen-Tsiang, 27, 64
Honavar, 372
Hooghly district, 433
Hooli, 119
Horse trading, 113, 379
Hoskote, 375
Hospice, 74
House of Wisdom, 124
Hoysala, 351–353
Hoysala architecture, 58, 167
Hoysala Empire, 41, 55, 65, 108, 148, 158, 200, 240, 300, 352, 361, 364, 365, 382, 454, 466
Hoysalas, 30, 119, 149, 198, 340
Hoysaleswara temple, 37, 286, 443
Hull (watercraft), 372
Humayun, 389
Huna people, 4, 7, 9, 11, 18, 93, 130
Hund, Khyber Pakhtunkhwa, 8
Hussain Shahi dynasty, 390

Iarchive:KavyaPrakash, 74
IAST, 101
Ibn Battuta, 309, 319, 320, 419, 426
Ibn Khaldun, 140
Ibn Khordadbeh, 297
Ibn Taymiyyah, 315
Ibrahim Lodi, 270, 282, 335
Iconoclasm, 284
Idar, 288
Ikhtiyar Uddin Muhammad Bin Bakhtiyar Khalji, 262
I. K. Sarma, 243
Ilamchetchenni, 143, 188
Ilango Mutharaiyar, 192
Iltumish, 295
Iltutmish, 272, 273, 292
Ilyas Shahi dynasty, 389
India, 9, 48, 73, 75, 77, 90, 101, 124, 142, 173, 187, 221, 270, 274, 290, 292, 296, 307, 329, 361, 364, 388, 404, 408, 445
Indian art, 11
Indian astronomy, 11
Indian civilization, 271

Indian continental debate: an intra- and inter-Dharmic dialectic, 11
Indian copper plate inscriptions, 241, 379
Indian culture, 271
Indian history, 341
Indian Independence Act 1947, 42
Indian inscriptions, 101, 102, 112
Indian literature, 11, 124
Indian logic, 11
Indian maritime history, 190
Indian mathematics, 11
Indian Navy, 208
Indian Ocean, 16
Indian painting, 124
Indian people, 269, 274, 308
Indian philosophy, 11, 124
Indian religion, 11
Indian religions, 27
Indian subcontinent, 6, 10, 11, 17, 18, 40, 42, 43, 76, 90, 91, 101, 124, 262, 270, 271, 296, 432
Indica (Megasthenes), 344
Indo-Gangetic Plain, 9, 93, 95, 102
Indo-Gangetic plains, 10
Indo-Greek Kingdom, 3
Indo-Islamic architecture, 271
Indonesia, 187, 190
Indo-Parthian Kingdom, 4
Indo-Sasanians, 6
Indo-Scythians, 2
Indra, 448
Indra III, 32, 91, 95, 101, 106
Indra IV, 100, 101
Indra Pala, 21
Indus River, 4, 78, 90, 97
Industry in ancient Tamil country, 358
Infantry, 73
International Standard Book Number, 39, 43, 44, 68, 69, 77, 85, 86, 89, 99, 121, 122, 141, 171, 172, 186, 217–220, 243, 259, 260, 288, 295, 304, 305, 359, 360, 384–387, 403, 423, 431
International Standard Serial Number, 360
Ionians, 4
Iran, 93
Iraq, 52, 292
Irfan Habib, 298, 305, 469, 471
Iron Age, 339
Irrawaddy delta, 394
Irrigation tank, 371
Isami (historian), 247, 304, 311
Islam, 124, 291, 329, 388
Islamic, 113, 379
Islamic Caliphate, 7
Islamic cosmology, 398
Islamic Golden Age, 271, 282

Islamic invasions of India, 364
Islamicization, 271
Islam Shah Suri, 401
Ismailism, 272
Italian cuisine, 110

Jabalpur, 107, 121, 461
Jadunath Sarkar, 44
Jaffna kingdom, 107, 339, 340, 353
Jagadhekamalla II, 154
Jagannath Temple (Puri), 19
Jagannath Temple, Puri, 41
Jaggadala, 124
Jain, 24, 48, 83, 102, 164, 343, 379
Jainism, 10, 22–24, 27, 47, 66, 100, 102, 112, 113, 148, 160, 163, 214, 221, 224, 230, 246, 249, 256, 338, 359
Jains, 287, 340
Jaisalmer, 80
Jalaluddin Ahsan Khan, 354
Jalaluddin Fateh Shah, 401
Jalal ud din Firuz Khalji, 273, 274, 292, 296, 297, 299, 304
Jalaluddin Khalji, 273
Jalaluddin Lodi, 336
Jalal-ud-din Mangabarni, 293
Jalaluddin Muhammad Shah, 389, 391, 396, 400
Jalore, 83
Jamal-ud-Din Yaqut, 293
James Fergusson (architect), 211
Janna, 454
Jataka, 191
Jatavarman Kulasekaran I, 349
Jatavarman Parakrama Pandyan, 339
Jatavarman Sundara Pandyan, 201, 340, 351
Jatavarman Sundara Pandyan I, 351, 353
Jatavarman Vira Pandyan II, 351
Jāti, 256
Jatila Parantaka Nedunjadayan, 349
Jat people, 294, 309
Jauhar, 365
Jaunpur Sultanate, 281, 334, 392, 397
Jaunpur, Uttar Pradesh, 336
Java, 10, 18, 38, 373
Jayadeva, 266
Jayamkondar, 213
Jayantavarman, 349
Jaya Pala, 21
Jayasimha II (Western Chalukya dynasty), 152
Jayasimha (Vatapi Chalukya dynasty), 50
Jayatirtha, 379
Jessore, 394
Jhain, 288
Jharkhand, 18, 432
Jihad, 315

Jimutavahana, 134
Jinasena, 112, 117, 236
Jivaka-chintamani, 212
Jizya, 277, 280, 287, 301, 313, 316, 318
João de Barros, 391
Jodhpur, 81, 107
Jogeswar Singha, 407
John Faithfull Fleet, 447
John Keay, 41, 43, 49
Joishtho, 265
Jorhat, 404
JSTOR, 68, 85, 99, 259–261, 337, 415
Julian the Apostate, 345
Jumna, 12
Jumuah, 113, 379
Junaid, 14, 97
Junayd ibn Abd al-Rahman al-Murri, 77

Kabul, 3, 8, 79, 336
Kachari kingdom, 409
Kadamba dynasty, 47–49, 65, 107, 150, 158, 177, 225, 240
Kadambas, 24, 64, 153
Kadava, 201
Kadava dynasty, 351, 352
Kadungon, 182, 338, 340, 349, 456
Kaikolar, 205–207
Kailasa temple, Ellora, 103
Kaitabheshvara Temple, Kubatur, 168
Kaithal, 294
Kakatiya dynasty, 33, 35, 41, 55, 148, 149, 244, 270, 285, 300, 361, 365, 416, 417, 421, 424, 425, 429, 439
Kakatiya Kala Thoranam, 258, 285
Kakustha (Gurjara-Pratihara dynasty), 98
Kakusthavarma, 25
Kalabhra, 28, 54
Kalabhra dynasty, 173, 178
Kalabhras, 24, 182, 192, 340, 359
Kalachuri, 33, 118
Kalachuri dynasty, 35
Kalachuris of Kalyani, 35, 65, 108, 149, 155, 158, 162, 198, 240
Kalachuris of Tripuri, 36, 41, 85, 90, 95, 127, 128
Kalamukha, 256
Kalhana, 76
Kalidasa, 11, 346
Kalinga (historical kingdom), 7, 9, 18, 33
Kalinga (historical region), 42, 124, 153, 222, 340, 343, 367, 419, 420, 427, 428, 432
Kalinganagar, 198
Kalki Krishnamurthy, 216
Kalki (Tamil magazine), 216
Kalleshvara Temple, Aralaguppe, 239
Kalleshvara Temple, Bagali, 149, 168

Kalleshwara Temple, Hire Hadagali, 151
Kalyana, 154
Kalyani Chalukyas, 119
Kamarupa, 7, 18, 20, 70, 124, 128–130, 404
Kamarupa kingdom, 410
Kamata Kingdom, 392
Kambadahalli, 27, 112, 160, 224, 228, 379
Kamban, 213
Kamboja Kingdom, 18
Kamboja Pala dynasty, 127, 130
Kambojas, 4, 130
Kampili, 354
Kampili kingdom, 247, 365
Kanakachalapathi Temple, Kanakagiri, 384
Kanakadasa, 374, 379, 381
Kanauj, 79, 87
Kanchi, 51, 224, 288, 384
Kanchi Kailasanathar Temple, 175, 176
Kanchipuram, 22, 23, 26, 28, 29, 173–176, 178, 179, 181, 194, 206, 345, 352, 417, 425
Kandahar, 336
Kandhar, 246
Kandy, 181
Kangar union, 290, 307
Kangra valley, 80, 129
Kanhadade Prabandha, 44
K. A. Nilakanta Sastri, 91, 177, 219, 348, 385, 457
K.A. Nilakanta Sastri, 455, 456
Kanishka, 435
Kanker, Chhattisgarh, 246
Kannada, 24, 28, 36, 41, 50, 54, 68, 102, 112, 116, 120, 149, 154, 157, 224, 226, 227, 450, 461
Kannada language, 23, 24, 26, 34, 47, 100, 104, 115, 119, 148, 221, 247, 250, 361, 364
Kannada literature, 48, 55, 63
Kannada literature in Vijayanagara empire, 381
Kannada people, 263
Kannada script, 51
Kannadiga, 41, 42, 104, 149, 364, 439
Kannadigas, 440
Kannanur, 352
Kannauj, 12, 15, 27, 32, 70, 74, 76, 89, 90, 101, 105, 124, 126, 436
Kannur, 372
Kanva dynasty, 9
Kanyakubja, 7
Kapilendradeva, 432
Kapilendra Deva, 432, 434
Kapisa Province, 8
Kappe Arabhatta, 28, 51, 63
Karaikal District, 202
Kara-Khanid dynasty, 290, 307
Kara-Khanid Khanate, 290, 307
Kara, Uttar Pradesh, 275
Kareng Ghar, 409
Karikala, 143, 188
Karikala Chola, 192, 249
Karka II, 33, 101, 152
Karkala, 384
Karka II, 54
Karkota dynasty, 79
Karkota Empire, 7
Karkoṭa Empire, **75**
Karluk Yabgu State, 290, 307
Karna (Chaulukya dynasty), 16
Karnataka, 24, 26, 34–36, 41, 42, 48, 49, 51, 53, 101, 102, 104, 115, 118, 119, 149, 150, 166, 168, 222, 246, 262, 263, 364, 365
Karrani dynasty, 390
Kartikeya, 66
Kārttikeya, 135
Karur, 24
Kashipur, Uttarakhand, 96
Kashi Vishwanath Temple, 285
Kashmir, 2, 76, 81, 153
Kashmiri people, 50
Kashyapa, 250
Kasivisvesvara Temple, 149, 168
Kataha, 200
Kathiawar, 16, 79, 82
Kathleen Gough, 203, 217
Katoch, 14
Kātyāyana, 5
Kautilya, 164, 227
Kaveri, 10, 26, 27, 48, 54, 224, 432
Kaveripattinam, 192
Kaveri River, 29, 33, 105, 106, 120, 149, 190, 224, 229
Kavirajamarga, 102, 116, 236, 438
Kavitrayam, 422, 430
Kavya, 120
Kayalpattanam, 113
Kayastha, 125
Kedah, 199
Kedareshvara Temple, Balligavi, 163, 168
Keel, 372
Kekeya Kingdom, 4
Keladi (India), 369
Keladi Nayaka, 369
Keling, 10
Keraites, 291, 308
Kerala school of astronomy and mathematics, 382
Keshava Sena, 261, 265
Khajuraho, 91, 96
Khalaj language, 297
Khalid Yahya Blankinship, 81, 85

505

Khalji dynasty, 270, 274, 290–292, 294, **296**, 305, 307–309
Khambhat, 113
Khandesh, 109
Kharaj, 301, 303, 318
Kharavela, 9, 343
Khazars, 290, 307
Khidr Khan(Bengal), 401
Khizr Khan, 281, 329, 330
Khokhar, 272
Khosrau II, 27
Khosrau II, 51
Khottiga, 101
Khottiga Amoghavarsha, 106
Khums, 300
Khusrau Khan, 253, 273
Khusro Khan, 275, 301, 304, 309, 353
Khwarazmian dynasty, 291, 308
Killivalavan, 143, 188
Kimek confederation, 291, 308
King, 142, 187
Kingdom of Ava, 392
Kingdom of Axum, 357
Kingdom of Funan, 186
Kingdom of Mrauk U, 388, 392
Kingdom of Mysore, 42, 66, 108, 158, 241, 361, 369
Kingdom of Polonnaruwa, 351
Kipchak people, 273
Kirtimukha, 163, 169, 238
Kirtivarman II, 47, 101
Kirtivarman I, 440
Kirtivarman II, 54
Kocengannan, 192
Kochadaiyan Ranadhiran, 349
Kochchenganan, 143, 188
Koch dynasty, 413
Koch Hajo, 410
Koh-i-Noor, 253, 275, 300, 301
Kolar, 26, 196, 221, 224, 225
Kolar district, 224
Kolhapur, 113
Konark, 18, 19, 433
Konark Sun Temple, 18, 19, 41
Kondapalli, 417, 425
Kondavid Fort, 416, 424
Kondavidu, 417, 425
Koneswaram temple, 181, 348
Kongu Nadu, 224, 351
Konkan, 51, 105, 152
Koppal district, 58, 151, 168
Kopperunchinga II, 352
Kopperunchinga I, 201
Kopperuncholan, 143, 188
Korkai, 338, 339, 358
Kosala, 104, 105, 159, 213

Kosala Kingdom, 27
Kota Vamsa, 247
Kozhikode, 372
Krishna, 194, 249, 442, 451
Krishnadevaraya, 362, 364, 367, 380
Krishna Deva Raya, 418, 426
Krishna district, 177
Krishna I, 101, 105
Krishna II, 101, 106
Krishna III, 32, 101, 106, 117, 120, 248, 448, 451, 461, 464
Krishna River, 33, 106, 152, 181, 254, 300, 365, 366, 419, 422, 427, 430
Kshatriya, 50, 113, 125, 235, 247, 255
K. S. Lal, 305, 360
Kubja Vishnuvardhana, 13, 55, 440
Kudalasangama, 35
Kukkanur, 461
Kuknur, 119, 120
Kulakkottan, 143, 188
Kulīna System, 20
Kulothunga Chola I, 143, 146, 153, 188, 190
Kulothunga Chola II, 143, 188
Kulothunga Chola III, 143, 188, 351
Kulothunga Chola II, 215
Kulothunga Chola III, 198
Kulottunga Chola I, 348
Kulottunga Chola III, 199
Kumara Gupta I, 10
Kumarapala (Pala king), 139
Kumaravishnu I, 182
Kumaravishnu II, 182
Kumaravishnu III, 182
Kumara Vyasa, 381
Kumbakonam, 202, 352, 384
Kumudam, 217
Kundavai Pirāttiyār, 147
Kurnool, 109
Kuru (kingdom), 129
Kuru Kingdom, 4
Kurukshetra War, 165
Kushan Empire, 4, 6, 8
Kutch, 81, 82
K. V. Ramesh (archaeologist), 49, 386

Lad Khan Temple, 57
Lahore, 269, 292, 309
Lajja Gauri, 66
Lakkundi, 58, 149, 157, 169
Lakshadweep, 38, 195
Lakshmana, 91
Lakshmana Pandita, 382
Lakshmana Sena, 262, 265
Lakshman Sen, 20
Lakshmeshwar, 66
Lakshmi, 212

Lalitaditya Muktapida, 7, 75, 76, 81, 94
Lamghan, 297
Lanka, 199
Lapis lazuli, 159
Lashkargah, 298
Lata (region), 27, 140, 159
Late modern period, 1
Later Chola, 146, 192
Later Cholas, 2, 143, 148, 188
Lathe, 168
Launggyet, 392
Lepakshi, 384
Levant, 292
Library of Congress Control Number, 68, 121, 171, 243, 385
Library of Congress Country Studies, 39
Lilatilakam, 353
Lingayat, 36, 454
Lingayatism, 169, 374, 381
Lingayats, 162
Lingua franca, 284
Lion, 394
List of countries and outlying territories by area, 306
List of Indian inventions and discoveries, 11
List of Rajput dynasties and states, 42
List of rivers in Bangladesh, 391
List of Solesvara temples, 144, 189
List of Tamil monarchs, 339
Literature, 210
Lodi dynasty, 270, 329, 330, **333**, 338
Lodi Gardens, 329
Lodi (Pashtun tribe), 281
Logic, 63
Lord Elphinstone, 14, 98
Lord Rishabha, 116
Lord Shiva, 162

Machilipatnam, 372
Madanapala (Pala dynasty), 20, 123, 139
Madan Kamdev, 21
Madayyagari Mallana, 382
Madhava-kara, 134
Madhava of Sangamagrama, 382
Madhvacharya, 379, 381
Madhya Pradesh, 5, 11, 15, 34–36, 42, 121, 315, 432
Madra, 4, 129
Madrasa, 317, 397
Madurai, 24, 27, 30, 37, 178, 194, 225, 288, 300, 338–340, 345, 365, 369, 419, 426
Maduraikkanci, 345
Madurai Nayak dynasty, 339, 340, 361, 369
Madurai Nayaks, 354
Madurai Sultanate, 340, 354, 361, 365, 380
Madura Vijayam, 380

Magadh, 159
Magadha, 9, 64, 72, 95
Magas of Cyrene, 343
Magnesia (regional unit), 4
Mahabalipuram, 174, 179, 180
Mahaballipuram, 23
Mahabharata, 5, 32, 105, 116, 133, 134, 164, 341, 345, 346, 380, 419, 422, 427, 430
Mahabharatha, 341
Mahadeva Temple (Itagi), 58, 149, 168
Mahajan, 64
Mahajanapadas, 17
Mahajanas, 159
Mahakavya, 166
Mahakoshal, 95
Mahakuta group of temples, 28, 56
Mahakuta Pillar, 51
Mahalakshmi Temple (Kolhapur), 113
Maharaja, 43, 47, 91, 100, 221, 404
Maharashtra, 2, 5, 11, 30, 34–36, 41, 42, 51, 101, 102, 104, 117, 246, 277, 313
Mahavamsa, 191, 192, 201, 456
Mahavira, 112
Mahavira (mathematician), 112, 116
Mahāvīra (mathematician), 115
Mahayana, 17, 123, 124
Mahayana Buddhism, 18, 132
Mahdi, 280
Mahenderpal I, 95
Mahendrapala, 139
Mahendrapala I, 91, 98
Mahendrapala II, 98
Mahendravadi, 181
Mahendravarman I, 29, 174, 182, 185
Mahendravarman II, 174, 182, 185
Mahendravarman (Varman dynasty), 20
Mahipala, 18, 38, 139, 145, 190
Mahipala I, 95, 98, 124
Mahipala II, 139
Mahi River, 82
Mahishasura, 67
Mahmud al-Kashgari, 298
Mahmud of Ghazni, 16, 91, 95, 127, 271, 287
Mahmud Shah II, 401
Mahmud Shah (Sultan of Bengal), 401
Mainland Southeast Asia, 11
Maitraka, 79, 81, 83
Maize, 229
Malabar coast, 379
Malacca sultanate, 210
Malaprabha, 28, 56
Malay Peninsula, 18, 38
Malay people, 195
Malaysia, 159, 187, 190
Maldives, 10, 142, 187, 190
Malik Altunia, 294

Malik Kafur, 253, 275, 285, 300, 353
Malik Kafurs invasion of the Pandya kingdom, 353
Mallikarjuna Raya, 362
Mallikarjuna Temple, Kuruvatti, 149, 168
Malnad, 37, 228, 371
Malwa, 5, 15, 27, 72, 81, 93, 102, 104, 149, 153, 226, 275
Malwa Sultanate, 298
Mamallapuram, 29, 183
Mamluk, 270–273, 284, 291, 310
Mamluk dynasty (Delhi), **289**, 291, 308
Mamluk dynasty of Delhi, 296, 299
Mamluk dynasty of Iraq, 273
Mamluk Egypt, 396
Mamluk Sultanate, 271
Mamluk Sultanate (Cairo), 271, 273, 291, 308
Mamluk Sultanate (Delhi), 270
Mamluk Sultanate of Egypt, 284
Manasollasa, 166
Manas river, 410
Mandalam, 203
Mandapa, 57, 354
Mandore, 79
Mandya district, 224
Mangalesha, 51, 440
Mangalore, 372
Mangulam, 343
Manigramam, 159
Manikkavacakar, 347
Manimekalai, 23, 176, 342
Manipur, 404
Mañjuśrī-mūla-kalpa, 125
Mansura (Brahmanabad), 79, 83, 97
Mantapa, 57
Manu (Hinduism), 225
Manusmṛti, 5
Manyakheta, 26, 30, 33, 100–102, 104, 105, 107, 148, 149, 226
Mappila, 113
Maratha, 104
Maratha Empire, 42
Marathi language, 34
Marathi people, 34
Maravarman Kulasekara Pandyan I, 351, 353
Maravarman Rajasimha I, 349
Maravarman Rajasimha II, 349
Maravarman Sundara Pandyan, 340, 351
Maravarman Sundara Pandyan II, 351
Marco Polo, 30, 160, 251, 345, 465
Maritime Southeast Asia, 10, 11
Martand Sun Temple, 76
Māru-Gurjara architecture, 96
Masjid, 113, 379
Massagetae, 3
Masulipatnam, 465

Matha, 164
Mathura, 5, 10, 281
Mathuraikkanci, 342
Matriarchy, 23
Matrika, 52, 239
Matrikas, 66
Matsya Kingdom, 129
Mattavilasa Prahasana, 182
Maues, 2
Maurya Empire, 2, 9, 129, 190
Mauryan Empire, 9
Mauryas, 25
Mayurasharma, 25
Mayurkhandi, 447
Mecca, 372, 397
Medes, 3
Medieval, 306
Medieval Cholas, **142**, 143, 188, 191
Medieval history, 1
Medieval India, 2, **40**, 80, 283, 416, 424, 432
Medieval Near East, 1
Medina, 397
Meenakshi, 341
Meenakshi Amman Temple, 30, 340, 354
Meenakshi Temple, 285, 341, 385
Megasthenes, 340, 344, 359
Mehrauli, 293, 295
Mehrauli Archaeological Park, 295
Melakadambur, 144, 189
Melkote, 162
Melting pot, 395
Mercenary, 140
Metropolitan Museum of Art, 215
Mewar, 15, 81
Middle Ages, 1, 2, 40, 142, 187, 270, 282
Middle East, 271
Middle Indo-Aryan languages, 284
Middle kingdoms of India, 1, **1**, 78, 89, 261, 283
Mid-Imperial China, 210
Mihira Bhoja, 15, 85, 91, 95, 96, 98, 130
Mihirakula, 8
Mihrab, 399
Miller Atlas, 395
Minaret, 279
Ming China, 392
Ming dynasty, 395
Minhaj-i-Siraj, 298
Mint (facility), 393
Mir Jumla II, 410
Mitakshara, 62, 166
Mithila (ancient), 265
Mleccha, 2
Mlechchha dynasty, 20
Moamoria rebellion, 404, 408, 410
Modern history, 1

508

Modernity, 1
Modhera Sun Temple, 16
Mogaung, 414
Mohammed of Ghor, 15
Moksha, 74
Molding (decorative), 238
Molla (poet), 374, 375
Momai Tamuli Borbarua, 414
Monarch, 148, 361
Monarchy, 3, 47, 75, 89, 100, 123, 142, 148, 173, 187, 221, 244, 261, 333, 338, 361, 416, 424, 432
Mong Mao, 408
Mongol Empire, 270, 271, 274, 284
Mongol invasion of China, 284
Mongol invasion of Europe, 284
Mongol invasion of India, 292
Mongol invasion of Persia, 284
Mongol invasions, 284
Mongol invasions of India, 271, 275, 284, 297
Mongols, 284, 293
Monolithic architecture, 384
Mori Rajputs, 85
Mosque, 317
Mount Abu, 12, 52, 93
Mounted infantry, 73
Mubarak Shah (Sayyid dynasty), 329, 330
Mueang, 408
Mughal architecture, 384
Mughal Bengal, 389
Mughal Emperor, 93
Mughal Empire, 40, 42, 246, 270, 271, 282, 283, 287, 333, 335, 374, 388–390, 392, 393, 408, 410
Muhammad bin Bakhtiyar Khalji, 287, 288
Muhammad bin Bakhtiyar Khilji, 285, 292
Muhammad bin Qasim, 79, 97
Muhammad bin Tughluq, 254, 276, 287, 306, 309, 311, 323, 353, 354, 365
Muhammad ibn Qasim, 84
Muhammad Khan Sur, 401, 402
Muhammad of Ghor, 270, 272, 273, 292
Muhammad Shah (Sayyid dynasty), 329, 330, 334
Muiz ud din Bahram, 272, 294
Muiz ud din Qaiqabad, 273, 289, 292, 294
Multan, 84, 273, 292, 322, 330, 331
Multicultural, 282
Mumbai, 23, 84, 118
Munger, 124, 126
Munshiram Manoharlal, 99
Murshidabad, 394
Music, 210
Musk, 375
Musket, 370

Muslim, 19, 20, 37, 95, 270, 296, 308, 365, 389, 391
Muslim conquest in the Indian subcontinent, 13
Muslim conquest of the Indian subcontinent, 389
Muslim conquests, 357
Muslim lands, 271
Muslim Rajput, 78
Muslim world, 271
Muslin, 109
Mustard seed, 384
Musunuri Nayak, 313
Musunuri Nayaks, 244, 245, 257, 270, 361
Muthuraja, 192
Muttarayar, 194, 348
Muziris, 344
Myanmar, 18, 38, 388
Mymensingh, 393
Mysore, 105, 110, 192, 200
Mysore district, 26, 224
Mysore State, 153, 160, 451

Nabadwip, 20, 261, 262
Nadia, 394
Nāga, 374
Nagabhata I, 77, 78, 83, 85, 90, 92, 93, 98
Nagabhata II, 85, 90, 94, 98, 126
Nagaland, 404
Naga (mythology), 125
Nagananda, 73, 74
Nagaon, 413
Nagapattinam, 215
Nagapattinam District, 202
Nagappattinam, 202
Nagarattar, 159
Nagarjunakonda, 419, 427
Nagavarma I, 170, 237
Nagavarma II, 164
Nageshvara Temple, Begur, 239
Nagore, 113
Naimans, 291, 308
Nainativu, 176
Nalanda, 18, 124, 132, 133, 285, 287, 288
Nalanda Gedige, 181
Nalankilli, 143, 188, 191
Nanadesis, 159
Nandi (bull), 233, 354, 384
Nandi Hills, India, 233
Nandinagari, 464
Nandipuri, 81
Nandi Thimmana, 382
Nandivarman I, 182
Nandivarman II, 174, 184, 185
Nandivarman III, 174, 184, 185
Nandivarman II, 54
Nandol, 79

Nanjangud, 225, 233
Nannaya, 422, 430
Naraharitirtha, 379
Narakasura, 20
Narasimha, 57, 377, 422, 430
Narasimhadeva I, 19
Narasimha I, 155
Narasimha III, 352
Narasimha Raya II, 362
Narasimhavarman, 53
Narasimhavarman I, 28, 29, 174, 182, 183, 185
Narasimhavarman II, 29, 174, 180–182, 184, 185
Narasimhavarman I, 216
Narayanapala, 127
Narayanapala (Kamboja), 127
Narayan Pala, 139
Narmada, 91
Narmada River, 12, 22, 27, 33, 34, 48, 53, 54, 70, 73, 94, 106, 149, 254, 441
Nasir ud din Mahmud, 272, 294
Nasir-ud-Din Mahmud Shah Tughluq, 280, 323
Nasiruddin Nasrat Shah, 390, 399, 401
Nasir-ud-din Nusrat Shah Tughluq, 280, 323
Nasir-ud-Din Qabacha, 292
Nataraja, 57, 212, 215
Natavadi, 247
National Museum, New Delhi, 96
Navalinga Temple (Kukkanur), 119
Navsari, 82
Navy, 392
Nayakas of Chitradurga, 66, 108, 158, 241, 361, 369
Nayakas of Keladi, 66, 108, 158, 241, 361
Nayak dynasty, 43
Nayaks of Gingee, 361, 369
Nayaks of Tanjore, 375
Nayak (title), 256
Nayanars, 181
Naya Pala, 139
Naya Pala (Kamboja), 127
Nedunalvadai, 345
Nedunjeliyan I, 346
Nedunjeliyan II, 347
Nedunkilli, 143, 188, 191
Nellaiappar Temple, 30, 340, 354, 355
Nellore, 55, 253
Nellore district, 177
Nepal, 124, 159, 270, 307
Nerbudda, 441
Netunalvatai, 342
Niccolò Da Conti, 364
Niccolo De Conti, 397
Nicolaus of Damascus, 345
Nidadavolu, 252

Nilakanta Sastri, 182
Nilakantha Somayaji, 382
Nitish Sengupta, 141
Niyogi, 227
Nolamba, 233, 462, 463
Nolambas, 233, 238
Nomad, 271
North Bengal, 20
Northeast India, 408
Northern India, 12, 14, 76, 291
North Gauhati, 21
North Guwahati, 20, 21
North India, 6, 14, 70, 73, 224, 284
North Karnataka, 35, 36

OCLC, 68, 69, 121, 122, 171, 243, 260, 305, 328, 360, 385
Odantapuri, 132, 287
Odia language, 432
Odia people, 433
Odisha, 13, 18–20, 26, 41, 104, 195, 222, 262, 366, 418, 426, 432
OECD Development Centre, 469
Official language, 398
Oghuz Turks, 298
Oghuz Yabgu State, 291, 308
Oilseed, 229
Okha, India, 81
Old Great Bulgaria, 290, 307
Old Kannada, 120, 170
Onyx, 159
Open Library, 86, 243
Orissa, 420, 428
Orissa, India, 42, 127, 255
Orissa Subah, 390
Ottakuttan, 213
Ottoman Empire, 291, 308
Outline of ancient India, 40, 439
Outline of South Asian history, 1

Padmakshi Temple, 256
Padmavati (Jainism), 246
Pagoda (coin), 157
Paik system, 410, 413
Paithan, 109
Pakhal Lake, 251
Pakistan, 75, 78, 124, 270, 296, 307, 322, 329
Pala Dynasty, 32, 195
Pala dynasty (Kamarupa), 20, 21
Pala Empire, 17, 20, 22, 41, 79, 87, 91, 94, 101, 105, **123**, 145, 153, 190, 261, 267
Palestine (region), 372
Pali, 102, 123
Pallava, 22, 52, 53, 104, 222, 340, 341
Pallava alphabet, 174
Pallava dynasty, 5, 26, 41, **173**, 174, 192, 221

510

Pallavas, 24, 27, 29, 52, 105, 145, 224, 341, 348
Palnadu, 418, 425
Pampa Bharata, 92
Panam City, 388
Panchakuta Basadi, Kambadahalli, 239
Panchala, 4
Pandava, 32, 237, 341
Pandu, 341
Pandua, Malda, 393
Pandya, 22, 23, 54, 159, 182, 341
Pandya coinage, 348
Pandya Empire, 466
Pandyan, 117
Pandya Nadu, 339
Pandyan dynasty, 10, 24, 187, 190, 191, 253, **338**, 361, 382
Pandyan Empire, 357, 365
Pandyan Kingdom, 24, 358
Pandyas, 22, 24, 27, 55, 105, 145, 174, 343
Pāṇini, 237
Pannonian Avars, 3
Parada Kingdom, 3
Parakrama Pandyan I, 349
Parakrama Pandyan II, 351
Parama Kamboja Kingdom, 3
Paramara, 32, 33, 93, 95, 106, 149, 226
Paramara dynasty, 14, 90, 270
Paramesvaravarman I, 174, 182, 185
Paramesvaravarman II, 174, 184, 185
Parantaka Chola II, 143, 145, 147, 188, 349
Parantaka I, 143, 145, 147, 188, 348
Parantaka Viranarayanan, 349
Parantaka I, 194
Parashurama, 247
Pargana, 265
Parihaspore, 75
Parihaspur, 76
Parimelazhagar, 191
Parthia, 3
Parthian language, 5
Parthians, 52
Parthiban Kanavu, 216
Parvathi, 117
Parvati, 73, 233, 359, 381, 384
Pashto language, 297
Pashtunization, 274
Pashtun people, 336
Pashtuns, 281
Pataliputra, 24, 124, 190
Patan, Gujarat, 16, 286
Patkai, 408
Pattadakal, 23, 28, 50, 51, 56, 61, 64, 102, 110, 115, 118
Pattupattu, 342
Pazhaiyaarai, 142, 187

P. B. Desai, 476
Peanut, 384
Pearson Education, 469
Pechenegs, 291, 308
Pegu, 366
Peninsula, 13
Pennar, 181
Penukonda, 361
Peoples Republic of China, 408
Perak, 211
Perambalur district, 202
Percy Brown (scholar), 443, 478
Periplus, 357
Periplus of the Erythraean Sea, 5, 191, 340, 344, 358
Periyalvar, 382
Periyapuranam, 456
Persia, 109, 159, 372
Persian alphabet, 303
Persianate, 389
Persianate society, 391
Persian Empire, 27
Persian language, 269, 270, 289, 291, 296, 306, 329, 333, 388, 398
Persian literature, 399
Persian people, 4, 372, 398
Perunarkilli, 143, 188
Peter Jackson (historian), 259, 288, 305, 360
Philosopher king, 15
Pietro Della Valle, 459
Pillars of Ashoka, 191, 343
Pingali Surana, 382
Pipeline transport, 371
Piracy, 159
Plantain (cooking), 229
Poignard, 370
Poland, 109
Political history of medieval Karnataka, 65, 107, 158, 240
Politics of Andhra Pradesh, 245, 416, 424
Polity, 224
Polo, 292
Polymath, 15
Ponds, 399
Ponniyin Selvan, 216
Poompuhar, 144, 187, 189
Portal:Assam, 407
Portuguese India, 364
Portuguese people, 379
Portuguese settlement in Chittagong, 389, 390, 396
Post and lintel, 239
Post-classical history, 1
Potana, 422, 430
Prabandha, 83
Prabhakarvardhana, 70

511

Prabhu, 159
Pragjyotisha, 127
Prakrit, 88, 89, 112, 123, 181
Prakrit language, 173
Pramatta Singha, 409
Prambanan, 210
Prashasti, 159, 176
Prataap Singha, 414
Prataparudra Deva, 432, 434
Prataparudra II, 252
Prataprudra Deva, 432
Pratap Singha, 410
Prathihara, 22, 102
Pratihara, 14, 18, 32, 105, 226
Pratihara Empire, 87
Pratiharas, 14, 79
Praudha Raya, 362, 382
Pre-Columbian era, 1
Prehistory, 1
Pre-modern coinage in Sri Lanka, 348
Primogeniture, 411
Prince, 29
Princely state, 258
Princely States, 42
Principality, 365
Prithviraj Chauhan, 16
Prithvi Raj Chauhan, 15
Prithviraj III, 14, 15
Prithviraj Raso, 52, 93
Priyadarsika, 74
Prophet Muhammad, 330
Prophets Mosque, 397
Prose, 236
Prosody (poetry), 237
Ptolemaic dynasty, 357
Ptolemaic Egypt, 345
Ptolemy, 4, 191, 340
Ptolemy II Philadelphus, 343
Pudukkottai district, 202
Pulakeshin I, 27, 47
Pulakeshin II, 12, 13, 27, 71, 73
Pulakeshin I, 49, 53
Pulakeshin II, 48, 51
Pulicat, 373
Pulse (legume), 157, 371
Punch-marked coins, 343, 356
Punjab, 76, 79
Punjab region, 2, 3, 43, 104, 330, 334
Purana, 240
Purananuru, 342, 345
Puranas, 2, 5, 164
Purandaradasa, 379, 381
Purandar Singha, 407
Puranic, 478
Puri, 27, 64, 288, 432, 433
Purushottama Deva, 432, 434

Pushkalavati, 3
Pushyavarman, 20
P. V. Parabrahma Sastry, 246, 260
Pyre, 114, 163

Qalandariyya, 312
Qalat, Zabul Province, 274
Qaraunas, 309
Qarlughids, 291, 308
Qazi Fazilat, 401
Qocho, 290, 307
Questia, 260
Quilon, 366
Quli Qutb Mulk, 367
Qutb al-Din Aibak, 270, 273, 289, 291, 292, 295
Qutb complex, 273, 275, 303
Qutb Minar, 292, 293, 295, 319
Qutb Shahi dynasty, 361
Qutb-ud-din Aibak, 272, 285
Qutb-ud-din Aybak, 286
Qutb ud din Mubarak Shah, 276, 296, 301, 304
Qutb-ud-din Mubarak Shah, 273
Qutub Minar, 273
Quwwat-ul-Islam mosque, 292

Rachamalla II, 222
Raghavanka, 162
Raghuvamsha, 346
Rai dynasty, 7, 79
Raja, 41, 419, 427
Raja Chulan, 211
Raja Dahir, 79
Rajadhiraja Chola, 107, 143, 146, 188, 190
Rajadhiraja Chola I, 146, 147
Rajadhiraja Chola II, 143, 188
Rajadhiraja Chola II, 199
Rajaditya, 145, 147
Raja Ganesha, 389, 400
Rajahmundry, 416, 417, 424, 425
Rajahnate of Cebu, 144, 189
Rajamundry, 30
Raja Nahar Khan, 288
Rajaraja Chola, 38, 195, 200
Raja Raja Chola, 145, 147
Rajaraja Chola I, 143, 152, 188, 190, 226
Rajaraja Chola II, 143, 188
Rajaraja Chola III, 143, 188, 351
Rajaraja Cholan, 217
Rajaraja Chola I, 55
Rajaraja Chola II, 200
Rajaraja Chola III, 201
Rajaraja Narendra, 199, 451
Rajasthan, 2, 5, 12, 27, 35, 42, 77, 79, 84, 107
Rajasuya, 113
Rajatarangini, 7, 8, 76

Rajendra Chola, 18, 38, 145
Rajendra Chola I, 127, 143, 147, 152, 188, 190
Rajendra Chola II, 143, 146, 147, 188
Rajendra Chola III, 2, 143, 187, 188, 351–353
Rajendra Chola III, 200
Rajeswar Singha, 409
Rajgir, 10
Rajkumar (actor), 68
Rajput, 9, 14, 22, 42, 93
Rajputana, 14, 95
Rajuvula, 5
Rajyapala, 127, 139
Rajyapala Kamboja, 127
Rajyavardhana, 70
Rama, 91, 237, 247, 346
Ramabhadra, 91, 98
Ramachandra of Devagiri, 274
Ramachandra Raya, 362
Ramacharitam, 128, 134, 140
Rama Deva Raya, 363
Ramanuja, 215
Ramanujacharya, 67, 162, 433
Ramapala, 18, 124, 125, 139
Ramappa Temple, 249, 251
Ramarajabhushanudu, 382
Ramavataram, 213
Ramayana, 5, 23, 133, 164, 213, 346, 380, 422, 430
Ramesh Chandra Majumdar, 139
Rameshvara Temple, Narasamangala, 239
Rampart (fortification), 251
Ram Sharan Sharma, 260
Ranaraga, 50
Rang Ghar, 409
Rangpur (Ahom capital), 404
Rangpur District, 394
Rani ki vav, 286
Ranjit Singh, 43
Ranna, 63, 150, 164, 170, 236, 442, 451
Ranthambore Fort, 273, 299
Rarh region, 128
Rashidun Caliphate, 6
Rashtrakuta, 22, 24, 31, 51, 54, 82, 91, 97, 123, 124, 126, 148, 149, 156, 248, 442
Rashtrakuta Dynasty, 26, 41, 48, 65, **100**, 101, 108, 126, 148, 158, 194, 224, 240, 417, 425
Rashtrakuta Empire, 87
Rashtrakutas, 22, 48, 94, 145
Rathore, 107
Ratna Pala, 21
Ratnavali, 74
Ratta dynasty, 107
Ravana, 117
Rayalaseema, 456
Razia Sultana, 270, 272, 273, 292, 293

R. C. Majumdar, 13, 44, 86, 89, 434, 442, 467
Reconquest of Arakan, 392
Recorded history, 1
Reddi, 104
Reddy, 257, 365, 425
Reddy dynasty, 42, 244, 361, **416**
Red Sea, 357, 372
Relief, 348, 384
Religion, 210, 224, 249
Religion in Assam, 407
Religious pluralism, 391
Renaissance, 339
Rice, 157, 228
Richest country, 30
Rishikas, 3
River basin, 254
Robert Caldwell, 341
Romance (heroic literature), 237
Roman emperor, 345
Roman Empire, 5, 30, 340, 358
Rome, 357
Romila Thapar, 219, 386
Rose water, 375
Roxana, 4
Rudrama Devi, 251, 252
Rudra Mahalaya Temple, 286
Rudrasimha III, 3
Rudra Singha, 409, 414
Rukn-e-Alam, 309
Rukn ud din Firuz, 273, 292, 293
Rukn-ud-din Firuz, 272
Rukunuddin Barbak Shah, 401
Ryotwari, 206

Sabarmati River, 16
Sacred Books of the East, 435
Sadashiva Raya, 367
Sadasiva Raya, 363
Sagala, 3
Saifuddin Firuz Shah, 401
Saifuddin Hamza Shah, 400
Sailendra, 18
Saindhava, 78, 79, 82, 84
Saiva, 134
Saka, 2, 9
Saliya, 206
Sallekhana, 106, 163, 235
Salt pan (evaporation), 372
Saluva, 376
Saluva dynasty, 362
Saluva Narasimha Deva Raya, 362
Samana, Punjab, 288
Samanta, 249
Samanta Sena, 262
Samarkand, 281
Sambuvaraya, 339

Samma dynasty, 78
Samraat, 75
Samudragupta, 10, 11, 20, 26
Samudra Gupta, 224
Sanctum sanctorum, 233
Sandalwood, 375
Sandhyakar Nandi, 128, 134, 140
Sandilyan, 217
Sandstone, 56
Sanduru, 57
Sangama dynasty, 258, 362, 364, 366
Sangam literature, 23, 24, 176, 191
Sangam period, 24, 181, 191, 226, 341
Sanjan (Gujarat), 113
Sanskrit, 22, 23, 27, 50, 89, 100, 102, 112, 116, 123, 124, 134, 148, 149, 182, 187, 221, 224, 246, 261, 265, 287, 334, 338, 341, 364, 380, 422, 430
Sanskrit language, 47, 173, 361, 433
Sanskrit literature, 20, 55
Santaraksita, 133
Saraha, 133
Sarala Dasa, 434
Sarasvati, 62, 134
Saraswati, 117
Sari, 235
Sarma (Tibetan Buddhism), 133
Sarnath, 435
Sarvajna, 374
Sasanian Empire, 6, 391
Sassanian Empire, 5
Sassanid Empire, 14
Satavahana, 9, 11, 29, 64, 452
Satavahana dynasty, 2
Satavahanas, 25, 174
Satgaon, 389, 393, 400
Sati (practice), 66, 114, 163, 235, 374
Satiyaputras, 343
Satyashraya, 152, 196
Saundatti, 107, 110
Saurashtra (region), 5, 13, 79, 81, 159
Sayana, 380, 382
Sayyid, 312, 330
Sayyid dynasty, 270, 281, 307, **329**, 333, 334
Science and technology in ancient India, 11
Scribes, 369
Sculpture, 210, 372
Sculpture in South Asia, 124
Scythians, 3
Second Battle of Tarain, 15
Sedentary, 271
Seleucid Empire, 52
Seleucus I Nicator, 4
Self-immolation, 114, 163
Seljuk Empire, 291, 308

Sena dynasty, 20, 41, 123, 124, 129, 153, **261**, 264
Sena Empire, 290
Senguttuvan, 456
Seuna, 454
Seuna (Yadava) dynasty, 42, 148, 270, 466
Seuna Yadavas of Devagiri, 33, 55, 149, 155, 365
Shah Muhammad Sagir, 399
Shahnameh, 298, 399
Shahrukh Mirza, 330, 397
Shah Turkan, 293
Shahzada Barbak, 401
Shailodbhava dynasty, 127
Shaiva, 376
Shaivaites, 340
Shaivism, 23, 66, 73, 113, 123, 142, 147, 187, 230, 256, 359, 456
Shakti, 66
Shaktism, 113
Shamsuddin Ahmad Shah, 400
Shamsuddin Firoz Shah, 311
Shams ud din Iltutmish, 292
Shamsuddin Ilyas Shah, 389, 400
Shamsuddin Muzaffar Shah, 401
Shamsuddin Yusuf Shah, 401
Shankha, 135
Shantinatha, 249
Sharia, 317
Sharqi dynasty, 334
Shashanka, 72, 125
Sheldon Pollock, 104, 150
Sher Shah Suri, 389, 390
Shesha, 57
Shia, 280
Shia Islam, 306
Shibi (king), 191
Shihabuddin Bayazid Shah, 395, 400
Shihab-ud-din Omar, 296, 304
Shihabuddin Omar, 273, 274
Shiladitya, 72
Shimoga district, 163, 383
Shipbuilding in Bangladesh, 392
Shiraz, 398
Shiva, 7, 16, 23, 57, 66, 73, 95, 113, 117, 134, 181, 211, 214, 259, 359, 376, 422, 430, 454
Shivamara II, 222, 225
Shore Temple, 29, 174, 181, 182
Shravanabelagola, 27, 106, 112, 160, 224, 226, 232, 238–240, 242, 379
Shudra, 50, 114, 235, 247, 255
Shunga Empire, 9
Shurapala I, 139
Shurapala II, 139
Siberia, 2

Sibi Jataka, 191
Sibsagar, 409
Siddheshwar, 165
Siddhesvara Temple, 58, 168
Sidhpur, 288
Siege of Dwarasamudra, 353
Siege of Warangal, 1310, 253
Siege of Warangal, 1318, 253
Siege of Warangal, 1323, 254
Sikandar Lodi, 281
Sikandar Shah, 390, 400
Sikandar Shah II, 401
Sikhara, 238
Sikh Empire, 43
Silambam, 205
Silapathikaram, 342
Silk Road, 2, 357
Simhachalam, 419, 427
Simhavarman I, 173, 182
Simhavarman II, 182
Simhavarman III, 174, 182
Simhavishnu, 29, 174, 182, 185, 456
Simuka, 2
Sindh, 5, 7, 14, 77, 78, 91, 95, 309, 315
Sindh River, 299
Singapore, 187
Sinhalese people, 199, 353
Siphon, 371
Siraf, 160
Sirajul Islam, 266
Sirhind, 334
Sita, 346
Sivaji Ganesan, 217
Siwalik, 273
Siyaka, 106
Skandavarman, 182
Skandavarman II, 182
Skandavarman III, 182
Skandavarman IV, 182
S. Krishnaswami Aiyangar, 184
Sluice, 371
Soapstone, 168
Sogal, 119
Sogdia, 2
Solar dynasty, 125, 247
Somapura, 124
Somapura Mahavihara, 18, 124, 133, 137
Somavaṃśī dynasty, 128
Someshvara (Chahamana dynasty), 17
Someshvara I, 33, 149, 152, 196, 263
Someshvara II, 153
Someshvara III, 62, 166, 453
Someshvara IV, 148, 155, 198
Someshwara Temple, Kolar, 384
Somesvara I, 154
Somesvara IV, 154

Somnath, 95, 288
Somnath Patan, 16
Somnath Temple, 284
Sonargaon, 393, 398, 400
Song Dynasty, 160, 209
Soomra dynasty, 78
South Arcot, 353
South Asia, 3, 190
South Canara, 53
South-east Asia, 18, 190
Southeast Asia, 22, 23, 142, 160, 190, 389
South East Asia, 145
Southern India, 149, 190, 357
South India, 5, 10, 13, 24, 26, 29, 37, 38, 41,
  48, 82, 101, 142, 149, 190, 222, 224,
  245, 254, 364, 374, 417, 425, 466
South Indian, 30
Spinning wheel, 283
Spread of Islam, 271

Śrauta, 66

Srikakulam, 433
Srikalahasti, 384
Sri Lanka, 10, 11, 38, 105, 142, 145, 173, 181,
  187, 190, 340, 351, 357, 366
Srimara Srivallabha, 349
Srimukhalingam, 18
Srinagar, 75
Srinatha, 382, 422, 430
Sringeri, 365, 376, 384
Sripadaraya, 379
Sri Ponna, 63, 116, 453
Sripurusha, 222, 225
Sriranga I, 363
Sriranga II, 363
Sriranga III, 361, 363
Srirangam, 37, 162, 382, 384
Srirangapatnam, 214
Srisailam, 104, 417, 419–421, 425, 427, 429
Srivijaya, 30, 145, 190, 195, 340
Srivijaya Empire, 124
S. Srikanta Sastri, 74
Stable, 384
Stanley Wolpert, 220
State religion, 391
States Reorganisation Act, 1956, 466
Steppes, 271
Stepwell, 286
Stone masonry, 372
Storax, 110
Strabo, 340, 357
Stupa, 74
Sualkuchi, 21
Subhasita Ratnakosa, 140
Subinphaa, 406, 414

Sudangphaa, 406
Sudingphaa, 404, 407
Sudoiphaa, 406

Śudra, 125

Sudras, 113
Sufi, 312, 389, 398, 399
Sufism, 309, 398
Sugarcane, 229
Sugriva, 346
Suhenphaa, 406
Suhitpangphaa, 407
Suhung, 406
Suhungmung, 406, 408, 409, 411
Sujangphaa, 406
Sujinphaa, 406
Sukaphaa, 404, 406, 408, 411
Sukhaamphaa, 406
Sukhaangphaa, 406
Sukhrangpha, 406
Sukhrungphaa, 406
Sukkur, 7
Suklamphaa, 406
Suklenmung, 406, 410
Suklingphaa, 407
Sulaiman Khan Karrani, 403
Sulikphaa, 406
Sultan, 252, 270, 289, 296, 306, 329, 330, 389
Sultan Abu Bakr Shah Tughluq, 323
Sultanate, 269, 270, 289, 296, 306, 329
Sultanate of Delhi, 286
Sultanate of Rum, 291, 308
Sultan Feroze Shah Tughluq, 323
Sultan Ghari, 293, 295
Sultan Muhammad Shah Tughluq, 323
Sultan of Delhi, 292, 328
Sumatra, 10, 18, 38, 134
Sundarban, 265
Sunenphaa, 406
Sunni, 272
Sunni Islam, 269, 289, 296, 306, 333
Sunni Muslim, 337
Sun Temple, 433
Sunyatphaa, 406
Sunyeophaa, 407
Supangmung, 406
Suphakphaa, 406
Supimphaa, 406
Suramphaa, 406
Suremphaa, 407
Sur Empire, 401
Suresvara, 134
Surface-water hydrology, 370
Suri Empire, 388
Surya, 66, 73, 113, 233

Suryanath U. Kamath, 49, 385
Suryavansha, 102, 433
Susenghphaa, 406, 411
Susenphaa, 406
Sutamla, 404, 406
Sutanphaa, 406
Suteuphaa, 406
Sutingphaa, 406
Sutlej River, 12
Sutuphaa, 406
Svarupananda Desikar, 382
Swargadeo, 404, 411, 412
Swayambhunath, 279
Syed Sultan, 399
Syncretism, 2
Syria, 97

Tabula Peutingeriana, 344
Tadpatri, 384
Tai folk religion, 404
Tai language, 409
Tailapa II, 33, 54, 87, 101, 106, 148–150, 156
Tailapa III, 154
Tai peoples, 408
Taj al-Din Yildiz, 273
Tājika, 82
Taj Khan Karrani, 403
Tajuddin Elduz, 292
Tajuddin Yildoz, 292
Talagunda, 150, 235
Talakad, 25, 26, 37, 53, 105, 221, 225
Talakadu, 224
Talakkad, 196
Talatal Ghar, 409
Taluqdar, 389
Tamarind, 372
Tambralinga, 199, 348
Tamerlane, 319
Tamilakam, 119, 190, 339, 356, 358
Tamil-Brahmi, 343, 356
Tamil language, 23, 24, 142, 173, 187, 216, 338, 341, 364, 382
Tamil literature, 23
Tamil Nadu, 24, 41, 175, 202, 224, 225, 384
Tamil people, 24, 190, 339, 341, 357
Tamil Sangams, 340
Tamim ibn Zaid al-Utbi, 77
Tamin, 97
Tamralipta, 124
Tamraparni, 343
Tandah, 394
Tang dynasty, 7, 73, 209
Tang Empire, 160
Tanintharyi Division, 366
Tanjavur, 26, 224
Tanjore, 149

Tantric Buddhism, 134
Tapti River, 27
Taranatha, 125, 141
Tarikh-i Sistan, 298
Tattuvarayar, 382
Taxila, 3, 24
Telangana, 35, 245, 246, 311, 416, 421, 424, 429
Teli ka Mandir, 96
Telugu Cholas, 144, 189, 193, 250, 352, 456
Telugu language, 56, 173, 244, 246, 248, 254, 361, 364, 379, 416, 422, 424, 430, 439, 466
Telugu literature, 48, 63
Telugu people, 30, 35, 41, 174, 245, 381, 416, 424
Template:Ahom Dynasty, 407
Template:Chalukyas, 52, 152
Template:Chola history, 144, 189
Template:Culture of Assam, 407
Template:Delhi Sultanate, 272, 299, 308, 330, 333
Template:History of Andhra Pradesh, 245, 416, 424
Template:History of Bengal, 262
Template:History of the Turkic peoples pre-14th century, 291, 308
Template:Human history, 1
Template:Karnataka History, 66, 108, 159, 241
Template:Part of History of India, 76, 87, 90, 145, 351, 364
Template:Sena dynasty, 265
Template talk:Ahom Dynasty, 407
Template talk:Chalukyas, 52, 152
Template talk:Chola history, 144, 189
Template talk:Culture of Assam, 407
Template talk:Delhi Sultanate, 272, 299, 308, 330, 333
Template talk:History of Andhra Pradesh, 245, 416, 424
Template talk:History of Bengal, 262
Template talk:History of the Turkic peoples pre-14th century, 291, 308
Template talk:Human history, 1
Template talk:Karnataka History, 66, 108, 159, 241
Template talk:Part of History of India, 76, 87, 90, 145, 351, 364
Template talk:Sena dynasty, 265
Template talk:TNhistory, 189, 339
Template talk:Western Ganga kings, 222
Template:TNhistory, 189, 339
Template:Western Ganga kings, 222
Temple car, 384
Temples, 210
Tenali Ramakrishna, 382

Tenant farmer, 372
Tenkasi, 338, 340
Terracotta, 399
Textile, 283
Tezpur, 20
Thailand, 10
Thamirabarani, 340
Thane, 84, 109
Thanesar, 70–72, 441
Thanjavur, 38, 142, 144, 145, 187, 189, 194, 195, 348, 351, 352
Thanjavur District, 202
Thanjavur Nayak kingdom, 361
Thanjavur Nayaks, 369
The History and Culture of the Indian People, 44, 434
The History of India as told by its own Historians, 43
The History of India, as Told by Its Own Historians, 472
The History of India, as Told by Its Own Historians. The Muhammadan Period, 43, 288
The Imperial Gazetteer of India, 295, 470
The Indian Antiquary, 450
Theophilos (king), 4
The Pahlavas, 4, 9
The World Economy: Historical Statistics, 469
Thimma Bhupala, 362
Thiruchirapalli, 192
Thiruvarangam, 352
Thousand and One Nights, 399
Thousand Pillar Temple, 279
Three Crowned Kings, 190, 339, 356
Tianzhu (India), 344
Tibet, 18, 134
Tibetan Buddhism, 125, 133
Tibetan Empire, 7
Tibetan people, 73
Tilopa, 133
Timeline of the Turkic peoples (500–1300), 290, 307
Timmakka, 375
Timur, 280, 328, 330, 331
Timurid dynasty, 397
Timurid Empire, 280, 392
Timurids, 330
Tirtha (Hinduism), 346
Tirthankar, 232
Tirthankara, 115, 165, 249
Tirthankaras, 164
Tiruchirapalli District, 202
Tiruchirappalli, 352
Tiruchirappalli district, 354
Tirumala Deva Raya, 363
Tirumalamba, 374

Tirumala - Tirupati, 379
Tirumala Venkateswara Temple, 376, 384
Tirunelveli, 30, 197, 338, 340, 354
Tirutakkatevar, 212
Tiruvannamalai, 354
Tiruvarur, 144, 187, 189
Tiruvarur District, 202
Tomara dynasty, 290
Tomaras, 95
Tomaras of Delhi, 16
Tomb of Shah Rukn-e-Alam, 322
Tondaimandalam, 418, 426
Tondeswaram temple, 181
Tonnage, 372
Topaz, 110, 159
Tower, 384
Transcreation, 434
Treasure voyages, 395
Treaty of Yandabo, 408, 410
Trebuchet, 253
Tribe, 3
Tributary state, 353
Tribute, 209, 253
Trikuteshwara, 119
Trimurti, 66
Trincomalee, 181, 348
Tripadi, 63
Tripartite struggle, 32, **87**, 91, 102
Tripura, 21, 390, 404
Tripura Sundari, 135
Tughlaqabad, 276
Tughlaqabad Fort, 324
Tughlaq dynasty, 269, 270, 276, 291, 296, 303, **306**, 308, 328–330
Tughluq dynasty, 301
Tughluq Khan, 323
Tuluva, 376, 383
Tuluva dynasty, 362
Tuluva Narasa Nayaka, 362
Tumkur district, 224, 233
Tungabhadra, 34, 58, 190, 226, 229, 364, 365, 441
Tungabhadra River, 33, 149, 371
Tunic, 370
Turban, 114, 375
Turco-Mongol, 42, 319
Turgesh, 290, 307
Turkestan, 309
Turkey, 109
Turkic Khaganate, 290, 307
Turkic migration, 271
Turkic people, 281, 297, 309
Turkic peoples, 6, 95, 97, 262, 269–271, 273, 274, 284, 291, 308, 310, 389, 417, 425
Turkmenistan, 369
Turko-Afghan, 274

Turk Shahi, 290, 307
Turmeric, 371
Turushka, 246
T. V. Mahalingam, 477
Twipra Kingdom, 21
Tyagada Brahmadeva Pillar, 238
Tyao Khamti, 406
Tyrant, 276

Udayagiri and Khandagiri Caves, 10
Udayar (novel), 217
Udupi, 379, 380
Ujjain, 13, 32, 79, 81, 83, 85, 90, 93, 97, 109, 288
Ulster Museum, 213
Ulugh Khan, 287, 288
Umar II, 80
Umayyad, 79, 80
Umayyad Caliphate, 54, 77, 78
Umayyad campaigns in India, **77**
Umayyad Mosque, 400
Underwater diving, 208
UNESCO, 28, 57, 118, 212, 382, 474
UNESCO Heritage Site, 38
UNESCO World Heritage Site, 11, 29, 42, 91, 174
UNESCO World Heritage Sites, 32, 102
Unification of Karnataka, 66, 108, 158, 241
Unitary state, 404
Untouchability, 373
Upanishads, 9, 379
Upparapalli, 253
Uraiyur, 144, 189, 351
Urayur, 187, 192
Urdu, 270
Urdu language, 291
Usurper, 389
Uththama Chola, 147, 194
Utkala Kingdom, 18, 127, 130
Utpala dynasty, 75, 76
Uttama Chola, 143, 145, 188, 216
Uttara Kannada, 24
Uttaranchal, 42
Uttarandhra, 432
Uttar Pradesh, 42, 70
Uyghur Khaganate, 290, 307
Uzbekistan, 3

Vachana, 162
Vachanas, 36, 162, 164, 165
Vaddaradhane, 234
Vadirajatirtha, 379
Vaghela dynasty, 270, 296
Vahana, 249
Vaigai, 345
Vaishnava, 113, 147, 230, 376

Vaishnavism, 23, 66, 160, 230, 359
Vaishya, 72, 113, 235
Vajrayana, 17, 123, 124
Vakapatiraja, 88
Vakataka, 13
Vakatakas, 177
Vallabhi, 79, 82, 85
Valmiki, 213
Varaguna I, 349
Varagunavarman II, 349
Varaha, 57, 64, 67, 94, 136, 376
Varahamihira, 11
Varanasi, 20, 128, 262, 281, 288
Vardhana dynasty, 41, 70
Varendra, 18, 124, 125
Varendra Rebellion, 128
Varman dynasty, 20
Varna, 247
Varna (Hinduism), 23, 72, 255
Varna in Hinduism, 72
Varuna, 346
Vasant Kunj, 295
Vasco Da Gama, 396
Vasistha, 433
Vatapi, 28
Vatsaraja, 98
Vatsraj, 94
Vatsraja, 94, 126
Vatsyayana, 11
Vault (architecture), 384
Veda, 57, 120
Vedas, 164, 379, 380
Vedavati, 229
Vedic Brahmanism, 230
Vedic period, 114
Veera Ballala II, 37, 155
Veera Ballala III, 37, 353, 418, 426
Veera Ballala II, 198
Veerashaiva, 48, 162
Velama, 420, 428
Velama (caste), 257
Velanati Chodas, 244, 250, 392
Vellalar, 203, 205
Vellore, 384
Velurpalaiyam plates, 176
Vemana, 374
Vemulwada, Karimnagar District, 116, 117, 442, 451
Venetian Republic, 345, 397
Vengi, 29, 30, 33, 48, 87, 105, 106, 142, 149, 152, 196, 237
Venice, 372
Venkata I, 362
Venkata II, 363
Venkata III, 363
Venkateshwara, 376, 380
Venur, 384
Verandah, 57
Vernacular, 284
Vernacular literature, 23
Vesara, 37, 382
Vestibule (architecture), 57
Vidarbha, 84, 129
Vidyadhara (Chandela king), 95
Vidyakara, 140
Vidyaranya, 365, 376, 382
Vietnam, 10, 38
Vigrahapala I, 127
Vigrahapala II, 127, 139
Vigrahapala III, 139
Vigrahapala I (Pala dynasty), 139, 140
Vigraharaja IV, 17
Vihara, 18, 164
Vijapur, 288
Vijayaditya, 54
Vijayalaya, 194
Vijayalaya Chola, 142, 143, 145, 147, 187, 188, 192, 348
Vijayanagar, 387
Vijayanagara, 37, 340, 361, 364, 367, 382
Vijayanagara Architecture, 364
Vijayanagara coinage, 361
Vijayanagara Empire, 37, 42, 65, 108, 158, 241, 244, 258, 270, 279, 307, 313, 354, **361**, 362, 387, 416, 418, 420, 424–426, 428, 433, 458
Vijayanagar empire, 162
Vijaya Sena, 262, 265
Vijayawada, 417, 425
Vijay Sen, 20
Vijnaneshwara, 62, 166
Vikrama Chola, 143, 188, 199
Vikramaditya II, 28, 77, 78, 97, 451
Vikramaditya VI, 33, 128, 149, 153, 263, 438, 463
Vikramaditya I, 54
Vikramaditya II, 51, 54, 442
Vikramaditya VI, 54, 196
Vikramarjuna Vijaya, 116
Vikramashila, 18, 124, 132, 133, 138
Vimana (architectural feature), 354
Vimana (shrine), 167
Vimana (tower), 168
Vincent Arthur Smith, 276
Vindhya Range, 315
Vindhyas, 53
Vinukonda, 419, 427
Virabhadra, 384
Viranarasimha Raya, 362
Virarajendra Chola, 143, 146, 147, 188, 190
Virasena, 117
Virashaiva, 36, 162, 164, 379

519

Virashaivism, 160
Vira Someshwara, 351, 352
Viravarman (Pallava dynasty), 182
Vira Vijaya Bukka Raya, 362
Virupaksha Raya, 362
Virupaksha Raya II, 362
Virupaksha Temple, Hampi, 377, 384
Visakhapatnam, 55
Vishnu, 23, 57, 66, 94, 113, 134, 136, 212, 233, 249, 342, 376, 377, 382
Vishnukundin, 182
Vishnukundina, 29, 55
Vishnukundins, 53
Vishnu Sharma, 11
Vishnuvardhana, 37, 162, 198
Vishvarupa Sena, 265
Visnugopa, 182
Vizhinjam, 338
Vizier, 318
Volga Bulgaria, 290, 307
Vrishni, 249
Vyasakuta, 379
Vyasatirtha, 379, 381

Wang Xuance, 73
Warangal, 109, 244, 245, 257, 275, 288, 300, 313, 365, 417, 421, 425, 429
War elephant, 124, 140, 204
War elephants, 284, 392
Warship, 392
Water transportation, 371
Wax seal, 369
Weilüe, 39
Wendy Doniger, 74
West Asia, 93
West Bengal, 18, 20, 432
Western Asia, 271
Western Chalukya Architecture, 34, 149
Western Chalukya Empire, 33, 41, 65, 101, 108, 128, **148**, 158, 196, 226, 240, 244, 262, 263, 466
Western Chalukya literature, 150
Western Chalukyas, 30, 34, 48, 52, 87, 101, 106, 146, 244
Western Ganga Dynasty, 24, 25, 41, 53, 64, 65, 105, 107, 112, 116, 158, 160, 221, **221**, 240, 379
Western India, 14
Western Roman Empire, 357
Western Satraps, 3, 5, 9
Western Turkic Khaganate, 290, 307
West Godavari district, 30
What information to include, 211
Wikipedia:Citation needed, 3, 4, 11, 29, 30, 34, 35, 38, 75, 80, 84, 95, 97, 134, 137, 174, 181, 182, 191–193, 200, 202, 216, 217, 263, 276, 279, 281, 291, 323, 334–336, 338, 342, 343, 350, 456, 458
Wikipedia:Citing sources, 202, 212, 213
Wikipedia:Identifying reliable sources, 354
Wikipedia:Link rot, 386
Wikipedia:Please clarify, 11, 205, 214
Wikipedia:Verifiability, 132, 205, 417, 421, 425, 429
Wikisource, 74, 123, 387
Wootz steel, 205
World Heritage site, 18, 19, 28, 57, 137, 212, 364, 382
Worm gear, 283
WP:NOTRS, 3

Xuanzang, 13, 51, 71–74, 174, 179, 194, 345, 456
Xueyantuo, 290, 307

Yadu, 30, 129
Yahya bin Ahmad Sirhindi, 330
Yajvapala dynasty, 270
Yaksha, 239, 249
Yalli (motif), 239
Yamuna, 32
Yamuna River, 14, 102, 106
Yashovarman, 7, 70, 76, 79, 88, 94
Yavana, 129
Yavana Rani, 217
Yazid II, 80
Yerrapragada, 422, 430
Yojana, 343
Yona, 9
Yongle, 395
Yudhishthira, 225, 346
Yuezhi, 6
Yu Huan, 344
Yunnan, 408
Yusuf and Zulaikha, 399
Yusuf ibn Umar al-Thaqafi, 83

Zamindar, 389
Zamorin, 366
Zen, 29
Zheng He, 372
Ziauddin Barani, 310

www.ingramcontent.com/pod-product-compliance
Lightning Source LLC
Chambersburg PA
CBHW021147230426
43667CB00006B/291